Philosophy Through Science Fiction

D1244704

Philosophical investigation at its best shares some of the goals and methods of good science fiction. At the root of both of these disciplines is a belief in the richness of the human mind, a desire for theoretical explanation, and enjoyment through rational reflection.

Philosophy Through Science Fiction offers a fun, challenging, and accessible way in to the issues of philosophy through the genre of science fiction. Tackling problems such as the possibility of time travel, or what makes someone the same person over time, the authors take a four-pronged approach to each issue, providing:

- a clear and concise introduction to each subject by the authors
- a science fiction story that exemplifies a feature of the philosophical discussion
- historical and contemporary philosophical texts that investigate the issue with rigor, and
- pedagogical features including a glossary, plot profiles of pertinent science fiction stories and films, and questions for further reflection.

Philosophy Through Science Fiction includes stories from leading new science fiction writers including Greg Egan and Mike Resnick, as well as from world renowned authors like Philip K. Dick and Robert Heinlein. Philosophy readings in this book include historical pieces by René Descartes and David Hume, and contemporary pieces by John Searle and Mary Midgley.

The authors: **Ryan Nichols** is Assistant Professor at California State University, Fullerton. **Nicholas D. Smith** is Professor of Philosophy at Lewis and Clark College. **Fred Miller** is Professor of Philosophy and the Executive Director of the Social Philosophy and Policy Center at Bowling Green State University, Ohio.

Philosophy Through Science Fiction

A Coursebook with Readings

**Ryan Nichols,
Nicholas D. Smith,
and Fred Miller**

Routledge
Taylor & Francis Group

LONDON AND NEW YORK

First published 2009
by Routledge
2 Park Square, Milton Park, Abingdon, Oxon OX14 4RN
52 Vanderbilt Avenue, New York, NY 10017

Routledge is an imprint of the Taylor & Francis Group, an informa business

© 2009 Taylor & Francis

Typeset in Charter and Folio by
Keystroke, 28 High Street, Tettenhall, Wolverhampton

Library of Congress Cataloging in Publication Data
A catalog record has been requested for this book

ISBN13: 978-0-415-95756-4 (hbk)
ISBN13: 978-0-415-95755-7 (pbk)

Contents

List of boxes

Preface

If you love thinking about the big issues and have an interest in science fiction, this book is for you. We hope to interest people with a prior passion for philosophy in wonders of the imagination as envisioned in science fiction literature. We also hope to interest fans of science fiction in the pleasures of philosophical reflection and self-discovery.

We offer this book in the conviction that the study of philosophy and the appreciation of science fiction can be combined in a fruitful way. Our objective is to present some basic concepts and problems of philosophy in conjunction with stories that are well written and stimulating. Philosophy, like science fiction, can and should excite the interest of the beginner. And science fiction at its best, like philosophy, represents an intellectual challenge to the reader.

We have chosen stories that will help the reader understand central philosophical concepts and problems and develop critical thinking capacities. The reader is invited to consider selected problems about knowledge (philosophical method, knowledge and skepticism), the nature of reality (the problem of skepticism, the existence of God, the nature of space and time) and our human nature (the philosophy of mind, the problem of personal identity, the question of free will).

The chapters are formatted to begin with a brief thought experiment offered in the hopes that it will prompt the reader to think new, critical thoughts about the issue at hand. That is followed by a substantive discussion of the philosophical problem at the heart of the chapter. We place an emphasis in every chapter on developing our readers' critical thinking and reading skills, which is why we aim to construct and clarify philosophical arguments. We offset our discussion of these issues with boxes that often highlight areas of convergence between science fiction and philosophy. Following our discussion, each chapter offers the reader a set of supplementary readings: a science fiction short story, a reading (or two) from the history of philosophy, and an article drawn from contemporary philosophy.

The text has been designed so that it can serve different purposes. It can be used in introductory philosophical courses and in literature courses concerned with developing a philosophical appreciation of fiction. The book comes with its own apparatus of study questions, bibliographies and a glossary. We have written study and discussion questions for all the stories and for all the historical and contemporary philosophy readings. These questions are designed to help readers employ the skills that they have gained in analyzing and assessing problems, interpretations, and arguments contained in or suggested by the story and the essay. We hope to inspire readers to pursue these philosophical issues further, and we have tried to come to their aid with select bibliographies on the philosophical and science fiction literature relating to each chapter.

This apparatus is intended to make this book easy to use—for instructor and student alike—as a course text. Instructors can chart a straight path through the book from the introductory chapter to Chapter 7. But this same apparatus enables the general reader with an interest in philosophy or science fiction to pick up the book and read it profitably.

Our ultimate purpose is to help inspire in the reader appreciation for and attraction to a goal and a method which philosophy and science fiction share in common: the understanding of our human nature, the nature of reality, and human values by means of creative and critical thinking.

R.T.N.
F.D.M.
N.D.S.

Acknowledgments

I received generous help from people too numerous to mention in my development and composition of this book, and I thank those named and unnamed here for it. Extra special thanks go to anonymous referees, and Amy Coplan, Kevin Corcoran, Rick Groshong, Franz Kiekeben, JeeLoo Liu, Bill Melanson, Carol Nichols, Alasdair Richmond, Kevin Timpe, and Stephen Wykstra, all of whom read chapters of the manuscript. Special thanks go to James Gunn, Jeff Koperski, Al Lent, Dan Nichols, Chris McKitterick, Mark Silcox, Cathal Woods and George Zebrowski for conversations about these ideas. Participation at summer institutes at the Center for the Study of Science Fiction at University of Kansas were especially helpful to me. Countless students over the years have read earlier versions of this material in coursebook form. In particular I thank Brent Boos, Kyle Bova, Beata Bujalski, Matt Harper, Paige Van Hong, and Ryan Nunes for helpful comments.

I have fully rewritten this book from its earlier incarnation as *Thought Probes* (Prentice-Hall, 1981). The core concept, the design of the chapters and the topics addressed remain the same. The analysis and discussion of many of the arguments in the book closely resemble those in Nicholas Smith and Fred Miller's original text. But in addition to my goal of updating each chapter to account for new philosophical research in the last few decades, I have also put my stamp upon the arguments. The depth and breadth of the revisions merited a new title and new publisher, and I thank Routledge, especially Kate Ahl, for seeing the value in this project. It is left to me to lay claim to any flaws in the text. Last, I owe Fred and Nick great debts of gratitude for inviting me to re-compose and re-envision their creation. I have become a better teacher and a better philosopher and I have had a great deal of fun as a result of this unexpected and wonderful project.

Insofar as this book is mine to dedicate, I offer it to my mom, Carol Nichols, with gratitude and happiness and dreams.

Ryan Nichols

What is philosophy?

In this introduction we'll provide a framework for understanding the rest of the book by explaining the relationships between science fiction and philosophy. We'll also contrast the methods used in each. By creating a thought experiment, we'll introduce you to several sub-disciplines within philosophy.

After completing this chapter, you should be able to:

- Describe the similarities and differences between science fiction and philosophy
- Explain what thought experiments are
- Distinguish between sub-disciplines within philosophy
- Describe an intellectual problem arising within each sub-discipline.

0.0 SCIENCE FICTION AND PHILOSOPHY

Science fiction is a literature of ideas. This exciting genre bursts with creativity found in few others. Authors writing science fiction enrich our understanding of our relationship to the world, to other people, to other species and to science and technology. At the fundamental level, this genre explores the human condition—what it is and what it might become—while pushing us to consider what lies beyond the horizon of the present.

Science fiction authors accomplish this in part through crafting alternative worlds. As a rule, alternate worlds within science fiction (or simply "SF") conform to the laws of nature and do not use supernatural solutions to resolve conflict within the plots of the stories. This distinguishes the genre from fantasy literature. Gods, non-physical beings, and inexplicable powers do not enter science fiction plots to save the day. Some members of the SF community describe fantasy authors as "playing tennis without a net." SF makes use of conceptual boundaries within which to plot and populate stories. Through this narrow stretch of conceptual space, SF authors craft stories that prompt us to reflect critically upon our fundamental **beliefs** and the future of our species.

This may seem like a lofty description of SF. If your knowledge of SF stems from watching reruns of *Mystery Science Theater 3000*, then it may seem like a very lofty description of SF. In *Mystery Science Theater 3000*, a TV program from the 1990s, evil scientists torture an unlucky human being on the Satellite of Love by forcing him to watch Earth's worst SF films with his homemade robots! Very, very funny. Films like *The Brains that Wouldn't Die*, *The Killer Shrews* and *Santa Claus Conquers the Martians* can be a whole lot of fun. (*Rental*: You can rent these *MST3000* classics from major online DVD rental companies. If those aren't to taste, try *MST3000: Attack of the Killer Leeches*!) Hollywood SF blockbusters are a summer staple, and we'll all be entertained by dazzling special effects and CGI. But SF has moved beyond the pulp paperback, the B-movie and the blockbuster. On critically acclaimed best-seller lists you'll almost always find novels that clearly use conventions of the genre; perhaps they are set in the future, or in an alternative history, or bring as yet unknown technology into the plot. At the end of each chapter, we include a bibliography with handpicked science fiction and philosophy resources for further reading. You'll find a great deal of wonderful literature in those lists. The literature of SF typically trumps cinematic SF in richness and depth, but there are lots of wonderful SF films out there. We'll be highlighting countless films throughout the book through a series of parenthetical remarks directing you to recommended DVD rentals.

We believe that philosophical investigation at its best shares some of the goals and methods of good SF, which is the principal motivation for this book. Both of these forms of literature exemplify the richness of the human mind and an unquenchable desire for intellectual exploration. Plato, the ancient Greek father of Western philosophy, said, "Wonder is the feeling of a philosopher, and philosophy begins in wonder." People often enter into philosophical investigations of their own due to their intellectual curiosity. This sense of awe is captured in the titles of the early sci-fi magazines: *Amazing Stories*, *Astounding Science Fiction* and *Wonder Stories*.

This book is for two audiences. First, students approaching philosophy will find this book an accessible, fun, and challenging introduction to central issues in philosophy. Second, SF readers who are not content simply to read SF stories but who want to scrutinize their implications will enjoy this book. Working on this assumption we will use science fiction to conduct seven philosophical enquiries focused on a broad range of topics including **skepticism**, the existence of **God**, and human freedom.

Though we investigate ways in which SF can enrich philosophy, philosophy can inform SF as well. The conceptual sophistication of the genre's imagined universes has improved dramatically in the last 30 years, but plot inconsistencies remain—especially in time travel tales (see Chapter 4). Here's our favorite. Suppose you were able to travel back in time and steal all the Spanish bullion you could bring back to the future. When you return to the date at which you left, how could you confirm the historic pedigree of these coins? In *Timecop*, a 1980s Jean-Claude Van Damme flick, bandits travel to the past and do this. Once they get back they test the gold through carbon dating to confirm its historic value. The bandits need to satisfy their buyers that they didn't simply mint the gold with a forged, historic coin press. What is wrong with this picture?

Carbon dating can only be conducted upon objects that have a specific isotope of carbon. Gold, of course, is not an organic compound, so it can't be carbon-dated! We don't begrudge the writer of the screenplay or the fact-checker because we're not sure the film would have been much better without this blunder. The present point is that evaluating *stories* for internal consistency is remarkably similar to evaluating a philosophical *theory* for consistency. When we read philosophy, we do so critically, in order to discover what doesn't fit together.

In addition to being motivated by a sense of wonder, philosophy and SF both use the *thought experiment*. A thought experiment is a scenario in which an imagined environment contains some features that our world has and other features it doesn't. The differences in a thought experiment might have to do with political systems, natural laws, biological organisms, technological advancement, or moral codes. Philosophers use thought experiments to emphasize the central role of the analysis, definition, and criticism of concepts in philosophy.

BOX 0.A: MOLYNEUX'S QUESTION

William Molyneux, of Dublin, Ireland, couldn't understand some of the details of the theories of knowledge and perception in his day. So in 1693 he wrote a letter to a leading philosopher, John Locke. Molyneux proposed a thought experiment to Locke that Molyneux thought would clear up some of his misunderstandings.

> Suppose a man born blind, and now adult, and taught by his touch to distinguish between a cube and a sphere of the same metal, and [nearly] of the same bigness, so as to tell, when he felt one and the other, which is the cube, which the sphere. Suppose then the cube and sphere placed on a table, and the blind man be made to see: question, whether by his sight, before he touched them, he could now distinguish and tell which is the globe, which the cube?[1]

Molyneux is asking this: Suppose someone blind from birth has his sight surgically restored as an adult. Imagine a cube and a sphere sitting on a table at which the patient sits. The surgeon removes the bandages from the patient's eyes and the patient slowly opens them. What would he be able to see? Specifically, would the patient know which thing he sees is the cube and which is the sphere? (No touching allowed!)

This thought experiment made waves in philosophy in the eighteenth century. It went on to influence lots of psychologists too. People wanted to know answers to questions like these: Do humans have knowledge of objects prior to experiencing things? Do we touch the very same things we see, really? How does the loss of one sense affect our other senses?

Believe it or not, researchers still haven't found unanimous answers to Molyneux's questions—perhaps you can be the person to find them.

Reading: *Molyneux's Question: Vision, Touch and the Philosophy of Perception* (1977), by Michael Morgan studies this issue from philosophical and experimental perspectives (Cambridge: Cambridge University Press).

The purpose of the thought experiments philosophers create differs from that of SF thought experiments. The philosopher uses the contrasts brought to light in thought experiments to elaborate and investigate philosophical concepts and to draw attention to hidden assumptions within a philosophical theory.

The SF thought experiment is primarily literary. By placing a human character in an alien culture, for example, the SF author can explore the adaptability of human nature, or probe into issues of gender, or peek at life in a radically different political system. The SF author isn't mainly trying to prove a point or attack an alternative theory, even though famous sci-fi novels can be interpreted that way. Jonathan Swift's *Gulliver's Travels* puts sympathetic characters in alternate universes in order to criticize political regimes, as does George Orwell's *Nineteen Eighty-Four*. (*Rental*: John Hurt and Richard Burton star in the film *1984* (1984). See also *Brazil* (1985, directed by Terry Gilliam, starring Robert DeNiro), in which Orwellian absurdities are given a Monty Python twist.)

Here is a display of the differences between the way philosophers and SF authors use thought experiments:

BOX 0.B: FRAMING SF THOUGHT EXPERIMENTS

1   What if God were to destroy a planet populated with intelligent beings like us?
2   Should prisoners be allowed to pay their debts to society by donating their organs, or by growing new ones to donate?
3   What if a complete brain transplant were medically possible?
4   What if I could travel to the past?

FRAMING PHILOSOPHY THOUGHT EXPERIMENTS

1   Is anything that God does morally permissible simply because God does it?
2   Are we morally permitted to do anything we want to our bodies as long as what we do doesn't harm others?

3   Am I identical with my brain, my mind, my body or something else?
4   Does the very idea of time travel involve a conceptual inconsistency?

Some thought experiments are not what they appear to be. Suppose you were to fold a sheet of tissue paper 0.001 inches thick 50 times. Just how thick would it be? The answer: 17,770,000 miles thick, the product of $2^{50} \times 0.001$ (Sorenson, 1992: p. 31).

The lesson? Treat thought experiments with care. But how? We will approach a thought experiment by asking a set of critical questions. Here are some important ones:

- What is the author's purpose in posing this thought experiment?
- What facts are presupposed in the thought experiment?
- Are those presuppositions true?
- Is the scenario physically possible in our world?
- Is the scenario coherent, that is, are there conceptual conflicts created by the presuppositions of the thought experiment?
- What does the thought experiment reveal about our world, our practices, and our moral **intuitions**?

0.1 THOUGHT EXPERIMENTS

Let's now consider an extended thought experiment in order to explore the areas within philosophy. What if a science team on board a starship ventures into the outer reaches of the civilized galaxy? Suppose the ship reaches a new planet, Xong, and meets a new intelligent species. The director of the science team, Candice, writes back to her boss with a preliminary and informal update on her findings:

It is difficult for me to complete this report due to conflicting assessments of Xongians and their society from my team of scientists. First, the two linguists on my staff disagree about the language of the natives. One linguist claims to have translated the language satisfactorily and has served as an interpreter. The second linguist says that the irrationality of this species implies that, despite patterns in the sounds they make with their "mouths," they lack a language with determinate parts of speech. My second linguist says that, if what they speak is a language, then Xongians make many false or irrational **statements**. For example, according to the first linguist, Xongian—their language—lacks nouns that differentiate *people* from *things*, like rocks. Xongians might say "The house waits" and "The spouse waits." They believe that the world has a creator but that this "god" behaves haphazardly. They have no words for *mind* or *consciousness* and they lack first-person constructions. We surmise that Xongian people treat other Xongians as mere physical objects.

Closely related, Xongians do not hold one another responsible for their actions. The anthropologists on my team do not fully comprehend Xongian ideas of ethics and etiquette. If a native kills another native for whatever reason, Xongians exhibit no concern for the loss of life, but great concern for its proper burial. The seriousness with which they bury their dead resembles their adherence to their eating rituals. If a Xongian eats a dish with the wrong cutlery, they become distressed, as if a serious crime had been committed. My first linguist reports that the natives feel contempt for our confusion of serious moral matters of culinary etiquette with trivial issues of homicide.

My psychologists report that Xongians suffer irreversible amnesia at (at least) four points in their metabolic development into adulthood—when infant Xongians begin walking upright; at their first puberty, giving them the ability to conceive children; at their second puberty, giving them the ability to birth; and at menopause. Ongoing research by my psych officers aims to establish a correlation between these amnesiac events and an unusual decision-procedure. Each Xongian carries a wallet with them wherever they go. It contains the knucklebones of a local mammal. In order to make a judgment, he or she or it thinks of as many alternative hypotheses as possible, assigns each a configuration of knucklebones, and tosses out the bones to see which configuration comes up. That settles the matter. When the natives try to reach any **conclusions** about what ought to be done, they toss their bones together.

My political scientists and sociologists also report odd events. My staff is disputing whether there is any form of government amongst these strange people. Xongians do not have an organized police force or any national defense, even though what we would call "crime" occurs all the time. My biologists haven't thoroughly examined Xongians, but from what they tell me, these natives appear to have three, or maybe four, different genders represented in their species. The "male" impregnates the "female," who carries and births the fetus. A "caregiver" gender rears and feeds the infant. Current observations indicate that members of a fourth group appear to play no role in the reproductive cycle.

My chemists report that the natives have a periodic table much like ours. But many of the natives' mathematical concepts seem untranslatable. We have identified their arithmetical rules—in base 12. But their **logic** differs from ours because they do not recognize the law of non-contradiction. They think that some statement S can be true and false at the same time. My conceptual scientists try to explain that by saying that the Xongians must be using a fuzzy, multi-valent logic.

The natives make confident predictions about future events. Although they will not or cannot tell us the basis for these statements, they seem as confident about the future as about the present. But Xongians appear to dismiss any statement about the past—even about what happened yesterday—as false or unknowable.

This has been a serious obstacle in our attempts to understand them—and in my ability to complete my formal report. My unanswered questions include: What kind of worldview could they possibly have that would lead to such bizarre behavior? Are they **rational**? If they are not, is the second linguist on my team correct to argue that it would be impossible for any intelligent race to behave as this race does?

BOX 0.C: WHAT IS A "THOUGHT EXPERIMENT"?

Philosophers don't agree on what happens in a thought experiment. On one theory, proposed by Thomas Kuhn, scientific thought experiments give scientists the means to recall anomalies in data that they have noticed but ignored. But this doesn't apply to a great many thought experiments of things that are physically impossible. A second theory, by John Norton, suggests that thought experiments are nothing more than **deductive** and **inductive arguments** in a peculiar, prose form. But some thought experiments seem to require thinking that cannot be contained in propositional form. For example, David Hume tests his thesis about where our ideas come from by asking his readers to imagine an unseen shade of blue whose color fits naturally between two other seen shades of blue. A third account suggests that thought experiments are models of the world through which we can determine the **truth** of **conditional**, "if–then" statements. If the world were like . . ., would it follow that. . . . If the model is internally consistent, then we've identified a way the world could be. Some conceptual models of the world fail to identify a consistent **possible world**, which, on this third suggestion, make them poor thought experiments.

0.2 AREAS OF PHILOSOPHY: VALUE THEORY

Xongians differ from us about what things are good and bad, what acts are right or wrong, and how we should make decisions. **Value theory** is the part of philosophy that identifies and tries to assess those claims, but value theory is much more than this. Within this sub-field, philosophers discuss virtues and vices, the meanings and purposes of life, and answer questions about human nature. **Metaethics** raises questions about the ultimate nature of values, such as "What do terms like 'right' and 'moral' mean?" A Xongian might say that preserving intelligent life is less important than eating with the proper fork; eating properly is a more basic value for Xongians. The metaethicist might ask questions like: Is there any sense to be made of saying that Xongians are immoral because they don't conform to our values? How do we justify such a claim? What makes moral statements true or false?

Normative ethics seeks principles on which we can base moral judgments. Generally, normative ethics identifies the principles on which we base our ethical evaluations of things as "good" or "bad" and our evaluations of actions as "right" or "wrong." A normative theory offers a set of principles that are thought to demarcate good from bad and right from wrong. Consider this claim: You should stop to save your neighbor from choking to death rather than continuing to eat your meal. The ethicist wants to give reasons for thinking this moral claim is true or false. The ethicist might argue that it is true on the basis of the theory that whatever action creates the most pleasure for the most number of people is the action you are obligated to perform. But it is not as tidy as that. A Xongian might object by claiming that not finishing a meal causes more harm to self and others than would preventing a mere neighbor from choking to death. The normative ethicist asks questions including: Is abortion morally permissible? What sort of obligations do children have to their parents? Do I have any moral obligation to help the poor?

Aesthetics (the philosophy of art) also falls under the rubric of value theory since it is concerned with beauty. Suppose the Xongians hold that only natural items, like blades of grass and fossils, are beautiful, and hold that artifacts, like paintings and temples, of necessity have no aesthetic value. Could they be right about that? Suppose we want to argue that they are incorrect on these points. What is our standard of beauty such that we can show that they are incorrect?

Social and political philosophy explores the structures in which people interact—social structures like the family and political structures like the democratic process. The Xongians have no formal government and make collective decisions by tossing knuckle-bones. The political philosopher asks whether this sort of political structure is better or worse than ours, and how such a structure might be improved. Social and political philosophers use concepts such as justice, equality, autonomy, and power to explain social and political structures that will better serve our kind in its search for value. The Xongians appear to believe that a central government isn't needed for a happy life. Are they right? Social and political philosophers ask questions like: Is anarchy morally preferable to democratic government or monarchy? How should wealth be distributed in society? What human rights are there, if any?

Bioethics is an emerging area of study concerned with moral considerations surrounding the ethics of life, human and non-human. The Xongians seem not to value life intrinsically, which creates implications for bioethics. Perhaps making radical physical alterations to their bodies—growing another arm or changing genitalia—is acceptable and commonplace on Xong. Reflecting on the bioethical presuppositions that support the Xongians' decisions about the moral status of their bodies might help us think through our moral decisions. For example, whether xenotransplantation—the transplantation of organs farmed from non-human animals into human bodies—is morally permissible depends upon our moral beliefs about the inviolability of our bodies. If we had thought about the moral status of the Xongian practices, we would be better able to address questions raised about the moral status of our bodies. These include: When neo-natal doctors are faced with a choice of saving a mother or an unborn baby, what should they do? If the mother disagrees with the doctor's decision, should her preference trump the doctor's opinion? Do I really have a moral obligation to improve the environment?

BOX 0.D: *SOLARIS*

Solaris, written by Polish author Stanislaw Lem in 1961, is a novel about a group of scientists struggling to understand a world seemingly without a stable system of natural laws. "Solaris" is the name of the planet they orbit, and it harbors an intelligence that seems to cover its surface like a vast ocean. The nature of the organism's thought and consciousness is beyond human comprehension. But despite this narrative obstacle, Lem vividly portrays this world and the futile attempts by humanity to understand it. The radical otherness of alien life is a cherished theme in Lem's writings. The vision of unfathomable alien life portrayed in *Solaris* offers perhaps the sharpest contrast available to the world of *Star Trek*, in which aliens typically maintain human characteristics.

Rental: Andrei Tarkovsky's 1972 film (entitled *Solyaris*) closely mirrors the structure of the novel. Steven Soderbergh's (2002) version, with George Clooney, emphasizes the effects of the alien organism upon the human crew.

0.3 AREAS OF PHILOSOPHY: KNOWLEDGE AND REALITY

This book primarily focuses on philosophical arguments given on behalf of theories of knowledge and reality. Let's introduce issues in this area of philosophy.

Epistemology refers to the study of knowledge and belief and the processes by which statements are known. Most of us claim to know many things, and we base those claims on the observations we make with our sense organs. The Xongians express confidence about their beliefs, but they justify their beliefs by randomly tossing knucklebones. We might confront a Xongian's use of knucklebones by arguing that it is irrational, but the Xongian might respond by asking us to justify our use of our sense organs as rational.

Chapter 2 of this book introduces and explores the epistemological problem of skepticism. The skeptic raises many doubts about the reliability of our sense organs and about other ways in which we think we know things. The epistemologists also ask questions such as: Can we believe whatever we want to believe? Must all knowledge be ultimately based on perception? Can there be mystical knowledge without evidence? To know something, must we know that we know it?

Metaphysics deals with theories about the nature and constitution of reality. Five chapters in this book deal with questions placed under the broad category of metaphysics. Chapter 3 discusses God's existence. How justified are the Xongians in holding that the world has a creator, but one who is haphazard in managing things? Chapter 4 concerns the nature of time and its role in reality. The Xongians appear to believe that the past isn't real. Might they be right?

Chapter 5 raises questions about the philosophy of mind. Some philosophers agree with the Xongians that it makes no sense to refer to the "mind" or "soul" or to any "conscious" states as such. For some philosophers, the mind is nothing more than the complex arrangement of matter. For others, human minds stand out from the material world because minds experience non-physical states. In fact, some believe that minds are themselves non-physical things that are made of a spiritual substance.

Chapter 6 explores the conditions under which existing persons maintain their individuality and identity, in other words, the issue of "**personal identity**." When the Xongians undergo their periodic amnesia and rebirth, do they remain the same persons or do new persons come into existence? What should we say about a human being who suffers total amnesia after a car accident? These questions concern the **problem of personal identity**.

Chapter 7 investigates whether human beings have freedom. The Xongians appear to recognize that they have a form of free will. That's because they praise and blame others for violations of etiquette. But what if they both blamed a Xongian for this breach of etiquette and believed that the Xongian couldn't have avoiding doing it? That position appears to be inconsistent. We humans typically believe in free will, but when presented with evidence from the laws of science, we also believe that physical events are determined. This gives rise to a number of arguments for freedom (**libertarianism**), against freedom (**determinism**) and for a hybrid view according to which we are "free" in a nuanced sense of that term compatible with determinism (**compatibilism**). We'll study each of these positions below.

0.5 SUMMARY

In this introductory chapter, we described the bridges that bring philosophy and science fiction together—curiosity, a desire to understand, a sense of wonder, and the pleasure of learning new things. We used a thought experiment about an alien species to illustrate questions raised within areas of contemporary philosophy, including value theory, epistemology and metaphysics.

0.6 BIBLIOGRAPHY AND RECOMMENDED READING

*Barad, Judith and Ed Robertson. *The Ethics of Star Trek*. New York: Perennial Press, 2001. Accessible and informed philosophical analysis of moral issues raised in the Star Trek multiverse.

Bassham, Gregory and Eric Bronson, eds. *Lord of the Rings and Philosophy: One Book to Rule Them All*. Peru, IL: Open Court, 2003.

Brown, J. *The Laboratory of the Mind: Thought Experiments in the Natural Sciences*. London: Routledge, 1991.

Chaires, Robert and Bradley Chilton, eds. *Star Trek Visions of Law and Justice*. Dallas, TX: Adios Press, 2003.

Clark, Stephen K. *How to Live Forever: Science Fiction and Philosophy*. London: Routledge, 1995.

Cohen, M. *Wittgenstein's Beetle and Other Classic Thought Experiments*. Oxford: Blackwell, 2005.

Cooper, R. "Thought Experiments." *Metaphilosophy* 36 (2005): pp. 328–347.

DePaul, M. andnd W. Ramsey, eds. *Rethinking Intuition: The Psychology of Intuition and Its Role in Philosophical Inquiry*. Rowman and Littlefield, 2002.

Easton, Thomas, ed. *Gedanken Fictions: Stories on Themes in Science, Technology, and Society*. Wildside Press, 2000.

*Gunn, James, ed. *The Road To Science Fiction*. Vols. 1–6. New York: The Scarecrow Press, 2002. The definitive collection of SF short stories from ancient Rome to the present.

Haggqvist, S. *Thought Experiments in Philosophy*. Stockholm: Almqvist & Wiksell International. 1996.

*Hanley, Richard. *Is Data Human? The Metaphysics of Star Trek*. Basic Books, 1998. Philosophical analysis of metaphysics and epistemology in the *Star Trek* multiverse.

Irwin, William, ed. *The Matrix and Philosophy: Welcome to the Desert of the Real*. Peru, IL: Open Court, October 2002.

Norton, J. "Are Thought Experiments Just What You Thought?" *Canadian Journal of Philosophy* 26 (1996): pp. 333–66.

*Phillips, Michael, ed. *Philosophy and Science Fiction*. Amherst, NY: Prometheus Books, 1984. Dated, though well chosen, SF short stories with especially philosophical themes.

Schick, Theodore and Lewis Vaughn. *How to Think about Weird Things: Critical Thinking for a New Age*. 3rd ed. McGraw-Hill, 2001.

*Sorenson, Roy. *Thought Experiments*. Oxford: Oxford University Press, 1992. Advanced, fascinating analysis of thought experiments from a pre-eminent philosopher.

Tittle, Peg. *What If . . . : Collected Thought Experiments in Philosophy*. New York: Pearson Longman, 2005.

Weldes, Jutta. *To Seek Out New Worlds: Exploring Links between Science Fiction and World Politics*. Palgrave Macmillan, 2003.

Yeffeth, Glenn, ed. *Taking the Red Pill: Science, Religion, and Philosophy in the Matrix*. Dallas, TX: BenBella Books, 2003.

1 Philosophical method and philosophical disagreement

Imagine traveling to a world inhabited by a few other intelligent species with alien forms of communication and reasoning. Some of their scientists attempt to extract sunbeams from cucumbers, architects attempt to build houses starting with the roof and working down, and linguists oppose all use of words. Some biologists are doing experiments on humans to determine whether, if people eat crackers with words like "apple" or "cat" written on them, those people will come to think about apples and cats. One professor is creating a "literary engine." This machine is made of countless blocks of wood. On each side of each piece of wood is a word, and, taken altogether, every word of their language is represented on the wood blocks. The professor has bound the blocks of wood together with wires. When he gives the word, each of his pupils grab an iron handle and thrusts it forward, imprinting some of the words on their blocks on a large paper. The goal of the research project is to attempt to cut the work out of writing and, by doing so, write all the books that can ever be written. These are only some of the pursuits of the scholars of the island of Balnibarbi, in Jonathan Swift's *Gulliver's Travels* (Part 3, Chapter 5).

These scholars advocate odd learning methods and unusual scientific experiments. We think that our methods of learning about the world are more likely to get us to the truth. But you may be surprised to know that, at the time, Jonathan Swift was using these passages about the scientists of Balnibarbi to satirize what in his day (*Gulliver's Travels* was published in 1726) was the leading international organization for scientists, the Royal Society. What differences separate our methods of acquiring knowledge from those of the scientists of Balnibarbi? Or from scientists in 1726?

When explored properly, this question illustrates a problem in philosophical method. Scientists, philosophers and theologians from one culture to another assume very different first principles, which leads each group in each culture to adopt different methods for seeking the truth. Each group then produces different answers to the same questions. Some people believe that God exists and governs the physical world; others believe that the physical world is merely an illusion; others the physical cosmos is the only thing that has ever existed, and that God doesn't exist; yet others believe that, though God doesn't exist, many little spirits do, and they inhabit nature. Only one of those sets of beliefs can be true at any one time.

Wait, is that right? If it is, it may appear as though by selecting one set of beliefs we must condemn the people who differ with us. After all, if we are right, then their fundamental beliefs are simply wrong. Perhaps instead of that, we can claim that all of these beliefs can be true at the same time—the atheist, the theist and the polytheist all have true religious beliefs.

Does truth work like that? If it doesn't, must we condemn others' beliefs? In this chapter we'll provide conceptual tools needed to answer these important questions. First, we will explain some techniques for constructing and evaluating philosophical arguments, the main currency of philosophical exchange. To evaluate arguments, we discern whether their **premises** are *true*. So we'll briefly explain what "true" means, and what it doesn't mean. In the speculations of the previous few paragraphs we crept up to the edge of a debate about **relativism**. Relativism is a family of theories that have in common a commitment to a theory of truth on which the truth of statements depends upon what people or societies believe those statements. We'll explain relativism and build some arguments that lead us to think that relativist theories are unsatisfying. All told, this chapter will provide you with theoretical and practical knowledge of philosophical method and debate.

After completing this chapter, you should be able to:

- Identify and describe **deductive arguments**
- Explain the differences between validity and soundness
- Explain how to analyze arguments and what makes some of them fallacious
- Begin to understand rationality and its importance in philosophical discussion
- Begin to understand the **correspondence theory of truth**
- Explain the thesis of relativism, the arguments for it and the problems with those arguments.

1.0 LOGIC AND ARGUMENTS

Unlike biology, astronomy, and psychology, philosophy does not have a standard methodology by which theories can be tested through observation or experiment. But philosophers—or at least, an important group of them to which we belong—have a distinctive method. Our approach has two components. First, premises in philosophical arguments are, when possible, informed by our scientific knowledge of the world. For example, when we discuss personal identity, we inform our philosophical arguments with truths about human psychology drawn from introspection and from psychology. Second, philosophical theories are to be supported by arguments. In each chapter of this book, we will be constructing arguments—often including arguments for premises within other arguments.

Each philosophical argument has a formal structure, just as every building has a foundation. Different types of building have different foundations, just as different arguments use different types of formal structure. We will focus on three types of argument, which we'll explain briefly. But first, to understand what an argument is, let's first describe *logic*.

Logic is a sub-discipline of philosophy dedicated to the study of rules and patterns of inference, and to formal relationships between statements. Logicians create a formal language of symbols that map onto statements in a natural language, like English. Often their goal is to use the formal language to identify logical relations of statements in the natural language. Other times logicians study the relations between statements within the formal systems they create. For example, suppose it is true that (i) *If aliens land on Earth, then some people will be afraid*, and that (ii) *aliens land on Earth*. Logical rules of inference entail a conclusion, (iii) *some people will be afraid*.

This is a deductive argument. A deductive argument is a set of statements, some of which, the premises, are thought to entail another, the conclusion. Premises *entail* a conclusion when, if the premises are true, the conclusion *must* be true. *Rules of inference* is a term that refers to patterns of logical structure indicating which conclusions can be drawn from which premises. Most (but not all) of the arguments we will discuss are deductive arguments. *Good* deductive arguments are said to be **valid**, which means that, *if* the premises are true, the conclusion must be true. If an argument is *invalid*, then, even if its premises are true, the conclusion might not be true.

I can validly conclude this practice argument with the statement (iii) *some people will be afraid* because (iii) follows validly from (i) and (ii). When presented with our practice argument, a logician formalizes the pair of statements so that A = aliens land on Earth and B = some people will be afraid. With this in hand, the argument itself can be formalized as follows: (i) if A, then B; (ii) A; (iii) therefore, B.

So far, so good. But before we go further, let's state a few more definitions. A *statement* is a sentence that expresses a proposition that is either true or false. An *argument* is a set of statements in which one is the conclusion and the others are premises. A *premise* is a statement used as evidence to support the conclusion. *Conclusions* are those statements supported by premises.

An appreciation for the logical form of arguments helps philosophers in the construction of other arguments. *If* statements (i) and (ii) are true, then (iii) must be true. Think about it: if is a fact that *if* aliens land on Earth, *then* some people will be afraid, and it is also a fact that aliens actually land on Earth, then it clearly follows that some people will be afraid. Why? *Because the logical form of this argument corresponds to a valid rule of inference.* In other words, *any* statements substituted in for A and B will yield a valid argument so long as the pattern—in this case:

(1.1)   If A, then B

(1.2)   A

(1.3)   Therefore, B

—remains the same.

Arguments frequently contain "conditional" statements like 1.1, which have an if–then structure. "Antecedent" refers to the if-clause and "consequent" refers to the then-clause.

Consider two examples of this logical pattern:

If the Ford Motor Company owns the dealership, then it sells Ford cars. The Ford Motor Company owns the dealership. So it sells Ford cars.

If the moon is made of green cheese, then there is a man up there eating it. The moon is made of green cheese. Therefore there is a man up there eating it.

You may wonder whether that last argument is valid.

Yes, it is. The premises are clearly false, but valid arguments can have false premises. This shows that merely valid arguments are unpersuasive. In addition to validity, philosophers want arguments that are **sound**. A sound argument is an argument that is both valid *and* that contains true premises. Remember that validity is only a formal property of arguments. In other words, "validity" refers to the structure and logical relationships of premises. It does not refer to the content or meaning of premises.

Formally stating arguments by enumerating their premises and clearly stating their conclusions helps us understand their structure. And understanding the structure of arguments enables us to take a big step toward successfully evaluating the argument's validity and soundness. Analyzing arguments in this way describes what we'll be up to in this book. Typically soundness is a greater concern than validity, but we'll identify some invalid arguments along the way.

Even though we will almost exclusively use deductive arguments in this book, philosophical argumentation is not limited to them. Philosophers often use inductive arguments. An **inductive argument** is a set of statements, some of which, the premises or assumptions, are intended to make the conclusion probable. The key difference between inductive and deductive arguments lies in the way the sets of premises are alleged to relate to the conclusion. Inductive arguments merely make their conclusions probable. If a statement is probable, then it is more likely than not to be true. It is not made certain. In a properly formed deductive argument, if the premises are true, then the conclusion must be true.

Last, **abductive arguments**, or arguments to the best explanation, form a third type. Abductive arguments typically begin with a puzzling or unique fact in need of explanation. Imagine a puddle of yellow liquid in the corner of a classroom and consider a few possible explanations of that fact. These might include: a squirrel crawled in through the open window and urinated; an extra-terrestrial being arrived on campus and left an important message to Earthlings encoded in the liquid; or perhaps a student in the last class spilled his apple juice, which pooled there. How can we assess the relative probability of these competing explanations?

Deduction is useless here since our rules of inference do not allow us to infer any one of these hypotheses from our data. Induction is also unhelpful since we haven't witnessed the formation of puddles of yellow liquid in this context before. On the basis of our general knowledge we must find reasons to eliminate certain hypotheses. Abductive arguments aim to identify the best explanation for the fact, where "best explanation" implicitly means most adequate and simplest.

Given the size of the puddle, the explanation according to which a squirrel created it is far-fetched since a squirrel bladder couldn't create a pool that large. The claim that an alien created the puddle in order to communicate with us is not nearly as simple as the hypothesis that a student spilled his apple juice. If the hypothesis about aliens were true, a number of other highly improbable facts would also have to be true, including that there are aliens, that they traveled to Earth and that they have a liquid-based medium of communication. In contrast, the last explanation accounts for the data with a number of familiar truths, including that students bring drinks to class all the time; many of those drinks are apple juice; and spills happen. For these reasons, the first two hypotheses seem to be less cogent than the last. This is abductive reasoning—a less definitive enterprise than inductive or deductive reasoning, but more useful in certain contexts.

1.1 FALLACIES

Many logical patterns yield invalid arguments. Consider this set of statements:

(1.4)   If Jones is stung by a bee, then Jones dies within the hour. (If A then B)

(1.5)   Jones dies within the hour. (B)

(1.6)   So Jones is stung by a bee. (A)

Is this valid, that is, if the premises—1.4 and 1.5—are true, must the conclusion—1.6—be true? No. Jones might be hit by a truck or die in a botched alien abduction. This pattern of reasoning is fallacious. It exemplifies an invalid rule of inference known as **affirming the consequent**. Affirming the consequent is a **fallacy** according to which one affirms the consequent of a conditional statement, then concludes that the antecedent must be true.

One helpful way to determine whether an argument is valid or invalid is by using your imagination to create a counterexample that shows the premises can be made true and the conclusion made false. This is what we've just done with Jones.

BOX 1.A: INSTRUCTIONS FOR ANALYZING AN ARGUMENT

1   When reading the argument, look for key words. Some words indicate premises, such as "since," "because," and some "if–then" statements. Keywords for conclusions include "therefore," "so," and "hence."

2   Attempt to state the conclusion, which should be the author's main point.
3   Reconstruct the premises of the argument by listing them in their inferential order.
4   Assess the argument by determining whether it is a valid argument. You can do this by evaluating whether, *on the supposition that the premises are true*, the conclusion must be true.
5   If the argument is valid, then you can further assess the argument by determining whether it is a sound argument. You can do this by evaluating whether as a matter of fact the premises are true.

Arguments using invalid rules of inference—like the Jones/bee argument—are fallacious. The most prevalent forms of fallacious reasoning include the following five.

A **false dilemma** is a logical fallacy in which too few explanations are proposed (often merely two) and all but one are eliminated, yielding only one explanation. For example, a politician might say, "This waste of government money can only be explained by bad decision-making on the part of the program director, or by theft within the leadership of the opposing party." But other explanations not considered may better explain the waste of government money. By limiting alternatives to these two, the politician prevents blame being cast upon his or her party. Putting issues into "black or white" terms signals the improper use of the term "or" that characterizes this fallacy.

A second fallacy, called the **slippery slope** fallacy, is an attempted refutation of a statement on the grounds that, if it is true, a sequence of increasingly unacceptable events follows. For example, opponents of the legalization of hemp, a crop grown for commercial use, argue that *if* the government permits farmers to grow hemp, *then* we will see the destruction of our culture through increased drug use among youth. That inference is based upon a number of loose linking statements: the hemp plant is a member of the same genus as marijuana, a plant with psychotropic effects on human beings; hemp plants could be used to grow marijuana; if people have greater access to growing marijuana, more youths will smoke it; if more youths smoke it, then surely it will destroy our culture. The connection between the antecedent and the consequent—between the "if–clause" and the "then–clause"—is tenuous and mere conjecture. Some of the linking statements are false. This is an improper use of conditional statements.

Complex question, a third fallacy, combines two otherwise unrelated statements into a single statement. The advocate of complex question arguments expects the reader to accept or reject both parts together, when in reality one is acceptable while the other is not. Suppose that the government institutes a population-wide electronic surveillance program under the auspices of the "war on terrorism." After you voice opposition to the government's actions, a friend says, "Are you against the government and for terrorism?" In this case, the complex question illegitimately uses the "and." Your opposition to the government's policy doesn't imply that you advocate terrorism.

Popular during election season, the **ad hominem fallacy** (a Latin term for "attacking the person") occurs when someone criticizes a person who is giving an argument rather than criticizing the argument itself. This fallacy takes many forms. The advocate of a philosophical idea can be ridiculed, found guilty by association, or be accused of hypocrisy. But none of those types of objection address the **justification** for the philosophical idea. For example, if a critic dismisses an argument for affirmative action on the grounds that the advocate of that argument is a member of a minority who stands to benefit by the practice, then the critic commits an ad hominem fallacy.

Begging the question, the fifth and final fallacy, refers to a situation in which the advocate of an argument presupposes the truth of the conclusion of that argument within the premises. To "presuppose" means "to believe something in advance, often without disclosing this belief." Advocates of arguments are often themselves unaware of their presuppositions. Sometimes the advocate of an argument restates the conclusion in the premises in a different form. Other instances of begging the question are more difficult to identify. Suppose you ask a friend why he believes in the Bible, and he responds by saying, "I believe in the Bible because it is the divinely inspired word of God." Being the curious person you are, you now ask him why he believes in God. To this he responds by saying, "I believe in God because the Bible says God exists." He has begged the question by presupposing the truth of her conclusion within her premises.

1.3 TRUTH AND RATIONALITY

Logic is one means by which philosophers (and others) think critically. Philosophers aim to construct sound arguments. Sound arguments contain true premises. So we want to explain what "truth" means. Let's define this term and explain the implications of our definition.

In philosophical contexts "true" is an adjective that modifies statements. Statements are sentences that can be affirmed or denied and have what philosophers call a "truth-value"—they are true or false. Questions and exclamations are not statements because they are not true or false. Examples of statements about philosophical topics include "God exists," "Time travel is conceptually possible," and "Libertarianism is the optimal theory of political governance." A *belief* is simply a statement that is affirmed by a person.

A statement is *true* if and only if the state of affairs expressed by the statement corresponds to the way that the world is. In other words, *truth* is a relationship between statements and reality. This simple definition belongs within the family of theories known as the *correspondence theories of truth*. This family derives from Aristotle, who said, "To say of what is that it is not, or of what is not that it is, is false, while to say of what is that it is, and of what is not that it is not, is true" (*Metaphysics* 1011b25). For example, "In 2007 Czechs drank more beer per capita than citizens of any other country" is true if and only if, in 2007, it is a fact that Czechs drank the most beer per capita than citizens of any other country. "I like cookie dough ice cream" is true if and only if it is a fact that I like cookie dough ice cream. Our definition of "true" applies to all sorts of statements, including mathematical propositions, statements about someone's emotional state, scientific claims, and philosophical theses.

With this definition in hand, we'll turn to our discussion of rationality. To be rational in believing something does not require that the belief be true. Likewise, if you believe something false, that alone does not make you irrational. This simple insight should guard against misguided condemnation of others for their beliefs.

BOX 1.B: NECESSARY AND SUFFICIENT CONDITIONS

Philosophers increase conceptual clarity about murky definitions with **necessary** and **sufficient conditions**. You already know a great deal about necessary and sufficient conditions, even if you don't know that you know. For example, a **necessary condition** upon watching television is that your eyes are open. You cannot watch TV without being able to see the TV, and you cannot see the TV if your eyes are closed. If and only if A is a necessary condition for B then the falsity or non-existence of A is guaranteed to bring about the falsity or non-existence of B. A **sufficient condition** for, say, something's being an airplane is being a Boeing 777. This is to say, if something is a Boeing 777, then it is an airplane. A is a sufficient condition for B if and only if the truth or existence of A is guaranteed to bring about the truth or existence of B.

Consider two relationships between necessary and sufficient conditions. First, A can be a necessary condition of B *without* also being a sufficient condition of B. Being male is a necessary condition for being a bachelor, but it is not sufficient since not all males are bachelors. Second, A can be a sufficient condition of B *without* also being a necessary condition of B. Being a citizen of the United Kingdom is sufficient for being human but it is not necessary since there exist humans who are not citizens of the U.K.

Typically, sufficient conditions are harder to give than are necessary conditions. For you to watch TV, it is necessary that (i) you are positioned so a TV is in your line of sight, and (ii) your eyes are open; (iii) the TV must be on and (iv) within a certain distance of the eye; more exotic still, (v) the ambient light in the space between you and the TV must not be so bright as to prevent the light waves it emits from reaching your retina, and so on. No doubt you can think of further conditions. This example shows that necessary and sufficient conditions, though useful, can be difficult to identify.

We're raising the topic of rationality because many people disagree sharply about some of their most important beliefs, and reflecting upon rationality can improve the communication of philosophical ideas. In social settings like the classroom and the workplace, individuals typically refrain from expressing their actual feelings about their fundamental commitments. For example, someone might believe that Christianity is true and base his life on that belief, while the person in the cubicle opposite him might believe it is not only false but also pernicious. They work alongside one another for years, studiously avoiding their differences through efforts of self-censorship. Religious beliefs tend to play a big role in determining one's moral beliefs, scientific beliefs, and beliefs about the purpose of life. Perhaps they each think that expressing a difference of opinion on some moral issue to the other person will cause an emotional reaction with negative consequences for their relationship. We have all experienced the feeling of irritation or insecurity when someone tells us that one doesn't believe what we are saying, or that one believes we have done something wrong.

Challenging ourselves to be honest *and* open with others about what we really believe is true has the power to bring together people of different backgrounds into an intellectual intimacy that yields the profound pleasures of knowing and being known by others. Unfortunately, in order to make a friend out of an acquaintance two people need to communicate what they actually feel, believe and fear. Of course, we aren't kindergarten teachers and we won't pretend that philosophical discussion always brings people together. The open exchange of ideas often prompts visceral disagreements and even violence.

Nonetheless, an understanding of the nature of rationality can eliminate some of the obstacles to fruitful philosophical exchange by allowing us to appreciate the basis for others' beliefs. In common English the word "rational" is used as an adjective to modify words referring to people and to beliefs. For our purposes the phrases "belief P is rational for person A" and "person A is rational to believe P" have the same meaning. We'll say that a belief P is *rational* for a person A only if, *if* the beliefs upon which A believes P are true, *then* A is likely to be true. In this sense it is possible that A is rational to believe P *even though P is highly unlikely to be true, or absurd, or even a necessary falsehood.* P might be rational in believing that people live on the moon or in believing that *pi* = 7. Nine-year-old Danny might rationally believe that *pi* is 7 due to his background beliefs that *older brothers typically tell the truth* and that *my older brother told me pi = 7.* So long as Danny has background beliefs that, if they are true, make P likely to be true, Danny is rational in believing P. It is a further question whether P's background beliefs are themselves rational and whether the target belief is actually likely to be true. (See §2.0 where we distinguish justification from rationality.)

Let's look at an example to better appreciate the utility of an understanding of rationality in action. Commander Adama captains *Battlestar Galactica*, a starship. He suddenly orders his pilot to make an unscheduled starjump, causing the battleship to leave the rest of the vulnerable fleet. Though Adama is known for making decisions without consulting civilian authorities, in this case he has put his ship and others' ships at great risk. This appears irrational to those who have observed the situation. Specifically, his belief that

> (1.10) It is best that I make an unscheduled starjump away from the fleet.

seems irrational to us. Suppose Adama's belief 1.10 is based upon advice from a trusted spy on an enemy Cylon vessel. Amongst Adama's background beliefs is this one, based on testimony from his spy:

> (1.11) My spy gives me good counterintelligence about the Cylons.

Last, he may assent to

> (1.12) My spy tells me that Cylons have pinpointed the location of *Battlestar Galactica* but that Cylons don't know the locations of the rest of the vessels in the fleet.

Given that Adama believes 1.10 on the basis of his prior belief of 1.11 and 1.12, we infer that our first impression was mistaken. 1.10 is rational for Adama because if Adama believes 1.11 and 1.12 to be true, then he has adequate reason for believing 1.10 to be true. Adama believes he needs to starjump *Battlestar Galactica* away from the fleet to protect the fleet. The rationality of Adama's belief in 1.10 is conditional upon his belief of 1.11 and 1.12.

When his officers on the *Battlestar Galactica* discover that he jumped the ship away from the fleet, no doubt many of them will criticize him and blame him for abandoning the other, very vulnerable ships. To these crew members, Adama made an irrational decision, but they lacked his background knowledge.

Let's analyze this conflict. First, we haven't defined "rational" so that only true beliefs are rational. False or unjustified beliefs, even wildly false and wildly unjustified beliefs, can be rational. Adama's belief 1.10, that his spy thinks it best that he move the ship away from the other unarmed spacecraft in the fleet, is rational. It also seems to be true. But suppose that a Cylon enemy murdered, and then replaced, his spy. If so, although 1.10 is rational for Adama, 1.10 is also false. It would be best if he did not move the *Galactica* away from the fleet.

Second, Adama's commitment to 1.10 is dependent on his assent to 1.11 and 1.12—his faith in the spy himself and his belief in the plausibility of the counterintelligence. The same is true for 1.11 and 1.12 themselves. The conditional rationality of a belief is produced by a complex and interconnected set of logical and psychological relationships between other beliefs within someone's belief system. The brief model of rationality on offer conforms to this fact. The rationality of 1.12 depends on Adama believing statements like "The Cylons have used a similar attack pattern before." Naturally Adama's beliefs about his spy depend for their rationality on beliefs about his spy's past performance, trustworthiness, and so on.

Third, rationality is a quantitative property: beliefs have more or less rationality depending upon the degree of rationality of the beliefs from which they stem and depending upon the number of those supporting beliefs.

But under what circumstances would Adama's belief 1.10 be *irrational*? The obvious answer is that, if he believes either the denial of 1.11 or the denial of 1.12, then 1.10

would be irrational. If Adama believes 1.11 and 1.12, is 1.10 therefore rational? Not necessarily. Consider the interconnected structure of Adama's belief system. If Adama believes that the only belief that makes 1.11 and 1.12 rational is "A little birdie told me so" then 1.11 and 1.12 are not rational for Adama. Less fancifully, Adama might believe "The Cylons have shown an aptitude for infiltrating human intelligence networks." Assume that this belief has a fairly high degree of rationality for Adama—perhaps Adama received confirmation of this belief from other war veterans. If so, then 1.11 and 1.12 aren't rational for Adama. He'd be irrational to believe 1.11 and 1.12 in light of this new evidence.

Adama's rationality in believing these statements does not imply that the statements are true or likely to be true. Some beliefs can be believed rational, and one can be within one's rights to believe them, even if they are false. The practical lesson to be learned from this section is this. People—including you—adopt beliefs on the basis of other beliefs in the background, and typically those background beliefs were placed there by family, school, culture or religious institutions. Those background beliefs almost always make the foreground beliefs conditionally probable, even if they are false.

So when you disagree with someone, first be mindful of the ways in which your beliefs are or, at some point, were inherited. If you wish to avoid offending someone with whom you disagree, treat them as persons by showing them respect and gently explain the reasons for your disagreement, giving them opportunities to respond and explain. Then *listen*, for they will have their own arguments that contain reasons for which they disagree with your commitments. Unfortunately, philosophical disagreements in professional philosophy have frequently become little more than opportunities to express clever arguments in witty ways. We hope that our readers use philosophical discussions as occasions for mutual understanding and genuine self-exploration, in addition to using them to improve the clarity and rigor of analytical thought.

1.4 RELATIVISM

In the context of a philosophical disagreement, you can hide the fact that you disagree, play naïve and continue with the rest of your day. You can aggressively state your point at the risk of alienating or offending your friend. You can engage in an open conversation that recognizes disagreement but treat your dialogue partner as worthy of respect.

A common response to philosophical disagreement is the uncritical relativist response, in which each person's morality is separate and distinct from the moral beliefs of everyone else. For example, a friend who works in your unit decides to use the company computers to run a little ebay business for an hour each workday. He doesn't tell your boss. You think what he is doing is wrong. But you also believe that doing this is right *for your friend*. In this way, you ease the situation by implicitly saying that running his side-business is right for him but it would be wrong for you.

Philosophical discussion of relativism is more complex than we relate in this chapter. The simplified version of relativism we discuss is the most common version. This version resembles Protagorus' famous dictum "Man is the measure of all things—of things that are, that they are, and of things that are not, that they are not." In other words, truth depends upon us.

Brief analysis of a few different statements gives an indication of how versions of relativism can come about. Statements like "garlic tastes good to me" are in fact relative to a standard. When I utter "garlic tastes good to me" I implicitly invoke my own individual gustatory preferences as the standard. If I enjoy the taste of garlic, then that statement is subjectively true for me. But when Sam utters the statement, it may be false for him. According to our theory of what makes a statement true, the statement "garlic tastes good to me" is true if and only if it is a fact that garlic does indeed taste good to me. First-person statements of preference are *subjective*. As that term indicates, the *subject* uttering the sentence plays an important role in the truth of the statement. **Subjective statements** are those statements whose truth depends upon the statement's correspondence to facts about the utterer's state of mind. On this definition of "subjective statement," those statements conform to our correspondence theory. However, subjective statements stand apart from the majority of statements.

The majority of statements are *objective*. This term refers to statements whose truth does not depend upon facts found within the speaker's own mind. "14 = 22 – 8," "I was born on November 1st, 1982" and "Evolution has occurred on Earth" are **objective statements** that are true or made according to facts that are independent of what the speaker of those statements believes about them. Notice that I might lie about the date of my birth. I might even do so so frequently as to convince myself I'm not as old as I am. But that does not make my belief that "I was born on November 1st, 1982" true.

Subjective statements are not always true. You can be wrong about the truth of statements whose truth depends upon your thoughts and desires. For example, you might say that garlic tastes good to you even though it does not. Perhaps you've only convinced yourself that it does because every meal your dad ever cooks for you includes lots of garlic, and you are determined to enjoy it.

This fact illustrates the difference between the subjectivity of statements and the relativity of statements. A statement is *relative* if it is true whenever a person or a group believes it is true. **Relativism** is the theory that sets of statements are true whenever a person or group believes them to be true. Obviously many statements are subjectively true, as our garlic example illustrates. The truth of a great many (subjective) statements depends upon the statement's correspondence to facts within the subject's mind. But it is not obvious that there are sets of statements whose truth depends upon whether a person or a group *believes* that the statement is true.

A statement like "evolution has occurred on Earth" is not made false because I believe it is false, nor is it made false because the people I hang around with all believe it is false. It isn't relative. (Of course, a small class of tricky statements is relative. The statement "I believe that evolution has occurred on Earth" is made true by the fact that I do believe that evolution has occurred on Earth.) Most relativists appeal to moral statements to make their case. An implicit commitment to a form of moral relativism is at the root of comments like "I know that this guy in my unit at work is running his ebay store on the job, but that's his business. It is right for him, but I'd never do that."

This type of remark exemplifies **individual relativism**, which states that the truth of statements depends on whether or not the subject believes they are true. Truth becomes relative to a single person. **Group relativism** is the thesis that the truth of my statements depend on whether the group to which I belong believes they are true. The group that serves as the truth-making standard might be any group—sociological, economic, ethnic, or religious—of which I am a member. For example, you might hear someone say, "For Christians, God exists and Jesus is his son, but not for me." This means that "God exists" is true for Christians but it is not true for the speaker. In addition to distinguishing between local and group forms of relativism, ethical relativism forms another distinct type. This is the thesis that all statements about rightness and wrongness are relative to what I believe. Ethical relativism implies that if I believe that lying is morally wrong, then the statement "lying is morally wrong" is true for me. This individualistic form of relativism is often paired with *cultural relativism*. Cultural relativism implies that, if the majority of people in my culture believes "genital mutilation is morally permissible," then it is morally permissible for members of my culture. Likewise, if the majority of members in your culture believes that it is not morally permissible, then it is not morally permissible for members of your culture.

In the next section we're going to present arguments for and against relativism. The sum of our discussion yields the conclusion that relativism is false and its support misleading.

1.5 THE MORAL DISAGREEMENT ARGUMENT FOR RELATIVISM

Support for relativism comes from considerations drawn from facts about cultural differences, from a concern for tolerance, and from the nature of language. As with philosophical theories, one endorses the theory in part because of the reasons and arguments on its behalf and in part because of non-rational factors. For example, many people are drawn to relativism because they are motivated to be kind and tolerant to others, which is a noble motive to endorse a theory. We'll look at these motivations to assess whether they oblige us to endorse relativism. Let's use the group form of ethical relativism as a running example.

Different cultures advocate different moral codes. The practice of female circumcision, a lightning rod for debate in years past, illustrates the ethical relativist's point of view. In some Middle Eastern and sub-Saharan African cultures, girls become women in the eyes of the culture when all or part of their clitoris and/or labia are removed or surgically modified in a coming-of-age ceremony. In addition to pain during the procedure, the recipient of such a procedure will experience pain during sexual intercourse and an increased risk of health problems to mother and child during childbirth. However, in these cultures female genital mutilation contributes to cultural identity and womanhood, and serves as an important rite of passage. The World Health Organization estimates that, as of 2006, over 100 million women alive have received this procedure, most of whom were under 10 years old at the time.[1]

Many different groups, for example the group composed by the residents of Montana, consider this practice morally impermissible, whereas the majority of people in Mali think it is. A behavior considered abhorrent and awful in one culture might not only be morally permitted in another culture, but be obligatory or praiseworthy in another culture. Human beings differ widely in their moral beliefs. The unusual case of Khalid Adem highlights this clash of moral differences across cultures. In 2001 Khalid, an Ethiopian immigrant to the U.S., performed this ritual on his daughter in his home in the suburbs of Atlanta. He was tried and convicted for aggravated battery and cruelty to children. He was sentenced to 10 years in prison and another five on probation for performing an action that, in his home country, he might have been shunned and ridiculed for *not* performing.[2]

To appreciate the relativity of the morality surrounding this issue, turn your attention to male circumcision. Male circumcision refers to the cutting of all or part of the foreskin from the penis. Doctors in the West performing male circumcisions typically do not use anesthetic.[3] In addition to the pain of the procedure, controversial studies suggest decreased pleasure during intercourse is an effect. Many Europeans believe male circumcision is gruesome and harms the body and mind of young infants irrevocably. Others counter that health benefits achieved through male circumcision and/or that the religious importance of the ritual of male circumcision outweighs the pain of the process.

So we have a situation in which the majority of Group A practices male circumcision but condemns the practice of female circumcision in Group B. And the majority of Group B practices female circumcision but condemns the practice of male circumcision in Group A.

This situation gives rise to a **moral disagreement argument for relativism**. Such divergence in systems of moral beliefs held by various groups of people indicates that a moral statement is true in some cultures and false in others. In Mali it is true that "female circumcision is morally permissible" while that same statement is false in Montana. In Montana it is true that "male circumcision is morally permissible" while that same statement is false in Mali. From the fact of moral disagreement across cultures the relativist proceeds to a conclusion about value. Is the relativist correct that the fact of moral disagreement entails that the thesis of relativism is true?

The relativist argues as follows:

(1.13) There is no universal agreement across cultures about which moral statements are true.

(1.14) The best explanation of 1.13 is that the truth or falsity of moral statements is relative to cultures.

(1.15) Therefore, the truth or falsity of moral statements is relative to cultures.

First, does the conclusion follow if the premises are true? Second, are the premises true?

As to the first question, the conclusion appears too strong. According to 1.14 the thesis of ethical relativism best explains the fact of empirical disagreement. But because an hypothesis best explains a phenomenon, it doesn't follow that the hypothesis is true. As anyone who has watched a few crime dramas knows, what appear to be the best explanations frequently turn out false. To capture this feature of the argument, we could rewrite the conclusion as:

(1.15′) Therefore, probably, the truth or falsity of moral statements is relative to cultures.

This change clarifies the status of this argument. It is not a deductive argument, but rather an argument to the best explanation—an abductive argument. With the conclusion suitably weakened in 1.15′, the argument is able to avoid one major problem. Having said that, though, the degree of probability established by the premises is open to question.

On to our second question: are these premises true? To answer this, we need to insure that we understand the meaning of each premise. 1.13 seems to be true—in fact there are wide disagreements about which moral statements are believed to be true across cultures. But notice some ambiguities about the logical scope of 1.13. This premise could mean either that

(1.13′) The majority in all cultures disagree about the truth or falsity of all moral statements. (strong version); or

(1.13″) The majority in all cultures disagree about the truth or falsity of most moral statements. (weak version)

Some ethical relativists argue as though the strong form stated in 1.13′ is true, but anthropological studies only vindicate the weak version in 1.13′. A select handful of moral statements appears throughout extant cultures, including injunctions against murdering the innocent and advocacy of ethical reciprocity. By adopting the weaker 1.13′, the ethical relativist's case on behalf of the differences between cultural moral codes is weakened.

Opponents of relativism object to 1.14 by arguing that the fact that groups disagree about the truth of moral statements isn't sufficient reason to infer that moral statements are true for one group and not for another. Other explanations are at hand. Suppose that the majority of people in the Xong culture believe that murder is morally permissible whereas the majority in the Blong culture believe that murder is not morally permissible. One explanation of this disagreement is the hypothesis that either the Xong or the Blong believe something false. Taking a different tack, another explanation is that the majorities in the Xong and Blong cultures are false majorities; in other words, those majorities only believe what they do via coercion by a deceptive leader for example.

Think again of objective statements, which provide the clearest case against the inference to 1.14. Schoolchildren mistakenly believe false arithmetical statements. Because someone believes $1 + 1 = 3$ doesn't make it the case that $1 + 1 = 3$. The same is true of groups: because the majority of a group believes $1 + 1 = 3$ does not make it true. If we were to reformulate the argument so it was about mathematical statements rather than moral statements, it would be transparently unsound. If ethical relativists believe that ethical statements differ from mathematical statements in special ways, they must show why this is so (and why that is relevant to the argument at hand).

1.6   THE ARGUMENT FROM TOLERANCE FOR RELATIVISM

The second motivation for relativism stems from an **argument from tolerance** for different points of view held by other individuals and groups. A person exemplifies the vice of *intolerance* by acting, in word or deed, in a way that unjustifiably condemns others. Relativists allege that one becomes intolerant if one doesn't adopt the relativist thesis. Being intolerant is considered immoral. So, to be a moral person, one must endorse relativism.

BOX 1.C: *STAR TREK: ENTERPRISE*, "DEAR DOCTOR"

The central guiding principle of human exploration as envisioned in *Star Trek* is the "Prime Directive," which is a principle of non-interference: Starfleet vessels that encounter civilizations with significantly less technological sophistication than their own are required not to interfere in their development. If interference occurs, the human vessel must reverse or minimize the cultural and technological contamination. In effect, the Prime Directive is an official endorsement of a type of tolerance principle. This is because the purpose of the Prime Directive is to enable civilizations to develop on their own terms.

The principle behind the Prime Directive has been the focus of numerous *Star Trek* episodes, which raise questions for Starfleet personnel. A controversial application of the Prime Directive occurs in "Dear Doctor," an episode of the *Star Trek* series *Enterprise* (season 1, episode 13). The human vessel *Enterprise* encounters a planet with two humanoid species: the Valakians and the Menk. The ship's doctor, Dr. Phlox, is asked by the Valakians, the more developed and dominant of the two species, to save them from an epidemic that threatens their very existence. Doctor Phlox finds a cure for the epidemic but, as a result of his research, discovers that the Menk have the evolutionary potential to overtake the Valakians as the planet's most intelligent and dominant species.

Phlox presents this dilemma to the captain. If the cure is administered, then the continued presence of the Valakians will prevent the Menk from reaching their evolutionary potential. If it is not, then billions of Valakians will suffer the painful, lethal effects of the disease and their species may become extinct, *but* the Menk will then be able to reach their evolutionary potential.

The doctor argues that to administer the cure is to interfere with the course of nature and evolution, which would be morally wrong. Thus the captain is persuaded by the doctor, and the crew refrain from administering the cure to the Valakians.

Is this decision morally justified? If it is, it surely is not justified by the reasoning given by the doctor in the episode. Consider: if this were reason to refrain from administering the cure to the Valakians, it would also be reason to refrain from administering medical treatment to anyone, including members of his own crew. Medicine is in the business of preventing and curing the effects of natural, though harmful, micro-organisms, among other things. If the decision made by the captain in consultation with the doctor is not justified by this odd view of the sacredness of evolution, then can it be justified at all? If you disagree with Phlox, by what reasons would you attempt to persuade him that you are correct? Lastly, where is Captain Kirk when you need him? (Even better, where is Spock?)

But in the hands of the relativist, "intolerance" is often used with different definitions. Consider these examples of intolerance:

(1.16) Forcibly compelling individuals of other cultures to forsake their beliefs and practices and adopt beliefs and practices of another culture, for example conquistadors' behavior toward the native peoples of Central America in the sixteenth century.

(1.17) Failure to show respect for the beliefs and practices of individuals and groups, for example visiting a mosque without removing one's shoes.

(1.18) Believing that some beliefs held by individuals or by other cultures are false, for example holding that the animist beliefs of the !Kung tribe are false.

Of the three definitions, clearly acting in accord with the first sense of "intolerance" results in immoral behavior. 1.16 refers to coercion through the implementation of physical force, a morally indefensible practice.

However, actions described in 1.16 and 1.17 aren't always immoral. This is the first problem with the argument from tolerance. We can find cases in which using physical force described in 1.16 is prima facie (on first glance) morally justified. In effect, the Allied forces in World War II were forcibly compelling the Axis forces to forsake their cultures' ethnocentric beliefs and their practice of genocide. If the relativist objects to *every* instance of coercion through physical force, he makes a sweeping assertion. Surely the Allied forces were morally justified attempting to defeat the Axis powers (even if certain of their actions, such as dropping atomic bombs, were unjustified).

The form of intolerance in 1.17 also may or may not be immoral depending on how disrespect for another culture is shown. 1.17 refers not to physical coercion but to disrespect and cultural insensitivity. The relativist cannot argue that because immoral people advocate a given philosophical position that philosophical position is therefore false. This inference commits the ad hominem fallacy. Simply because a doctrine is associated with a disreputable person is no reason to think that the doctrine is false. (After all, evil people believe that Earth orbits the sun!) The relativist hasn't shown that even the strong forms of alleged intolerance in 1.16 and 1.17 are always immoral.

The second philosophical problem with this argument is more damaging to the relativist's cause. To put the problem concisely, someone who denies the relativist thesis isn't committed to either of the forms of alleged intolerance in 1.16 or 1.17. Non-relativists are only committed to the alleged form of intolerance in 1.18. By denying the relativist thesis, non-relativists are neither forcing people to believe what they believe nor actively disrespecting the social customs of other cultures.

So is 1.18 actually intolerant? It is difficult to understand why it would be. While some might intolerantly *convey* their belief that others' viewpoints are false, merely *believing* others' beliefs are false is not intolerant. When a boss corrects an employee's error on a legal document, the boss, far from being intolerant, is helping the employee.

I believe that spirits don't inhabit trees. In other words, I deny animism—the theory on which non-living objects are inhabited by spirits or souls. I am rational to deny the truth of animism. Merely by asserting that spirits don't inhabit trees, I am not *ipso facto* (by that fact) intolerant of animists. If I were intolerant of animists merely for believing that their doctrines are false, then presumably they would be intolerant of me for believing that my denial of animism is false. Since the non-relativist is only committed to 1.18, it follows that the non-relativist position is not intolerant.

The relativist worries that if he believes that the worldviews of other cultures are mistaken, then he implicitly claims that members of that other culture are his inferiors. But he needn't believe that members of other cultures are his inferiors simply because he believes that their beliefs are false. Our discussion of rationality assists in showing why. Members of cultures with other belief-systems, including animist belief-systems, can be rational in believing what they believe. Conditional on their background beliefs, belief in animism is often rational. If all the elders in the group tell me that there are spirits in trees and I know that the elders are very knowledgeable about many matters about which I am ignorant then, all other things being equal, I am rational in believing spirits inhabit trees. This provides the non-relativist with an explanation for why people in groups that have false beliefs are rational in believing them.

A theory of rationality is a better means to build tolerance than is a theory of relativism. A closely related point marks the third, more abstract problem associated with the relativist's appeal to tolerance. Ironically, the relativist's own position is less able to accommodate the virtue of tolerance than is the non-relativist's. According to group ethical relativism, the moral beliefs of any local group are true for them, even if they differ widely from what my group believes. The majority of Serbs in Bosnia once believed that "Muslims living there should be killed." The Serbs acted on this belief. Between 1999 and 2001 many mass graves were unearthed revealing gruesome evidence of Serbian acts of genocide against the local Muslim population.

According to the relativist, the standard by which the truth or falsity of the statement "Muslims should be killed" is determined by what the majority of Serbs believe. In this way the relativist has no way to object to these immoral actions of the Serbs. The relativist can't describe that belief, and the actions resulting from it, as immoral because the relativist from Group A has no philosophical means through which to dispute the moral judgment of the majority of Group B.

Here's another way to make this point. If the relativist from Group A recommends to the Serbs in Group B that they ought to practice tolerance to the Serbs, her recommendation is itself relative to her Group A culture. Her statement that "Serbs should not kill Moslems" is true only if the majority in her own Group A affirm it. It is not true in Serbia, where the majority repudiates it, because the relativist denies that there are any moral values independent of culture.

The objectivist and non-relativist who advocates a correspondence theory of truth can claim that this belief is objectively false and that genocide is immoral, even if it is the will of the majority in some groups. According to the objectivist, tolerance is virtuous independently of what people believe about tolerance. The objectivist believes that the truth or falsity of ethical statements does not depend upon facts found within the speaker's mind or, as in the case of group relativism, speakers' minds. The virtue of tolerance is a virtue for *all* cultures or individuals—even to those that are intolerant.

1.7 REDUCTIO AD ABSURDUM ARGUMENT AGAINST ETHICAL RELATIVISM

Now that we've analyzed considerations on behalf of relativism, let's consider a philosophical problem with the relativist thesis itself. These problems are separate from problems associated with the *justification* of the thesis.

We have the core of this problem before us already. One can mount a **reductio ad absurdum argument** against relativism. A reductio ad absurdum argument shows that a thesis implies absurd or irrational statements that render the original thesis false. Most of us believe that "it is wrong to torture innocent children." The group relativist says that if "it is right to torture innocent children" is asserted by the majority of a culture, it is true in that culture. The absurdity is that such a statement could ever be true. Any theoretical position that implies "it is right to torture innocent children" is true must itself be false.

Here's a concrete example of this argument. Joseph Stalin took control of the Soviet Union in the 1920s and led it in accordance with communist policies until his death in 1953. During this time he had killed an estimated 8 million people minimum, many of whom were executed because they endorsed (or were thought to have endorsed) political views opposed to his own. Stalin's governmental policies were immoral. But according to relativism, we lack a means through which to conclude that Stalin's governance was immoral. This is fodder for our reductio ad absurdum argument on the grounds that our conviction that Stalin's Soviet regime was so obviously immoral, that any moral theory that denies that belief is itself incorrect.

1.8 SUMMARY

In this chapter we have introduced tools of logical analysis and offered examples of good and bad reasoning. This was accomplished by a study of statements, and of the nature of deductive, inductive and abductive arguments. We argued that people can be rational in believing what they believe even though they do not have valid, sound arguments for their beliefs. The rationality of a belief is dependent upon the background beliefs to which a person assents.

This put us in a position to understand the difficult concept of truth as correspondence to reality. After seeing that correspondence theory can be applied to mind-independent or mind-dependent realities, we tackled relativism. Relativism asserts that statements—on a specific topic or for a specific group—are true because they correspond with facts that depend upon minds. Ethical relativism is supported by a number of arguments, including arguments from moral disagreement and from tolerance. We criticized these arguments and offered a few further arguments against ethical relativism.

This chapter raises a number of further questions about philosophical method, rationality, truth and relativism. Here's a conundrum about rationality in the history of science. In the early 1600s, scientists began to gather data that showed that Earth was not in the center of the solar system. This data was incomplete, confused, gathered with poor lab equipment and countered the dominant worldview. The statement "the sun is in the center of the solar system" was highly improbable given the background beliefs of the scientists themselves. The conundrum is this: the scientists who first gathered this data and first held to a heliocentric solar system appear to be irrational, despite the fact that they were correct and everyone else was incorrect! Is that an appropriate way to describe the beliefs of those scientists? Can you find a better way to describe the nature of rationality? Scientists throughout history have been in the business of proposing theories, refuting them, proposing new theories to replace the old, refuting those and so on. Consider any unifying theory of quantum physics today, for example, string theory. Is it rational for us to endorse string theory, given the fact that it is probably going to be proven false with further advances in science?

Our discussion of truth opens up a field of further questions too. Is the statement "unicorns have horns" true or false? Attempts to answer silly questions like this can reveal fascinating philosophical problems. In some conversational contexts it appears true and in others it appears false. We might interpret "unicorns have horns" so it means "there are unicorns and they have horns." Since it is a fact that there are no unicorns, it follows that this statement is false according to the correspondence theory. This interpretation clarifies the way in which a child can speak falsely when saying "unicorns have horns." A second interpretation of the statement uses the term "unicorn" to mean "an imaginary creature with the body of a horse and a horn." It is a fact that imaginary beings with bodies of horses and horns are called "unicorns." This definition makes the statement "unicorns have horns" a true statement about mythological beings.

Are both of these interpretations incorrect? Switch gears and imagine chemists creating the next man-made element on the periodic table, which will have an atomic number of 111. As they talk in the lab, they call this future element "elevenium," meaning simply an "element with atomic number 111." In this case the term "elevenium" clearly conveys something—we know exactly what these chemists mean—and yet there is nothing in reality (yet) to which "elevenium" corresponds. So are the chemists' sentences true or false?

Finally, consider relativism once again. Though we've argued against the relativist thesis, mysteries about the truth of ethical statements remain. "Murder is morally wrong" is true, but how? If we're right that the correspondence theory explains how it is true, clearly the way it is true differs sharply from the way "Earth orbits the sun" is true. The wrongness of murder cannot be discovered by scientific investigation, and this has led to many different explanations of the truth of ethical statements. Philosophers say "murder is wrong" doesn't express a proposition but rather expresses an emotion translatable as "murder: boo hoo!" Others stick to their guns by arguing that "murder is wrong" because there are moral facts to which that statement corresponds, but these philosophers must explain how these moral facts exist. But they can defend their position by appeal to a comparison with arithmetic. "1 + 1 = 2" is just as obviously true as is "murder is wrong," but its *truthmakers*—the facts that make it true—are just as obscure. Scientists can't find the number one in physical reality. So, what are we to do?

1.9 ABOUT THE READINGS

This chapter has three supplementary readings. The first is a science fiction story, the second is from the history of philosophy and the third is a contemporary philosophy article.

In our science fiction reading, "Kirinyaga," by Michael Resnick, a grave dilemma faces authorities that govern a new orbital colony. At a distant point in Earth's future, the world government grants the right to colonize new worlds to those cultural and ethnic groups that have experienced the most discrimination in the past. The Kikuyu people, from present-day Kenya, take this opportunity and create a new settlement far off in space. Led by a shaman named Koriba, the Kikuyu settle on an artificial habitat and establish a community in accordance with their traditional customs. "Maintenance," the oversight organization at this outpost, doesn't interfere with the Kikuyu . . . until Koriba's fateful decision to violate Maintenance protocols in the name of Kikuyu cultural values. This decision strains relations with Maintenance and creates internal strife within the Kikuyu community that threatens to turn into war. Resnick proposes for his readers' reflection the question: Are moral statements believed by the shaman Koriba true because he says they are, or is their truth dependent upon something else?

Plato takes a different tack in his famous thought experiment known by the name "The Ring of Gyges," which occurs in his *Republic*. The *Republic* is a book about the nature of justice in the individual and in society. It is written in the form of a discussion. The debate begins with a conversation between Socrates and others about whether the just life is also the best life. Socrates believes it is, but others, including Glaucon, doubt that it is. Glaucon argues that the description of certain behavior as "just" and "unjust" is produced when the weak in a society attempt to tame the strong. In his view, "justice" is a social construction. He argues that, if someone could avoid detection, that person would use this power to advance his own interests at the expense of others. So Glaucon relates a story about a ring of invisibility used for no good. This story gets a fantastic retelling in J. R. R. Tolkein's *Lord of the Rings*. Gollum, the former owner of an invisibility ring, appears as a mere shadow of his self because he has evidently been corrupted by using the ring. Tolkein seems strongly inclined toward Socrates' answer about the connection between the life of justice and the good life (but should he be?). H. G. Wells in *The Invisible Man* also explores issues about morality through this thought experiment.

In our final reading we learn a Japanese word, **tsujigiri**, which means "to try out one's new sword on a chance wayfarer." In "On Trying Out One's New Sword," Mary Midgley reflects on the samurai practice this word describes. She draws lessons about what she dubs "moral isolationism," which is the thesis that critical moral judgments cannot be made about other cultures. She offers a series of arguments that aim to show not only that moral isolationism is false, but that the position is self-refuting and internally inconsistent. Since she sets her argument in a cultural context, she reflects on the philosophical importance of the historical inheritance of moral commitments from one cultural to the next.

1.10 "KIRINYAGA," BY MICHAEL RESNICK

(AUGUST 2129)

In the beginning, Ngai lived alone atop the mountain called Kirinyaga. In the fullness of time He created three sons, who became the fathers of the Ivlaasai, the Mamba, and the Kikuyu races, and to each one He offered a spear, a bow, and a digging stick. The Maasai chose the spear, and was told to tend herds on the vast savannah. The Kamba chose the bow, and was sent to the dense forests to hunt for game. But Gikuyu, the first Kikuyu, knew that Ngai loved the earth and the seasons, and chose the digging stick. To reward him for this Ngai not only taught him the secrets of the seed and the harvest, but gave him Kirinyaga, with its holy fig tree and rich lands.

The sons and daughters of Gikuyu remained on Kirinyaga until the white man came and took their lands away, and even when the white man had been banished they did not return, but chose to remain in the cities, wearing Western clothes and using Western machines and living Western lives. Even I, who am a *mundumugu*—a witch doctor—was born in the city. I have never seen the lion or the elephant or the rhinoceros, for all of them were extinct before my birth; nor have I seen Kirinyaga as Ngai meant it to be seen, for a bustling, over-crowded city of three million inhabitants covers its slopes, every year approaching closer and closer to Ngai's throne at the summit. Even the Kikuyu have forgotten its true name, and now know it only as Mount Kenya.

To be thrown out of Paradise, as were the Christian Adam and Eve, is a terrible fate, but to live beside a debased Paradise is infinitely worse. I think about them frequently, the descendants of Gikuyu who have forgotten their origin and their traditions and are now merely Kenyans, and I wonder why more of them did not join with us when we created the Eutopian world of Kirinyaga.

True, it is a harsh life, for Ngai never meant life to be easy; but it is also a satisfying life. We live in harmony with our environment, we offer sacrifices when Ngai's tears of compassion fall upon our fields and give sustenance to our crops, we slaughter a goat to thank him for the harvest.

Our pleasures are simple: a gourd of pombe to drink, the warmth of a *boma* when the sun has gone down, the wail of a newborn son or daughter, the footraces and spear-throwing and other contests, the nightly singing and dancing.

Maintenance watches Kirinyaga discreetly, making minor orbital adjustments when necessary, assuring that our tropical climate remains constant. From time to time they have subtly suggested that we might wish to draw upon their medical expertise, or perhaps allow our children to make use of their educational facilities, but they have taken our refusal with good grace, and have never shown any desire to interfere in our affairs.

Until I strangled the baby.

It was less than an hour later that Koinnage, our paramount chief, sought me out.

"That was an unwise thing to do, Koriba," he said grimly.

"It was not a matter of choice," I replied. "You know that."

"Of course you had a choice," he responded. "You could have let the infant live." He paused, trying to control his anger and his fear. "Maintenance has never set foot on Kirinyaga before, but now they will come."

"Let them," I said with a shrug. "No law has been broken."

"We have killed a baby," he replied. "They will come, and they will revoke our charter."

I shook my head. "No one will revoke our charter."

"Do not be too certain of that, Koriba," he warned me. "You can bury a goat alive, and they will monitor us and shake their heads and speak contemptuously among themselves about our religion. You can leave the aged and the infirm out for the hyenas to eat, and they will look upon us with disgust and call us godless heathens. But I tell you that killing a newborn infant is another matter. They will not sit idly by; they will come."

"If they do, I shall explain why I killed it," I replied calmly.

"They will not accept your answers," said Koinnage. "They will not understand."

"They will have no choice but to accept my answers," I said. "This is Kirinyaga, and they are not permitted to interfere."

"They will find a way," he said with an air of certainty. "We must apologize and tell them that it will not happen again."

"We will not apologize," I said sternly. "Nor can we promise that it will not happen again."

"Then, as paramount chief, *I* will apologize."

I stared at him for a long moment, then shrugged. "Do what you must do," I said.

Suddenly I could see the terror in his eyes.

"What will you do to me?" he asked fearfully.

"I? Nothing at all," I said. "Are you not my chief?" As he relaxed, I added: "But if I were you, I would beware of insects."

"Insects?" he repeated. "Why?"

"Because the next insect that bites you, be it spider or mosquito or fly, will surely kill you," I said. "Your blood will boil within your body, and your bones will melt. You will want to scream out your agony, yet you will be unable to utter a sound." I paused. "It is not a death I would wish on a friend," I added seriously.

"Are we not friends, Koriba?" he said, his ebony face turning an ash-gray.

"I thought we were," I said. "But my friends honor our traditions. They do not apologize for them to the white man."

"I will not apologize!" he promised fervently. He spat on both his hands as a gesture of his sincerity.

I opened one of the pouches I kept around my waist and withdrew a small polished stone from the shore of our nearby river. "Wear this around your neck," I said, handing it to him, "and it shall protect you from the bites of insects."

"Thank you, Koriba!" he said with sincere gratitude, and another crisis had been averted.

We spoke about the affairs of the village for a few more minutes, and finally he left me. I sent for Mali, the infant's mother, and led her through the ritual of purification, so that she might conceive again. I also gave her an ointment to relieve the pain in her breasts, since they were heavy with milk. Then I sat down by the fire before my *boma* and made myself available to my people, settling disputes over the ownership of chickens and goats, and supplying charms against demons, and instructing my people in the ancient ways.

By the time of the evening meal, no one had a thought for the dead baby. I ate alone in my *boma*, as befitted my status, for the *mundumugu* always lives and eats apart from his people. When I had finished I wrapped a blanket around my body to protect me from the cold and walked down the dirt path to where all the other *bomas* were clustered. The cattle and goats and chickens were penned up for the night, and my people, who had slaughtered and eaten a cow, were now singing and dancing and drinking great quantities of *pombe*. As they made way for me, I walked over to the caldron and took a drink of *pombe*, and then, at Kanjara's request, I slit open a goat and read its entrails and saw that his youngest wife would soon conceive, which was cause for more celebration. Finally the children urged me to tell them a story.

"But not a story of Earth," complained one of the taller boys. "We hear those all the time. This must be a story about Kirinyaga."

"All right," I said. "If you will all gather around, I will tell you a story of Kirinyaga." The youngsters all moved closer. "This," I said, "is the story of the Lion and the Hare." I paused until I was sure that had everyone's attention, especially that of the adults. "A hare was chosen by his people to be sacrificed to a lion, so that the lion would not bring disaster to their village. The hare might have run away, but he knew that sooner or later the lion would catch him, so instead he sought out the lion and walked right up to him, and as the lion opened his mouth to swallow him, the hare said, 'I apologize, Great Lion.'

"'For what?' asked the lion curiously.

"'Because I am such a small meal,' answered the hare. 'For that reason, I brought honey for you as well.'

"'I see no honey,' said the lion.

"'That is why I apologized,' answered the hare. 'Another lion stole it from me. He is a ferocious creature, and says that he is not afraid of you.'

"The lion rose to his feet. 'Where is this other lion?' he roared.

"The hare pointed to a hole in the earth. 'Down there,' he said, 'but he will not give you back your honey.'

"'We shall see about that!' growled the lion.

"He jumped into the hole, roaring furiously, and was never seen again, for the hare had chosen a very deep hole indeed. Then the hare went home to his people and told them that the lion would never bother them again."

Most of the children laughed and clapped their hands in delight, but the same young boy voiced his objection.

"That is not a story of Kirinyaga," he said scornfully. "We have no lions here."

"It *is* a story of Kirinyaga," I replied. "What is important about the story is not that it concerned a lion and a hare, but that it shows that the weaker can defeat the stronger if he uses his intelligence."

"What has that to do with Kirinyaga?" asked the boy.

"What if we pretend that the men of Maintenance, who have ships and weapons, are the lion, and that the Kikuyu are the hares?" I suggested. "What shall the hares do if the lion demands a sacrifice?"

The boy suddenly grinned. "Now I understand! We shall throw the lion down a hole!"

"But we have no holes here," I pointed out.

"Then what shall we do?"

"The hare did not know that he would find the lion near a hole," I replied. "Had he found him by a deep lake, he would have said that a large fish took the honey."

"We have no deep lakes."

"But we do have intelligence," I said. "And if Maintenance ever interferes with us, we will use our intelligence to destroy the lion of Maintenance, just as the hare used his intelligence to destroy the lion of the fable."

"Let us think how to destroy Maintenance right now!" cried the boy. He picked up a stick and brandished it at an imaginary lion as if it were a spear and he a great hunter.

I shook my head. "The hare does not hunt the lion, and the Kikuyu do not make war. The hare merely protects himself, and the Kikuyu do the same."

"Why would Maintenance interfere with us?" asked another boy, pushing his way to the front of the group. "They are our friends."

"Perhaps they will not," I answered reassuringly. "But you must always remember that the Kikuyu have no true friends except themselves."

"Tell us another story, Koriba!" cried a young girl.

"I am an old man," I said. "The night has turned cold, and I must have my sleep."

"Tomorrow?" she asked. "Will you tell us another tomorrow?'

I smiled. "Ask me tomorrow, after all the fields are planted and the cattle and goats are in their enclosures and the food has been made and the fabrics have been woven."

"But girls do not herd the cattle and goats," she protested. "What if my brothers do not bring all their animals to the enclosure?"

"Then I will tell a story just to the girls," I said.

"It must be a long story," she insisted seriously, "for we work much harder than the boys."

"I will watch you in particular, little one," I replied, "and the story will be as long or as short as your work merits."

The adults all laughed and suddenly she looked very uncomfortable, but then I chuckled and hugged her and patted her head, for it was necessary that the children learned to love their *mundumugu* as well as hold him in awe, and finally she ran off to play and dance with the other girls, while I retired to my *boma*.

Once inside, I activated my computer and discovered that a message was waiting for me from Maintenance, informing me that one of their number would be visiting me the following morning. I made a very brief reply—"Article II, Paragraph 5," which is the ordinance forbidding intervention—and lay down on my sleeping blanket, letting the rhythmic chanting of the singers carry me off to sleep.

I awoke with the sun the next morning and instructed my computer to let me know when the Maintenance ship had landed. Then I inspected my cattle and my goats—I, alone of my people, planted no crops, for the Kikuyu feed their *mundumugu*, just as they tend his herds and weave his blankets and keep his *boma* clean—and stopped by Siboki's *boma* to deliver a balm to fight the disease that was afflicting his joints. Then, as the sun began warming the earth, I returned to my own *boma*, skirting the pastures where the young men were tending their animals. When I arrived, I knew the ship had landed, for I found the droppings of a hyena on the ground near my hut, and that is the surest sign of a curse.

I learned what I could from the computer, then walked outside and scanned the horizon while two naked children took turns chasing a small dog and running away from it. When they began frightening my chickens, I gently sent them back to their own *shamba*, and then seated myself beside my fire. At last I saw my visitor from Maintenance, coming up the path from Haven. She was obviously uncomfortable in the heat, and she slapped futilely at the flies that circled her head. Her blonde hair was starting to turn gray, and I could tell by the ungainly way she negotiated the steep, rocky path that she was unused to such terrain. She almost lost her balance a number of times, and it was obvious that her proximity to so many animals frightened her, but she never slowed her pace, and within another ten minutes she stood before me.

"Good morning," she said.

"*Jambo*, Memsaab," I replied.

"You are Koriba, are you not?"

I briefly studied the face of my enemy; middle-aged and weary, it did not appear formidable. "I am Koriba," I replied.

"Good," she said. "My name is—"

"I know who you are," I said, for it is best, if conflict cannot be avoided, to take the offensive.

"You do?"

I pulled the bones out of my pouch and cast them on the dirt. "You are Barbara Eaton, born of Earth," I intoned, studying her reactions as I picked up the bones and cast them again. "You are married to Robert Eaton, and you have worked for Maintenance for nine years." A final cast of the bones. "You are forty-one years old, and you are barren."

"How did you know all that?" she asked with an expression of surprise.

"Am I not the *mundumugu*?"

She stared at me for a long minute. "You read my biography on your computer," she concluded at last.

"As long as the facts are correct, what difference does it make whether I read them from the bones or the computer?" I responded, refusing to confirm her statement. "Please sit down, Memsaab Eaton."

She lowered herself awkwardly to the ground, wrinkling her face as she raised a cloud of dust.

"It's very hot on Kirinyaga," she noted uncomfortably.

"It is very hot in Kenya," I replied.

"You could have created any climate you desired," she pointed out.

"We *did* create the climate we desired," I answered.

"Are there predators out there?" she asked, looking out over the savannah.

"A few," I replied.

"What kind?"

"Hyenas."

"Nothing larger?" she asked.

"There *is* nothing larger anymore," I said.

"I wonder why they didn't attack me?"

"Perhaps because you are an intruder," I suggested.

"Will they leave me alone on my way back to Haven?" she asked nervously, ignoring my comment.

"I will give you a charm to keep them away."

"I'd prefer an escort."

"Very well," I said.

"They're such ugly animals," she said with a shudder. "I saw them once when we were monitoring your world."

"They are very useful animals," I answered, "for they bring many omens, both good and bad."

"Really?"

I nodded. "A hyena left me an evil omen this morning."

"And?" she asked curiously.

"And here you are," I said.

She laughed. "They told me you were a sharp old man."

"They were mistaken," I replied. "I am a feeble old man who sits in front of his *boma* and watches younger men tend his cattle and goats."

"You are a feeble old man who graduated with honors from Cambridge and then acquired two postgraduate degrees from Yale," she replied.

"Who told you that?"

She smiled. "You're not the only one who reads biographies."

I shrugged. "My degrees did not help me become a better *mundumugu*," I said. "The time was wasted."

"You keep using that word. What, exactly, is a *mundumugu*?'

"You would call him a witch doctor," I answered. "But in truth the *mundumugu*, while he occasionally casts spells and interprets omens, is more a repository of the collected wisdom and traditions of his race."

"It sounds like an interesting occupation," she said.

"It is not without its compensations."

"And *such* compensations!" she said with false enthusiasm as a goat bleated in the distance and a young man yelled at it in Swahili. "Imagine having the power of life and death over an entire Eutopian world!"

So now it comes, I thought. Aloud I said: "It is not a matter of exercising power, Memsaab Eaton, but of maintaining traditions."

"I rather doubt that," she said bluntly.

"Why should you doubt what I say?" I asked.

"Because if it were traditional to kill newborn infants, the Kikuyus would have died out after a single generation."

"If the slaying of the infant arouses your disapproval," I said calmly, "I am surprised Maintenance has not previously asked about our custom of leaving the old and the feeble out for the hyenas."

"We know that the elderly and the infirm have consented to your treatment of them, much as we may disapprove of it," she replied. "We also know that a newborn infant could not possibly consent to its own death." She paused, staring at me. "May I ask why this particular baby was killed?"

"That *is* why you have come here, is it not?"

"I have been sent here to evaluate the situation," she replied, brushing an insect from her cheek and shifting her position on the ground. "A newborn child was killed. We would like to know why."

I shrugged. "It was killed because it was born with a terrible *thahu* upon it."

She frowned. "A *thahu*? What is that?"

"A curse."

"Do you mean that it was deformed?" she asked.

"It was not deformed."

"Then what was this curse that you refer to?"

"It was born feetfirst," I said.

"That's it?" she asked, surprised. "That's the curse?"

"Yes."

"It was murdered simply because it came out feetfirst?'

"It is not murder to put a demon to death," I explained patiently. "Our tradition tells us that a child born in this manner is actually a demon."

"You are an educated man, Koriba," she said. "How can you kill a perfectly healthy infant and blame it on some primitive tradition?"

"You must never underestimate the power of tradition, Memsaab Eaton," I said. "The Kikuyu turned their backs on their traditions once; the result is a mechanized, impoverished, overcrowded country that is no longer populated by Kikuyu, or Maasai, or Luo, or Wakamba, but by a new, artificial tribe known only as Kenyans. We here on Kirinyaga are true Kikuyu, and we will not make that mistake again. If the rains are late, a ram must be sacrificed. If a man's veracity is questioned, he must undergo the ordeal of the *githani* trial. If an infant is born with a *thahu* upon it, it must be put to death."

"Then you intend to continue to kill any children that are born feetfirst?" she asked.

"That is correct," I responded.

A drop of sweat rolled down her face as she looked directly at me and said: "I don't know what Maintenance's reaction will be."

"According to our charter, Maintenance is not permitted to interfere with us," I reminded her.

"It's not that simple, Koriba," she said. "According to your charter, any member of your community who wishes to leave your world is allowed free passage to Haven, from which he or she can board a ship to Earth." She paused. "'Was the baby you killed given such a choice?"

"I did not kill a baby, but a demon," I replied, turning my head slightly as a hot breeze stirred up the dust around us.

She waited until the breeze died down, then coughed before speaking. "You do understand that not everyone in Maintenance may share that opinion?"

"What Maintenance thinks is of no concern to us," I said.

"When innocent children are murdered, what Maintenance thinks is of supreme importance to you," she responded. "I am sure you do not want to defend your practices in the Eutopian Court."

"Are you here to evaluate the situation, as you said, or to threaten us?" I asked calmly.

"To evaluate the situation," she replied. "But there seems to be only one conclusion that I can draw from the facts that you have presented to me."

"Then you have not been listening to me," I said, briefly closing my eyes as another, stronger breeze swept past us.

"Koriba, I know that Kirinyaga was created so that you could emulate the ways of your forefathers—but surely you must see the difference between the torture of animals as a religious ritual and the murder of a human baby."

I shook my head. "They are one and the same," I replied. "We cannot change our way of life because it makes *you* uncomfortable. We did that once before, and within a mere handful of years your culture had corrupted our society. With every factory we built, with every job we created, with every bit of Western technology we accepted, with every Kikuyu who converted to Christianity, we became something we were not meant to be." I stared directly into her eyes. "I am the *mundumugu*, entrusted with preserving all that makes us Kikuyu, and I will not allow that to happen again."

"There are alternatives," she said.

"Not for the Kikuyu," I replied adamantly.

"There *are*," she insisted, so intent upon what she had to say that she paid no attention to a black-and-gold centipede that crawled over her boot. "For example, years spent in space can cause certain physiological and hormonal changes in humans. You noted when I arrived that I am forty-one years old and childless. That is true. In fact, many of the women in Maintenance are childless. If you will turn the babies over to us, I am sure we can find families for them. This would effectively remove them from your society without the necessity of killing them. I could speak to my superiors about it; I think that there is an excellent chance that they would approve."

"That is a thoughtful and innovative suggestion, Memsaab Eaton," I said truthfully. "I am sorry that I must reject it."

"But why?" she demanded.

"Because the first time we betray our traditions this world will cease to be Kirinyaga, and will become merely another Kenya, a nation of men awkwardly pretending to be something they are not."

"I could speak to Koinnage and the other chiefs about it," she suggested meaningfully.

"They will not disobey my instructions," I replied confidently.

"You hold that much power?"

"I hold that much respect," I answered. "A chief may enforce the law, but it is the *mundumugu* who interprets it."

"Then let us consider other alternatives."

"No."

"I am trying to avoid a conflict between Maintenance and your people," she said, her voice heavy with frustration. "It seems to me that you could at least make the effort to meet me halfway."

"I do not question your motives, Memsaab Eaton," I replied, "but you are an intruder representing an organization that has no legal right to interfere with our culture. We do not impose our religion or our morality upon Maintenance, and Maintenance may not impose its religion or morality upon us."

"It's not that simple."

"It is precisely that simple," I said.

"That is your last word on the subject?" she asked.

"Yes."

She stood up. "Then I think it is time for me to leave and make my report."

I stood up as well, and a shift in the wind brought the odors of the village: the scent of bananas, the smell of a fresh caldron of *pombe*, even the pungent odor of a bull that had been slaughtered that morning.

"As you wish, Memsaab Eaton," I said. "I will arrange for your escort." I signaled to a small boy who was tending three goats and instructed him to go to the village and send back two young men.

"Thank you," she said. "I know it's an inconvenience, but I just don't feel safe with hyenas roaming loose out there."

"You are welcome," I said. "Perhaps, while we are waiting for the men who will accompany you, you would like to hear a story about the hyena."

She shuddered involuntarily. "They are such ugly beasts!" she said distastefully. "Their hind legs seem almost deformed." She shook her head. "No, I don't think I'd be interested in hearing a story about a hyena."

"You will be interested in *this* story," I told her.

She stared at me curiously, then shrugged. "All right," she said. "Go ahead."

"'It is true that hyenas are deformed, ugly animals,' I began, "but once, a long time ago; they were as lovely and graceful as the impala. Then one day a Kikuyu chief gave a hyena a young goat to take as a gift to Ngai, who lived atop the holy mountain Kirinyaga. The hyena took the goat between his powerful jaws and headed toward the distant mountain—but on the way he passed a settlement filled with Europeans and Arabs. It abounded in guns and machines and other wonders he had never seen before, and he stopped to look, fascinated. Finally an Arab noticed him staring intently and asked if he, too, would like to become a civilized man—and as he opened his mouth to say that he would, the goat fell to the ground and ran away. As the goat raced out of sight, the Arab laughed and explained that he was only joking, that of course no hyena could become a man." I paused for a moment, and then continued. "So the hyena proceeded to Kirinyaga, and when he reached the summit, Ngai asked him what had become of the goat. When the hyena told him, Ngai hurled him off the mountaintop for having the audacity to believe he could become a man. He did not die from the fall, but his rear legs were crippled, and Ngai declared that from that day forward, all hyenas would appear thus—and to remind them of the foolishness of trying to become something that they were not, He also gave them a fool's laugh."

I paused again, and stared at her. "Memsaab Eaton, you do not hear the Kikuyu laugh like fools, and I will not let them become crippled like the hyena. Do you understand what I am saying?"

She considered my statement for a moment, then looked into my eyes. "I think we understand each other perfectly, Koriba," she said.

The two young men I had sent for arrived just then, and I instructed them to accompany her to Haven. A moment later they set off across the dry savannah, and I returned to my duties.

I began by walking through the fields, blessing the scarecrows. Since a number of the smaller children followed me, I rested beneath the trees more often than was necessary, and always, whenever we paused, they begged me to tell them more stories. I told them the tale of the Elephant and the Buffalo, and how the *Maasai elmoran* cut the rainbow with his spear so that it never again came to rest upon the earth, and why the nine Kikuyu tribes are named after Gikuyu's nine daughters, and when the sun became too hot I led them back to the village.

Then, in the afternoon, I gathered the older boys about me and explained once more how they must paint their faces and bodies for their forthcoming circumcision ceremony.

Ndemi, the boy who had insisted upon a story about Kirinyaga the night before, sought me out privately to complain that he had been unable to slay a small gazelle with his spear, and asked for a charm to make its flight more accurate. I explained to him that there would come a day when he faced a buffalo or a hyena with no charm, and that he must practice more before he came to me again. He was one to watch, this little Ndemi, for he was impetuous and totally without fear; in the old days, he would have made a great warrior, but on Kirinyaga we had no warriors. If we remained fruitful and fecund, however, we would someday need more chiefs and even another *mundumugu*, and I made up my mind to observe him closely.

In the evening, after I ate my solitary meal, I returned to the village, for Njogu, one of our young men, was to marry Kamiri, a girl from the next village. The bride-price had been decided upon, and the two families were waiting for me to preside at the ceremony.

Njogu, his faced streaked with paint, wore an ostrich-feather headdress, and looked very uneasy as he and his betrothed stood before me. I slit the throat of a fat ram that Kamiri's father had brought for the occasion, and then I turned to Njogu.

"What have you to say?" I asked.

He took a step forward. "I want Kamiri to come and till the fields of my *shamba*," he said, his voice cracking with nervousness as he spoke the prescribed words, "for I am a man, and I need a woman to tend to my *shamba* and dig deep around the roots of my plantings, that they may grow well and bring prosperity to my house."

He spit on both his hands to show his sincerity, and then, exhaling deeply with relief, he stepped back.

I turned to Kamiri.

"Do you consent to till the *shamba* of Njogu, son of Muchiri?" I asked her.

"Yes," she said softly, bowing her head. "I consent."

I held out my right hand, and the bride's mother placed a gourd of *pombe* in it.

"If this man does not please you," I said to Kamiri, "I will spill the *pombe* upon the ground."

"Do not spill it," she replied.

"Then drink," I said, handing the gourd to her.

She lifted it to her lips and took a swallow, then handed it to Njogu, who did the same.

When the gourd was empty, the parents of Njogu and Kamiri stuffed it with grass, signifying the friendship between the two clans.

Then a cheer rose from the onlookers, the ram was carried off to be roasted, more *pombe* appeared as if by magic, and while the groom took the bride off to his *boma*, the remainder of the people celebrated far into the night. They stopped only when the bleating of the goats told them that some hyenas were nearby, and then the women and children went off to their *bomas* while the men took their spears and went into the fields to frighten the hyenas away.

Koinnage came up to me as I was about to leave.

"Did you speak to the woman from Maintenance?" he asked.

"I did," I replied.

"What did she say?"

"She said that they do not approve of killing babies who are born feetfirst."

"And what did *you* say?" he asked nervously.

"I told her that we did not need the approval of Maintenance to practice our religion," I replied.

"Will Maintenance listen?"

"They have no choice," I said. "And *we* have no choice, either," I added. "Let them dictate one thing that we must or must not do, and soon they will dictate all things. Give them their way, and Njogu and Kamiri, would have recited wedding vows from the Bible or the Koran. It happened to us in Kenya; we cannot permit it to happen on Kirinyaga."

"But they will not punish us?" he persisted.

"They will not punish us," I replied.

Satisfied, he walked off to his *boma* while I took the narrow, winding path to my own. I stopped by the enclosure where my animals were kept and saw that there were two new goats there, gifts from the bride's and groom's families in gratitude for my services. A few minutes later I was asleep within the walls of my own *boma*.

The computer woke me a few minutes before sunrise. I stood up, splashed my face with water from the gourd I keep by my sleeping blanket, and walked over to the terminal.

There was a message for me from Barbara Eaton, brief and to the point:

It is the preliminary finding of Maintenance that infanticide, for any reason, is a direct violation of Kirinyaga's charter. No action will be taken for past offenses.

We are also evaluating your practice of euthanasia, and may require further testimony from you at some point in the future.

Barbara Eaton

A runner from Koinnage arrived a moment later, asking me to attend a meeting of the Council of Elders, and I knew that he had received the same message.

I wrapped my blanket around my shoulders and began walking to Koinnage's *shamba*, which consisted of his *boma*, as well as those of his three sons and their wives. When I arrived I found not only the local Elders waiting for me, but also two chiefs from neighboring villages.

"Did you receive the message from Maintenance?" demanded Koinnage, as I seated myself opposite him.

"I did."

"I warned you that this would happen!" he said. "What will we do now?"

"We will do what we have always done," I answered calmly.

"We cannot," said one of the neighboring chiefs. "They have forbidden it."

"They have no right to forbid it," I replied.

"There is a woman in my village whose time is near," continued the chief, "and all of the signs and omens point to the birth of twins. We have been taught that the firstborn must be killed, for one mother cannot produce two souls—but now Maintenance has forbidden it. What are we to do?'

"We must kill the firstborn," I said, "for it will be a demon."

"And then Maintenance will make us leave Kirinyaga!" said Koinnage bitterly.

"Perhaps we could let the child live," said the chief "That might satisfy them, and then they might leave us alone."

I shook my head. "They will not leave you alone. Already they speak about the way we leave the old and the feeble out for the hyenas, as if this were some enormous sin against their god. If you give in on the one, the day will come when you must give in on the other."

"Would that be so terrible?" persisted the chief "They have medicines that we do not possess; perhaps they could make the old young again."

"You do not understand," I said, rising to my feet. "Our society is not a collection of separate people and customs and traditions. No, it is a complex system, with all the pieces as dependent upon each other as the animals and vegetation of the savannah. If you burn the grass, you will not only kill the impala who feeds upon it, but the predator who feeds upon the impala, and the ticks and flies who live upon the predator, and the vultures and maribou storks who feed upon his remains when he dies. You cannot destroy the part without destroying the whole."

I paused to let them consider what I had said, and then continued speaking: "Kirinyaga is like the savannah. If we do not leave the old and the feeble out for the hyenas, the hyenas will starve. If the hyenas starve, the grass eaters will become so numerous that there is no land left for our cattle and goats to graze. If the old and the feeble do not die when Ngai decrees it, then soon we will not have enough food to go around."

I picked up a stick and balanced it precariously on my forefinger.

"This stick," I said, "is the Kikuyu people, and my finger is Kirinyaga. They are in perfect balance." I stared at the neighboring chief. "But what will happen if I alter the balance, and put my finger *here*?" I asked, gesturing to the end of the stick.

"The stick will fall to the ground."

"And here?" I asked, pointing to a stop an inch away from the center.

"It will fall."

"Thus is it with us," I explained. "Whether we yield on one point or all points, the result will be the same: The Kikuyu will fall as surely as the stick will fall. Have we learned nothing from our past? We *must* adhere to our traditions; they are all that we have!"

"But Maintenance will not allow us to do so!" protested Koinnage.

"They are not warriors, but civilized men," I said, allowing a touch of contempt to creep into my voice. "Their chiefs and their *mundumugus* will *not* send them to Kirinyaga with guns and spears. They will issue warnings and findings and declarations, and finally, when that fails, they will go to the Eutopian Court and plead their case, and the trial will be postponed many times and reheard many more times." I could see them finally relaxing, and I smiled confidently at them. "Each of you will have died from the burden of your years before Maintenance does anything other than talk. I am your *mundumugu*; I have lived among civilized men, and I tell you that this is the truth."

The neighboring chief stood up and faced me. "I will send for you when the twins are born," he pledged.

"I will come," I promised him.

We spoke further, and then the meeting ended and the old men began wandering off to their *bomas*, while I looked to the future, which I could see more clearly than Koinnage or the Elders.

I walked through the village until I found the bold young Ndemi, brandishing his spear and hurling it at a buffalo he had constructed out of dried grasses.

"*Jambo*, Koriba!" he greeted me.

"*Jambo*, my brave young warrior," I replied.

"I have been practicing, as you ordered."

"I thought you wanted to hunt the gazelle," I noted.

"Gazelles are for children," he answered. "I will slay *mbogo*, the buffalo."

"*Mbogo* may feel differently about it," I said.

"So much the better," he said confidently. "I have no wish to kill an animal as it runs away from me."

"And when will you go out to slay the fierce *mbogo*?"

He shrugged. "When I am more accurate." He smiled up at me. "Perhaps tomorrow."

I stared at him thoughtfully for a moment, and then spoke: "Tomorrow is a long time away. We have business tonight."

"What business?" he asked.

"You must find ten friends, none of them yet of circumcision age, and tell them to come to the pond within the forest to the south. They must come after the sun has set, and you must tell them that Koriba the *mundumugu* commands that they tell no one, not even their parents, that they are coming." I paused. "Do you understand, Ndemi?"

"I understand."

"Then go," I said. "Bring my message to them."

He retrieved his spear from the straw buffalo and set off at a trot, young and tall and strong and fearless.

You are the future, I thought, as I watched him run toward the village. *Not Koinnage, not myself, not even the young bridegroom Njogu, for their time will have come and gone before the battle is joined. It is you, Ndemi, upon whom Kirinyaga must depend if it is to survive.*

Once before the Kikuyu have had to fight for their freedom. Under the leadership of Jomo Kenyatta, whose name has been forgotten by most of your parents, we took the terrible oath of Mau Mau, and we maimed and we killed and we committed such atrocities that finally we achieved Uhuru, for against such butchery civilized men have no defense but to depart.

And tonight, young Ndemi, while your parents are asleep, you and your companions will meet me deep in the woods, and you in your turn and they in theirs will learn one last tradition of the Kikuyu, for I will invoke not only the strength of Ngai but also the indomitable spirit of Jomo Kenyatta. I will administer a hideous oath and force you to do unspeakable things to prove your fealty and I will teach each of you, in turn, how to administer the oath to those who come after you.

There is a season for all things: for birth, for growth, for death. There is unquestionably a season for Utopia, but it will have to wait.

For the season of Uhuru is upon us.

STUDY AND DISCUSSION QUESTIONS

1 Suppose you are Secretary General of the United Nations, and the overseer of a program to select groups to settle a new world. On what considerations would you base your decision to select one group over another? How does your answer to that question compare or contrast with the rationale given in the story for the choice of the Kikuyu?

2 The Kikuyu medicine man and the central, conflicted character of all of Resnick's Kirinyaga stories is Koriba. Is the Kikuyu society on Kirinyaga based on a deception on the part of Koriba? If so, what is this deception?

3 On the world of Kirinyaga the tribal laws permit—actually, they require —female circumcision, polygamy, deception, and sexism. Are these practices morally permissible for the Kikuyu people? Would they be for us? Why or why not?

4 In Resnick's collection of stories about the Kikuyu's attempt to found a utopia he describes many other harrowing steps Koriba must take in order to preserve tribal law, including enforcing several tribal laws that are ruthlessly sexist. Suppose that another law amongst the Kikuyu is that Kikuyu are morally obligated to continuously and brutally torture and maim adults of other tribes and murder children and infants. They are required to do so in such a way that each of the other tribespeople remain alive for years. Now consider this statement: "Such actions by the Kikuyu are morally impermissible." Can the relativist show that this is false?

5 When the person from Maintenance exits her ship and enters the area of Kirinyaga used by the Kikuyu, to which culture does she belong, or primarily belong? Suppose that she violated a Kikuyu law by failing to wear appropriate clothing and, by doing so, showed great disrespect to the tribal chief. Are the Kikuyu morally permitted to punish her? How can a relativist answer this question?

6 If you work for Maintenance and are given the task of writing the charter which sets out the rules the Kikuyu people must abide by, what would you write? More importantly, which theory of truth described in this chapter would you presuppose for the charter?

1.11 "THE RING OF GYGES," FROM PLATO'S *REPUBLIC*

1. Now that those who practice justice do so involuntarily and because they have not the power to be unjust will best appear if we imagine something of this kind: having given both to the just and the unjust power to do what they will, let us watch and see whither desire will lead them; then we shall discover in the very act the just and unjust man to be proceeding along the same road, following their interest, which all natures deem to be their

good, and are only diverted into the path of justice by the force of law. The liberty that we are supposing may be most completely given to them in the form of such a power as is said to have been possessed by Gyges the ancestor of Croesus the Lydian. According to the tradition, Gyges was a shepherd in the service of the king of Lydia; there was a great storm, and an earthquake made an opening in the earth at the place where he was feeding his flock. Amazed at the sight, he descended into the opening, where, among other marvels, he beheld a hollow brazen horse, having doors, at which he stooping and looking in saw a dead body of stature, as appeared to him, more than human, and having nothing on but a gold ring; this he took from the finger of the dead and reascended.

2. Now the shepherds met together, according to custom, that they might send their monthly report about the flocks to the king; into their assembly he came having the ring on his finger, and as he was sitting among them he chanced to turn the collet of the ring inside his hand, when instantly he became invisible to the rest of the company and they began to speak of him as if he were no longer present. He was astonished at this, and again touching the ring he turned the collet outwards and reappeared; he made several trials of the ring, and always with the same result—when he turned the collet inwards he became invisible, when outwards he reappeared. Whereupon he contrived to be chosen one of the messengers who were sent to the court; where as soon as he arrived he seduced the queen, and with her help conspired against the king and slew him, and took the kingdom.

3. Suppose now that there were two such magic rings, and the just put on one of them and the unjust the other; no man can be imagined to be of such an iron nature that he would stand fast in justice. No man would keep his hands off what was not his own when he could safely take what he liked out of the market, or go into houses and lie with any one at his pleasure, or kill or release from prison whom he would, and in all respects be like a God among men. Then the actions of the just would be as the actions of the unjust; they would both come at last to the same point. And this we may truly affirm to be a great proof that a man is just, not willingly or because he thinks that justice is any good to him individually, but of necessity, for wherever any one thinks that he can safely be unjust, there he is unjust. For all men believe in their hearts that injustice is far more profitable to the individual than justice, and he who argues as I have been supposing, will say that they are right. If you could imagine any one obtaining this power of becoming invisible, and never doing any wrong or touching what was another's, he would be thought by the lookers-on to be a most wretched idiot, although they would praise him to one another's faces, and keep up appearances with one another from a fear that they too might suffer injustice. Enough of this.

STUDY AND DISCUSSION QUESTIONS

1 Suppose you had an invisibility ring. What would you actually do while wearing the ring that you don't now do as a part of your normal life?

2   Would you be wrong to use your ring like Gyges uses his? Why?
3   How much influence does society in general have on your actions? On your thoughts?
4   Do you think differently about performing an action if you know that no one will ever be able to see you do it? If so, explore the nature of that difference.
5   Several of these questions suggest a bigger and broader concern in moral philosophy (and science fiction). That is: Are there moral norms—rights and wrongs—independent of society?

1.12 "ON TRYING OUT ONE'S NEW SWORD," BY MARY MIDGLEY

All of us are, more or less, in trouble today about trying to understand cultures strange to us. We hear constantly of alien customs. We see changes in our lifetime which would have astonished our parents. I want to discuss here one very short way of dealing with this difficulty, a drastic way which many people now theoretically favour. It consists in simply denying that we can ever understand any culture except our own well enough to make judgments about it. Those who recommend this hold that the world is sharply divided into separate societies, sealed units, each with its own system of thought. They feel that the respect and tolerance due from one system to another forbids us ever to take up a critical position to any other culture. Moral judgment, they suggest, is a kind of coinage valid only in its country of origin.

I shall call this position "moral isolationism." I shall suggest that it is certainly not forced upon us, and indeed that it makes no sense at all. People usually take it up because they think it is a respectful attitude to other cultures. In fact, however, it is not respectful. Nobody can respect what is entirely unintelligible to them. To respect someone, we have to know enough about him to make a *favourable* judgment, however general and tentative. And we do understand people in other cultures to this extent. Otherwise a great mass of our most valuable thinking would be paralysed.

To show this, I shall take a remote example, because we shall probably find it easier to think calmly about it than we should with a contemporary one, such as female circumcision in Africa or the Chinese Cultural Revolution. The principles involved will still be the same. My example is this. There is, it seems, a verb in classical Japanese which means "to try out one's new sword on a chance wayfarer." (The word is *tsujigiri*, literally "crossroadscut.") A samurai sword had to be tried out because, if it was to work properly, it had to slice through someone at a single blow, from the shoulder to the opposite flank. Otherwise, the warrior bungled his stroke. This could injure his honour, offend his ancestors, and even let down his emperor. So tests were needed, and wayfarers had to be expended. Any wayfarer would do—provided, of course, that he was not another Samurai. Scientists will recognize a familiar problem about the rights of experimental subjects.

Now when we hear of a custom like this, we may well reflect that we simply do not understand it; and therefore are not qualified to criticize it at all, because we are not members of that culture. But we are not members of any other culture either, except our own. So we extend the principle to cover all extraneous cultures, and we seem therefore to be moral isolationists. But this is, as we shall see, an impossible position. Let us ask what it would involve.

We must ask first: Does the isolating barrier work both ways? Are people in other cultures equally unable to criticize us? This question struck me sharply when I read a remark in *The Guardian* [an esteemed British daily newspaper] by an anthropologist about a South American Indian who had been taken into a Brazilian town for an operation, which saved his life. When he came back to his village, he made several highly critical remarks about the white Brazilians' way of life. They may very well have been justified. But the interesting point was that the anthropologist called these remarks "a damning indictment of Western civilization." Now the Indian had been in that town about two weeks. Was he in a position to deliver a damning indictment? Would we ourselves be qualified to deliver such an indictment on the Samurai, provided we could spend two weeks in ancient Japan? What do we really think about this?

My own impression is that we believe that outsiders can, in principle, deliver perfectly good indictments—only, it usually takes more than two weeks to make them damning. Understanding has degrees. It is not a slapdash yes-or-no matter. Intelligent outsiders can progress in it, and in some ways will be at an advantage over the locals. But if this is so, it must clearly apply to ourselves as much as anybody else.

Our next question is this: Does the isolating barrier between cultures block praise as well as blame? If I want to say that the Samurai culture has many virtues, or to praise the South American Indians, am I prevented from doing *that* by my outside status? Now, we certainly do need to praise other societies in this way. But it is hardly possible that we could praise them effectively if we could not, in principle, criticize them. Our praise would be worthless if it rested on definite grounds, if it did not flow from some understanding. Certainly we may need to praise things which we do not *fully* understand. We say "there's something very good here, but I can't quite make out what it is yet." This happens when we want to learn from strangers. And we can learn from strangers. But to do this we have to distinguish between those strangers who are worth learning from and those who are not. Can we then judge which is which?

This brings us to our third question: What is involved in judging? Now plainly there is no question here of sitting on a bench in a red robe and sentencing people. Judging simply means forming an opinion, and expressing it if it is called for. Is there anything wrong about this? Naturally, we ought to avoid forming—and expressing—*crude* opinions, like that of a simple-minded missionary, who might dismiss the whole Samurai culture as entirely bad, because it is non-Christian. But this is a different objection. The trouble with crude opinions is that they are crude, whoever forms them, not that they are formed by the wrong people. Anthropologists, after all, are outsiders quite as much as missionaries. Moral isolationism forbids us to form any opinions on these matters. Its ground for doing so is that we don't understand them. But there is much that we don't understand in our own culture too. This brings us to our last question: If we can't judge other cultures, can we really judge our own? Our efforts to do so will be much damaged if we are really deprived of our opinions about other societies, because these provide the range of comparison, the spectrum of alternatives against which we set what we want to understand. We would have to stop using the mirror which anthropology so helpfully holds up to us.

In short, moral isolationism would lay down a general ban on moral reasoning. Essentially, this is the programme of immoralism, and it carries a distressing logical difficulty. Immoralists like Nietzsche are actually just a rather specialized sect of moralists. They can no more afford to put moralizing out of business than smugglers can afford to abolish customs regulations. The power of moral judgment is, in fact, not a luxury, not a perverse indulgence of the self-righteous. It is a necessity. When we judge something to be bad or good, better or worse than something else, we are taking it as an example to aim at or avoid. Without opinions of this sort, we would have no framework of comparison for our own policy, no chance of profiting by other people's insights or mistakes. In this vacuum, we could form no judgments on our own actions.

Now it would be odd if homo sapiens had really got himself into a position as bad as this—a position where his main evolutionary asset, his brain, was so little use to him. None of us is going to accept this sceptical diagnosis. We cannot do so, because our involvement in moral isolationism does not flow from apathy, but from a rather acute concern about human hypocrisy and other forms of wickedness. But we polarize that concern around a few selected moral truths. We are rightly angry with those who despise, oppress or steamroll other cultures. We think that doing these things is actually *wrong*. But this is itself a moral judgment. We could not condemn oppression and insolence if we thought that all our condemnations were just a trivial local quirk of our own culture. We could still less do it if we tried to stop judging altogether.

Real moral scepticism, in fact, could lead only to inaction, to our losing all interest in moral questions, most of all in those which concern other societies. When we discuss these things, it becomes instantly clear how far we are from doing this. Suppose, for instance, that I criticize the bisecting Samurai, that I say his behaviour is brutal. What will usually happen next is that someone will protest, will say that I have no right to make criticisms like that of another culture. But it is most unlikely that he will use this move to end the discussion of the subject. Instead, he will justify the Samurai. He will try to fill in the background, to make me understand the custom, by explaining the exalted ideals of discipline and devotion which produced it. He will probably talk of the lower value which the ancient Japanese placed on individual life generally. He may well suggest that this is a healthier attitude than our own obsession with security. He may add, too, that the wayfarers did not seriously mind being bisected, that in principle they accepted the whole arrangement.

Now an objector who talks like this is implying that it is possible to understand alien customs. That is just what he is trying to make me do. And he implies, too, that if I do succeed in understanding them, I shall do something better than giving up judging them. He expects me to change my present judgment to a truer one—namely, one that is favourable. And the standards I must use to do this cannot just be Samurai standards. They have to be ones current in my own culture. Ideals like discipline and devotion will not move anybody unless he himself accepts them. As it happens, neither discipline nor devotion is very popular in the West at present. Anyone who appeals to them may well have to do some more arguing to make *them* acceptable, before he can use them to explain the Samurai. But if he does succeed here, he will have persuaded us, not just that there was something to be said for them in ancient Japan, but that there would be here as well.

Isolating barriers simply cannot arise here. If we accept something as a serious moral truth about one culture, we can't refuse to apply it—in however different an outward form—to other cultures as well, wherever circumstance admit it. If we refuse to do this, we just are not taking the other culture seriously. This becomes clear if we look at the last argument used by my objector—that of justification by consent of the victim. It is suggested that sudden bisection is quite in order, *provided* that it takes place between consenting adults. I cannot now discuss how conclusive this justification is. What I am pointing out is simply that it can only work if we believe that *consent* can make such a transaction respectable and this is a thoroughly modern and Western idea. It would probably never occur to a Samurai; if it did, it would surprise him very much. It is *our* standard. In applying it, too, we are likely to make another typically Western demand. We shall ask for good factual evidence that the wayfarers actually do have this rather surprising taste—that they are really willing to be bisected. In applying Western standards in this way, we are not being confused or irrelevant. We are asking the questions which arise *from where we stand*, questions which we can see the sense of. We do this because asking questions which you can't see the sense of is humbug. Certainly we can extend our questioning by imaginative effort. We can come to understand other societies better. By doing so, we may make their questions our own, or we may see that they are really forms of the questions which we are asking already. This is not impossible. It is just very hard work. The obstacles which often prevent it are simply those of ordinary ignorance, laziness and prejudice.

If there were really an isolating barrier, of course, our own culture could never have been formed. It is no sealed box, but a fertile jungle of different influences—Greek, Jewish, Roman, Norse, Celtic and so forth, into which further influences are still pouring—American, Indian, Japanese, Jamaican, you name it. The moral isolationist's picture of separate, unmixable cultures is quite unreal. People who talk about British history usually stress the value of this fertilizing mix, no doubt rightly. But this is not just an odd fact about Britain. Except for the very smallest and most remote, all cultures are formed out of many streams. All have the problem of digesting and assimilating things which, at the start, they do not understand. All have the choice of learning something from this challenge, or alternatively, of refusing to learn, and fighting it mindlessly instead.

This universal predicament has been obscured by the fact that anthropologists used to concentrate largely on very small and remote cultures, which did not seem to have this problem. These tiny societies, which had often forgotten their own history, made neat, self-contained subjects for study. No doubt it was valuable to emphasize their remoteness, their extreme strangeness, their independence of our cultural tradition. This emphasis was, I think, the root of moral isolationism. But, as the tribal studies themselves showed, even there the anthropologists were able to interpret what they saw and make judgments—often favourable—about the tribesmen. And the tribesmen, too, were quite equal to making judgments about the anthropologists—and about the tourists and Coca-Cola salesmen who followed them. Both sets of judgments, no doubt, were somewhat hasty, both have been refined in the light of further experience. A similar transaction between us and the Samurai might take even longer. But that is no reason at all for deeming it impossible. Morally as well as physically, there is only one world, and we all have to live in it.

STUDY AND DISCUSSION QUESTIONS

1   What is "moral isolationism"? Can you offer any examples of this position from your own reading or conversation?

2   What is required in order for someone to respect someone else from another culture? What, according to Midgley, is *respect*?

3   Where does the title come from? What does Midgley use the example of *tsujigiri* to show?

4   In your opinion, is committing *tsujigiri* immoral? Can you answer that question without knowing who it is—you or a Samurai, for instance—who is to commit *tsujigiri*?

5   Midgley offers a tacit argument against moral isolationism according to which it prevents moral judgments even about our own culture. What is her reasoning on behalf of her assertion that moral isolationism leads to a "general ban on moral reasoning"?

6   Midgley cites a way in which moral isolationism undermines itself. Explain this point. Is this similar to the way that cultural relativism undermines itself?

7   Is it possible to offer conclusive reasons against a practice of another culture and still remain a moral isolationist? Could morality be a property that is culturally-specific? What would this amount to?

8   What's the point of the third-to-last paragraph beginning "Isolating barriers simply cannot arise here"?

9   Midgley concludes her paper by making a factual point about culture, namely, that all major world cultures are the products of many other historical cultures. What is the utility of this point in her overall case against moral isolationism?

1.13 BIBLIOGRAPHY AND RECOMMENDED READING

Entries with an asterisk indicate highly recommended readings.

Science fiction

*Atwood, Margaret. *The Handmaid's Tale*. McClelland and Stewart, 1985. Militaristic fundamentalists enforce a totalitarian regime in which women are severely subjugated.

Biggle, Lloyd. *The World Menders*. Doubleday, 1971. Human observers on alien world witness slavery, but all isn't as it seems.

Carr, Terry. *Cirque*. Bobbs-Merrill, 1977. Strange citizens take action to save decadent city; metaphysical questions.

Chalker, Jack. *Dancers in the Afterglow*. New York: Ballantine, 1978. Self as social product in world of polarized societies. Happiness highest value?

Delany, Samuel. *Triton*. New York: Bantam, 1983. An individual must orient himself in culture where social role and gender is by choice.

Delany, Samuel, and Neil Gaiman. *The Einstein Intersection*. Wesleyan University Press, 1998. Tour de force of the imagination in which non-human inhabitants of future Earth return to its classics for meaning

Heinlein, Robert. *The Moon is a Harsh Mistress*. New York: Orb Books, 1997. Colonists on moon declare independence from Earth, and explore new models of social organization; libertarianism?

Kingsbury, Donald. *Courtship Rite*. Timescape Books, 1982. Colony world existing in extreme conditions must adopt peculiar anthropological traits.

LeGuin, Ursula. *The Dispossessed*. New York: Eos, 1994. Contrasts poverty stricken world with rich neighbor. Serious discussion of moral political issues.

*——. *The Left Hand of Darkness*. New York: Barnes & Noble Books, 2004. Moderately intelligent humanoid male struggles negotiating the changing gender identities of the people of planet Gethen.

Lynn, Elizabeth A. *The Sardonyx Net*. New York: Ace, Reissue Edition, February 2001. Slavery survives on at least one planet in the galaxy, and the protagonist faces a conflict between principles.

McHugh, Maureen F. *Nekropolis*. New York: Eos, Reprint Edition, November 2002. Set in future Morocco, which is ruled by a Moslem theocratic government, Hariba has been chemically bonded to her master by a process that ensures she will serve him obsessively.

Merrill, Judith. "That Only a Mother." *Astounding*, June 1948. A husband leaves his pregnant wife for an extended business trip and returns to find his baby is nothing like the normal infant he expected.

*Moorcock, Michael. *The Dancers at the End of Time*. Gollancz 2003. At the end of time immortals with vast power find ways to amuse themselves and find meaning in life, with or without morality.

Pohl, Frederik. "The Day After the Day the Martians Came." In *Dangerous Visions*, ed. Harlan Ellison, Garden City, NY: Doubleday 1967. Written in the 1960s, Pohl wonders how human prejudices like racism and sexism might inform our reaction to Martians.

*Resnick, Michael. *Kirinyaga*. New York: Ballantine Del Rey, 1998. Also published in *The Magazine of Fantasy and Science Fiction*. November 1998. pp. 6–25. In this short story collection, which includes our feature story, Resnick juxtaposes the moral teachings of ancient Kikuyu culture and future United Nations protocols to confront the reader with repeatedly fascinating moral dilemmas.

Russell, Eric Frank. *The Great Explosion*. Dobson, 1962. When Earth achieves light-speed travel, our explorers reach other populated worlds but find that they are politically unlike our own by virtue of lacking governmental leadership.

Sheckley, Robert. *Untouched by Human Hands*. New York: Ballantine, 1954. This collection of stories includes "The Monsters," which explores cultural relativism through a look at sharply different visions of beauty in humanity and in aliens.

Spinrad, Norman. *The Iron Dream*. Pocket, 1982 Fantasy novel written from Hitler's perspective.

Sucharitkul, Somtow. *Starship and Haiku*. Del Rey, 1988. Messiah figure urges future Japanese nation to expiate historical sins in seppuku.

Philosophy

Benedict, Ruth. *Patterns of Culture*. Boston, MA: Houghton Mifflin, 1934.

Bloor, David. *Knowledge and Social Imagery*. Chicago, IL: University of Chicago Press, 2nd ed., 1992.

Bricmont, Jean and Alan Sokal. *Fashionable Nonsense: Postmodern Intellectuals' Abuse of Science*. New York: Picador USA, 1998.

Davidson, Donald "On the Very Idea of a Conceptual Scheme." *Proceedings and Addresses of the American Philosophical Association* (1974): pp. 5–20. Reprinted in his *Inquiries into Truth and Interpretation*. Oxford: Oxford University Press, 1984.

Feyerabend, Paul. *Against Method: Outline of an Anarchist Theory of Knowledge*. 3rd ed. London: Verso, September 1993.

Geertz, Clifford. *The Interpretation of Cultures*. New York: Basic Books. New ed. January 2000.

James, William. *Pragmatism: A New Name for Some Old Ways of Thinking*. Indianapolis, IN: Hackett Publishing Company, 1907.

Kuhn, Thomas. *The Structure of Scientific Revolutions*. 2nd ed. (1st ed. 1962). Chicago, IL: University of Chicago Press, December 1996.

Laudan, Larry. *Progress and its Problems. Towards a Theory of Scientific Growth*. Berkeley: University of California Press, October 1978.

Midgley, Mary. "On Trying Out One's New Sword." *Heart and Mind: The Varieties of Moral Experience*. Brighton, U.K.: Harvester Press, 1981.

*Nagel, Thomas. *The Last Word*. Oxford: Oxford University Press, 1996.

*Nietzsche, Friedrich. *The Portable Nietzsche* (Viking Portable Library). Ed. and trans. Walter Kaufmann. New York: Penguin, 1977.

——. *The Will to Power* (*Der Wille zur Macht*). Trans. Walter Kaufmann. New York: Random House, 1967.

Plato. "The Ring of Gyges" (from Chapter 1). *Republic*. 2nd ed. Trans. G. M. A. Grube, revision C. D. C. Reeve. Indianapolis: Hackett Publishing, 1992, pp. 34–36. Originally published *c*.380 BCE.

Winch, Peter. "Understanding a Primitive Society." *American Philosophical Quarterly* 1 (1964): pp. 307–24.

2 Knowledge and skepticism

Red pill or blue? In the eponymous groundbreaking film, Neo takes the red pill and exits the "matrix." Once out of the matrix Neo realizes he had been living his life in a virtual reality world created by **artificial intelligences**. Of course, people who've not yet taken red pills don't know that they inhabit a virtual reality world. It appears real to them . . . just as our present world appears real to us.

The life to be lived within the matrix isn't bad at all. Residents live in nice houses and have interesting jobs. They eat delicious meals—steak is a favorite. They read books, watch television, and listen to music. They take trips to New York, have sex and play volleyball. Residents in the matrix have interests and beliefs identical to ours.

When considering alternatives open to people in the matrix, life looks comfy. If you take the red pill, you wake up rudely and you thrash around in an amniotic sac. After choking on the fluid, you realize you have no idea where you are. You occupy an isolated pod, one amongst millions, set deep underground. Someone might pick you up to enlist you in the fight against the AI's, but this means you'll be serving on a cramped battle craft, always on alert for preying AI attack vessels. You'll lose all your matrix-family. Your meals will be nutrimeat and yeast cultures. You'll never sit in a Lazy Boy, eat a pizza and watch Direct TV again.

So would you really—*really*—want to take the red pill?

The ancient philosopher Plato offers a clear answer to this question in his "Allegory of the Cave" (see §2.11). If you knowingly don't take the red pill, you are living a lie. You believe that your matrix-steak came from a cow, but it didn't; that you are going to sleep in your room, but you don't have one; that your spouse loves you, but you don't have a spouse. Instead, you wallow in that fluid-filled sac all alone.

Whether you want to be in the matrix or not, you probably can't know whether you are in one now or not. Of course, we *think* we know we're in the real world. However, a number of philosophers, upon investigating the nature of knowledge, have concluded that we know very little, if anything. What can we know?

After completing this chapter, you should be able to do the following:

- Explain the concept of **knowledge** operative when we claim to know a statement is true
- Explain why, according to the skeptic, we cannot or do not have knowledge of various kinds
- Assess the skeptic's principal arguments
- Explain **foundationalism**, **fallibilism**, and **closure principles**.

2.0 THE CONCEPT OF KNOWLEDGE

The question "What can we know?" can't be answered fully until a prior question is answered, namely, "What is knowledge?" Though the concept of knowledge seems clear, *epistemologists*—philosophers of knowledge—find that giving an adequate definition is no easy task. "Knowledge" has many uses and many sources. Jones knows his next-door neighbor, Smith; knows *that* Smith is a reservist in the National Guard; knows *what* Smith does on Saturdays; knows *how* to annoy Smith; and knows *why* Smith is a social worker rather than a programmer or a server.

The primary concept of knowledge is knowledge *that* some statement is true. Many uses of the concept can be put in terms of knowledge *that*. Jones' knowing *what* Smith does on Saturdays is nothing other than Jones' knowing *that* she reads home improvement books on Saturdays. "Knowledge that" is **propositional knowledge** since what you know is a statement that expresses a proposition about something. So epistemologists address the question "What is knowledge?" by answering the question "What is propositional knowledge?"

What conditions must someone fulfill to have propositional knowledge? Something like the following three conditions must be met. For an **agent** A, Agatha, to know some statement P,

(2.1)   P must be *true*

(2.2)   A must *believe* P, and

(2.3)   A must be *justified* in believing P.

We have already defined *truth* as correspondence to reality. *Belief* is simply one's mental assent to a statement. Knowledge requires that condition 2.1 is appropriately related to condition 2.2. Not just any true belief deserves the honorific title of knowledge, after all. *Justification* refers to evidence for a belief that increases the likelihood that the belief is true.

This characterization of justification distinguishes A's *justification* for believing P from A's *rationality* in believing P. There is an extremely important difference between the two. If A is justified in believing P, then A's belief P is rational. But the converse is not true. If A is rational in believing P, it does not follow that A is justified in believing P. "Rationality" refers to the conditional probability of a belief on the basis of background beliefs. Suppose I believe that aliens will attack Earth tomorrow because I also believe that I met the aliens last year, and I believe that they told me many true things, including things about this attack. Since these are my background beliefs, I am rational in believing that aliens will attack tomorrow.

However, I can be rational in this belief even if none of these background beliefs are true and even if these background beliefs are themselves unjustified by further beliefs. The mere fact *that I believe* that I met aliens last year and that they told me these things doesn't evidentially support—doesn't make it likely to be true—that aliens will attack tomorrow. To be *justified* in believing that the aliens will attack tomorrow, I need background beliefs that offer evidential support for my belief in the attack by actually increasing the likelihood that my belief in the attack is true.

Philosophical definitions of the key term "justification" oscillate between two different meanings. On one theory, **internalism**, justification takes the form of evidence or reasons possessed by the agent. This type of justification converts true belief into knowledge. Agatha knows P because *she herself* has *reasons to believe* P. Internalism states that justification is constituted by certain kinds of mental states internal to A, which provide A with a reason to think P is true. Naturally the internalist must say much more about justification than we have on his behalf, but this is sufficient to contrast the view with its major alternative, **externalism**.

We can characterize externalism as a theory of justification on which justification depends upon the features that produce the belief, rather than on reasons possessed by the agent. On one externalist proposal the reliability of the process that causes belief P is what justifies belief P for person A. Thus A's belief P is justified, on the "reliabilist" form of externalism, only if P is produced by a reliable process. A *reliable* belief forming process is a process that would produce more true beliefs than false beliefs over the long run. According to reliabilist externalism, A's perceptual beliefs will be justified because perception is a reliable belief-forming process. A's guesses or A's beliefs based upon her horoscope will not be justified on this theory because guessing and astrology do not produce more true beliefs than false beliefs. One benefit of externalist theories is that we can be justified to believe many widely held beliefs. The standards of internalist theories are higher, but they yield smaller quantities of known beliefs.

One alleged problem with externalism is that it doesn't take philosophical problems of knowledge as seriously as does internalism. One often-quoted understanding of internalism comes from W. K. Clifford. He says, "To sum up; it is wrong always, every-where, and for anyone, to believe anything upon insufficient evidence."[1] Internalism recommends—in Clifford's version, demands—that individual believers undertake a quest to justify their beliefs with evidence that is accessible to the believers themselves. But externalism threatens the internalist's picture of the philosopher deep in critical thought about the problems of knowledge. Some venerable problems in epistemology are solved too easily on externalism. If externalism is true, then whether Agatha thinks critically about the sources of the reliability of her belief bears little relation to her justification for it. When confronted with a skeptical scenario—she might be in a simulation of reality—the internalist's fundamental question is: "What reasons has she to justify her belief that she is not in a virtual reality environment?" The externalist's fundamental question is: "Are her beliefs generated by cognitive processes that produce more true beliefs than false beliefs?"

Science fiction stories often exemplify externalism by enhancing the minds of their characters, whether through technology, pharmacology or through some super-special "psionic" power. The award-winning short story called "Flowers for Algernon" explores externalism through a drug treatment given to the protagonist, Charlie Gordon. Charlie, a mentally retarded janitor, volunteers for an intelligence-enhancing drug, which causes a steep rise in his intelligence. At points in the story, Charlie can't understand how he knows that he knows, even though his beliefs are true. Daniel Keyes, the author, writes the story in the first-person, deftly conveying the rise and the precipitous fall in Charlie's intelligence as the drug's effects fade. (*Rental*: *Charly* (1968) stars Cliff Robertson, who won the Academy Award for Best Actor.)

In the Philip K. Dick short story "Minority Report," set in 2054, three individuals possess the ability to foresee glimpses of the future. (*Rental*: *Minority Report* (2002), directed by Steven Spielberg and starring Tom Cruise.) These three "pre-cogs," as they are called, glimpse images of the near-term future in which citizens are in imminent danger of losing their lives—this seems to be the only information that their pre-cognition faculty gives them. The sources of their incredibly valuable foreknowing ability remain somewhat mysterious. But this belief-forming faculty works. Mostly. The criminal justice system of the future uses this special form of knowing to its advantage; Dick imagines a division of the police force devoted to "pre-crime." The pre-cogs telepathically receive images, which are translated into data and fed to the police information technology system. The system automatically dispatches teams to intercept the individual about to commit murder.

By using this exotic belief forming faculty, do these three people *know* who is about to commit murder? The reliabilist externalist would answer "Yes" because it is sufficient for knowledge that the belief is true and is caused by a reliably truth-conducive faculty of the mind. Someone might reply with any number of objections, including: Scientists do not know how their exotic belief-forming faculty works so well. The pre-cogs themselves don't understand how they have come to have this power. The origins of this faculty appear in tension with standard evolutionary theories about the origins of the components of our brains. Only three people in the world appear to have this special capacity. Taken together, these objections go some way toward undermining confidence in our judgment about the faculty.

These objections are voiced from an internalist perspective, one according to which we need more information about belief-forming faculties before we give them our credence. For example, we need a larger test group to determine that the very small results are not a statistical fluke. But the externalists will insist that, despite the many things that we do not know about the faculty, the most important fact we do know is that it works reliably to produce more true than false beliefs.

As described, this scenario raises a host of epistemological questions, and the life-and-death setting of this gadget story forces the characters to make difficult ethical decisions based directly upon the justificatory status of their beliefs about what will happen. But Dick puts a further twist in our epistemic intuitions about the faculty of pre-cognition when he reveals the meaning of the title. In some cases the triumvirate of pre-cogs fail to reach unanimity about what will happen. When there is disagreement, the "minority report"— the one report of three that disputes the beliefs formed by the other two—is given careful analysis. The story unfolds into an internal affairs mystery about corrupt officers who have tainted the minority reports in some key investigations.

BOX 2.A: CLAIRVOYANCE AND EXTERNALISM

Externalism attempts to define "knowledge" in a way that implies that the justification for a known belief can come in the form of its connections to the facts that make it true. On reliabilist externalism, if the process that produces the belief is reliable, then it is known. In contrast, the internalist says that the justification for a belief arises from the reasons that a person has to believe that it is true. This difference gives rise to a line of criticism against externalism that can be illustrated with the help of science fiction examples.

In the re-imagined *Battlestar Galactica* series, President Laura Roslin battles her terminal illness through a psychotropic remedy, "chamalla." After taking chamalla, Roslin experiences hallucinations that she interprets as prophecies about the future, which are given to her by the gods. The beliefs induced by chamalla are more often true than false. This meets the reliabilist externalist's criterion for justified belief. (*Rental: Battlestar Galactica* season one episodes "Flesh and Bone," "The Hand of God," and "Kobol's Last Gleaming, Part I" all feature Roslin making important decisions based in part or whole upon chamalla-induced visions.)

So, is Roslin justified in believing them? Within an epistemological context, Laurence BonJour's thought experiments convinced many philosophers that externalism was false. This is one of his cases:

> Samantha believes herself to have the power of clairvoyance, though she has no reasons for or against this belief. One day she comes to believe, for no apparent reason, that the President is in New York City. She maintains this belief, appealing to her alleged clairvoyant power, even though she is at the same time aware of a massive amount of apparently cogent evidence, consisting of news reports, press releases, allegedly live television pictures, etc., indicating that the President is at that time in Washington, D.C. Now the President is in

fact in New York City, the evidence to the contrary being part of a massive official hoax mounted in the face of an assassination threat. Moreover, Samantha does in fact have completely reliable clairvoyant power, under the conditions that were then satisfied, and her belief about the President did result from the operation of that power.

(BonJour, 1980: pp. 59–60)

According to the externalist, Samantha knows that the President is in New York City. Not only does she not have a reason to believe this, but she also has reasons against this. Does she know?

We will be working with an internalist account of justification in the remainder of the chapter, though we will say more about this controversy in our conclusion. Meantime, though, one needn't take a stand on this issue to see what is amiss in our definition of knowledge.

This three-part, "**justified true belief**" or "JTB" definition of knowledge held sway for ages. But Bertrand Russell and, later, Edmund Gettier, devised clever counterexamples to it—"Gettier cases." Imagine that every day for a decade Agatha has passed by a grandfather clock on the landing of her stairway. She has many true and well justified background beliefs, including: the clock has told time accurately for the past decade; my eyes are in great working condition, allowing me to read the clock face; I know how to tell time; etc. These background beliefs are all true, she has good evidence for thinking that these beliefs are true and the set of her background beliefs makes it likely that her belief that it is 10 a.m. is also true. One morning Agatha looks at the grandfather clock, sees that its hands indicate that it is 10 o'clock. Unbeknownst to her, the clock stopped precisely twelve hours earlier. But it so happens that it is 10 a.m. at the moment she forms the belief that it is 10 a.m. Her evidence for her belief is impeccable and it does make it likely to be true that it is 10 a.m. so her belief that it is 10 a.m. is justified.

However, we are reluctant to attribute to Agatha *knowledge* that it is 10 a.m. Something seems amiss. It is only by a serendipitous accident that Agatha happened to glance at the clock just when she did, which happened to be exactly 12 hours from the time the clock happened to stop working. Her belief depends on a number of coincidences; she got very lucky this time. This Gettier case and others like it have convinced many people of the deficiency of the justified, true belief definition of knowledge.

The creation of Gettier cases prompted the search for a "fourth condition" for knowledge. Added to the previous three, a fourth condition involves specifying just what is missing from the JTB account. Epistemologists disagree widely about the content of the fourth condition. One such condition might read:

(2.4)   There is no true statement that would render A's belief P unjustified, were A to be aware of that true statement.

In this Gettier case, Agatha's justification for the belief that it is 10 a.m. depends on her belief that the clock works well. Though it has in the past, it doesn't now work well. We can call 2.4 a *no false belief condition* for it specifies that Agatha will have knowledge provided she meets the first three conditions, *and* her justification for the belief doesn't depend on a false belief.

In the thought experiment under discussion Agatha's circumstances fail to meet condition 2.4. The true proposition that defeats Agatha's justification for believing that it is 10 a.m. is "The clock is not functioning." Were Agatha to be apprised of this fact, she would no longer be justified in believing that it is 10 a.m. Since she is not justified in believing proposition P, she does not have knowledge of P.

BOX 2.B: GETTIER CASES AND THE DEFINITION OF KNOWLEDGE

In order to gain a better understanding of the JTB definition of knowledge, it is helpful to create cases of purported knowledge in which the agent believes statement P, P is true and A is justified in believing P, but in which A does *not* know P. Here is the most famous such case, created by Edmund Gettier.[2]

Suppose that Smith is justified in believing the belief "Jones owns a Ford," even though this belief is false. (Imagine that Smith saw someone in Jones' driveway who looked exactly like Jones washing a Ford.) Smith draws the valid inference that "either Jones owns a Ford, or Brown is in Barcelona." This is a valid inference because if you know P is true, then you also know that either P or Q is true.

Smith does not have any evidence to think that Brown is actually in Barcelona, but by sheer luck Brown is in Barcelona. So Smith's belief is true because it is true that "either Jones owns a Ford, or Brown is in Barcelona." Furthermore, Smith has evidence for this disjunctive statement—his original evidence that Jones owns a Ford. So on the JTB definition, even though he has inferred it from a false belief, Smith *knows* that "either Jones owns a Ford, or Brown is in Barcelona." But surely Smith doesn't really know this—it is by a stroke of luck that he is justified in believing it.

2.1 SKEPTICISM

What we have said about the term "knowledge" in 2.0 assists us in understanding epistemological challenges to knowledge claims. For every kind of knowledge claim that has been offered, it seems there has been a skeptic who attempts to argue that the claim fails to meet the requirements for knowledge. A skeptic who denies that we can have any knowledge is called a *global skeptic*.

The knowledge claims that skeptical arguments target include claims

* about religious and other supernatural matters
* about the thoughts, feelings, and sensations of other people
* about ethical and moral judgments
* about memories
* about the laws and makeup of the world around us
* about abstract principles, such as the laws of logic and mathematics
* about ourselves and our own thoughts, feelings, and characteristics.

The global skeptic holds that we have no knowledge of statements within any of those topics. Someone who holds that we lack knowledge of statements in some but not in all of the topics above is a *local skeptic*. For example, the story included in this chapter, Philip K. Dick's "We Can Remember It for You Wholesale," portrays one man's struggle with a form of local memory skepticism. The protagonist tries to identify which of his memory beliefs are truthful and which are not, but in the process he becomes skeptical of just about all his memories.

In denying that we have knowledge, the skeptic does *not* deny that some beliefs are better than others. Even the most extreme global skeptic can agree that we are *less justified* to believe that the moon is made of green cheese than to believe that it is made of rock.

BOX 2.C: ORSON WELLES, MARTIANS AND UNJUSTIFIED BELIEFS

Orson Welles was responsible for what must be one of the biggest practical jokes of the twentieth century. On October 30, 1938, under his direction, CBS radio interrupted the broadcast of an orchestral concert to alert listeners to the landing of a Martian spacecraft in New Jersey. (The description of the invasion was based largely upon the book *War of the Worlds*, authored by H. G. Wells.) The number of people convinced that a Martian invasion was taking place is often blown out of proportion to the point that people believe that the majority of listeners were duped. (There were, after all, several announcements that the broadcast was a radio play, not a newscast.) Nonetheless many acted as though they believed it by driving hundreds of miles to be with loved ones and holding impromptu religious services. Were they epistemically justified in believing there was an invasion?

When this stunt was repeated in February 1949, in Quito, Ecuador, a larger portion of the listening audience was fooled. This time listeners became so angry at having been deceived that a violent horde of people began rioting in the city and burned to the ground the radio station that broadcast the play.

(*Rental*: Tom Cruise stars in a remake of H. G. Wells' *War of the Worlds* (2005).)

The skeptic attacks the third condition of the above analysis of knowledge, statement 2.3. The skeptic allows that your belief may be rational for you, in the sense of rationality defined in §1.3. But the skeptic denies that you have sufficient evidence to be justified, so the skeptic will conclude that you do not have knowledge.

In the seventeenth century René Descartes added a number of arguments for and against several forms of skepticism in his important work *Meditations on First Philosophy*. His goal was not to wreak havoc in the then-current belief systems, even though the *Meditations* had that effect. Instead, Descartes wanted to give our knowledge claims a trial by fire, putting them through rigorous tests so that they would be better able to withstand skeptical attacks.

In the first of Descartes' *Meditations* (see reading §2.12) he creates a succession of arguments for skeptical positions. His skeptical considerations successively increase in scope, so that each skeptical argument calls into doubt more beliefs than the prior argument. Descartes starts by noticing that the propositions he had devoutly believed in the past have turned out to be false. He decides to discard any belief that is based on any evidence that is less than certain. If the evidence is less than certain, the conclusions drawn from the evidence cannot constitute knowledge, for they too will be uncertain.

Descartes realizes that much of what we believe is based on sense experience. We make judgments based on what we see, hear, feel, and so forth. Each of us, however, has experienced some form of sensory illusion.

BOX 2.D: BLIND SPOTS

So you don't think you need to worry about perceptual skepticism because your sensory systems work well? Ever considered the possibility that your sensory systems are systematically causing false perceptions? Let us help: put your left hand over your left eye. With your face about two feet away from the page, stare with your right eye at the heart and slowly move toward the book.

Figure 1 Heart and spade

The spade should disappear at some point and be replaced by a background of the same color that the page is printed on. You have found your blind spot.

At the back of each eye is the location at which an optic nerve enters the retina. This blind spot has no light receptors, therefore no light is registered by your eye and brain as being present in the location in your field of vision directly opposite your blind spots. Therefore, no light is picked up there. The reason you do not detect it normally is because both eyes working together help to minimize the effects of the blind spot. Your brain deceives you by filling in the blind spot with the colors nearest the blind spot.

When we experience an illusion, we form a false belief about the way the world is because our perceptions do not correspond to the world. I see what appears to be a body of water across the desert highway, but on approach I realize that there was no body of water and that, instead, my eyes were playing tricks on me. Descartes offers another example: from across the fields, I see what appears to be a round tower but closer in I see that it is square. Descartes infers that, since his senses sometimes deceive him, he is not justified in believing anything his senses tell him. In his words, "Whatever I have up till now accepted as most true I have acquired either from the senses or through the senses. But from time to time I have found that the senses deceive, and it is prudent never to trust completely those who have deceived us even once" (Meditation I, Descartes, 1984: p. 12).

Descartes provisionally endorses this skeptical argument about the senses. But in the cultural and historical context of his time, Descartes wants to clear away all the opinions he accepted blindly upon testimony. In the early 1600s, when Descartes was thinking about these problems, the scientist Galileo was condemned by the Catholic Church twice because Galileo dared assert that the Sun was in the center of the solar system, not Earth. The Catholic Church exerted considerable control over peoples' beliefs, and it had taught false beliefs about science and the world. Descartes wanted a fresh start for epistemology.

This provides Descartes his motivation for using what he calls the "Method of Doubt." He illustrates the method with a simile. Our set of beliefs is like a barrel of apples, some good, some rotten.

> Suppose [someone] had a basket full of apples and, being worried that some of the apples were rotten, wanted to take out the rotten ones to prevent the rot spreading. How would he proceed? Would he not begin by tipping the whole lot out of the basket? And would not the next step be to cast his eye over each apple in turn, and pick up and put back in the basket only those he saw to be sound, leaving the others?
> (Replies to the Objections to the Meditations, Descartes, 1984: p. 324)

One rotten apple can spoil the whole barrel of them, so the best way to prevent that from happening is by tipping over the whole barrel. In much the same way, one false perceptual belief can be used as a basis for many other false perceptual beliefs. Descartes recommends that we reject all the beliefs produced by some belief-forming process—in this case, vision—as being methodologically false.

2.2 DREAM SKEPTICISM

By using skeptical arguments, Descartes intends to tip the barrel over and call into question as many beliefs as possible. But perceptual skepticism didn't go far enough and didn't cause him to doubt enough beliefs. For example, even if I can't know any perceptual beliefs, I can still be justified in beliefs based on testimony from others, beliefs based on my memories and beliefs based on mathematical reasoning. So, next, he broadens the scope of skepticism with another argument having to do with dreams.

In (at least some of) our dreams, our minds create vivid experiences that can seem real to us. In some cases they appear so real that they can be mistaken for waking experience. Because dream experience can appear indistinguishable from waking experience, the skeptic argues that any waking experience I seem to have might be dream experience instead. Descartes builds a skeptical argument from these considerations about dreams.

BOX 2.E: *STAR TREK: THE NEXT GENERATION*, "SHIP IN A BOTTLE"

In "Ship in a Bottle," (season 6, episode 12) the android Commander Data is involved in a role-playing, virtual reality detective game based on the Sherlock Holmes stories. Data commands the computer to create a criminal worthy of Data's detective abilities and it does so—with startling results. Captain Picard and Data are deceived by Moriarty, Data's computer-created, virtual reality opponent (and Holmes' literary nemesis). Moriarty deceives the two into believing that they are on the bridge of the *Enterprise* when in truth they are in a virtual reality holodeck simulation of a bridge created by Moriarty himself. Fear not: Picard and Data eventually realize the deception in time to save the ship and her crew. They escape by tricking Moriarty in the same way he tricked them.

For some time while in the simulation, Picard and Data believed that they were actually operating the real ship. Though they were in the holodeck, they did not know they were. Likewise, we have various beliefs when we are dreaming about the dream-scenarios. But while in a dream, we do not know that we are. The skeptic seeks to build an argument, inspired by these situations, for the conclusion that one cannot know that one is not now dreaming.

We'll put this argument in the first person for obvious reasons. Begin with a factual claim:

(2.5)   There is a qualitative similarity between what seems to be my dream experience and what seems to be my waking experience.

This is a statement of the empirical fact that one's dream experience greatly resembles one's waking experience at least some of the time. Descartes draws some inferences from this observation.

(2.6)   If (2.5) is true, then there are no certain indications by which I can distinguish what seem to be dream experiences from what seem to be waking experiences.

(2.7)   If there are no such certain indications, then I cannot *know* I'm not dreaming right now.

(2.8)   So, I do not know that I'm not dreaming right now.

So far this argument has the following valid structure:

(2.5)   P

(2.6)   If P, then Q

(2.7)   If Q then not K

(2.8)   So, not K

This conclusion, that I cannot know that I'm not dreaming right now, is the thesis of **dream skepticism**. But what does Descartes mean by "knowledge"?

According to Descartes, for agent A to know proposition P, A must believe P, P must be true and A must be justified in believing P. So far, so good. But Descartes has his own special definition of "justification." To be justified a belief must be *indubitable*; this term means "unable to be doubted."

This type of skepticism offers two possibilities: I am in the real world or I am in a virtual world. In the *Matrix* films, characters seem to know something exceedingly important: *they know that they are either in the matrix or in the real world.* This notion that there might be a *plurality* of worlds—many virtual worlds and one real one— instead of merely a duality of worlds is not explored well in the films. The characters are given a clear and simplistic choice between two and only two alternatives. This point crystallizes in the observation that none of the characters ever appear to take seriously the hypothesis that what they think of as their non-matrix world—in which they move around in their hovercraft and subterranean caves—*might itself be part of the matrix.*

Let's return to Descartes' conclusion in the dream argument: I cannot know that I am not now dreaming. At this point in Descartes' dream argument, we have a similar phenomenon going on. On common interpretations of Descartes' dream skepticism, he too allows us to presume that we are either in a dream world or in the real world. There are only two options there, just as in *The Matrix*. Once they take the red pill, characters in the film are given knowledge of the difference between appearance and reality. For these people, they refute global skepticism by the simple act of swallowing!

Descartes takes the argument further. He realizes that if he can't know that he isn't now dreaming, then he also can't know that any of the perceptual beliefs he has are true. His perceptual beliefs—about what he sees, say—might instead be caused by computer programmers who are writing Descartes' simulation. They might be caused by Descartes' mental delusions.

> All these considerations are enough to establish that it is not reliable judgement but merely some blind impulse that has made me believe up till now that there exist things distinct from myself which transmit to me ideas or images of themselves through the sense organs or in some other way.
>
> (Meditation III, Descartes, 1984: p. 27)

In this passage Descartes is adding another obvious observation, and follows it with further conclusions:

(2.9)   In dreams, the mind-independent physical objects I believe cause my experiences are not causing my experiences.

(2.10) If (2.8) and (2.9), then I cannot know that there is a mind-independent, physical world.

Since premises 2.8 and 2.9 are in place, the antecedent—the if–clause—of 2.13 is true. This implies 2.11:

(2.11) So, I cannot know that there is an external, mind-independent world.

This conclusion is stronger than the earlier claim that I can't know that I'm not dreaming now. This argument for dream skepticism has now called into doubt beliefs about the physical world due to premises 2.9 and 2.10. The scope of this conclusion is now much wider than 2.8. Now this argument is quite strong, but not strong enough.

2.3 EVIL DEMON SKEPTICISM

We mentioned that in the tumultuous cultural and historical context of the early seventeenth century, Descartes wanted to clear away as many previous beliefs and biases as he could in order to put philosophy and science on firmer footing. The dream argument created doubt about many more types of beliefs than did his earlier perceptual skepticism argument. However, dream skepticism still didn't create doubt about all beliefs. Descartes thought that even if the full dream argument is sound, some knowledge would be left intact. Specifically, knowledge of all sorts of mathematical beliefs would remain even if he can reach the conclusion in 2.11. Agent A's belief that $1 + 1 = 2$ will be known so long as A can entertain the meaning of the terms in the belief. And this is something that she can do in dreams (says Descartes). On this basis, Descartes sought—and found—an even more pervasive form of skepticism. He hypothesized that an all-powerful evil God might exist and deceive us all. In order not to offend religious authorities at the time, Descartes redescribes the skepticism as being caused by an evil demon or evil genius.

It seems possible that there is a terrifically powerful being that controls all our thoughts and experiences, and deceives us into thinking all sorts of things that are untrue. We might be deceived in our thoughts about basic abstract principles. Each time we add $1 + 1$ we might be getting different results—and yet we might be manipulated in such a way as to be permanently unaware that we are getting different results. The evil demon could induce in us a strong feeling of regularity, consistency, and certainty in our abstract thought even when we were pitifully mistaken. The evil demon (or deceiving God) might be altering the basic metaphysics of the universe and structuring our thoughts to misrepresent it. Here is Descartes' own description of this thought experiment:

> [F]irmly rooted in my mind is the long-standing opinion that there is an omnipotent God who made me the kind of creature that I am. How do I know that he has not brought it about that there is no earth, no sky, no extended thing, no shape, no size, no place, while at the same time ensuring that all these things appear to me to exist just as they do now?
>
> (Descartes, 1984: p. 21)

BOX 2.F: INFLUENCES ON DESCARTES' EVIL DEMON ARGUMENT

Suppose you believe that demons can inhabit and control human beings. Demons do bad stuff, so it is only natural that people inhabited with demons would eventually be brought to trial. In the 1630s in a famous case in Loudon, France, a priest named Grandier was alleged to be possessed by a demon, and to have infested a convent of nuns with a legion of demons. This made headlines at the time, and Descartes was well aware of the trial and reflected upon the fascinating philosophical problems to which it gives rise.

Wouldn't Grandier's apprehension by the police be evidence against his being possessed, since demons are presumably so powerful that they could escape apprehension? Couldn't the demon control those around him so as to manipulate court proceedings of any kind? Could Grandier's own testimony ever be taken as veridical—even if he swore to tell the truth on a Bible?

Further reading: None other than author Aldous Huxley was so intrigued by this trial that he wrote a book about it called *The Devils of Loudon* (New York, 1952). Huxley's interest in social deception and control arises in his much more famous dystopian SF novel *Brave New World* (1932).

Rental: Director Ken Russell's *The Devils* (1971) was based on the Huxley book. It delves into the political machinations behind the trial, as well as the epistemological problems.

Descartes' evil demon hypothesis is the statement that *it is possible that there is an evil demon that systematically deceives me about all of my beliefs*. Here is one way to reframe this hypothesis and its accompanying thought experiment as a skeptical argument.

(2.12) I know any statement S only if I know that the evil demon hypothesis is false.

(2.13) I cannot know that the evil demon hypothesis is false.

(2.14) Therefore, I do not know any statement S, in other words, I know nothing.

The truth of premise 2.12 depends upon Descartes' definition of the key term "knowledge" as requiring indubitable justification.

2.13 is justified on the grounds that there is no first-person criterion for determining whether or not I am being deceived by an evil demon. Any evidence to which I appeal to disprove the evil demon hypothesis will fail. Arguing that I have no reason to believe that an evil demon actually exists does *not* disprove the evil demon hypothesis. True, I don't have reason to believe that any evil demon exists. But more importantly, I don't have good reasons to believe that it is *not possible* that an evil demon exists. The evil demon hypothesis only appeals to the *possible* existence of an evil demon. If I cannot disprove the evil demon hypothesis, then I am unable to prove that I know anything.

We can appreciate Descartes' skeptical arguments by a comparison with science fiction scenarios. One interesting debate regards whether skeptical science fiction scenarios parallel dream skepticism more than they do **evil demon skepticism**. When describing *The Matrix* just now, we wrote that the humans in the film seem to themselves to live the humdrum sorts of lives that we on Earth actually do live. How do I know, given the conceivability of such developments, that I am not deceived just as the characters in such stories are deceived?

One necessary condition for evil demon skepticism is that agents are unable to determine the difference between appearance and reality. I know the difference between dreaming and waking experience, but I simply don't know, at a given point in time, which I am having at that moment. We just observed that in *The Matrix*, the main characters not only can know the difference but in fact do know the difference between real and virtual experience. The same is eventually true of Captain Picard in "Ship in a Bottle."

The film *Existenz* stands apart from *The Matrix* and *Star Trek* because only *Existenz* makes the point that a virtual reality environment can itself contain other virtual environments. (*Rental*: *Existenz* (1999) directed by David Cronenberg and starring Jude Law and Jennifer Jason Leigh.) This makes *Existenz* epistemically challenging in ways that *The Matrix* films are not. In *Existenz*, candidates are selected for a special beta-test of a new virtual reality game. They assemble and begin playing in one virtual world, only to be shifted from one world to the other, never knowing which amongst those worlds is the real world. But once in the virtual environment they cannot determine which of countless "worlds" is real. In other words, *Existenz* illustrates strong evil demon skepticism whereas *The Matrix* only illustrates a weaker form of dream skepticism.

2.4 ASSESSING THE SKEPTICAL ARGUMENTS

Consider again the argument from dreaming. The first premise states that there is some qualitative similarity between what seems to be dream experience and what seems to be waking experience. But perhaps I have a test for determining whether I'm dreaming: in dreams I do not feel pain. So I can pinch myself and determine whether I'm dreaming based on whether I feel pain as a result. This shows that the claim about qualitative similarity in premise 2.5 is false.

But to this the skeptic has a ready response. For any test that I consider, it is possible to *dream* that I perform the test. And, furthermore, I can dream any result to any such test. Therefore, I can't rule out the possibility that, at any given moment, I am dreaming. This objection to premise 2.5 begs the question and presupposes that premise 2.5 is false. The critic claims that in dreams I do not experience pain—but this is only to assume that I know when I am dreaming and when I am not!

The same sort of point can be made in response to a slightly different qualitative test. A critic might observe that in what seems to be waking experience, there is a greater degree of coherence and regularity than there is in what seems to be dream experience. For examples, in what appears to be waking life, laws of nature are not violated and I don't find myself performing actions wholly out of my character. But again, this type of objection only presupposes that we know the difference between dreaming and waking experience. Perhaps, the skeptic retorts, it is my dreaming experience that is the more coherent and regular. This points to the insidiousness of skeptical arguments; they are intellectual quicksand.

A famous response to global skepticism was offered by Descartes himself, in the second of his *Meditations*. It begins with a question: are there any beliefs whatsoever about which I can be certain? Suppose I am in a virtual world, wherein the intelligence that deceives me can even make false my belief that $1 + 1 = 2$. Is there anything at all that I can know with certainty?

Descartes believes that I know one statement with certainty: that I exist. (We can see why Descartes chooses to write in the first-person.) Even if I might be deceived in all I think, says Descartes, still I am certain of this: I think, I am. For even if *what* I think is false and deceptive, *that* I think cannot be doubted, for to doubt is to think, and, even if my thoughts are deceived, they are still thoughts. If I think, then I am, I exist. This thought is called the **cogito**, from the Latin "I think." It rests upon the fact that statements such as this are *self-verifying*: by doubting the statement in question, by doubting that I think, I thereby think. In other words, since doubting is a form of thinking, I make the statement true by doubting it.

Establishing this belief as true and sufficiently justified marks the first half of Descartes' move out of global skepticism. From this foundation, as small as it may seem, Descartes proceeds to argue that we can once again come to know most of the beliefs that he initially subjected to doubt. Descartes believes that from this modest beginning he can offer arguments that give us certain knowledge of the existence of God, and of the physical world.

But there are other interesting ways to respond to evil demon skepticism. First, the premises of the argument depend upon a privileged definition of "know": for Descartes, to know a statement entails that the statement is indubitable for you. You cannot doubt it. If we simply lower those demanding standards for knowledge, we can deny his claims that we do not "know" certain statements. For example, in order to know something perhaps I only need to have pretty good evidence on its behalf. If so, then my knowledge of beliefs from memory, perception or mathematics are known *even though* I can't show that it is impossible an evil demon is deceiving me. (We explore this response to skepticism shortly in section 2.7.)

BOX 2.G: DID DESCARTES PLAGIARIZE ST. AUGUSTINE?

It wasn't common practice to cite sources in the 1640s as it is today. But we shouldn't forget that Saint Augustine (b. 354–d. 430 AD) raised the skeptical worries Descartes did, and solved them in the same ways too. Saint Augustine writes,

> In regard to this [being deceived about our knowledge that we live] we are absolutely without any fear unless we are perhaps being deceived by some resemblance of the truth; since it is certain, that he who is deceived, yet lives . . . The knowledge by which we know that we live is the most inward of all knowledge, of which even the Academic [skeptic] cannot insinuate: Perhaps you are asleep, and do not know it . . . Nor can the academic again say, in confutation of this knowledge: Perhaps you are mad, and do not know it: . . . but he who is mad is alive. Therefore he who says he knows he is alive, can neither be deceived nor lie. Let a thousand kinds of deceitful objects of sight

be presented to him who says, I know I am alive; yet he will fear none of them, for he who is deceived yet is alive.

(*De Trinitate* XV.xii.21)

Not only does Augustine concisely explain the epistemological status of self-verifying propositions, but he also seems to take up just those skeptical considerations Descartes later does: about bodily senses, sleep and dreaming, and insanity.

The refutation of global skepticism from the indubitability of self-verifying propositions like "I think" is most clear in Augustine's most famous work, *The City of God*:

In the face of these truths, the quibbles of the skeptics lose their force. If they say, "What if you are mistaken?"—well, if I am mistaken, I am. For, if one does not exist, he can by no means be mistaken. Therefore, I am, if I am mistaken. Because, therefore, I am, if I am mistaken, how can I be mistaken that I am, since it is certain that I am, if I am mistaken? and because, if I could be mistaken, I would have to be the one who is mistaken, therefore, I am most certainly not mistaken in knowing that I am. Nor, as a consequence, am I mistaken in knowing that I know. For, just as I know that I am, I also know that I know.

(*The City of God*, book XI, c.26)

Augustine rarely receives the credit he deserves for foreseeing this "Cartesian" solution to global skepticism. Not only has he foreseen the epistemological utility of self-verifying statements, he seems to be better attuned to the subtlety of such statements than Descartes himself. You can be the judge as to whether Descartes is guilty of plagiarism. Perhaps a better question is: Did a demon make him do it?

2.5 FOUNDATIONALISM

The structure of Descartes' replies to his own skeptical arguments influences contemporary epistemology. Because he starts from a few fundamental truths and builds from these a broad structure of knowledge, Descartes is called a foundationalist. **Foundationalism** is the thesis that special statements called *basic beliefs* are known and that basic beliefs allow us to justify further beliefs based upon them. What is special about basic beliefs is that they are known but their knowledge does not depend upon the knowledge of any other beliefs. In geometry, one starts with a few basic beliefs called "axioms," and one uses these axioms to construct theorems. Using the axioms, one can generate a very sophisticated system of thought. The foundationalist thinks that a similar structure can be constructed for ordinary knowledge claims, on the basis of a few basic beliefs.

The central motivation for foundationalism involves the **regress of knowledge** problem. My belief B is justified and true, and so is knowledge. The justification for B is another belief P. P justifies B for me because P is also justified and true: I know P too. But we have a similar pattern with respect to the justification of P. P is justified by my belief that Q, which is in turn justified and true. But how do I justify Q, and the beliefs upon which Q is itself justified? This sequence of beliefs can take one of only a few forms. It may (i) loop back upon itself; (ii) may continue on indefinitely; (iii) stop in beliefs that are themselves unknown; or (iv) it may stop in basic beliefs that are known independently of knowledge of yet other beliefs.

The most plausible responses to the regress of knowledge problem are (i) and (iv). *Coherentists* are those philosophers who adopt a form of option (i). Foundationalists opt for (iv). Few philosophers are attracted to options (ii) and (iii) because it is thought that neither of those options achieves the desired result—showing that I know B.

Coherentists opt for a form of (i), but this option can be given different logical structures. The loop might be a linear circle: Q justifies P, which justifies B, and B justifies Q, which . . . This chain-like structure does not seem to justify all its component beliefs. If that were the structure of my justification for B, the justification would be inadequate to convert belief B into knowledge. But coherentists argue for a version of (i) in which the structure of our beliefs resembles a spider's web. In a spider's web each filament is connected to every other filament through very strong ties. The overall result is a stable, well engineered structure. The coherentist holds that our network of beliefs is similarly interconnected and produces a stable structure. Member beliefs bear numerous inferential relationships with other beliefs, producing a coherent nexus of beliefs to support knowledge.

Foundationalists argue, in contrast, that option (iv) best solves the regress problem. Foundationalists are led to find basic beliefs that are known, but whose knowledge does not depend on the knowledge of other beliefs. Basic beliefs serve as the foundation for the superstructure of beliefs that we build on top of them. When we construct a big, multi-storey building, the only way it can be made to stand is by pouring a solid foundation. Reflect on the enormously layered nature of your belief system. The foundationalist suggests that beliefs in those upper layers—layers containing no basic beliefs at all—crucially depend for their justification upon lower layers that are well grounded and well justified.

If a skeptic shows that foundational beliefs are uncertain, he effectively shows that all beliefs in the structure are uncertain. Such a skeptic might argue in this way against Descartes by attempting to raise doubts about whether Descartes knows with certainty that he exists.

BOX 2.H: PUTNAM ON RESOLVING BRAIN-IN-A-VAT SKEPTICISM

A contemporary philosopher, Hilary Putnam, describes what he calls *brain-in-a-vat skepticism* and articulates a novel response to it. His response uses resources from the philosophy of language to make a point about the limits of the ability to refer to objects with words.

> Imagine that a human being (you can imagine this to be yourself) has been subjected to an operation by an evil scientist. The person's brain (your brain) has been removed from the body and placed in a vat of nutrients which keeps the brain alive. The nerve endings have been connected to a super-scientific computer which causes the person whose brain it is to have the illusion that everything is perfectly normal. There seem to be people, objects, the sky, etc., but really all the person (you) is experiencing is the result of electronic impulses traveling from the computer to the nerve endings. The computer is so clever that if the person tries to raise his hand, the feedback from the computer will cause him to "see" and "feel" the hand being raised. Moreover, by varying the program, the evil scientist can cause the victim to "experience" (or hallucinate) any situation or environment the evil scientist wishes. He can also obliterate the memory of the brain operation, so that the victim will seem to himself to have always been in this environment. It can even seem to the victim that he is sitting and reading these very words about the amusing but quite absurd supposition that there is an evil scientist who removes people's brains from their bodies and places them in a vat of nutrients which keeps the brains alive.
>
> (Putnam, 1981: pp. 5–6)

Putnam argues that he can refute brain-in-a-vat skepticism on grounds having to do with the nature of language.

Suppose that the meanings of the words used by the envatted person are fixed by their causal connections with objects in the mind-independent world, as opposed to being fixed by networks of mental states in the mind. So his thoughts about fire hydrants have the structure and content that they do in part because he has experienced causal interactions with fire hydrants. If so, then, if he were a brain-in-a-vat, it would be impossible for him to form the thought that he is a brain-in-a-vat since that thought fails to bear the appropriate causal connections to the mind-independent world! When a brain-in-a-vat thinks "that's a fire hydrant," the term "fire hydrant" means something different in brain-in-a-vat-English than it does in normal English. This argument is based upon a theory in the philosophy of language known as *semantic externalism*.

There are a number of different proposals on how to use semantic externalism to prove that brain-in-a-vat skepticism is false. The most commonsensical one is this: (i) Brains in vats fail to have concepts through which they can think about things like cars, Mars and candy bars; (ii) I, though, have just the sorts of concepts needed to think about those things; (iii) therefore, I know I am not a brain-in-a-vat. Concerns about this use of semantic externalism to refute skepticism have focused upon (ii), for just how the non-skeptic justifies this premise without begging the question against the skeptic is unclear.

Despite its apparent decisiveness in refuting skepticism, there are actually several questions we can raise about the *cogito*. Foremost among these is: What is its precise logical status? Many have thought that the *cogito* and other propositions like it are *self-verifying*, that is, known in virtue of being believed. But is the *cogito* self-verifying? Descartes states the *cogito* in two different ways. In the *Meditations*, he puts it as we have above: "I think, I am." But in a lesser known book, *The Rules for the Direction of Mind*, he further writes, "I think, therefore I am" (in Latin *Cogito, ergo sum*). The way of putting the point in *The Rules* makes it seem as though the *cogito* is an inference: "I think" is the premise, and "I am" is the conclusion. If interpreted in this way, though, "I think, so I exist" begs the question since my existence, the conclusion, is presupposed in the premise.

Yet another way in which a skeptic might argue against Descartes' foundationalist approach is to say that, even if the foundation is indubitable and certain, it is inadequate to support anything beyond itself. The foundationalist needs to have basic knowledge of statements that are both certain and sufficiently numerous to be able to use them to infer further truths. If all I can rightly claim to know is that I think and exist, I am not far from being a global skeptic. The global skeptic will ask, "When you make inferences from knowing that you exist to knowing statements about what your dog ate yesterday, how do you know that your reasoning isn't confused by the manipulations of the evil demon?" The content of my belief in my existence doesn't lend any evidential support to my belief about my dog—they are about wholly different things. Descartes must find a set of basic beliefs from which he can build an epistemological bridge from what he knows to what he does not yet know. No bridge between these two beliefs is apparent. So it seems Descartes may need more beliefs in his foundations for knowledge. But "I think" and other beliefs very similar to it are the only beliefs capable of meeting Descartes' indubitability requirement for knowledge.

2.6 CLOSURE PRINCIPLES

The skeptic insists that I can't know that skeptical hypotheses, like the evil demon hypothesis, are false. We see this in premise 2.12: I know some statement P only if I know that the skeptical hypothesis is false. This wouldn't be a problem if it weren't for the fact that, as stated in 2.13, I cannot know that the skeptical hypothesis is false. It is the combination of 2.12 with 2.13 that justifies the conclusion that I have no knowledge. Implicitly, these two premises are bound logically together by a conditional statement of the form:

(2.15) If I do not know that skeptical hypotheses are false, then I do not know most of the beliefs I think I know.

Typically, the first line of attack on skeptical arguments is to argue against premises like 2.12 by giving specific refutations of each type of skeptical hypothesis. This is what we have been engaged in doing (so far, unsuccessfully) when assessing forms of skepticism. But there is another important second line of attack open to the non-skeptic in which he targets the logical relationship represented in 2.15.

This line of attack uses **closure principles** about knowledge. *Closure principles* specify the conditions under which one is justified to move from some known belief P to knowledge of another belief Q. They can also specify conditions under which one is not justified to move from some known belief P to knowledge of another belief Q.

The non-skeptic may turn the tables on the skeptic's reasoning in 2.12 to 2.15 by using a closure principle like this:

(2.16) If an agent knows P, and knows that if P then Q, then the agent knows Q.

This principle can be used in a refutation of skepticism. Consider the following two statements:

(P)   I see that snow is falling in New York City.

(Q)   I am not now dreaming.

Suppose I know P because I am in New York City, and I see snow falling all around me. If P—that is, if I am actually seeing snow falling in New York City—then I cannot be dreaming. In dreams, I do not actually see anything and I am not actually in New York City. In dreams I only *seem* to see and *appear* to be somewhere else. In this case, if 2.16, then P and Q combine to justify the conclusion that dream skepticism is false.

When we attempt to assess whether an agent knows a proposition, the agent is thought to need to rule out alternative beliefs that, if true, would defeat the agent's knowledge of the proposition. Consider an alternative to P, namely:

(S)   All my perceptual beliefs, including the belief that it is snowing in New York City, are the products of a virtual reality simulation I am now running.

If the context in which P is asserted is a local radio station's weather report, then the skeptical possibility presented in S is not relevant. Alternatives are deemed relevant or irrelevant in part upon the context in which the statement is asserted. But if the context in which P is asserted is a complex science fiction story involving artificial intelligences that harbor prejudices against humanity, then S becomes relevant.

On the basis of this use of the non-skeptic's closure principle, non-skeptics argue that in order to know most of the beliefs I think I know, I do not need to know that skeptical hypotheses are false because such skeptical hypotheses are irrelevant to my knowledge of most of what I know. Therefore, the non-skeptic alleges, the problem of global skepticism is overcome.

But the skeptic has a reply at hand. In the context of a radio station's weather report, other alternatives are relevant. Consider this one:

(R)   I see that fine flakes of white ash emitted by a factory are falling in New York City.

Let's set the context. It is a balmy July in New York, where the daytime temperature hasn't dropped below 85 for weeks. It happens that there was an industrial accident in the city that morning that has emitted 30 tonnes of white ash into the sky. One radio station's local weather watchers report to the station that it is snowing. In addition, many background beliefs play important epistemic roles in making a judgment about R. These include the beliefs that snow only falls when it is cold outside, for example.

With the context and background assumptions in mind, R is relevant given the context. The local weather watcher's report is not justified because he has failed to rule out R as an alternative explanation of his sensory perception. So there are circumstances in which some alternatives are relevant, and serve to scuttle the knowledge that one claims to possess. The skeptic directs us to contexts in which an alternative like S is relevant to my belief that P. What would such a context be? One strong candidate for a context in which S is a relevant alternative to P is the very context we're in now—doing philosophy. The skeptic will argue that the use of 2.16 makes a travesty of the problems of epistemology. Skepticism is refuted in one exceedingly simple step if the non-skeptic's closure principle is true. But, the skeptic argues, this refutation is much too easy. Invoking the non-skeptic's closure principle is tantamount to dissolving the skeptical challenge, and does not take the problem seriously. The non-skeptic wins the bet only by fixing the race, or so epistemologists have argued.

2.7 CERTAINTY AND FALLIBILISM

Perhaps, after considering skeptical arguments, you thought that they were fanciful and unrealistic, that they took the problem of knowledge too seriously in the first place. If so, you are in good company. *Fallibilists* in epistemology attempt to restructure our thinking about knowledge by arguing that person A can know statement P even if A's justification for P is not certain or indubitable. Fallibilists argue that Descartes took epistemology down a dead-end with his exceedingly strong requirements on knowledge. Most knowledge claims do not meet the requirements set out by Descartes. But fallibilists take this as a reason to reject those requirements in the first place.

Fallibists differ from skeptics on an important point. Skeptics claim that beliefs fail to meet a high standard for knowledge, and they conclude that we lack knowledge. Fallibilists claim that beliefs fail to meet a high standard for knowledge, but they do not conclude that we have no knowledge. Fallibilists just endorse different standards for knowledge. Typically, if someone were to ask you, "Do you know that you are reading a book?," you would answer, "Of course!" But then he asks, "Couldn't it be the case that an evil demon was deceiving you into thinking that you are reading a book, when in fact you are not?" Now you might answer, "Well, it's possible that I am mistaken in such a way, but I never claimed to be *infallible*. Nonetheless, I still believe that I know I am reading a book." If you answer in this way, you are a fallibilist. According to **fallibilism**, you can have knowledge of P even if P is not certain for you. The fallibilist is then able to argue that we can know most of what we think we know.

But, as might be expected, many are not convinced that this answer defeats skepticism. We can imagine a case in which the majority of people used a term incorrectly. For example, the proper definition of "Martian" might be "an intelligent creature from Mars." Now that we have landed very sophisticated equipment on Mars and have found it to be devoid of life, we might conclude that there are no Martians. But then someone might come along and say that most people use the term "Martian" to refer to any alien from another world, as a synonym for "extraterrestrial being." Does that mean that when we say, "There are no Martians because there is no life on Mars," we have employed a poor analysis of the term "Martian?" No, it only means that, in ordinary usage, people use the term "Martian" carelessly.

Similarly, the skeptic might argue that the fact that people use the word "knowledge" in all sorts of careless ways does not show that the analysis of knowledge used by the skeptic is incorrect. It may only show that a careless use of the term is common. The skeptic would conclude that, on a proper understanding of the term, it refers to few (if any) actual cases. If we choose to use the word "knowledge" in a fallibilist way, we are simply using another concept. We are not refuting the skeptic's arguments.

The skeptic challenges us to defend our claim that we have a large amount of knowledge about various subjects (or, in the case of global, evil demon skepticism, about anything at all). The skeptic's strategy is to point out that many of the beliefs we have that we think are knowledge do not qualify as knowledge. Many of our beliefs about scientific matters are false, for example, but I rely equally on them all and count them all as knowledge. We must grant to the skeptic that at least some of what we currently count as knowledge is not. Then the question becomes: *Which* of our beliefs are known?

2.8 SUMMARY

Chapter 2 began with a discussion of the concept of knowledge and a definition of that term. Propositional knowledge is our focus, and we offered a justified-true-belief definition of it. This, however, was subject to the Agatha counterexample. Her belief *that it is 10 a.m.* is justified and true, but it is insufficient for knowledge since its truth depends upon a lucky accident.

We examined dream and evil demon skepticisms, which Descartes uses in his *Meditations*. We presented and evaluated arguments on behalf of those forms of skepticism. Criticisms of those arguments included appeals to the "cogito," to foundationalism and to closure principles.

According to foundationalism there are basic beliefs, and they are self-justifying. The regress of justification—the demand to justify all those beliefs that justify other beliefs— stops when it reaches basic beliefs, so says the foundationalist. Descartes himself was a foundationalist whose only foundational principle was the cogito. That has limited success in stopping skepticism, however, because that foundation is ineffective at justifying a wide selection of other beliefs.

This led us into a discussion of closure principles. Closure principles about knowledge specify the conditions under which one is justified in inferring an unknown belief from a known belief. Both skeptics and non-skeptics use these principles to debate the burden of proof. We concluded the chapter by discussing the role of certainty in refutations of skepticism. Descartes sets the bar for knowledge very high indeed; philosophers since his time have adopted weaker definitions of knowledge and fallible foundations in their continuing engagement with skepticism.

2.9 ABOUT THE READINGS

This chapter includes four readings, one of science fiction, one from ancient philosophy, one from early modern philosophy and a final contemporary philosophy paper.

Our science fiction selection, "We Can Remember It for You Wholesale," is perhaps the best Philip K. Dick exploration of the boundaries between appearance and reality. Like other Dick stories, this was produced as a film under the title *Total Recall* (1990). Douglas Quail is a miserable salaried employee for the West Coast Emigration Bureau, but he has one abiding dream—to visit Mars before he dies. He can't afford the trip, so he settles for implanted memories of such a trip, which he buys at Rekal Inc. But after the doctors at Rekal begin the procedure, they discover that Quail has a number of apparently false memories embedded in his brain already. They hustle him out the door with a refund, but the procedure has brought back to Quail fragmentary memories of a Mars trip. Which are real and which are fake? Neither he nor Rekal seems to know. Quail learns the truth when police from the security agency Interplan hunt him down. Or does he?

Plato, in *Republic* book VII, explores appearance/reality with a brief story of his own. In the "Allegory of the Cave," Plato offers compelling visual imagery to describe the inability of the human mind to gain knowledge of reality as it is in itself. He believed that the physical world was illusory. Knowledge, he said, must be of things that do not change. But we are surrounded by a physical environment that changes every moment. We are like prisoners who see only shadows on the wall. And shadows of what? Puppets. We are benighted and deceived.

This allegory can be compared and contrasted with Descartes' skepticism. Descartes also believed that our senses do not give us knowledge of the world and, like Plato, believed that reason was infinitely better than the senses at acquiring knowledge. In the 1640s, when the *Meditations* were published, questioning the prejudices and presuppositions of the authorities was punishable by death. For example, shortly before Descartes' career as an author, Galileo was brought a second time before an inquisition by the Catholic Church on the grounds that he believed in a heliocentric solar system, which contradicted the Church's teachings and conflicted with the Bible. With stakes so high, Descartes adopted a literary form that allowed him some freedom to speak his mind in order to achieve his goal of laying waste to the inherited beliefs passed down by the Catholic Church of his day. This philosophical treatise was put in the form of six daily meditations, and the selection here includes the first and part of the second. There he presents the case for dream skepticism, evil demon skepticism and his response to those arguments with the claim that "I think, I exist."

Contemporary philosophers have found ways to amplify the force of skepticism by appeal to the power of computer simulations. The simulation argument, developed by Nick Bostrom of the Future of Humanity Institute at Oxford University, contends that one of the following claims must be true: (1) intelligent beings won't reach a level of technology at which they create simulations so sophisticated that they are indistinguishable from reality; (2) species that do reach such a level refrain from creating them; or (3) it is highly probable that we are living in a simulation, not in the real world. In our reading, Alasdair Richmond, of Edinburgh University, analyzes the simulation argument, compares its content with other skeptical arguments in the history of philosophy (including Descartes'), and diagnoses some problems with it.

2.10 "WE CAN REMEMBER IT FOR YOU WHOLESALE," BY PHILIP K. DICK

He awoke—and wanted Mars. The valleys, he thought. What would it be like to trudge among them? Great and greater yet: the dream grew as he became fully conscious, the dream and the yearning. He could almost feel the enveloping presence of the other world, which only Government agents and high officials had seen. A clerk like himself? Not likely.

"Are you getting up or not?" his wife Kirsten asked drowsily, with her usual hint of fierce crossness. "If you are, push the hot coffee button on the darn stove."

"Okay," Douglas Quail said, and made his way barefoot from the bedroom of their conapt to the kitchen. There, having dutifully pressed the hot coffee button, he seated himself at the kitchen table, brought out a yellow, small tin of fine Dean Swift snuff. He inhaled briskly, and the Beau Nash mixture stung his nose, burned the roof of his mouth. But still he inhaled; it woke him up and allowed his dreams, his nocturnal desires and random wishes, to condense into a semblance of rationality.

I will go, he said to himself. *Before I die I'll see Mars.*

It was, of course, impossible, and he knew this even as he dreamed. But the daylight, the mundane noise of his wife now brushing her hair before the bedroom mirror—everything conspired to remind him of what he was. *A miserable little salaried employee*, he said to himself with bitterness. Kirsten reminded him of this at least once a day and he did not blame her; it was a wife's job to bring her husband down to Earth. *Down to Earth*, he thought, and laughed. The figure of speech in this was literally apt.

"What are you sniggering about?" his wife asked as she swept into the kitchen, her long busy-pink robe wagging after her. "A dream, I bet. You're always full of them."

"Yes," he said, and gazed out the kitchen window at the hover-cars and traffic runnels, and all the little energetic people hurrying to work. In a little while he would be among them. As always.

"I'll bet it has to do with some woman," Kirsten said witheringly.

"No," he said. "A god. The god of war. He has wonderful craters with every kind of plant-life growing deep down in them."

"Listen." Kirsten crouched down beside him and spoke earnestly, the harsh quality momentarily gone from her voice. "The bottom of the ocean—*our* ocean is much more, an infinity of times more beautiful. You know that; everyone knows that. Rent an artificial gill-outfit for both of us, take a week off from work, and we can descend and live down there at one of those year-round aquatic resorts. And in addition," She broke off. "You're not listening. You should be. Here is something a lot better than that compulsion, that obsession you have about Mars, and you don't even listen!" Her voice rose piercingly. "God in heaven, you're doomed, Doug! What's going to become of you?"

"I'm going to work," he said, rising to his feet, his breakfast forgotten. "That's what's going to become of me."

She eyed him. "You're getting worse. More fanatical every day. Where's it going to lead?"

"To Mars," he said, and opened the door to the closet to get down a fresh shirt to wear to work.

Having descended from the taxi Douglas Quail slowly walked across three densely-populated foot runnels and to the modern, attractively inviting doorway. There he halted, impeding mid-morning traffic, and with caution read the shifting-color neon sign. He had, in the past, scrutinized this sign before . . . but never had he come so close. This was very different; what he did now was something else. Something which sooner or later had to happen.

Rekal, Incorporated

Was this the answer? After all, an illusion, no matter how convincing, remained nothing more than an illusion. At least objectively. But subjectively—quite the opposite entirely.

And anyhow he had an appointment. Within the next five minutes. Taking a deep breath of mildly smog-infested Chicago air, he walked through the dazzling polychromatic shimmer of the doorway and up to the receptionist's counter. The nicely-articulated blonde at the counter, bare-bosomed and tidy, said pleasantly, "Good morning, Mr. Quail."

"Yes," he said. "I'm here to see about a Rekal course. As I guess you know."

"Not 'rekal' but *recall*," the receptionist corrected him. She picked up the receiver of the vidphone by her smooth elbow and said into it, "Mr. Douglas Quail is here, Mr. McClane. May he come inside, now? Or is it too soon?"

"Giz wetwa wum-wum wamp," the phone mumbled.

"Yes, Mr. Quail," she said. "You may go on in; Mr. McClane is expecting you." As he started off uncertainly she called after him, "Room D, Mr. Quail. To your right."

After a frustrating but brief moment of being lost he found the proper room. The door hung open and inside, at a big genuine walnut desk, sat a genial-looking man, middle-aged, wearing the latest Martian frog-pelt gray suit; his attire alone would have told Quail that he had come to the right person.

"Sit down, Douglas," McClane said, waving his plump hand toward a chair which faced the desk. "So you want to have gone to Mars. Very good."

Quail seated himself, feeling tense. "I'm not so sure this is worth the fee," he said. "It costs a lot and as far as I can see I really get nothing." *Costs almost as much as going*, he thought.

"You get tangible proof of your trip," McClane disagreed emphatically. "All the proof you'll need. Here; I'll show you." He dug within a drawer of his impressive desk. "Ticket stub." Reaching into a manila folder he produced a small square of embossed cardboard. "It proves you went—and returned. Postcards." He laid out four franked picture 3-D full-color postcards in a neatly-arranged row on the desk for Quail to see. "Film. Shots you took of local sights on Mars with a rented movie camera." To Quail he displayed those, too. "Plus the names of people you met, two hundred poscreds worth of souvenirs, which will arrive—from Mars—within the following month. And passport, certificates listing the shots you received. And more." He glanced up keenly at Quail. "You'll know you went, all right," he said. "You won't remember us, won't remember me or ever having been here. It'll be a real trip in your mind; we guarantee that. A full two weeks of recall; every last piddling detail. Remember this: if at any time you doubt that you really took an extensive trip to Mars you can return here and get a full refund. You see?"

"But I didn't go," Quail said. "I won't have gone, no matter what proofs you provide me with." He took a deep, unsteady breath. "And I never was a secret agent with Interplan." It seemed impossible to him that Rekal, Incorporated's extra-factual memory implant would do its job—despite what he had heard people say.

"Mr. Quail," McClane said patiently. "As you explained in your letter to us, you have no chance, no possibility in the slightest, of ever actually getting to Mars; you can't afford it, and what is much more important, you could never qualify as an undercover agent for Interplan or anybody else. This is the only way you can achieve your, ahem, life-long dream; am I not correct, sir? You can't be this; you can't actually do this." He chuckled. "But you can *have been* and *have done*. We see to that. And our fee is reasonable; no hidden charges." He smiled encouragingly.

"Is an extra-factual memory that convincing?" Quail asked.

"More than the real thing, sir. Had you really gone to Mars as an Interplan agent, you would by now have forgotten a great deal; our analysis of true-mem systems— authentic recollections of major events in a person's life—shows that a variety of details are very quickly lost to the person. Forever. Part of the package we offer you is such deep implantation of recall that nothing is forgotten. The packet which is fed to you while you're comatose is the creation of trained experts, men who have spent years on Mars; in every case we verify details down to the last iota. And you've picked a rather easy extra-factual system; had you picked Pluto or wanted to be Emperor of the Inner Planet Alliance we'd have much more difficulty . . . and the charges would be considerably greater."

Reaching into his coat for his wallet, Quail said, "Okay. It's been my life-long ambition and I can see I'll never really do it. So I guess I'll have to settle for this."

"Don't think of it that way," McClane said severely. "You're not accepting second-best. The actual memory, with all its vagueness, omissions and ellipses, not to say distortions—that's second-best." He accepted the money and pressed a button on his desk.

"All right, Mr. Quail," he said, as the door of his office opened and two burly men swiftly entered. "You're on your way to Mars as a secret agent." He rose, came over to shake Quail's nervous, moist hand. "Or rather, you have been on your way. This afternoon at four-thirty you will, um, arrive back here on Terra; a cab will leave you off at your conapt and as I say you will never remember seeing me or coming here; you won't, in fact, even remember having heard of our existence."

His mouth dry with nervousness, Quail followed the two technicians from the office; what happened next depended on them.

Will I actually believe I've been on Mars? he wondered. *That I managed to fulfill my lifetime ambition?* He had a strange, lingering intuition that something would go wrong. But just what—he did not know.

He would have to wait to find out.

The intercom on McClane's desk, which connected him with the work area of the firm, buzzed and a voice said, "Mr. Quail is under sedation now, sir. Do you want to supervise this one, or shall we go ahead?"

"It's routine," McClane observed. "You may go ahead, Lowe; I don't think you'll run into any trouble." Programming an artificial memory of a trip to another planet—with or without the added fillip of being a secret agent—showed up on the firm's work-schedule with monotonous regularity. *In one month,* he calculated wryly, *we must do twenty of these . . . ersatz interplanetary travel has become our bread and butter.*

"Whatever you say, Mr. McClane," Lowe's voice came, and thereupon the intercom shut off.

Going to the vault section in the chamber behind his office, McClane searched about for a Three packet—trip to Mars—and a Sixty-two packet: secret Interplan spy. Finding the two packets, he returned with them to his desk, seated himself comfortably, poured out the contents—merchandise which would be planted in Quail's conapt while the lab technicians busied themselves installing the false memory.

A one-poscred sneaky-pete side arm, McClane reflected; *that's the largest item. Sets us back financially the most.* Then a pellet-sized transmitter, which could be swallowed if the agent were caught. Code book that astonishingly resembled the real thing . . . the firm's models were highly accurate: based, whenever possible, on actual U.S. military issue. Odd bits which made no intrinsic sense but which would be woven into the warp and woof of Quail's imaginary trip, would coincide with his memory: half an ancient silver fifty cent piece, several quotations from John Donne's sermons written incorrectly, each on a separate piece of transparent tissue-thin paper, several match folders from bars on Mars, a stainless steel spoon engraved PROPERTY OF DOME-MARS NATIONAL KIBBUZIM, a wire tapping coil which—

The intercom buzzed. "Mr. McClane, I'm sorry to bother you but something rather ominous has come up. Maybe it would be better if you were in here after all. Quail is already under sedation; he reacted well to the narkidrine; he's completely unconscious and receptive. But—"

"I'll be in." Sensing trouble, McClane left his office; a moment later he emerged in the work area.

On a hygienic bed lay Douglas Quail, breathing slowly and regularly, his eyes virtually shut; he seemed dimly—but only dimly—aware of the two technicians and now McClane himself.

"There's no space to insert false memory-patterns?" McClane felt irritation. "Merely drop out two work weeks; he's employed as a clerk at the West Coast Emigration Bureau, which is a government agency, so he undoubtedly has or had two weeks vacation within the last year. That ought to do it." Petty details annoyed him. And always would.

"Our problem," Lowe said sharply, "is something quite different." He bent over the bed, said to Quail, "Tell Mr. McClane what you told us." To McClane he said, "Listen closely."

The gray-green eyes of the man lying supine in the bed focused on McClane's face. The eyes, he observed uneasily, had become hard; they had a polished, inorganic quality, like semi-precious tumbled stones. He was not sure that he liked what he saw; the brilliance was too cold. "What do you want now?" Quail said harshly. "You've broken my cover. Get out of here before I take you all apart." He studied McClane. "Especially you," he continued. "You're in charge of this counter-operation."

Lowe said, "How long were you on Mars?"

"One month," Quail said gratingly.

"And your purpose there?" Lowe demanded.

The meager lips twisted; Quail eyed him and did not speak. At last, drawling the words out so that they dripped with hostility, he said, "Agent for Interplan. As I already told you. Don't you record everything that's said? Play your vid-aud tape back for your boss and leave me alone." He shut his eyes, then; the hard brilliance ceased. McClane felt, instantly, a rushing splurge of relief.

Lowe said quietly, "This is a tough man, Mr. McClane."

"He won't be," McClane said, "after we arrange for him to lose his memory-chain again. He'll be as meek as before." To Quail he said, "So *this* is why you wanted to go to Mars so terribly bad."

Without opening his eyes Quail said, "I never wanted to go to Mars. I was assigned it—they handed it to me and there I was: stuck. Oh yeah, I admit I was curious about it; who wouldn't be?" Again he opened his eyes and surveyed the three of them, McClane in particular. "Quite a truth drug you've got here; it brought up things I had absolutely no memory of." He pondered. "I wonder about Kirsten," he said, half to himself. "Could she be in on it? An Interplan contact keeping an eye on me . . . to be certain I didn't regain my memory? No wonder she's been so derisive about my wanting to go there." Faintly, he smiled; the smile—one of understanding—disappeared almost at once.

McClane said, "Please believe me, Mr. Quail; we stumbled onto this entirely by accident. In the work we do—"

"I believe you," Quail said. He seemed tired, now; the drug was continuing to pull him under, deeper and deeper. "Where did I say I'd been?" he murmured. "Mars? Hard to remember—I know I'd like to see it; so would everybody else. But me—" His voice trailed off. "Just a clerk, a nothing clerk."

Straightening up, Lowe said to his superior, "He wants a false memory implanted that corresponds to a trip he actually took. And a false reason which is the real reason.

He's telling the truth; he's a long way down in the narkidrine. The trip is very vivid in his mind—at least under sedation. But apparently he doesn't recall it otherwise. Someone, probably at a government military-sciences lab, erased his conscious memories; all he knew was that going to Mars meant something special to him, and so did being a secret agent. They couldn't erase that; it's not a memory but a desire, undoubtedly the same one that motivated him to volunteer for the assignment in the first place."

The other technician, Keeler, said to McClane, "What do we do? Graft a false memory-pattern over the real memory? There's no telling what the results would be; he might remember some of the genuine trip, and the confusion might bring on a psychotic interlude. He'd have to hold two opposite premises in his mind simultaneously: that he went to Mars and that he didn't. That he's a genuine agent for Interplan and he's not, that it's spurious. I think we ought to revive him without any false memory implantation and send him out of here; this is hot."

"Agreed," McClane said. A thought came to him. "Can you predict what he'll remember when he comes out of sedation?"

"Impossible to tell," Lowe said. "He probably will have some dim, diffuse memory of his actual trip, now. And he'd probably be in grave doubt as to its validity; he'd probably decide our programming slipped a gear-tooth. And he'd remember coming here; that wouldn't be erased—unless you want it erased."

"The less we mess with this man," McClane said, "the better I like it. This is nothing for us to fool around with; we've been foolish enough to—or unlucky enough to—uncover a genuine Interplan spy who has a cover so perfect that up to now even he didn't know what he was—or rather is." The sooner they washed their hands of the man calling himself Douglas Quail the better.

"Are you going to plant packets Three and Sixty-two in his conapt?" Lowe said.

"No," McClane said. "And we're going to return half his fee."

"Half! Why half?"

McClane said lamely, "It seems to be a good compromise."

As the cab carried him back to his conapt at the residential end of Chicago, Douglas Quail said to himself, *It's sure good to be back on Terra.*

Already the month-long period on Mars had begun to waver in his memory; he had only an image of profound gaping craters, an ever-present ancient erosion of hills, of vitality, of motion itself. A world of dust where little happened, where a good part of the day was spent checking and rechecking one's portable oxygen source. And then the life forms, the unassuming and modest gray-brown cacti and maw-worms.

As a matter of fact he had brought back several moribund examples of Martian fauna; he had smuggled them through customs. After all, they posed no menace; they couldn't survive in Earth's heavy atmosphere.

Reaching into his coat pocket he rummaged for the container of Martian maw-worms—

And found an envelope instead.

Lifting it out he discovered, to his perplexity, that it contained five hundred and seventy poscreds, in 'cred bills of low denomination.

Where'd I get this? he asked himself. *Didn't I spend every 'cred I had on my trip?*

With the money came a slip of paper marked: *one-half fee ret'd. By McClane.* And then the date. Today's date.

"Recall," he said aloud.

"Recall what, sir or madam?" the robot driver of the cab inquired respectfully.

"Do you have a phone book?" Quail demanded.

"Certainly, sir or madam." A slot opened; from it slid a microtape phone book for Cook County.

"It's spelled oddly," Quail said as he leafed through the pages of the yellow section. He felt fear, then; abiding fear. "Here it is," he said. "Take me there, to Rekal, Incorporated. I've changed my mind; I don't want to go home."

"Yes sir, or madam, as the case may be," the driver said. A moment later the cab was zipping back in the opposite direction.

"May I make use of your phone?" he asked.

"Be my guest," the robot driver said. And presented a shiny new emperor 3-D color phone to him.

He dialed his own conapt. And after a pause found himself confronted by a miniature but chillingly realistic image of Kirsten on the small screen. "I've been to Mars," he said to her.

"You're drunk." Her lips writhed scornfully. "Or worse."

"'S God's truth."

"When?" she demanded.

"I don't know." He felt confused. "A simulated trip, I think. By means of one of those artificial or extra-factual or whatever it is memory places. It didn't take."

Kirsten said witheringly, "You *are* drunk." And broke the connection at her end. He hung up, then, feeling his face flush. *Always the same tone,* he said hotly to himself. *Always the retort, as if she knows everything and I know nothing. What a marriage. Keerist,* he thought dismally.

A moment later the cab stopped at the curb before a modern, very attractive little pink building, over which a shifting, polychromatic neon sign read: *Rekal, Incorporated.*

The receptionist, chic and bare from the waist up, started in surprise, then gained masterful control of herself. "Oh hello Mr. Quail," she said nervously. "H-how are you? Did you forget something?"

"The rest of my fee back," he said.

More composed now the receptionist said, "Fee? I think you are mistaken, Mr. Quail. You were here discussing the feasibility of an extra-factual trip for you, but—" She shrugged her smooth pale shoulders. "As I understand it, no trip was taken."

Quail said, "I remember everything, miss. My letter to Rekal, Incorporated, which started this whole business off. I remember my arrival here, my visit with Mr. McClane. Then the two lab technicians taking me in tow and administering a drug to put me out." No wonder the firm had returned half his fee. The false memory of his "trip to Mars" hadn't taken—at least not entirely, not as he had been assured.

"Mr. Quail," the girl said, "although you are a minor clerk you are a good-looking man and it spoils your features to become angry. If it would make you feel any better, I might, ahem, let you take me out . . . '

He felt furious, then. "I remember you," he said savagely. "For instance the fact that your breasts are sprayed blue; that stuck in my mind. And I remember Mr. McClane's promise that if I remembered my visit to Rekal, Incorporated I'd receive my money back in full. Where is Mr. McClane?"

After a delay—probably as long as they could manage—he found himself once more seated facing the imposing walnut desk, exactly as he had been an hour or so earlier in the day.

"Some technique you have," Quail said sardonically. His disappointment—and resentment—were enormous, by now. "My so-called 'memory' of a trip to Mars as an undercover agent for Interplan is hazy and vague and shot full of contradictions. And I clearly remember my dealings here with you people. I ought to take this to the Better Business Bureau." He was burning angry, at this point; his sense of being cheated had overwhelmed him, had destroyed his customary aversion to participating in a public squabble.

Looking morose, as well as cautious, McClane said, "We capitulate, Quail. We'll refund the balance of your fee. I fully concede the fact that we did absolutely nothing for you." His tone was resigned.

Quail said accusingly, "You didn't even provide me with the various artifacts that you claimed would 'prove' to me I had been on Mars. All that song-and-dance you went into— it hasn't materialized into a damn thing. Not even a ticket stub. Nor postcards. Nor passport. Nor proof of immunization shots. Nor—"

"Listen, Quail," McClane said. "Suppose I told you—" He broke off. "Let it go." He pressed a button on his intercom. "Shirley, will you disburse five hundred and seventy more 'creds in the form of a cashier's check made out to Douglas Quail? Thank you." He released the button, then glared at Quail.

Presently the check appeared; the receptionist placed it before McClane and once more vanished out of sight, leaving the two men alone, still facing each other across the surface of the massive walnut desk.

"Let me give you a word of advice," McClane said as he signed the check and passed it over, "Don't discuss your, ahem, recent trip to Mars with anyone."

"What trip?"

"Well, that's the thing." Doggedly, McClane said, "The trip you partially remember. Act as if you don't remember; pretend it never took place. Don't ask me why; just take my advice: it'll be better for all of us." He had begun to perspire. Freely. "Now, Mr. Quail, I have other business, other clients to see." He rose, showed Quail to the door.

Quail said, as he opened the door, "A firm that turns out such bad work shouldn't have any clients at all." He shut the door behind him.

On the way home in the cab Quail pondered the wording of his letter of complaint to the Better Business Bureau, Terra Division. As soon as he could get to his typewriter he'd get started; it was clearly his duty to warn other people away from Rekal, Incorporated.

When he got back to his conapt he seated himself before his Hermes Rocket portable, opened the drawers and rummaged for carbon paper—and noticed a small, familiar box. A box which he had carefully filled on Mars with Martian fauna and later smuggled through customs.

Opening the box he saw, to his disbelief, six dead maw-worms and several varieties of the unicellular life on which the Martian worms fed. The protozoa were dried-up, dusty, but he recognized them; it had taken him an entire day picking among the vast dark alien boulders to find them. A wonderful, illuminated journey of discovery.

But I didn't go to Mars, he realized.

Yet on the other hand—

Kirsten appeared at the doorway to the room, an armload of pale brown groceries gripped. "Why are you home in the middle of the day?" Her voice, in an eternity of sameness, was accusing.

"*Did I go to Mars?*" he asked her. "You would know."

"No, of course you didn't go to Mars; *you* would know that, I would think. Aren't you always bleating about going?"

He said, "By God, I think I went." After a pause he added, "And simultaneously I think I didn't go."

"Make up your mind."

"How can I?" He gestured. "I have both memory-tracks grafted inside my head; one is real and one isn't but I can't tell which is which. Why can't I rely on you? They haven't tinkered with you." She could do this much for him at least—even if she never did anything else.

Kirsten said in a level, controlled voice, "Doug, if you don't pull yourself together, we're through. I'm going to leave you."

"I'm in trouble." His voice came out husky and coarse. And shaking. "Probably I'm heading into a psychotic episode; I hope not, but—maybe that's it. It would explain everything, anyhow."

Setting down the bag of groceries, Kirsten stalked to the closet. "I was not kidding," she said to him quietly. She brought out a coat, got it on, walked back to the door of the conapt. "I'll phone you one of these days soon," she said tonelessly. "This is goodbye, Doug. I hope you pull out of this eventually; I really pray you do. For your sake."

"Wait," he said desperately. "Just tell me and make it absolute; I did go or I didn't— tell me which one." *But they may have altered your memory-track also*, he realized.

The door closed. His wife had left. Finally!

A voice behind him said, "Well, that's that. Now put up your hands, Quail. And also please turn around and face this way."

He turned, instinctively, without raising his hands.

The man who faced him wore the plum uniform of the Interplan Police Agency, and his gun appeared to be UN issue. And, for some odd reason, he seemed familiar to Quail; familiar in a blurred, distorted fashion which he could not pin down. So, jerkily, he raised his hands.

"You remember," the policeman said, "your trip to Mars. We know all your actions today and all your thoughts—in particular your very important thoughts on the trip home from Rekal, Incorporated." He explained, "We have a tele-transmitter wired within your skull; it keeps us constantly informed."

A telepathic transmitter; use of a living plasma that had been discovered on Luna. He shuddered with self-aversion. The thing lived inside him, within his own brain, feeding, listening, feeding. But the Interplan police used them; that had come out even in the homeopapes. So this was probably true, dismal as it was.

"Why me?" Quail said huskily. What had he done—or thought? And what did this have to do with Rekal, Incorporated?

"Fundamentally," the Interplan cop said, "this has nothing to do with Rekal; it's between you and us." He tapped his right ear. "I'm still picking up your mentational processes by way of your cephalic transmitter." In the man's ear Quail saw a small white-plastic plug. "So I have to warn you: anything you think may be held against you." He smiled. "Not that it matters now; you've already thought and spoken yourself into oblivion. What's annoying is the fact that under narkidrine at Rekal, Incorporated you told them, their technicians and the owner, Mr. McClane, about your trip—where you went, for whom, some of what you did. They're very frightened. They wish they had never laid eyes on you." He added reflectively, "They're right."

Quail said, "I never made any trip. It's a false memory-chain improperly planted in me by McClane's technicians." But then he thought of the box, in his desk drawer, containing the Martian life forms. And the trouble and hardship he had had gathering them. The memory seemed real. And the box of life forms; that certainly was real. Unless McClane had planted it. Perhaps this was one of the "proofs" which McClane had talked glibly about.

The memory of my trip to Mars, he thought, *doesn't convince me—but unfortunately it has convinced the Interplan Police Agency. They think I really went to Mars and they think I at least partially realize it.*

"We not only know you went to Mars," the Interplan cop agreed, in answer to his thoughts, "but we know that you now remember enough to be difficult for us. And there's no use expunging your conscious memory of all this, because if we do you'll simply show up at Rekal, Incorporated again and start over. And we can't do anything about McClane and his operation because we have no jurisdiction over anyone except our own people. Anyhow, McClane hasn't committed any crime." He eyed Quail. "Nor, technically, have you. You didn't go to Rekal, Incorporated with the idea of regaining your memory; you went, as we realize, for the usual reason people go there—a love by plain, dull people for adventure." He added, "Unfortunately you're not plain, not dull, and you've already had too much excitement; the last thing in the universe you needed was a course from Rekal, Incorporated. Nothing could have been more lethal for you or for us. And, for that matter, for McClane."

Quail said. "Why is it 'difficult' for you if I remember my trip—my alleged trip—and what I did there?"

"Because," the Interplan harness bull said, "what you did is not in accord with our great white all-protecting father public image. You did, for us, what we never do. As you'll presently remember—thanks to narkidrine. That box of dead worms and algae has been sitting in your desk drawer for six months, ever since you got back. And at no time have you shown the slightest curiosity about it. We didn't even know you had it until you remembered it on your way home from Rekal; then we came here on the double to look for it." He added, unnecessarily, "Without any luck; there wasn't enough time."

A second Interplan cop joined the first one; the two briefly conferred. Meanwhile, Quail thought rapidly. He did remember more, now; the cop had been right about narkidrine. They—Interplan—probably used it themselves. Probably? He knew darn well they did; he had seen them putting a prisoner on it. Where would *that* be? Somewhere on Terra? More likely Luna, he decided, viewing the image rising from his highly defective—but rapidly less so—memory.

And he remembered something else. Their reason for sending him to Mars; the job he had done.

No wonder they had expunged his memory.

"Oh god," the first of the two Interplan cops said, breaking off his conversation with his companion. Obviously, he had picked up Quail's thoughts. "Well, this is a far worse problem, now; as bad as it can get." He walked toward Quail, again covering him with his gun. "We've got to kill you," he said. "And right away."

Nervously, his fellow officer said, "Why right away? Can't we simply cart him off to Interplan New York and let them—"

"*He* knows why it has to be right away," the first cop said; he too looked nervous, now, but Quail realized that it was for an entirely different reason. His memory had been brought back almost entirely, now. And he fully understood the officer's tension.

"On Mars," Quail said hoarsely, "I killed a man. After getting past fifteen body-guards. Some armed with sneaky-pete guns, the way you are." He had been trained, by Interplan, over a five year period to be an assassin. A professional killer. He knew ways to take out armed adversaries . . . such as these two officers; and the one with the ear-receiver knew it, too.

If he moved swiftly enough—

The gun fired. But he had already moved to one side, and at the same time he chopped down the gun-carrying officer. In an instant he had possession of the gun and was covering the other, confused, officer.

"Picked my thoughts up," Quail said, panting for breath. "He knew what I was going to do, but I did it anyhow."

Half sitting up, the injured officer grated, "He won't use that gun on you, Sam; I pick that up, too. He knows he's finished, and he knows we know it, too. Come on, Quail." Laboriously, grouting with pain, he got shakily to his feet. He held out his hand. "The gun," he said to Quail. "You can't use it, and if you turn it over to me I'll guarantee not to kill you; you'll be given a hearing, and someone higher up in Interplan will decide, not me. Maybe they can erase your memory once more; I don't know. But you know the thing I was going to kill you for; I couldn't keep you from remembering it. So my reason for wanting to kill you is in a sense past."

Quail, clutching the gun, bolted from the conapt, sprinted for the elevator. *If you follow me*, he thought, *I'll kill you. So don't.* He jabbed at the elevator button and, a moment later, the doors slid back.

The police hadn't followed him. Obviously they had picked up his terse, tense thoughts and had decided not to take the chance.

With him inside the elevator descended. He had gotten away—for a time. But what next? Where could he go?

The elevator reached the ground floor; a moment later Quail had joined the mob of peds hurrying along the runnels. His head ached and he felt sick. But at least he had evaded death; they had come very close to shooting him on the spot, back in his own conapt.

And they probably will again, he decided. *When they find me. And with this transmitter inside me, that won't take too long.*

Ironically, he had gotten exactly what he had asked Rekal, Incorporated for. Adventure, peril, Interplan police at work, a secret and dangerous trip to Mars in which his life was at stake—everything he had wanted as a false memory.

The advantages of it being a memory—and nothing more—could now be appreciated.

On a park beach, alone, he sat dully watching a flock of perts: a semi-bird imported from Mars' two moons, capable of soaring flight, even against Earth's huge gravity.

Maybe I can find my way back to Mars, he pondered. But then what? It would be worse on Mars; the political organization whose leader he had assassinated would spot him the moment he stepped from the ship; he would have Interplan and *them* after him, there.

Can you hear me thinking? he wondered. Easy avenue to paranoia; sitting here alone he felt them tuning in on him, monitoring, recording, discussing . . . He shivered, rose to his feet, walked aimlessly, his hands deep in his pockets. *No matter where I go,* he realized. *You'll always be with me. As long as I have this device inside my head.*

I'll make a deal with you, he thought to himself—and to them. *Can't you imprint a false-memory template on me again, as you did before, that I lived an average, routine life, never went to Mars? Never saw an Interplan uniform up close and never handled a gun?*

A voice inside his brain answered, "As has been carefully explained to you: that would not be enough."

Astonished, he halted.

"We formerly communicated with you in this manner," the voice continued. "When you were operating in the field, on Mars. It's been months since we've done it; we assumed, in fact, that we'd never have to do so again. Where are you?"

"Walking," Quail said, "to my death." *By your officers' guns,* he added as an after-thought. "How can you be sure it wouldn't be enough?" he demanded. "Don't the Rekal techniques work?"

"As we said. If you're given a set of standard, average memories you get—restless. You'd inevitably seek out Rekal or one of its competitors again. We can't go through this a second time."

"Suppose," Quail said, "once my authentic memories have been cancelled, something more vital than standard memories are implanted. Something which would act to satisfy my craving," he said. "That's been proved; that's probably why you initially hired me. But you ought to be able to come up with something else—something equal. I was the richest man on Terra but I finally gave all my money to educational foundations. Or I was a famous deep-space explorer. Anything of that sort; wouldn't one of those do?"

Silence.

"Try it," he said desperately. "Get some of your top-notch military psychiatrists; explore my mind. Find out what my most expansive daydream is." He tried to think. "Women," he said. "Thousands of them, like Don Juan had. An interplanetary playboy—

a mistress in every city on Earth, Luna and Mars. Only I gave that up, out of exhaustion. Please," he begged. "Try it."

"You'd voluntarily surrender, then?" the voice inside his head asked. "If we agreed to arrange such a solution? *If* it's possible?"

After an interval of hesitation he said, "Yes." *I'll take the risk*, he said to himself, *that you don't simply kill me.*

"You make the first move," the voice said presently. "Turn yourself over to us. And we'll investigate that line of possibility. If we can't do it, however, if your authentic memories begin to crop up again as they've done at this time, then—" There was silence and then the voice finished, "We'll have to destroy you. As you must understand. Well, Quail, you still want to try?"

"Yes," he said. Because the alternative was death now—and for certain. At least this way he had a chance, slim as it was.

"You present yourself at our main barracks in New York," the voice of the Interplan cop resumed. "At 580 Fifth Avenue, floor twelve. Once you've surrendered yourself we'll have our psychiatrists begin on you; we'll have personality-profile tests made. We'll attempt to determine your absolute, ultimate fantasy wish—and then we'll bring you back to Rekal, Incorporated, here; get them in on it, fulfilling that wish in vicarious surrogate retrospection. And—good luck. We do owe you something; you acted as a capable instrument for us." The voice lacked malice; if anything, they—the organization—felt sympathy toward him.

"Thanks," Quail said. And began searching for a robot cab.

"Mr. Quail," the stern-faced, elderly Interplan psychiatrist said, "you possess a most interesting wish-fulfillment dream fantasy. Probably nothing such as you consciously entertain or suppose. This is commonly the way; I hope it won't upset you too much to hear about it."

The senior ranking Interplan officer present said briskly, "He better not be too much upset to hear about it, not if he expects not to get shot."

"Unlike the fantasy of wanting to be an Interplan undercover agent." the psychiatrist continued, "which, being relatively speaking a product of maturity, had a certain plausibility to it, this production is a grotesque dream of your childhood; it is no wonder you fail to recall it. Your fantasy is this: you are nine years old, walking alone down a rustic lane. An unfamiliar variety of space vessel from another star system lands directly in front of you. No one on Earth but you, Mr. Quail, sees it. The creatures within are very small and helpless, somewhat on the order of field mice, although they are attempting to invade Earth; tens of thousands of other such ships will soon be on their way, when this advance party gives the go-ahead signal."

"And I suppose I stop them," Quail said, experiencing a mixture of amusement and disgust. "Single-handed I wipe them out. Probably by stepping on them with my foot."

"No," the psychiatrist said patiently. "You halt the invasion, but not by destroying them. Instead, you show them kindness and mercy, even though by telepathy—their mode of communication—you know why they have come. They have never seen such humane traits exhibited by any sentient organism, and to show their appreciation they make a covenant with you."

Quail said, "They won't invade Earth as long as I'm alive."

"Exactly." To the Interplan officer the psychiatrist said, "You can see it does fit his personality, despite his feigned scorn."

"So by merely existing," Quail said, feeling a growing pleasure, "by simply being alive, I keep Earth safe from alien rule. I'm in effect, then, the most important person on Terra. Without lifting a finger."

"Yes indeed, sir," the psychiatrist said. "And this is bedrock in your psyche; this is a life-long childhood fantasy. Which, without depth and drug therapy, you never would have recalled. But it has always existed in you; it went underneath, but never ceased."

To McClane, who sat intently listening, the senior police official said, "Can you implant an extra-factual memory pattern that extreme in him?"

"We get handed every possible type of wish-fantasy there is," McClane said. "Frankly, I've heard a lot worse than this. Certainly we can handle it. Twenty-four hours from now he won't just *wish* he'd saved Earth; he'll devoutly believe it really happened."

The senior police official said, "You can start the job, then. In preparation we've already once again erased the memory in him of his trip to Mars."

Quail said, "What trip to Mars?"

No one answered him, so, reluctantly, he shelved the question. And anyhow a police vehicle had now put in its appearance; he, McClane, and the senior police officer crowded into it, and presently they were on their way to Chicago and Rekal, Incorporated.

"You had better make no errors this time," the police officer said to heavy-set, nervous-looking McClane.

"I can't see what could go wrong," McClane mumbled, perspiring. "This has nothing to do with Mars or Interplan. Single-handedly stopping an invasion of Earth from another star-system." He shook his head at that. "Wow, what a kid dreams up. And by pious virtue, too; not by force. It's sort of quaint." He dabbed at his forehead with a large linen pocket handkerchief.

Nobody said anything.

"In fact," McClane said, "it's touching."

"But arrogant," the police official said starkly. "Inasmuch as when he dies the invasion will resume. No wonder he doesn't recall it; it's the most grandiose fantasy I ever ran across." He eyed Quail with disapproval. "And to think we put this man on our payroll."

When they reached Rekal, Incorporated the receptionist, Shirley, met them breathlessly in the outer office. "Welcome back, Mr. Quail," she fluttered, her melon-shaped breasts—today painted an incandescent orange—bobbing with agitation. "I'm sorry everything worked out so badly before; I'm sure this time it'll go better."

Still repeatedly dabbing at his shiny forehead with his neatly-folded Irish linen handkerchief, McClane said, "It better." Moving with rapidity he rounded up Lowe and Keeler, escorted them and Douglas Quail to the work area, and then, with Shirley and the senior police officer, returned to his familiar office. To wait.

"Do we have a packet made up for this, Mr. McClane?" Shirley asked, bumping against him in her agitation, then coloring modestly.

"I think we do." He tried to recall; then gave up and consulted the formal chart. "A combination," he decided aloud, "of packets Eighty-one, Twenty, and Six." From the vault section of the chamber behind his desk he fished out the appropriate packets, carried them to his desk for inspection. "From Eighty-one," he explained, "a magic healing rod given him—the client in question, this time Mr. Quail—by the race of beings from another system. A token of their gratitude."

"Does it work?" the police officer asked curiously.

"It did once," McClane explained. "But he, ahem, you see, used it up years ago, healing right and left. Now it's only a memento. But he remembers it working spectacularly." He chuckled, then opened packet Twenty. "Document from the UN Secretary General thanking him for saving Earth; this isn't precisely appropriate, because part of Quail's fantasy is that no one knows of the invasion except himself, but for the sake of verisimilitude we'll throw it in." He inspected packet Six, then. What came from this? He couldn't recall; frowning, he dug into the plastic bag as Shirley and the Interplan police officer watched intently.

"Writing," Shirley said. "In a funny language."

"This tells who they were," McClane said, "and where they came from. Including a detailed star map logging their flight here and the system of origin. Of course it's in *their* script, so he can't read it. But he remembers them reading it to him in his own tongue." He placed the three artifacts in the center of the desk. "These should be taken to Quail's conapt," he said to the police officer. "So that when he gets home he'll find them. And it'll confirm his fantasy. SOP—standard operating procedure." He chuckled apprehensively, wondering how matters were going with Lowe and Keeler.

The intercom buzzed. "Mr. McClane, I'm sorry to bother you." It was Lowe's voice; he froze as he recognized it, froze and became mute. "But something's come up. Maybe it would be better if you came in here and supervised. Like before, Quail reacted well to the narkidrine; he's unconscious, relaxed and receptive. But—"

McClane sprinted for the work area.

On a hygienic bed Douglas Quail lay breathing slowly and regularly, eyes half-shut, dimly conscious of those around him.

"We started interrogating him," Lowe said, white-faced. "To find out exactly when to place the fantasy-memory of him single-handedly having saved Earth. And strangely enough—"

"They told me not to tell," Douglas Quail mumbled in a dull drug-saturated voice. "That was the agreement. I wasn't even supposed to remember. But how could I forget an event like that?"

I guess it would be hard, McClane reflected. *But you did—until now.*

"They even gave me a scroll," Quail mumbled, "of gratitude. I have it hidden in my conapt; I'll show it to you."

To the Interplan officer who had followed after him, McClane said, "Well, I offer the suggestion that you better not kill him. If you do they'll return."

"They also gave me a magic invisible destroying rod," Quail mumbled, eyes totally shut, now. "That's how I killed that man on Mars you sent me to take out. It's in my drawer along with the box of Martian maw-worms and dried-up plant life."

Wordlessly, the Interplan officer turned and stalked from the work area.

I might as well put those packets of proof-artifacts away, McClane said to himself resignedly. He walked, step by step, back to his office. *Including the citation from the UN Secretary General. After all—*

The real one probably would not be long in coming.

STUDY AND DISCUSSION QUESTIONS

1   Before you think about the implications of the story about knowledge and skepticism, first ask yourself this: What sort of desire does one have that would prompt going to Rekal, Inc.? Mr. McClane, a Rekal executive and salesman, asks Doug Quail a fascinating question, "So you want to have gone to Mars?" Are subjunctive desires formed in this way coherent and sensible?

2   One way to sharpen that question is by asking another related one: Suppose that you are faced with a choice either to take a $2,500 vacation to Hawaii or to take a, say, $1,250 Rekal "vacation to Hawaii." Imagine that your memories of your time in Hawaii will be identical in both cases. Which do you do? How much more valuable is having a real vacation in Hawaii to you, for example twice as much, five times as much, etc.? Why?

3   Quail seems to desire to escape reality—his job, his wife, and even his planet. In this case Rekal can help. Rekal's guarantee: If you doubt that you went to Mars, Rekal will fully refund your purchase. Descartes also uses a criterion of doubt. How does Descartes employ the concept of doubt in the *Meditations*?

4   This story raises the epistemologically frightening prospect that false memories could be not merely as believable but *more* believable than true memories. When Quail hesitates before purchasing a Rekal treatment, Mr. McClane explains why Rekal memory is better than real memory: "The actual memory, with all its vagueness, omissions and ellipses, not to say distortions—that's second best." How does this create a hurdle for the justification of memory beliefs?

5   After the failed procedure at Rekal, Quail says to his wife, "By God, I think I went. And simultaneously I think I didn't go." By what criteria can Quail determine whether or not he went to Mars? Is introspection useful in justifying his belief? Why/why not?

6   Quail's skepticism is originally restricted to his memory beliefs. But he then realizes that, if his memories are unreliable about having gone to Mars, they are by implication unreliable about his wife. For that matter, his wife's memories may also have been tampered with. This raises a question: Can forms of local skepticism (in this case, skepticism about memory) be contained, or do all or most forms of local skepticism call into question the reliability of other types of beliefs?

2.11 "THE ALLEGORY OF THE CAVE," FROM PLATO'S *REPUBLIC*

Note on Plato's dialogue form: The discussion that follows is a small excerpt about an allegory that Plato uses in *Republic* Book VII to describe his opinions about the nature of human knowledge. In it two characters are having a discussion. These characters are Socrates and Glaucon. Here Socrates is a character in Plato's book, but Socrates was also a real historical person—in fact, Socrates was Plato's philosophy teacher.

Socrates: And now, I said, let me show in a figure how far our nature is enlightened or unenlightened: — Behold! human beings living in a underground den, which has a mouth open towards the light and reaching all along the den; here they have been from their childhood, and have their legs and necks chained so that they cannot move, and can only see before them, being prevented by the chains from turning round their heads. Above and behind them a fire is blazing at a distance, and between the fire and the prisoners there is a raised way; and you will see, if you look, a low wall built along the way, like the screen which marionette players have in front of them, over which they show the puppets.

Glaucon: I see.

Socrates: And do you see, I said, men passing along the wall carrying all sorts of vessels, and statues and figures of animals made of wood and stone and various materials, which appear over the wall? Some of them are talking, others silent.

Glaucon: You have shown me a strange image, and they are strange prisoners.

Socrates: Like ourselves, I replied; and they see only their own shadows, or the shadows of one another, which the fire throws on the opposite wall of the cave?

Glaucon: True, he said; how could they see anything but the shadows if they were never allowed to move their heads?

Socrates: And of the objects which are being carried in like manner they would only see the shadows?

Glaucon: Yes, he said.

Socrates: And if they were able to converse with one another, would they not suppose that they were naming what was actually before them?

Glaucon: Very true.

Socrates: And suppose further that the prison had an echo which came from the other side, would they not be sure to fancy when one of the passers-by spoke that the voice which they heard came from the passing shadow?

Glaucon: No question, he replied.

Socrates: To them, I said, the truth would be literally nothing but the shadows of the images.

Glaucon: That is certain.

Socrates: And now look again, and see what will naturally follow if the prisoners are released and disabused of their error. At first, when any of them are liberated and compelled suddenly to stand up and turn his neck round and walk and look towards the light, he will suffer sharp pains; the glare will distress him, and he will be unable to see the realities of which in his former state he had seen the shadows; and then conceive some one saying to him, that what he saw before was an illusion, but that now, when he is approaching nearer to being and his eye is turned towards more real existence, he has a clearer vision,—what will be his reply? And you may further imagine that his instructor is pointing to the objects as they pass and requiring him to name them,—will he not be perplexed? Will he not fancy that the shadows which he formerly saw are truer than the objects which are now shown to him?

Glaucon: Far truer.

Socrates: And if he is compelled to look straight at the light, will he not have a pain in his eyes which will make him turn away to take and take in the objects of vision which he can see, and which he will conceive to be in reality clearer than the things which are now being shown to him?

Glaucon: True, he said.

Socrates: And suppose once more, that he is reluctantly dragged up a steep and rugged ascent, and held fast until he's forced into the presence of the sun himself, is he not likely to be pained and irritated? When he approaches the light his eyes will be dazzled, and he will not be able to see anything at all of what are now called realities.

Glaucon: Not all in a moment, he said.

Socrates: He will require to grow accustomed to the sight of the upper world. And first he will see the shadows best, next the reflections of men and other objects in the water, and then the objects themselves; then he will gaze upon the light of the moon and the stars and the spangled heaven; and he will see the sky and the stars by night better than the sun or the light of the sun by day?

Glaucon: Certainly.

Socrates: Last of all he will be able to see the sun, and not mere reflections of him in the water, but he will see him in his own proper place, and not in another; and he will contemplate him as he is.

Glaucon: Certainly.

Socrates: He will then proceed to argue that this is he who gives the season and the years, and is the guardian of all that is in the visible world, and in a certain way the cause of all things which he and his fellows have been accustomed to behold?

Glaucon: Clearly, he said, he would first see the sun and then reason about him.

Socrates: And when he remembered his old habitation, and the wisdom of the den and his fellow-prisoners, do you not suppose that he would felicitate himself on the change, and pity them?

Glaucon: Certainly, he would.

Socrates: And if they were in the habit of conferring honours among themselves on those who were quickest to observe the passing shadows and to remark which of them went before, and which followed after, and which were together; and who were therefore best able to draw conclusions as to the future, do you think that he would care for such honours and glories, or envy the possessors of them? Would he not say with Homer,

Better to be the poor servant of a poor master, and to endure anything, rather than think as they do and live after their manner?

Glaucon: Yes, he said, I think that he would rather suffer anything than entertain these false notions and live in this miserable manner.

Socrates: Imagine once more, I said, such a one coming suddenly out of the sun to be replaced in his old situation; would he not be certain to have his eyes full of darkness?

Glaucon: To be sure, he said.

Socrates: And if there were a contest, and he had to compete in measuring the shadows with the prisoners who had never moved out of the den, while his sight was still weak, and before his eyes had become steady (and the time which would be needed to acquire this new habit of sight might be very considerable) would he not be ridiculous? Men would say of him that up he went and down he came without his eyes; and that it was better not even to think of ascending; and if any one tried to loose another and lead him up to the light, let them only catch the offender, and they would put him to death.

Glaucon: No question, he said.

Socrates: This entire allegory, I said, you may now append, dear Glaucon, to the previous argument; the prison-house is the world of sight, the light of the fire is the sun, and you will not misapprehend me if you interpret the journey upwards to be the ascent of the soul into the intellectual world according to my poor belief, which, at your desire, I have expressed whether rightly or wrongly God knows. But, whether true or false, my opinion is that in the world of knowledge the idea of good appears last of all, and is seen only with an effort; and, when seen, is also inferred to be the universal author of all things beautiful and right, parent of light and of the lord of light in this visible world, and the immediate source of reason and truth in the intellectual; and that this is the power upon which he who would act rationally, either in public or private life must have his eye fixed.

Glaucon: I agree, he said, as far as I am able to understand you.

Socrates: Moreover, I said, you must not wonder that those who attain to this beatific vision are unwilling to descend to human affairs; for their souls are ever hastening into the upper world where they desire to dwell; which desire of theirs is very natural, if our allegory may be trusted.

Glaucon: Yes, very natural.

Socrates: And is there anything surprising in one who passes from divine contemplations to the evil state of man, misbehaving himself in a ridiculous manner; if, while his eyes are blinking and before he has become accustomed to the surrounding darkness, he is compelled to fight in courts of law, or in other places, about the images or the shadows of images of justice, and is endeavouring to meet the conceptions of those who have never yet seen absolute justice?

STUDY AND DISCUSSION QUESTIONS

1   Draw as best you can Plato's cave. As you do so, try to place everything in the allegory in its proper physical place.
2   There are two groups of people in the cave, one of which is tied down and facing a wall. Why do you think Plato portrays them as unable to move, and generally as having many bodily restrictions?
3   What are the prisoners seeing? Specifically, how many levels removed from reality is what they are seeing? Why is Plato using this motif to communicate to his readers about the knowledge of human beings?
4   What is the prisoner's experience upon escaping out of the cave and up to the surface intended to convey? The escapee, now knowledgeable about what lies outside the cave, returns to the cave in order to tell his friends but gets spurned. Is Plato saying that people who achieve true knowledge about reality are often disliked by people who prefer to live lives based upon false beliefs? If so, is he right? Why/why not? Can you identify any examples of this in your culture?
5   Plato's "Allegory of the Cave" can be interpreted in straightforwardly episte-mological terms as being about knowledge and reality. But it can also be given a more personal reading. Socially, we often project images of ourselves, consciously or not, which have the effect of distancing others' opinion of us from the way we really are. On the flipside, we often acquiesce in the false or creative self-presentations given us by others. You probably have examples of ways in which you had thought you were "seeing" another person truly, but found out later that he or she was only presenting a "shadow" (or even a "shadow of a shadow") of him or herself to you. What might Plato say about such a form of self-deception?
6   What is the main point that Plato is attempting to get across?

2.12 'MEDITATIONS ON FIRST PHILOSOPHY' (I AND II), BY RENÉ DESCARTES

Meditations on first philosophy in which the existence of God and the distinction between the soul and the body are demonstrated

Meditation I: Concerning those things that can be called into doubt

1. Several years have now passed since I first realized how numerous were the false opinions that in my youth I had taken to be true, and thus how doubtful were all those that I had subsequently built upon them. And thus I realized that once in my life I had to

raze everything to the ground and begin again from the original foundations, if wanted to establish anything firm and lasting in the sciences. But the task seemed enormous, and I was waiting until I reached a point in my life that was so timely that no more suitable time for undertaking these plans of action would come to pass. For this reason, I procrastinated for so long that I would henceforth be at fault, were I to waste the time that remains for carrying out the project by brooding over it. Accordingly, I have today suitably freed my mind of all cares, secured for myself a period of leisurely tranquility, and am withdrawing into solitude. At last I will apply myself earnestly and unreservedly to this general demolition of my opinions.

2. Yet to bring this about I will not need to show that all my opinions are false, which is perhaps something I could never accomplish. But reason now persuades me that I should withhold my assent no less carefully from opinions that are not completely certain and indubitable than I would from those that are patently false. For this reason, it will suffice for the rejection of all of these opinions, if I find in each of them some reason for doubt. Nor therefore need I survey each opinion individually, a task that would be endless. Rather, because undermining the foundations will cause whatever has been built upon them to crumble of its own accord, I will attack straightaway those principles which supported everything I once believed.

3. Surely whatever I had admitted until now as most true I received either from the senses or through the senses. However, I have noticed that the senses are sometimes deceptive; and it is a mark of prudence never to place our complete trust in those who have deceived us even once.

But perhaps, even though the senses do sometimes deceive us when it is a question of very small and distant things, still there are many other matters concerning which one simply cannot doubt, even though they are derived from the very same senses: for example, that I am sitting here next to the fire, wearing my winter dressing gown, that I am holding this sheet of paper in my hands, and the like. But on what grounds could one deny that these hands and this entire body are mine? Unless perhaps I were to liken myself to the insane, whose brains are impaired by such an unrelenting vapor of black bile that they steadfastly insist that they are kings when they are utter paupers, or that they are arrayed in purple robes when they are naked, or that they have heads made of clay, or that they are gourds, or that they are made of glass. But such people are mad, and I would appear no less mad, were I to take their behavior as an example for myself.

4. This would all be well and good, were I not a man who is accustomed to sleeping at night, and to experiencing in my dreams the very same things, or now and then even less plausible ones, as these insane people do when they are awake. How often does my evening slumber persuade me of such ordinary things as these: that I am here, clothed in my dressing gown, seated next to the fireplace—when in fact I am lying undressed in bed! But right now my eyes are certainly wide awake when I gaze upon this sheet of paper. This head which I am shaking is not heavy with sleep. I extend this hand consciously and deliberately, and I feel it. Such things would not be so distinct for someone who is asleep. As if I did not recall having been deceived on other occasions even by similar thoughts in my dreams! As I consider these matters more carefully, I see so plainly that there are no

definitive signs by which to distinguish being awake from being asleep. As a result, I am becoming quite dizzy, and this dizziness nearly convinces me that I am asleep.

5. Let us assume then, for the sake of argument, that we are dreaming and that such particulars as these are not true: that we are opening our eyes, moving our head, and extending our hands. Perhaps we do not even have such hands, or any such body at all. Nevertheless, it surely must be admitted that the things seen during slumber are, as it were, like painted images, which could only have been produced in the likeness of true things, and that therefore at least these general things—eyes, head, hands, and the whole body— are not imaginary things, but are true and exist. For indeed when painters themselves wish to represent sirens and satyrs by means of especially bizarre forms, they surely cannot assign to them utterly new natures. Rather, they simply fuse together the members of various animals. Or if perhaps they concoct something so utterly novel that nothing like it has ever been seen before (and thus is something utterly fictitious and false), yet certainly at the very least the colors from which they fashion it ought to be true. And by the same token, although even these general things—eyes, head, hands and the like could be imaginary, still one has to admit that at least certain other things that are even more simple and universal are true. It is from these components, as if from true colors, that all those images of things that are in our thought are fashioned, be they true or false.

6. This class of things appears to include corporeal nature in general, together with its extension; the shape of extended things; their quantity, that is, their size and number; as well as the place where they exist; the time through which they endure, and the like.

7. Thus it is not improper to conclude from this that physics, astronomy, medicine, and all the other disciplines that are dependent upon the consideration of composite things are doubtful, and that, on the other hand, arithmetic, geometry, and other such disciplines, which treat of nothing but the simplest and most general things and which are indifferent as to whether these things do or do not in fact exist, contain something certain and indubitable. For whether I am awake or asleep, two plus three make five, and a square does not have more than four sides. It does not seem possible that such obvious truths should be subject to the suspicion of being false.

8. Be that as it may, there is fixed in my mind a certain opinion of long standing, namely that there exists a God who is able to do anything and by whom I, such as I am, have been created. How do I know that he did not bring it about that there is no Earth at all, no heavens, no extended thing, no shape, no size, no place, and yet bringing it about that all these things appear to me to exist precisely as they do now? Moreover, since I judge that others sometimes make mistakes in matters that they believe they know most perfectly, may I not, in like fashion, be deceived every time I add two and three or count the sides of a square, or perform an even simpler operation, if that can be imagined? But perhaps God has not willed that I be deceived in this way, for he is said to be supremely good. Nonetheless, if it were repugnant to his goodness to have created me such that I be deceived all the time, it would also seem foreign to that same goodness to permit me to be deceived even occasionally. But we cannot make this last assertion.

9. Perhaps there are some who would rather deny so powerful a God than believe that everything else is uncertain. Let us not oppose them; rather, let us grant that everything

said here about God is fictitious. Now they suppose that I came to be what I am either by fate, or by chance, or by a connected chain of events, or by some other way. But because being deceived and being mistaken appear to be a certain imperfection, the less powerful they take the author of my origin to be, the more probable it will be that I am so imperfect that I am always deceived. I have nothing to say in response to these arguments. But eventually I am forced to admit that there is nothing among the things I once believed to be true which it is not permissible to doubt—and not out of frivolity or lack of forethought, but for valid and considered reasons. Thus I must be no less careful to withhold assent henceforth even from these beliefs than I would from those that are patently false, if I wish to find anything certain.

10. But it is not enough simply to have realized these things; I must take steps to keep myself mindful of them. For long-standing opinions keep returning, and, almost against my will, they take advantage of my credulity, as if it were bound over to them by long use and the claims of intimacy. Nor will I ever get out of the habit of assenting to them and believing in them, so long as I take them to be exactly what they are, namely, in some respects doubtful, as has just now been shown, but nevertheless highly probable, so that it is much more consonant with reason to believe them than to deny them. Hence, it seems to me I would do well to deceive myself by turning my will in completely the opposite direction and pretend for a time that these opinions are wholly false and imaginary, until finally, as if with prejudices weighing down each side equally, no bad habit should turn my judgment any further from the correct perception of things. For indeed I know that meanwhile there is no danger or error in following this procedure, and that it is impossible for me to indulge in too much distrust, since I am now concentrating only on knowledge, not on action.

11. Accordingly, I will suppose not a supremely good God, the source of truth, but rather an evil genius, supremely powerful and clever, who has directed his entire effort at deceiving me. I will regard the heavens, the air, the earth, colors, shapes, sounds, and all external things as nothing but the bedeviling hoaxes of my dreams, with which he lays snares for my credulity. I will regard myself as not having hands, or eyes, or flesh, or blood, or any senses, but as nevertheless falsely believing that I possess all these things. I will remain resolute and steadfast in this meditation, and even if it is not within my power to know anything true, it certainly is within my power to take care resolutely to withhold my assent to what is false, lest this deceiver, however powerful, however clever he may be, have any effect on me. But this undertaking is arduous, and a certain laziness brings me back to my customary way of living. I am not unlike a prisoner who enjoyed an imaginary freedom during his sleep, but, when he later begins to suspect that he is dreaming, fears being awakened and nonchalantly conspires with these pleasant illusions. In just the same way, I fall back of my own accord into my old opinions, and dread being awakened, lest the toilsome wakefulness which follows upon a peaceful rest must be spent thenceforward not in the light but among the inextricable shadows of the difficulties now brought forward.

Meditation II: Concerning the nature of the human mind: That it is better known than the body

12. Yesterday's meditation has thrown me into such doubts that I can no longer ignore them, yet I fail to see how they are to be resolved. It is as if I had suddenly fallen into a deep whirlpool; I am so tossed about that I can neither touch bottom with my foot, nor swim up to the top. Nevertheless I will work my way up and will once again attempt the same path I entered upon yesterday. I will accomplish this by putting aside everything that admits of the least doubt, as if I had discovered it to be completely false. I will stay on this course until I know something certain, or, if nothing else, until I at least know for certain that nothing is certain. Archimedes sought but one firm and immovable point in order to move the entire Earth from one place to another. Just so, great things are also to be hoped for in succeeding in finding just one thing, however slight, that is certain and unshaken.

13. Therefore I suppose that everything I see is false. I believe that none of what my deceitful memory represents ever existed. I have no senses whatever. Body, shape, extension, movement, and place are all chimeras. What then will be true? Perhaps just the single fact that nothing is certain.

14. But how do I know there is not something else, over and above all those things that I have just reviewed, concerning which there is not even the slightest occasion for doubt? Is there not some God, or by whatever name I might call him, who instills these very thoughts in me? But why would I think that, since I myself could perhaps be the author of these thoughts? Am I not then at least something? But I have already denied that I have any senses and any body. Still I hesitate; for what follows from this? Am I so tied to a body and to the senses that I cannot exist without them? But I have persuaded myself that there is absolutely nothing in the world: no sky, no Earth, no minds, no bodies. Is it then the case that I too do not exist? But doubtless I did exist, if I persuaded myself of something. But there is some deceiver or other who is supremely powerful and supremely sly and who is always deliberately deceiving me. Then too there is no doubt that I exist, if he is deceiving me. And let him do his best at deception, he will never bring it about that I am nothing so long as I shall think that I am something. Thus, after everything has been most carefully weighed, it must finally be established that this pronouncement "I am, I exist" is necessarily true every time I utter it or conceive it in my mind.

15. But I do not yet understand sufficiently what I am—I, who now necessarily exist. And so from this point on, I must be careful lest I unwittingly mistake something else for myself, and thus err in that very item of knowledge that I claim to be the most certain and evident of all. Thus, I will meditate once more on what I once believed myself to be, prior to embarking upon these thoughts. For this reason, then, I will set aside whatever can be weakened even to the slightest degree by the arguments brought forward, so that eventually all that remains is precisely nothing but what is certain and unshaken.

16. What then did I used to think I was? A man, of course. But what is a man? Might I not say a "rational animal"? No, because then I would have to inquire what "animal" and "rational" mean. And thus from one question I would slide into many more difficult ones. Nor do I now have enough free time that I want to waste it on subtleties of this sort. Instead, permit me to focus here on what came spontaneously and naturally into my

thinking whenever I pondered what I was. Now it occurred to me first that I had a face, hands, arms, and this entire mechanism of bodily members: the very same as are discerned in a corpse, and which I referred to by the name "body." It next occurred to me that I took in food, that I walked about, and that I sensed and thought various things; these actions I used to attribute to the soul. But as to what this soul might be, I either did not think about it or else I imagined it a rarified I—know not what—like a wind, or a fire, or ether, which had been infused into my coarser parts. But as to the body I was not in any doubt. On the contrary, I was under the impression that I knew its nature distinctly. Were I perhaps tempted to describe this nature such as I conceived it in my mind, I would have described it thus: by "body," I understand all that is capable of being bounded by some shape, of being enclosed in a place, and of filling up a space in such a way as to exclude any other body from it; of being perceived by touch, sight, hearing, taste, or smell; of being moved in several ways, not, of course, by itself, but by whatever else impinges upon it. For it was my view that the power of self-motion, and likewise of sensing or of thinking, in no way belonged to the nature of the body. Indeed I used rather to marvel that such faculties were to be found in certain bodies.

STUDY AND DISCUSSION QUESTIONS

1   Descartes says that he wants to rid himself of all his former opinions. What about Descartes' historical and cultural context would make him say something like that? Satisfactorily answering that question may require some Internet research on the religious and scientific context in mid-seventeenth century Europe.

2   As a method, Descartes' *method of doubt* is extremely rigorous in its demand to dismiss previously held beliefs. What do you think: is that an unreasonable way to begin a philosophy book, or is it just how such a book should read? Underlying your answer to this question will probably be concerns about whether philosophical inquiry should be objective and unbiased, and about whether total objectivity is possible. Is it?

3   Descartes offers the following analogy for his *method of doubt* on display in his First Meditation. Suppose I want to find the good apples in a barrel full of apples, many of which are bad. Amongst the methods open to me, the most efficient means to my goal is to dump the barrel over and, in one glance, identify the brown, rotten apples from the bright red apples. What does this tell you about Descartes' use of skepticism here—is he a skeptic at heart, or is it merely a means to an end? Why?

4   En route to calling all his beliefs into question, he offers a brief argument in paragraph 3 that his senses are not to be trusted. What is this argument? Is it valid and sound?

5   Paragraph 4 places a constraint or caveat on his enquiries. What is this constraint? What is its philosophical importance?

6 Descartes next mounts an argument from dreams for skepticism. Is Descartes concluding that it is possible that I might always be dreaming, or that it is possible that I might be dreaming right now? What is the philosophical difference between these two conclusions?

7 What beliefs does the dream argument call into question, and what beliefs does it fail to call into question?

8 In paragraphs 10 and 11, Descartes discusses God's role in quelling Descartes' skeptical doubts. Many Christian philosophers throughout the ages also appeal to God as being a guarantor of our knowledge. But in paragraph 12 Descartes subverts the traditional appeal to a good God by replacing it with a deceiving God. From this follows an unholy form of total skepticism. First, how do you think people in Descartes' day would react to this form of skepticism? Second, what beliefs does this "evil demon" skepticism show are unknown that dream skepticism did not show are unknown?

9 In Meditation II, Descartes attempts to answer the skeptical worries from his previous reflections. What is his central response to total skepticism? Why is this response considered a great work of philosophical genius?

10 Think critically about Descartes' alleged solution to his skeptical doubts. Is it as great as people often think it is? What sorts of philosophical problems does his solution have?

2.13 "THE SIMULATION ARGUMENT AND SIMULATION HYPOTHESES," BY ALASDAIR RICHMOND

1. Demons, vats, Sims

Nick Bostrom argues that some plausible ideas about computing and consciousness might imply that reality has a structure rather unlike what we ordinarily imagine. His "Simulation Argument" may sound like Descartes' "Evil Demon" or Putnam's "Brain-in-a-vat" scenarios but really it's quite unlike either, raising interesting metaphysical and epistemic issues all its own. Before tackling Bostrom's argument, let's revisit skepticism and consider some philosophy of mind.

In Descartes' thought experiment, an "Evil Demon" has been feeding all your senses a systematically false model world throughout your life. If no empirical evidence can distinguish "real world" from "evil demon" experiences and all your senses could be simultaneously demon-compromised, maybe all your beliefs about reality are false. If totally demon-managed lives are indistinguishable from "real world" lives, how do you know you aren't an evil demon dupe right now?

Descartes thought some certainties survive radical skepticism. Nothing can deceive him into thinking he exists if he doesn't: *Cogito, ergo sum*. (Descartes also concluded he *was* his mind but *inhabited* his body—he can doubt his physical self exists but not his thinking self. Furthermore, souls are indivisible and so naturally immortal.) Next, Descartes argued, his idea of God proves such a being must exist—neither experience nor finite minds could yield the idea of an omnipotent and perfectly good being. So an omnipotent, omnibenevolent God exists and created (at least some of) our ideas. No such God would create us and our senses, only to leave us in thrall to an evil demon. Hence Evil Demon skepticism must be false. (Many philosophers suspect Descartes inadvertently helped skepticism more than hindered it.)

In Putnam's "Brain-in-a-vat" ("BiV") story, your brain has always lived in a vat and been artificially stimulated with appearances of an external world. Putnam says: thinking you're a BiV is incoherent, because meaning involves preserving correct causal links between signs and things signified. If it's the causal chains that determine their meanings, BiV-words don't mean the same things as our words. A BiV who thinks "I'm a brain in a vat" is *wrong*. How can a BiV falsely assert its own BiV-ness? For a BiV, the word "brain" refers, not to grey matter in a skull, but to a vat-*image* of a brain. (Likewise, for the word "vat" and perhaps for "in.") Words uttered by BiVs are not, and never were, causally linked to brains and vats. A BiV who thinks "I'm a brain in a vat" doesn't mean what we mean by this sentence. Instead, it means (e.g.) "I'm a brain* in a vat*," where "brain*" means "BiV-image of a brain" and "vat*" means "BiV-image of a vat." Thus, a BiV can't truly think "I'm a brain in a vat" because it's a BiV, *not* a brain-image in a vat-image. So, a non-BiV thinking "I'm a brain in a vat" is wrong but a BiV thinking "I'm a brain in a vat" is wrong too. Putnam concludes: a BiV can't *correctly* think "I'm a brain in a vat." (Note newly-envatted brains might retain sufficient causal traces of external objects to let them think "I'm a brain in a vat" with the same reference we possess.) Descartes thought Evil Demon victims massively duped but Putnam thinks BiVs needn't be deceived. A BiV could still gather all available empirical evidence. So, Descartes thought his hypothesis coherent but skeptical; Putnam thinks his hypothesis self-undermining but non-skeptical. However, Bostrom argues for outcomes which should be neither incoherent nor skeptical.

Now some philosophy of mind: *functionalists* think minds stand to brains as computer software does to hardware. Thus, mind is a product of brain-function and consciousness just *is* performing the right sort of operations. Just as software can move between hard-drives without impairment, so human consciousness could function on different substrates. Thus, mind might be "substrate independent," i.e. not dependent on the particular hardware it runs on. Your mind presumably now runs on synaptic hardware but you could think exactly the same thoughts while your mind ran on a properly-configured computer. The contents of your experience don't infallibly reveal the substrate you run on. Your mind could survive changing substrate, and even achieve immortality by adopting an infinite succession of physical substrates. Your mind (*qua* software) could survive forever, even if all its substrates were mortal.

After Weatherson (2003), let conscious simulations be "Sims." Making Sims is beyond us now but our computing capability is far from its theoretical limits. Advanced ("posthuman") beings might already run Sims on vastly better computers than ours. Indeed, there may be more posthuman-run Sims than there are non-Sims.

The Simulation Argument says: functionalists who (a) accept substrate-independence and (b) believe posthumans will run many Sims, should also believe (c) they're probably Sims. Why should (a) and (b) jointly imply (c)? Philosophers often model reasons for belief as guidelines for rational betting. Imagine you believe you have a sign on your back which is either green or red. You can't inspect your own sign but you believe 90 percent of people wear green signs and 10 percent, red. If you've no other information, you should think it 90 percent probable your sign is green. Why? Your evidence concerns relative preponderance of two states. You don't know which is yours but you know you're in one state, and one state is nine times more common than the other. You ought to proportion your degree of belief to what you consider the most populous state. Rational gamblers seek maximal winnings, and "Bet green" promises nine times the winners of "Bet red."

Replace "wearing a green sign" and "wearing a red sign" with "being a Sim" and "being a non-Sim" respectively. Your evidence doesn't determine whether or not you're a Sim. (You haven't received messages from your simulators or glimpsed any programming glitches.) If you think 90 percent of all minds are Sims, your indicated strategy is: give your Sim-hood 90 percent personal probability. Putnam and Descartes only require their hypotheses to be empirically indistinguishable from an external world, and *don't* need any positive evidence for their hypotheses. Instead, Bostrom thinks some assumptions about computing and mind make Sim-hood not only possible but *probable*.

Bostrom says functionalists who accept his argument face a trilemma: (1) posthumans are rare, (2) posthumans run few Sims, or (3) we're probably Sims. Bostrom defends only this trilemma, and does *not* claim that we're probably Sims. The Simulation *Argument* differs from Simulation *Hypotheses*. The former is a probabilistic disjunction; the latter are metaphysical theories about what lies beneath sensory appearances (e.g. we live in a computer simulation). Simulation Hypotheses say our world resembles The Matrix: a virtual realm simultaneously shared by many humans but with an intelligently-controlled computational substratum which we (ordinarily) can't access. (Simulation Hypotheses imply reality is computational at some level, but the reverse implication needn't hold. Reality might have a computational substratum without this substratum being under conscious control. For ease, we'll assume all computationally-generated worlds are simulations.)

Neither Simulation Argument nor Simulation Hypothesis implies the other. You can accept Bostrom's argument but reject your Sim-hood. (You might believe **functionalism** is false or few posthumans exist.) You might reject Bostrom's argument but believe you're a Sim. (Maybe your simulators place a pop-up menu of instructions in your visual field.) The Simulation Argument commits you to the Simulation Hypothesis only if you think Sims out-number non-Sims.

2. Simulation, Doomsday and anthropic reasoning

Compare Bostrom's argument with Brandon Carter and John Leslie's "Doomsday Argument" (see Leslie 1998). Both use the "Anthropic Principle," coined by Carter to express how our nature as observers relates to the physical conditions we observe. As only certain kinds of physical conditions support observers, only certain kinds of conditions get observed. (I bet you're reading this in a temperate oxygen-bearing environment and not inside a star.) Doomsday applies anthropic reasoning to our position in human history, not our spatial or physical location.

Doomsday suggests we should give low probability to human population expanding (or holding steady), and high probability to our population irreversibly declining. Perhaps 10 percent of all people who have ever lived are alive now, so our *c.* 6 billion contemporaries have birth-ranks *c.* 60 billion. If this 10 percent is a significant fraction of everyone who ever *will* live (i.e. humanity nears extinction), our current position is fairly unexceptional. (Almost all birth-ranks will equal, or be less than, ours.) If Doom is deferred and most people live after us, we're unusually early humans. (Birth-ranks below 60 billion are then atypical, because most birth-ranks will exceed 60 billion.) If we should prefer explanations that maximize our location's probability, we should assume imminent extinction is likely. (Strictly, "Doomsday" is misnamed, as the argument is compatible not only with our extinction but our evolving into something else. Both Doomsday and Simulation arguments have disjunctive conclusions. For a fictional treatment of Doomsday, see Baxter (2000).)

Leslie illustrates Doomsday thus: (i) Your name is written on a slip of paper and placed in an urn. Assume the urn either holds ten names or a million names. Names are drawn randomly from the urn, and aren't replaced. If your name is drawn third, this datum favors the "ten name" hypothesis. (ii) You draw balls randomly from an urn (without replacement) and the first 100 balls you draw are all green. You have two hypotheses: H1—the urn holds 1,000 green balls; H2—the urn holds 100 green balls and 900 red ones. If you assume a random draw, you should favor H1, because H1 confers higher probability on your data. If H2 is true, your sample is atypical, containing the only green balls from an urn 90 percent full of red balls.

Like all anthropic arguments, Doomsday assumes we ought to favor whichever hypothesis makes our location as observers probable. Bostrom accepts this assumption but rejects Doomsday. He says knowing our approximate birth-ranks (i.e. that we live *c.* 2007 CE) means we can't treat ourselves as random humans. We don't possess any direct evidence as to whether or not we're Sims but we do have abundant population data.

3. Simulation hierarchies

Bostrom thinks our creating Sims would suggest (1) posthumans aren't rare and/or (2) posthumans run many Sims. If/when we create Sims, this would tell heavily against two options in Bostrom's trilemma and suggest we're probably Sims. Presumably properly simulating a civilization would involve simulating all its Sims. If functionalism is correct, simulated Sims would themselves be conscious. So, if we start running Sims, we should think we probably live in a nested hierarchy of simulating simulators (like Sawyer's auto-homicide hierarchy in "Iterations').

Each level in a Sim-hierarchy can effectively be its own world with its own laws. Presumably, simulators at the bottom bear the costs of simulating all higher layers. If basement simulators have only finite resources, presumably there can be only finite Sim-hierarchies. Even if only finitely many Sim-levels can exist, a hierarchy might hold many levels and each level, many Sims. (If the basement simulator is a god-like being of infinite resources then reality could be infinitely-layered and extend indefinitely.)

Causal and evidential asymmetries will exist between lower and higher levels. Higher levels are causal descendents of lower ones, but not *vice-versa*. Levels must know about any simulations they run, but needn't know if anyone is simulating them. Bostrom requires these asymmetries, e.g. so we can't dismiss our Sim-hood because we see no-one simulating us. Lower levels might effectively act as gods to those above them, e.g. monitoring and controlling their lives and physical environments. Bostrom (2003a: p. 254) thinks the mere *possibility* of a multi-layered reality might induce moral behavior in all levels. Any level might reasonably fear detection and punishment of its moral failings from levels lower down. If no level can be sure that it is the bottom, all levels have an incentive to treat other beings well.

4. Skepticism: Truman Burbank, Glaroons and Cthulhu

Can you believe you're a Sim without being metaphysically confused? Could everyday knowledge survive such a belief? It seems as if Sims occupy the same shaky footing as BiVs or Evil Demon dupes, and that Simulation Hypotheses are radically skeptical. Sims, BiVs and Evil Demon dupes all inhabit artificial worlds where appearance and reality can diverge.

However, this skeptical appearance may be deceptive. If you're an Evil Demon dupe, there may be no reliable memories in your mind, no other people, no physical objects as you imagine them, no space or time, no mathematical truths—all could be Demon-spawned illusions. Maybe you and the Demon exhaust the sum total of existence. However, if Simulation Hypotheses are correct, there can still be other human minds in a shared (computational) space. Simulation Hypotheses may just be novel stories about what underlies the objects we perceive. Sims may preserve all the correct causal links to computers, other minds etc., necessary for meaningfully thinking "I'm a Sim." So, Sims need be neither metaphysically incoherent (like BiVs) nor massively deceived (like Evil Demon dupes). Indeed, we might even have good reason to think Sim-hood is our current state.

Fictional scenarios might illustrate which Sim-worlds are, and aren't, radically skeptical. Consider Truman Burbank, titular hero of the film *The Truman Show* and the 24-hour reality TV show within the film. Truman lives in a perpetually stage-managed world, dedicated solely to keeping him functioning and telegenic. He is the victim of a massive conspiracy and his view of reality is comprehensively skewed. (His supposed friends and neighbors are all actors, charged with keeping him happy and slipping a little product-placement into the show under his unsuspecting nose.) Bostrom thinks that while "Truman worlds" could be governed by exactly the same physical laws we think govern our world, such worlds are nonetheless genuinely skeptical—no one is trustworthy, all is not as it appears. "Truman world" engineering might become necessary if a Sim-world malfunctioned and threw up glitches its Sims could observe. Simulators might intervene to erase memories of glitches or encourage Sims to dismiss glitches as hallucinations. So, even if your local simulation failed, you wouldn't necessarily remember such failures and so you can't infer such things don't happen just because you don't recall them. A lack of observed glitches in our environment doesn't prove we aren't Sims but this suggestion buys the Simulation Hypothesis compatibility with experience at a skeptical price.

The protagonist of Robert Heinlein's story "They" is in a mental institution, having concluded that neither everyday, scientific nor religious explanations for human existence make any sense. He believes the inconsistencies of human behavior prove we're being manipulated by other beings with agendas of their own. In fact, he's right; his world is studded with beings called "Glaroons," who continually scrutinize him disguised as doctors and nurses. So, Glaroons belong to the same space-time manifold as us but control the fundamentals of perception. "Glaroon" worlds too seem deeply skeptical—your perceptions and environment are continually monitored and controlled by hidden powers.

In Heinlein's "The Unpleasant Profession of Jonathan Hoag," Hoag returns from work every evening with no recollection of what his job entails. Hoag gradually discovers he is not human but merely inhabits a human shell. This immersion has occurred because Hoag is a critic, making an in-depth assessment of a work of art, i.e. our world and all its contents. Completing his task obliges Hoag to make adjustments to our reality. So our world is an artifact whose laws bind its inhabitants, but not its creators. Hoag-worlds don't seem *radically* skeptical—in Hoag-worlds, our physical laws are real and (normally) apply everywhere we can observe but such laws can be over-ridden by the world's makers.

In H. P. Lovecraft's "Cthulhu Mythos" stories, our world is an orderly island in an otherwise chaotic universe, beset by alien and/or extra-dimensional beings. The laws governing our matter, geometry and colors are real hereabouts but needn't obtain everywhere. Lovecraft worlds exemplify what D. M. Armstrong (1975: p. 104) called "cosmic epoch" skepticism; a non-radical skepticism whereby our local laws are correct but not spatio-temporally invariant.

Simulation could be Hoagian, Glaroonian or Lovecraftian. In a Matrix, our (local) physics may be real qua our shared perceptual world but it can be over-ridden and needn't apply to all existence. In the *Matrix* trilogy, Neo grows from passive consumer of Sim-reality to Hoagian world-shaper, (like Morpheus and Trinity). Agent Smith's hostile editing of Sim-reality is Glaroonian. The trilogy explains the Matrix's existence in Glaroonian/Lovecraftian fashion: hostile Machines built the Matrix to hold our minds in thrall so they can use our bodies as batteries. (Is thermodynamics different in reality-at-large?) However, there's no *intrinsic* reason why simulators need be hostile. For example, imagine a benign

Matrix, (e.g.) wherein benevolent powers feed human survivors of nuclear war a simulated world more pleasant than scorched reality

Simulation can have theological dimensions. Consider the problem of evil, i.e. reconciling God's omnipotence and omnibenevolence with the existence of suffering. Bostrom offers this (admittedly far-fetched) Sim-answer to the problem of evil: "There is no suffering in this world and all memories of suffering are illusions," (2003a: p. 254). Besides inciting skepticism about the past and other minds, this answer faces the problem that delusory memories of suffering are still evils. Is it consoling to think suffering is genuinely painful but has a delusory cause? (Offered this Matrix "solution" to suffering, one might want neither red nor blue pills, but a refund.) Generally, philosophical accounts of evil don't dismiss suffering as unreal but argue that suffering is a real but inescapable accompaniment of greater goods, e.g. personal growth, moral autonomy or free will. In *The Matrix: Reloaded*, Neo asks the Matrix's Architect why the Matrix is so bleak if it was built to keep humans entertained. The Architect replies: original Matrices were Utopian but their inhabitants found perfection boring and became ungovernable. Sim-humans seemingly need pain in order to keep their mental wheels turning.

5. Simulationism as revisionary metaphysics

David Chalmers thinks the Matrix hypothesis is not a *skeptical* hypothesis that undermines our beliefs about the physical world but a *metaphysical* hypothesis about what underlies the physical world. Chalmers compares the Matrix Hypothesis to Berkelian immaterialism and quantum theory—neither denies the existence of familiar objects but offers a new account of what reality is. In quantum theory, events can lack causes, a particle's position and velocity cannot simultaneously be known with arbitrary precision (cf. Heisenberg's "uncertainty principle"), and objects may exist in "superpositions" of contradictory states, (cf. Schrödinger's cat). Philosophy too has a long history of revisionary metaphysics. Like his mentor Parmenides, Zeno of Elea (*fl. c.*370 BCE) held that all reality is One, and hence motion and change are impossible. Thomas Hobbes (1588–1679) argued, contrary to Cartesian dualism, that all existence is material, including thoughts, souls and even God. J. M. E. McTaggart (1866–1925) thought time cannot exist and all temporal appearances are false.

According to George Berkeley (1685–1753), only minds and their ideas exist. Non-thinking things exist if (and only if) they are presented to consciousness. Berkeley thought his metaphysics was *not* revisionary, because commonsense would agree with him that *Esse est percipi* ("To be is to be perceived"). Berkeley accepted the existence of chairs, tables and mountains but rejected the idea of Matter, conceived as an imperceptible material substratum beneath what we perceive and which somehow causes our ideas. Thus, a tree is the sum of all the (actual and possible) perceptions of it that exist in minds. Beyond our perceptions, no extra imperceptible "real" tree exists. Does the tree outside disappear if I close my eyes? No, Berkeley says, the tree still appears to God's omnipresent perception and won't disappear even if all finite minds stop perceiving it. Berkeley saw

Nature as not unlike a vast theistic simulation or virtual reality, a gigantic language of signs orchestrated by God for our benefit.

Chalmers says Simulation Hypotheses offer a kind of Cartesian mind/body dualism—our selves might be confined to a Sim-world now but could survive uploading into another world. On this view, our consciousness might genuinely be distinct from any of the (simulated) physical processes we can observe. But unlike Cartesian dualism, simulation can allow a strictly materialistic immortality—Chalmers' selves don't need any *immaterial* substratum to be able to survive Sim-death indefinitely.

Immanuel Kant (1724–1804) distinguished between the "phenomenal realm" and "noumenal realm" (i.e. respectively the world as we perceive it and the world as it is in itself). He thought space and time were real properties of the phenomenal world, but that the noumenal world is not spatio-temporal. Space and time are inescapable categories of our grasp of the world but don't apply to reality-at-large. Chalmers thinks the relation between simulators and Sims resembles that between Kantian noumena and phenomena. Simulators determine the structure of Sim-reality but need not themselves be bound by that structure. Simulation Hypotheses mean our level's noumenal realm may be a phenomenal realm to another level. Our simulators may have noumenal attributes for *us* (e.g. metaphysical foundations beneath our perceptions that can't be accessed directly), but they're presumably phenomena to *themselves*. There may be a *regress* of levels; each level seeming noumenal to its Sims but merely phenomenal to itself and its simulators.

The *Matrix* trilogy gives reality only two levels: the Matrix level and the Zion/Machine level. However, for all its inhabitants can tell, the latter may itself be a simulation run by still deeper levels, which in turn . . . Where the trilogy offers a simple, stable Sim-hierarchy (early on, we learn how many levels there are and which level is which), Simulation Hypotheses allow a regress of levels. David Cronenberg's 1999 film *Existenz* and Christopher Priest's novels *A Dream of Wessex* (1978) and *The Extremes* (1998) brilliantly portray disturbing regressive virtual realities. Many of Philip K. Dick's stories are virtuoso exercises in appearance/reality discords, but see particularly his novels *Time Out of Joint* (1959), *Martian Time-Slip* (1964) and *Ubik* (1969).

6. Skepticism redux?: kinds of Sim, history and truth-tracking

Can skepticism be kept at bay in a Sim-world? It might depend on the kind of simulation we live in and how we come to be in it. Eight arguments (of varying plausibility) follow, some of which suggest that Sim-hypotheses can be skeptical.

(i) If we live in a Matrix, the natural laws we observe may be contingent on our world's programming. Hence none of the laws we think really govern reality may actually do so. How do we know we're generalizing correctly from our experience? Maybe in unsimulated reality-at-large, cold makes water boil, and only in Sim-worlds does cold accompany freezing. However, the problem of how to generalize correctly from experience is the traditional problem of *induction*. Induction is extrapolating from data to a conclusion that goes beyond what the data strictly imply. You might observe a million white swans and conclude inductively "All swans are white." However, the next swan you observe could prove to be black. Future observations need not conform to past observations and even well-supported inductions can go astray.

David Hume (1711–1776) asked what *rational* warrant we have for induction. Saying the future must resemble the past because it has always done so before is to argue in a circle, assuming the inductive principle at stake. Hume thought induction couldn't be given non-circular justification but was nonetheless inescapable if we want to survive. We can't prove the future will resemble the past or the unobserved will resemble the observed. We have no *logical* guarantee that Nature won't spring nasty surprises or that the laws we think govern the world aren't plain wrong. However, Hume says, we must assume the unobserved will resemble the observed, otherwise we can't live. With respect to induction, Sims and non-Sims are in the same boat. Sims can't prove that reality-at-large must conform to their expectations but neither can non-Sims. Any argument that Sim-hypotheses are skeptical must show that Sims face skeptical problems non-Sims don't. *General* skeptical challenges don't threaten any particular hypothesis.

(ii) Maybe the Sim-hypothesis is skeptical because it makes unfalsifiable claims, i.e. no empirical evidence can prove we aren't Sims. However, many non-skeptical metaphysical claims seem unfalsifiable. I can imagine observations that could falsify the hypothesis "There is a rhinoceros under my desk"; it's harder to imagine how to falsify the hypotheses "Other people exist" or "There is an external world." The Sim-hypothesis may be unfalsifiable but this doesn't necessarily make it skeptical.

(iii) In one sense, Sim-life is like BiV-life: Sim-language will probably have different referents from ours. In the Matrix, Neo has hair but in reality-at-large he's bald—so for Neo, "virtual hair" stands in for our "hair." "Hair" in the Matrix means (e.g.) "flexible stuff that grows out of follicles" but at the next level up, "hair" means (e.g.) "sub-routine X." And so it goes, with each level having a different sub-routine that acts as place-holder for the thing experienced in the Matrix as hair. However, because the inhabitants of the Matrix share a communal and stable virtual world, they can possess a stable, rule-governed language—it just may not have the same referents as ours. Sims needn't be BiVs.

(iv) Our simulators might simulate many alternative histories, so the different levels resemble the branching worlds hypothesized by physicists. (Although quantum worlds are effectively causally isolated from each other once they've branched, whereas simulators are causally linked to the worlds they simulate.) Might a multi-level Sim reality lead to *historical* skepticism? Sims like us might wrongly think they occupy a 21st century pre-Sim period. However, while such uncertainty induces some skeptical unease, it might not support radical skepticism. We may be unsure as to our place in history-at-large but still confident about our place in local (simulated) history. I'm sure I live roughly 90 years after *a* First World War, but my confidence in this proposition needn't falter if not all my contemporaries share this property. How disturbing we find historical divergences between our world and reality-at-large may have a lot to do with what our simulators are like and how long our simulation lasts. Nothing seems more dreadful than this (simulated) life ceasing and our waking up to (e.g.) a Nazi-dominated world. Fortunately, we've no reason to think (a) reality-at-large is totalitarian or (b) our present simulation is transitory. However, even benevolent simulation might not prevent reality-at-large from striking us as very strange indeed. The Matrix trilogy barely hints at how far reality and appearance might diverge—for example in or out of the Matrix, Neo looks like Keanu, space has three dimensions and time runs one way. Philosophy, physics and fiction have all entertained more exotic possibilities.

(v) Consider *holographic* versus *depth* simulation—the former encodes details about objects' surfaces but the latter simulates underlying microstructure too. Holographic simulation suffices for most purposes. Why waste computing resources simulating light-rays passing between chair and eye if you can implant chair-grasping cognitive results directly into Sim-consciousness? If we live in a surface-only holographic simulation then physical objects and their causal powers drop out of the equation. Considerations of economy favor holographic simulation over depth-simulation and thus prompt a measure of skepticism. Thus, most Sims only perceive surface simulations, whose objects have a discontinuous existence. Holographic simulation seems Berkelian: objects exist fully only when perceived and otherwise exist only as potentially perceived.

(vi) Putnam's argument that certain BiV-beliefs are incoherent needn't work for recently-envatted brains. Likewise, short-term immersion in Sim-worlds might raise skeptical worries. Dainton (2002) talks of "day-simulations": short-term rewirings of our neural network that give us a transitory full-immersion visit to another life. Just as Sim-hood and non-Sim-hood are empirically indistinguishable, likewise there may be no detectable differences between being lifetime Sims and daytripper Sims.

How different can parent and simulated selves be before they become different persons? The self typing this likes far-fetched British 1960s TV spy series *The Avengers*. If I chose from a menu of simulated selves, how come I got a "nondescript lecturer" module and not a "John Steed, debonair secret agent" module? If I'm now a daytripper-Sim for my parent self, my parent self's tastes differ from mine. Skepticism looms because I can't safely reason from my Sim-tastes to "my" tastes in reality-at-large. Maybe when this module runs out, my current preferences will too and I'll find myself inhabiting not merely a history but a *self* this self wouldn't recognize. Perhaps Sim-me reads about Lovecraft monsters because (one level down) I am a Lovecraft monster. (Sim-me devoutly hopes not. Monster-me may rejoice in its unspeakable condition but fear that it's pitifully human another level down.) If I'm not a Sim, a BiV or dreaming, only a huge disruption of natural laws could make human-type experiences be succeeded by Cthulhu-type experiences.

If I'm a research-Sim and run to help check a hypothesis about life in 2007, then why *this* particular (pleasantly unexciting) existence? Dainton suggests posthumans might be most interested in the period when simulation began to be discussed. But why should this period be more interesting than any other? Perhaps an observer selection-effect operates instead, so wondering if you're a recreational Sim makes it *less* likely that such is your condition. Any life interesting enough to be a popular choice of Sim-module probably wasn't spent pondering the Simulation Argument.

(vii) Consider Gettier cases, i.e. justified true beliefs which fail to be knowledge. Robert Nozick tried defeating Gettier cases with a "truth-tracking" theory of knowledge. Nozick's theory replaces JTB's justification requirement with two conditionals. Thus, a proposition ("P") counts as knowledge if it fulfils four conditions:

1   P is true.
2   You believe P.
3   If P stopped being true, you would stop believing P.
4   If P were to remain true, you would still believe P.

Thus, Nozick says a belief qualifies as knowledge if it is sensitive to the truth of the proposition believed. Here we might get a diagnosis of why the BiV hypothesis seems skeptical. If I was a BiV, I needn't believe I was a BiV, so my beliefs about BiV-hood needn't track the truth. Likewise, if I were a newly-embodied ex-BiV, I might not notice any change and keep thinking I was a BiV. Like beliefs in BiV-hood, beliefs in Sim-hood needn't track truth. If Sim-hood is indistinguishable from non-Sim-hood, you could move between them and not notice. (Substrate-independence makes this a real possibility.) Bostrom requires such failure of truth-sensitivity, because his argument must treat Sim-hood and non-Sim-hood as plausibly indistinguishable. If failing to track truth makes hypotheses skeptical, the Simulation Argument uses a skeptical hypothesis after all.

(viii) While Simulation Hypotheses needn't be nightmarish, they still do violence to ordinary metaphysics. Revisionary metaphysicians can (broadly) make two claims: (i) the revisionary theory has explanatory advantages over its competitors, and/or (ii) competing theories are incoherent. (Quantum theory's unparalleled empirical success reconciled scientists to its metaphysical oddities; Zeno and McTaggart thought motion and time respectively would have to combine logically incompatible properties and therefore *couldn't* exist.) Neither claim seems compelling in the Sim case. By hypothesis, Sim-life is empirically indistinguishable from non-Sim life, and no one has proposed any reason why the non-Sim hypothesis is incoherent.

However, the epistemologist's "total evidence requirement" says we should take into account *all* available evidence before weighing up competing hypotheses. We can't tell whether or not we're Sims but we may have some evidence that bears on our Sim-hood. Bostrom says if we run Sims, we should be more inclined to believe we're Sims ourselves and that reality is a Sim hierarchy. Presumably, such a hierarchy must build up a from a primary "basement" level of non-simulated simulators and terminate in a unique layer of non-simulating Sims. If we are non-simulating Sims, we presumably occupy this unique terminus. However, the more levels reality has, the less likely such a location seems. If we want our level of reality to appear likely, we ought to think that reality doesn't boast other (undetectable) levels below ours. If Bostrom's argument induces a probability-shift towards our Sim-hood, thinking about our non-simulating location can induce an opposing probability-shift.

7. Summary and conclusions

Although not entirely convinced by Bostrom's conclusions, I find his Simulation Argument a fascinating addition to the metaphysical and epistemic literature on computation, probability and even reality. It's also one of the most interesting products to date of the two-way traffic of ideas between philosophy and science fiction. It can't be repeated often enough that you might find an argument of lasting interest and importance even if you find yourself not in complete sympathy with its conclusions. If nothing else, Bostrom's argument can serve as a fine ice-breaker and intuition-tester for lectures on such diverse topics as probability, induction, knowledge and the anthropic principle.

We can certainly grant Bostrom that his argument differs significantly in its methods and conclusions from Cartesian or BiV hypotheses. However, with that granted, we might still be wary of the claim that functionalism plus a belief in achieved posthumanity should make us think that we're Sims. Updating our beliefs in favor of Sim-hood is no small revision of our beliefs and we would need to put such an updating in a broader epistemic context before we contemplated such a step.

Although not all Simulation Hypotheses are radically skeptical, many have skeptical implications, and compelling reasons for entertaining such revisionary metaphysics aren't yet forthcoming. However, there doesn't seem to be any incoherence in the Simulation Argument, or Simulation Hypotheses. How many levels reality contains, and how they relate to one another, are still open questions. Plenty of hitherto-unobserved but perfectly imaginable *Matrix*-style phenomena may yet be found to occur, and so drive us (or our descendents) towards entertaining something like the Simulation Hypothesis. Maybe in the various realms of quantum mechanics, cosmic fine-tuning and human self-awareness we have already encountered processes that only a computational model of reality can explain.

STUDY AND DISCUSSION QUESTIONS

1   What is the simulation argument's conclusion? Do you find it plausible? What sort of argument is it that Bostrom offers? In other words, is it deductive or inductive or an argument from elimination?

2   What assumptions must the advocate of the argument make about (i) computing, (ii) the nature of consciousness and (iii) how to derive beliefs from probabilities?

3   How does the simulation argument differ from the simulation hypothesis? Does the world portrayed in the films of the *Matrix* trilogy provide a good model of the simulation hypothesis?

4   The simulation argument might have something in common with Doomsday and anthropic arguments. What similarities do these arguments show and how do they differ?

5   David Chalmers thinks that the simulation hypothesis isn't a skeptical hypothesis. What does Chalmers think the simulation hypothesis is and do you agree? What reasons might there be for thinking the simulation hypothesis is skeptical after all?

6   Bostrom suggests his argument might have moral and even theological implications. What might these implications be? Do you find them convincing? What other implications (philosophical or otherwise) might Bostrom's argument have?

7   How, if at all, might life as a Sim differ from life as a normally-embodied mind? Would being a Sim be like being a Putnam-style brain-in-a-vat or a victim of Descartes' evil demon? If not, how do these scenarios differ?

8   If you could choose to live as a Sim, would you do so? If not, why not? I invite you not to dismiss this question as having an obvious answer. Think about it: if you are in a Sim world—one that offers you some control over your virtual reality—wouldn't you find more enjoyment living in it? You can eat exactly what you want, have the job you really want (or not have one at all), have the sexual experiences you really want, etc., all at the merest whim.

2.14 BIBLIOGRAPHY AND RECOMMENDED READING

Science fiction

*Baxter, Stephen. *Time: Manifold 1*. London: HarperCollins, 2000. Nominated for the 2000 Arthur C. Clarke award, this highly philosophical novel engages in topics including the Doomsday argument and genetic engineering. People attempt to change time, and events in it, in order to prevent the extinction of post-humanity.

Dick, Philip K. *Eye in the Sky*. New York: Vintage Books; reprint ed., 2003. The mental lives of several people are cast into the mind of a single person through an accident at a particle accelerator. Dick plays with issues of solipsism, as well as McCarthyite political surveillance in this heady novel.

——. *Martian Time-Slip* (1964, many subsequent editions). Mental illness, the physics of time and the perception of alternate realities blend thematically as colonists on Mars attempt to become self-sufficient.

*——. *A Scanner Darkly*. New York: Vintage Books; reprint ed., 1977. Drawn from a verse in 1 Corinthians 13, the scanner which is seen through darkly refers to a holographic recording device allowing people to view their own lives. The characteristic blending of the real and unreal occurs on many levels in this novel, beginning with the protagonist, who is a double agent, a hallucinogenic drug addict and a user of scanners. Indeed, the drug, Substance D, in effect separates the two hemispheres of the brain, rending one person into two. The novel is semi-autobiographical.

——. *The Three Stigmata of Palmer Eldritch*. Gollancz, reprint ed., 2003. Colonists must take a concoction of drugs to acclimate to the Martian world and preserve their sanity. Eldritch supplies them with a new drug which not only changes the perception of reality, but also, apparently, recreates reality.

——. *Time Out of Joint* (1959, many subsequent editions). Ragle Gumm slowly realizes that he is living in a virtual reality environment as objects he sees fade in and out of existence. He realizes that there is much more to his world than he had thought, à la *The Truman Show* (1998). But, characteristic of Dick's frenetic plotting, this is much more than a story about appearance/reality distinctions. Themes of military exploitation of an innocent civilian for success on the battlefield predate and influence subsequent novels, like *Ender's Game*.

——. *Ubik* (1969, many subsequent editions). The protagonist is engaged by a corporation to do some espionage regarding telepaths and their influence on business. He is double-crossed, and put in an unusual form of cognitive stasis.

——. "We Can Remember It for You Wholesale." *The Magazine of Fantasy and Science Fiction*. April 1966.

Galouye, Daniel. *Dark Universe*. Gollancz, new ed., 1961. Rich and detailed Hugo nominee is about herbivorous human beings who inhabit another world in the conditions quite like Plato's Cave. They live in a lightless environment, which leads them to worship light, and must indirectly infer everything about their surroundings.

Haldeman, Joe W. *A Mind of His Own*. Analog, 1974. Focuses on problems with distinguishing dreams from reality.

*Heinlein, Robert A. "They" and "The Unpleasant Profession of Jonathan Hoag." *The Fantasies of Robert A. Heinlein* New York: Tom Doherty Associates, 1999.

Jaeger, Muriel. *The Man with Six Senses*. London: Hogarth Press, 1927. Especially philosophical novel in which the protagonist attempts to craft a new sense.

Jeter, K. W. *Noir*. Bantam Spectra, 1999. A misanthropic L.A. detective, given the cringe-worthy name of McNihil (literally, "son of nothing"), gets his eyes surgically "enhanced" so that he sees everything as though it were a black and white noir film from the 1930s. The plot picks up on the theme about perception and knowledge as it sinks into a murder mystery involving a runaway suspect who has fled into virtual reality.

Kaul, Fedor. *Contagion to this World*. Bles, 1933. Imagine a world in which everyone got amnesia and lost all memory knowledge. A rogue scientist creates just such a plague, and the result is catastrophic for our species.

Kepler, Johannes. *Somnium: The Dream, or Posthumous Work on Lunar Astronomy*. Trans. Edward Rosen. Dover Publications, 2003. Kepler uses the medium of what we now know as science fiction as the ideal vehicle for his Galilean understanding of the solar system. The story relates a journey to the moon and, from that site, the observation of the solar system and its celestial bodies. Often considered the first work of the genre.

Lovecraft, H. P. *The Call of Cthulhu and Other Weird Stories*. S. T. Joshi, ed. New York: Penguin, 2001.

Priest, Christopher. *A Dream of Wessex*. London: Faber, 1977. A group of British futurists undertake an experiment to create a virtual-reality society. Once in, members forget who they had been by undergoing a form of hypnosis. In addition to working with themes of the perception and reality of space and time, the novel includes intriguing ethical dimensions that lead to thoughts of John Rawls and the "veil of ignorance."

——. *The Extremes*. St. Martin's Press, 1999. 393pp. Virtual reality technology, branded "Extreme Experience," is used extensively by an FBI agent who is attempting to reconstruct and understand two simultaneous massacres, one in Texas, in which her husband was killed, and the other in England. She travels to England to investigate any connection, and begins using ExEx extensively. Priest draws this to his characteristically stunning conclusion by revealing connections between technology and consciousness.

Sturgeon, Theodore. *Not Without Sorcery*. New York: Ballantine, 1948. "The Ultimate Egoist," contained in this collection, explores ideas in skepticism and solipsism.

Swanwick, Michael. "Scherzo with Tyrannosaur." *Asimov's Science Fiction* 282: July, 1999. A formal dinner, a fascinated boy glued to the window, packs of dinosaurs for entertainment, and much more.

*Zelazny, Roger. *The Dream Master*. New York: Ace, 1966. Based on the Nebula winning "He Who Shapes" (*Amazing*, 1965). *The Dream Master* portrays a psychologist who enters his patient's awareness and "shapes" vivid dreams as part of the therapy. By doing this, the psychologist runs the risk of losing contact with the real world.

Philosophy

Armstrong, D. M. *What is a Law of Nature?* Cambridge: Cambridge University Press, 1975.

Ayer, A. J. *The Problems of Knowledge*. New York: Penguin, 1957.

Berkeley, George. *The Works of George Berkeley, Bishop of Cloyne*. Ed. A. A. Luce and T. E. Jessop. London: Thomas Nelson and Sons, 1948–1957. 9 vols.

*——. *A Treatise Concerning the Principles of Human Knowledge* and *Three Dialogues Between Hylas and Philonous*. J. Dancy, ed. Oxford: Oxford University Press, 1998.

BonJour, Laurence. "Externalist Theories of Empirical Knowledge." *Midwest Studies in Philosophy* 5 (1980): pp. 59–60.

——. *The Structure of Empirical Knowledge*. Cambridge: Harvard University Press, 1985.

Bostrom, Nick. "Are We Living in a Computer Simulation?" *The Philosophical Quarterly* 53 (2003): pp. 243–55. See also: www.simulation-argument.com/simulation.html [Bostom 2003a].

*——. "The Simulation Argument: Why the Probability that You Are Living in a Matrix is Quite High." *Times Higher Education Supplement*, May 16, 2003. See also: www.simulation-argument.com/matrix.html [Bostrom 2003b].

*Chalmers, David. "The Matrix as Metaphysics," 2002, at: http://consc.net/papers/matrix.html

Chisholm, Roderick. *Theory of Knowledge*. 3rd. ed., Englewood Cliffs, NJ: Prentice Hall, 1989.

*Dainton, Barry. "Innocence Lost: Simulation Scenarios: Prospects and Consequences," 2002, at: www.simulation-argument.com/dainton.pdf

Dancy, Jonathan. *Introduction to Contemporary Epistemology*. Oxford: Blackwell, 1985.

Davidson, Donald. "On the Very Idea of a Conceptual Scheme." *Inquiries into Truth and Interpretation*. Oxford University Press, 2001.

Descartes, René. *Meditations on First Philosophy*, I and II (in Chapter 1). *Discourse on Method and Meditations on First Philosophy*, 3rd ed. Trans. Donald Cress. Indianapolis: Hackett Publishing, 1998. Originally published in 1641.

DeRose, Keith and Ted Warfield. *Skepticism: A Contemporary Reader*. Oxford: Oxford University Press, 1999.

Dretske, Fred. *Perception, Knowledge, and Belief*. Cambridge University Press, 2003.

Feldman, Fred. *A Cartesian Introduction to Philosophy*. New York: McGraw Hill, 1986.

Greco, John and Ernest Sosa, eds. *The Blackwell Guide to Epistemology*. Oxford: Blackwell, 1998.

Hegel, G. W. F. *Phenomenology of Mind* (also known as *Phenomenology of Spirit*). Multiple editions in print.

Hirst, R. J. *Perception and the External World*. Macmillan, 1965.

Howson, Colin. *Hume's Problem: Induction and the Justification of Belief*. Oxford University Press, 2003.

Hume, David. *A Treatise of Human Nature*. Multiple editions in print.

——. *Enquiry Concerning Human Understanding*. Multiple editions in print.

Kant, Immanuel. *Critique of Pure Reason*. Multiple editions in print.

Kelley, David. *The Evidence of the Senses: A Realist Theory of Perception*. Louisiana State University Press, 1988.

Kripke, Saul. *Naming and Necessity*. Cambridge, MA: Harvard University Press, 1980.

Lehrer, Keith. *Theory of Knowledge.* Boulder, CO: Westview Press, 1990.

*Leslie, John. *The End of the World: The Science and Ethics of Human Extinction*. London: Routledge, 1996; revised paperback ed., 1998.

Moore, G. E. *Philosophical Papers*. Allen & Unwin, 1959.

Morick, H. ed. *Wittgenstein and the Problem of Other Minds*. McGraw Hill, 1967.

*Nozick, Robert. *Philosophical Explanations*. Cambridge: Cambridge University Press, 1981.

*Plantinga, Alvin. *Warrant: The Current Debate*. Oxford: Oxford University Press, 1993.

Plato. "The Allegory of the Cave" (from Chapter 2). *Republic*. 2nd ed. Trans. G. M. A. Grube, revision C. D. C. Reeve. Indianapolis: Hackett Publishing, 1992. pp. 186–92. Originally published *c.*380 BCE.

Putnam, Hilary. *Reason, Truth, and History*. Cambridge: Cambridge University Press, 1981.

Reid, Thomas. *An Inquiry into the Human Mind on the Principles of Common Sense*. Derek R. Brookes, ed. University Park: Pennsylvania State University Press, 1997.

Unger, Peter. *Ignorance*. Oxford University Press, 1979.

Weatherson, Brian. "Are You A Sim?" *The Philosophical Quarterly* 53 (2003): pp. 425–31.

3 Religion and belief in God

Imagine a scientist who creates a primitive multi-cellular life form and seeds its DNA with the potential for accelerated development so that its evolutionary timescale is thousands and thousands of times faster than that of our species. She designs these creatures, "Neoterics," so small that she can contain them in a sterile, shatterproof enclosure in her lab. The Neoterics evolve emotions and intelligence; they begin to communicate with her; they eventually worship her. She uses their talents and powers to help her develop new chemical compounds and inventions. When the Neoterics obey her, she rewards them; when they do not, she punishes them. Periodically she kills an entire generation to remind them that escape is futile and deathly. Neoterics have concepts of morality, but they believe that their moral rules do not apply to their creator. They debate amongst themselves whether their God is a moral being. Most Neoterics who survive the genocidal cataclysms continue to worship the scientist that created them as a perfect God.

This plot comes from the fecund mind of Theodore Sturgeon, from his short story "Microcosmic God." For most people walking around on the surface of our spinning planet, we human beings are to God as the Neoterics are to the scientist. Just as the God of the Bible exterminated the human race but for the people and animals on Noah's ark, so the scientist kills off the population of Neoterics. Like the Neoterics, we observe features of design in our world and, many of us, infer that an intelligent being created it. We're going to explore this and several other issues raised by this thought experiment in this chapter.

The philosopher approaches religious issues in a peculiar way, which seems at times almost sacrilegious to some religious believers. Some believers regard their faith in God as private and personal, tied up with the performance of rituals and membership in a religious community. But the philosopher, whether religious or not, wants to know what people mean by the word "God" and whether evidence can be found that will prove or support the claim of the *theist* that God exists or the claim of the *atheist* that there is no God. Although the way we will approach the existence of God may seem somewhat abstract and conceptual, these issues are nonetheless of deep personal concern for many philosophers.

Debate about God's existence, extending over thousands of years, yields lots of theories. We will select a few choice arguments to explain and evaluate.

After completing this chapter, you should be able to do the following:

- Explain the concept of **God**
- Understand and evaluate evidence in support of **theism**, particularly as manifest in the design argument
- Understand and evaluate the problem from evil as a criticism of theism
- Describe ways in which epistemological theories have influenced the justificatory status of belief in God

3.0 THE CONCEPT OF GOD

You might think that any attempt to define the name "God" is doomed to failure. Many theists believe that God surpasses all understanding. God is an immaterial, supernatural being fundamentally unlike anything in the natural world studied by scientists. "God" cannot be defined the way other words can.

If we don't clarify some characteristics of God, then our efforts to determine whether God exists won't get off the ground. Many traditional theistic religions agree that God has these traits: unique, incorporeal, eternal and uncreated, omnipotent, omniscient, purposive, and omni-benevolent (all-good). God has created moral rules for human beings and transmitted them to us by sacred texts. Given this concept of God, we can turn to the question of how to understand and evaluate evidence that is advanced for or against the claim that something in reality answers to this description.

Before we dig into the arguments, let's ask a simple question: is it possible that the traits we have just listed can be possessed by a single being? Suppose I said that a "Merfer" is a geometrical figure that is both a circle and a square at the same time. You probably wouldn't want to spend much time debating with me whether a Merfer exists. The concept is incoherent, so it cannot exist.

Perhaps the set of traits we have used to describe God are also incoherent taken together. The "Paradox of Omnipotence" draws just this conclusion. It starts with a question: Is it true or false that God can create a stone so big He cannot lift it? Either way it seems as though God isn't omnipotent since either way there is something God can't do. If God can create a stone *that* big, then there is something God is powerless to do—lift it. But if God can't create the stone in the first place, then there is also something God is powerless to do. So if God were to exist, there is an action that God is incapable of performing. The paradox concludes that a being with the characteristic of omnipotence does not (and perhaps cannot) exist.

So does "omnipotence" require the ability to do everything, as the term seems to imply? Some theists argue God's power has limits. God can't do *what is logically impossible,* e.g. create married bachelors or make $1 + 1 = 3$. God is all-powerful, but the concept of a "power" only refers to what it is possible to do.

Other theists have added another restriction: God cannot do *what is inconsistent with the nature of God*. Given that God is all-loving, God cannot hate himself or commit suicide, for examples. By restricting God's actions to the realm of logically possible actions, theists argue that the statement "God can create a stone so big God cannot lift it" is logically incoherent.

BOX 3.A: A ROBOT'S PROOF OF GOD

In a wickedly clever story, "Reason," Isaac Asimov has a character deliver an argument for God's existence that mirrors an argument given by René Descartes in his Third Meditation. QT1 is an artificial intelligence whose components were designed and manufactured on Earth. Powell and Donovan, two human engineers, assemble "QT" out on a satellite. QT's job is to regulate and transmit the energy received from a network of other satellites, but, once assembled and activated, QT doesn't want to cooperate. In fact, it doubts the story told it by Powell and Donovan. Those two tell QT that it is surrounded by infinite emptiness containing massive globes of energy; that there is a cold spinning ball occupied by billions of humans twenty light years away; and that QT is their creation.

To Powell and Donovan's "explanation," QT responds incredulously, "Do you expect me to believe any such complicated, implausible hypothesis as you have just outlined?" QT says it only knows one thing, "I, myself, exist because I think." QT could not create itself since something can't come from nothing. QT assumes that physically and cognitively inferior beings, like humans, could not create QT. So a being superior to QT that created QT must exist. QT identifies that being as the satellite's energy converter and calls it the "Master." As the Master's prophet, Cutie founds a new religion and converts the other robots on the satellite. Predictably, Asimov brings this tale to a delightfully unpredictable conclusion.

This argument is modeled upon Descartes' argument in the Third Meditation of his *Meditations*. He rules out being his own creator. If he were, "I should have bestowed upon myself every perfection of which I possess the idea, and I should thus be God." Just like QT, Descartes rejects the possibility that he could create himself. And like QT, Descartes rejects the idea that any being inferior to Descartes could create him. But Descartes masks this assumption in his terminology by saying,

But perhaps this being is not God, and perhaps I was produced either by my parents or by other causes less perfect than God. No; for as I have said before, it is quite clear that there must be at least as much in the cause as in the effect. And therefore whatever kind of cause is eventually proposed, since I am a thinking thing and have within me some idea of God, it must be admitted that what caused me is itself a thinking thing and possesses the idea of all the perfections which I attribute to God.

(Descartes, 1985: p. 34)

The conclusion to both of their arguments is that, in order to explain their own existences, QT and Descartes must infer that a vastly superior intelligence must exist and must have created each of them. But what sort of argument is this—an abductive argument to the best explanation, or a deductive argument? What about the key premise that the inferior cannot create the superior?

3.1 A DESIGN ARGUMENT FOR GOD'S EXISTENCE

The Neoterics and the future robots we create with consciousness and other intelligent creatures around the galaxy may offer design arguments for the existence of a superior creator. Historically, design arguments, sometimes called "**teleological arguments**," are the most popular proofs for God's existence. The design argument makes use of our knowledge of the conditions under which something is designed. Cameras, ships and symphonies all have telltale signs of design. Let's call those signs of design "apparent design." When we use a digital camera, we realize that the camera can be used to take pictures or record events. When we dissect it, we find lots of tiny parts—memory chips, lenses, electrical circuits, etc.—all of which work together to take photos. The purposive nature of the camera and the intricate, interworking parts combine to yield the appearance of design. We don't infer that it is designed; we see that it is.

Cameras not only *appear* to be designed; they *are* designed. So why focus on apparent design? Whether or not certain objects are designed is an open question. Imagine hiking through a forest to find a formation of overgrown rocks in broadly circular pattern. They might be remnants of an ancient fire pit. They might have arisen through forces of nature. Consider the signs of design we perceive when using a digital camera. They greatly resemble the signs of design in our human eyes. The eye, like the camera, produces visual images of its surroundings. Coupled with features of the brain, our brain can record information about those visual images for subsequent recollection. The distinction between *apparent* and *actual* design can be used to identify tough cases in which we aren't sure whether design is present or merely apparent.

The awe of the world around us is often a product of the perception of apparent design in nature. This is captured quite well in the words of David Hume here:

> Look round the world; contemplate the whole and every part of it: You will find it to be nothing but one great machine, subdivided into an infinite number of lesser machines, which again admit of subdivisions to a degree beyond what human senses and faculties can trace and explain. All these various machines, and even their most minute parts, are adjusted to each other with an accuracy which ravishes into admiration all men who have ever contemplated them. The curious adapting of means to ends, throughout all nature, resembles exactly, though it much exceeds, the pro-ductions of human contrivance; of human design, thought, wisdom, and intelligence. Since, therefore, the effects resemble each other, we are led to infer, by all the rules of analogy, that the causes also resemble; and that the Author of Nature is somewhat similar to the mind of man, though possessed of much larger faculties, proportioned to the grandeur of the work which he has executed. By this argument *a posteriori*, and by this argument alone, do we prove at once the existence of a Deity, and his similarity to human mind and intelligence.
>
> (Hume, 1998: p. 45)

The design argument for God's existence harnesses and articulates this insight, then uses it to justify conclusions about our beliefs about when a natural object is designed.

The version of the design argument offered in the above quotation (which, by the way, is the first paragraph of our historical reading for this chapter) is an **analogical argument**. Analogical arguments aim to draw conclusions about thing A by comparing thing A to thing B. In the design argument, things in nature (or nature itself) are identified and described as sharing *apparent design* or "**designedness**" with artifacts, man-made objects.

Philosophers often use arguments by analogy, but they present some difficulties. Consider these tips and questions when you reflect on an argument by analogy:

- What is the force of the conclusion of the analogy? Comparing two watches might lead me to a number of different conclusions, including that the watch is designed, that the watch is designed well, that the watch is designed in China, or that the watch is designed by a 34 year-old father of two named Shen. The more detailed the conclusion, the more extensive must the analogy be.
- How many instances of each of the two objects have been observed?
- Were a variety of watches—different styles from different manufacturers from different periods of history—examined? A sundial—which might be little more than piece of wood stuck into the ground with markings around it—does not seem to possess designedness. Or does it?
- Are there a great many similarities between the two products being compared? Are there many dissimilarities? The fewer the number of similarities, and the greater the number of dissimilarities, the weaker the analogy will be.

- Are the traits that are shared by the two products relevant to the comparison at hand? If I want to know whether black Timex watches are high quality products, I should not compare them to other black watches since color is irrelevant to justifying conclusions about the quality of the watch.

Analogical forms of the design argument for God's existence break down into a few stages. The first stage aims to identify apparent design in nature. This is followed by an inference from the presence of apparent design to the existence of a designer. A third stage in good design arguments involves inferring that the designer, whose existence is established at the second stage, is or must be God. Here is one interpretation of the design argument as presented by David Hume in reading §3.13.

(3.1)   Some natural object O resembles human artifact A by exhibiting apparent design.

(3.2)   Artifact A has apparent design because it is designed by an intelligent being.

(3.3)   If two objects resemble one another by exhibiting apparent design, then their causes probably resemble one another.

(3.4)   So, probably natural object O is also designed by an intelligent being.

(3.5)   O, probably, was designed by a very intelligent, very powerful, non-human designer.

3.1 asserts a resemblance between some natural object, like the human eye, and some human artifact, like a camera. They both possess the "curious adapting of means to ends" of which Hume speaks. Furthermore, both do similar and remarkable things: they create visual representations of our world. Since 3.1 only posits the apparent design of natural object O, it is a plausible premise. The next premise is uncontroversial; 3.2 explains the appearance of design in the artifact in terms of the fact that it has been designed by human beings.

One powerful principle in the analogical design argument is 3.3, which links together natural object O and artifact A. The aim of 3.3 is to justify the inference from the facts (i) that both O and A have apparent design and (ii) that A is designed to the claim (iii) that, probably, their causes are similar. Since the cause of A is an intelligent designer, 3.3 suggests we draw 3.4 as a conclusion: O is also, probably, produced by design. 3.3 is stated in very general form, and includes the term "probably" to indicate that just because two effects resemble one another it does not deductively follow that their causes must also resemble one another.

The proponent of this design argument cannot conclude by inferring that God exists since the premises do not establish that an omnipotent, omniscient, and all-loving being designed O. To infer that God exists from these premises, we would need another argument from elimination proving that *no other designer* better explains the existence and nature of the natural objects with apparent design. Despite this, the proponent of the argument could rest content with 3.5 as it is stated since it does establish an important thesis.

BOX 3.B: *STAR TREK: VOYAGER*, "Q2"

David Hume, in his *Dialogues Concerning Natural Religion*, disputes the design argument by noting poor designs. No omnipotent, omniscient and omnibenevolent God could have made a world with appendixes, atomic weapons, and destructive hurricanes. Hume then says,

> This world, for aught [we know], is very faulty and imperfect, compared to a superior standard; and was only the first rude essay of some infant Deity, who afterwards abandoned it, ashamed of his lame performance: it is the work only of some dependent, inferior deity; and is the object of derision to his superiors.
>
> (Hume, 1998: p. 37)

Star Trek has taken its turn in casting just such a character as Hume's Infant Deity. "Q2" (season 7, episode 19, series episode 165) marks the return visit of the mercurial, omnipotent entity in *Star Trek*'s multiverse known as "Q." But this time, Q has brought his son, Q2—an infant omnipotent deity. Havoc ensues. Q2 gives the computer a rebellious personality, starts a war, removes Seven-of-Nine's unitard— typical stuff for an adolescent god. Q repeatedly disciplines his son but nothing works. So Q turns his son into an amoeba. Q2 is given a second chance and things work out for the better, but only after Q2 is humanized somewhat. Oddly, these omnipotent beings look to humans as a source of moral conduct, not vice-versa. The philosophical question is this: is it more likely that the Earth and everything in it was designed by a god like Q2, or by God, capital "G"?

3.2 ASSESSING THE DESIGN ARGUMENT FOR GOD'S EXISTENCE

Let's turn briefly to critical discussion of the argument. (Hume offers additional criticisms in §3.13.)

The first is a criticism of 3.4, which we can call "the 'purpose' problem." A critic might argue that even if we know that O exhibits *apparent* design, O *is not designed* because O may not have an identifiable purpose. Suppose that O refers to the universe itself, and suppose that the universe itself exhibits apparent design. The present criticism argues that, since the universe has no identifiable purpose, its apparent design is only apparent. To know that something is designed, we must know what its purpose is, or at least *that it has a purpose*. But the purpose of the universe is not obvious. Thus, says the critic, we cannot infer that the universe is designed.

However, one might respond to this point by arguing that we need not know the *purpose* of an object, or even *that it has a purpose*, in order to know that it was designed.

For example, consider Arthur C. Clarke's "The Sentinel." (*Rental*: This was the story upon which (the novel and) the film *2001: A Space Odyssey* (1968) was based. Stanley Kubrick directed the film. Kubrick and Clarke co-authored the screenplay.) Human explorers on the moon find a mysterious black monolith buried under the surface. They infer it was designed intelligently, despite the fact that it appears to have no inter-working parts and despite the fact that its purpose is, to them, shrouded in complete obscurity. The inference that the monolith is designed appears justified even though the astronauts have limited information. This counterexample shows that we needn't know the purpose of some object O in order to know that O is designed.

The "purpose" problem aims at 3.4, but the second criticism is aimed at 3.3. This is the "similarity criticism." Suppose you are standing at the end of the factory line at a BMW plant. You see a pair of X5 models coming off the line. These cars are identical—both have the same engine, same body, the same tires, etc. Because they are similar in nearly all respects, it follows that we are justified in inferring that it is highly likely that they have the same designer. We make this inference with confidence because the two things we compare are so very similar. But when we compare a camera and an eye or compare a watch and the universe we compare two things that are utterly dissimilar. Hume makes this point in a different way:

> Exact similarity of the cases gives us a perfect assurance of a similar event, and a stronger evidence is never desired nor sought after. But wherever you depart, in the least, from the similarity of the cases, you diminish proportionably the evidence; and may at last bring it to a very weak *analogy*, which is confessedly liable to error and uncertainty.
>
> (Hume, 1998: p. 16)

The greater *number* of similarities between the two things being compared is proportional to the *amount* of justification we have in inferring that the causes of the two things are the same. One might argue that, since a universe and a watch have a great number of different properties, the probability that they have the same cause is quite low. Thus, premise 3.3 is false.

This similarity criticism has problems of its own. Someone may respond to it by noting that the sheer *number* of properties that two objects possess in common is not important to determining whether they have the same cause. If we were to compare a BMW X5 with a Cadillac Escalade, they may share countless properties in common—having an automatic five-speed transmission, a wheelbase of 111 inches, a height of 70 inches, etc. In addition, they are made of steel, plastic, leather, etc. The X5 and the Escalade may share more properties in common than does the X5 with a small BMW coupe. But the BMW coupe and the X5 are designed by the same team. In addition, some properties—such as being to my left—are utterly irrelevant to an object's causes. If two objects share many properties that are irrelevant to their causes, this does not increase our justification for inferring that the two objects have the same designer. What is important for premise 3.3, then, is not the sheer *number* of properties shared by two objects that exemplify apparent design, but the number of properties *relevant to their causes* that exemplify apparent design. The similarity criticism must be reformed so that the main point isn't concerned merely with the number of unshared but rather with the number of relevant but unshared properties.

Here is a third criticism. Some critics attempt to discredit the justification for the inference to 3.4 by observing that evolution through natural selection can explain the apparent design in biological forms without recourse to a designing agent. Throughout unfathomable millions of years, mutations in the genes of unicellular organisms caused slight advantages in the competition for resources. Organisms became increasingly diversified and increasingly complex as mutations continued and generations of creatures joined in evolutionary competition in changing environments. This led to the appearance of design. The plausibility of explaining apparent design by positing a non-human intelligent designer should be assessed relative to alternative explanations that appeal to natural processes like evolution. Those explanations are cogent, thorough and persuasive, so explanations for apparent design that invoke a supernatural being are not highly plausible.

BOX 3.C: INTELLIGENT DESIGN THEORY

Intelligent design theory is a contemporary outgrowth of design arguments. Advocates of "ID" assert that, because the natural world was created by a supernatural intelligence, evidence of that intelligence will be manifest through the scientific study of the natural world. Advocates have argued that certain biological systems, for example, cilia in a cell, cannot be adequately explained by appeal to naturalistic forces. ID recommends that a new, different method be allowed in scientific inquiry—a method that allows for appeal to agency and purpose (teleology) in the scientific explanation of natural systems. ID isn't an argument for the existence of God. Rather, it presumes the intelligibility of nature through the prism of design, and proposes a scientific methodology in accordance with that commitment.

Criticisms against this proposal have blossomed. One objection is that it is unclear how a new method for scientific investigation would differ from the current, naturalistic method. ID theory grants that we don't know anything specific about the designing agent. (Knowing specific traits of the designer would require us to do theology.) It seems that all we know of the designer is that it is a designer. But how can we use this point in a new scientific method? It seems as though this claim will not be useful in making predictions or scientific explanations. In order to establish a distinctive scientific method on the basis of ID Theory, we need more information about the designer. But using information about a designer to structure our scientific explanations is the method employed in "creation science," which isn't scientific at all.

3.4 THE ARGUMENT FROM EVIL

The primary argument against God's existence has its origins in the presence of evil and misfortune on Earth. If you believe in God, your faith might be troubled by the unfortunate events that befall humanity. A hurricane meanders through the Caribbean killing thousands of people and destroying billions of dollars worth of property. A close friend suffers from a debilitating, eventually fatal, case of breast cancer. Your parents enter their retirement only to begin suffering from dementia at the onset of Alzheimer's. Our world contains an enormous number of horrendous evils.

Imagine you are one of two finalists in a contest to win $100,000. You learn you lose. In that situation someone might describe your fate with a number of interesting idioms: "it wasn't in the stars" or "you've been dealt a bad hand." Take note of the literal meanings of these colloquialisms. The first implies that nothing and no one is in control of the event; your failure to win the money is purely random. The second idiom—being dealt a bad hand—has the connotation that someone is in control, but only insofar as he randomly deals cards.

For the traditional theist these idioms don't convey the purposive nature of events in a world governed by God. God is in control of and knowledgeable about worldly events, and God is all-good. If God exists, the presence of evil, and the quantity and horrid qualities of evil, is deeply perplexing.

The events described thus far can be distinguished from another type of misfortune. For we also suffer at the hands of our fellow human beings through acts of jealousy, anger, negligence and war. If a neighborhood boy slices my tires with a knife, then he—rather than some arbitrary force of nature—does me harm. Thieves, murderers and other evil-doers cause lots of pain in our world.

The term **moral evil** refers to harm done by human beings who could have done other than they did. Actions are described as instances of moral evil because *agents*, like that neighborhood kid, perform actions that are morally wrong. In contrast, when a *hurricane* destroys one's house, that event is not capable of being appraised as moral or immoral. Unfortunate, yes, but—as that very term makes clear—such an event is the result of fortune, not the result of an agent's decision. We will refer to this and like events as instances of **natural evil**. The theist is troubled by evil states of affairs in general, and deploys different defensive arguments at moral evil and at natural evil, as we shall see.

Both types of evil include items that we don't label as "evil" in our ordinary use of that term. While we don't often describe slicing one's finger open with a knife as "evil," under these definitions it is evil because it is a state of affairs that creates pain, suffering or harm. "Evil" in this context is a grab-bag of assorted, disvaluable states and events.

Philosophers have used observations about evil to mount arguments against God's existence. First, philosophers articulate *deductive arguments* that conclude that God does not exist because God's existence is logically incompatible with the existence of evil. Second, they have argued that the particular depth and breadth of the evil on Earth warrants an *inductive argument* that the existence of God is improbable. The deductive argument is more ambitious than the inductive argument, but as a result it is more vulnerable to criticism. In the next section we will explicitly discuss a deductive argument from evil and several criticisms of it.

In reading §3.14, Stephen Wykstra discusses an inductive argument from evil and several criticisms of that argument. The inductive argument replaces deductive certainty with a probability judgment. The probability judgment—that it is unlikely that God exists— depends upon a premise about there being much more evil than is necessary for any further goods. The intuition behind the adoption of an inductive, as opposed to deductive, argument, is that even if certain criticisms of the deductive argument from evil are cogent, it nonetheless follows that God need not allow *as much* evil as God does. In one sense the inductive argument can be taken as an atheist's heavily fortified retreat position, should the deductive argument from evil not succeed. The principal response to inductive arguments from evil involves setting out conditions under which we are justified in believing that God would or could have no reason for allowing large quantities of evil and horrific evils.

David Hume restated the most succinct summary of the deductive argument from evil, which Epicurus (341–270 BC) originally articulated. "Epicurus's old questions are yet unanswered. Is he [God] willing to prevent evil, but not able? then he is impotent. Is he able, but not willing? then he is malevolent. Is he both able and willing? whence then is evil?" (Hume, 1998: p. 63).

To see how such queries can be recast into a challenging argument for atheism, let's apply the techniques we've developed above. First, we assume that God's properties include not only omnipotence and omniscience, but also benevolence. If you believe that God is an amoral force, or that God is not all-powerful, you shouldn't be bothered much by this argument. The argument can be understood as follows:

(3.6)   The term "God" is defined as "a being which is omniscient, omnipotent and omnibenevolent."

(3.7)   If God exists, then He knows of evil, can eliminate evil and would want to eliminate evil.

(3.8)   Hence, if God exists, there would be no evil. (inference from 3.6 and 3.7)

(3.9)   There is evil.

(3.10) Therefore, God does not exist.

Premise 3.6 simply states our definition of "God." It is typically thought that the God of the Bible possesses the traits mentioned in 3.6. Given this analysis of God's nature, the proponent of the argument infers 3.7 from 3.6. The reasoning for this inference is straightforward. The inference from 3.6 and 3.7 to 3.8 may also seem commonsensical. Given God's nature, not only does God know about and have the power to eliminate evil, but God would want to do so. Hence, if God exists, 3.8 concludes, there would be no evil. But as we have defined it, there is evil. Since if God exists there would be no evil, and there is evil, it follows that it is false that God exists.

Theists have tried in various ways to show that these premises are false. Premises 3.7 and 3.8 form the core of the argument from evil because the traditional theist believes that God is omniscient, omnipotent and omnibenevolent, and believes that there is evil in the world.

3.5 ASSESSING THE ARGUMENT FROM EVIL: IF GOD DOES IT, IT IS GOOD

Some theists suggest that using the term "evil" in 3.7 and elsewhere in this argument implicitly judges God according to human moral concepts. This attitude is suggested in the biblical book of Job, well worth reading for further reflection about the problem of evil. In the story of Job the Devil makes a bet with God regarding the faithfulness of one of God's people, Job. The Devil bets that he can turn Job against God. God antes up and says that Job's faith will remain intact. God then gives the Devil permission to cause Job all the suffering the Devil wants to cause him. The Devil then causes Job to lose his land, his fortune, and his family in death and destruction.

At one point, when Job feels like condemning God for his fate, God says, "I will question you, and you declare to me. Will you ever put me in the wrong? Will you condemn me that you may be justified? Have you an arm like God, and can you thunder with a voice like his?" (Job 40:7–9). Human beings don't compare with God in power or knowledge. Job acquiesces in God's declaration and its implicit message. Job believes he should accept as God's will whatever happens, and not presume to pass moral judgment on God and God's actions. Job concludes that we humans aren't able to determine whether or not what God allows to occur is actually evil. It may seem evil but be good since God's plan is far beyond our comprehension.

This problem should be placed in the context of the nature of God. Above we characterized "God" as referring to a being that is, among other things, omnibenevolent. With that word we attribute to God the trait of being all-good, though we didn't pause to define "good." The theist faces a dilemma. Either "good" and "omnibenevolent" (a) are defined independently of God or (b) they are defined in terms of God's own nature. Both options present problems (see Box 3.D).

Consider option (a). Our definition of "good" implies that the destruction of someone's property, the loss of his land, his animals and his fortune, and the death of his immediate family is not "good." On the contrary, this is the worst form of suffering that can befall a human being. Therefore, since God has allowed the Devil to play around with Job, like a cat toys with a mouse, evil events occur even though God could have prevented them. So God has allowed evil actions. (Question for further thought: Should God be let off the hook since God did not (but the Devil did) cause Job this suffering?) Given our definition of "God" as omnibenevolent, clearly option (a) needs to be avoided or repaired.

Now consider option (b). Rather than resting the claim that "evil" is misused in the argument, the critic argues that goodness is *dependent on God's will*. In other words, a state of affairs is good only if it is willed by God, and is evil only if it is not willed by God.

If morality is dependent upon God, then premises in our argument that invoke the concept of evil—including 3.9—are doubtful. We can use the term "good" and "evil" properly so long as we use those terms to refer to only to those things of which God approves (and disapproves).

BOX 3.D: GOD AND MORALITY

In a dialogue written by Plato called the *Euthyphro*, Socrates questions someone by that name about matters of justice. Euthyphro is prosecuting his father for a crime, and claims that he is doing so because it is good and right. Why? Socrates wants to know (a) whether some action is good because the gods say that it is, or (b) whether the gods say an action is good for some further reason. If (b), then claiming that the gods say an action is good does not help us understand what the good-making feature of the action is. If (a), then it seems as though the gods can create or make actions good simply by saying that actions—which appear evil to us—are actually good.

Socrates was working in a polytheistic environment when presenting his argument against Euthyphro, but the example can be revised for monotheism. Consider events performed by God that seem by all counts to be evil, like this one recorded in the Jewish scriptures and the Christian Church's Old Testament. Just after prophet Elisha sees prophet Elijah transfigured into heaven, Elisha starts a long walk to Bethel.

> And as he was going up by the way, some youths came out of the city and mocked him, and said to him, Go up, you baldy; go up, you baldhead. He looked behind him and saw them, and cursed them in the name of Yahweh. Two female bears came out of the woods, and mauled forty-two of those youths. He went from there to Mount Carmel, and from there he returned to Samaria.
>
> (2 Kings 2:23–25)

Because a group of boys called this gentleman "baldy," God commanded two bears to maul forty-two of them to death. If Euthyphro believes that whatever God does is good because God does it, then the murders of these boys is good. This marks a reason to be skeptical that "good" and "evil" can be successfully defined as relative to God. The parallels with violent religious fundamentalism today are transparent.

Rental: Famed Italian filmmaker Roberto Rossellini directed *Socrates* in 2000. It is a forthright look at Plato's early dialogues about Socrates, including Euthyphro. In Italian with subtitles.

This clarification of the meaning of the (b) criticism creates new problems, though. First, consider that the states of affairs on Earth have always been under the complete control of God, given 3.6. Thus, the events that have taken place are presumably only those events that God has willed, either directly or indirectly. (To "indirectly will" an event E is to have had the power to prevent E from occurring, but nonetheless to have allowed E to occur.) But in the wake of this response, every event that we heretofore have thought evil is actually good, since God has either directly or indirectly willed it. Once one contemplates some of the more horrifying events of human history, it is clear that any account of goodness and badness that implies such events are all good is troubling.

So option (a) says that "good" and "evil" are defined independently of God and (b) says they are defined in terms of God's own will; but is there a third option? On the third option, (c) the theist endorses moral **agnosticism**. *Moral agnosticism* is the thesis that one cannot know what is good and bad, right and wrong. Sometimes it appears as though the character Job is endorsing moral agnosticism. This option resonates with Job's comments that he cannot know what is right and wrong. Job imagines that the deaths of his family and loss of land might be good, depending upon what happens in the future. That might have an air of plausibility, but think more about it and you'll find several serious problems.

The theist wishes to know that God is good. But if the theist takes a position of moral agnosticism, then the theist cannot know what is good and what is evil. Thus, the theist arguably cannot know that God himself is good. Not only that, but the theist who takes this defense cannot know that other events in our world are good, or are bad. So when a miracle takes place in which one is healed of third-degree burns, that event cannot be properly described as "good" since it is under God's control and His morals are not our morals. This implication effectively reduces this criticism to absurdity, for the inability knowingly to apply moral concepts would devastate our way of life.

Let's step back from the details surrounding the theist's difficulty upholding the omnibenevolence of God. Notice the close connection between a moral theory that links goodness and badness to God's will and a moral theory that links goodness and badness to the will of human beings. In Chapter 1 we described individual ethical relativism as being the thesis that the truth of moral claims is dependent upon what a human being wills. The type of theory suggested by the objection under discussion would seem to be a form of *divine* relativism. Many of our reasons for rejecting ethical relativism would apply to the divine form as well as the human form. For example, we argued that ethical relativism makes it possible for the most horrifying events to be morally permissible so long as you think that they are. You are encouraged to explore the similarities and differences between these two forms of relativism. Specifically, might the theist have a way of showing that divine relativism does not lead to this result, perhaps by appeal to the necessity of God's goodness? If so, then God is unable to do anything but good. So does God lack free will?

3.6 ASSESSING THE ARGUMENT FROM EVIL: EVIL FOR GOODNESS' SAKE

Some theists argue that human suffering does exist, but that such suffering creates further goods. In sketching this proposal, the theist constructs a **theodicy**. The goal of a *theodicy* is to vindicate God's moral character by explaining how God uses evil events to create goods that depend upon those prior evils. For example, bravery is a virtue. But to develop this virtue, you or your loved ones must be subjected to harm or the possibility of harm. Inculcating bravery as a virtue outweighs the evils needed to enable the development of bravery.

The philosophical aims at work in theodicies contrast with the aims of what are called *defenses*. A **defense** against the problem of evil aims only to propose ways in which God *might* use certain evils to acquire certain goods. If theodicies work, then we know the reasons God has for allowing certain evils. If defenses work, we still do not know God's reasons. Instead, we only learn what possible sorts of goods might outweigh certain evils.

Imagine the following scenario: a man is cast unwillingly into a basement to live in filthy confinement and utter misery, forever outside society, never eating what he wants, never sleeping when he wants. This seems like an evil, disvaluable state of affairs to be sure. However, appearances can be deceiving. This critic of the argument from evil claims that, though this appears to be evil, it is not. Far from being evil, this state of affairs might be good, given other circumstances. Unbeknownst to you, this individual is a murderer who was placed in a prison. His punishment will deter others from committing similar crimes. He experiences retribution for his crime and is also prevented from murdering other people, which makes what seemed to be a bad situation a good situation, on balance. Thus, premise 3.8 that "If God exists, there would be no evil" is false. God may allow *some* evil states of affairs because they are necessary for a more just world.

In effect this objection argues that evil exists for goodness' sake. To understand this point we need to introduce a distinction between **instrumental** and **intrinsic goods** and evils. Broadly speaking, instrumental states of affairs are means to ends, whereas intrinsic states of affairs are ends in themselves. Consider the experience of a doctor resetting a dislocated shoulder. Typically this consists in a brief moment of very intense pain. But you're likely to accept this "evil" happily given the consequences. For if you do *not* have your shoulder reset, you will go without full usage of that arm and experience continued physical pain. Thus, what at first blush seemed like an evil state of affairs is actually instrumentally good since the moment of pain is a necessary step to a valuable end.

BOX 3.E: HICK'S WORLD WITH FLEXIBLE LAWS OF NATURE

One objection to the problem of evil aims at explaining that evil is a consequence of the laws of nature, then that the laws of nature are either intrinsically good or are necessary for some intrinsic goods. John Hick makes this point through a thought experiment:

> Suppose, contrary to fact, that this world were a paradise from which all possibility of pain and suffering were excluded. The consequences would be very far-reaching. . . . No one would ever be injured by accident: the mountain-climber, steeplejack, or playing child falling from a height would float unharmed to the ground; the reckless driver would never meet with disaster . . . There would be no call to be concerned for others in time of need or danger, for in such a world there could be no real needs or dangers.
>
> (Hick 1963, 44–45)

To make possible this continual series of individual adjustments, nature would have to work by "special providences" instead of running according to general laws which men must learn to respect on penalty of pain or death. The laws of nature would have to be extremely flexible: sometimes gravity would operate, sometimes not; sometimes an object would be hard and solid, sometimes soft. There could be no sciences, for there would be no enduring world structure to investigate.

If God had created a world in which he would violate the "laws" of nature routinely to prevent evils, then we as a species would hardly be able to live in it. What assumptions does this thought experiment rest upon? Is it successful in its dialectical goals?

An evil is instrumentally good if its existence is necessary for the production of a net amount of good in the world. Intrinsically evil states of affairs are states that are not instrumentally good. Intrinsically evil states are not necessary for the production of future goods that outweigh those evils. Being mercilessly tortured to death every day over your 90-year lifetime would qualify as intrinsically evil—barring strange scenarios such that, by your miserable death, millions of people are given immensely pleasurable lives.

To return to the objection at hand, some evils, as in the examples given, seem evil but in fact they are instrumentally good for a host of reasons. The critic of the argument from evil claims that 3.8 is false. The defender of the argument rephrases 3.8 as follows:

(3.8')   Hence, if God exists, there would be no evil that is not also an **instrumental good**.

In other words, if God exists, there would be no intrinsically evil states of affairs. To complete this criticism, the defender of the argument would argue that, in fact, there is no evil that is not also instrumentally good. We stated 3.9 as "There is evil." But the defender counters: either "evil" in 3.9 refers to *intrinsic evils* or *to evils that are instrumentally good*. If it refers to instrumentally good evil, then 3.9 is true. But if it refers to intrinsic evil, then it is false.

Clearly this objection hits upon something important: many evils—natural and moral—can be turned to our advantage to create a net quantity of good, contrary to first impressions. Any dental treatment requires moments of pain, but those are vastly outweighed by the pleasure (or the avoidance of greater pain) that results. But if this objection is to succeed in refuting the argument from evil, the defender of the argument must show that events that seem to be intrinsically evil are actually instrumentally good.

Many evils appear to be unnecessary for the production of goods that outweigh the evils required for its production. Being tortured to death over a long period of time seems to produce no good at all, let alone some good greater than that evil itself. Examples from the history of our world can serve as evidence of some evils that are not instrumentally good. Perhaps catastrophic natural disasters and mass genocides do produce some isolated goods, like inculcating virtues of courage and perseverance. However, it is difficult to understand how such events produce a net balance of good. For what we are saying when claiming that an event produces a net balance of good is that the world would have been a worse place had such events not occurred. But it seems possible to produce whatever goods were produced by cataclysmic natural disasters—for example, 812 people doubling their reserves of courage—without all the collateral evil produced by such disasters.

3.7 ASSESSING THE ARGUMENT FROM EVIL: EVIL FOR FREEDOM'S SAKE

Many of the worst evils seem to be visited on us by our fellow human beings. The injury inflicted upon humanity by genocides, wars and armed conflicts would be worse than the injury inflicted by a natural disaster, were it to have precisely the same body count, because of the psychological and emotional damage done to participants of war. The theist argues that when God created humanity, He could have avoided all this only by creating a pair of robots programmed always to do the right thing. In this case, the theist proposes a theodicy to explain why there is moral evil: human freedom requires it. God did not want fleshy robots. He wanted persons who would love Him and do the right thing of their own free will. An agent who acts virtuously and freely is preferable by God to a piece of clockwork, no matter how efficient it is. Furthermore, it is a better thing to be someone with free will than someone (or something) without free will. These thoughts support the first step in an objection to premise 3.8, that "if God exists, there would be no evil." The first step in this criticism reads:

(3.11) That our world contains people with free wills makes it a better place, all things considered, than if our world did not contain such people.

A person who is free to do the right thing is also free to do the wrong thing. It would be a contradiction to suggest that God could have created people so that they were free to do right but were programmed not to do wrong. God could not prevent us from causing evil unless he somehow takes away our free will. But, the critic continues, taking away our free will is worse, on balance, than allowing humans to perform actions. This is because, though free will is *used as* an instrument for evil, its *possession* is intrinsically good. This is to say that the world is a better place in virtue of there being creatures on it with genuinely free wills. Thus we have another premise in this objection:

(3.12) If we are to have free will, then we must be able to do evil.

The atheist will quickly counter: merely being able to do evil is one thing, but doing it quite another. I am able to cheat on my girlfriend, but that doesn't mean I thus do it. Minding this distinction, the atheist suggests that God could have created human beings with free will and yet selected a world in which they simply did not perform evil actions.

The theist might respond by arguing that free will in an environment without any evil would constitute a second-rate type of free will. Imagine I have free will to do evil but never see any evil or hear about any evil. It seems that, even though it is broadly possible for me to do evil, it is not a live option. This represents an initial qualitative distinction between forms of free will. Consider the statement that it is possible for you to fly on a NASA mission to the moon station in 2045. With the right training and education, this is possible for you: physically, your body can withstand the demands of space flight; socially and economically, you have the citizenship and resources needed to acquire the conditions of possibility for the flight; etc. But now imagine a little girl who lives in a war-ravaged rural village in the African hinterland. She doesn't have any hope for an education and hasn't heard about the United States, let alone NASA. Clearly there is an important quantitative difference between the way in which flying a NASA mission is an option for young U.S. citizens and for her. The theist is then drawing a distinction between *free will* and *genuine free will*, whereby genuine free will requires the presence of at least some evil. This leads to a revision of 3.12:

(3.12') If we are to have genuine free will, then there must be some evil.

Now the theist may seek to combine the appeal to free will with the appeal to the greater good. Some evil states of affairs are necessary in order that people develop virtues through the exercise of genuine free will. If so, this would mark a further reason for 3.11 and, derivatively, 3.12 and 3.12'. The theist's line of reasoning can be summarized like this: Our possession of genuine free will tips the balance in our world over from net bad to net good. Since genuine free will requires the existence of some evil, God has reason to allow some evil in our world. So, 3.8 is false.

However, each of the premises in this objection to the argument from evil is subject to criticism. How might the advocate of the problem of evil respond to this line of thinking? The atheist might argue that the shift from 3.12 to 3.12' is unjustified. A philosophical understanding of free will shows that what is significant about free will does not depend on the existence of some evil. (Developing the concept of free will must wait until Chapter 7.) The atheist may grant that freedom of the will requires the *possibility* of doing evil. The concept of freedom is intimately tied to alternative courses of action open to us, after all. But evil needn't exist in order for us to have free will. Perhaps the presence of evil would make our acting in evil ways more probable. But, in the contexts of the deductive argument from evil—in which we are interested in the purely logical, not epistemic, features of the premises—this objection seems to fall short.

In addition, the world might be a better place if there didn't exist the people with free will that there are. The caveat in 3.11—"all things considered"—is important. It might be the case that, even if free will is intrinsically good, its horrible misuse by a set of people in this world produced such a great quantity of evil that it would be better if there weren't people with free will. Addicts require great force of will to overcome debilitating behaviors. Developing a will of one's own is a good thing, to be sure. But for many addicts who destroy themselves and those around them, it would have been better had they been programmed for good and never had free will at all.

Here is one final criticism of the free will objection to the argument from evil. Recall our distinction between moral evil and natural evil. Moral evil is the product of freely willed choices with evil consequences, but natural evil is not the product of any freely willed choice. Suppose, then, that the appeal to free will succeeded in accounting for the consistency of God's existence and moral evil: God allows evil only because preventing evil would require violating our free will, which would be worse than allowing the moral evil in the first place. The appeal to free will is shortsighted in the sense that, even if correct, it does not go far enough. For the appeal to free will cannot make the existence of *natural evil* consistent with God's existence. God thus seems to have no good reason to allow natural evils to occur, since He could prevent them without violating anyone's free will.

BOX 3.F: FALSE GODS OF *STARGATE SG-1*

In *Stargate SG-1*, a long-running and award-winning science fiction television series, a network of gates joins a number of solar systems. The U.S. military begins exploring these gates and, among many other wonders, they eventually learn about a species called the Ori ("Or-eye"). The Ori live as energy beings and have remarkable physical and parapsychological powers. Intelligent species on countless planets worship the Ori as gods. In fact, the Ori evolved from lower form and only late in their species' history did they "ascend" to a higher form. Intelligent peoples across the universe are mistaken in their religious beliefs about the Ori, but the Ori do everything in their power to maintain their flock of believers by empowering those who worship them and killing those who do not. The Ori make a fascinating species of god for many reasons, including their complicated past; their relationship with the Alterans, a sister-species; their steadfast and thoroughgoing belief in free will; and their ruthless treatment of those with whom they disagree.

3.8 GOD'S EXISTENCE VS. KNOWLEDGE OF GOD'S EXISTENCE

Often the conceptual gap between debate about God's existence and debate about *knowledge of* God's existence goes unrecognized. Recent trends in analytic philosophy have put new emphasis on the epistemological question, "Can I know that God does or does not exist?" as distinct from the metaphysical question, "Does God exist or not?"

We know we needn't have any sound argument to be *rational* in believing in God's existence. But must we have a sound argument for God's existence in order to be *justified in believing that* God exists? Many epistemologists and philosophers of religion believe that the bar has been set too high for the justification of religious beliefs, and they answer this question negatively. Most religious believers would too since they don't base their religious beliefs upon arguments. Addressing this question requires a return to concepts of knowledge and their applicability to the statement *that God exists*.

Recall that *internalism* is the thesis that an agent's belief is justified only if the agent is in possession of sufficient evidence for the belief. Descartes nicely exemplifies internalism, as discussed in Chapter 2, §2.0. Religious beliefs are not self-evident, which implies that their evidence must be in the form of non-religious beliefs from which religious beliefs can be inferred. If those non-religious beliefs are justified, and they imply religious beliefs, then their justification will transfer to religious beliefs. This is precisely the pattern employed by arguments for God's existence. If we are successful in creating an argument for God's existence that is sound, then our religious beliefs will meet the internalist condition for justification. Religious believers can meet the internalist condition for justification without necessarily having a sound argument. Perhaps they have cogent reasons that give them access to conclusive evidence on behalf of their belief that God exists. Either way, religious philosophers have been in the business of giving arguments for the existence of God for millennia, in part because they have endorsed internalism about justification.

If internalism is true, then 3.13 follows:

(3.13) In order to be justified in believing that God exists one must have conclusive evidence in support of that belief.

Internalism is a thesis that cuts across the theist/atheist divide: some theists endorse it, others don't; some atheists endorse it, others don't. The theists endorsing internalism go on to mount arguments for God's existence. But the atheist internalist would continue, arguing that:

(3.14) There is no conclusive evidence for the belief that God exists.

(3.15) Therefore, belief that God exists is not justified.

But the theist who is an externalist opposes this argument by denying internalism and by arguing that one can be justified in believing that God exists even if one does not have conclusive evidence in support of that belief. The externalist theist suggests that internalism is unfairly biased against religious belief. Alvin Plantinga presents a version of this objection. He argues that the nature of belief in God has the same justificatory status as does our belief in the existence of the minds of others. Let's state Plantinga's analogical argument in support of the claim that religious believers are justified in believing in God's existence in the absence of sound arguments for that conclusion.

The **problem of other minds** is the epistemological problem of proving that the beings you think are people—your co-workers and classmates—do have minds of their own. We all believe that the things we call "human beings" have emotions, intellectual capacities and a panoply of other mental states. But there is no conclusive evidence for this belief, Plantinga argues. There are arguments, yes, but just as is the case with arguments for the existence of God, the arguments for the existence of other minds fail. Consider the historically prominent analogical argument for other minds:

(3.16) I know that *I* have a mind.

(3.17) Others are like me in shape, composition, behavior, and in many other ways.

(3.18) Therefore, probably, the things I call "human beings" have minds.

When I am given a physical stimulus, I react in a characteristic manner. When I'm poked, I jump. Likewise, when I observe other beings get poked, I also observe that they jump. Their observable behavior resembles mine, so, I infer, their unobservable mental events also resemble mine.

As we know from our analysis of the analogical form of the design argument, arguments from analogy often contain structural problems. In an argument such as this, the sample size of the test group—from which an inference is made—is a single case: my experience of my own mind is the evidence base. Suppose I infer that all squirrels are white on the basis of seeing one that is white. My belief is false but, more important in this context, my belief is unjustified. Unfortunately the remaining arguments for other minds are no better, argues Plantinga.

But we believe there exist other minds even though this fails to satisfy the internalist requirement. Many other beliefs we commonly take for granted appear difficult to justify on internalist criteria—that there is an external world (which Descartes struggled with in Chapter 1), that time is not an illusion (see Chapter 4), that we have free will (see Chapter 7). *Nonetheless*, we think that these beliefs are justified. If these beliefs—beliefs very near the foundational levels of our belief-structure—were not justified, then we might not have many other justified beliefs. But, Plantinga argues, surely we do have many justified beliefs. Thus Plantinga adopts a form of externalism that results in our having justification for believing that there are other minds, that there is an external world *and* that God exists.

So we confront a dilemma: *either* (a) we accept that we are justified in assenting to such beliefs as that there are other minds, etc., without conclusive evidence, *or* (b) we maintain the internalist's requirement and concede that we are not justified in holding such beliefs. Through (b) the critic attempts to show that internalism leads to absurdity because it leads to skepticism. If we maintain the high epistemological standards of internalism, then we are unjustified in believing our most basic beliefs, which violates common sense. If instead we choose option (a), then it seems that at least some people are justified in believing that God exists.

BOX 3.G: BELIEF WITHOUT EVIDENCE?

W. K. Clifford argued that it is wrong always, everywhere, and for anyone to believe anything upon insufficient evidence. This internalist theory of epistemic justification was criticized by the philosopher William James (1842–1910) in an essay entitled "The Will to Believe" (James 1956) James argues that, although we have no conclusive evidence for or against the existence of God, this issue is crucially important for our well-being. He says, "We cannot escape the issue by remaining skeptical and waiting for more light, because, although we do avoid error in that way if religion be untrue, we lose the good, if it be true, just as certainly as if we positively chose to disbelieve." Skepticism offers us no escape from this dilemma, because we have to take a stand for or against belief. Hence, James reasons, you have the right to believe in God even without sufficient evidence. Indeed, the skeptic is in the same boat:

> *Better risk loss of truth than chance of error*,—that is your faith-vetoer's exact position. He is actively playing his stake as much as the believer is; he is backing the field against the religious hypothesis, just as the believer is backing the religious hypothesis against the field. To preach skepticism to us as a duty until "sufficient evidence" for religion be found, is tantamount therefore to telling us, when in the presence of the religious hypothesis, that to yield to our fear of its being error is wiser and better than to yield to our hope that it may be true . . . Dupery for dupery, what proof is there that dupery through hope is so much

worse than dupery through fear? I, for one, can see no proof; and I simply refuse obedience to the scientist's command to imitate his kind of option, in a case where my own stake is important enough to give me the right to choose my own form of risk.[1]

How would you rephrase the main point of this passage in your own words? Has he provided a convincing rebuttal to the skeptic, or is he just making a plea for wishful thinking? Given his argument, should a person facing a terminal disease believe in a "miracle" cure even if there is no evidence that it will work?

3.9 SUMMARY

"God" is a concept, a name and a term that is used in multiple ways. To single out the meaning used by philosophers was the job of the first section of this chapter: "God" refers to a divine person who is omnipotent, omniscient and omni-benevolent. After clarifying the meaning of this term, we posed a paradox—the "paradox of omnipotence"—which called into question the coherence of the very concept of omnipotence.

We next examined a proof for God's existence, the design argument, in its analogical form. The argument proceeds from an empirical premise about the nature and extent of order in the world, through a principle stating that like effects must proceed from like causes, to a conclusion that the world is the product of intelligent design. Criticisms of the argument included the observation that variance between effects leads to variance between causes, which undermines a principle of the argument. We examined the character of arguments from analogy, and also compared the design argument to intelligent design theory.

Arguments against God's existence came next, and we featured a discussion of the argument from evil. After settling on a broad definition of the term "evil," we proceeded to distinguish between moral and natural evil. This enabled us to put the argument into form and offer criticisms of it. These criticisms included the claim that there can be no evil unless God exists, since God is the progenitor of all moral value; that the evil that God allows is necessary for bringing about specific goods in the world; and that some degree of evil is necessary in order for us to have free will.

Last, we distinguished proving that God exists from knowing that God exists. Considerable attention is now paid to the justification of belief in God. Externalists and internalists make competing claims about the evidence required to justify God's existence. One important argument on this front derives from Alvin Plantinga's *God and Other Minds*, in which he argues that we have the same reason to believe that there exist minds other than our own as we have to believe that God exists.

3.10 ABOUT THE READINGS

Our science fiction story is "Hell is the Absence of God," by Ted Chiang. Chiang portrays aspects of the problem of evil through an unusual, compelling thought experiment. Imagine a world in which a literal interpretation of the Bible is not only true, but is played out before us in full color: bystanders witness human souls dragged up to heaven and down to hell when people die; God grants prayer requests in ways that make them instantly verifiable; people are struck down and killed by the sheer glory of God and his angels. What would we think of God if we had much greater knowledge of his actions?

Neil, the protagonist, witnesses the death of his wife in a manifestation of angelic glory. Though his wife was immediately taken up to heaven, Neil can't understand what has befallen him. He embarks on a quest to become reunited with her by being transfigured into heaven, as was she. He meets a number of other curious persons on his journey, each of whom is trying to understand the will of God in the face of the good and evil that has been his or her lot.

One of several proofs for God's existence we haven't an opportunity to discuss in this chapter is the **ontological argument**. Below we include the earliest statement of that argument, written by Saint Anselm. Anselm was a monk who lived in Canterbury, England, in the eleventh century (1033–1109). His version of the argument begins with commonsense reflection upon God's nature. God appears to be a perfect being, in other words, a being than which no greater can be conceived. This much establishes the presence of the concept of God in our minds. Anselm then argues that in order to be the greatest possible being, than which no greater can be conceived, God must not only exist in our minds as a concept but must also exist in reality. This is because the greatest possible being would exist necessarily. In this argument, God is proven to exist by way of reflection upon the concept of God. Many bright philosophers have attempted to refute this argument over the centuries. Whether you become an adherent of the argument, or whether you struggle to identify just what is wrong with this provocative piece of philosophy, we hope you enjoy stretching your mind by thinking critically about it.

David Hume (1711–1776) is a Scottish philosopher and historian who played a big role in the Enlightenment. I mentioned earlier in the chapter that this reading from Hume contains an analogical design argument for God's existence. This reading, like §2.11, is in dialogue form. Two characters take part in the debate—Cleanthes, who advocates on behalf of the argument, and Philo, who advocates against it.

Our contemporary philosophy reading, by Stephen Wykstra, faces down the threat of the evidential problem of evil. Wykstra is a pioneer of the "epistemic" response to the problem of evil. He is interested in determining the conditions under which we are justified in inferring, from knowledge of evil events, the conclusion that it is improbable that God exists. In this paper he analyzes the evidential problem of evil and argues that the pain and suffering that we know of are not sufficient to justify the conclusion that God does not exist.

3.11 "HELL IS THE ABSENCE OF GOD," BY TED CHIANG

This is the story of a man named Neil Fisk, and how he came to love God. The pivotal event in Neil's life was an occurrence both terrible and ordinary: the death of his wife Sarah. Neil was consumed with grief after she died, a grief that was excruciating not only because of its intrinsic magnitude, but because it also renewed and emphasized the previous pains of his life. Her death forced him to reexamine his relationship with God, and in doing so he began a journey that would change him forever.

Neil was born with a congenital abnormality that caused his left thigh to be externally rotated and several inches shorter than his right; the medical term for it was proximal femoral focus deficiency. Most people he met assumed God was responsible for this, but Neil's mother hadn't witnessed any visitations while carrying him; his condition was the result of improper limb development during the sixth week of gestation, nothing more. In fact, as far as Neil's mother was concerned, blame rested with his absent father, whose income might have made corrective surgery a possibility, although she never expressed this sentiment aloud.

As a child Neil had occasionally wondered if he was being punished by God, but most of the time he blamed his classmates in school for his unhappiness. Their nonchalant cruelty, their instinctive ability to locate the weaknesses in a victim's emotional armor, the way their own friendships were reinforced by their sadism: he recognized these as examples of human behavior, not divine. And although his classmates often used God's name in their taunts, Neil knew better than to blame Him for their actions.

But while Neil avoided the pitfall of blaming God, he never made the jump to loving Him; nothing in his upbringing or his personality led him to pray to God for strength or for relief. The assorted trials he faced growing up were accidental or human in origin, and he relied on strictly human resources to counter them. He became an adult who—like so many others—viewed God's actions in the abstract until they impinged upon his own life. Angelic visitations were events that befell other people, reaching him only via reports on the nightly news. His own life was entirely mundane; he worked as a superintendent for an upscale apartment building, collecting rent and performing repairs, and as far as he was concerned, circumstances were fully capable of unfolding, happily or not, without intervention from above.

This remained his experience until the death of his wife.

It was an unexceptional visitation, smaller in magnitude than most but no different in kind, bringing blessings to some and disaster to others. In this instance the angel was Nathanael, making an appearance in a downtown shopping district. Four miracle cures were effected: the elimination of carcinomas in two individuals, the regeneration of the spinal cord in a paraplegic and the restoration of sight to a recently blinded person. There were also two miracles that were not cures: a delivery van, whose driver had fainted at the sight of the angel, was halted before it could overrun a busy sidewalk; another man was caught in a shaft of Heaven's light when the angel departed, erasing his eyes but ensuring his devotion.

Neil's wife Sarah Fisk had been one of the eight casualties. She was hit by flying glass when the angel's billowing curtain of flame shattered the storefront window of the cafe in which she was eating. She bled to death within minutes, and the other customers in the café—none of whom suffered even superficial injuries—could do nothing but listen to her cries of pain and fear, and eventually witness her soul's ascension toward Heaven.

Nathanael hadn't delivered any specific message; the angel's parting words, which had boomed out across the entire visitation site, were the typical *Behold the power of the Lord.* Of the eight casualties that day, three souls were accepted into Heaven and five were not, a closer ratio than the average for deaths by all causes. Sixty-two people received medical treatment for injuries ranging from slight concussions to ruptured eardrums to burns requiring skin grafts. Total property damage was estimated at $8.1 million, all of it excluded by private insurance companies due to the cause. Scores of people became devout worshipers in the wake of the visitation, either out of gratitude or terror.

Alas, Neil Fisk was not one of them.

After a visitation, it's common for all the witnesses to meet as a group and discuss how their common experience has affected their lives. The witnesses of Nathanael's latest visitation arranged such group meetings, and family members of those who had died were welcome, so Neil began attending. The meetings were held once a month in a basement room of a large church downtown; there were metal folding chairs arranged in rows, and in the back of the room was a table holding coffee and doughnuts. Everyone wore adhesive name tags made out in felt-tip pen.

While waiting for the meetings to start, people would stand around, drinking coffee, talking casually. Most people Neil spoke to assumed his leg was a result of the visitation, and he had to explain that he wasn't a witness, but rather the husband of one of the casualties. This didn't bother him particularly; he was used to explaining about his leg. What did bother him was the tone of the meetings themselves, when participants spoke about their reaction to the visitation: most of them talked about their newfound devotion to God, and they tried to persuade the bereaved that they should feel the same.

Neil's reaction to such attempts at persuasion depended on who was making it. When it was an ordinary witness, he found it merely irritating. When someone who'd received a miracle cure told him to love God, he had to restrain an impulse to strangle the person. But what he found most disquieting of all was hearing the same suggestion from a man named Tony Crane; Tony's wife had died in the visitation too, and he now projected an air of groveling with his every movement. In hushed, tearful tones he explained how he had accepted his role as one of God's subjects, and he advised Neil to do likewise.

Neil didn't stop attending the meetings—he felt that he somehow owed it to Sarah to stick with them—but he found another group to go to as well, one more compatible with his own feelings: a support group devoted to those who'd lost a loved one during a visitation, and were angry at God because of it. They met every other week in a room at the local community center, and talked about the grief and rage that boiled inside of them.

All the attendees were generally sympathetic to one another, despite differences in their various attitudes toward God. Of those who'd been devout before their loss, some struggled with the task of remaining so, while others gave up their devotion without a second glance. Of those who'd never been devout, some felt their position had been validated, while others were faced with the near impossible task of becoming devout now. Neil found himself, to his consternation, in this last category.

Like every other nondevout person, Neil had never expended much energy on where his soul would end up; he'd always assumed his destination was Hell, and he accepted that. That was the way of things, and Hell, after all, was not physically worse than the mortal plane.

It meant permanent exile from God, no more and no less; the truth of this was plain for anyone to see on those occasions when Hell manifested itself. These happened on a regular basis; the ground seemed to become transparent, and you could see Hell as if you were looking through a hole in the floor. The lost souls looked no different than the living, their eternal bodies resembling mortal ones. You couldn't communicate with them—their exile from God meant that they couldn't apprehend the mortal plane where His actions were still felt—but as long as the manifestation lasted you could hear them talk, laugh, or cry, just as they had when they were alive.

People varied widely in their reactions to these manifestations. Most devout people were galvanized, not by the sight of anything frightening, but at being reminded that eternity outside paradise was a possibility. Neil, by contrast, was one of those who were unmoved; as far as he could tell, the lost souls as a group were no unhappier than he was, their existence no worse than his in the mortal plane, and in some ways better: his eternal body would be unhampered by congenital abnormalities.

Of course, everyone knew that Heaven was incomparably superior, but to Neil it had always seemed too remote to consider, like wealth or fame or glamour. For people like him, Hell was where you went when you died, and he saw no point in restructuring his life in hopes of avoiding that. And since God hadn't previously played a role in Neil's life, he wasn't afraid of being exiled from God. The prospect of living without interference, living in a world where windfalls and misfortunes were never by design, held no terror for him.

Now that Sarah was in Heaven, his situation had changed. Neil wanted more than anything to be reunited with her, and the only way to get to Heaven was to love God with all his heart.

This is Neil's story, but telling it properly requires telling the stories of two other individuals whose paths became entwined with his. The first of these is Janice Reilly.

What people assumed about Neil had in fact happened to Janice. When Janice's mother was eight months pregnant with her, she lost control of the car she was driving and collided with a telephone pole during a sudden hailstorm, fists of ice dropping out of a clear blue sky and littering the road like a spill of giant ball bearings. She was sitting in her car, shaken but unhurt, when she saw a knot of silver flames—later identified as the angel Bardiel—float across the sky. The sight petrified her, but not so much that she didn't notice the peculiar settling sensation in her womb. A subsequent ultrasound revealed that the unborn Janice Reilly no longer had legs; flipperlike feet grew directly from her hip sockets.

Janice's life might have gone the way of Neil's, if not for what happened two days after the ultrasound. Janice's parents were sitting at their kitchen table, crying and asking what they had done to deserve this, when they received a vision: the saved souls of four deceased relatives appeared before them, suffusing the kitchen with a golden glow. The saved never spoke, but their beatific smiles induced a feeling of serenity in whoever saw them. From that moment on, the Reillys were certain that their daughter's condition was not a punishment.

As a result, Janice grew up thinking of her legless condition as a gift; her parents explained that God had given her a special assignment because He considered her equal to the task, and she vowed that she would not let Him down. Without pride or defiance, she saw it as her responsibility to show others that her condition did not indicate weakness, but rather strength.

As a child, she was fully accepted by her schoolmates; when you're as pretty, confident, and charismatic as she was, children don't even notice that you're in a wheelchair. It was when she was a teenager that she realized that the able-bodied people in her school were not the ones who most needed convincing. It was more important for her to set an example for other handicapped individuals, whether they had been touched by God or not, no matter where they lived. Janice began speaking before audiences, telling those with disabilities that they had the strength God required of them.

Over time she developed a reputation, and a following. She made a living writing and speaking, and established a nonprofit organization dedicated to promoting her message. People sent her letters thanking her for changing their lives, and receiving those gave her a sense of fulfillment of a sort that Neil had never experienced.

This was Janice's life up until she herself witnessed a visitation by the angel Rashiel. She was letting herself into her house when the tremors began; at first she thought they were of natural origin, although she didn't live in a geologically active area, and waited in the doorway for them to subside. Several seconds later she caught a glimpse of silver in the sky and realized it was an angel, just before she lost consciousness.

Janice awoke to the biggest surprise of her life: the sight of her two new legs, long, muscular, and fully functional.

She was startled the first time she stood up: she was taller than she expected. Balancing at such a height without the use of her arms was unnerving, and simultaneously feeling the texture of the ground through the soles of her feet made it positively bizarre. Rescue workers, finding her wandering down the street dazedly, thought she was in shock until she—marveling at her ability to face them at eye level—explained to them what had happened.

When statistics were gathered for the visitation, the restoration of Janice's legs was recorded as a blessing, and she was humbly grateful for her good fortune. It was at the first of the support group meetings that a feeling of guilt began to creep in. There Janice met two individuals with cancer who'd witnessed Rashiel's visitation, thought their cure was at hand, and been bitterly disappointed when they realized they'd been passed over. Janice found herself wondering, why had she received a blessing when they had not?

Janice's family and friends considered the restoration of her legs a reward for excelling at the task God had set for her, but for Janice, this interpretation raised another question. Did He intend for her to stop? Surely not; evangelism provided the central direction of her life, and there was no limit to the number of people who needed to hear her message. Her continuing to preach was the best action she could take, both for herself and for others.

Her reservations grew during her first speaking engagement after the visitation, before an audience of people recently paralyzed and now wheelchair-bound. Janice delivered her usual words of inspiration, assuring them that they had the strength needed for the challenges ahead; it was during the Q&A that she was asked if the restoration of her legs meant she had passed her test. Janice didn't know what to say; she could hardly promise them that one day their marks would be erased. In fact, she realized, any implication that she'd been retarded could be interpreted as criticism of others who remained afflicted, and she didn't want that. All she could tell them was that she didn't know why she'd been cured, but it was obvious they found that an unsatisfying answer.

Janice returned home disquieted. She still believed in her message, but as far as her audiences were concerned, she'd lost her greatest source of credibility. How could she inspire others who were touched by God to see their condition as a badge of strength, when she no longer shared their condition?

She considered whether this might be a challenge, a test of her ability to spread His word. Clearly God had made her task more difficult than it was before; perhaps the restoration of her legs was an obstacle for her to overcome, just as their earlier removal had been.

This interpretation failed her at her next scheduled engagement. The audience was a group of witnesses to a visitation by Nathanael; she was often invited to speak to such groups in the hopes that those who suffered might draw encouragement from her. Rather than sidestep the issue, she began with an account of the visitation she herself had recently experienced. She explained that while it might appear she was a beneficiary, she was in fact facing her own challenge: like them, she was being forced to draw on resources previously untapped.

She realized, too late, that she had said the wrong thing. A man in the audience with a misshapen leg stood up and challenged her: was she seriously suggesting that the restoration of her legs was comparable to the loss of his wife? Could she really be equating her trials with his own?

Janice immediately assured him that she wasn't, and that she couldn't imagine the pain he was experiencing. But, she said, it wasn't God's intention that everyone be subjected to the same kind of trial, but only that each person face his or her own trial, whatever it might be. The difficulty of any trial was subjective, and there was no way to compare two individuals' experiences. And just as those whose suffering seemed greater than his should have compassion for him, so should he have compassion for those whose suffering seemed less.

The man was having none of it. She had received what anyone else would have considered a fantastic blessing, and she was complaining about it. He stormed out of the meeting while Janice was still trying to explain.

That man, of course, was Neil Fisk. Neil had had Janice Reilly's name mentioned to him for much of his life, most often by people who were convinced his misshapen leg was a sign from God. These people cited her as an example he should follow, telling him that her attitude was the proper response to a physical handicap. Neil couldn't deny that her leglessness was a far worse condition than his distorted femur. Unfortunately, he found her attitude so foreign that, even in the best of times, he'd never been able to learn anything from her. Now, in the depths of his grief and mystified as to why she had received a gift she didn't need, Neil found her words offensive.

In the days that followed, Janice found herself more and more plagued by doubts, unable to decide what the restoration of her legs meant. Was she being ungrateful for a gift she'd received? Was it both a blessing and a test? Perhaps it was a punishment, an indication that she had not performed her duty well enough. There were many possibilities, and she didn't know which one to believe.

There is one other person who played an important role in Neil's story, even though he and Neil did not meet until Neil's journey was nearly over. That person's name is Ethan Mead.

Ethan had been raised in a family that was devout, but not profoundly so. His parents credited God with their above-average health and their comfortable economic status, although they hadn't witnessed any visitations or received any visions; they simply trusted that God was, directly or indirectly, responsible for their good fortune. Their devotion had never been put to any serious test, and might not have withstood one; their love for God was based in their satisfaction with the status quo.

Ethan was not like his parents, though. Ever since childhood he'd felt certain that God had a special role for him to play, and he waited for a sign telling him what that role was. He'd have liked to have become a preacher, but felt he hadn't any compelling testimony to offer; his vague feelings of expectation weren't enough. He longed for an encounter with the divine to provide him with direction.

He could have gone to one of the holy sites, those places where—for reasons unknown—angelic visitations occurred on a regular basis, but he felt that such an action would be presumptuous of him. The holy sites were usually the last resort of the desperate, those people seeking either a miracle cure to repair their bodies or a glimpse of Heaven's light to repair their souls, and Ethan was not desperate. He decided that he'd been set along his own course, and in time the reason for it would become clear. While waiting for that day, he lived his life as best he could: he worked as a librarian, married a woman named Claire, raised two children. All the while, he remained watchful for signs of a greater destiny.

Ethan was certain his time had come when he became witness to a visitation by Rashiel, the same visitation that—miles away—restored Janice Reilly's legs. Ethan was by himself when it happened; he was walking toward his car in the center of a parking lot, when the ground began to shudder. Instinctively he knew it was a visitation, and he assumed a kneeling position, feeling no fear, only exhilaration and awe at the prospect of learning his calling.

The ground became still after a minute, and Ethan looked around, but didn't otherwise move. Only after waiting for several more minutes did he rise to his feet. There was a large crack in the asphalt, beginning directly in front of him and following a meandering path down the street. The crack seemed to be pointing him in a specific direction, so he ran alongside it for several blocks until he encountered other survivors, a man and a woman climbing out of a modest fissure that had opened up directly beneath them. He waited with the two of them until rescuers arrived and brought them to a shelter.

Ethan attended the support group meetings that followed and met the other witnesses to Rashiel's visitation. Over the course of a few meetings, he became aware of certain patterns among the witnesses. Of course there were those who'd been injured and those who'd received miracle cures. But there were also those whose lives were changed in other ways: the man and woman he'd first met fell in love and were soon engaged; a woman who'd been pinned beneath a collapsed wall was inspired to become an EMT after being rescued. One business owner formed an alliance that averted her impending bankruptcy, while another whose business was destroyed saw it as a message that he change his ways. It seemed that everyone except Ethan had found a way to understand what had happened to them.

He hadn't been cursed or blessed in any obvious way, and he didn't know what message he was intended to receive. His wife Claire suggested that he consider the visitation a reminder that he appreciate what he had, but Ethan found that unsatisfying, reasoning that every visitation—no matter where it occurred—served that function, and the fact that he'd witnessed a visitation firsthand had to have greater significance. His mind was preyed upon by the idea that he'd missed an opportunity, that there was a fellow witness whom he was intended to meet but hadn't. This visitation had to be the sign he'd been waiting for; he couldn't just disregard it. But that didn't tell him what he was supposed to do.

Ethan eventually resorted to the process of elimination: he got hold of a list of all the witnesses, and crossed off those who had a clear interpretation of their experience, reasoning that one of those remaining must be the person whose fate was somehow intertwined with his. Among those who were confused or uncertain about the visitation's meaning would be the one he was intended to meet.

When he had finished crossing names off his list, there was only one left: JANICE REILLY.

In public Neil was able to mask his grief as adults are expected to, but in the privacy of his apartment, the floodgates of emotion burst open. The awareness of Sarah's absence would overwhelm him, and then he'd collapse on the floor and weep. He'd curl up into a ball, his body racked by hiccuping sobs, tears and mucus streaming down his face, the anguish coming in ever-increasing waves until it was more than he could bear, more intense than he'd have believed possible. Minutes or hours later it would leave, and he would fall asleep, exhausted. And the next morning he would wake up and face the prospect of another day without Sarah.

An elderly woman in Neil's apartment building tried to comfort him by telling him that the pain would lessen in time, and while he would never forget his wife, he would at least be able to move on. Then he would meet someone else one day and find happiness with her, and he would learn to love God and thus ascend to Heaven when his time came.

This woman's intentions were good, but Neil was in no position to find any comfort in her words. Sarah's absence felt like an open wound, and the prospect that someday he would no longer feel pain at her loss seemed not just remote, but a physical impossibility. If suicide would have ended his pain, he'd have done it without hesitation, but that would only ensure that his separation from Sarah was permanent.

The topic of suicide regularly came up at the support group meetings, and inevitably led to someone mentioning Robin Pearson, a woman who used to come to the meetings several months before Neil began attending. Robin's husband had been afflicted with stomach cancer during a visitation by the angel Makatiel. She stayed in his hospital room for days at a stretch, only for him to die unexpectedly when she was home doing laundry. A nurse who'd been present told Robin that his soul had ascended, and so Robin had begun attending the support group meetings.

Many months later, Robin came to the meeting shaking with rage. There'd been a manifestation of Hell near her house, and she'd seen her husband among the lost souls. She'd confronted the nurse, who admitted to lying in the hopes that Robin would learn to love God, so that at least she would be saved even if her husband hadn't been. Robin wasn't at the next meeting, and at the meeting after that the group learned she had committed suicide to rejoin her husband.

None of them knew the status of Robin's and her husband's relationship in the afterlife, but successes were known to happen; some couples had indeed been happily reunited through suicide. The support group had attendees whose spouses had descended to Hell, and they talked about being torn between wanting to remain alive and wanting to rejoin their spouses. Neil wasn't in their situation, but his first response when listening to them had been envy: if Sarah had gone to Hell, suicide would be the solution to all his problems.

This led to a shameful self-knowledge for Neil. He realized that if he had to choose between going to Hell while Sarah went to Heaven, or having both of them go to Hell together, he would choose the latter: he would rather she be exiled from God than separated from him. He knew it was selfish, but he couldn't change how he felt: he believed Sarah could be happy in either place, but he could only be happy with her.

Neil's previous experiences with women had never been good. All too often he'd begin flirting with a woman while sitting at a bar, only to have her remember an appointment elsewhere the moment he stood up and his shortened leg came into view. Once, a woman he'd been dating for several weeks broke off their relationship, explaining that while she herself didn't consider his leg a defect, whenever they were seen in public together other people assumed there must be something wrong with her for being with him, and surely he could understand how unfair that was to her?

Sarah had been the first woman Neil met whose demeanor hadn't changed one bit, whose expression hadn't flickered toward pity or horror or even surprise when she first saw his leg. For that reason alone it was predictable that Neil would become infatuated with her; by the time he saw all the sides of her personality, he'd completely fallen in love with her. And because his best qualities came out when he was with her, she fell in love with him too.

Neil had been surprised when Sarah told him she was devout. There weren't many signs of her devotion—she didn't go to church, sharing Neil's dislike for the attitudes of most people who attended—but in her own, quiet way she was grateful to God for her life. She never tried to convert Neil, saying that devotion would come from within or not at all. They rarely had any cause to mention God, and most of the time it would've been easy for Neil to imagine that Sarah's views on God matched his own.

This is not to say that Sarah's devotion had no effect on Neil. On the contrary, Sarah was far and away the best argument for loving God that he had ever encountered. If love of God had contributed to making her the person she was, then perhaps it did make sense. During the years that the two of them were married, his outlook on life improved, and it probably would have reached the point where he was thankful to God, if he and Sarah had grown old together.

Sarah's death removed that particular possibility, but it needn't have closed the door on Neil's loving God. Neil could have taken it as a reminder that no one can count on having decades left. He could have been moved by the realization that, had he died with her, his soul would've been lost and the two of them separated for eternity. He could have seen Sarah's death as a wake-up call, telling him to love God while he still had the chance.

Instead Neil became actively resentful of God. Sarah had been the greatest blessing of his life, and God had taken her away. Now he was expected to love Him for it? For Neil, it was like having a kidnapper demand love as ransom for his wife's return. Obedience he might have managed, but sincere, heart-felt love? That was a ransom he couldn't pay.

This paradox confronted several people in the support group. One of the attendees, a man named Phil Soames, correctly pointed out that thinking of it as a condition to be met would guarantee failure. You couldn't love God as a means to an end, you had to love Him for Himself. If your ultimate goal in loving God was a reunion with your spouse, you weren't demonstrating true devotion at all.

A woman in the support group named Valerie Tommasino said they shouldn't even try. She'd been reading a book published by the humanist movement; its members considered it wrong to love a God who inflicted such pain, and advocated that people act according to their own moral sense instead of being guided by the carrot and the stick. These were people who, when they died, descended to Hell in proud defiance of God.

Neil himself had read a pamphlet of the humanist movement; what he most remembered was that it had quoted the fallen angels. Visitations of fallen angels were infrequent, and caused neither good fortune nor bad; they weren't acting under God's direction, but just passing through the mortal plane as they went about their unimaginable business. On the occasions they appeared, people would ask them questions: Did they know God's intentions? Why had they rebelled? The fallen angels' reply was always the same: *Decide for yourselves. That is what we did. We advise you to do the same.*

Those in the humanist movement had decided, and if it weren't for Sarah, Neil would've made the identical choice. But he wanted her back, and the only way was to find a reason to love God.

Looking for any footing on which to build their devotion, some attendees of the support group took comfort in the fact that their loved ones hadn't suffered when God took them, but instead died instantly. Neil didn't even have that; Sarah had received horrific lacerations when the glass hit her. Of course, it could have been worse. One couple's teenage son had been trapped in a fire ignited by an angel's visitation, and received full-thickness burns over eighty percent of his body before rescue workers could free him; his eventual death was a mercy. Sarah had been fortunate by comparison, but not enough to make Neil love God.

Neil could think of only one thing that would make him give thanks to God, and that was if He allowed Sarah to appear before him. It would give him immeasurable comfort just to see her smile again; he'd never been visited by a saved soul before, and a vision now would have meant more to him than at any other point in his life.

But visions don't appear just because a person needs one, and none ever came to Neil. He had to find his own way toward God.

The next time he attended the support group meeting for witnesses of Nathanael's visitation, Neil sought out Benny Vasquez, the man whose eyes had been erased by Heaven's light, Benny didn't always attend because he was now being invited to speak at other meetings; few visitations resulted in an eyeless person, since Heaven's light entered the mortal plane only in the brief moments that an angel emerged from or reentered Heaven, so the eyeless were minor celebrities, and in demand as speakers to church groups.

Benny was now as sightless as any burrowing worm: not only were his eyes and sockets missing, his skull lacked even the space for such features, the cheekbones now abutting the forehead. The light that had brought his soul as close to perfection as was possible in the mortal plane had also deformed his body; it was commonly held that this illustrated the superfluity of physical bodies in Heaven. With the limited expressive capacity his face retained, Benny always wore a blissful, rapturous smile.

Neil hoped Benny could say something to help him love God. Benny described Heaven's light as infinitely beautiful, a sight of such compelling majesty that it vanquished all doubts. It constituted incontrovertible proof that God should be loved, an explanation that made it as obvious as $1 + 1 = 2$. Unfortunately, while Benny could offer many analogies for the effect of Heaven's light, he couldn't duplicate that effect with his own words. Those who were already devout found Benny's descriptions thrilling, but to Neil, they seemed frustratingly vague. So he looked elsewhere for counsel.

Accept the mystery, said the minister of the local church. If you can love God even though your questions go unanswered, you'll be the better for it.

Admit that you need Him, said the popular book of spiritual advice he bought. When you realize that self-sufficiency is an illusion, you'll be ready.

Submit yourself completely and utterly, said the preacher on the television. Receiving torment is how you prove your love. Acceptance may not bring you relief in this life, but resistance will only worsen your punishment.

All of these strategies have proven successful for different individuals; any one of them, once internalized, can bring a person to devotion. But these are not always easy to adopt, and Neil was one who found them impossible.

Neil finally tried talking to Sarah's parents, which was an indication of how desperate he was: his relationship with them had always been tense. While they loved Sarah, they often chided her for not being demonstrative enough in her devotion, and they'd been shocked when she married a man who wasn't devout at all. For her part, Sarah had always considered her parents too judgmental, and their disapproval of Neil only reinforced her opinion. But now Neil felt he had something in common with them—after all, they were all mourning Sarah's loss—and so he visited them in their suburban colonial, hoping they could help him in his grief.

How wrong he was. Instead of sympathy, what Neil got from Sarah's parents was blame for her death. They'd come to this conclusion in the weeks after Sarah's funeral; they reasoned that she'd been taken to send him a message, and that they were forced to endure her loss solely because he hadn't been devout. They were now convinced that, his previous explanations notwithstanding, Neil's deformed leg was in fact God's doing, and if only he'd been properly chastened by it, Sarah might still be alive.

Their reaction shouldn't have come as a surprise: throughout Neil's life, people had attributed moral significance to his leg even though God wasn't responsible for it. Now that he'd suffered a misfortune for which God was unambiguously responsible, it was inevitable that someone would assume he deserved it. It was purely by chance that Neil heard this sentiment when he was at his most vulnerable, and it could have the greatest impact on him.

Neil didn't think his in-laws were right, but he began to wonder if he might not be better off if he did. Perhaps, he thought, it'd be better to live in a story where the righteous were rewarded and the sinners were punished, even if the criteria for righteousness and sinfulness eluded him, than to live in a reality where there was no justice at all. It would mean casting himself in the role of sinner, so it was hardly a comforting lie, but it offered one reward that his own ethics couldn't: believing it would reunite him with Sarah. Sometimes even bad advice can point a man in the right direction. It was in this manner that his in-laws' accusations ultimately pushed Neil closer to God.

More than once when she was evangelizing, Janice had been asked if she ever wished she had legs, and she had always answered—honestly—no, she didn't. She was content as she was. Sometimes her questioner would point out that she couldn't miss what she'd never known, and she might feel differently if she'd been born with legs and lost them later on. Janice never denied that. But she could truthfully say that she felt no sense of being incomplete, no envy for people with legs; being legless was part of her identity. She'd never bothered with prosthetics, and had a surgical procedure been available to provide her with legs, she'd have turned it down. She had never considered the possibility that God might restore her legs.

One of the unexpected side effects of having legs was the increased attention she received from men. In the past she'd mostly attracted men with amputee fetishes or sainthood complexes; now all sorts of men seemed drawn to her. So when she first noticed Ethan Mead's interest in her, she thought it was romantic in nature; this possibility was particularly distressing since he was obviously married.

Ethan had begun talking to Janice at the support group meetings, and then began attending her public speaking engagements. It was when he suggested they have lunch together that Janice asked him about his intentions, and he explained his theory. He didn't know how his fate was intertwined with hers; he knew only that it was. She was skeptical, but she didn't reject his theory outright. Ethan admitted that he didn't have answers for her own questions, but he was eager to do anything he could to help her find them. Janice cautiously agreed to help him in his search for meaning, and Ethan promised that he wouldn't be a burden. They met on a regular basis and talked about the significance of visitations.

Meanwhile Ethan's wife Claire grew worried. Ethan assured her that he had no romantic feelings toward Janice, but that didn't alleviate her concerns. She knew that extreme circumstances could create a bond between individuals, and she feared that Ethan's relationship with Janice—romantic or not—would threaten their marriage.

Ethan suggested to Janice that he, as a librarian, could help her do some research. Neither of them had ever heard of a previous instance where God had left His mark on a person in one visitation and removed it in another. Ethan looked for previous examples in hopes that they might shed some light on Janice's situation. There were a few instances of individuals receiving multiple miracle cures over their lifetimes, but their illnesses or disabilities had always been of natural origin, not given to them in a visitation. There was one anecdotal report of a man being struck blind for his sins, changing his ways, and later having his sight restored, but it was classified as an urban legend.

Even if that account had a basis in truth, it didn't provide a useful precedent for Janice's situation: her legs had been removed before her birth, and so couldn't have been a punishment for anything she'd done. Was it possible that Janice's condition had been a punishment for something her mother or father had done? Could her restoration mean they had finally earned her cure? She couldn't believe that.

If her deceased relatives were to appear in a vision, Janice would've been reassured about the restoration of her legs. The fact that they didn't made her suspect something was amiss, but she didn't believe that it was a punishment. Perhaps it had been a mistake, and she'd received a miracle meant for someone else; perhaps it was a test, to see how she would respond to being given too much. In either case, there seemed only one course of action: she would, with utmost gratitude and humility, offer to return her gift. To do so, she would go on a pilgrimage.

Pilgrims traveled great distances to visit the holy sites and wait for a visitation, hoping for a miracle cure. Whereas in most of the world one could wait an entire lifetime and never experience a visitation, at a holy site one might only wait months, sometimes weeks. Pilgrims knew that the odds of being cured were still poor; of those who stayed long enough to witness a visitation, the majority did not receive a cure. But they were often happy just to have seen an angel, and they returned home better able to face what awaited them, whether it be imminent death or life with a crippling disability. And of course, just living through a visitation made many people appreciate their situations; invariably, a small number of pilgrims were killed during each visitation.

Janice was willing to accept the outcome whatever it was. If God saw fit to take her, she was ready. If God removed her legs again, she would resume the work she'd always done. If God let her legs remain, she hoped she would receive the epiphany she needed to speak with conviction about her gift.

She hoped, however, that her miracle would be taken back and given to someone who truly needed it. She didn't suggest to anyone that they accompany her in hopes of receiving the miracle she was returning, feeling that that would've been presumptuous, but she privately considered her pilgrimage a request on behalf of those who were in need.

Her friends and family were confused at Janice's decision, seeing it as questioning God. As word spread, she received many letters from followers, variously expressing dismay, bafflement, and admiration for her willingness to make such a sacrifice.

As for Ethan, he was completely supportive of Janice's decision, and excited for himself. He now understood the significance of Rashiel's visitation for him: it indicated that the time had come for him to act. His wife Claire strenuously opposed his leaving, pointing out that he had no idea how long he might be away, and that she and their children needed him too. It grieved him to go without her support, but he had no choice. Ethan would go on a pilgrimage, and at the next visitation, he would learn what God intended for him.

Neil's visit to Sarah's parents caused him to give further thought to his conversation with Benny Vasquez. While he hadn't gotten a lot out of Benny's words, he'd been impressed by the absoluteness of Benny's devotion. No matter what misfortune befell him in the future, Benny's love of God would never waver, and he would ascend to Heaven when he died. That fact offered Neil a very slim opportunity, one that had seemed so unattractive he hadn't considered it before; but now, as he was growing more desperate, it was beginning to look expedient.

Every holy site had its pilgrims who, rather than looking for a miracle cure, deliberately sought out Heaven's light. Those who saw it were always accepted into Heaven when they died, no matter how selfish their motives had been; there were some who wished to have their ambivalence removed so they could be reunited with their loved ones, and others who'd always lived a sinful life and wanted to escape the consequences. In the past there'd been some doubt as to whether Heaven's light could indeed overcome all the spiritual obstacles to becoming saved. The debate ended after the case of Barry Larsen, a serial rapist and murderer who, while disposing of the body of his latest victim, witnessed an angel's visitation and saw Heaven's light. At Larsen's execution, his soul was seen ascending to Heaven, much to the outrage of his victims' families. Priests tried to console them, assuring them on the basis of no evidence whatsoever that Heaven's light must have subjected Larsen to many lifetimes' worth of penance in a moment, but their words provided little comfort.

For Neil this offered a loophole, an answer to Phil Soames's objection; it was the one way that he could love Sarah more than he loved God, and still be reunited with her. It was how he could be selfish and still get into Heaven. Others had done it; perhaps he could too. It might not be just, but at least it was predictable.

At an instinctual level, Neil was averse to the idea: it sounded like undergoing brainwashing as a cure for depression. He couldn't help but think that it would change his personality so drastically that he'd cease to be himself. Then he remembered that everyone in Heaven had undergone a similar transformation; the saved were just like the eyeless except that they no longer had bodies. This gave Neil a clearer image of what he was working toward: no matter whether he became devout by seeing Heaven's light or by a lifetime of effort, any ultimate reunion with Sarah couldn't re-create what they'd shared in the mortal plane. In Heaven, they would both be different, and their love for each other would be mixed with the love that all the saved felt for everything.

This realization didn't diminish Neil's longing for a reunion with Sarah. In fact it sharpened his desire, because it meant that the reward would be the same no matter what means he used to, achieve it; the shortcut led to precisely the same destination as the conventional path.

On the other hand, seeking Heaven's light was far more difficult than an ordinary pilgrimage, and far more dangerous. Heaven's light leaked through only when an angel entered or left the mortal plane, and since there was no way to predict where an angel would first appear, light-seekers had to converge on the angel after its arrival and follow it until its departure. To maximize their chances of being in the narrow shaft of Heaven's light, they followed the angel as closely as possible during its visitation; depending on the angel involved, this might mean staying alongside the funnel of a tornado, the wavefront of a flash flood, or the expanding tip of a chasm as it split apart the landscape. Far more light-seekers died in the attempt than succeeded.

Statistics about the souls of failed light-seekers were difficult to compile, since there were few witnesses to such expeditions, but the numbers so far were not encouraging. In sharp contrast to ordinary pilgrims who died without receiving their sought-after cure, of which roughly half were admitted into Heaven, every single failed light-seeker had descended to Hell. Perhaps only people who were already lost ever considered seeking Heaven's light, or perhaps death in such circumstances was considered suicide. In any case, it was clear to Neil that he needed to be ready to accept the consequences of embarking on such an attempt.

The entire idea had an all-or-nothing quality to it that Neil found both frightening and attractive. He found the prospect of going on with his life, trying to love God, increasingly maddening. He might try for decades and not succeed. He might not even have that long; as he'd been reminded so often lately, visitations served as a warning to prepare one's soul, because death might come at any time. He could die tomorrow, and there was no chance of his becoming devout in the near future by conventional means.

It's perhaps ironic, that, given his history of not following Janice Reilly's example, Neil took notice when she reversed her position. He was eating breakfast when he happened to see an item in the newspaper about her plans for a pilgrimage, and his immediate reaction was anger: how many blessings would it take to satisfy that woman? After considering it more, he decided that if she, having received a blessing, deemed it appropriate to seek God's assistance in coming to terms with it, then there was no reason he, having received such terrible misfortune, shouldn't do the same. And that was enough to tip him over the edge.

Holy sites were invariably in inhospitable places: one was an atoll in the middle of the ocean, while another was in the mountains at an elevation of twenty thousand feet. The one that Neil traveled to was in a desert, an expanse of cracked mud reaching miles in every direction; it was desolate, but it was relatively accessible and thus popular among pilgrims. The appearance of the holy site was an object lesson in what happened when the celestial and terrestrial realms touched: the landscape was variously scarred by lava flows, gaping fissures, and impact craters. Vegetation was scarce and ephemeral, restricted to growing in the interval after soil was deposited by floodwaters or whirlwinds and before it was scoured away again.

Pilgrims took up residence all over the site, forming temporary villages with their tents and camper vans; they all made guesses as to what location would maximize their chances of seeing the angel while minimizing the risk of injury or death. Some protection was offered by curved banks of sandbags, left over from years past and rebuilt as needed. A site-specific paramedic and fire department ensured that paths were kept clear so rescue vehicles could go where they were needed. Pilgrims either brought their own food and water or purchased them from vendors charging exorbitant prices; everyone paid a fee to cover the cost of waste removal.

Light-seekers always had off-road vehicles to better cross rough terrain when it came time to follow the angel. Those who could afford it drove alone; those who couldn't formed groups of two or three or four. Neil didn't want to be a passenger, reliant on another person, nor did he want the responsibility of driving anyone else. This might be his final act on Earth, and he felt he should do it alone. The cost of Sarah's funeral had depleted their savings, so Neil sold all his possessions in order to purchase a suitable vehicle: a pickup truck equipped with aggressively knurled tires and heavy-duty shock absorbers.

As soon as he arrived, Neil started doing what all the other light-seekers did: crisscrossing the site in his vehicle, trying to familiarize himself with its topography. It was on one of his drives around the site's perimeter that he met Ethan; Ethan flagged him down after his own car had stalled on his return from the nearest grocery store, eighty miles away. Neil helped him get his car started again, and then, at Ethan's insistence, followed him back to his campsite for dinner. Janice wasn't there when they arrived, having gone to visit some pilgrims several tents over; Neil listened politely while Ethan— heating prepackaged meals over a bottle of propane—began describing the events that had brought him to the holy site.

When Ethan mentioned Janice Reilly's name, Neil couldn't mask his surprise. He had no desire to speak with her again, and immediately excused himself to leave. He was explaining to a puzzled Ethan that he'd forgotten a previous engagement when Janice arrived.

She was startled to see Neil there, but asked him to stay. Ethan explained why he'd invited Neil to dinner, and Janice told him where she and Neil had met. Then she asked Neil what had brought him to the holy site. When he told them he was a light-seeker, Ethan and Janice immediately tried to persuade him to reconsider his plans. He might be committing suicide, said Ethan, and there were always better alternatives than suicide. Seeing Heaven's light was not the answer, said Janice; that wasn't what God wanted. Neil stiffly thanked them for their concern, and left.

During the weeks of waiting, Neil spent every day driving around the site; maps were available, and were updated after each visitation, but they were no substitute for driving the terrain yourself. On occasion he would see a light-seeker who was obviously experienced in off-road driving, and ask him—the vast majority of the light-seekers were men—for tips on negotiating a specific type of terrain. Some had been at the site for several visitations, having neither succeeded nor failed at their previous attempts. They were glad to share tips on how best to pursue an angel, but never offered any personal information about themselves. Neil found the tone of their conversation peculiar, simultaneously hopeful and hopeless, and wondered if he sounded the same.

Ethan and Janice passed the time by getting to know some of the other pilgrims. Their reactions to Janice's situation were mixed: some thought her ungrateful, while others thought her generous. Most found Ethan's story interesting, since he was one of the very few pilgrims seeking something other than a miracle cure. For the most part, there was a feeling of camaraderie that sustained them during the long wait.

Neil was driving around in his truck when dark clouds began coalescing in the southeast, and the word came over the CB radio that a visitation had begun. He stopped the vehicle to insert earplugs into his ears and don his helmet; by the time he was finished, flashes of lightning were visible, and a light-seeker near the angel reported that it was Barakiel, and it appeared to be moving due north. Neil turned his truck east in anticipation and began driving at full speed.

There was no rain or wind, only dark clouds from which lightning emerged. Over the radio other light-seekers relayed estimates of the angel's direction and speed, and Neil headed northeast to get in front of it. At first he could gauge his distance from the storm by counting how long it took for the thunder to arrive, but soon the lightning bolts were striking so frequently that he couldn't match up the sounds with the individual strikes.

He saw the vehicles of two other light-seekers converging. They began driving in parallel, heading north, over a heavily cratered section of ground, bouncing over small ones and swerving to avoid the larger ones. Bolts of lightning were striking the ground everywhere, but they appeared to be radiating from a point south of Neil's position; the angel was directly behind him, and closing.

Even through his earplugs, the roar was deafening. Neil could feel his hair rising from his skin as the electric charge built up around him. He kept glancing in his rearview mirror, trying to ascertain where the angel was while wondering how close he ought to get.

His vision grew so crowded with afterimages that it became difficult to distinguish actual bolts of lightning among them. Squinting at the dazzle in his mirror, he realized he was looking at a continuous bolt of lightning, undulating but uninterrupted. He tilted the driver's-side mirror upward to get a better look, and saw the source of the lightning bolt, a seething, writhing mass of flames, silver against the dusky clouds: the angel Barakiel.

It was then, while Neil was transfixed and paralyzed by what he saw, that his pickup truck crested a sharp outcropping of rock and became airborne. The truck smashed into a boulder, the entire force of the impact concentrated on the vehicle's left front end, crumpling it like foil. The intrusion into the driver's compartment fractured both of Neil's legs and nicked his left femoral artery. Neil began, slowly but surely, bleeding to death.

He didn't try to move; he wasn't in physical pain at the moment, but he somehow knew that the slightest movement would be excruciating. It was obvious that he was pinned in the truck, and there was no way he could pursue Barakiel even if he weren't. Helplessly, he watched the lightning storm move further and further away.

As he watched it, Neil began crying. He was filled with a mixture of regret and self-contempt, cursing himself forever thinking that such a scheme could succeed. He would have begged for the opportunity to do it over again, promised to spend the rest of his days learning to love God, if only he could live, but he knew that no bargaining was possible and he had only himself to blame. He apologized to Sarah for losing his chance at being reunited with her, for throwing his life away on a gamble instead of playing it safe. He prayed that she understood that he'd been motivated by his love for her, and that she would forgive him.

Through his tears he saw a woman running toward him, and recognized her as Janice Reilly. He realized his truck had crashed no more than a hundred yards from her and Ethan's campsite. There was nothing she could do, though; he could feel the blood draining out of him, and knew that he wouldn't live long enough for a rescue vehicle to arrive. He thought Janice was calling to him, but his ears were ringing too badly for him to hear anything. He could see Ethan Mead behind her, also starting to run toward him.

Then there was a flash of light and Janice was knocked off her feet as if she'd been struck by a sledgehammer. At first he thought she'd been hit by lightning, but then he realized that the lightning had already ceased. It was when she stood up again that he saw her face, steam rising from newly featureless skin, and he realized that Janice had been struck by Heaven's light.

Neil looked up, but all he saw were clouds; the shaft of light was gone. It seemed as if God were taunting him, not only by showing him the prize he'd lost his life trying to acquire while still holding it out of reach, but also by giving it to someone who didn't need it or even want it. God had already wasted a miracle on Janice, and now He was doing it again.

It was at that moment that another beam of Heaven's light penetrated the cloud cover and struck Neil, trapped in his vehicle.

Like a thousand hypodermic needles the light punctured his flesh and scraped across his bones. The light unmade his eyes, turning him into not a formerly sighted being, but a being never intended to possess vision. And in doing so the light revealed to Neil all the reasons he should love God.

He loved Him with an utterness beyond what humans can experience for one another. To say it was unconditional was inadequate, because even the word "unconditional" required the concept of a condition and such an idea was no longer comprehensible to him: every phenomenon in the universe was nothing less than an explicit reason to love Him.

No circumstance could be an obstacle or even an irrelevancy, but only another reason to be grateful, a further inducement to love. Neil thought of the grief that had driven him to suicidal recklessness, and the pain and terror that Sarah had experienced before she died, and still he loved God, not in spite of their suffering, but because of it.

He renounced all his previous anger and ambivalence and desire for answers. He was grateful for all the pain he'd endured, contrite for not previously recognizing it as the gift it was, euphoric that he was now being granted this insight into his true purpose. He understood how life was an undeserved bounty, how even the most virtuous were not worthy of the glories of the mortal plane.

For him the mystery was solved, because he understood that everything in life is love, even pain, especially pain.

So minutes later, when Neil finally bled to death, he was truly worthy of salvation.

And God sent him to Hell anyway.

Ethan saw all of this. He saw Neil and Janice remade by Heaven's light, and he saw the pious love on their eyeless faces. He saw the skies become clear and the sunlight return. He was holding Neil's hand, waiting for the paramedics, when Neil died, and he saw Neil's soul leave his body and rise toward Heaven, only to descend into Hell.

Janice didn't see it, for by then her eyes were already gone. Ethan was the sole witness, and he realized that this was God's purpose for him: to follow Janice Reilly to this point and to see what she could not.

When statistics were compiled for Barakiel's visitation, it turned out that there had been a total of ten casualties, six among light-seekers and four among ordinary pilgrims. Nine pilgrims received miracle cures; the only individuals to see Heaven's light were Janice and Neil. There were no statistics regarding how many pilgrims had felt their lives changed by the visitation, but Ethan counted himself among them.

Upon returning home, Janice resumed her evangelism, but the topic of her speeches has changed. She no longer speaks about how the physically handicapped have the resources to overcome their limitations; instead she, like the other eyeless, speaks about the unbearable beauty of God's creation. Many who used to draw inspiration from her are disappointed, feeling they've lost a spiritual leader. When Janice had spoken of the strength she had as an afflicted person, her message was rare, but now that she's eyeless, her message is commonplace. She doesn't worry about the reduction in her audience, though, because she has complete conviction in what she evangelizes.

Ethan quit his job and became a preacher so that he too could speak about his experiences. His wife Claire couldn't accept his new mission and ultimately left him, taking their children with her, but Ethan was willing to continue alone. He's developed a substantial following by telling people what happened to Neil Fisk. He tells people that they can no more expect justice in the afterlife than in the mortal plane, but he doesn't do this to dissuade them from worshiping God; on the contrary, he encourages them to do so. What he insists on is that they not love God under a misapprehension, that if they wish to love God, they be prepared to do so no matter what His intentions. God is not just, God is not kind, God is not merciful, and understanding that is essential to true devotion.

As for Neil, although he is unaware of any of Ethan's sermons, he would understand their message perfectly. His lost soul is the embodiment of Ethan's teachings.

For most of its inhabitants, Hell is not that different from Earth; its principal punishment is the regret of not having loved God enough when alive, and for many that's easily endured; For Neil, however, Hell bears no resemblance whatsoever to the mortal plane. His eternal body has well-formed legs, but he's scarcely aware of them; his eyes have been restored, but he can't bear to open them. Just as seeing Heaven's light gave him an awareness of God's presence in all things in the mortal plane, so it has made him aware of God's absence in all things in Hell. Everything Neil sees, hears, or touches causes him distress, and unlike in the mortal plane this pain is not a form of God's love but a consequence of His absence. Neil is experiencing more anguish than was possible when he was alive, but his only response is to love God.

Neil still loves Sarah, and misses, her as much as he ever did, and the knowledge that he came so close to rejoining her only makes it worse. He knows his being sent to Hell was not a result of anything he did; he knows there was no reason for it, no higher purpose being served. None of this diminishes his love for God. If there were a possibility that he could be admitted to Heaven and his suffering would end, he would not hope for it; such desires no longer occur to him.

Neil even knows that by being beyond God's awareness, he is not loved by God in return. This doesn't affect his feelings either, because unconditional love asks nothing, not even that it be returned.

And though it's been many, years that he has been in Hell, beyond the awareness of God, he loves Him still. That is the nature of true devotion.

STUDY AND DISCUSSION QUESTIONS

1   Suppose you were a theist. Would this change what you believe about the events that befall Neil? In other words, if you believe in God, does that bias you against the story in a way? Or, instead, do you feel as though the story is biased against theism?

2   How would you describe the differences theologically between Christian religious beliefs and the theistic beliefs represented in the story?

3   Janice appears to be cursed, but she transforms that into a blessing through her ministerial activities. She is "healed" and then asks, "Why have I received a blessing and others did not?" Psychologically, what is going on in her mind? What is her answer to her question? Is it immoral for her to have and express this desire?

4   Do human conceptions of justice and morality apply to God, or not? Why or why not?

5 Take for granted that God does miracles often. The story raises the following question: Under what conditions is God justified to withhold performing a miracle for someone in great need?

6 Compare and contrast Neil in this story with the character of Job in the biblical story of Job.

7 What is the meaning of Neil's claim that God is "not responsible" for his leg problem? How is this God's "responsibility"? How is it not?

8 Neil is struck by a bolt of heaven's light, but is not taken up. Instead he is sent to hell. Is whatever God does, including sending Neil to hell, morally permissible simply because God does it?

9 "Predestination" is a term that refers to a theological doctrine of certain Christian believers according to which humans are chosen by God to enter heaven and enter hell solely on the basis of God's preferences. What does Neil's experience—and those of Janice and Ethan—say about the morality of the doctrine of predestination? In this light, consider Ethan's means of evangelizing non-believers.

10 Would it be more intellectually difficult to be a Christian in the story's world than in our world? Would it be more emotionally and psychologically difficult to be a Christian in the story's world?

11 Suppose that, as in the world of the story, God's existence was obvious and manifest in countless ways in our world. What further conditions are required to make a divinity worthy of our worship, if any?

3.12 "THE CLASSICAL ONTOLOGICAL ARGUMENT FOR GOD'S EXISTENCE," FROM SAINT ANSELM'S *PROSLOGION*

Chapter 2

God truly exists.

Therefore, O Lord, You who give understanding to faith, grant me to understand—to the degree You know to be advantageous—that You exist, as we believe, and that You are what we believe. Indeed, we believe You to be something than which nothing greater can be thought. Or is there, then, no such nature, for the Fool has said in his heart that God does not exist? [Psalms 14:1] But surely when this very same Fool hears my words "something than which nothing greater can be thought," he understands what he hears. And what he understands is in his understanding, even if he does not understand it to exist. For that a thing is in the understanding is distinct from understanding that the thing exists. For example, when a painter envisions what he is about to paint, he indeed has in his understanding that which he has not yet made, but he does not yet understand that it exists. But after he has painted it, he has in his understanding that which he has made, and he understands that it exists. So even the Fool is convinced that something than which nothing greater can be thought is at least in his understanding; for when he hears of a being [than which nothing greater can be thought], he understands, and whatever is understood is in the understanding. But surely that than which a greater cannot be thought cannot be only in the understanding. For if it were only in the understanding, it could be thought to exist also in reality—something which is greater. Therefore, if that than which a greater cannot be thought were only in the understanding, then that than which a greater cannot be thought would be that than which a greater can be thought! But surely this is impossible. Hence, without doubt, something than which a greater cannot be thought exists both in the understanding and in reality.

Chapter 3

God cannot be thought not to exist.

Assuredly, this being exists so truly that it cannot even be thought not to exist. For there can be thought to exist something which cannot be thought not to exist; and this thing is greater than that which can be thought not to exist. Therefore, if that than which a greater cannot be thought could be thought not to exist, then that than which a greater cannot be thought would not be that than which a greater cannot be thought—which is contradictory. Hence, something than which a greater cannot be thought exists so truly that it cannot even be thought not to exist. And You are this, 0 Lord our God. Therefore, 0 Lord my God, You exist so truly that You cannot even be thought not to exist. And this is rightly the case. For if any mind could think of something better than You, the creature would rise above the Creator and would sit in judgment over the Creator—something which is utterly absurd. Indeed, except for You alone, whatever else exists can be thought not to exist. Therefore, You alone exist most truly of all and thus most greatly of all; for whatever else exists does not exist as truly and thus exists less greatly [than do You]. Since, then, it is so readily clear to a rational mind that You exist most greatly of all, why did the Fool say in his heart that God does not exist?—why except because he is foolish and a fool!

STUDY AND DISCUSSION QUESTIONS

1   Anselm (2000) employs the concept of "greatness" in the statement of God's nature—God is that being than which no greater can be thought. Does he mean by "greater" what we might mean by that term when we say, for example, that one amount of money is greater than another?

2   According to Anselm, we can think of something's existence in two ways: I can think of something as existing in my understanding (in Latin, *esse in intellectu*) or I can think of something existing in reality (*esse in re*). What does he mean by this distinction? Is he right?

3   Anselm pits himself against someone he calls "the Fool" (from *Psalms*). The Fool can think of a being than which no greater can be thought, and the Fool believes that this being exists in the understanding. But the Fool does not infer from that claim that such a being exists in reality. Why not?

4   In response to the Fool, Anselm offers a very compact *reductio ad absurdum* argument. What is its premises and conclusion?

5   A contemporary of Anselm's, another monk called Gaunilo, offered an objection through an argument by analogy. Gaunilo suggests that we replace instances of "that [being] than which nothing greater can be thought" with "that island than which no greater can be thought." If we can think of a being than which no greater can be thought, then we can also think of an island than which no greater can be thought. Furthermore, if this is true, then the analogical argument yields the absurd conclusion that there exists (in reality) a perfect island. Can you explain this objection in your own words? What might Anselm say in reply?

3.13 "PROBLEMS WITH THE DESIGN ARGUMENT," BY DAVID HUME (1779)

1. [From Book II] *Cleanthes*: Look round the world: contemplate the whole and every part of it: You will find it to be nothing but one great machine, subdivided into an infinite number of lesser machines, which again admit of subdivisions, to a degree beyond what human senses and faculties can trace and explain. All these various machines, and even their most minute parts, are adjusted to each other with an accuracy, which ravishes into admiration all men, who have ever contemplated them. The curious adapting of means to ends, throughout all nature, resembles exactly, though it much exceeds, the productions of human contrivance; of human designs, thought, wisdom, and intelligence. Since therefore the effects resemble each other, we are led to infer, by all the rules of analogy, that the causes also resemble; and that the Author of Nature is somewhat similar to the mind of man; though possessed of much larger faculties, proportioned to the grandeur of the work, which he has executed. By this argument a posteriori, and by this argument alone, do we prove at once the existence of a Deity, and his similarity to human mind and intelligence.

2. *Philo*: What I chiefly scruple in this subject, said Philo, is not so much, that all religious arguments reduced to experience, as that they appear not to be even the most certain and irrefragable of that inferior kind. That a stone will fall, that fire will burn, that

the earth has solidity, we have observed a thousand and a thousand times; and when any new instance of this nature is presented, we draw without hesitation the accustomed inference. The exact similarity of the cases gives us a perfect assurance of a similar event; and a stronger evidence is never desired nor sought after. But where-ever you depart, in the least, from the similarity of the cases, you diminish proportionably the evidence; and may at last bring it to a very weak analogy, which is confessedly liable to error and uncertainty. After having experienced the circulation of the blood in human creatures, we make no doubt that it takes place in Titius and Maevius: but from its circulation in frogs and fishes, it is only a presumption, though a strong one, from analogy, that it takes place in men and other animals. The analogical reasoning is much weaker, when we infer the circulation of the sap in vegetables from our experience, that the blood circulates in animals; and those, who hastily followed that imperfect analogy, are found, by more accurate experiments, to have been mistaken.

3. . . . That all inferences, Cleanthes, concerning fact, are founded on experience, and that all experimental reasonings are founded on the supposition, that similar causes prove similar effects, and similar effects similar causes; I shall not, at present, much dispute with you. But observe, I entreat you, with what extreme caution all just reasoners proceed in the transferring of experiments to similar cases. Unless the cases be exactly similar, they repose no perfect confidence in applying their past observation to any particular phenomenon. Every alteration of circumstances occasions a doubt concerning the event; and it requires new experiments to prove certainly, that the new circumstances are of no moment or importance. A change in bulk, situation, arrangement, age, disposition of the air, or surrounding bodies; any of these particulars may be attended with the most unexpected consequences: And unless the objects be quite familiar to us, it is the highest temerity to expect with assurance, after any of these changes, an event similar to that which before fell under our observation. The slow and deliberate steps of philosophers, here, if anywhere, are distinguished from the precipitate march of the vulgar, who, hurried on by the smallest similitudes, are incapable of all discernment or consideration.

4. But can you think, Cleanthes, that your usual phlegm and philosophy have been preserved in so wide a step as you have taken, when you compared to the universe houses, ships, furniture, machines; and from their similarity in some circumstances inferred a similarity in their causes? Thought, design, intelligence, such as we discover in men and other animals, is no more than one of the springs and principles of the universe, as well as heat or cold, attraction or repulsion, and a hundred others, which fall under daily observation. It is an active cause, by which some particular parts of nature, we find, produce alterations on other parts. But can a conclusion, with any propriety, be transferred from parts to the whole? Does not the great disproportion bar all comparison and inference? From observing the growth of a hair, can we learn any thing concerning the generation of a man? Would the manner of a leaf's blowing, even though perfectly known, afford us any instruction concerning the vegetation of a tree?

5. But allowing that we were to take the operations of one part of nature upon another for the foundation of our judgment concerning the origin of the whole (which never can be admitted) yet why select so minute, so weak, so bounded a principle as the reason and

design of animals is found to be upon this planet? What peculiar privilege has this little agitation of the brain which we call thought, that we must thus make it the model of the whole universe? Our partiality in our own favor does indeed present it on all occasions; but sound philosophy ought carefully to guard against so natural an illusion.

6. So far from admitting, continued Philo, that the operations of a part can afford us any just conclusion concerning the origin of the whole, I will not allow any one part to form a rule for another part, if the latter be very remote from the former. Is there any reasonable ground to conclude, that the inhabitants of other planets possess thought, intelligence, reason, or any thing similar to these faculties in men? When Nature has so extremely diversified her manner of operation in this small globe; can we imagine, that she incessantly copies herself throughout so immense a universe? And if thought, as we may well suppose, be confined merely to this narrow corner, and has even there so limited a sphere of action; with what propriety can we assign it for the original cause of all things? The narrow views of a peasant, who makes his domestic economy the rule for the government of kingdoms, is in comparison a pardonable sophism.

7. A very small part of this great system, during a very short time, is very imperfectly discovered to us: and do we then pronounce decisively concerning the origin of the whole?

8. Admirable conclusion! Stone, wood, brick, iron, brass, have not, at this time, in this minute globe of Earth, an order or arrangement without human art and contrivance: therefore the universe could not originally attain its order and arrangement, without something similar to human art. But is a part of nature a rule for another part very wide of the former? Is it a rule for the whole? Is a very small part a rule for the universe? Is nature in one situation, a certain rule for nature in another situation, a certain rule for nature in another situation, vastly different from the former?

[Following Philo's criticisms of Cleanthes' first version of the Design Argument (contained in the first paragraph above), Cleanthes offers an analogy that illustrates the epistemic status of the inference that the universe is intelligently designed.]

9. Book III: *Cleanthes*: Suppose, therefore, that an articulate voice were heard in the clouds, much louder and more melodious than any which human art could ever reach: Suppose, that this voice were extended in the same instant over all nations, and spoke to each nation in its own language and dialect: Suppose, that the words delivered not only contain a just sense and meaning, but convey some instruction altogether worthy of a benevolent being, superior to mankind: could you possibly hesitate a moment concerning the cause of this voice? and must you not instantly ascribe it to some design or purpose? Yet I cannot see but all the same objections (if they merit that appellation) which lie against the system of Theism, may also be produced against this inference.

10. Might you not say, that all conclusions concerning fact were founded on experience: that when we hear an articulate voice in the dark, and thence infer a man, it is only the resemblance of the effects, which leads us to conclude that there is a like resemblance in the cause: but that this extraordinary voice, by its loudness, extent, and flexibility to all languages, bears so little analogy to any human voice, that we have no

reason to suppose any analogy in their causes: and consequently, that a rational, wise, coherent speech proceeded, you know not from whence, from some accidental whistling of the winds, not from any divine reason or intelligence? You see clearly your own objections in these cavils; and I hope too, you see clearly, that they cannot possibly have more force in the one case than in the other.

[Philo does not explicitly address Cleanthes' analogy, but he does articulate further problems with the analogical version of the design argument.]

11. Book 5: *Philo*: But to show you still more inconveniences, continued Philo, in your anthropomorphism; please to take a new survey of your principles. Like effects prove like causes. This is the experimental argument; and this, you say too, is the sole theological argument. Now it is certain, that the liker the effects are, which are seen, and the liker the causes, which are inferred, the stronger is the argument. Every departure on either side diminishes the probability, and renders the experiment less conclusive. You cannot doubt of the principle: neither ought you to reject its consequences.

12. . . . Now, Cleanthes, said Philo, with an air of alacrity and triumph, mark the consequences. First, by this method of reasoning, you renounce all claim to infinity in any of the attributes of the Deity. For as the cause ought only to be proportioned to the effect, and the effect, so far as it falls under our cognizance, is not infinite; what pretensions have we, upon your suppositions, to ascribe that attribute to the divine Being? You will still insist, that, by removing him so much from all similarity to human creatures, we give in to the most arbitrary hypothesis, and at the same time weaken all proofs of his existence.

13. Secondly, You have no reason, on your theory, for ascribing perfection to the Deity, even in his finite capacity; or for supposing him free from every error, mistake, or incoherence in his undertakings. There are many inexplicable difficulties in the works of Nature, which, if we allow a perfect Author to be proved a priori, are easily solved, and become only seeming difficulties, from the narrow capacity of man, who cannot trace infinite relations. But according to your method of reasoning, these difficulties become all real; and perhaps will be insisted on, as new instances of likeness to human art and contrivance. At least, you must acknowledge, that it is impossible for us to tell, from our limited views, whether this system contains any great faults, or deserves any considerable praise, if compared to other possible, and even real systems. Could a peasant, if the Aeneid were read to him, pronounce that poem to be absolutely faultless, or even assign to it its proper rank among the productions of human wit; he, who had never seen any other production?

14. But were this world ever so perfect a production, it must still remain uncertain, whether all the excellences of the work can justly be ascribed to the workman. If we survey a ship, what an exalted idea must we form of the ingenuity of the carpenter, who framed so complicated, useful, and beautiful a machine? And what surprise must we feel, when we find him a stupid mechanic, who imitated others, and copied an art, which, through a long succession of ages, after multiplied trials, mistakes, corrections, deliberations, and controversies, had been gradually improving? Many worlds might have been botched and

bungled, throughout an eternity, ere this system was struck out: much labour lost: many fruitless trials made: and a slow, but continued improvement carried on during infinite ages in the art of world-making. In such subjects, who can determine, where the truth; nay, who can conjecture where the probability, lies; amidst a great number of hypotheses which may be proposed, and a still greater number which may be imagined?

15. And what shadow of an argument, continued Philo, can you produce, from your hypothesis, to prove the unity of the Deity? A great number of men join in building a house or ship, in rearing a city, in framing a commonwealth: why may not several Deities combine in contriving and framing a world? This is only so much greater similarity to human affairs. By sharing the work among several, we may so much further limit the attributes of each, and get rid of that extensive power and knowledge, which must be supposed in one deity, and which, according to you, can only serve to weaken the proof of his existence. And if such foolish, such vicious creatures as man can yet often unite in framing and executing one plan; how much more those deities or daemons, whom we may suppose several degrees more perfect?

16. To multiply causes, without necessity, is indeed contrary to true philosophy: but this principle applies not to the present case. Were one deity antecedently proved by your theory, who were possessed of every attribute, requisite to the production of the universe; it would be needless, I own (though not absurd) to suppose any other deity existent. But while it is still a question, Whether all these attributes are united in one subject, or dispersed among several independent beings: by what phenomena in nature can we pretend to decide the controversy? Where we see a body raised in a scale, we are sure that there is in the opposite scale, however concealed from sight, some counterpoising weight equal to it: but it is still allowed to doubt, whether that weight be an aggregate of several distinct bodies, or one uniform united mass. And if the weight requisite very much exceeds any thing which we have ever seen conjoined in any single body, the former supposition becomes still more probable and natural. An intelligent being of such vast power and capacity, as is necessary to produce the universe, or, to speak in the language of ancient philosophy, so prodigious an animal, exceeds all analogy, and even comprehension.

17. But farther, Cleanthes; men are mortal, and renew their species by generation; and this is common to all living creatures. The two great sexes of male and female, says Milton, animate the world. Why must this circumstance, so universal, so essential, be excluded from those numerous and limited deities? Behold then the theogony of ancient times brought back upon us.

18. And why not become a perfect Anthropomorphite? Why not assert the deity or deities to be corporeal, and to have eyes, a nose, mouth, ears, &c.? Epicurus maintained, that no man had ever seen reason but in a human figure; therefore the gods must have a human figure. And this argument, which is deservedly so much ridiculed by Cicero, becomes, according to you, solid and philosophical.

19. In a word, Cleanthes, a man, who follows your hypothesis, is able, perhaps, to assert, or conjecture, that the universe, sometime, arose from something like design: but beyond that position he cannot ascertain one single circumstance, and is left afterwards

to fix every point of his theology, by the utmost license of fancy and hypothesis. This world, for aught he knows, is very faulty and imperfect, compared to a superior standard; and was only the first rude essay of some infant Deity, who afterwards abandoned it, ashamed of his lame performance: it is the work only of some dependent, inferior deity; and is the object of derision to his superiors: it is the production of old age and dotage in some superannuated deity; and ever since his death, has run on at adventures, from the first impulse and active force, which it received from him.

20. From the moment the attributes of the Deity are supposed finite, all these have place. And I cannot, for my part, think, that so wild and unsettled a system of theology is, in any respect, preferable to none at all.

STUDY AND DISCUSSION QUESTIONS

1   In paragraph 1, the character of Cleanthes states a version of the design argument. How would you rephrase that argument in your own words?

2   Philo responds in paragraph 2 by arguing that "The analogical reasoning is much weaker, when we infer the circulation of the sap in vegetables from our experience that the blood circulates in animals." What is his point? Does it apply to Cleanthes' argument?

3   In paragraph 4 Philo poses a question to Cleanthes: "But can a conclusion, with any propriety, be transferred from parts to the whole?" Explain the importance of this question in the context of the design argument.

4   After listening to Philo's objections, Cleanthes appears to believe that they result in skepticism. Cleanthes thinks that, if Philo is right, then even the most convincing and unimpeachable evidence for the existence of an intelligent deity wouldn't justify belief in God. But that is absurd. Cleanthes attempts to convince Philo of this point in paragraphs 9 and 10. How does he attempt to do this? Does he convince you?

5   Cleanthes' design argument includes an appeal to the principle that "like effects yield like causes." What does that mean? Philo tries to show that Cleanthes may have taken on more than he bargained for when Cleanthes endorsed that principle. How does Philo argue for that point in paragraph 13?

6   Even if the core of the design argument were successful, Philo thinks that the argument would prove very little about the character of the intelligent designer—other than that the designer was intelligent! How does Philo make this point in paragraphs 15–20?

3.14 "SUFFERING, EVIDENCE, AND ANALOGY: NOSEEUM ARGUMENTS VS. SKEPTICAL GAMBITS" BY STEPHEN WYKSTRA

"Theism," in the traditional sense used here, is the claim that *God exists*—where by "God" is meant a personal being who created and sustains the universe, who is all-powerful and all-knowing, and who is entirely good, and in this goodness loves and tends for all creatures. Theism is a big claim, and this alone, for some, makes it hard to believe. But often we feel it made even harder to believe by the suffering in the world. Such suffering is often prolonged and tormenting, and caused by events with little evident plan, purpose, or pattern. If theism is already hard to believe, events causing such suffering can make it even harder. They may not conclusively disprove theism, but they do seem to be evidence against theism—evidence making theism improbable or implausible.

But exactly what facts about suffering are supposed to make theism improbable, and how do they do so? Philosophers have developed several lines of thought here, but none has gotten more attention than a simple but powerful approach of philosopher William Rowe. Rowe calls attention to the fact that many instances of suffering are in a special sense *inscrutable*: no matter how hard we look, we can *see no* point served by them that would justify God in allowing them. Rowe's argument is that our *seeing no* such point is strong evidence for there *being no* such point, and therefore—since God wouldn't allow such suffering if it were pointless—is also strong evidence for there being no God.

But can our seeing no point for some suffering *really* be strong evidence that there is no point, and hence, no God? After all, if God does exist, aren't His purposes just the sort of thing we should expect to often fail to see? And if theism "predicts" this, then shouldn't our not seeing such purposes be, if anything, evidence in favor of theism?

I shall here call Rowe's type of argument, giving such bite to what we cannot see, a "Noseeum Argument"; and I shall call the reply just described a "Skeptical Gambit Critique" of Rowe's argument.[2] I begin this paper by explaining in detail Rowe's Noseeum Argument and my own Skeptical Gambit Critique of it. In dialogue over the years, Rowe and I have sought the best objections we could to our views, and considered whether these objections have cogent defenses. I will here explain four objections ("daggers") that Rowe has directed at my Skeptical Gambit Critique, and sketch my best "shields" against these. Your mission is to evaluate whether these shields (or better ones that you can think of) allow the Skeptical Gambit Critique to hold against Rowe's daggers, or whether finding fault with Rowe's Noseeum Argument requires some better critique.

In philosophy, the method of objections and replies—or of "daggers versus shields," as I call it—is not a matter of winning a debate. It is instead a way of seeking the truth, by enabling rival positions to evolve in ways that brings out their real strengths and weaknesses. Dialogue with Rowe has been, for me, a continuing source of new insights not only into the evidential problem of suffering, but also into evidence, probability, and other key topics in current epistemology. (See Rowe 2006 for his own account.) By joining our dialogue, I hope that you will come to appreciate the method of philosophy, and come to your own new insights on these topics. For here there are, I believe, still new insights to be had at every turn of the argument.

Rowe's Noseeum Argument. Evidential arguments from suffering rely on a tension between three basic ideas. The first idea is since God (in the theist's sense) is good, God would *prefer not* to have any creature suffer intensely—just as a good mother or father would prefer not to have a dearly loved child suffer intensely. A good God, like a good parent, will deem such suffering, *considered in itself,* a bad thing, a "negative," and so will allow such suffering only when doing so is required for[3] some outweighing positive thing—some "outweighing good," as philosophers put it. The second idea is that God—*unlike* a human parent—is all-powerful: God therefore won't, it seems, as easily be in a bind where getting some outweighing good requires His allowing intense suffering. This can happen only if the outweighing good is of a special sort—one so intimately linked to the suffering that even an all-powerful being can't have the good without allowing the bad. The third idea is that certain facts about suffering make it improbable that each instance of suffering serves some outweighing good of this special sort (and hence, improbable that there is a God).

But what facts about suffering allow one to show this, and by what argument? Rowe's overall argument has three stages. The first stage focuses on a particular instance of suffering—a deer, caught in forest fire set by lightning, is burned horribly, and lies several days in agony before dying. Rowe argues that when we review in our minds the various goods that such suffering might serve, we see no good that suffices to justify an all-powerful and all-good God in allowing the deer's suffering. As shorthand, let's say that an instance of suffering "serves a Point" when there is some outweighing good that suffices to justify an all-good and all-powerful God in allowing it. Rowe's claim is then that we *see no Point* served by the deer's suffering. And our *seeing no* such Point—our "noseeum data," as I will call it—is, Rowe argues, strong evidence for there *being no* such Point served by this particular instance of suffering.

Rowe's second stage urges that there are *many* instances of suffering like this: their sheer number, he urges, makes it even more probable (very probable) that for at least one of the instances, there is no Point.

Rowe's third stage asserts that if God exists, each instance of intense suffering must serve some Point. Adding this to the second stage (that very probably, at least one instance serves no Point), he gets the conclusion that very probably, God does not exist.

The main steps of the argument are depicted in Figure 2.

Rowe's Underlying Principles. In Rowe's first stage, the central inference is from our *seeing no* Point for the deer's suffering, to there probably *being no* Point served by it. What sort of inference is this, and on what general principles does it rely?

Rowe has two approaches here. In his earliest work (see Rowe 1979) he uses what I'll call an "indirect" approach, making use of an intermediate "does not appear" claim. He begins from

(1) We see no Point served by the deer's suffering.

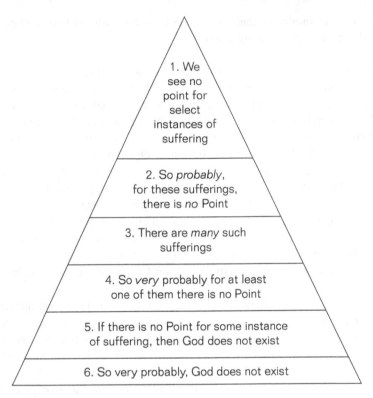

Figure 2 Nosecone of suffering

He goes from this to an intermediate conclusion

(1.5)   It does not *appear* that the deer's suffering serves a Point.

And from this he concludes

(2)   It is reasonable to believe the deer's suffering *does not* serve a Point.

In going from (1.5) to (2), Rowe's inference is best seen as relying on a highly regarded general principle that epistemologists call the Credulity Principle. The Credulity Principle says that if it *appears* to you that something is the case, then it is, other things being equal, reasonable for you to believe that it *is* the case. For example, suppose you are lying in bed napping with the blinds drawn, and you hear a familiar friendly pitter-patter on the window such that it *appears* to you that it is raining outside. The Credulity Principle says that given this, it is (other things being equal[4]) reasonable for you to believe that it *is* raining outside. At core, the Credulity Principle says that how things *appear* is—other things being equal—strong evidence for how they *are*.

In later papers (see Rowe 1996) Rowe shifts to a direct approach to the same inference. Again he selects a specific instance of suffering—this time, an actual case of a little girl savagely beaten to death in Flint, Michigan. And again, he asks us to consider possible goods to see if they suffice to justify a God's allowing this instance. He defines "J" as the property a good has just in case the good *suffices* to justify a God in allowing the suffering involved in that particular event in Flint. He then begins from the claim that when we consider possible goods that might be involved, we see the following:

(1) All goods *we know of* lack J.

This, he then argues, makes it reasonable to conclude that

(2) All goods *there are* lack J.

Here (2) is saying that no good has the property of being sufficient to justify God's allowing the suffering of the little girl in Flint. And the inference from (1) to (2), Rowe says, uses a principle at the heart of all inductive reasoning from data about a sample to a larger population. The principle, called the "straight rule," is this: if in a fairly selected sample, *a certain percentage* has some characteristic C, then the most reasonable conclusion is that *the same percentage* of the larger population has characteristic C. Suppose, for example, that in a fairly selected sample of 100 pit bulls, 90 percent *of your sample* gets vicious when taunted and poked with a stick. (Don't try this at home.) Then the most reasonable conclusion is that 90 percent *of all* pit bulls get vicious when taunted and poked with a stick. Or, suppose you are looking for a good electrical conductor, test a large number of pieces of gold, and find that 100 percent of the pieces *in this sample* are conductors. Then the most reasonable conclusion is then that 100 percent *of all* gold in the universe conducts electricity.

Seeability Requirements. So Rowe's first stage claims to use the same principles of reasoning that we use in other areas of life. But when considered carefully, how strong is this evidence, and how good are the inferences?

Consider first the indirect version. The most vulnerable step, I suggest, is the step from (1) to (1.5). This step moves from our seeing no God-justifying outweighing good served by the deer's suffering to the claim that it does not appear that this suffering serves any God-justifying outweighing good. Seeing this as vulnerable may seem surprising. After all, if we see no Point for the deer's suffering, isn't it almost trivial to go on to say that "there does not appear to be" any such Point? Indeed, isn't this "does not appear" claim pretty much just repeating the claim that we don't see any such Point for it?

No, it's not. Here we must see that "does not appear" can have either a modest meaning or a more ambitious meaning. Suppose you call me and ask me if it is raining outside, not knowing that I am deep underground in a bank vault and have no idea what the current weather is. Now, suppose I answer you by asserting "Well, it does not appear to be raining." I might later defend myself by saying that I was using "does not appear" in a modest sense to mean just "It isn't the case that it appears to me to be raining." And in this modest sense, my assertion would be true. But you'd probably feel miffed, for you understood me to be using "does not appear" in the ordinary way, on which my assertion was saying "It appears *not to be raining*." And in this more ambitious sense, my assertion was of course false: in the vault, it didn't appear to me *not* to be raining outside.

Now for Rowe's overall argument to work, his first stage must use "does not appear" in this more ambitious sense—otherwise, he can't, in the second stage, use the Credulity Principle to get to the conclusion that probably there is no Point to the suffering. But once we see this, we can see that the inference from (1) to (1.5) needs careful scrutiny. Sometimes inferences of this sort are reasonable; but sometimes they aren't reasonable. For example, if you are on the bleachers looking down at a basketball court, and see no elephants on the court, it is reasonable enough for you to say, "There appear to be no elephants on the basketball court." But if you look around and see no sand fleas, it isn't reasonable for you to say "There appear to be no sand fleas on the court." We must carefully consider, then, what relevant features make the former reasonable and the latter unreasonable, and in this light ask whether Rowe's inference is more like the elephant inference, or more like the sand flea inference.

So in the scenario sketched above, what makes a noseeum inference reasonable for elephants but not for sand fleas? I propose that the difference is due to the "seeability" of elephants and sand fleas. Elephants have high "seeability": if some elephants were in the gym, then it's pretty likely you would have seen them from your seat in the bleachers. And this is why *not seeing* them entitles you to say "It appears there are no elephants here." Sand fleas, in contrast, have low "seeability." Even if they're there, it's entirely likely that you, from up in the bleachers, wouldn't see them. And that's why not seeing them doesn't entitle you to say "It doesn't appear that there are sand fleas there."

Keeping these examples in mind, let's try to turn the idea into a general requirement that any reasonable noseeum argument must meet. I'll call it a "Seeability Requirement" or "Seeability Rule"—for short, a SEER. For indirect noseeum arguments relying on an intermediate "does not appear" claim, a workable first approximation is this:

SEER-1: Seeing no X in a situation after carefully looking makes it reasonable to say "It appears that no X is here" *only if* it's reasonable for you to think that in that situation, *X is pretty "seeable"*—that is, that *if X were there, it's pretty likely that you would have seen it*.

And for direct noseeum arguments, a good first formulation is this:

SEER-2: Finding that *all X's we know lack a property P* gives one strong evidence that *all X's lack P, only if* it is reasonable for one to believe that if some X has P, this would likely fall within our experience.

Applying SEER: The Parent Analogy. Do Rowe's Noseeum Arguments satisfy these requirements? Do we, on balance, have good reason to think that outweighing goods purposed by God, if they did exist, would have high seeability? Or is it, instead, just as reasonable to suppose[5] that even if God-purpose goods exist, we likely would often not see them?

Against Rowe, I've defended the latter. I've relied heavily on what I call the Parent Analogy. The idea is that if there is a God, his Mind will be vastly deeper than our minds, much as a parent's mind is deeper than a mind of a child who is very young—say, one year old. By analogy, then, that we should see most of God's purposes seems about as likely as that a one-year old would discern most of her parents' purposes—that is to say, it is not likely at all. We thus have substantial reason to think that if God does exist, his Purposes for allowing many instances of suffering would often be beyond our ken. Like sand fleas viewed from the bleachers, they'd be things we humans are not well situated to detect— things to which we wouldn't have very good "epistemic access."

Thus, the Skeptical Gambit Critique[6] rests on two claims. The first claim, based on examples, is that any reasonable noseeum inference must satisfy appropriate seeability requirements; the second claim, based on the Parent Analogy, is that Rowe's argument does not meet such requirements. We now turn to Rowe's objections against each claim.

Rowe's First Dagger: SEER Yields Absurdities. Though Rowe's first objection to my Skeptical Gambit is somewhat technical, beginning with it offers insights about probabilistic evidence that are crucial for clear thinking in this area and many others. Rowe argued that the "Seeability Requirement" cannot be right, because it leads to absurdities when combined with a second principle that is an established part of probability theory. The second principle, called the Consequence Condition (or CC for short), says this:

(CC): If evidence disconfirms or makes improbable some hypothesis H, then it also must disconfirm or make improbable any "bigger" (i.e., more informative) hypothesis H' that has H as an entailed consequence.

For example, suppose that H is the hypothesis that the President is now somewhere in the United States, and suppose that H' is the more informative hypothesis the President is now at the White House in Washington. Now H is clearly an entailed consequence of H': if H' is true, then H *must* be true too. Hence, applied to H and H', CC says this: if we have evidence E that "disconfirms" H to some degree, then H' must be disconfirmed to at least this same degree. Perhaps, for example, E is the fact that the *New York Times* says that the President plans to be at the G8 summit in Berlin today; and suppose we judge that on this evidence, there is a probability of well under 1 percent (0.01) that the President is in the United States. Then CC tells us that H' (which entails H) must have a probability of well under 0.01 too. A good way to grasp this is to think of H as a "component" within H': CC is then saying that as a chain can't be stronger than its weakest link, so also the probability of a hypothesis can never be higher than its least probable component.

Now CC, Rowe argued, is an established theorem in probability theory, so must be embraced. But suppose we've also accepted the Seeability Rule. We then, Rowe argued, quickly get the absurd result that no probabilistic evidence *ever* disconfirms any hypothesis. An example will make clear why. Let your hypothesis of interest be

(W)   "Wykstra is Catholic."

And suppose you were then to discover the following evidence:

(E)   Wykstra taught for years at Calvin College and is a member of Eastern Avenue Christian Reformed Church.

Now here, intuitively, we surely want to say that E makes W improbable. But consider the bigger hypothesis W' that you get when you *combine* W *with* E (and here we will add a little parenthetical "binder" to help hold the two together):

(W')   Wykstra is Catholic; in addition, Wykstra teaches at Calvin College and is a member of Eastern Avenue Christian Reformed Church. (Wykstra is keeping his Catholicism a secret, thinking this will allow him to secretly subvert the Protestant convictions of others.)

Using examples something like this, Rowe argues in three short steps that the Seeability Rule can't be right. The first step is to note that the Seeability Rule *forces* us to say that E does *not* make W' improbable (for if W' were true, E is clearly just what we would expect). The second step says that given this, CC forces the further result that that E cannot make W improbable either. (W' entails or contains W, so if E made W improbable, it would—as a "weak link"—make W' at least this improbable too.) The third step is that this result is absurd: E clearly *does* make W improbable. Since the Seeability Rule leads to an absurd result here, it can't be right. Worse yet, the Seeability Rule yields this absurdity for *any* hypothesis confronting disconfirming evidence, for we can always expand any hypothesis in a similar way to get a similarly absurd result.

A Proposed Shield: Carnap's Distinction. Rowe's first objection was daunting, but my gut level instincts were that it is based on confusion. Even in the example, it seemed to me that both principles are saying something right. In cases like this, confusions come from neglecting a key distinction, and a few days of reading and reflection yielded a new key insight. Rowe's argument, I saw, is overlooking a distinction between two senses of the verb "confirm" and "disconfirm," a distinction stressed by Rudolf Carnap in his classic *Logical Foundations of Probability*.

What Carnap saw is that "confirms" (and "disconfirms") can be used in either a static or a dynamic sense (my terms, not his). In the static sense, some *body* of evidence (which I shall designate with an upper-case "E") confirms H just in case, *on* E, H *has* a probability of over 0.5 (it is more likely true than false). And E statically "disconfirms" H just in case, on E, H has a probability of under 0.5 (it is more likely false than true). In the dynamic sense, a new bit of evidence e (lowercase) "confirms" H when learning of e *raises* the probability of H from what it was on our previous evidence. Similarly, e dynamically disconfirms H when, by adding e to our previous evidence, the probability of H is lowered from what it was on our previous evidence.

To illustrate, suppose you are playing poker: you have the standard knowledge of cards, and you know that a new deck is being used and that everyone has been dealt a fair hand. Call this body of evidence "E." You now consider the probability that (H) your friend Fritz is holding four aces. On E, H is of course very improbable: E statically disconfirms H. You now glance at your own hand, and gain a new bit of evidence—call it "e"—that you do not yourself hold *any* aces. Now, on e, it is also very improbable that Fritz holds four aces: again, e statically disconfirms H. But in the *dynamic* sense, e *confirms* H. For clearly, learning that you hold no aces *increases* somewhat the probability that Fritz is holding four aces, making this a bit *more* probable than it was previously, on E alone. So in the first or static sense, e does not confirm H, but in the second dynamic sense, e does confirm H.

This distinction allows a decisive answer to Rowe's first objection, for it exposes a misunderstanding. When CC says that if E makes improbable some hypothesis H, then E makes improbable any hypothesis H' entailing H, the phrase "makes improbable" means the same as "disconfirm" in the static sense. That is, if H' entails H, then when, on evidence E, H has a probability under some value (say, 0.5), it must also be the case that H' has, on E, a probability under this same value. In contrast, the Seeability Requirement is talking about dynamic disconfirmation: it is saying that whenever H makes some new piece of evidence e expectable, our learning about e cannot *dynamically* disconfirm H—cannot *decrease* the probability of H from whatever it was on our previous evidence. Once this confusion is rooted out, we can see that Rowe's second step rests on an **equivocation**. For his first step shows that E does make H' improbable in the dynamic sense: E does not reduce the probability of H'. Hence, his second step can't use CC to get the alleged absurd consequence from this, because CC addresses only the static sense.

The No-Free-Lunch Law. Going more deeply, the shield against Rowe's first dagger opens the way to a fundamental insight about *why* we can't effectually protect a pet hypothesis from disconfirming evidence just by expanding it into a bigger hypothesis. To open this up, let's put our illustration in story form. Imagine that you are a Catholic, and that you have a certain body of evidence E that makes very probable that (W) Wykstra is a Catholic. Your evidence is this: at Mass, you observed Wykstra going to the front, kneeling, and receiving the bread and wine of communion;[7] and as a Catholic loyal to Vatican teaching, you know that only confirmed Catholics are supposed to do this. On this basis, you judge that there is a probability of well over 95 percent (0.95) that Wykstra is a Catholic. (You're pleased to see Wykstra as one of the flock.)

But the next day, you acquire new evidence, which we'll call (e): you overhear Wykstra tell someone that he teaches at Calvin College and is a member of Eastern Avenue Christian Reformed Church, both of which are enthusiastically Protestant. You are taken aback, for (e) seems to indicate that you must now hugely lower the probability of W. But then you have a bright idea. Why not protect your belief that Wykstra is a fellow Catholic, simply by shifting to an "expanded" hypothesis that combines W together with e (using a little parenthetical binder to hold the two together):

(W')   Wykstra is a Roman Catholic; he also teaches at Calvin and is a member of Eastern Avenue Christian Reformed Church. (He is keeping his Catholicism a secret in a misguided effort to secretly subvert the convictions of as many Calvinists as he can.)

Since this new hypothesis (W') makes it totally expectable that Wykstra teaches at Calvin and belongs to EACRC, your new information does not at all disconfirm W', and you can go on, as before, believing that Wykstra is a fellow Catholic.

Most of us, I think, will feel intuitively that that there is something terribly wrong with maintaining our pet beliefs by such a strategy. Carnap's distinction helps us see clearly why this is so. By expanding, you have indeed (in accord with our Seeability Rule!) purchased effective protection against *dynamic* disconfirmation by the new evidence e. But this "protection" has a price tag. For on your initial evidence E (seeing Wykstra receive the sacrament), you rightly gave a very high probability of 0.95 to W (that Wykstra is a Catholic). But suppose you had, on E, assigned a probability to W'—that Wykstra is a Catholic; that he also teaches at Calvin College and belongs to a Protestant church, and that he keeps this secret (except for occasional visits to Mass of course) to subvert Calvinism from within. This *expanded* hypothesis, on your old evidence (seeing Wykstra take communion) has an extremely low probability—well under a hundredth of a percent (0.0001), you might reasonably judge. So shifting to W' gives "protection" against the new evidence that W didn't have, but only because W started out with a hugely lower probability than W. What your left hand has given (protection against losing probability), your right hand had already taken away! Rowe himself, dropping his first dagger and embracing this insight, put the point neatly: "It seems that in philosophy, as in economics, there is no such thing as a free lunch."

Rowe's Second Dagger: The Distant-Future Gap. Granting my Seeability Requirement, Rowe next probed my "Parent Analogy" case that his Noseeum Argument violates this requirement. Rowe analyzed my reasoning as having three main steps. Wykstra begins (he said) with the ground-zero claim (as I'll call it) that

(0)   "God (if He exists) has an intellect that is vastly greater than ours."

From this, Rowe saw me as inferring that

(1)   "God grasps many goods that are beyond our ken."

And from this, Rowe saw me as inferring that

(2)   "The goods for which God (if He exists) allows many present sufferings are beyond our ken."

Working from this analysis, Rowe agreed with ground-zero claim (0). He also accepted the inference from (0) to (1): if God exists, Rowe granted, God surely sees many goods in the very distant future (say, a billion years from now) that are beyond our grasp. The problem, Rowe urged, is that (1) doesn't allow us to get to (2): there is a big gap between them. The gap—let's call it "the Distant-Future Gap"—arises because (2) is a claim about the goods served by sufferings *in the present world* (like the fawn's suffering). To go legally from (1) to (2), Rowe urged, we thus need the *further assumption* that the goods served by *present* sufferings are, or often are, goods that are in the distant future (or are for some other reason inaccessible to us). Put diagrammatically:

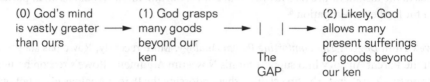

Figure 3 Wykstra's knowledge of God table

But, Rowe continued, Wykstra gives no reason for this Distant-Future Assumption, and theism itself gives us "no reason whatever" to accept it (Rowe, 1990: p. 164). If this is so, the Distant-Future Gap becomes an unbridgeable chasm, stopping any inference from (1) to (2). For this reason, Rowe urged, the Parent Analogy doesn't show the Seeability Rule is violated by his Noseeum Inference.

A Proposed Shield: the Improved Parent Analogy. Rowe's second dagger, like the first, is a stimulus for further clarification. The first thing to notice is that his dagger does not mention the Parent Analogy—perhaps viewing it merely as a colorful way to illustrate the claim that God's mind is far deeper and larger than our minds. But I meant the analogy as an *argument*, and the question is now whether it can be improved so as to bridge the Distant-Future Gap.

   One important question here is whether the similarities between the parent–child relation and the God–human relation give us reason to think that God, if God exists, would indeed, in His *present* dealings with us, often be motivated by goods that are, to us, in an inscrutably distant future. This is, after all, true of parent–child relations: parents allow a beloved infant to suffer the insertion of painful needles by the Man in the White Coat, for the sake of goods in a future which is, to the child, inscrutably distant. Do the analogies in the God–human relation give us reason to expect the same here?

   When parents allow a child to suffer for the sake of goods too far in the future for the child to see, this is partly because they, with their superior knowledge, can discern these goods in a way the child cannot. But it is also because they *care* about the future; they are not myopically concerned only about the present. And it is also because their abilities allow them to steer things in the present so as to help bring about desirable consequences in the future. These characteristics, and others besides, are also possessed even more by God. Appealing to such similarities allows us to use the Parent Analogy to address the Gap noticed by Rowe, and to support the Distant-Future Assumption that God (if God exists) will likely, in a significant number of His present dealings with us, be motivated by goods in the distant future (see Russell and Wykstra, 1988: pp. 144–47; and Wykstra, 1996: pp. 142–45).

At the same time, it is possible—as Rowe recently has suggested—that there are dissimilarities between the parent–child relation and the God–human relation that point in the opposite direction. God, for example, being vastly more powerful than human parents, might be less likely to need to allow pain in the present for the sake of great goods in the distant future (see Rowe 1996; 2006). Sorting this out remains an important area for further investigation.[8]

Rowe's Third Dagger: The Comforting Parent Analogy. More recently, Rowe has sought to turn the Parent Analogy into support for his Noseeum Argument. Rowe's reasoning here rests on two key claims. The first claim is that endorsing the Parent Analogy gives not only the implication that the theist desires, but a further undesired implication as well. The theist's desired implication is that the goods purposed by God in allowing present sufferings will often be in the distant inscrutable future or for some other reason beyond our ken. The *further* implication is that if God is like a good parent, then God will behave as good parents do when they allow a child to suffer for reasons beyond the child's grasp. A good mother, in such a case, does all she can to be *present* to the child, to assure the child of her love, and to assure the child that there *is* a purpose for the suffering, even if the child can't grasp it. If God is indeed like a good parent, God will do the same: when allowing us to suffer for reasons beyond our ken, God will do all He can to be present to us in the suffering, to assure us of his love, and so on. This, to Rowe's mind, is an inevitable *extension* of the Parent Analogy. But—Rowe's second key claim—we know from experience that human beings in their suffering very often do *not* experience God as close and present, or experience assurances that the suffering has a Point. Instead, God seems especially absent and hidden.

And how exactly does Rowe think his two key claims bear on the issue at hand? A close reading shows that he makes a *double* use of it—his dagger is here a two-pronged dagger—a forked dagger as it were. The first is that the Parent Analogy, although "very much favored by theists, is actually unfavorable to theism." It is unfavorable, in part, because if endorsed it brings theism into conflict with a widespread inability to experience God's presence, especially in times of intense suffering. Here, Rowe's suggestion is that widespread "non-experience" of God's presence during times of inscrutable suffering is a new independent argument for atheism (Rowe, 2006).

But this, however interesting, is not relevant to whether his original noseeum argument holds up against the Skeptical Gambit critique. What is relevant is the second prong. As Rowe sees it, the Parent Analogy, in its further implication that God would draw close to us during times of inscrutable suffering, means that in *that special subset of cases* of suffering where we don't experience God as drawing close to us, we should, if theism is true, expect the Point for God's allowing this suffering to be one we can see. For this *special subset* of cases, therefore, our not seeing any such Point for the suffering will—even given the Seeability Requirement—be strong evidence for there being no Point (and hence of there being no God).

Shielding Against the Third Dagger: The Infection Analogy. Let's briefly review so as to bring into sharp focus the relevant issue. The overall question concerning us is whether Rowe's Noseeum Argument works: does Rowe's noseeum data—our not seeing a Point served by many instances of suffering—give us strong evidence that there is no Point (and hence no God). To answer this, we proposed our Seeability Requirement, defending it against Rowe's first dagger, and we used the Parent Analogy to argue that a God-purposed good for suffering would likely often not be seeable. Against Rowe's second dagger, we improved the Parent Analogy to support the claim that God-purposed goods for present suffering would likely often be in the distant future. Rowe's third dagger is that improving the Parent Analogy actually works against theism, because if God is like a good parent, God will draw discernibly close to us during times of inscrutable intense suffering; when God doesn't do so, the purpose for the suffering should thus be one we can see.

Is Rowe's claim here right? In my judgment, it's not quite right. Rowe's claim is that God, if God is like a good parent, will always "draw close" to his children when He allows them to suffer for the sake of goods that they cannot grasp. But it's not true that a good parent always does this. What is true is that a good parent draws close *provided that* this does not sacrifice any outweighing good. But there are times when a good parent will, nevertheless, refrain from drawing close in the way the child might expect—perhaps the child, due to radiation therapy, is very vulnerable to infections, and must be kept in isolation due to risk of a fatal infection. So what the Parent Analogy really implies is something more subtle: that during times of inscrutable suffering we should expect God to draw close to us, unless God's remaining hidden is itself vital for some outweighing good.

But this means that for Rowe's third dagger to work, Rowe must support the claim that there is no Point served by God's remaining often hidden from us, in those cases where we suffer intensely and can't see any Point for this. I don't see Rowe as having done this yet, and I don't myself see a way for him to do it. He can't do it, I think, by appealing to the mere fact that we see no Point served by God's remaining hidden during such times: that would be another Noseeum Inference, which would beg the very question at issue. For now, it seems to me, this means Rowe's third dagger is not lethal to the Skeptical Gambit.

Rowe's Fourth Dagger: The Ineffectualness of Expansion. I come now to Rowe's fourth dagger, which will return us to earlier issues about evidence and probability. The Skeptical Gambit argues that Rowe's noseeum data isn't strong evidence against theism, because if theism is true, this noseeum data is pretty much what we should expect. Rowe's fourth dagger is that this isn't so: in making noseeum data "expectable" on theism, the theist is relying on more than the core claim of "theism itself." For in thinking that God allows a human to suffer for the sake of goods in the distant future, the theist is typically taking for granted certain further doctrines—typically, doctrines peculiar to some specific Christian versions of theism, such as the view that our earthly lives are a preparation for an afterlife in which humans (some of them, anyway) enjoy great goods such as eternal fellowship with God.

It may be true, Rowe argues, that on theism plus additional doctrines like this, it is expectable that we'd often fail to see the Point served by many instances of suffering. But, says Rowe, this is ineffectual against noseeum evidence, because it means that one is now shifting to an "expanded" version of theism. And such expansions are ineffectual, Rowe urges, for exactly the reasons that emerged in our grappling with Rowe's first dagger: the expansion "protects" theism against the new data only by making it vastly less probable on the old evidence. Twisting the knife, Rowe adds that while some theists may personally embrace the further doctrines due to credulous faith in some special revelation in the Bible, this can hardly be part of a "rational philosophical response" to the problem.

Confronting Rowe's Fourth Dagger. It's easy, I think, for traditional theists to not appreciate the real force of Rowe's fourth dagger. To do so, let's consider how it applies to someone who expands theism by adding to it a very *non-traditional* doctrine. Consider someone— Bug Man, let's call him—who seeks to meet Rowe's argument by adding to theism the following "Karma-Insect" doctrine:

(K): Each of us is a soul that has lived many past lives as various types of insects; we cannot now remember these past lives; much present suffering is connected by "karma" to choices made in past insect-lives, which is thus inscrutable to us.

Let's refer to the combination of theism and this insect-karma doctrine as *Karma-Insect-Theism* (or, for short, *KIT*). Now, is inscrutable human suffering evidence against KIT? In one sense, the answer is that it is not. For if KIT is true, this data is just what we should expect. So, given our Seeability Requirement, this data cannot be evidence against KIT. But does this mean that a theist can answer Rowe's Noseeum Argument simply by taking theism and adding the insect-karma doctrine? Of course not, and we saw why earlier. For in expanding theism by adding to it this new doctrine, we have produced a version of theism that is, on our previous body of evidence, vastly less probable than "mere theism" by itself. And if Bug Man defends his karma-insect doctrine by appealing to private mystical revelations, we might well see him as no longer giving—in Rowe's terms—a "rational philosophical response" to noseeum evidence.

Rowe's fourth dagger thus has a sharp point. And it relies, interestingly, on the very insight by which I shielded the Skeptical Gambit from his first dagger. I argued there that the "Loyal Catholic," by expanding her pet hypothesis that Wykstra is a Catholic, gets a hypothesis with protection against *new* disconfirming evidence only at the high price of being vastly less improbable *on* her old body of evidence. Rowe's claim is now that Skeptical Gambit is also "expanding" theism, and is similarly ineffectual. And this fourth dagger is—ironically, so to speak—forged from the same steel I'd used in my shield against his first dagger!

Is Rowe right here? Does the Skeptical Gambit rely on an "expansion" of theism? And if it does, is it on a par with the clearly ineffectual expansions we've analyzed? Rowe thinks so. But is he here, perhaps, underestimating the degree to which modest claims about divine revelation might have genuine *independent* evidential support, and so inform a rational philosophical response to the problem? For suppose one has good evidence that *if* God exists, it is very likely certain persons are genuine agents of revelation. Could this help the Skeptical Gambiteer differentiate her expansions from those of a clearly ineffectual sort?

For Rowe's earlier daggers, I've proposed shields and left you to evaluate whether they adequately hold against Rowe's daggers. But for Rowe's Fourth Dagger, I leave you the challenge of finding the best shield as well of evaluating whether it holds. In philosophy, positions are tested by this dialectical process of seeing if it can survive the most worrisome objections, and through this process of iron sharpening iron we gain deeper insights into philosophical problems. With Rowe's fourth dagger, I have brought you to a cutting edge of investigation on the problem of suffering, and invited you to work alongside us.

STUDY AND DISCUSSION QUESTIONS

1   William Rowe is a philosopher that Wykstra has engaged in a very longstanding, important debate about the problem of evil. What are the stages of Rowe's Noseeum Argument? What is its conclusion?

2   There are two different versions of Rowe's argument. How do they differ?

3   Wykstra discusses Rowe's inference from *seeing no point* of suffering to the conclusion that *there is no point* to suffering. He uses an example about being asked whether it is raining while you are deep in a bank vault. What is the point of this example?

4   Can you explain the "Seeability Requirement" (SEER) in your own words? What about the "Consequence Condition" (CC)?

5   Wykstra describes an argument by Rowe that puts SEER and CC together to show that SEER is false. How does that argument go?

6   What is the difference between "dynamic" disconfirmation of a theory "by" certain evidence and "static" disconfirmation "on" a body of evidence? How does this distinction help answer Rowe's objection?

7   Rowe objects that Wykstra's Parent Analogy argument only shows that God grasps goods we don't know in the distant future. Why isn't it enough to show this: what "Gap" hurts Wykstra's case here? How might a theist try to improve the argument and plug the gap?

8   To address the Distant-Future problem, Wykstra suggests improving the analogy between a parent and a one-year-old. What is the point of the improvements? Do they help?

9   Rowe objects to the parent/child analogy on the grounds that it actually works against theism, not for theism. Why does he say this? What is Wykstra's response to that objection?

10   The last stage of the conversation between Wykstra and Rowe involves the "expansion" of the doctrine of theism. Approximately what is the issue here?

3.15 BIBLIOGRAPHY AND RECOMMENDED READING

Science fiction

*Asimov, Isaac. "Nightfall." *Science Fiction Hall of Fame Vol. I*. Ed. Robert Silverberg. Doubleday, 1970. In "Nightfall" (originally published in 1941) a planet in a six-star system sees the darkness only once every two thousand years, and its culture is repeatedly destroyed by its superstitious response. Asimov later expanded the story into a full-length novel, collaborating with Robert Silverberg.

*———. "Reason." *I Robot*. Bantam Spectra, 2004. "Reason," included in this collection of short stories by Asimov, explores the idea of intelligent machines which are converted to humanlike religious faith

Benford, Gregory and Gordon Ekland. *If the Stars Are Gods*. New York: Ace Books, 1998. Contrasts the religious views of a canine-like species with our human outlook.

*Blish, James. *A Case of Conscience*. New York: Ballantine, 1958. In this Hugo-winning novel, a crocodile-like alien species has a high intelligence but is incapable of appreciating human religious concerns and seems to the protagonist, a Jesuit priest, to embody moral evil.

Chiang, Ted. "Hell is the Absence of God." *Starlight 3*. Tor Books, 2001. pp. 15–47. Also published in Chiang, Ted. *Stories of Your Life and Others*. Tor Books, 2002.

*Clarke, Arthur C. "Nine Billion Names of God." *Science Fiction Hall of Fame Vol 1*. Ed. Robert Silverberg. Advanced computer technology is utilized by Tibetan mystics with an arresting outcome.

Cooper, Edmund. *A Far Sunset*. Walker, 1967. Human beings become entangled in alien religions.

Del Rey, Lester. *The Eleventh Commandment*. Regency, 1962. After a nuclear war, a variant of the Catholic Church, which values life intrinsically, urges humanity to be fruitful. The result of the application of this basic religious principle leads to overpopulation and economic devastation.

Dick, Philip K. *The Divine Invasion*. Vintage, 1991. Even if Dick didn't set out to write a sequel to the Bible set in the far future, this comes close. Human beings inhabited by a newly reincarnate God return to Earth from a space colony, and in the process unleash forces of light and of darkness to recreate religious havoc on our planet.

———. *Galactic Pot-Healer*. Vintage, 1994. An anti-hero, a repairer of crockery by trade, is called to service by a godlike alien, Glimmung. But the Kalends are at work on a history of the future that is routinely proven to be correct, raising philosophical worries about fatalism and meaning in life.

———. *A Maze of Death*. Vintage, 1994. Portrays a set of paranoid colonists who, after failing to understand the uniqueness of their new world, turn to an idiosyncratic religion for succor and meaning.

Ellison, Harlan. "Deathbird." *Deathbird Stories*. Collier Books, 1993. Employs a variety of literary techniques to redefine the cosmic conflict between God and Satan and to challenge our traditional assumptions that God is good and all-powerful.

*——. "I Have no Mouth and I Must Scream." *Alone against Tomorrow*. Macmillan, 1971. In Hugo Award winning short story, a sadistic supercomputer, AM, is self-deceived to believe that it is God, or Satan. Though AM's intelligence is vast, its power is weak, which has led AM to preserve and artificially extend the lives of the only five humans it has not annihilated in order to torture them mentally and physically for eternity.

Heinlein, Robert. *Stranger in a Strange Land*. New York: Ace, 1991. Valentine Michael Smith is the star of this Hugo Award winning story in which the eponymous figure, who was raised on Mars, returns to Earth and unintentionally initiates a trend of revolutionary behavior by being cast in the role of a religious messiah figure.

Herbert, Frank. *Destination: Void*. Berkley, 1966. An AI is constructed by the crew of a long-range colony ship in order to assist them to reach their destination, but once it is activated, it believes it is a god and demands worship for its service to humanity. This and its three sequels form a complex and fascinating meditation on the nature and morality of worship.

*Kelly, James Patrick. *Look into the Sun*. Tor, 1989. An American artist is commissioned by aliens to build a shrine for a goddess from another planet. Kelly's portrayal of the alien religion is fascinating.

Kessel, John. *Good News from Outer Space*. Orb Books, 1995. I have filed this within the subject of philosophy of religion for a particular reason: this book contains the remarkable portrayal of aliens who have made oblique contact with Earth, but whose motives remain entirely beyond our ken—in much the way that some theists approach the problem of evil.

*Le Guin, Ursula K. "The Ones Who Walk Away From Omelas." In *New Dimensions 3*. Robert Silverberg, ed. SF Book Club, 1973. A child is kept in horrible conditions in a basement forever so that others in that city can live in harmony.

Lewis, C. S. *Out of the Silent Planet*. New York: Scribner, 2003. The world-famous author of the *Chronicles of Narnia* wrote an SF trilogy, of which this book is the first, about a man abducted to Mars. He realizes that life on Mars is in effect Eden-like, and that Earth has become "bent," or infused by original sin. The theological parallels are plain for all readers to see. The trilogy continues to attack a physicalist, non-Christian worldview in *Perelandra* and *That Hideous Strength*.

Lieber, Fritz. *Gather, Darkness!* Pelligrini & Cudahy, 1950. Scientists fight for freedom by taking on the trappings of a Satanic cult in the midst of an authoritarian Catholic dictatorship.

Malzberg, Barry. *The Cross of Fire*. New York: Ace, 1982. A witty novel in which the protagonist gets psychiatric treatment that constructs illusions that he is Jesus Christ. He attempts to find meaning and peace in a self-sacrificial life but fails miserably.

Martin, George R. R. "A Song for Lya." *A Song for Lya: and Other Stories*. Babbage Press, 2001. In this story an alien species' biology gives its members special reason to believe in life after death.

McDonald, Ian. *The Broken Land*. New York: Bantam Spectra, 1992. From this esteemed Northern Irish author is a book about the division between the Proclaimers and the Confessors. Though biotechnology allows people to grow homes and raise the dead (as plants), religious divisions in this far future continue unabated, and with that conflict follows suffering and evil.

*Moorcock, Michael. *Behold the Man*. Overlook TP; Reprint ed., 2007. This Nebula award winning work features a protagonist who time travels to witness first-hand the ministry of Jesus Christ, but discovers that Jesus is so ill-suited to the job that he must take Jesus' place. Draws heavily on Carl Jung's psychological theories of religion.

Niven, Larry and Jerry Pournelle. *Inferno*. Pocket Books, 1976. Niven and Pournelle offer a tongue-in-cheek science fiction reconstruction of Dante's account of the afterlife.

——. *Lucifer's Hammer*. Del Rey, 1985. A novel about the collision of a comet with Earth. Following the catastrophe, a religious brotherhood seeks the total demolition of surviving technology.

Rankin, Robert. *Armageddon: The Musical*. Bloomsbury, 1990. Time-traveling brussel sprout? Christeen, sister of Jesus Christ? In this romp through the genre, readers learn that Earth has been the set of a wide-angle reality TV show produced by aliens for aliens, and only Elvis can save us.

Sawyer, Robert. *Calculating God*. New York: Tor, 2000. An intelligent alien visits to Earth to examine our paleological history. Its analysis yields the surprising discovery that our great extinction events precisely parallel the extinction events of its planet's history. The alien uses the data to develop a proof for God's existence.

Shiel, M. P. *The Purple Cloud*. BiblioBazaar, 2006. This final installment of a trilogy places Adam Jeffson as the last man on Earth after a gas has annihilated the population while he was on a polar expedition. The book serves as a modern retelling of the biblical story of Job and as a meditation on God and evil.

Silverberg, Robert. *Downward to Earth*. Gollancz, 2004. Edmund Gunderson seeks forgiveness from an alien population, called Nildoror, over which he ruled long ago, but this process compels him to participate in an alien rebirthing ritual with morpho-logical consequences. A striking novel about a protagonist seeking transcendence.

Simac, Clifford. *A Choice of Gods*. Putnam, 1971. In this pastoral SF novel, Earth has been de-populated for unknown reasons, and a small band of humans in America's Midwest live out their lives with assistance from robots. Robots undertake humanity's religious quest, since the remnant of remaining people are uninterested in religion, but they eventually face the title's fateful choice.

——. *Project Pope*. New York: Ballantine, 1982. On a colony world a religion is created that unifies disparate faiths; a pope is constructed in a supercomputer, but heaven throws a knot in it.

*Stapledon, Olaf. *Star Maker*. New York: Penguin, 1973. Stapledon offers a view of the nature of God that is in many ways comparable to that of the twentieth-century philosopher Alfred North Whitehead. In his odyssey to fathom the star maker, the unnamed narrator finds a philosophical solution to the problem set forth in Clarke's "The Star," but it involves a view of God which some will find unaccceptable.

Vidal, Gore. *Messiah*. New York: Penguin Classics, 1998. An erudite exploration of religion flipped on its side. This new religion deifies death and suicide, and investigates the psychology behind the spreading of mindless fanaticism.

Philosophy

Abernathy, G. L. and T. L. A. Langford. *Philosophy of Religion: A Book of Readings*. Macmillan, 1962.

Adams, Robert M. "A Modified Divine Command Theory of Ethical Wrongness." *Divine Commands and Morality*. Helm, Paul, ed. Oxford University Press, 1981. pp. 83–108.

Adams, Robert M. and Marilyn M. Adams. *The Problem of Evil*. Oxford University Press, 1990.

Anselm, Saint. "The Classical Ontological Argument for God's Existence." *Complete Philosophical and Theological Treatises of Anselm of Canterbury*. Hopkins, Jasper and Herbert Richardson, eds. Trans. Arthur J. Banning. Minneapolis: University of Minnesota Press, 2000.

Augustine, Saint. *On Free Choice of the Will*. Trans. A. Benjamin and L. H. Hackstaff. New York: Prentice Hall, 1964.

Davies, Brian. *An Introduction to the Philosophy of Religion*. 2nd ed. Oxford: Oxford University Press, 1993. 272pp.

Draper, Paul. "Cosmic Fine-Tuning and Terrestrial Suffering: Parallel Problems for Naturalism and Theism." *American Philosophical Quarterly* 41 (2004): pp. 311–21.

Flew, Anthony. "Pain and Pleasure: An Evidential Problem for Theists." *Nous* 23 (1989): pp. 331–50.

——. *Body, Mind, and Death*. Macmillan, 1976.

——. *God and Philosophy*. Hutchinson, 1966.

Fischer, John Martin, ed. *God, Foreknowledge, and Freedom*. Stanford University Press, 1998. 351pp.

Hick, John. *Faith and Knowledge*. Cornell University Press, 1957.

——. *Philosophy of Religion*. Prentice Hall, 1989. Concise and clear survey, which is sympathetic to the religious viewpoint.

*Howard-Snyder, Daniel, ed. *The Evidential Problem of Evil*. Bloomington, IN: University of Indiana Press, 1996.

Hume, David. *Dialogues Concerning Natural Religion*. J. Gaskin, ed. New York: Oxford University Press, 1998. Originally published in 1779.

——"Problems with the Design Argument." *Dialogues Concerning Natural Religion*. First published 1779. Urbana, IL: Project Gutenberg, 2003. Online source: www.gutenberg.org/etext/4583. Originally published in 1854.

James, William. *The Varieties of Religious Experience*. Routledge, 2002.

——. *The Will to Believe: Human Immortality*. Dover Publications, 1956.

Mackie, J. L. *The Miracle of Theism: Arguments For and Against the Existence of God*. Oxford: Oxford University Press, 1982.

Martin, C. B. *Religious Belief*. Cornell University Press, 1956.

Meeker, Kevin and Philip Quinn, eds. *The Philosophical Challenge of Religious Diversity*. Oxford: Oxford University Press, 2000.

Mitchell, Basil, ed. *The Philosophy of Religion*. Oxford University Press, 1971.

*Murray, Michael J. and Eleonore Stump, eds. *Philosophy of Religion: The Big Questions*. Oxford: Blackwell, 1999. A broad and inclusive anthology of readings in philosophy of religion.

Peterson, Michael, William Hasker, Bruce Reichenbach and David Basinger. *Reason and Religious Belief: An Introduction to the Philosophy of Religion*. Oxford: Oxford University Press, 2003.

Peterson, Michael, William Hasker, Bruce Reichenbach and David Basinger, eds. *Philosophy of Religion: Selected Readings*. Oxford: Oxford University Press, 2006.

Phillips, D..Z. "Religious Beliefs and Language Games." *The Philosophy of Religion*. Ed. Basil Mitchell. Oxford University Press, 1971.

*Plantinga, Alvin. *God, Freedom and Evil*. Grand Rapids, MI: Wm. B. Eerdman Publishing Co., 1977.

Quinn, Philip L. and Charles Taliaferro, eds. *Companion to Philosophy of Religion*. Oxford: Blackwell, 1997. A helpful and comprehensive reference work for philosophy of religion.

Rowe, William. *The Cosmological Argument*. Fordham University Press, 1975.

*——. "Evil and the Theistic Hypothesis: A Response to Wykstra." (pp. 61–88). *International Journal for Philosophy of Religion* 16 (1984): pp. 95–100. Republished in Adams, Robert M. and Marilyn M. Adams. *The Problem of Evil*. Oxford University Press, 1990. pp. 161–67.

*——. *Can God be Free?* New York: Oxford University Press, 2006.

Stace, W.T. *Mysticism and Philosophy*. Macmillan, 1961.

Swinburne, Richard. *Is There a God?* Oxford University Press, 1996.

Wykstra, Stephen. "The Humean Obstacle to Evidential Arguments from Suffering: On Avoiding the Evils of 'Appearance.'" *International Journal for Philosophy of Religion* 16 (1984): pp. 73–93. Republished in Adams, Robert M. and Marilyn M. Adams. *The Problem of Evil*. Oxford University Press, 1990. pp. 138–60.

*——. "Rowe's Noseeum Arguments from Evil". In Howard-Snyder, Daniel, ed. *The Evidential Problem of Evil*. Bloomington, IN: University of Indiana Press, 1996. pp. 126–50.

4 Spacetime and time travel

Imagine taking a lunch break and traveling south. By traveling in that direction on your world, your experience of time passes much more slowly than it would have had you stayed at work. In fact, while in the south you meet someone, get married and have children. But then you receive a message indicating that you're needed back at work in the north. You return to work and discover that only half an hour has passed. This is the plot of David Masson's "Traveller's Rest."

Such a story plays upon a theory of spacetime that may not be all that different, in principle, than the theory of spacetime proposed by contemporary physicists. In Masson's story, the qualities of spacetime vary in different areas. We know that spacetime is warped in gravity wells created by objects in space. The phenomenon of what physicists call "frame-dragging" exemplifies presuppositions made in the story. Massive gravitational forces in rotational motion drag nearby objects out of the locations that they should occupy according to Newtonian physics. According to the theory of general relativity, Earth's gravity and rotation warps spacetime through frame-drag in observable ways. A pair of reflective spheres was put in orbit and their velocities were measured over the course of 11 years with lasers. They were each six feet short of where they should have been had Earth not dragged them through spacetime. Spacetime, as it has been toyed with in science fiction, is bizarre, but physicists are also fascinated by the oddity of properties of spacetime.

This chapter examines the nature of time and, to a lesser extent, the nature of space. Time figures in many major philosophical debates today, including debates about personal identity, free will, ethical obligations and straightforward metaphysical arguments about the nature of reality. In spite of its importance, you may find it hard to explain just what time is. If you have ever pondered your experience of time or discussed it with your friends, you may have come to the conclusion that time is very mysterious. Philosophers have long been conscious of the mysterious nature of time. The early Christian philosopher Augustine (354–430) confessed his perplexity:

> What is time? Who can explain it easily and briefly? Who can get a hold of it, even in thought, so that they can give an explanation in words of it? Yet what do we talk about more knowingly than time? We certainly understand it when we talk about it. We even understand it when we hear another person speaking about it. What, then, is time? If no one asks me, I know; but if I want to explain it to a questioner, I do not know.[1]

Augustine starts from commonsense notions about time: Time is passing, and only the present time is real. But this leads to paradoxical consequences. How can you have obligations to your future self or future generations if they have no reality? But, if you have no obligations to them, don't you have the right to squander the world's resources all you please? Augustine finds that his commonsense notions about time lead him to dizzying conclusions. He soon doubts whether anything as weird as time could even exist. Many other philosophers argue time is contradictory and that our belief that we are conscious of time passing is an illusion.

These philosophical worries about the nature and reality of time can be brought into sharper focus by considering the hypothesis (championed by science fiction writers and philosophers) that it is in principle possible to "travel" to the past or future. A study of time travel paradoxes, the bread and butter of many science fiction writers, clarifies our ideas about the nature of time. And a serious consideration of the possibility of time travel may help us decide whether or not to agree with Augustine's worries about time. We'll do this through a discussion of two theories of time, **presentism** (Augustine's theory) and **four-dimensionalism**.

After completing this chapter, you should be able to:

- Explain the difference between presentism and four-dimensionalism
- Explain why time seems to be unreal on presentism, and how Augustine's paradoxes are avoided on four-dimensionalism
- Describe the **time traveler's hypothesis** and indicate how it bears on the controversy between four-dimensionalism and presentism
- Explain the importance of the theory that time is "relative" for the time traveler's hypothesis
- Understand some of the key contributions of contemporary physics to the debate about time travel
- Explain how the notion of time travel is hard to reconcile with our notions of cause and effect.

BOX 4.A: TIME TRAVELER CONVENTION

First things first: in the famous words of Douglas Adams, don't panic. The convention "was" on May 7, 2005, 10:00 p.m. EDT (08 May 2005 02:00:00 UTC). But if you are eligible to attend, then presumably you can return to that time frame and enjoy the festivities. This event was sponsored and hosted by students at MIT, whose biggest problem was getting the word out. Their budget compelled them to publicize the event by writing down the details about the conference's location in spacetime on slips of paper and putting them into obscure books in university libraries. They made a special plea for time travelers from other points of spacetime to bring some proof of their travels, like a cold fusion reactor or a cure for AIDS. Unfortunately, they did not (yet?) have any visitors from other frames of reference. Thankfully, they don't need to make this an annual event!

4.0 PRESENTISM

Augustine's *Confessions* contains a fascinating discussion of the puzzling nature of time. He has a commonsense theory of time that we will call *presentism* on which time "passes." The future continually decreases or is "eaten up," and the past continually increases or is fed. The presentist theory assumes a fundamental difference between space and time. Space is an externally existing receptacle of matter, but time is perpetually changing. Because this theory treats time as conceptually distinct from space, commonsense favors it over the main alternative. The main alternative is the "four-dimensionalist" theory of time, which says space and time are inseparable and static.

To illustrate the nature of time on presentism, consider an event such as your first kiss. For a very long time it was in your future, then, for a tantalizing brief while, it was in your present; now, alas, it is in your dead past. Time flows relentlessly in one direction, "like a river." Your experience of time's passage can be a source of anxiety, especially when you realize that one of the approaching future events is your own death. According to presentism, a steady succession of temporal events is coming into and going out of existence while time passes. Augustine expresses this clearly in this chapter's historical reading, §4.11.

Augustine's basic question is this: How do those two parts of time, the past and the future, exist since the past has already ceased to exist and the future has not yet come into existence? Augustine doesn't understand how the past or future *could* exist. He says, "If the past and future exist, I would like to know where they are." But even the present moment isn't immune from difficulty. He says,

The present would not pass over into the past, if it were *always* present. But then it would be eternity, not time. So, if the present really is time, it must pass over into the past. But then how can we say that it exists? For the sole reason for its existence is the fact that it will stop existing. Is it not the case that time exists only because it tends *not to exist*?" Our human idea of time seems self-contradictory! Our natural human understanding of that part of reality called time is limited, according to Augustine. We encounter such drastic difficulties when we think about them that we cannot solve them on our own (that is, without God's help).

(*Confessions*)

Augustine also contends that, although we have various means of measuring time, the idea of measuring time is nonsensical. To measure a spatial length, such as a fish just caught, we place the existing fish alongside an existing measuring device. Obviously, we can't carry out the measurement if the length to be measured or the measuring stick does not exist. For example, we cannot measure a non-existent fish. So we can't possibly measure a stretch of time that has ceased to exist or has not come into existence. Suppose it is a "present" length of time, for example, the time it takes you to read this chapter— say, an hour. But Augustine has an argument to show that even "the present hour" cannot be said to exist in the sense required.

This hour passes by means of little parts. The part that is gone is the past; the part that is left is the future. If you can think of a part of time that could not be divided into even the tiniest parts, then this part is *the present*. It darts from the future into the past so quickly that it does not have any length. For, if it has length, it has past and future parts. The present has no length. By this "whittling argument," Augustine chips away the past and future portions of any stretch of time leaving nothing but an unextended moment. By saying that the remaining moment is "unextended," we mean that it has no temporal parts into which it can be divided further. This means that no length of time exists to be measured!

Augustine concludes time resists our full understanding. But it would be inaccurate to say that he thinks time is unreal. He regards time as a *mysterious* reality inscrutable to human beings and comprehensible only to God. God is all-knowing but also eternal, so that God can know all things in time without remembering a past or expecting the future. Our time is real in a sense, but unreal when contrasted with the eternal reality of God.

4.1 FROM PRESENTISM TO FOUR-DIMENSIONALISM

Problems plague presentism. (If it is correct, time travel is impossible, but this does not serve as a reason to reject the dynamic view since time travel itself is at least as controversial as the dynamic view of time.) Augustine's paradoxical arguments conclude, first, that time exists only because it does not exist, and that there is no length of time that can be measured. He arrives at those conclusions through the following reasoning process:

(4.1)   The present is only the point at which past and future meet.

(4.2)   So any stretch of time is composed exclusively of past or future parts.

(4.3)   But the past is unreal (because it no longer exists), and

(4.4)   The future is unreal (because it does not yet exist).

(4.5)   So no stretch of time is real and no stretch of time can be measured (since you can't measure what doesn't exist).

The paradoxicality of 4.5 gives us an implicit reason to reject it. After all, not even Augustine is satisfied with his conclusions; they are to him evidence that he doesn't understand time.

In addition to the paradoxical results of Augustine's conclusion, another reason to reject his assumptions concerns his misuse of language. Augustine argues for presentism on the basis of the use of ordinary language. Augustine believes that only what exists in the present instant can be real. His puzzles depend on assumptions 4.3 and 4.4, which assume that the statement that something "is real" or "exists" *always* means that it "is real *now*" or "exists *now*." Only on an unusual interpretation of English words are these assumptions plausible. Our use of the term "is real" is tensed. Augustine exploits this to argue that the past and future, and the events that they are said to contain, are unreal. For some might assume that what is real is either timeless or always existent; if it lapses from reality, then it isn't—and wasn't—really real.

Though Augustine relies upon this fact about natural language, we can deny that there is anything of lasting philosophical importance about this aspect of the structure of language. By denying these assumptions and the intuition that natural language must reflect reality, one can deny Augustine's conclusions and reject presentism.

Two further facts about presentism are these. First, if presentism is true then no sentences about the past or the future have any truth-value. Since the future doesn't exist, it is neither true nor false to say that "I'll be there in five minutes." Statements about the past and future have the same status as claims made about gods that do not exist; such statements don't refer to anything at all, and are therefore meaningless. Second, discoveries made by twentieth-century physicists challenge assumptions of presentism. According to Einstein's special theory of relativity, time is not a momentary reality as it is for Augustine. Einstein draws on the analysis of space to argue that time is best conceived as another dimension. Rather than reality being composed of length, width and breadth, it has a fourth dimension—time. In the wake of Einstein's successes, physicists now speak of *spacetime* instead of *space* and *time*. We call the theory that emerged from those discoveries the *four-dimensionalist theory of time*.

According to the four-dimensionalist theory of time, the spatial and temporal relations of everything in the universe form a unified manifold of four dimensions: three spatial dimensions and a temporal dimension. Any event has a precise location within this spacetime manifold. Different events stand at certain "distances" from each other as measured in spatial *and* temporal terms. For example, the location of one volcanic eruption might be 2,000 miles due north from and 12 years after another eruption.

To many people four-dimensionalism seems wildly counterintuitive. It represents the universe as a forbidding, unchanging "block universe." Our experience of the perpetual flux of time, of one event's coming into existence after another, seems too real to deny. But four-dimensionalism receives favorable representation in one of the greatest of all thought experiments, H. G. Wells's science fiction novel *The Time Machine* (1895). (*Rental*: A film based on the novel was released in 2002 starring Guy Pearce.) A character called "The Time Traveler" lectures a number of guests in his home on his theory of space and time. He argues that just as "a mathematical line, a line of thickness *nil*, has no real existence . . . neither has a mathematical plane. These things are mere abstractions. . . . Nor, having only length, breadth, and thickness can a cube have a real existence." When a guest objects that "of course a solid body may exist," the Time Traveler responds,

Can a cube that does not last for any time at all have a real existence? Any real body must have extension in four directions: it must have Length, Breadth, Thickness, and—Duration. But through a natural infirmity of the flesh . . . we incline to overlook this fact. There are really four dimensions, three of which we call the three planes of Space, and a fourth, Time. There is, however, a tendency to draw an unreal distinction between the former three dimensions and the latter, because it happens that our consciousness moves intermittently in one direction along the latter from the beginning to the end of our lives.

The Time Traveler explains how the relation of time to space can be represented by a four-dimensional geometry:

Space, as our mathematicians have it, is spoken of as having three dimensions, which one may call Length, Breadth, and Thickness, and is always definable by reference to three planes, each at right angles to the others. But some philosophical people have been asking why *three* dimensions particularly—why not another direction at right angles to the other three?—and have even tried to construct a Four-Dimension geometry. Professor Simon Newcomb was expounding this to the New York Mathematical Society only a month or so ago. You know how on a flat surface, which has only two dimensions, we can represent a figure of a three-dimensional solid, and similarly they think that by models of three dimensions they could represent one of four—if they could master the perspective of the thing. . . . For instance, here is a portrait of a man at eight years old, another at fifteen, another at seventeen, another at twenty-three, and so on. All these are evidently sections, as it were, Three-Dimensional representations of his Four-Dimensional being, which is a fixed and unalterable thing.

This view of space and time has important implications for the way in which you look at yourself. Consider the idea of a geometric "slice," as shown in Figure 4.

A straight line has one dimension; it can be sliced (length-wise) at a point on it, which has no dimension. Likewise, a two-dimensional plane figure like a circle can be sliced (breadth-wise) along a one-dimensional line, and a three-dimensional solid object like a sphere can be sliced (depth-wise) along a two-dimensional surface. But can't the three-dimensional object itself be viewed as a "slice" of a four-dimensional object? You at this present instant are a time-slice of a four-dimensional object that is the "real you." This four-dimensional object contains many other time-slices of you.

This doesn't lend itself to visual representation, which gives this observation its impossible, abstract feeling. Perhaps one of the most thorough representations of the cross-temporal nature of reality occurs in *Slaughterhouse Five*. There Kurt Vonnegut describes an alien species, the Tralfamadorians, who perceive everything non-sequentially. For them the nighttime heaven is filled not with points of light but with "rarefied, luminous spaghetti." Tralfamadorians see human beings as "great millipedes—with babies' legs at one end and old people's legs at the other." They and they alone perceive us as we are—beings traveling through four dimensions.

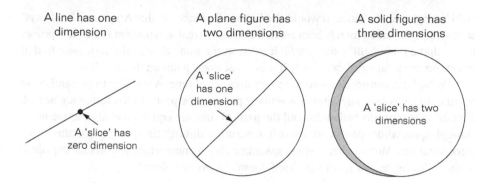

A line has one dimension	A plane figure has two dimensions	A solid figure has three dimensions

A 'slice' has zero dimension

A 'slice' has one dimension

A 'slice' has two dimensions

A physical object has four dimensions: three spatial and one temporal

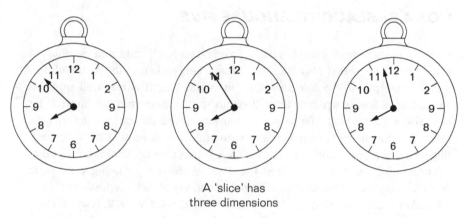

A 'slice' has three dimensions

Figure 4 Clocks

We noted that presentism appeals to facts about language in building its case, and we noted that language does not necessarily reflect reality. How does four-dimensionalism stand with respect to ordinary language? We need to take care in describing the senses in which the past and future are real on four-dimensionalism. On this view, an historical event such as Neil Armstrong's first setting foot on the moon's surface is just as real or existent as the event of your reading this sentence. But, from the fact that both events are equally real, it does not follow that both events are simultaneous.

Confusion arises from the fact the word "exists" in ordinary English is in the present tense. But it is possible (on four-dimensionalism) to distinguish between the existence of a thing or event and the time when it exists. An event or thing exists provided that it has some location within the unified manifold of spacetime. An event like the Chicago Cubs winning the World Series in the last century does not exist because they didn't win the World Series at any time during the last century. The date of an event depends on where it is located in time. So you can recognize that the event of stepping on the moon exists as truly as that of your reading this sentence, without having to claim that Armstrong is "still" stepping on the moon. It would also be a confusion to say that Armstrong is "always" stepping on the moon merely because that event is as real as a present event. It is proper to say that a thing "still" exists only if it exists at the same time as the statement to that effect. An event "always" exists only if it exists at every point on the time line.

We've been considering two proposed theories of time. According to presentism an event exists or is real only when it is actually present; the past and the future are unreal. According to four-dimensionalism all the parts of time are equally real. Just as we move through space while space stays where it is, we move through time, only in a limited, one-directional way. Motion occurs within spacetime (in a manner which you will see explained in the following section), but time itself doesn't "move" or "flow."

BOX 4.B: *SLAUGHTERHOUSE FIVE*

Kurt Vonnegut's novel *Slaughterhouse Five* juxtaposes human and non-human characters in a way that illustrates the different conceptions of the nature of time and its perception. The human soldier in World War II is removed from his experience of linear, dynamic time. Previous to that moment, time "flowed" for him. His first-person experience was of moments of time that passed one after the other. But the aliens, Tralfamadorians, encounter time directly in its static, four-dimensionalist form. In other words, for these beings time does not even appear to be presentist. Vonnegut describes the Tralfamadorians as being capable of "experiencing" any moment of their lives. The entirety of their lifetime's line is laid out before them. (*Rental*: A good film version was released in 1972. It won a Hugo Award for Best Dramatic Presentation and the Jury Prize at the Cannes film festival.)

Ted Chiang's "Understand" is a recent, elegant SF story about the perception of time. In this first-contact story, a human linguist attempts to understand the language of aliens who have landed on Earth. The language of the aliens makes unusual use of temporal concepts, which befuddles the linguist. Over the course of this novelette, the linguist does learn the language, but as she does so, she realizes that the aliens experience time in a way indescribable on presentism. In short, they experience time much in the way that Vonnegut's Tralfamadorians do. By virtue of her burgeoning fluency in their language, the linguist's personality is permanently changed in an opaque and mystical way.

4.2 THE TIME TRAVELER'S HYPOTHESIS

Of course, the theory that time is static and conjoined with space doesn't imply that it is possible to travel back through time. The Time Traveler's hypothesis is that travel to the past by some object is both logically and physically possible. An event is *logically possible* if and only if its occurrence is consistent with logical laws. Logical laws include "statement A and statement Not-A cannot both be true at the same time" and "if statement B is true, then statement B is true." An event is *physically possible* if and only if its occurrence is consistent with the conjunction of known physical laws, like the law of the conservation of matter and energy. After explaining this hypothesis, we will explain and assess attempts by advocates of the Time Traveler's hypothesis to defend it against objections.

As the Time Traveler is expounding his theory in H. G. Wells' *Time Machine*, a guest asks a challenging question, "Why cannot we move in Time as we move about in the other dimensions of Space?" The Time Traveler responds by defending the hypothesis that it is logically and physically possible to travel through time. He offers an analogy of a man in a balloon. (The first draft of Wells' story was written fifteen years before the first successful airplane flight.) Ordinarily we are confined to motion in just two dimensions, but a balloon enables us to travel upward as well. Perhaps a time machine could let us move in a temporal direction as well. Someone objects, "You cannot move at all in Time, you cannot get away from the present moment." The Time Traveler replies, "My dear sir, that is just where you are wrong. That is just where the whole world has gone wrong. We are always getting away from the present moment. Our mental existences, which are immaterial and have no dimensions, are passing along the Time-Dimension with a uniform velocity from the cradle to the grave." His point can be illustrated by a variation on the balloon metaphor.

You drift through time like a person in a balloon borne by the wind at uniform velocity. Why couldn't you attach a propeller to your time travel vehicle and accelerate or decelerate? Or why couldn't you stop or reverse your drift along the time-dimension? As a demonstration, the Time Traveler claims to be sending a small-scale time machine into the past. After it disappears the guests object that it could not have moved into the past or future: "if it traveled into the future it would still be here all this time, since it must have traveled through this time . . . But if it traveled into the past it would have been visible when we came first into this room." The Time Traveler replies that they cannot

> appreciate this machine, any more than we can the spoke of a wheel spinning, or a bullet flying through the air. If it is traveling through time fifty times or a hundred times faster than we are, if it gets through a minute while we get through a second, the impression it creates will of course be only one-fiftieth or one-hundredth of what it would make if it were not traveling in time.

Thus, whereas you ordinarily travel through time at the plodding rate of a minute per minute, a time machine would enable you to soar along at a year a minute. Later, the Time Traveler describes his vivid visual experiences as the world seems to speed up before his eyes.

Wells' discussion of the Time Traveler's hypothesis brings out a crucial theoretical difference between the presentism and four-dimensionalism. For, if the future and the past have no reality, as Augustine contends, then it is absurd to speak of traveling to them. The Time Traveler's hypothesis rests firmly on four-dimensionalism. It is hard to see how it could be coherently stated otherwise. The view that you could move into the future at an accelerated or decelerated rate seems to assume that the temporal dimension is fundamentally similar to spatial dimensions. The fact that one theory of time, but not the other, falsifies the Time Traveler's hypothesis enables us to appreciate the depth of the difference between them.

Let's now look at whether the concept of time travel to the past is logically coherent.

BOX 4.C: *STAR TREK: THE NEXT GENERATION*, "TIME'S ARROW I AND II"

Star Trek: The Original Series' "City on the Edge of Forever" is the most famous time travel episode in the *Star Trek* multiverse. No wonder why: it was written by award-winning SF author Harlan Ellison and it guest-starred Joan Collins. But the most philosophically interesting *Star Trek* time travel episode is "Time's Arrow" (season 5, episode 26; and season 6, episode 1), a two-part episode in the TNG series.

The starship *Enterprise* is summoned to San Francisco because android Commander Data's severed head—old and worn—has been found in a cavern there. Evidently, backward causation through time is possible. The mystery about how it got there takes the crew to a planet with shape-shifting, time-traveling beings who threaten nineteenth-century Earth. Data beams down and soon disappears.

He reappears in nineteenth-century San Francisco and builds a device that would allow him to send a signal to the *Enterprise*. Soon the *Enterprise* crew also transport back to that period to meet Data, vanquish the aliens and save humanity! Ahem. Needless to say, they succeed. *Enterprise* crew members confront the aliens in a melee in the cavern, at which point one of the aliens activates their time-traveling device in an explosion that severs Data's head from his body.

4.3 THE SIMPLE LOGICAL PROBLEM OF TIME TRAVEL

We'll now investigate two logical problems with time travel. The first is the more simple problem, the second the more complex. By "logical problem" we refer to philosophical objections to the **logical possibility** of time travel. The thrust of logical objections can be encapsulated as follows. Time travel (from the present to the past) implies that logically impossible events can occur. But logically impossible events cannot occur in any possible world. So, since time travel implies what is logically impossible, time travel itself is logically impossible.

Though that's the form of the objections, we need to set up some scaffolding for them. First consider how we understand movement or change. Suppose a student is walking on a college campus from the student union to the library in three minutes, passing a dormitory and a class building on the way. At *different instants* the student is at *different places* along the path. We can represent the student's movements like this:

Place	Union	Dorm	Class building	Library
Time	3:00	3:01	3:02	3:03

Movement refers to change in spatial and temporal locations. As with Vonnegut's Tralfamadorians (see Box 4.B), movement can be represented four-dimensionally as a sequence of locations with precise coordinates in spacetime. If you are "at rest," your time line will connect locations that are at the same spatial coordinates but different temporal coordinates:

Place	Union	Union	Union	Union
Time	3:00	3:01	3:02	3:03

Philosopher Donald Williams has formed one argument out of these considerations against the logical possibility of time travel.

> True motion is motion at once in time and space. Nothing can "move" in time alone anymore than in space alone, and time itself cannot "move" anymore than space itself. "Does this road go anywhere?" asks the city tourist. "No, it stays right along here," replies the countryman. Time travel, *prima facie,* then, is analyzable either as the banality that at each different moment we occupy a different moment from the one we occupied before, or the contradiction that at each different moment we occupy a different moment from the one which we are then occupying—that five minutes from now, for example, I may be a hundred years from now.[2]

Rephrased as a paradox, if time travel is possible then five minutes might be one hundred years.

His argument seems to be this:

(4.6) It is logically impossible to travel to a point one hundred years into the past in a period of five minutes.

(4.7) But if time travel is logically possible, then it is logically possible to travel to a point one hundred years into the past in a period of five minutes.

(4.8) So time travel is logically impossible.

Premises 4.6–4.8 have the form: not B; if A then B; therefore, not A. This is valid in form. But the argument is unsound because 4.6 is false. Let's explain why.

Consider how we might represent travel through time on two time-keeping devices. The first measures **internal time**. "Internal time" refers to the length of time a person ages. The time traveler's wristwatch does a good job measuring this. When he opens its clock function, he can see a readout counting up in seconds, minutes and hours. When one year of personal time has elapsed, the traveler has gotten one year older. In English we refer to internal time in periods, for example, when I say "I'll be there in five minutes." When I say this, I mean that I'll be there in a *duration of* five minutes as measured *from the moment I uttered the sentence* "I'll be there in five minutes."

The second time device measures **external time**. "External time," also called "historical time," refers to time as it is measured from outside of the flow of time. External time is, as it were, measured from a timeless, ageless God's point of view. Imagine God has a cosmic calendar that charts the timeline of all of spacetime itself, from the big bang to the heat death of the universe. He can pinpoint the epoch in which planet Earth solidified through gravitational forces on stellar dusts and he can pinpoint events that occur long after the human species goes extinct. In English the best we can do to refer to external time is by referring to points in the past or future. Phrases like "one hundred years ago" don't refer to *durations of* time; they refer to temporal *points on* God's calendar.

Before we apply this distinction to the argument in 4.6–4.8, we want to make a comparison between temporal and spatial concepts. Internal time and external time are examples of frames of reference. A *frame of reference* is a set of axes relative to a privileged point of view that are useful for measurement. We measure time in frames of reference so often that we don't even know that is what we're doing. People travel across time-zone lines all the time. One might say, "I've gained two hours on this journey." On the assumption behind the Simple Logical Problem, this is contradictory. While it does have the appearance of contradiction—after all, you can't add two hours of internal time to your life by flying across a couple of time-zones—this is only because such a statement implicitly invokes two different frames of reference. The first is the time at the place of departure and the second is the time at the destination. But frames of reference are useful for sorting out common spatial concepts too. The uses of terms like "left" and "right," and "up" and "down" are also relative to a frame of reference. If someone across the room asks you to pick up the book "on the left" this is ambiguous. You can clarify the frame of reference by asking "Your left or mine?"

This juxtaposition of two frames of spatial reference compares to the juxtaposition of two frames of temporal reference in premise 4.6. If I go from 2012 to 1912, I have traveled one hundred years through external time. If my time machine works properly, that journey might only take me five minutes of internal time. When I arrive one hundred years into the past in the year 1912, my watch informs me that five minutes have elapsed from the time I set out. These two facts are not contradictory and their conjunction is not logically impossible. 4.6 is false.

4.4 THE CHANGING THE PAST OBJECTION TO TIME TRAVEL

The *changing the past objection* is an objection based on what we can and cannot do in the past if time travel is logically possible. (Often this is called the "grandfather paradox," but it is easier to understand without involving grandpas.)

To state the argument in support of this problem, we'll need to construct more scaffolding. *Possible worlds* are logical constructions made of sets of statements, some true, others false. Every statement is either true or false in a possible world. Possible worlds exist in logical space; they are not in spacetime and so are not on the other side of the galaxy. Our world is not only possible, but actual, because, since our world exists, it contains facts that make statements true. We can identify a possible world by virtue of setting certain statements as false in it. Logicians use possible worlds to categorize and analyze the status of statements in three categories. Statements can be *contingently true*, meaning true in some possible worlds, but false in others; statements can be *necessarily true*, meaning true in every possible world; or statements can be *logically impossible*, meaning true in no possible world. For example, the statement *1 + 1 = 2* is necessarily true but the statement *The 9/11 terrorist attacks did happen* is contingent because it is true in some possible worlds (namely ours) but not true in other possible worlds. It is contingent because there is nothing about the structure of that statement that would make it either necessary or impossible. Some statements, though, such as *The basketball appears red and green all over at the same time*, are logically impossible because it cannot be made true in any possible world.

The argument is straightforward:

(4.9)   It is logically possible to time travel.

(4.10) If 4.9, then it is logically possible that I return to the past as an adult and kill my infant self.

(4.11) But it is not logically possible that I return to the past as an adult and kill my infant self.

(4.12) So, it is not logically possible to time travel.

This argument takes a reductio ad absurdum form because it assumes in 4.9 what it will reject. This argument is valid. 4.11 is justified by the fact that, if I were to have killed my infant self in the past, I would not exist as an adult. If I were not to exist as an adult, I would not be able to return to the past and kill my infant self.

It certainly appears that 4.10 is justified and true. Continuing with the first-person structure of the argument, if I am able to return to the past through time travel, then it appears as though I will take with me all the abilities I currently have. I am able to kill an infant child because I'm an adult—bigger, stronger and smarter than babies. Since I am able to do this, it appears to follow that it would be logically possible for me to kill any infant at all, including my infant self. One way of bringing out the paradoxical nature of the argument at hand is to juxtapose two statements, both of which appear obviously true. I am (a) able to kill my infant self, and I am (b) not able to kill my infant self. Since the logical possibility of time travel implies this contradiction, time travel is not logically possible.

However, this way of putting the point reveals an equivocation on the term "am able to." In (a) "able to" refers to my physical abilities to end the life of a child, which in this case happens to be an earlier version of myself upstream in the timeline. In (b) "able to" refers to what is logically possible; (b) says that it is not logically possible for me as a time traveling adult to kill my infant self. Both (a) and (b) are true once their meanings are separated, but they cannot both be true if we use the same meaning of "am able to." Explaining this **equivocation** (using one word for two different meanings) assists in diagnosing why 4.10 is false.

Though it may appear strange, once I time travel to the past there are certain actions that it is logically impossible for me to perform. This is because the past is fixed and determined. This is not to say that the time traveler doesn't act and interact with events in the past to which he travels. He behaves just like we do, and, presumably, he has a sense of purpose and freedom as he acts. However, all the events in the past have already occurred in the only way that they will ever occur, which is what makes the past the past. Many people hastily infer from that observation that time travel is impossible. They do this by making an unstated assumption that when a time traveler *performs actions* in the past, the time traveler *will change* the past.

This assumption is false, though. If I travel back in time as an adult to the year 1980 and see my infant self, then the year 1980 has always included my presence as an infant and has always included my presence as an adult. By traveling to the past I do not change it. This explains why I can't kill my infant self. I cannot change the past. So, if in the past I grew from infancy into adulthood, then it is logically impossible for me to prevent me from growing from infancy into adulthood.

It is strange to think that I might return to the past as an adult and hover over my infant self with malicious, murderous intent and nonetheless be unable to kill myself. This strangeness is in part conjured up due to our equivocation on sense of "able" and "possible." The argument does not show that time travel is logically impossible. Strange? Yes. Logically impossible? No.

4.5 THE CAUSAL LOOP PROBLEM OF TIME TRAVEL

This sense of strangeness won't go away, either. The final problem with time travel—**the causal loop problem**—is as bizarre as the previous problem. But, as in that case, what is strange is not, therefore, impossible. Causal loops are sequences of events in which A causes B, B causes C and C causes A.

The reason traveling to the past appears preposterous to us is due to our previous experience of the directional flow of time. Causes precede their effects in all our experience. It seems physically impossible that an effect precede its cause. An event is *physically impossible* if and only if it is consistent with the conjunction of known physical laws of our world. David Hume claimed that when we say that one event c causes another event d— for example, swallowing cyanide causes death—we imply several things: event c occurs *before d* in time (priority), events c and d are connected in space (propinquity), and, other things being equal, events like c are generally followed by events like d (constant conjunction). We also take for granted two general principles in trying to explain natural phenomena: *Every event has a cause* (the law of causality) and, *in similar circumstances, similar causes have similar effects* (the law of uniformity). Those compact principles explain most of our pre-theoretical beliefs about the pattern of temporal order in cause and effect relationships. People don't die first and then ingest poison.

Advocates of time travel accept the law of causality and the law of uniformity but deny that it is logically or physically necessary that the cause must always precede its effect. The causal loop problem emerges from the conceptual conflict between our intuitions about causation and the temporal order, and the implications of time travel.

A nasty version of the causal loop problem occurs in a *Futurama* episode called "Roswell That Ends Well," in which Fry travels to the past, kills his paternal 'grandpa' (before the conception of his father) and, once aware of the stakes, has sex with his grandma. Fry thereby fathers his own father and becomes his own grandpa.

The late Douglas Adams illustrates the causal loop problem quite well. In his book *Life, the Universe and Everything*, chapter 15, a poet named Lallafa is described as having written the finest poems ever to exist in any language, *Songs of the Long Land*. Lallafa wrote them about his unrequited love. He wrote them on dried Habra leaves in primitive conditions without benefit of word processors, typewriters, computers or even correcting fluid. But after the advent of time travel, enterprising correcting fluid manufacturers "wondered whether his poems might have been better still if he had had access to some high-quality correcting fluid, and whether he might be persuaded to say a few words to that effect." These businessmen traveled back in time and successfully persuaded Lallafa to endorse their product. They paid him handsomely. But as a result, Lallafa had the money to move out of the squalor of his forest encampment and into proper housing. He could buy transportation, luxury goods and other niceties, like shoes. The upshot is that Lallafa didn't lose his girlfriend after all. But the loss of his girlfriend inspired his poetry in the first place. So he never wrote the poems.

Once the correcting-fluid businessmen came back to their own time they realized their mistake. They had to return to Lallafa's time to fix the problem. When the went back, they packed Lallafa off for a week's vacation—with dried Habra leaves and copies of his poems brought from the future. Lallafa dutifully recopied all of them. But who wrote them?

In this closed "time loop" each event is caused by other events within the loop. Lallafa's poems were created because people from his future came back and gave the poems to him to write. But the correcting-fluid personnel from Lallafa's future only knew his poems because his poems made their way through recorded history. *Either* Lallafa wrote *Songs of the Long Land or* he did not. In the scenario described by Adams, he did not write them. He only *recopied* poems brought to him from the future—poems which he was credited with writing.

We can put this into form as follows:

(4.13) It is physically necessary that every event in spacetime must have a cause. (law of causality)

(4.14) The writing of *Songs* is an event in spacetime.

(4.15) But if time travel is physically possible, then it is physically possible that *Songs* has no cause in spacetime.

(4.16) But it is not physically possible that *Songs* has no cause in spacetime.

(4.17) So, it is false that time travel is physically possible.

4.13 takes the law of causality as a universal general law of our universe. The law of causality is physically necessary because it must be true in our world, even though it might be false in other possible worlds. So let's accept 4.13 and 4.14 as true. (Don't get hung up on the fact that the thing created is a set of poems and not some physical object. The argument works the same way if you substitute the name for a physical object for the poems.)

The crux of the argument is premise 4.15. It conveys the oddity that Lallafa didn't write *Songs* and the correcting-fluid businessmen didn't write *Songs*. *Songs* has no beginning or end. Given the law of causality, it must have a cause in spacetime. Here we have a serious conundrum.

To this challenging argument, a few responses come to mind, but they are tentative and each comes with its own further problems. First, one might argue, along with a famous defender of the logical possibility of time travel, David Lewis, that the writing of *Songs* is physically anomalous. In effect, this objection is directed against 4.16. The causal loop here is inexplicable in just the way that the Big Bang is inexplicable. The Big Bang violates the principle that something cannot come from nothing. Likewise, *Songs* appears to have been written by no one and come from nowhere. This response to the problem rests content with the oddity of the causal loop and the inexplicability of the authorship of *Songs*. Time travel is mysterious, and we knew that already. If events like the Big Bang are physically possible, causal loops are too. Odd and improbable, yes, but not physically impossible.

Second, another response to this argument is to defend the claim that the **physical possibility** of some instances of time travel *does not* imply the physical possibility of causal loops. This response reframes the logical relationship between the possibilities of time travel and the possibilities of the creation of closed causal loops.

When reading the engaging but complex short story in §4.10, "—All You Zombies—," you might notice that author Robert A. Heinlein portrays a clear, singular timeline without any resort to contradiction, miracles or *deus ex machina* plot twists. In other words, Heinlein uses no ad hoc explanations to fashion his time-travel story. The timeline fits snugly within the confines of four-dimensionalism. The story does involve a causal loop but does not involve any **logical impossibility**. There's funny business in the story alright, but the logic and the metaphysics of spacetime presupposed in the story are sound.

BOX 4.D: AD HOC FALLACY

One commits an ad hoc fallacy when, in response to a problem with a theory, one creates a solution for no other reason than to save the favored theory. This form of explanation is a mark of poor reasoning because the response to the problem is improperly motivated. Here's a wonderful example: Galileo turned his telescope to the moon and clearly observed a cratered, mottled surface. Church leaders instead believed that the surface of the moon and all other planets in our solar system had to be perfectly smooth (due to their commitments to Aristotle's ancient theories). How, though, could they dispute the unambiguous observations through the telescope?

They offered an ad hoc hypothesis of staggering bravado. They claimed that, though we cannot see it, the moon's cratered surface we see lay under another layer of transparent material, which happens to be perfectly smooth. This is ad hoc because their suggestion is explicitly tailored to preserve their theory, is not supported by evidence and in fact contradicts available evidence.

This example should not be taken to imply that all ad hoc hypotheses are false. Sometimes people have good intuitions as to how to account for anomalies in their theories. Famously, Einstein added the cosmological constant to his theory of relativity in order to allow for the physical possibility that the universe conforms to a steady-state model (as opposed to a Big Bang model). Though Einstein regarded this as a great blunder, subsequent physicists have realized that Einstein's hunch conforms remarkably well with developing research about the roles given to dark energy in cosmology!

4.6 CONTEMPORARY PHYSICS AND TIME TRAVEL

The discussion of time travel so far, and about its logical and causal problems, has not incorporated or extrapolated from contemporary discoveries about quantum physics. In this section we will examine the implications of the theories of relativity on time travel, and two results of mathematical models of quantum physics on time travel—closed timelike curves and the branching universe interpretation of quantum indeterminacy. Though these are highly complex theoretical constructions, understanding the basics of these issues helps show how time travel might be physically possible. In fact, debates about the last two insights from quantum physics have taken center stage in attempts to resolve causal paradoxes.

The theories of relativity make physically possible at least one form of time travel— *time travel into the future*. If a starship were to leave the gravitational system of Earth and travel to another star system at a very rapid rate, and were to return to Earth at a later date, it would experience a detectable distortion in the flow of time. This forms the premise for many SF stories. One of the earliest and best of these, Robert Heinlein's *Time for the Stars*, concerns young Tom Bartlett, who leaves his twin Pat on Earth and travels to nearby stars in the torchship *Elsie* at speeds close to the speed of light. As a former physics student, he knows that according to the "Lorentz contraction formula," ship time should pass at a much slower rate from the rate at which time passes on Earth. (The Lorentz equations, by the way, have been proven true and are part of our scientific knowledge.) Suppose the *Elsie* were to pass Earth at a velocity of one half the speed of light as measured on Earth on January 1, 3001. And suppose that Tom and Pat were to synchronize calendars then. If the *Elsie* continued to travel through space and reappeared on January 1, 3002, on Pat's Earth calendar, Tom's ship calendar would read only November 12, 3001. "That's just the special case, of course, for constant speeds," a friend reminds Tom. "It is more complicated for acceleration." Tom is very disconcerted to learn that the "time dilation" theory has not been tested.

He reflects, "But *everybody* said that once we got up near the speed of light the months would change like days. The equations *said* so." The crew members of the *Elsie* are, in effect, guinea pigs. Tom is worried: "Dying of old age in the *Elsie* was not what I had counted on. It was a grim thought, a life sentence shut up inside these still walls." Tom is relieved to learn that the equations are correct. He helps to confirm them by maintaining instantaneous telepathic contact with his twin brother, Pat. When Tom finally returns to Earth after what seems to him a few months, he finds Pat an old man of almost 90. The reason why Pat has aged so much more than Tom is that Tom quickly moved from one reference frame to the other. Tom and his shipmates are called "Rip Van Winkles" by people on Earth, and he ends the story by marrying his own great-grandniece.

Thus, if you could construct a starship and find an energy source powerful enough to accelerate your starship to a velocity close to the speed of light, you could travel through time at decelerated speed. But there is no way to travel into the past on this theory—or to recover the time you lost by traveling in space. As such, the use of the term "time travel" to describe what happens in these situations is a stretch.

However, two more recent developments in quantum physics seem to indicate that time travel *to the past* might be physically possible. Theoretical work in physics on closed timelike curves, or "CTCs," indicates that it is physically possible for a quantum object to travel from one point of spacetime to another earlier point. A closed timelike curve is a curvature of spacetime that has the structure of a loop. To understand closed timelike curves, recall that in spacetime an object or person endures as a four-dimensional "worm." The mass of certain objects, like stars, black holes and other interstellar phenomena can be great enough to cause distortions in the worms of other smaller objects. The way many physicists understand the relevant equations leads them to conclude that it is possible these distortions could result in a closed timelike curve. This implies that at some point in the spacetime worm of an object, an object may enter a loop that reconnects with an earlier point in the spacetime trajectory of that very same object's worm.

Right now the physical possibility of closed timelike curves follows from the interpretations of the general and special theories of relativity, and various formulas in quantum mechanics. This is so far a purely theoretical enterprise; no one has solid evidence that there are closed timelike curves in the natural world, let alone that information or objects have traveled through closed timelike curves to an earlier point in spacetime.

David Deutsch and Michael Lockwood have argued that quantum physics may provide a key to showing time travel is physically possible. This is because some analyses of quantum physics propose that, at the quantum level, the structure of spacetime is permeated by numerous closed timelike curves. If so, then time travel at the subatomic level may be routinely taking place.

These authors make another salient point about the role of quantum physics in this context, specifically about *quantum indeterminacy*. This term refers to the thesis that, for some events at the quantum level, certain physical laws might fail. Instead, the physicist must resort to statistical generalizations. One helpful example of this phenomenon regards neutron decay. The quantum physicist can make an accurate generalization about a certain neutron that its decay will most likely occur in one hour. Some neutrons of this type will decay immediately upon exposure while others will remain stable for an indefinite period. There is no fact of the matter when a given neutron will decay because its behavior is random.

How do we account for this indeterminacy at the level of the building blocks of physical reality? We can't say that different neutrons (of the same type) contain different internal properties because all neutrons (of the same type) possess no internal differences. Deutsch and Lockwood favor an interpretation of this phenomenon according to which there are many universes, which collectively inhabit a "multiverse." Their interpretation calls for a radical restructuring of our intuitions about the universe. Our universe is not all there is, was, and ever will be because, in this interpretation of quantum mechanics, there are an infinite number of universes. For every point at which the neutron could decay, it does decay—whether in our universe or in some other parallel universe. Let's call this very counterintuitive theory the "branching universe" interpretation of quantum physics. This position contains important resources for making time travel physically possible.

If the branching universe interpretation can be applied to physical events above the quantum level, then this can be used to show that time travel is possible without the creation of causal loops. Any movement out of a spacetime line would effectively generate a new spacetime line. This means that if I depart from the spacetime line that I have inhabited thus far and travel through a closed timelike curve, I would not be able to travel to a point earlier in this same spacetime line. By virtue of reaching that point, I would generate a new spacetime line.

So suppose I travel through a CTC and find what appears to be my infant self sleeping in a crib. I say that it "appears" to be me because the baby is in what appears to be my old room and cared for by people who appear to be my parents. In this instance of travel to the past, there is nothing preventing me from killing the person that appears to be my infant self. That is because, despite appearances, it isn't my infant self. It is possible for me to kill this infant baby because that copy of me occupies a different spacetime line, a different universe, than I do—or rather, than I did until I entered the closed timelike curve.

As strange as it may seem, I could remain in this spacetime line to which I traveled and meet my parallel self. This assumes that all other things are equal, for example that my life span allows it and that I don't kill *his* grandfather!

This is the way the branching universe interpretation successfully avoids the causal loop problem. But that gain comes at a cost. While I may travel to a past, *it is not my very own past*. More exactly, if we assume that I am identical to my four-dimensional spacetime worm, then I do not travel back to *my* past. (For personal identity, see Chapter 6.) In this context I would be traveling back to a different universe. So our response to the changing the past objection still holds: the past is fixed and determinate. You cannot change your past. You cannot change any past. However, if you travel to another universe and muck around there, you are ipso facto not changing the past of that universe—you are merely causing events in that universe just as you cause events in our universe today. For this reason we shouldn't even describe this form of travel as time travel since it is not travel back in time to a point earlier along our own timeline.

Examples of the use of a multiverse abound in science fiction. The designers of the MYST franchise of games use the multiverse as a central plotting feature for actions of the characters. One universe will be described, but characters must find a way to open up that universe and explore it. In *The One*, the lead character, Yu-Law, was working for a global police force charged with the task of managing the network of wormholes on Earth that lead to other parallel universes. Now, however, he has become a super-criminal and is hunting down and killing all the other versions of himself in nearby parallel universes. (*Rental*: *The One*, with Jet Li. Action and special effects, with interesting speculation about the bureaucracy that would grow up around the discovery of wormholes.)

4.7 PHILOSOPHERS ON ABSOLUTE AND RELATIVE SPACE

We've used the terms "spacetime" and "relativity" in this chapter so far. In this section we'll explain why space is **relative** and not absolute. The historical development of theories of space runs parallel to the development of debates about time, since positions in both debates concern whether time and space are relative to us (or to someone) or are absolute and fixed.

Scientists like Isaac Newton conceived of space as absolute and fixed, as though it were created and placed where it is by a deity. Newton (1643–1727) developed a unified theory about the mechanical relationships between bodies and forces acting upon them in his *Mathematical Principles of Natural Philosophy* (1687). To help you see problems about the nature of space from Newton's point of view, consider this problem he was facing. Earth moves in several different ways: (a) Earth wobbles on its axis (the "Chandler wobble"); (b) it rotates on its axis at about 0.5 kilometers per second at the equator; (c) it revolves around the sun at 30 kps; (d) the entire solar system is flying around relative to our Milky Way galaxy at about 250 kps; (e) the Milky Way is moving in its own direction within our galaxy cluster, the "Local Group," at about 300 kps; and (f) the Local Group is speeding towards an incredibly dense stellar formation called the "Great Attractor" at 600 kps—that is a whopping 1.34 million miles per hour.

To measure speeds, we measure the movement of objects relative to other objects. When a policewoman pulls you over for speeding, she'll tell you how fast you were driving by telling you your distanced traveled per unit of time. That ratio will be relative to something moving zero miles on the surface of Earth per hour. The ratio the policewoman gives you is relative to objects which are stationary on Earth. You are actually hurtling through space at more than a million miles an hour since your speed can be measured as relative to the "stationary" Great Attractor.

In the car example, we have two distinct spaces. The driver of the car is moving at 70 mph but the onlooker, standing at the side of the highway, is stationary. *From the point of view of the onlooker* the driver is moving at 70 mph, and *from the point of view of the driver* the onlooker is stationary. From the point of view of someone on the Sun, the velocities of the onlooker and the driver are the same. In our discussion of time travel we distinguished between different frames of reference from within which time can be measured. Likewise, space and motion can be measured from within different frames of reference.

Newton's goal was to identify the laws that govern movements of bodies, but now we can ask an important question: in which frame of reference did Newton want his laws to hold? This is hard to answer since his laws cannot hold in all frames of reference. Newton's First Law of Motion says that objects in uniform motion tend to stay in that motion and objects at rest tend to stay at rest, unless an outside force acts on them. This is known as the "law of inertia." But Newton's concept of an object in motion as it appears in this law doesn't specify any frame of reference. This implies that an analysis of a car's motion down the highway through Newton's laws of motion will yield different results depending upon which frame of reference we choose.

One solution available to Newton is to suppose for the sake of argument that there is at least one frame of reference that was absolute and not relative. This is called **absolute space**. Even if everything in the universe is moving, even if the universe is itself moving, absolute space implies that the boundaries of space are unmoving and invariant. On this model space is a container inhabited by the cosmos. Space is independent and not defined by the bodies that it contains. Newton's laws of motion are fashioned to apply to objects moving in absolute space.

BOX 4.E: FOUCAULT'S PENDULUM

French physicist Leon Foucault (1819–1868) created a pendulum, a device that allows an object to swing freely under the influence of gravity, in order to display the effects of the rotation of Earth. (He also invented the gyroscope.) Bodies on Earth inhabit a *rotating* frame of reference, and when other forces are eliminated—

wind drag, for example—this Coriolis effect can be observed in carefully crafted pendula.

Foucault's pendulum cleverly illustrates the fact that we occupy a rotating frame of reference. Imagine placing the pendulum at a latitude of 30 degrees in the northern hemisphere, where the centripetal force of the Earth's rotation upon the bodies is substantial. Suppose the bob—the metal ball at the end of the pendulum's wire—was dropped toward due north at a fixed star like Polaris. The inertia of the bob causes it to move due north and back due south. But the centripetal force of Earth's rotation causes the bob slowly to alter direction as it circumnavigates Earth's axis. A better way to describe this effect is to say that Earth is rotating under the pendulum! This bob proceeds clockwise at the noticeable rate of 7.5 degrees per hour.

Now imagine suspending a pendulum over the North Pole. Despite Earth's spinning underneath such a pendulum, it would maintain the same angular oscillation throughout its life. If initially dropped directly facing the sun, the bob on the pendulum will move toward and away from the sun as Earth spins under it. The period of oscillation of a polar pendulum would be precisely 24 hours. (What would the pendulum do at the equator?)

The relevance of Foucault's pendulum for the present chapter is that this device allows someone on Earth to perceive the effects of her rotating frame of reference. This is quite a feat since the uniform motion of everything on Earth prevents us from obtaining a fixed reference point from which the effects of our mutual rotational motion can be observed. The effects demonstrated by Foucault's pendulum offer an experimental response to the medieval belief in the stationary Earth. The pendulum shows that the behavior of bodies deviates from Newton's assumption that there is an absolute space.

From a philosophical point of view, a central challenge to the hypothesis of absolute space is its unverifiability through experiment. That is, through no experiment can we determine whether we inhabit an absolute space. In the absence of such a test, philosophers objected to the existence of absolute space with the following thought experiment. For the purposes of a reductio ad absurdum argument, suppose space is absolute. Now imagine a god looks down on the "container" of absolute space and rotates it 180 degrees. From this god's point of view, the side of the container that was formerly on her left is now on her right, and vice-versa. Newton must say that all the bodies in space have changed their locations, despite the fact that it is in principle impossible to discern this change experimentally. This implies that Newton commits himself to an unempirical methodological principle. In other words, science experiments can't test his theory of absolute space even though the job of science is to test such theories.

Gottfried Leibniz (1646–1716), a brilliant German polymath, first offered that thought experiment as an argument against absolute space. But Leibniz develops it differently.

Rather than state the argument through an appeal to the unverifiability of absolute space, Leibniz crafts his argument in a theological idiom. He accomplishes this with the help of supplementary principles, including the *principle of sufficient reason*. In brief form, this grand principle states that "nothing happens without a reason why it should be so, rather than otherwise." Leibniz applies his understanding of God's perfect rationality displayed through the principle of sufficient reason to absolute space by arguing that God would have reason to orient the container of absolute space in one way rather than another. Concepts such as "east" and "west" take meaning from their use within our space; they make no sense applied to absolute space itself. When God creates and sets the container of absolute space into the void, God can have no reason to orient it one way or the other. Since there is no reason that explains the orientation of absolute space, absolute space violates the principle of sufficient reason. So, absolute space does not exist. Though Leibniz states this argument in theological terms, the point closely resembles arguments against absolute space from considerations about unverifiability.

This controversy did not prevent scientists from using Newton's mechanics to great effect in efforts to understand the movements of bodies. This is in part because this debate, at that time, had no discernible experimental consequences. Newton's laws operate quite well when restricted to an earthly environment (see Box 4.E). Nonetheless, the assumption of absolute space created a clear conceptual tension with work on the relativity of spacetime in the early twentieth century.

Leibniz argues instead that space and time are both defined relationally, in other words, they are characterized in terms of their contents. Time is the succession of sequences of moments and space is the arrangement of bodies. Since the early eighteenth century, scientific developments have supported that theory over Newton's. At the end of the nineteenth century, physics was ready for Einstein's special theory of relativity, unveiled in 1905. Einstein affirmed that measurements of distance and duration are relative to the observer's frame of reference. The results include such counterintuitive effects as "time dilation," mentioned in §4.5 in the context of Robert Heinlein's *Time for the Stars*. Less well known are parallel consequences about space. For example, special relativity creates the ladder paradox. At rest our ladder is too long to fit inside the garage, but moving at one tenth (or more) of the speed of light, the ladder contracts and thus can fit into the garage!

4.8 SUMMARY

We've developed two theories of time—presentism and four-dimensionalism—and have assessed their plausibility. Presentism implies that the only time is the present, and four-dimensionalism implies that time is a stable fourth dimension. We resolved Augustine's paradoxical thoughts about time by endorsing four-dimensionalism. We then explored the possibility of time travel given four-dimensionalism. This required us to introduce the concept of a frame of reference.

To time travel to the past requires sending an object or person back to an earlier point along its own timeline. We analyzed three conceptual problems with time travel: the simple logical problem, on which time travel implies that I can travel 100 years through time in five minutes, which is alleged to be logically impossible; the changing the past objection, on which time travel implies I could return to the past and kill my earlier self, which is alleged to be metaphysically impossible; and the causal loop problem, on which objects reintroduced at earlier points along a timeline may have no cause, which violates the law of causality. We argued that none of these objections show that time travel is logically, metaphysically or physically impossible. Nonetheless, the final problem in particular suggests that time travel must be mysterious.

Following a discussion of these conceptual issues, we introduced the branching universe interpretation of quantum physics and developed its relevance to the question of time travel. If you were to travel through a closed timelike curve, as described by quantum physics, you would return to an "earlier" point. But the scare quotes are important since the point in the past to which you traveled would not be a point on the same timeline that you had earlier occupied. Travel through a CTC leads to a destination of a different spacetime frame of reference. This form of time travel offers a different response to the changing the past objection: you can change the past if you arrive at a different universe after you time travel since *that* past is not *your* past. However, for that very reason, many do not consider this form of "time travel" time travel at all.

Last, we discussed an historical dialogue about absolute and relative theories of space and time. Debate about these issues arose in the terms of the physics of the seventeenth and eighteenth centuries. Participants in those conversations used theological terms to explain space and time. For Isaac Newton, absolute space was God's "sensorium," or sensory apparatus, but for Gottfried Leibniz, the hypothesis that space is absolute was an offense against God's perfect rationality.

4.9 ABOUT THE READINGS

Like Philip K. Dick, multiple-award winning Robert Heinlein (1907–1988) is an author of rock star proportions. "—All You Zombies—" is a classic time travel tale that takes every imaginable twist such a story could. As is typical of stories in this sub-genre, part of the fun lies in figuring them out, so we won't spoil it for you here. Heinlein sets out to show that it is not only possible to be your own grandfather, but it is also possible to be much, much more. However, be warned: the plotting of this story is complex, and it may require multiple readings. And ready your minds for the contemplation of the nearly impossible— "nearly" because, if time travel is logically and physically possible, then so is the conclusion of this story.

Saint Augustine (354–430), of course, would hold that this is impossible. In the historical reading for this chapter, you'll see for yourselves exactly why he says so. Augustine's concept of time is born of introspection about commonsense concepts of "past" and "future." As you read this excerpt from Augustine's landmark *Confessions*, do your best to track his definitions of those and similar terms. (Since this work takes the form of a confession or meditation, Augustine frequently uses the second person to refer to God.)

The popularity of time travel as a research topic in contemporary analytic philosophy has grown and grown ever since David Lewis published "The Paradoxes of Time Travel" in 1976. In that work, he argued that a certain form of time travel to the past was possible by disarming several paradoxes alleging that it was not. In the 30 or so years since that work, a number of new insights and developments have been made in philosophical thinking about time travel. Franz Kiekeben, of The Ohio State University, walks us through three problems. The questions he addresses are: What can time travelers change about the past? Are causal loops, of the kind seen in the story to follow, possible? Last, is it possible that the entire universe travel back in time?

4.10 "—ALL YOU ZOMBIES—," BY ROBERT HEINLEIN

2217 Time Zone V (EST) 7 Nov. 1970-NTC—"Pop's Place": I was polishing a brandy snifter when the Unmarried Mother came in. I noted the time—10:17 P. M., zone five, or eastern time, November 7th, 1970. Temporal agents always notice time and date; we must.

The Unmarried Mother was a man twenty-five years old, no taller than I am, childish features and a touchy temper. I didn't like his looks—I never had—but he was a lad I was here to recruit, he was my boy. I gave him my best barkeep's smile.

Maybe I'm too critical. He wasn't swish; his nickname came from what he always said when some nosy type asked him his line: "I'm an unmarried mother." If he felt less than murderous he would add: "at four cents a word. I write confession stories."

If he felt nasty, he would wait for somebody to make something of it. He had a lethal style of infighting, like a female cop—one reason I wanted him. Not the only one.

He had a load on, and his face showed that he despised people more than usual. Silently I poured a double shot of Old Underwear and left the bottle. He drank it, poured another.

I wiped the bar top. "How's the 'Unmarried Mother' racket?"

His fingers tightened on the glass and he seemed about to throw it at me; I felt for the sap under the bar. In temporal manipulation you try to figure everything, but there are so many factors that you never take needless risks.

I saw him relax that tiny amount they teach you to watch for in the Bureau's training school. "Sorry," I said. "Just asking, 'How's business?' Make it 'How's the weather?'"

He looked sour. "Business is okay. I write 'em, they print 'em, I eat."

I poured myself one, leaned toward him. "Matter of fact," I said, "you write a nice stick—I've sampled a few. You have an amazingly sure touch with the woman's angle."

It was a slip I had to risk; he never admitted what pen-names he used. But he was boiled enough to pick up only the last: "'Woman's angle!'" he repeated with a snort. "Yeah, I know the woman's angle. I should."

"So?" I said doubtfully. "Sisters?"

"No. You wouldn't believe me if I told you."

"Now, now," I answered mildly, "bartenders and psychiatrists learn that nothing is stranger than truth. Why, son, if you heard the stories I do—well, you'd make yourself rich. Incredible."

"You don't know what 'incredible' means!"

"So? Nothing astonishes me. I've always heard worse."

He snorted again. "Want to bet the rest of the bottle?"

"I'll bet a full bottle." I placed one on the bar.

"Well—" I signaled my other bartender to handle the trade. We were at the far end, a single-stool space that I kept private by loading the bar top by it with jars of pickled eggs and other clutter. A few were at the other end watching the fights and somebody was playing the juke box—private as a bed where we were.

"Okay," he began, "to start with, I'm a bastard."

"No distinction around here," I said.

"I mean it," he snapped. "My parents weren't married."

"Still no distinction," I insisted. "Neither were mine."

"When—" He stopped, gave me the first warm look I ever saw on him. "You mean that?"

"I do. A one-hundred-percent bastard. In fact," I added, "no one in my family ever marries. All bastards."

"Don't try to top me—*you're* married." He pointed at my ring.

"Oh, that." I showed it to him. "It just looks like a wedding ring; I wear it to keep women off." It is an antique I bought in 1985 from a fellow operative—he had fetched it from pre-Christian Crete. "The Worm Ouroboros . . . the World Snake that eats its own tail, forever without end. A symbol of the Great Paradox."

He barely glanced at it. "If you're really a bastard, you know how it feels. When I was a little girl—"

"Wups!" I said. "Did I hear you correctly?"

"'Who's telling this story? When I was a little girl—Look, ever hear of Christine Jorgenson? Or Roberta Cowell?"

"Uh, sex-change cases? You're trying to tell me—"

"Don't interrupt or so help me, I won't talk. I was a foundling, left at an orphanage in Cleveland in 1945 when I was a month old. When I was a little girl, I envied kids with parents. Then, when I learned about sex—and, believe me, Pop, you learn fast in an orphanage—"

"I know."

"—I made a solemn vow that any kid of mine would have both a pop and a mom. It kept me 'pure,' quite a feat in that vicinity—I had to learn to fight to manage it. Then I got older and realized I stood darn little chance of getting married—for the same reason I hadn't been adopted." He scowled. "I was horse-faced and buck-toothed, flat-chested and straight-haired."

"You don't look any worse than I do."

"Who cares how a barkeep looks? Or a writer? But people wanting to adopt pick little blue-eyed golden-haired morons. Later on, the boys want bulging breasts, a cute face, and an Oh-you-wonderful-male manner." He shrugged. "I couldn't compete. So I decided to join the W.E.N.C.H.E.S."

"Eh?"

"Women's Emergency National Corps, Hospitality & Entertainment Section, what they now call 'Space Angels'—Auxiliary Nursing Group, Extraterrestrial Legions."

I knew both terms, once I had them chronized. We use still a third name, it's that elite military service corps: Women's Hospitality Order Refortifying & Encouraging Spacemen. Vocabulary shift is the worst hurdle in time-jumps—did you know that "service station" once meant a dispensary for petroleum fractions? Once on an assignment in the Churchill Era, a woman said to me, "Meet me at the service station next door"—which is not what it sounds; a service station (then) wouldn't have a bed in it.

He went on: "It was when they first admitted you can't send men into space for months and years and not relieve the tension. You remember how the wowsers screamed?—that improved my chance, since volunteers were scarce. A gal had to be respectable, preferably virgin (they liked to train them from scratch), above average mentally, and stable emotionally. But most volunteers were old hookers, or neurotics who would crack up ten days off Earth. So I didn't need looks; if they accepted me, they would fix my buck teeth, put a wave in my hair, teach me to walk and dance and how to listen to a man pleasingly, and everything else—plus training for the prime duties. They would even use plastic surgery if it would help—nothing too good for Our Boys.

"Best yet, they made sure you didn't get pregnant during your enlistment—and you were almost certain to marry at the end of your hitch. Same way today, A.N.G.E.L.S. marry spacers—they talk the language.

"When I was eighteen I was placed as a 'mother's helper.' This family simply wanted a cheap servant, but I didn't mind as I couldn't enlist 'til I was twenty-one. I did housework and went to night school—pretending to continue my high school typing and shorthand but going to a charm class instead, to better my chances for enlistment.

"Then I met this city slicker with his hundred-dollar bills." He scowled. "The no-good actually did have a wad of hundred-dollar bills. He showed me one night, told me to help myself.

"But I didn't. I liked him. He was the first man I ever met who was nice to me without trying games with me. I quit night school to see him oftener. It was the happiest time of my life.

"Then one night in the park the games began."

He stopped. I said, "And then?"

"And then *nothing*! I never saw him again. He walked me home and told me he loved me—and kissed me good-night and never came back." He looked grim. "If I could find him, I'd kill him!"

"Well," I sympathized, "I know how you feel. But killing him—just for doing what comes naturally—hmm . . . Did you struggle?"

"Huh? What's that got to do with it?"

"Quite a bit. Maybe he deserves a couple of broken arms for running out on you, but—"

"He deserves worse than that! Wait till you hear. Somehow I kept anyone from suspecting and decided it was all for the best. I hadn't really loved him and probably would never love anybody—and I was more eager to join the W.E.N.C.H.E.S. than ever. I wasn't disqualified, they didn't insist on virgins. I cheered up.

"It wasn't until my skirts got tight that I realized."

"Pregnant?"

"He had me higher 'n a kite! Those skinflints I lived with ignored it as long as I could work—then kicked me out, and the orphanage wouldn't take me back. I landed in a charity ward surrounded by other big bellies and trotted bedpans until my time came.

"One night I found myself on an operating table, with a nurse saying, 'Relax. Now breathe deeply.'

"I woke up in bed, numb from the chest down. My surgeon came in. 'How do you feel?' he says cheerfully.

"'Like a mummy.'

"'Naturally. You're wrapped like one and full of dope to keep you numb. You'll get well—but a Cesarean isn't a hangnail.'

"'Cesarean,' I said. 'Doc—*did I lose the baby*?'

"'Oh, no. Your baby's fine.'

"'Oh, Boy or girl?'

"'A healthy little girl. Five pounds, three ounces.'

"I relaxed. It's something, to have made a baby. I told myself I would go somewhere and tack 'Mrs.' on my name and let the kid think her papa was dead—no orphanage for *my* kid!

"But the surgeon was talking. 'Tell me, uh—' He avoided my name. '—did you ever think your glandular setup was odd?'

"I said, 'Huh? Of course not. What are you driving at?'

"He hesitated. 'I'll give you this in one dose, then a hypo to let you sleep off your jitters. You'll have 'em.'

"'Why?' I demanded.

"'Ever hear of that Scottish physician who was female until she was thirty-five?— then had surgery and became legally and medically a man? Got married. All okay.'

"'What's that got to do with me?'

"'That's what I'm saying. You're a man.'

"I tried to sit up. '*What*?'

"'Take it easy. When I opened you, I found a mess. I sent for the Chief of Surgery while I got the baby out, then we held a consultation with you on the table—and worked for hours to salvage what we could. You had two full sets of organs, both immature, but with the female set well enough developed for you to have a baby. They could never be any use to you again, so we took them out and rearranged things so that you can develop properly as a man.' He put a hand on me. "Don't worry. You're young, your bones will readjust, we'll watch your glandular balance—and make a fine young man out of you.'

"I started to cry. 'What about my *baby*?'

"'Well, you can't nurse her, you haven't milk enough for a kitten. If I were you, I wouldn't see her—put her up for adoption.'

"'No!'

"He shrugged. 'The choice is yours; you're her mother—well, her parent. But don't worry now; we'll get you well first.'

"Next day they let me see the kid and I saw her daily—trying to get used to her. I had never seen a brand-new baby and had no idea how awful they look—my daughter looked like an orange monkey. My feelings changed to cold determination to do right by her. But four weeks later that didn't mean anything."

"Eh?"

"She was snatched."

"'Snatched?"

The Unmarried Mother almost knocked over the bottle we had bet. "Kidnapped—stolen from the hospital nursery!" He breathed hard. "How's that for taking the last a man's got to live for?"

"A bad deal," I agreed. "Let's pour you another. No clues?"

"Nothing the police could trace. Somebody came to see her, claimed to be her uncle. While the nurse had her back turned, he walked out with her."

"Description?"

"Just a man, with a face-shaped face, like yours or mine." He frowned. "I think it was the baby's father. The nurse swore it was an older man but he probably used makeup. Who else would swipe my baby? Childless women pull such stunts—but whoever heard of a man doing it?"

"What happened to you then?"

"Eleven more months of that grim place and three operations. In four months I started to grow a beard; before I was out I was shaving regularly . . . and no longer doubted that I was male." He grinned wryly. "I was staring down nurses' necklines."

"Well," I said, "seems to me you came through okay. Here you are, a normal man, making good money, no real troubles. And the life of a female is not an easy one."

He glared at me. "A lot you know about it!"

"So?"

"Ever hear the expression 'a ruined woman'?"

"Mmm, years ago. Doesn't mean much today."

"I was as ruined as a woman can be; that bum *really* ruined me—I was no longer a woman . . . and I didn't know *how* to be a man."

"Takes getting used to, I suppose."

"You have no idea. I don't mean learning how to dress, or not walking into the wrong rest room; I learned those in the hospital. But how could I *live*? What job could I get? Hell, I couldn't even drive a car, I didn't know a trade; I couldn't do manual labor—too much scar tissue, too tender.

"I hated him for having ruined me for the W.E.N.C.H.E.S., too, but I didn't know how much until I tried to join the Space Corps instead. One look at my belly and I was marked unfit for military service. The medical officer spent time on me just from curiosity; he had read about my case.

"So I changed my name and came to New York. I got by as a fry cook, then rented a typewriter and set myself up as a public stenographer—what a laugh! In four months I typed four letters and one manuscript. The manuscript was for *Real Life Tales* and a waste of paper, but the goof who wrote it sold it. Which gave me an idea; I bought a stack of confession magazines and studied them." He looked cynical. "Now you know how I get the authentic woman's angle on an unmarried-mother story . . . through the only version I haven't sold—the true one. Do I win the bottle?"

I pushed it toward him. I was upset myself, but there was work to do. I said, "Son, you still want to lay hands on that so-and-so?"

His eyes lighted up—a feral gleam.

"Hold it!" I said. "You wouldn't kill him?"

He chuckled nastily. "Try me."

"Take it easy. I know more about it than you think I do. I can help you. I know where he is."

He reached across the bar. "*Where is he*?"

I said softly, "Let go my shirt, sonny—or you'll land in the alley and we'll tell the cops you fainted." I showed him the sap.

He let go. "Sorry. But where is he?" He looked at me. "And how do you know so much?"

"All in good time. There are records—hospital records, orphanage records, medical records. The matron of your orphanage was Mrs. Fetherage—right? She was followed by Mrs. Gruenstein—right? Your name, as a girl, was 'Jane'—right? And you didn't tell me any of this—right?"

I had him baffled and a bit scared. "What's this? You trying to make trouble for me?"

"No indeed. I've your welfare at heart. I can put this character in your lap. You do to him as you see fit—and I guarantee that you'll get away with it. But I don't think you'll kill him. You'd be nuts to—and you aren't nuts. Not quite."

He brushed it aside. "Cut the noise. Where is he?"

I poured him a short one; he was drunk, but anger was offsetting it. "Not so fast. I do something for you—you do something for me."

"Uh . . . what?"

"You don't like your work. What would you say to high pay, steady work, unlimited expense account, your own boss on the job, and lots of variety and adventure?"

He stared. "I'd say, 'Get those goddamn reindeer off my roof!' Shove it, Pop—there's no such job."

"Okay, put it this way: I hand him to you, you settle with him, then try my job. If it's not all I claim—well, I can't hold you."

He was wavering; the last drink did it "When d'yuh d'liver 'im?" he said thickly.

"If it's a deal—*right now*!"

He shoved out his hand. "It's a deal!"

I nodded to my assistant to watch both ends, noted the time—2300—started to duck through the gate under the bar—when the juke box blared out: "I'm My Own Grandpaw!" The service man had orders to load it with Americana and classics because I couldn't stomach the "music" of 1970, but I hadn't known that tape was in it. I called out, "Shut that off! Give the customer his money back." I added, "Storeroom, back in a moment," and headed there with my Unmarried Mother following.

It was down the passage across from the johns, a steel door to which no one but my day manager and myself had a key; inside was a door to an inner room to which only I had a key. We went there.

He looked blearily around at windowless walls. "Where is 'e?"

"Right away." I opened a case, the only thing in the room; it was a U.S.F.F. Co-ordinates Transformer Field Kit, series 1992, Mod. II—a beauty, no moving parts, weight twenty-three kilos fully charged, and shaped to pass as a suitcase. I had adjusted it precisely earlier that day; all I had to do was to shake out the metal net which limits the transformation field.

Which I did. "What's that?" he demanded.

"Time machine," I said and tossed the net over us.

"Hey!" he yelled and stepped back. There is a technique to this; the net has to be thrown so that the subject will instinctively step back *onto* the metal mesh, then you close the net with both of you inside completely—else you might leave shoe soles behind or a piece of foot, or scoop up a slice of floor. But that's all the skill it takes. Some agents con a subject into the net; I tell the truth and use that instant of utter astonishment to flip the switch. Which I did.

1030-VI-3 April 1963—Cleveland, Ohio-Apex Bldg.: "Hey!" he repeated. "Take this damn thing off!"

"Sorry," I apologized and did so, stuffed the net into the case, closed it. "You said you wanted to find him."

"But—you said that was a time machine!"

I pointed out a window. "Does that look like November? Or New York?" While he was gawking at new buds and spring weather, I reopened the case, took out a packet of hundred-dollar bills, checked that the numbers and signatures were compatible with 1963. The Temporal Bureau doesn't care how much you spend (it costs nothing) but they don't like unnecessary anachronisms. Too many mistakes, and a general court-martial will exile you for a year in a nasty period, say 1974 with its strict rationing and forced labor. I never make such mistakes, the money was okay.

He turned around and said, "What happened?"

"He's here. Go outside and take him. Here's expense money." I shoved it at him and added, "Settle him, then I'll pick you up."

Hundred-dollar bills have a hypnotic effect on a person not used to them. He was thumbing them unbelievingly as I eased him into the hall, locked him out. The next jump was easy, a small shift in era.

7100-VI-10 March 1964—Cleveland-Apex Bldg.: There was a notice under the door saying that my lease expired next week; otherwise the room looked as it had a moment before. Outside, trees were bare and snow threatened; I hurried, stopping only for contemporary money and a coat, hat, and topcoat I had left there when I leased the room. I hired a car, went to the hospital. It took twenty minutes to bore the nursery attendant to the point where I could swipe the baby without being noticed. We went back to the Apex Building. This dial setting was more involved, as the building did not yet exist in 1945. But I had precalculated it.

0100-VI-20 Sept. 1945—Cleveland-Skyview Motel: Field kit, baby, and I arrived in a motel outside town. Earlier I had registered as "Gregory Johnson, Warren, Ohio," so we arrived in a room with curtains closed, windows locked, and doors bolted, and the floor cleared to allow for waver as the machine hunts. You can get a nasty bruise from a chair where it shouldn't be—not the chair, of course, but backlash from the field.

No trouble. Jane was sleeping soundly; I carried her out, put her in a grocery box on the seat of a car I had provided earlier, drove to the orphanage, put her on the steps, drove two blocks to a "service station" (the petroleum-products sort) and phoned the orphanage, drove back in time to see them taking the box inside, kept going and abandoned the car near the motel—walked to it and jumped forward to the Apex Building in 1963.

2200-VI-24 April 1963—Cleveland-Apex Bldg.: I had cut the time rather fine—temporal accuracy depends on span, except on return to zero. If I had it right, Jane was discovering, out in the park this balmy spring night, that she wasn't quite as "nice" a girl as she had thought. I grabbed a taxi to the home of those skinflints, had the hackie wait around a comer while I lurked in shadows.

Presently I spotted them down the street, arms around each other. He took her up on the porch and made a long job of kissing her good night—longer than I thought. Then she went in and he came down the walk, turned away. I slid into step and hooked an arm in his. "That's all, son." I announced quietly. "I'm back to pick you up."

"*You!*" He gasped and caught his breath.

"Me. Now you know who *he* is—and after you think it over you'll know who you are . . . and if you think hard enough, you'll figure out who the baby is . . . and who I am."

He didn't answer; he was badly shaken. It's a shock to have it proved to you that you can't resist seducing yourself. I took him to the Apex Building and we jumped again.

2300-VIII, 12 Aug. 1985—Sub Rockies Base: I woke the duty sergeant, showed my I.D., told the sergeant to bed my companion down with a happy pill and recruit him in the morning. The sergeant looked sour, but rank is rank, regardless of era; he did what I said—thinking, no doubt, that the next time we met he might be the colonel and I the sergeant. Which can happen in our corps. "What name?" he asked.

I wrote it out. He raised his eyebrows. "Like so, eh? *Hmm—*"

"You just do your job, Sergeant." I turned to my companion.

"Son, your troubles are over. You're about to start the best job a man ever held—and you'll do well. I *know*."

"That you will!" agreed the sergeant. "Look at me—born in 1917—still around, still young, still enjoying life." I went back to the jump room, set everything on preselected zero.

2301-V-7 Nov. 1970-NYC—'Pop's Place': I came out of the storeroom carrying a fifth of Drambuie to account for the minute I had been gone. My assistant was arguing with the customer who had been playing *I'm My Own Grandpaw!* I said, "Oh, let him play it, then unplug it." I was very tired.

It's rough, but somebody must do it, and it's very hard to recruit anyone in the later years, since the Mistake of 1972. Can you think of a better source than to pick people all fouled up where they are and give them well-paid, interesting (even though dangerous) work in a necessary cause? Everybody knows now why the Fizzle War of 1963 fizzled. The bomb with New York's number on it didn't go off, a hundred other things didn't go as planned—all arranged by the likes of me.

But not the Mistake of '72; that one is not our fault—and can't be undone; there's no paradox to resolve. A thing either is, or it isn't, now and forever amen. But there won't be another like it; an order dated "1972" takes precedence any year.

I closed five minutes early, leaving a letter in the cash register telling my day manager that I was accepting his offer to buy me out, to see my lawyer as I was leaving on a long vacation. The Bureau might or might not pick up his payments, but they want things left tidy. I went to the room in the back of the storeroom and forward to 1993.

2200-VII-12 Jan. 1993—Sub Rockies Annex-HQ Temporal DOL: I checked in with the duty officer and went to my quarters, intending to sleep for a week. I had fetched the bottle we bet (after all, I won it) and took a drink before I wrote my report. It tasted foul, and I wondered why I had ever liked Old Underwear. But it was better than nothing; I don't like to be cold sober, I think too much. But I don't really hit the bottle either; other people have snakes—I have people.

I dictated my report; forty recruitments all okayed by the Psych Bureau—counting my own, which I knew would be okayed. I was here, wasn't I? Then I taped a request for assignment to operations; I was sick of recruiting. I dropped both in the slot and headed for bed.

My eye fell on "The By-Laws of Time," over my bed:

Never Do Yesterday What Should Be Done Tomorrow.

If at Last You Do Succeed, Never Try Again.

A Stitch in Time Saves Nine Billion.

A Paradox May Be Paradoctored.

It Is Earlier When You Think.

Ancestors Are Just People.

Even Jove Nods.

They didn't inspire me the way they had when I was a recruit; thirty subjective-years of time-jumping wears you down. I undressed, and when I got down to the hide I looked at my belly. A Cesarean leaves a big scar, but I'm so hairy now that I don't notice it unless I look for it. Then I glanced at the ring on my finger.

The Snake That Eats Its Own Tail, Forever and Ever. I *know* where I *came* from—but *where did all you zombies come from?*

I felt a headache coming on, but a headache powder is one thing I do not take. I did once—and you all went away.

So I crawled into bed and whistled out the light.

You aren't really there at all. There isn't anybody but me—Jane—here alone in the dark.

I miss you dreadfully!

STUDY AND DISCUSSION QUESTIONS

1 Understanding the nature of time as portrayed in the story involves first figuring out the timeline of the story itself, which is no easy task! First, who tells the story? What is/are his relationship/s with the "Unmarried Mother"?

2 How did the narrator of Heinlein's story get recruited into the Temporal Bureau? Why was he selected?

3 What would Augustine say about Heinlein's story? Why would he say this?

4 At one point in the story, a song called *I'm My Own Grandpaw!* comes on the juke box. Is it metaphysically possible to be your own grandpaw? Is that what's going on in the story?

5 Does Heinlein's story involve changing past events? If so, which one(s)? If not, explain how each event in the story that appears to be altered is really not altered.

6 The "Mistake of '72" is not the fault of the Temporal Bureau and can't be undone. As the narrator of the story puts it, "A thing either is, or it isn't. Now and forever amen." Yet, slightly later, he reads in "The By-Laws of Time": ". . . A Paradox May Be Paradoctored." What do these phrases mean? Are they compatible?

7 Which theory of time discussed in the chapter does Heinlein presuppose in his story?

8 Imagine that I have a U.S.F.F. Co-ordinates Transformer Field Kit, series 1992, Mod. II. I shake out the metal net, throw it over myself, and jump into the future, twenty years hence. I get out, and look about me, and see nothing but desolation. The countryside is blackened. My Geiger counter clicks wildly, and I know what has happened . . . World War III has finally come to pass, and everyone was killed. I jump back into my net, and take a series of small jumps backward until I find the moment of the destruction. I see myself being blown to smithereens by the nuclear holocaust. But wait . . . how can I be dead? Doesn't dying mean that I cease to exist (at least in an embodied human form)? Yet I am alive, after my own death, standing there in my net seeing my own body in charred bits. How can I be dead, but alive, after my own death? How can it be that I live on, after I have been blown to pieces? Does such a time machine entail that, though I will die, I can live forever . . . and, if I use my machine properly, *will* live forever? How can I most certainly die in a nuclear holocaust, yet live forever? Can't I just set my time machine, and travel continuously into the future, until the end of time? Explain how this story must be resolved, or why there is no reason to suppose that any resolution is needed.

4.11 "TIME IS BEYOND THE UNDERSTANDING OF HUMAN MINDS," FROM SAINT AUGUSTINE'S *CONFESSIONS*

(18) . . . [W]e say that time is long and time is short; we do not say this except about the past and the future. A hundred years ago, for example, we call a long time past; similarly, a hundred years from now [we call] a long time to come. But ten days ago we call a short time past; and ten days from now, a short time to come. But in what sense is the non-existent either long or short? For the past is not now, and the future is not yet. Therefore, we should not say, "It is long," but we should say of the past, "It was long," and of the future, "It will be long." O my Lord, my light, shall not even here Your truth jest at man? For that past time which was long, was it long when it was already past, or when it was as yet present? For then it might be long when something existed to be long, but when it was past it no longer was. Hence, it could not be long if it was not at all. We should not say, therefore, "Time past was long," for we will not find anything that was long—since it was past, it was not. Let us say that present time was long, because when it was present it was long. For it had not as yet passed away so as not to be, and therefore something existed to be long. But after it passed away, there also ceased to be long since what was long was no more.

(19) Let us see, therefore, O human soul, whether present time can be long; for you [the human soul] perceive and measure periods of time. What will you [the human soul] reply to me? Is a hundred years when present a long time? See, first, whether a hundred years can be present. For if the first year of these is current, that year is present, and the other ninety-nine years are future; so they do not exist yet. But if the second year is current, one is already past, the other present, and the rest are future. And thus, if we identify any middle year of these hundred as present, those before it are past and those after it are future. Hence, a hundred years cannot be present.

See, at least, if the current year can be present. If its first month is current, the rest are future. If the second [is current], the first has already passed, and the rest are not yet. Therefore neither is the current year wholly present, and if not wholly present, then the year is not present. For twelve months make the year, of which only the current month is present, but the rest are either past or future. And neither is even the current month present, but one day only—if the first, then the rest of the days are yet to come; if the last, then the other days are past; if any of the middle, then it is between past and future.

(20) See how the present time, which alone could be called long, is shortened to the duration of scarcely a day. But let us discuss even that, for there is not one day present as a whole. One day is made up of twenty-four hours of night and day, of which the first has the rest future, the last has them past, but any one of the intervening has those before it past and those after it future. And that one hour, too, passes in fleeting parts. Whatever of it has flown away is past, whatever remains is future. If any portion of time is conceived which cannot now be divided into even the smallest parts of moments, this [portion] only is what may be called present. This, however, flies so rapidly from future to past that it

cannot be extended by any duration. For if it were extended, it would be divided into past and future. The present has no duration.

So where is the time that we may call long? Is it future? No, for we do not say, "It is long" [of the future] because it is not yet anything that can be long. Instead we say, "It will be long." When, then, will it be? If even then it is future it will not be long, because what may be long does not yet exist. But it will be long when, from the future, which as yet does not exist, it will already have begun to be, and will have become present, so that there could exist something to be long. But then the present time cries out in the above words that it cannot be long.

Time can only be perceived or measured while it is passing.

(21) And yet, O Lord, we perceive intervals of time, and we compare them to others and say that some are longer and others are shorter. We even measure by how much shorter or longer this time may be than that; and call [a given interval] two or three times as long as another, or two others equal in length. But we measure times passing when we measure them by perceiving them. But who can measure past times, which now are not, or future times, which as yet are not, unless someone dares to say that what does not exist can be measured? When, therefore, time is passing, it can be perceived and measured; but when it is passed, it cannot, since it is not.

STUDY AND DISCUSSION QUESTIONS

1 What are Augustine's definitions of "current," "past" and "future?"
2 Is Augustine correct that language (both English and his original Latin) continually misrepresents the nature of time to us as something it is not?
3 We found a problem in the use of ordinary language as a guide to philosophy in our discussion about skepticism. There some people claim to "know" facts because the word "know" is used to describe their apprehension of those facts. But philosophers are using that and other terms in different, and more specific, ways. Is using language as a guide for philosophical thinking prudent, or misleading?
4 Is Augustine correct to say that "Time can only be perceived or measured while it is passing"?
5 From this selection, how would you summarize Augustine's theory about the nature of time?

4.12 "THREE TIME TRAVEL PROBLEMS," BY FRANZ KIEKEBEN

Of all concepts commonly found in science fiction, perhaps the most intriguing is that of time travel. What could be more romantic a prospect than to revisit one's own past, or to experience some remote era? It is no wonder, then, that so many stories have been concerned with travels through time. Not everyone, however, regards all of this as mere science fiction. Many scientists and philosophers take the possibility of travel to the past seriously. Some go further and even argue that all that's left is for physicists to work out the details on how to accomplish it. But in spite of such optimism, I believe that there are reasons for regarding travel to the past as extremely unlikely. In this paper, I expand upon two of the better known arguments against its possibility, and introduce a third.

There are two common ways of understanding time travel, which can be understood as two different answers to the following problem:

> Time travel is logically impossible. For if someone or something travels to the past, they may succeed in changing it. And of course any change to the past involves a contradiction, for it implies that at some particular time and location some event both did and did not occur.

One view, usually associated with the many-worlds interpretation of quantum mechanics, is that we live in a branching universe, with multiple time lines, and that time travelers therefore either create or simply go to one of these other time lines. This way, if they do something that did not occur in our past, such as prevent World War II, there is no contradiction, for it just means that World War II was prevented in some other branch of time.

On the second view, time travelers affect the past, but they cannot succeed in changing it. Whatever occurred in the past includes the effects produced by the time travelers. Thus, no time traveler can successfully prevent World War II. The time traveler is in effect merely playing his or her role in the past, and so there is no paradox. The underlying principle behind this view, called the *principle of self-consistency*, states that the set of all events must be internally consistent, and therefore something must always prevent a paradox from occurring.

I will only be considering the second type of time travel. In a sense, that is the only genuine kind of time travel, for it is the only one involving a journey to what we ordinarily think of as the past.

Many time travel stories include changes to the past. One classic in this category is Ray Bradbury's "A Sound of Thunder", in which a time traveler accidentally kills a butterfly in prehistoric times and alters all of future history. But in many such works it is unclear whether authors are writing about our past or about the creation of a new time line.

There are also examples of science fiction that exemplify the principle of self-consistency. One such example (perhaps surprisingly) is the movie *Bill and Ted's Excellent*

Adventure, in which two time traveling high school students bring back famous historical figures from the past.

1. Why can't time travelers succeed in changing the past?

As already mentioned, the changing-the-past objection to the *logical* possibility of time travel does not work, for one can maintain that time travelers merely play their role in the past. However, if one is considering the physical, as opposed to the mere logical, possibility of time travel, things begin to appear suspicious. For suppose that a time traveler has the intention of changing the past. Suppose, for example, that Tim intends to go back and kill his own grandfather before the latter had conceived any children, as in the famous paradox discussed by David Lewis (1976). What will prevent him from doing so?

The time travel proponent must maintain that for *some* reason, Tim will not be able to kill his grandfather. Maybe he will experience a loss of nerve at the last moment, or maybe his gun will jam, or he will merely injure his grandfather and mistakenly believe that he has succeeded. But whereas this explanation makes perfectly good sense when considering one attempt at changing the past, it seems lacking when we consider that *every* such attempt by every time traveler will fail—including repeated attempts by any one time traveler. For instance, if Tim realized that he missed, he might simply get into his time machine and try again on the previous day. But no matter how persistent and capable he is, no matter how many opportunities he has, something will always happen that will cause him to fail. And this appears to require an unusual set of coincidences. As some commentators have put it, time travelers would always have to be slipping on banana peels.

Now this by itself does not conclusively show that time travel is physically impossible. Sets of coincidences, even ones that we might regard with suspicion, *could* occur (see Sider 2002). But notice that we have a choice of two hypotheses here:

(1)   Time travel is not physically possible.

(2)   Time travel is physically possible and attempts to change the past will always fail.

Given that the kinds of coincidences required by (2) appear to be unlikely, and that we have never observed time travel, hypothesis (1) seems preferable. The essential idea may be put in argument form as follows:

1   If time travel is physically possible, then attempts to change the past always fail.
2   If attempts to change the past always fail, unusual sets of coincidences occur.
3   It is extremely unlikely for unusual sets of coincidences to occur.
4   Therefore, it is extremely unlikely that time travel is physically possible.

An objection to the above argument is that the attempts to change the past must themselves be very rare. People like Tim, who would be that persistent in the face of repeated failure, are themselves rather unlikely (see the argument in Smith 1997). If we further consider that time travelers ought to be aware that they cannot succeed in changing the past (especially after failing more than once), the probability of someone like Tim becomes even smaller.

This objection is not very convincing, however. For is it really inconceivable that, say, scientists who have discovered how to time travel might want to conduct experiments to see *how* they would be prevented from changing the past? (Perhaps such experiments would carry with them a certain risk, given that they must in some way involve failure. But other explorers have likewise taken risks.)

The autonomy principle

The changing-the-past argument can be improved by combining it with a principle about human abilities known as the *Autonomy Principle*. As stated by Theodore Sider, the principle is as follows:

> If a person in local circumstances, C, is able to bring about some configuration of matter, M, then any other intrinsically similar person in physically possible circumstances C' that are intrinsically similar to C is able to bring about configuration M, regardless of what goes on in the universe outside of circumstances C'.
>
> (Sider 1997)

Thus, if Tim could have succeeded in killing someone in the present, then in sufficiently similar circumstances he could have succeeded in killing his grandfather. But if, as consistency requires, Tim cannot succeed, then the Autonomy Principle appears to be false.

A time travel proponent might of course challenge the applicability of this principle to time travelers. After all, it is possible that time travelers do not find themselves in intrinsically similar circumstances, or are themselves not intrinsically similar to non-time travelers. Thus, even if one accepts the Autonomy Principle, it does not follow that time travel is impossible.

But let's consider the situation in Tim's case once more in light of this. We assume first, that the Autonomy Principle is true, second, that Tim could have succeeded in killing someone in the present, and third, that if he travels back in time, he will attempt to kill his grandfather before the latter had conceived any children. Then, in order for time travel to be possible, we must also accept the following:

(3)   The circumstances surrounding Tim's attempt on his grandfather *cannot be* intrinsically similar to circumstances surrounding any successful murder he might have committed in the present.

But why couldn't they be? Aside from the *ad hoc* reason of safeguarding the possibility of time travel, there appears to be no reason for accepting (3). It seems that the time travel proponent must claim that, *because* Tim cannot succeed in killing his grandfather, it therefore must be the case that Tim's circumstances, either with respect to something in his surroundings or to something within himself, will be different from the circumstances in a successful attempt. But this simply begs the question. *If* time travel is possible, then time travelers will not be able to perform certain apparently ordinary actions. But that might just mean that time travel is not possible. Once again, we have a choice of hypotheses. And it seems that (1) is more likely to be true than (3).

What time travelers cannot avoid doing

Nor do we have to stop here. Instead of considering merely what a time traveler cannot succeed in doing, we might also consider what he cannot succeed in *avoiding*. For, it will be remembered, time travelers perform actions that are part of the past. Since these events did in fact occur, then, by the principle of self-consistency, the time travelers who perform them cannot end up *not* doing them.

And yet it seems obvious that, if ordinarily one can refrain from doing certain things, then time travelers should be able to do likewise. The following slightly modified autonomy principle may be used to state the idea more precisely:

> If a person in local circumstances, C, is able to refrain from bringing about some configuration of matter, M, then any other *intrinsically similar* person in physically possible circumstances C' that are intrinsically similar to C is able to refrain from bringing about configuration M, regardless of what goes on in the universe outside of circumstances C'.

To explain the difference this makes, compare the following two examples. First, suppose that there is a scientist with a time machine at his disposal who wishes to carry out certain experiments involving attempts to change the past. One experiment might be an attempt to cause something that he knows did not occur. So, for instance, he plans to go back in time one hour and meet with his younger self. He knows where he was at the time, and knows that he had no encounter with his older self. What will happen? For some reason, he cannot succeed. Perhaps he has an accident on the way to his planned encounter and is taken to the hospital and kept there until well after his younger self enters the time machine. Whatever the reason is, it can certainly be something beyond his control.

Now consider a second experiment. This time he tries to avoid doing something that he knows he did in fact do. For example, suppose he does in fact meet with his older self. He therefore knows that he will soon travel back in time and meet his younger self. What happens if he tries to skip the meeting? Once again, he cannot succeed. Only this time, his failure will be the result of something that he does, rather than being merely the result of something that he fails to do. He will be at the appointed meeting, even though he does not intend to be. How might that come about?

There are, of course, possible explanations for such a strange occurrence. Perhaps he will be forced by time traveling terrorists not only to attend the meeting but also to pretend everything is okay, or else. But nothing like that is plausible as a general explanation, for something like it would, once again, have to be true of every similar scenario, every time such an experiment was carried out. The upshot of all this is that time travel seems to make possible sequences of events that are inconsistent with abilities we believe human agents to possess.

2. Are object loops possible?

A second common objection to time travel is that it allows—some even believe requires—the existence of causal loops (also known as time loops). Causal loops, according to Lewis, are "closed causal chains in which some of the causal links are normal and others are reversed." (Lewis 1976) Here's an example. Suppose that you receive a phone call one night from someone who tells you how to build a time machine. You follow the instructions and eventually, say a year later, complete the project. You then go back one year and decide to call your own number. Suddenly it occurs to you that this is the night when you originally received the time machine instructions, so you proceed to give the instructions to your younger self. But where did that information—the knowledge required to build a time machine—come from? Each part of the loop has a causal explanation, but the loop as a whole does not.

There are many different types of causal loops, and many examples of them in science fiction. [See page 207 above for a quirky time travel causal loop having to do with the marketing of correcting fluid.] One of the best is in Robert Heinlein's "—All You Zombies—", where one individual is both his own mother and father, and thus has no ancestors. Since this individual has no ancestors he only has human characteristics by coincidence, and his existence is as unexplained as that of the time machine instructions in the first example. He has no place in the human family tree.

Another type of causal loop is the object loop. This is a causal loop consisting of an item, such as the pocket watch in the movie *Somewhere in Time*. At the beginning of the story, an old woman gives the time traveler a watch. He then goes back in time and gives the watch to the same woman when she was young. She keeps it during the intervening sixty years until we are back at the beginning of the story, when she gives it to him. Each stage of the watch can be causally accounted for by its previous stage, but the watch as a whole has no cause. It was never manufactured.

Could a watch exist uncaused? It's at least logically possible. After all, as Lewis pointed out, other things, such as the universe or God, may exist uncaused. But at the very least it must be extremely unlikely. The fact that it would have the characteristics of a watch—that it would resemble watches that have been manufactured by human beings—would be mere coincidence. In fact, it is so improbable for something like a watch to exist uncaused that if we find one, we automatically assume that there must have been a watchmaker.

There are other problems with object loops. Consider the fact that each moment in the life of the watch is a unique event. When the watch in the above story is given by the time traveler to the woman, it is in a particular state, S1. The woman then keeps it for many years, during which it undergoes certain changes. It loses many of its molecules through normal wear, and so on. When she gives it to the time traveler, then, the watch is almost certainly in a different state, S2. The time traveler then takes it back in time to give it to the woman, upon which it somehow has returned back to state S1. How could that be?

Note that S1 (as well as any other state) is a unique state. The watch has to somehow return to that state *exactly*, even as far as its subatomic particles are concerned.[3] I'll call this, following Richard Hanley, the *restoration problem* (Hanley 2004). But for such a thing to be true of a watch, or any other even minimally complex object, is so extremely improbable that we can safely assume it will never happen. On the other hand, if time travel is possible, why wouldn't the above scenario, or some other involving an object loop, be possible?

A third and perhaps even more serious problem caused by the possibility of object loops is the following. Consider the question of the age of the watch at any moment during its existence. I don't mean merely its *state* at any given moment (which is, at most, evidence of its age), but its actual age relative to other moments in its existence. The age we assign to a specific point in the watch's existence is arbitrary, but for illustration purposes, suppose we say that it is zero at the moment that it is given by the time traveler to the woman. Now, if it is zero at that moment, then one hour later it seems that it should be one hour old, which can be confirmed by, among other things, the watch's own time keeping (provided it is accurate). And sixty years later, when it is given back to the time traveler, it should be sixty years old. But now what happens when the watch is taken back in time?

To fully appreciate the problem, it will help to keep in mind what happens to the time traveler when he takes the journey. He will, of course, be going sixty years back in external time. But in his own personal time, he will nevertheless age by however long the journey takes for him. If the journey takes five minutes, then he will be five minutes older when he arrives in the past than he was when he began. The important thing is that he does age. Likewise, the watch that he is taking along with him also appears to age. It keeps on ticking. (This assumes that the journey is not instantaneous. But even if that were the case the watch would only remain the same age.)

However, when it is given to the woman, the watch is not sixty years old, but zero years old. It somehow becomes younger. It doesn't merely return to its former state S1, it actually *is* back at what we arbitrarily designated the beginning of its existence, for that is a unique event in the life of the watch. Is such a thing possible?

Well, it is possible, insofar as the watch taken by itself is concerned, provided that circular time is possible. But that may certainly be questioned. Furthermore, the watch does not exist in a temporal vacuum. It exists within the rest of the world, which means that it is also undergoing linear time.[4] Would it not be incorrect to deny that during that first hour after it was given to the woman the watch aged by one hour (and likewise for any other time span in its existence)? After all, it underwent an hour of time. What more could it possibly take for something to age one hour? However, as far as its own circular time is concerned, it does not age, for in circular time every moment is both before and after every other moment. And the combination of both claims appears to be inconsistent, for it amounts to claiming that the watch both ages and does not age during any segment of its existence.

Possible solutions

Richard Hanley offers the following solution to the restoration problem: "If an object is composed of replaceable parts, such as in the case of the watch, then the object itself can have a "path in space-time" that is a causal loop, and yet restoration is avoided, as long as its parts do not have looped paths" (Hanley, 2004: p. 135). In other words, if the parts out of which the watch is made get replaced by their own earlier selves, then each part avoids being an object loop, even though the watch as a whole may still be regarded as one. This might happen as follows. Suppose that the watch is taken back in time and given to someone in 1912. During the next sixty years, each component of the watch is replaced by a brand new part. For example, let's say that a spring is replaced in 1926. This means that the spring is manufactured sometime before it is placed in the watch, sticks around (inside the watch) until 1972, at which time it is taken back to 1912, and is finally discarded in 1926. This spring, then, is not an object loop. It has a beginning and an end. And every part of the watch could be like that.

This would not only solve the restoration problem, but the other ones as well. Since no component of the watch is an object loop, no entity would have to return to its former state, nor exist uncaused, nor undergo circular time.

Unfortunately, even if in some cases object loops could undergo replacement of parts in this way, that does not rule out the possibility of cases where that does not happen. Consider again our scientist who has a time machine at his disposal and wishes to carry out experiments, only this time involving object loops. There appears to be nothing preventing him from carrying them out in such a way as to avoid any replacement of parts. He might, for instance, go back one minute and give an object to his own younger self. During that minute he ought to be able to ensure that no parts get replaced. There might not even be enough time to do so anyway. (There is a different problem related to this experiment, however, which will be considered at the end of this section.)

Another way that the restoration problem might be avoided is if the objects involved do not change, or at least do not change in such a way as to lose any of their parts, including subatomic ones. If the item in question is a functioning watch, then it obviously cannot avoid all change. But perhaps it is not made of ordinary atoms, or if it is, they are arranged in such a way that none will be lost, no matter how much it is put through during its existence. After all, object loops are strange entities in the first place, only coincidentally sharing properties with other entities, so perhaps they are different in other respects as well.

The problem with this solution is that it replaces one very unlikely scenario with another, for, as far as we know, no complex objects exist with the above unusual properties, nor do we have any other reason for believing that they exist. This solution might work, however, for simple entities, such as electrons. An electron could exist in a causal loop without undergoing any changes, since presumably electrons do not change. Even so, this is at best only a solution to the restoration problem.

But perhaps there is a more general and simpler solution to all of the problems raised by object loops. Perhaps, it may be argued, they simply never occur. For how is it that they are supposed to come about? Consider once again our scientist. Two hours before he enters the time machine, he decides that he will travel back one hour from the moment of departure and give his younger self some object, which he will then take with him in the machine to give to his younger self. If one hour before he enters his time machine he is visited by his older self and given the object, then he has succeeded in carrying out his experiment. But what happens if he is not visited by his older self? Then he knows that he will not be able to succeed. To insist that the scientist ought to be able to carry out the experiment is to say that somehow he can make it the case that an object loop will be created. But that would mean that someone can cause an object loop. However, as has already been pointed out, an object loop has no external cause!

To further understand the problem, consider that the scientist in the above experiment does not yet have the object at the time he makes the plans. The object does not yet exist. Now, exactly what characteristics will the object have if he succeeds? This is obviously not something he can plan. And the same thing applies to the very existence of the object. Object loops, then, may simply never occur. If they do, it is entirely by chance, and even putting the other problems with object loops aside, the chances are very small. The same general point, incidentally, can be made regarding certain other causal loops, such as the time machine instructions mentioned at the beginning of this section.

A final problem

There remains one difficulty, however, a version of the basic problem discussed in section 1. If time travel is physically possible then the Autonomy Principle implies that a time traveler should be able to give his younger self some object, and also that his younger self should be able to take it with him when he travels back in time. If the scientist already has a watch in his possession, what is to prevent him from taking it with him and giving it to his younger self? And if he does, what is to prevent his younger self from taking *that* object and giving it to his younger self later on in his personal time? And yet, this story cannot be made consistent if the object was already in the scientist's possession before he was visited by his older self. Thus, it seems that time travelers are both able to and unable to make it the case that object loops occur. Once again, therefore, time travel, when combined with the Autonomy Principle and plausible assumptions regarding the circumstances time travelers would find themselves in, leads to a contradiction.

3. The paradox of the supersized universe

If someone or something can travel back in time, then presumably so can anything else, and so can any combination of things. It might therefore be interesting to consider whether the entire universe could travel back in time. As it turns out, supposing that it is possible leads to a paradox, at least under certain conditions.

Let's start with an ordinary example of time travel. Timea departs from time T2 and arrives at some earlier time T1. She then stays around until at least her (younger self's) original point of departure at T2. Thus, between T1 and T2, there are two Timeas around. This means that, unless there are any other changes to the total mass in the universe, the amount of matter in the universe between these two points has increased by Timea's mass at T2. Now this by itself is not a logical problem. It might not even be a problem for the physical possibility of time travel. It might just mean that time travel results in a violation of certain conservation laws. But a universe where time travel is possible might very well be different in several respects from the universe we believe we are in.

But now suppose, instead of it being merely Timea who travels back at T2, that the entire universe does so. (I am ignoring here complications arising from the relativity of simultaneity.) Then between T1 and T2, it apparently is the case that the mass of the universe has doubled, whereas after T2 the entire universe has vanished. This may sound rather strange, but that is not yet the problem I have in mind. The first real problem arises when we consider just how much mass has in fact traveled back at T2. For one can argue both that the mass of the universe at T1 equals the mass of the universe at T2, and also that the mass of the universe at T1 does *not* equal the mass of the universe at T2.

Let's say that T0 is a time prior to T1. Also, to keep things simple, let's make three assumptions. First, that other than the departure at T2 and the arrival at T1, no other time travel occurs between T0 and T2. Second, that when there are no time travel arrivals or departures, the total amount of mass in the universe remains constant. And third, that the mass of the universe at all three times, T0, T1, and T2, is some positive number (we're supposing that the universe remains until T2, and only then travels back in time).

Now since at T2 the entire universe travels back to T1, it follows that at T1 the universe acquires the mass of the universe at T2. And since the mass of the universe prior to T1 is the mass at T0, the mass at T1 equals the mass at T0 plus the mass at T2.

Here is the argument that the mass at T1 $\neq$ the mass at T2:

1. Let the mass at T0 = m

2. Let the mass at T2 = n

3. Then the mass at T1 = m + n

4. But m + n $\neq$ n

5. Therefore, the mass at T1 $\neq$ the mass at T2

In other words, since at T2 the entire universe travels back to T1, the mass at T1 is greater than that at T2, for it includes both that which was already around and that which arrived from the future.

Here is the argument that the mass at T1 = the mass at T2:

1. From T1 to T2 (inclusive), the mass of the universe remains constant

2. Therefore, the mass at T1 = the mass at T2

Since there are no other cases of time travel in our scenario, and since without time travel the mass of the universe remains constant, it follows that whatever mass the universe has at T1 remained unchanged all the way until T2.

But of course, the mass at T1 cannot be both equal and unequal to the mass at T2. How can this paradox be resolved?

The problem arises when we suppose that the entire universe travels back to T1 and then hangs around until the time of departure, T2.[5] As already pointed out, if our time traveler Timea goes from T2 to T1 and then does not time travel until at least T2, there are two copies of her from T1 to T2. Therefore, if each entity in the universe does the same, then between T1 and T2 it seems there are two copies of each entity in the universe. The universe becomes "supersized" all the way until T2. That is, if the universe had mass m at T0, then between T1 and T2 it apparently has mass 2m.

But then, since the entire universe at T2 travels back to T1, what travels back in time, contrary to our original supposition, is not merely one copy of each thing at T0 (mass m), but two copies of each thing at T0 (mass 2m). Or so it might at first seem, except that the same inconsistency arises once again. For now we have said the universe at T1 acquires two copies of each thing, which, added to the original copy already at T0, is three copies! So there are three copies between T1 and T2, which then travel back to T1, making a total of four copies, and so on and so on, ad infinitum. Therefore, if the entire universe travels back in time from T2 to T1 and hangs around until T2, the mass that travels back in time has to be infinite.

If the universe between T1 and T2 has infinite mass, then one problem is resolved. For infinity plus any finite number is still infinity. In other words, if we substitute infinity for n in the above argument, we no longer have a proof that the mass of T1 does not equal the mass of T2. Instead, we have

1. Let mass at T0 = m

2. Let mass at T2 = ∞

3. Then the mass at T1 = m + ∞

4. m + ∞ = ∞

5. Therefore, the mass at T1 = the mass at T2.

However, there is a deeper paradox here. For whatever may be true of infinity, it remains the case that at T1, those entity stages that have not yet reached T2 are joined by those that have reached T2 and then traveled back in time. And that means that there have to be entity stages at T1 that did not travel back in time at T2. The entity stages that do travel back in time at T2 therefore are not every entity stage that ends up being at T1, and that is a contradiction.

The solution is perhaps found in the fact that, in order for there to be an infinite number of copies of each entity at T2 (each older than its immediately younger version by T2–T1 years), the oldest ones would have to be infinitely older than the youngest ones. That means that in their personal time they would have taken an infinite amount of time since T1 to reach their current state. That, however, amounts to saying that they will never reach that state. Therefore it is impossible for the entire universe to travel back from some time T2 to some time T1 and then stay around until T2.

However, when looked at another way, it seems that it should be possible in principle for the entire universe to travel back in time, if it is possible for any part of it to do so. So a problem remains.

Conclusion

Travel to the past appears to be ruled out for a variety of reasons. It would require the occurrence of unusual coincidences and seems to be inconsistent with the Autonomy Principle. Object loops introduce several problems that cannot be solved without abandoning some very reasonable assumptions. In addition, the Autonomy Principle suggests that time travelers would be able to bring about object loops, whereas other considerations suggest that they would not. Finally, under certain conditions it is impossible for the entire universe to travel back in time. But the concept of time travel seems to imply that it is possible in principle. If this is the case, then there is something wrong with the concept itself.

STUDY AND DISCUSSION QUESTIONS

1   What are the two common ways of understanding time travel?
2   How does the autonomy principle strengthen the changing of the past objection?
3   What are the three main problems with object loops?
4   Explain the difficulty brought about by combining object loops with the autonomy principle.
5   In the paradox of the supersized universe, why does the mass that travels back in time have to be infinite?

4.13 BIBLIOGRAPHY AND RECOMMENDED READING

Science fiction

*Abbott, Edwin. *Flatland: A Romance in Many Dimensions*. Perseus Publishing, 2003. Though space travel has been a topic for science fiction authors since Lucian's *A True Story*, this early novel about the life of its two-dimensional protagonist offers the reader a systematic exploration of the nature of space. "A. Square" meets friends in Lineland and reaches out to Spaceland. The broad question raised: how narrow and limited is our experience? This theme is taken up again, and homage is paid, by Rudy Rucker in *Spaceland: A Novel of the Fourth Dimension* (Tor, 2002).

Aldiss, Brian. *Cryptozoic*. House of Stratus, 2001. The idea that time is dependent upon human consciousness is explored in a very strange, ruthlessly logical story.

Anderson, Paul. *Tau Zero*. Doubleday, 1970. The starship *Leonora Christine* speeds out of control after colliding with a nebula. After the malfunction there are no means of stopping the propulsion of the ship to near light speeds. The crew realize that their friends and family back on Earth will have long since died by the time they return. But as their inability to decelerate the ship continues, they take the radical step of steering the ship outside the galaxy. Another problem besets them: spacetime seems to be collapsing. Finally they awaken to the realization that the effects of relativistic time have obscured the fact that they are at the end of time and the universe is contracting . . .

Asimov, Isaac. *The End of Eternity*. Fawcett Publications, 1971. Uses the device of a region of "eternity" which is outside of the stream of historical time and is not subject to the changes that are produced by an elite corps of time travelers.

Ballard, J. G. "The Garden of Time." *Chronopolis and Other Stories*. Putnam, 1971. Theme is the subjectivity of time.

*Baxter, Stephen. *The Time Ships*. HarperCollins, 1995. This book—winner of the John W. Campbell and Philip K. Dick awards—is a sequel to H. G. Wells' *The Time Machine*. The protagonist sets out to explore the same world and rescue the same girl, but that timeline has changed. The nineteenth-century traveler, and a loyal Morlock companion, make a number of stops at different points in Earth's time line, and is confronted by several startling alterations. This novel offers a sense of remarkable open-endedness about humanity and its place in the universe.

*Benford, Gregory. *Timescape*. Simon & Schuster, 1980. John W. Campbell and Nebula award winning novel offering a detailed portrait of scientists at work. Time travel is not an idle fancy but the key to saving Earth as physicists in 1998 attempt to transmit a message back to physicists in 1962 in the hopes that it will save humanity.

Bradbury, Ray. "A Sound of Thunder." *A Sound of Thunder and Other Stories*. Harper Perennial, 2005. Presents the famous example of a dinosaur hunter who obliterates his own history by stepping on a butterfly.

*Butler, Octavia. *Kindred*. Doubleday, 1979. Dana, a contemporary African American woman, travels repeatedly back to the Civil War-era Confederate South. She does not know when she will travel back in time, and these trips take a huge emotional toll on her. During Dana's trips to the past, she saves the life of an ancestor, Rufus, who is white. Over the course of her many trips to the past, each of which is unexpected and painful, she learns that Rufus was a slave owner. This wrenching story forces the reader to come to terms with the juxtaposition of the past and present in contemporary African American life.

Delany, Samuel. *Dhalgren*. Bantam, 1975. In this complex, non-linear novel, its main character is the city Bellona, which experiences frequent distortions of spacetime. Arguably, the novel, and "Kid," the narrator, capture some symptoms of schizophrenia.

Dunn, J. R. *Days of Cain*. Eos, 1998. A guild of time travelers has pledged to preserve the integrity of the past, but Alma Lewin takes the Jewish holocaust into her own hands by journeying to 1943 Germany. This story offers a meditation about the ethics of **consequentialism**.

Edmondson, G. C. *The Ship that Sailed the Time Stream*. New York: Ace, 1981. Time travel yarn.

Eklund, Gordon. *All Times Possible*. DAW, 1974. Operates on the premise that time branches. Rather than "changing" history the time traveler finds himself or herself on a different branch.

Finney, J. *Time and Again*. New York: Scribner, 1970. Romance via time travel; scrupulous research.

Gerrold, Davod. *The Man Who Folded Himself*. Random House, 1973. By traveling back and forth through time, and each time replicating himself, the traveler must face several ontological paradoxes.

*Haldeman, Joe. *Forever War*. Ballantine, 1976. Describes an interstellar war with warships flying at near-light speeds. The crew undergoes repeated culture shock whenever they return to Earth, where centuries have passed.

Heinlein, Robert A. *Time for the Stars*. Scribner, 1956. The relationship between identical twin brothers with a telepathic connection is transformed as one shoots off into space at near light speeds and the other remains on Earth to endure time more quickly.

——. "—All You Zombies—." *The Magazine of Fantasy and Science Fiction*. March 1959.

Holdstock, Robert. *Where Time Winds Blow*. Faber, 1981. This novel, weighted with philosophical discussion by the characters, concerns a people whose planet experiences a type of wind that blows time and that leaves articles from other cultures and other times in its wake.

Joseph, M. *The Hole in the Zero*. Avon, 1969. Surreal SF in which characters exist outside space and time and create their own realities. Kantian. Compare Dick's *Ubik* and Stableford's *Man in a Cage*.

Masson, David. "Traveler's rest." *The Traps of Time*. Ed. Michael Moorcock. New York: Penguin, 1979. The story is set on a world at war in which different parts of the world experience time at different rates.

Powers, Tim. *The Anubis Gates*. New York: Ace, 1983. This Philip K. Dick Award winning novel places a present-day English professor in England in 1810. Powers assiduously avoids time-travel paradoxes, and his prose displays the refined elegance befitting his subjects, including Victorian poets and authors.

Priest, Christopher. *Inverted World*. Faber, 1974. City Earth is run by guilds who keep their secrets, but Helward Mann pieces together the unusual status of this unusual, moving city. Priest plays with concepts of space and time (residents of the city measure their age in miles travelled) and offers his readers opportunities to understand the how's and why's, all the while conveying an exquisite sense of wonder.

Silverberg, Robert. *Up the Line*. Ballantine, 1969. The picaresque hero obliterates himself by indulging in time travel paradoxes, for example, with a beautiful female ancestor.

*Stross, Charles. *Singularity Sky*. New York: Ace, 2003. A group of planets have limited technology, but when faced with a radical alien presence, they time travel back in order more effectively to make war. But the Eschaton, a god-like power, has limited time travel events and punishes those who disobey.

Swanwick, Michael. *Bones of the Earth*. New York: HarperCollins, 2002. A paleonotologist travels back to the age of dinosaurs at the government's mysterious behest, but unforeseen fissures in time cause effects in the present. Unusually thoughtful treatment of time travel paradoxes.

Tucker, Wilson. *The Year of the Quiet Sun.* New York: Ace, 1970. In an effort to evade a cataclysmic end to the planet, time travelers attempt to travel back to prevent events leading up to it, but they appear to be causing it. Religious themes about tribulation and end-times are dealt with extensively.

Twain, Mark. *A Connecticut Yankee in King Arthur's Court.* Adamant, 2000. Time travel romance and biting satire as only Twain could write.

Varley, John. *Millennium.* Berkley, 1983. Made into a feature film; people of the future use time travel to return to Earth at specific points to snatch other human beings needed to repopulate the dreary, decimated Earth of the future. Varley's style is infused with a wink and a nod to several earlier time travel yarns, making it a special delight for science fiction aficionados.

*Vonnegut, Kurt. *Slaughterhouse Five (The Children's Crusade).* New York: Dell Publishing, 1991. Billy Pilgrim is a POW from World War II whose traumatic witnessing of the Dresden bombings leads to his becoming unstuck in time, and taking an existential tour of his own life. He is seen and kidnapped by Tralfamadorians, beings who know every moment of their lives (and for whom notions of "past" and "future" make little sense).

Wells, H. G. *The Time Machine.* New York: Pocket Books, 1895. This is the story that nobly began a genre. Wells offers social criticism, biological speculation and presents an ethical consciousness throughout the narrative.

Willis, Connie. *Doomsday Book.* Bantam, 1992. A Hugo and Nebula Award winning novel, this story involves an Oxford student who travels back to the fourteenth century for a practical exam, but the Black Plague is in full force. With other hurdles to overcome—at both times, Kivrin struggles to make it back.

Wilson, Robert Anton. "The Universe Next Door." *Schrödinger's Cat Trilogy.* Dell, 1988. This novel and its companions, other books in the series, explore consequences of the strange implications of the subatomic world by portraying simultaneous alternate realities.

Philosophy

Augustine, Saint. "Time Is Beyond the Understanding of Human Minds." *Confessions.* *c.*397. This text and translation are in the public domain.

Davies, Paul. *How to Build a Time Machine.* New York: Penguin, 2003.

Dowe, Phil. "The Case for Time Travel." *Philosophy: The Journal of the Royal Institute of Philosophy* 75, 293 (July 2000): pp. 441–51.

——. "The Coincidences of Time Travel." *Philosophy of Science* 70, 3 (July 2003): pp. 574–89.

Earman, John. "Recent Work on Time Travel." *Time's Arrows Today: Recent Physical and Philosophical Work on the Direction of Time.* Cambridge: Cambridge University Press, 1995. pp. 268–324.

*Gale, Richard. *The Philosophy of Time.* Doubleday, 1967. A useful anthology, focused on metaphysical and epistemological speculation on the nature of time.

Gardner, Marvin. *The Relativity Explosion.* Vintage, 1976. A helpful introduction to the modern scientific view of space and time for the general reader without a strong background in mathematics.

Gott, J. Richard. *Time Travel in Einstein's Universe: The Physical Possibilities of Travel Through Time*. Boston, MA: Houghton Mifflin, 2001.

Grey, William. "Troubles with Time Travel." *Philosophy* 74 (1999): pp. 55–70.

Hanley, Richard. "No End in Sight: Causal Loops in Philosophy, Physics and Fiction." *Synthese: An International Journal for Epistemology, Methodology and Philosophy of Science* 141, 1 (July 2004): pp. 123–52.

——. "Identity Crisis: Time Travel and Metaphysics in the DC Multiverse." *Superheroes and Philosophy: Truth, Justice, and the Socratic Way*. Ed. Tom Morris. Chicago: Open Court, 2005.

Hawking, Stephen. "Chronology Protection: Making the World Safe for Historians." *The Future of Spacetime*. S. Hawking et al., eds. New York: W. W. Norton, 2001.

Horwich, Paul. "Closed Causal Chains." In S. Savitt, ed. *Time's Arrows Today*. Cambridge: Cambridge University Press, 1995. pp. 259–67.

——. "Time Travel." *Asymmetries in Time: Problems in the Philosophy of Science*, Cambridge, MA: MIT Press, 1987.

*Lewis, David. "The Paradoxes of Time Travel." *American Philosophical Quarterly* 13 (1976): pp. 145–52.

Nahin, Paul J. *Time Machines: Time Travel in Physics, Metaphysics, and Science Fiction*. Springer Verlag, 1991.

*Richmond, Alasdair M. "Time-Travel Fictions and Philosophy." *American Philosophical Quarterly* 38, 4 (October 2002): pp. 305–18.

——. "Gödelian Time-Travel and Anthropic Cosmology." *Ratio: An International Journal of Analytic Philosophy* 17, 2 (June 2004): pp. 176–90.

*Sider, Theodore. "A New Grandfather Paradox?" *Philosophy and Phenomenological Research* 57 (1997): pp. 139–44.

——. "Time Travel, Coincidences and Counterfactuals." *Philosophical Studies* 110 (2002): 115–38.

Smart, J. J. C., ed. *Problems of Space and Time*. Macmillan, 1964. A useful anthology; dealing with scientific approaches and the philosophical implications of modern science.

Smith, Nicholas J. J. "Bananas Enough for Time Travel?" *British Journal of Philosophy* 48 (1997): pp. 363–89.

5 Mind

Imagine Earth in the far, far future, long after the extinction of human beings. A handful of artificial intelligences—in the form of robots, satellites and computers—remain. And they get curious about humanity. First they launch a successful mission to find human artifacts. Then one among them, who goes by the name "Frost," wants to understand the biology and psychology of human beings. He finds and processes lots of data about our species, but he finds it incomplete. The data don't show him what it was like to be a human being. Through discussing this with his friends, he decides that this is what he really wants to know.

With the help of some, with the scorn of others, and with the fears of all the artificial intelligences, Frost takes steps to achieve that goal. He finds some bodies in the frozen tundra and excavates them. He uses his knowledge of human neuroscience to study the brain and how to pass electrical signals through it just as humans did. Frost then reanimates a human body and builds a complicated interface so that he can send and receive data from the brain. With all the preparations in place, he downloads his entire consciousness into the human body.

The results are mixed. After only a minute or two, Frost transfers himself back into his original wetware. He's clueless as to whether or not his experiment was a success. His description of the event appears confused and he is psychologically shaken by it. His friends who observed the event assure him that he was successful at experiencing what it is like to be a human being. But he remains uncertain. (This is the plot of Roger Zelazny's "For a Breath I Tarry.")

How would Frost know whether he did experience what it is like to be a human being? If humans are nothing more than physical objects, then, some say, all our experiences can be explained by reference to the minute interactions between physical particles—neurotransmitters, synapses, nerves and the electrical signals that pass through them. Perhaps if Frost knows everything there is to know about those features of the human brain and body, then he already knew what it was like to be a human being before transferring himself into the human body. You might think that if our brains are merely complex systems of minute physical parts operating together, and the artificially intelligent brains of robots are similar systems built out of different materials, then intelligence and consciousness can arise out of artificial brains too.

On the other hand, you might think that even if Frost knew everything about the human brain and body, and even if Frost transferred his consciousness into the brain of the human body that he reanimated, he *still* wouldn't know what it was like to be a human being. There is something mysterious about humanity that will always resist replication. If you take this position, you might believe that humans have souls—immaterial spirits—or that the human mind is not reducible to the physical matter that it is made from.

This leads to the broad question explored in this chapter: What is the mind, and how does it relate to the body? This can be broken down into several more specific questions: What arguments are there for and against dualism, the theory that each human being is part matter and part spirit? Is **physicalism**, the theory that everything that there is is physical, true? If so, then all the mental properties of the mind should reduce to physical properties. What is consciousness?

After completing this chapter, you should be able to do the following:

- Define and contrast the various philosophical theories of mind, including **substance dualism**, **physicalism**, functionalism and **eliminitivism**
- Assess these theories
- Understand key concepts in the philosophy of the mind, including consciousness, intentional and qualitative states, **multiple realizability** and the Turing Test
- Describe artificial intelligence and tell how it relates to the argument from simulation
- Explain how the argument from simulation supports or undercuts each of the philosophical positions
- Evaluate evidence for or against the various philosophical positions on the basis of a thought experiment.

5.0 THE MIND: WHAT IT DOES

We want to establish some vocabulary for this chapter up front. Consider these statements:

A: We have minds.

B: We have bodies.

C: Minds and bodies are different substances.

D: The different substances of minds and bodies causally interact.

We will be encountering several theories about the mind in this chapter, and nearly all of them can be characterized in terms of their positions with respect to those four statements.

But theories of the mind typically define the mind in their own idiosyncratic ways, which makes comparing and contrasting theories challenging. Minds can be defined in terms of *what they do*—think, feel and perceive—or in terms of *what they are*—spirit, soul or matter. Bodies in the most general case are physical objects in spacetime. *Human* bodies are physical objects in spacetime that bear privileged relationships to our minds.

When a theory is characterized in terms of substances (more on which in a moment), the theory aims to define minds in terms of what they are. The theory known as *substance dualism* holds that A, B and C are all true. Substance dualist **interactionism** holds that all four are true. *Physicalists* hold that B is true and C and D are false. A subset of physicalists, *eliminitivists*, can be interpreted as holding that A is false. *Idealists*, a dying breed, hold that only A is true. The most important theories have intriguing ways of describing the relationship between A and B. We will be revisiting these theories throughout this chapter.

A mind can be described by what it does or by what it is. First we'll explain what minds do by describing different forms of thinking that concern philosophers. In the next section, we'll enter the debate about what minds are by discussing substance dualism.

Mental states can be divided into two exhaustive categories: conscious and unconscious states. We're most interested in conscious states, but a word on unconscious states first. Consider dreaming. In normal dreams our minds think and imagine, and yet we are unaware our minds are doing what they are doing. So unconscious mental states do exist. Whereas mental states in dreams appear confused and vague, other unconscious mental states exhibit amazing precision and clarity. Suppose someone asks you what 1,374 times 7,118 equals. As you prepare an answer, you might use a stepwise method and ask yourself, consciously, how many times four must be multiplied to make 18, then ask how may times four must be multiplied to make 100, etc. But some people are able to "see" that the answer is 953,812. They perform that calculation rapidly and unconsciously.

Must minds have unconscious mental states? Alternatively, must minds have at least *some* conscious mental states? If unconscious cognition were all there were to having a mind, then software programs would be minds. To us, though, conscious mental states are dearer. Before we provide a taxonomy of forms of consciousness, note that the problem of sorting out types of consciousness and properly identifying them is a philosophical problem over which much ink has been spilled. This implies that philosophers of mind do not fully agree on what it is that they disagree about!

If, playing football, one gets hit and knocked to the ground someone might say "I can't believe he's still conscious after that." By the word "conscious" this bystander means that the football player remains awake and aware. If you are knocked unconscious, or knocked out, this means that your conscious mind has been turned off, as it is in sleep. To be conscious here means to be, at a given moment in time, in the possession of a basic capacity for cognition. We can dub this type of consciousness **creature consciousness**. This use of the term "conscious" describes a person rather than a mental state. The football *player* has creature consciousness, or, when knocked out, lacks it.

This contrasts with the other forms of consciousness we will be discussing. Typically, in the context of artificial intelligence, philosophers want to know not only whether the AI has creature consciousness, but also whether certain of the AI's states are themselves conscious. The cognitive feats of "human calculators," like current *Guinness Book of World Records* record holder Scott Flansburg, illustrate the utterly unconscious levels of cognitive processing at work deep below the surface of the conscious mind. Flansburg can calculate sums, divisions, multiples, square roots, etc., faster than accountants with computers. If we were to program an AI to duplicate Flansburg's feats, this would not show that the AI's mental states are conscious and it would not show that the AI itself has creature consciousness. In contrast to creature consciousness is *state consciousness*, a term which refers to the characteristics of specific mental states.

Forms of state consciousness present to the person that experiences them a way in which something seems to them. For example, if you are conscious of the red hue of a painting, then there is a way in which that painting's color appears to you at that moment. If you are conscious of the warmth of the wood fire, then there is a complex experience of heat that you are feeling via your skin. These experiences contain an ineffable "what-it-is-like-ness" to them.

Several familiar forms of consciousness are forms of state consciousness. These forms include self-consciousness, **qualitative consciousness** and **intentionality**. The term "self-consciousness" can refer to one of two phenomena. First, sometimes we are "self-conscious" when we commit a faux pas. You might make a post on a friend's Myspace about the beautiful woman you met at the party Saturday, which is then read by your girlfriend. This meaning of the term connotes embarrassment and shame; it isn't the sense of self-consciousness we wish to explore here. Second, "self-conscious" refers to our capacity to represent our own mental states to ourselves. Philosophers call this an "inner sense" or **"reflexive consciousness"** because, when we are self-conscious in this way, it is as if we are perceiving our own perceptions. *Reflexive consciousness*, then, is exemplified when I think about my desire to go camping. This differs from merely desiring to go camping.

Of special interest to us are two other types of consciousness. Compare your forms of consciousness with those of a sophisticated robot. This robot can represent information about the temperature of its environment, it can use its camera eyes to "see" and measure wavelengths of light, and it exhibits motor control over its appendages. By employing its speedy and powerful CPU, complex audio system and its voice recognition and generation software, it can "talk" to you. Indeed, it may be capable of representing its own inner states to itself by compiling its own code—thus having a rudimentary form of reflexive consciousness. If you asked it what it was doing right now, it would respond precisely and accurately. Despite all that, there is a sense in which it is not conscious. The robot has no qualitative experiences.

Qualitative sensory states are difficult to describe. As you turn the pages of this book, the causal interaction between the paper, your fingers and your nervous system produce something—a feeling of the texture of the pages. When you look at a painting, your conscious visual experience presents its colors to you in a specific way—a way that changes as the lighting in the room changes. We can call this form of consciousness *qualitative consciousness*. The qualitative states we have been speaking of are simply states that exemplify this type of consciousness. The concept of qualitative consciousness eludes easy characterization in language.

The final form of state consciousness comes under the name *intentionality*. I might say that "I am conscious *of* the table in front of me" or "I am conscious *that* Sputnik 1 was the first satellite into orbit." These states of consciousness are intentional states. Here "conscious" refers to mental states in which agents are *aware of something or other*. It is helpful, even though partially misleading, to use spatial terminology to explain something important about intentional states: these states are *directed* states. One's belief that "Taipei 101 is the tallest building in the world" somehow picks out and refers to the Taipei 101 building. Beliefs are always intentional mental states because they refer to a state of affairs.

States of qualitative consciousness, though, like the pain I experience as I stub my toe, do not appear to be intentional states since my pain is not about anything else. However, serious philosophical dispute about the character of qualitative states focuses upon whether pains are intentional. If we characterize intentionality not as "aboutness" or "other-directedness" but instead as "information-carrying," then pains are intentional. Pains can be understood to represent information about the body's nervous system.

Attempts of philosophers and psychologists to understand consciousness are discordant. Some deny that there are certain types of consciousness since they reduce to more fundamental mental states. Others will be unhappy with the classification we have before us because it is incomplete or mistaken. Some think that intentional states need not be conscious; others think that intentional states must be conscious; and yet others that conscious states must be intentional. A difficulty facing participants in this debate lies in agreeing on just what it is that is being debated in the first place.

Through the dialectical haze, though, an initial question confronts us: Can mere matter—physical particles in spacetime—bear all these forms of consciousness? Must human minds be composed out of something that is immaterial? Dualism affirms that a non-material mental substance—a mind—houses these forms of conscious mental states. Let's explain substance dualism now. Then we'll offer an argument for it.

BOX 5.A: NAGEL'S BAT

I assume we all believe that bats have experience. After all, they are mammals, and there is no more doubt that they have experience than that mice or pigeons or whales have experience . . .

. . . Now we know that most bats (the microchioptera, to be precise) perceive the external world primarily by sonar, or echo location, detecting the reflections, from objects within range, of their own rapid, subtly modulated, high-frequency shrieks. Their brains are designed to correlate the outgoing impulses with the subsequent echoes, and the information thus acquired enables bats to make precise discriminations of distance, size, shape, motion, and texture comparable to those we make by vision . . .

. . . I want to know what it is like for a *bat* to be a bat.[1]

5.1 THE MIND: WHAT IT IS—THE SUBSTANCE DUALIST ANSWER

According to substance dualism, each human being has two different characteristics. We have rich mental lives—we feel, think and sense. We have physical bodies—organs, limbs and brains. The two aspects relate with one another. When I think "I want a cup of coffee" various physical events follow. Neurons in those parts of my brain that govern gross motor functions become active. Then the muscles in my legs extend and contract as I walk to the coffee maker. Finally, my arm extends towards a cup, my fingers grasp its handle, and I pour coffee from the pot. As routine as such a sequence of events seem, the connection between my desire and my action is baffling. How does an event in my mind that appears to be non-physical cause physical events in my body?

If we are interested in crafting a theory to explain the connections between our two aspects, we need to identify the facts that merit analysis, then select a method to show that those facts are mutually consistent. When we have commonsense observations that yield conclusion C, we must choose whether to structure our theory to preserve C or to explain C in terms of more fundamental structures. The previous chapter on time provides a test case. Augustine's commonsense observations of time led him to a conclusion that time was unreal and illusory. He rested content with that conclusion, and left the details up to God. Others who were discontent with Augustine's claim thought that they could explain our perception of time in more detailed physical terms having to do with space and relativity.

One historically venerable approach to the philosophy of mind resembles the method Augustine used to reflect on time. *Substance dualism* embraces the twofold aspect of our nature and builds a theory around it. The substance dualist offers an account of our mental and physical aspects that conforms to our commonsense observations and deeply held intuitions. Intuitively, we believe we are mental beings. That is, whatever else may be true of us, we have minds and consciousness. Thus, substance dualists accept that a human being has both a mental and a physical component. The mental component is constituted by a mental substance, while the physical component is constituted of matter. The dualist believes that one's mental substance houses states like beliefs, emotions and perceptions. Our arms and legs, organs, bones, and nervous systems are housed in our body—the material part of us. The dualist is convinced that persons are composite entities, made of both an immaterial mind and a material body. The thesis of *substance dualism* is: each human person is composed of two distinct substances, a mental substance (a mind) and a physical substance (a body).

What is a substance? This term has a long history in philosophy, and so its use is complicated by two different meanings. Both meanings share the implication that a *substance* (from the Latin *substantia*) refers to that which stands under another thing—as a form of support. On the first meaning, "substance" is a general term referring to a type of being; it is *stuff*. For example, physicalism is a philosophical theory according to which there is only one substance, matter, out of which everything that exists must be constituted. On this general use of the term, "matter" is used to refer to things (my desk is made of bits of matter) and to a type of thing (matter, as opposed to spirit).

On the second meaning, "substance" is a term that refers to individual *things*. It is because a horse has a substance that we are able to attribute properties to it in a sentence like "The horse is gray, fast and young." Individual substances such as that of the horse are metaphysically fundamental because the property of *grayness* cannot exist on its own; *grayness* requires something to which it attaches. That and other properties depend upon substances for their existence, but substances do not depend upon anything else for their own existence.

Return to our definition of substance dualism. Advocates of this theory typically say that matter is a substance on the general, first definition, but that mind is a substance in the specific, second definition. Matter is stuff, and mind—rather, minds—are things. This represents Descartes' form of substance dualism (see reading §5.12).

5.2 THE CONCEIVABILITY ARGUMENT FOR DUALISM

Philosophers have offered a variety of arguments on behalf of forms of dualism over the millennia. Some stem from the mysteriousness of the mind/body relation. While much mystery remains, neuroscience has given us knowledge that has answered many historical questions about the mind. Other arguments for dualism depend instead upon conceptual considerations, like Descartes' argument about conceivability. (See this chapter's supplementary readings.) This argument can be stated in its historical form as follows:

(5.1)   I can conceive of myself existing without a body.

This means that I can imagine that my identity is preserved in a non-material form. Traditional religious doctrines, for example, suggest that not only *can* we conceive of ourselves as existing as an immaterial soul, but that in fact we will exist in that form after death. This premise appears uncontroversial.

Descartes puts a twist on this idea by claiming "I can doubt the existence of my body, but I cannot doubt the existence of my mind." The rest of the argument reads as follows:

(5.2)   If I can conceive of scenario X then X is possible.

(5.3)   It is possible that I exist without a body.

(5.4)   Therefore, having a body is not an essential property of myself.

In this context "essential" does not mean "most important," as it does in ordinary language. 5.4 follows from 5.3 if we assume that an *essential property* of some thing is a property of an object that, if lost, implies that the object ceases to be that type of object. For example, *being unmarried* is an essential property of a bachelor: without that property, he won't be a bachelor. Essential properties are not merely necessary properties. The bachelor also has the property of *wearing or not wearing clothes*. That is a *necessary* property of the bachelor because in every possible world, he either wears or does not wear clothes. But that property is not an essential property of the bachelor since whether or not he wears clothes, he is still a bachelor.

This argument falls short of concluding that dualism is true. 5.4 is compatible with **idealism**—the thesis that minds are the only things that exist—being true. But the important point about the argument is that the truth of the conclusion is incompatible with physicalism, the theory that nothing exists that is not physical and in spacetime. This exemplifies a common bootstrapping technique in philosophical argumentation: offer arguments to think that a competing theory is false, then build upon that success to increase the justification for believing one's own theory.

Philosophers have attempted to show that the conceivability argument is unsound by showing that 5.1 and 5.2 are false. Consider the use of "conceive" in 5.1 and 5.2. That term might mean that I can conceive of the statement "I exist without a body." In other words, I conceive that this statement has a clear and determinate meaning. Clearly I can do this. For example, I can conceive "1 + 1 = 4." After all, when I read the statement "1 + 1 = 4," I know precisely what that means—only because I have conceived of its meaning do I know that it is false. If I know what a statement means, then in one sense of the word "conceive," I conceive that statement.

The seeds of a fallacy grow right around here. *Equivocation* is a fallacy according to which an ambiguous word or sentence is used to mean one thing in one statement, but is used to mean another thing in another statement. For example, consider this statement: "I heard the weatherman forecasting extremely high winds today, but I guess since we're down in the valley we'll be okay." The first instance of the word "high" refers to fast speeds, but the second instance refers to large elevations. In our argument "conceive" also has two meanings:

> Linguistic conception (in 5.1): "conceive" means "to understand the meaning of the statement"

> Object conception (in 5.2): "conceive" means "to understand the statement in such a way that I am justified in believing that it is possibly true"

The linguistic and object meanings of "conceive" differ. I can conceive that "1 + 1 = 4" in the first sense of "conceive," but I cannot conceive "1 + 1 = 4" in the second sense. This is because "1 + 1 = 4" is necessarily false. So, even though I know what that statement means, I do not know that the statement is possibly true. But of course the argument mistakenly asserts that what I can conceive is possibly true.

5.1 appears true given the linguistic definition, and 5.2 appears true given the object definition. But they cannot both be made true using a single definition of "conceive," an instance of equivocation. The inference is invalid. For the success of the argument, "conceive" mustn't be linguistic. Perhaps by conceiving of some scenario S, I hypothesize that S is real. There are two noteworthy problems associated with employing this sort of definition of "conceive" in the argument. First of all, 5.1 may be false with this definition. Try imagining that you exist without physical embodiment in spacetime. In other words, try imagining yourself as a non-physical being, as opposed merely to stringing a sequence of words together describing yourself as a non-physical being. We are so attuned to our bodies that this is not as easy to do as you might have thought. It is tempting to imagine oneself floating through space, but of course you cannot float if you are non-spatial.

So premise 5.1 may or may not be true when we employ the non-linguistic, object-oriented definition of "conceive." But is 5.2 true on this definition? Many philosophers believe it is not true on the basis of certain counterexamples. Suppose I have perceptual experiences of (what used to be known as) the Morning Star and the Evening Star. I then imagine or conceive of a scenario in which the Morning Star exists and the Evening Star does not exist. But unbeknownst to me, the Morning Star and the Evening Star are one and the same object, the planet Venus. Despite the fact that I can conceive of a scenario in which the Morning Star exists and the Evening Star doesn't, such a scenario is impossible. Thus 5.2 is false.

5.3 ASSESSING DUALISM: CAUSAL INTERACTION

Further problems for dualism arise when we begin to probe the putative relation between our two aspects. We suppose that bodily events cause some of our mental states. You have the belief that you are reading a book because the book is before your eyes, which reflects light in certain ways into your eyes, which stimulates various photoreceptors on your retinae, which leads to responses in your optical nerve, which eventually stimulates cells in your visual cortex. So your awareness of reading a book can be explained in part through physiological causes. To accept this is to accept what might be called the **thesis of physical-to-mental causality**, the view that physical states cause certain mental states to arise. We also find intuitive the view that what our bodies do can be causally explained in part by an appeal to mental objects or processes. You often do things because you want to do them, because you think that doing them is a good idea. To accept this is to accept the **thesis of mental-to-physical causality**, the view that mental states cause physical states. The dualist philosophers who accept both lines of causality are *interactionists* since they believe that though minds and bodies are distinct entities, mind and body interact with one another. Events in your mind cause events in your body to occur and vice-versa. The question is: How and where do these causal interactions take place?

It is one thing to suppose that a physical event can cause another physical event, or in other words, to endorse physical-to-physical causation. The dualist also holds that our minds are not physical things, i.e. they are not made of matter. If the mind is non-physical, how can the interaction between it and a body occur? How can a non-physical thing be affected by something physical? To fully appreciate the dualist interactionist's difficulty in successfully answering these questions, we must understand a fundamental feature of causation. On a commonsensical explanation of causation, physical events routinely cause other physical events. While playing pool I thrust my stick at the cue ball and the momentum (i.e. the mass times velocity) of the stick propels the ball in a direction determined by physical features of the stick, the ball and their relative position. The cue ball in turn hits another ball, and the momentum of the cue ball is transferred, in part, to the second ball in strict accord with scientific laws.

Our understanding of the concept of causation is tied to the physicality of objects in spacetime. The movement of the pool stick cannot cause an imaginary ball to move. Nor can an imaginary pool ball cause anything else to move. The dualist interactionist is faced with the problem of showing that alterations in a mental substance—by definition, a substance without any material parts—can cause physical effects. But, on this picture, mental and physical substances are distinct types of things. This makes it difficult to understand how causal interaction can work, in either direction, on the dualist interactionist's theory.

To appreciate this point, consider cases of brain damage. When one's brain is severely damaged due to head trauma, one typically loses certain mental abilities, for example one might develop amnesia and become unable to remember events. If the mind just is the brain, as it is according to the physicalist, then a straightforward explanation is at hand: damage to my physical brain is identical to damage to my mind. But the dualist interactionist must have a very different explanation in mind. Since the mind is constituted by an immaterial substance, it seems as though the mind's abilities would not be damaged simply because there is damage to the material brain. It is thus not clear how the dualist can explain the very tight connection between the brain's health and our mental abilities.

We can exemplify this point in a jocular way through an observation about ghost stories. Ghosts are non-physical entities made from mental or spiritual stuff. You have seen films portraying ghosts haunting houses. The ghosts can do things that material objects cannot, like pass directly through walls without knocking them down. This makes perfect sense if ghosts have no material parts whatsoever. But if ghosts are non-physical, how can they pass through walls *and* make the floorboards creak with their weight? For that matter, how do they keep from passing through the floors if they have no mass whatsoever? The dualist faces closely related questions, for on dualism we are like ghosts living inside bodies.

For the same reasons that most ghost stories flounder on incoherent premises, dualist interactionism flounders on the problem of causation. Problems with causation call into question the basic assumption of dualism, namely that mental and physical objects and states must be categorically different sorts of entities. Dualists insist that mental objects and states must not be physical or explicable in terms of the physical and vice-versa. If the two sorts of entities are so fundamentally different, however, it is not at all clear how they could interact causally. This marks a substantial problem with substance dualism.

Historically, several philosophers attempted to maintain substance dualism but deny causal interaction by holding that there is mind and matter and the two never causally interact. The apparent interactions that we witness day to day are not examples of causal interaction. I desire ice cream, so my body moves its way to the freezer and grabs it, which is an example of mental to physical causal interaction. I cut my arm, and I feel pain, which is an example of physical to mental causal interaction. But according to Gottfried Leibniz's theory, when God created the world, he created two parallel tracks on which it ran: one mental and one physical. Leibniz called this **pre-established harmony** because God arranged the future so that the two tracks ran in perfect harmony, so that no one could tell that causal interaction was not happening. This resembles the way films are recorded on analog tape. Each reel of tape contains two separate recorded tracks, one for audio and one for video.

The main problems of pre-established harmony are, first, that it is a relatively complex theory. Since simplicity is generally a virtue in a theory, this marks a deficit with pre-established harmony. It is complex because there are two substances rather than one, because there are two streams of events rather than one, and because the world that Leibniz envisions requires God's existence and God's planning. Second, pre-established harmony denies a plausible feature of our experience since it implies that mental-to-physical causation and physical-to-mental causation don't occur.

In contemporary research on this problem, the theory of **epiphenomenalism** has gained the allegiance of many leading philosophers. **Epiphenomenalism** is the thesis that mental events are caused by physical events, but that mental events have no causal influence upon any physical events. Epiphenomenalism suggests that the brain causes mental events in the same way that a steam engine causes a whistle to blow. The sound of the whistle plays no causal role in the production of power by the engine. Likewise, mental events play no role causing any physical events.

Epiphenomenalism is not necessarily tied either to physicalism or dualism. In fact, pre-established harmony, a substance dualist theory about mental and physical causation, can be construed as a form of epiphenomenalism on the grounds that mental events have no causal efficacy whatsoever. But as the debate has progressed in contemporary times, epiphenomenalism is construed as a physicalist theory motivated by the claim that physical events are only caused by other physical events. This may seem counterintuitive since physicalism implies that all mental events are identical to physical events. But epiphenomenalism can be taken to describe the causal inefficacy of the mental properties of brain events. The principle support for epiphenomenalism is found in the conjunction of support for physicalism along with a commitment to the *causal closure of the physical*. The causal closure of the physical is the thesis that no non-physical event is capable of causing a physical event.

Arguments against epiphenomenalism often decry the theory as absurd. After all, it appears from the first-person point of view that my beliefs and feelings play causal roles in my actions. When and only when I want to drink a soda do I go get one. Epiphenomenalists must conclude that any influence of the mental on the physical is illusory, so they must deny that my belief that there is soda in the fridge and my desire to drink a soda cause my bodily action. Many, many more arguments for and against epiphenomenalism are available to those who want to find them.

5.4 THE MIND: WHAT IT IS—THE PHYSICALIST ANSWER

We'll use this section to set up a framework for physicalist theories by offering contrasts with dualist theories and by explaining the basic features of all forms of physicalism. In the following sections we will delve into greater explanatory detail about specific physicalist theories.

Philosophers use the term "physicalism" to describe members of a family of theories sympathetic to the basic physicalist thesis. *Basic physicalism* is the thesis that everything is or comes from the physical. This is an ontological thesis—a claim about what there is. Since everything is made of and only of physical ingredients, physicalism offers a monist (not dualist) ontology. This is why neurosurgeons can stimulate a patient's memory cortex and elicit from the person recollection of swimming at a summer camp long ago. We will investigate the arguments for the claim that everything, including mental states, is physical. But first we need to identify what this claim means.

The "to be" verb is notoriously vague and many key points hinge upon its meaning. Consider this sentence: *This book is wood pulp, glue and ink*. But *is* the book anything *over and above* wood pulp and ink? At one level, this book is much more than wood pulp, glue and ink. Suppose you were to slice this book and its pages into microscopic pieces, and put them in a big pile. The pile and the book would be composed of the same exact physical material—the same amounts of wood pulp, glue and ink, but the physical arrangement of the parts changes. The book has many properties that the pile does not: it is in English, it is about the central problems of philosophy, it is something we wrote. The wood pulp, glue and ink aren't any of these things, so the book is more than the sum of its physical parts.

Basic physicalists argue that the physical world is to the mental world like the wood pulp, glue and ink are to the book. Explaining this relationship has become one of the biggest concerns in contemporary philosophy of mind. One explanation uses the concept of **supervenience**. The fact that the book is written in English *supervenes* upon its physical constitution. If some property A supervenes on another property B, then if an object has property A it must have property B. A helpful way to understand supervenience is by thinking about an implication of this definition, which is that any change to A requires a change to B. The sentences in this book supervene upon the distribution of ink on its pages. Changes to the sentences of the book necessitate changes in the distribution of ink on its pages. The image of a stately mansion in an impressionist painting supervenes upon the tiny dots that make it up. If a painter wants to change the image of the mansion on his canvas, then he must change some of the tiny dots.

Supervenience is a relation common in scientific contexts. Many features of the physical world do not seem to be made of matter. For example, magnetic forces and gravitational forces aren't "things" that we can see, hear, touch, taste or smell. But this does not mean they are non-physical. Instead, the physicalist argues that magnetic forces supervene upon molecular composition, since a change in the molecular composition of an object—say, from aluminum to iron—produces a corresponding change in the magnetic force exerted by the object.

Mental properties supervene upon physical base properties, namely electrical and chemical activity in the brain. The basic physicalist asserts that properties of the mind supervene upon its physical constitution. The rich cocoa taste I experience while eating dark chocolate is a mental event—no doubt about that. But the physicalist insists that the mental event supervenes upon the physical constitution of my brain. The supervenience relationship implies that *no pair of things can be physically identical and have different mental properties*. Physical properties in my brain and nervous system determine all my mental properties. Anything with mental properties must be realized or instantiated through more basic physical properties.

At this point reductive and non-reductive forms of physicalism begin to diverge. Types of physicalism can be differentiated in terms of the extent to which each aims to allow a place for mental states in its ontology. Non-reductive physicalists are monists: everything that exists is made out of a single substance, matter. However, non-reductive physicalists hold that the mental properties that emerge from physical base properties have distinct features that are not shared by the physical base properties. Supervenience physicalism is a form of non-reductive physicalism. By denying that all facts about the mental events that arise from physical base properties can be expressed in physical terms, it denies a key feature of reductive physicalism.

Reductive physicalists believe that mental events are nothing over and above physical base properties. Reductive physicalism asserts a strict identity between mental states and corresponding physical states. The theory implies that a mental state is identical with a physical state, which means that mental states have no properties or characteristics other than those possessed by the corresponding physical state.

BOX 5.B: LEIBNIZ ON REDUCTIVE PHYSICALISM

Gottfried Wilhelm Leibniz (1646–1716) was a German mathematician, logician, and philosopher. He invented calculus independently of Sir Isaac Newton. Leibniz made first-rate, lasting contributions in most of the areas of inquiry he studied, which also included law, history, statesmanship and theology. In addition to his advocacy of pre-established harmony, Leibniz famously believed that the fundamental unity of explanation in the philosophy of mind is the monad. A monad is an immaterial, indivisible, mind-like essence. Monads think and perceive; in fact, I am a monad. He fiercely opposed physicalism, and had this to say in objection to what we today know as reductive physicalism:

> If we imagine that there is a machine whose structure makes it think, sense, and have perceptions, we could conceive it enlarged, keeping the same proportions, so that we could enter into it, as one enters into a mill. Assuming

that, when inspecting its interior, we will only find parts that push one another, and we will never find anything to explain a perception. And so, we should seek perception in the simple substance and not in the composite or in the machine.[2]

Can you identify the conclusion of his thought experiment? What are his premises? Leibniz seems to be making unstated assumptions in his reasoning. What are these?

Now we'll examine two theories in the historical development of physicalism in the twentieth century, **type identity theory** and functionalism. Doing this will fill in the physicalist framework we have set up.

5.5 TYPE IDENTITY THEORY

Type identity theory is the thesis that a type or kind of mental state is identical to a type or kind of physical event. To explain this theory, let's explain what "identity" means in this context, and then explain what a "type" is.

Here is a clear, succinct statement of a necessary condition for the identity relation. For any X and any Y, if X is identical to Y then X and Y have all of their intrinsic properties in common. Suppose a philosopher says that the pain I experience at this moment as coming from a cut on a finger *is identical to* C-fibers firing at rate R in my cerebral cortex. This means that that pain and those C-fibers share all their intrinsic properties. Intrinsic properties are non-relational properties of things. Seth may be *taller than* Caleb, which is a relational property. But that Seth is 6' 1" is an intrinsic property since being 6' 1" depends on nothing other than Seth.

Type identity theory is the claim that the mental type *pain* is identical to some neurological type, which we can name "C-fibers firing." This implies that type identity theory differs from basic physicalism. Whereas on basic physicalism, my pain only supervenes upon C-fibers firing, on type identity theory my pain is identical to C-fibers firing. The identity relation is considerably stronger than the supervenience relation. For example, the supervenience of some mental state M on some physical state P leaves open that M might have properties or traits that P lacks. But, given the potency of the identity relation, if some M is identical to some P, then M cannot have any (intrinsic) properties that P lacks.

This is tantamount to saying that type identity theory is a form of reductive physicalism. For our sakes, the term "reductive physicalism" is equivalent to the claim that mental events are identical to physical events in the sense of identity explained above. This makes reductive physicalism an ontological thesis about what there is; specifically, mental states have no intrinsic properties that the physical base properties lack.

This point can be amplified by introducing two terms, "type" and "token," which we'll do with an example. When your boss assigns you a 2,000-word report, she means that there must not be more than 2,000 words in your assignment. This means that the total number of words mustn't exceed 2,000. It does not mean that you can only use a total of 2,000 different words. You might use "and" 60 times and "the" 40 times, and count those 100 words as only two words. (Ahem.) In this context, you conceive of "and" and "the" as *types* of words, while the boss conceives of them as *token* words, or *instances* of word use.

Mental states can be divided between types and tokens, just as words can. Pain considered abstractly is a *type* of mental state, but the pain from a cut in my right index finger is a *token* pain. That token pain is an instance of the type of mental state *pain*. Likewise, belief is a type of mental state, and my belief that *Ottawa is the capital of Canada* is a token of that type.

This point is important for understanding the impetus behind the development of type identity theory. The psycho-physical identity relations hypothesized by the type identity theory are intended to enable scientists to investigate the relationships between mental types and physical, neurological types. Though they are far from a total success, neuroscientists have made significant strides, for example, toward identifying relations between memories and specific electrical patterns recorded in the anterior frontal lobes of our brains.

More success can be achieved if they were to find general laws that correlate mental events of remembrance with precise patterns of neurological activity in different human brains. Scientific laws are general and universal. The law of gravity states that every object in the universe attracts every other object with a force proportional to their masses and inversely proportional to the square of the distance between them. Laws must be general in order to offer explanations and predictions. Type identity theory aspires to foster scientific inquiry and enable neuroscientists to produce testable results about mind–brain relationships.

We might rest content with *token identity theory*, which is the banal claim that each individual mental event is identical to a particular physical event. Token identity theory says only this, and does not offer any further generalization. The token identity of each mental event with a physical event is implied by basic physicalism. Since physicalism asserts that everything is physical or supervenes on something that is physical, it implies the truth of the token identity theory. But token identity theory is not ambitious, it offers scientists no recipe for a research program and it is uncertain how it is to be proved true.

The contrast between type identity theory and token identity theory gives us a glimpse of the motivations on behalf of type identity theory. Now let's contrast type identity theory with substance dualism.

The dualist sees a correlation between mental and physical states: every time you have a thought, there are two simultaneous events, one mental and one physical. But the type identity theorist suggests a simpler hypothesis, namely that mental types of events are identical to physical types of events. From the type identity theorist's point of view, it seems rather odd to describe event M and event P as occurring at the same time with the same causes and effects, and yet to add, as the dualist does, that M and P are not identical.

We've established that type identity theory is more parsimonious than is dualism. This becomes important because both type identity theory and substance dualism are attempting to achieve the same explanatory goals. To say type identity theory is more parsimonious than substance dualism is to say that, where substance dualism sees two things, type identity theory sees only one. The total list of things that exist is for type identity theory much smaller than for dualism since dualism implies minds exist independent from brains. This benefits type identity theory. Or rather, this benefits type identity theory if it achieves the same results as does dualism but with fewer ingredients. Consider this: jet airplanes today are built without propellers. Of course, Boeing could build jet aircraft with propellers, but doing so is beside the point. The simpler the better.

With these contrasts in place, we can turn to a critical evaluation of type identity theory. I'll offer three criticisms of the theory. First, an initial puzzle concerns the way we talk about brain states and mental states. It certainly seems as though the meanings of the terms "pain" and "C-fibers firing" differ considerably. But the advocate of type identity can offer a few responses to this worry. True, the meanings of physical terms and mental terms differ, but that is at most evidence that we have learned improper ways of using language. As mentioned, the terms "the morning star" and "the evening star" have a lengthy history in European culture, and they were used in very different contexts to mean different things. But with the advent of astronomy, Europeans discovered that both terms picked out the same thing, Venus. Philosophers deal with this conundrum by drawing a distinction between the sense of the word and the referent of the word. The *sense* of a word is determined by contextual and cultural factors, while the *referent* of the word is determined by what the word picks out in the world. In this case, the two terms have different senses but the same referent.

The same is true of the term "pain" and the term "C-fibers firing," says the type identity theorist: different senses, same referent. They have the same referent because the mental type *pain* is identical to the physical type *C-fibers firing*. Because they have different senses, we reflect upon pains in a very different way than we reflect upon C-fibers firing. For example, I might assess whether someone is in pain by observing his or her behavior, as opposed to scanning his or her C-fibers with an MRI. But the type identity theory is content with this situation because it is offering a metaphysical reduction, and not a semantic reduction. Type identity theory does not imply that "pain" means the same thing as, or has the same sense as, "C-fibers firing." Instead, the type identity theory implies that my pain *is* my C-fibers firing in just the way that Superman *is* Clark Kent.

Here we mustn't get tripped up upon the English verb "to be." "Is" is often interpreted as having meanings other than identity. Typically "is" conjoins a subject with a predicate that is used to describe the subject, for example "Bilal is from Pakistan" or "Bilal is happy." Bilal is not identical to happy, of course. When writing that "Superman is Clark Kent" I use "is" to join those two nouns: this is the "is" of identity. (For more on identity, see §6.0.)

Here is the second criticism. Return to our necessary condition on identity relations: if X is identical to Y then X and Y have all of their intrinsic properties in common. Frequently the use of the term "identity" in philosophical contexts is slippery, and this is one of those occasions. When I experience a pain, it appears to feel a certain unpleasant way. This way that the pain feels is definitive of a mental state's being *a pain* and not some other mental state, like a daydream or a desire. Daydreams and desires do not feel like pains. But C-fibers firing also don't feel like pains. Here is another example: I look directly at the sun then shut my eyes. I experience a mental state that is presented visually as a bright yellow afterimage. The type identity theory says that this kind of experience is identical to a neurological type: A-fibers firing. But here too, A-fibers firing and yellow afterimages do not share all intrinsic properties. A-fibers are not yellow, but my afterimage is. So the firing of types of neurons in my brain is not identical with pains, afterimages or other mental states.

The third and final criticism of type identity theory is the most forceful. It is best understood through a thought experiment. Type identity theory is committed to certain type-identities, such as "pain is identical to the firing of C-fibers at rate R." But suppose that there are aliens who don't have C-fibers in their brains. Suppose C-fibers are made from chains of carbon-based molecules and aliens have no carbon-based molecules in their silicon-based brains. If so, then type identity theory implies it is impossible that such aliens experience pain. This is because pain is identical to C-fibers firing, which is to say that if and only if C-fibers are firing is there pain. But beings without C-fibers—aliens, or animals, or even other humans—can experience pain. This consequence of type identity theory is extremely counterintuitive.

If this argument is sound, then type identity theory must be false. The problem underlying this argument is known as the problem of *multiple realizability*. Certain mental states are "realizable," i.e. are able to be brought about, through different physical property types. Some pains might be identical to C-fibers firing, while others might be identical to D-synapses firing, and yet other pains might be the product of a certain charge streaming through a silicon computer chip at a certain frequency. Pain is in principle realizable in many different physical types, but type identity theory does not allow for this.

5.6 FUNCTIONALISM

In light of these problems, especially the last, many physicalists gave up type identity theory and crafted a theory called *functionalism*. To use a metaphor from computer science, functionalists recognize that the same software can be run on different hardware. Functionalism is a form of basic physicalism since it does not attempt to make a mental state identical (in the strong sense defined above) with a physical state. In other words, it is a non-reductive form of physicalism. It is a form of physicalism because the causal relationships constituting functional states are thought to be, at bottom, physical in nature.

Functionalism is the thesis that *mental states are identical to functional roles*. Mental states are characterized by the job that they do. Functionalists typically just assume basic physicalism, which implies that they have moved beyond the need to address substance dualism. A functional role is specified by the causal relations a state bears to inputs and outputs in the network of which it is a part. Pain in my body is thus not identical to C-fibers firing at rate R, and is not identical to certain bodily behaviors exhibited by humans.

Mental states, for the functionalist, are defined as a certain ordered set of inputs, interactions with other functional states, and outputs. According to the functionalist, pain is a distinct network of causal relations between mental and sensory inputs and behavioral outputs. What seemed to have been simple mental states now appear rather complex. For example, pain is not identical merely with a feeling of pain. Instead, the functionalist thinks of pain as a set of events, for example, lodging a splinter in my palm, wishing I had not been so careless handling the wood, and yelling "ouch!"

Though this is a good start, this simplified schematic fails to capture the functionalist's vision of the subtlety of the inputs and outputs constituting a mental state. Pains are caused by countless numbers of inputs, they bear much richer functional roles in our network of mental states, and they cause countless numbers of outputs. Think about the events that can cause us pain that just have to do with splinters (lodging a splinter in my right index finger, lodging a splinter in my right pinky . . .). It seems that there are an indefinitely large number of such inputs. In addition those inputs have innumerable outputs of qualitative consciousness, including feeling a sharp, momentarily piercing pain, yelling "*+%&!," or feeling a pulsing, throbbing pain of low intensity, and other cognitive and behavioral outputs, including wishing I had used oak and not poplar, regretting that I hadn't worn gloves, or taking better precautions next time. As you can see, identifying a mental state—any old mental state—by specifying its functional role becomes a very complex activity if functionalism is correct.

Mental states are like engines in this respect. We specify engines by their function, and not by their fuel or by their physical composition. An engine is something into which we place a fuel of some kind, and from which power is generated. Engines can be placed in different physical systems, for example motorcycles and submarines, just like mental states can be placed in different physical systems, for example animals and aliens. Furthermore, engines can be made from different physical components, such as ceramic engines and engines of metal alloys. Engines can be powered by heating water to make steam, igniting gasoline, sunlight, ion streams, liquefied hydrogen or other electromagnetic means. In short, engines take different fuel sources as inputs, have a variety of material configurations and produce power in very different forms. Mental states, for the functionalist, share in this amazing variability and complexity.

Its versatility differentiates functionalism from prior physicalist theories. Only the functionalist can accommodate multiple realizability. The mental event associated with anyone's pricking her left index finger is a physical event, whether it is realized in human, carbon-based neurons or by alien brains that have none of the molecules that our brains have. The alien's experience of pain and my experience of pain are the same type of experience in virtue of the functional, causal roles those experiences play in the greater network of human, and alien, mental events. The way in which functionalism allows for the multiple realizability of mental states gives it a further advantage: mental events can in principle be instantiated in the physical states of circuits on computer chips. Functionalism thus gives a conceptual foundation to the possibility of building an artificial intelligence.

BOX 5.C: *STAR TREK: THE NEXT GENERATION*, "MEASURE OF A MAN"

In "Measure of a Man" (season 2, season episode 9, series episode 35) the USS *Enterprise* docks at a new starbase in deep space, and Captain Bruce Maddox receives permission to disassemble and retro-engineer android Commander Data. In the face of "death" by dissection, Data resigns from Starfleet. But Maddox challenges even this on the grounds that, since Data is a piece of computer equipment, he cannot resign. Captain Picard intends to fight this decision, but the judge advocate general presiding over the new base is an old acquaintance with a chip on her shoulder. Due to a lack of other legal staff on the new base, the JAG officer appoints Picard to defend Data and Commander Riker to prosecute. If the prosecution is successful, Data will cease functioning. In addition, Maddox has plans to build an army of replicas of Data—one for every ship in the fleet.

Suppose you are the JAG officer presiding over this trial. What precisely is the issue? Is it whether or not Data has a consciousness, or has emotions, or has intelligence? Once you figure out the question, what ruling would you make? During the lengthy and dramatic court scene, Picard and Riker make several arguments. How plausible are they?

5.7 ARTIFICIAL INTELLIGENCE

Artificial intelligence (or "AI") refers both to a theoretical discipline aiming to understand intelligence and related mental states by designing machines (usually computer systems) that model the states that are believed to give rise to thought, and to the machines designed to give rise to thought. Physicalist theories of the mind are in principle sympathetic to the creation of an artificial intelligence. Dualist theories are generally not. (In order for human beings to build an AI, they need to build it of material parts. But on dualism, minds are not material.)

Naturally, depending upon what one takes as intelligence, the answer to the question "Can a man-made computer system be intelligent?" may be more or less obvious. If responding to changes in the environment, for example, is all one requires for a thing to qualify as intelligent, the simplest organisms will count as intelligent, as will photographic paper and thermostats. If performing certain chains of reasoning is enough, pocket calculators will qualify.

Intelligence is usually defined, in human terms, by appeal to propositional mental states and their logical relationships. Perhaps if some X is intelligent, then X must be capable of manipulating propositional mental states in ways that model inferential relations. We can imagine that to have intelligence, X must be capable of (i) recognizing a certain symbolic state, and (ii) adding, removing, or rearranging it to produce a new state. Of course, intelligence is not all there is to the life of the mind. But cognitive scientists attempting to create AIs have focused on modeling intelligence and have largely avoided the more difficult problem of creating a being that feels—that possesses qualitative states. What we want to investigate now is how successful the field of AI has been in achieving the goal of modeling intelligence.

BOX 5.D: HAL 9000

Artificial intelligences have been a principal vehicle of science fiction writers who wish to pose questions about the rationality of humanity and the consequences of technological advancement. One of the most famous is HAL 9000, star of the film *2001: A Space Odyssey*. This was directed by Stanley Kubrick and co-written by Arthur C. Clarke (and based upon Clarke's 1951 short story "The Sentinel").

HAL was developed as an on-board AI for the starship *Discovery*. On an exploratory mission in space, the crew members are unaware of findings on Earth's moon that reveal advanced alien technology. Apparently HAL is ordered not to reveal this to the crew, and takes steps to insure they do not discover this truth. The conflict between HAL and the human crew escalates and HAL murders all but one member. This was explained in the sequel, *2010: Odyssey Two*, as arising from cognitive dissonance: HAL, programmed to tell the truth, could lie to the human crew only by virtue of sacrificing its sanity.

Can what HAL did to the human crew be called murder, since that term implies moral responsibility? Presumably, to be morally responsible for an action requires that the agent have a mind. Does HAL? The surviving crew member eventually shuts HAL down. Now consider that action. Is it more like executing a criminal who has committed murder, or more like putting to sleep a dog because it has bit someone? Is it possible for an artificial intelligence to have a psychological breakdown?

Descartes raises questions about artificial intelligence as early as the 1640s. Descartes, a dualist, considers the question of whether human beings could be regarded as machines. He believes animals are very elaborate automata. He says, in his *Discourse on Method*, that the animal's body is a "machine which, having been made by the hands of God, is incomparably better ordered than any machine that can be devised by man, and contains in itself movements more wonderful than those in any such machine."[3] He continues on to argue that we couldn't tell the difference between a real monkey and an artificial monkey because of the ease with which a monkey's behavior can be simulated. But in the case of human beings, our behavior can't be simulated easily by an artificial creation.

He offers two "very certain tests" by which machines could be distinguished from humans, the first of which is the *language user* test. We could make a machine that would emit a word-like sound when we press a button, but it would not be able to use language as a human can. The second, the *general problem solver* test, says that artificial minds can't display the variability and intricacy of the real human mind. In Descartes' words,

> Although many animals show more skill than we do in some of their actions, yet the same animals show none at all in many others; so what they do better does not prove that they have any intelligence, for if it did then they would have more intelligence than any of us and would excel us in everything. It proves rather that they have no intelligence at all.[4]

One forthright response to Descartes' challenges to artificial intelligence comes from A. M. Turing.[5] The development of the computer in the twentieth century, to which Turing contributed, opened new avenues of reply to Cartesian skepticism about artificial intelligence. Like Descartes, Turing tackles an abstruse question by defining a specific test with observable results. Turing's question is, "Can machines think?" His test involves the *imitation game.* Suppose you are playing this game with a number of different individuals, whom you can't observe. You need to determine their identities by means of written questions and answers. Imagine that you are instant-messaging them. You can ask participants to supply information or to perform various tasks. Some of the players are human beings and others are AIs. Could you distinguish between the machine player and the human player? Suppose the machine player could answer factual questions about the past or present just as well as the human player, and suppose that it could perform tasks of the same level of difficulty, such as adding sums, playing card games, reciting rhymes, solving riddles, and so forth. And suppose it did this so well that you were no better at picking it out than you were at picking out the human player it replaced. Turing judges that, if people cannot distinguish the machine players from the human players, then the machine players qualify as artificially intelligent.

Turing's imitation game seems to be a restatement of Descartes' two tests. In order to play the game a machine must be a language user and a general problem solver. Turing accepts Descartes' challenge with a prediction made in 1950 for the year 2000: "I believe that in about fifty years' time it will be possible to program computers . . . [and] make them play the imitation game so well that an average interrogator will not have more than a 70% chance of making the right identification after five minutes of questioning." If you attempt to chat online with the best of the natural language chat bots, you cannot fail to be impressed. Several software programs can pass the Turing test—and much more. (Check out the Loebner Prize winners online.)

You may still wonder how the fact that a machine can imitate what you do proves anything about *how* you do it. Turing maintains that, even though a human nervous system differs from a digital computer, you cannot assume that the "thought" processes in the machine differ from those in the brain because "if we adhere to the conditions of the imitation game, the interrogator will not be able to take any advantage of this difference."[6] Although the physical processes differ in that the human's occur in organic tissue and the AI's occur in silicon chips, they do not differ in their functional capability. If the results of the machine's cognitive processes resemble ours, the processes by which we produce these results must be similar.

You might be skeptical about this. It seems that similar effects could result from quite different causes. For example, you could solve a mathematics problem through the agonizing application of your conscious wits, whereas a machine works it out in a different and quite painless way. Merely looking at the *results* of alleged thinking does not reveal whether thinking actually occurs. So the dualist might respond by arguing that, even if Descartes' "very certain tests" were satisfied, machines do not fully satisfy the tests. They simulate thinking, but do not think.

In contemporary philosophical work, this debate has taken shape in the form of arguments for and against *strong AI*. Strong AI is the thesis that it is physically possible to build and program a computer so that the computer exhibits cognitive processing across problem types. *Weak AI*, its counterpart, asserts the more modest thesis that it is physically possible to build and program a computer in order to study specific problem-solving functions of the human mind: for example, by building computer-based visual recognition systems, we can model how the eye sees.

Computer programs are recipes for processing code, and the programs themselves are written in code. At a foundational level, code is written in a binary language, a symbolic language that uses only two syntactic items: "1" and "0." (The philosopher Gottfried Leibniz, whose ideas we have studied above, invented the binary system for encoding data.) Sets of 1s and 0s can be used to represent any sentence occurring in a natural language, including this one. The relevant feature of computer code for this context is the fact that it is composed of syntactic symbols. 1s and 0s are meaningless without an interpretation. "Syntax" refers to the arrangements of symbols, and "semantic" refers to the meaning derived from an understanding of symbols. The black marks at which you are looking now are, at bottom, syntax. You happen to be able to understand the meaning of the symbols that we know as "letters." So to you these ink marks have semantic content—they mean something to you. But to someone unfamiliar with any Indo-European language, the words in this sentence will not only not be recognized as words in English, but they will not be recognized as words at all. In other words, for such a person, these words will be mere blotches of ink on paper, mere syntax.

In the philosophy reading for this chapter, John Searle uses the observation that software is programmed with syntactic symbols in an argument for the conclusion that strong AI is impossible. He believes that the mere processing of syntax does not enable a computer to think. In the most fascinating portion of his article he creates a thought experiment, one of the most famous in all of philosophy, called the Chinese Room Thought Experiment. If you understand that thought experiment, you will understand his objection to strong AI.

BOX 5.E: *GHOST IN THE SHELL*

Ghost in the Shell is the title of a series of Japanese *manga* created by Masamune Shirow, which has since broadened into a series of films, anime television shows, video games and novels. The series is cyberpunk with a great deal of philosophical sensibility. In this world of a global computer network, several types of AIs, unexpected biotechnology, etc., Shirow manages to create interest in the viewer in the persons/AIs by allowing them to converse and muse about their status as human beings.

One plot arc involves the search by Public Security Section 9 for the Puppeteer, an apparently artificial entity that has the ability to hack through cybernetic implants into the minds of "humans." The "ghost" of the title refers to an individual's mind. The etiology of the title traces back to the work of philosopher Gilbert Ryle, who attempted to ridicule dualism by referring to it as a theory upholding the existence of a ghost in a machine. In the hands of Shirow, people notionally hold onto their "ghosts" as a last-ditch effort to maintain their humanity in a world where many people—including the lead character, Motoko Kusanagi—are almost entirely mechanized.

Countless philosophical questions are posed in the series. What is the meaning of the term "mind'? The Puppeteer is an incredibly intelligent, and therefore dangerous AI, but does it have any rights? Is the government morally justified in hunting it down and deleting (or killing) it? What results when the Puppeteer merges with Kusanagi's "mind'? At that point in the film, the fused being is given a new body, but whose is it? In the series, Tachikoma AIs appear to share a mind. Is this possible? When a cyborg commits a crime in this future world, are they responsible for their actions if their actions result from an algorithm they are running? What sort of social relationships would develop in a world in which you can, if allowed, directly access the thoughts of your friends and co-workers?

5.8 PROBLEMS WITH PHYSICALISM: THE KNOWLEDGE ARGUMENT

We have construed basic physicalism as an *ontological* thesis about what there is. Physicalists are substance monists since they assert that everything that exists is particles or waves in spacetime. But one point of attack against physicalism lies in showing that it has unacceptable *epistemological* implications. In other words, given a certain theory about *what there is* in the world, one might argue that it follows that *we cannot know* things we think we can know. For example, in Chapter 3, I argued that a certain ontological thesis about God leads to epistemic consequences, namely it leads to our inability to know the truth about moral statements.

This roughly characterizes the approach taken by some opponents of physicalism, most notably Frank Jackson. He employs his famous "Mary the scientist" thought experiment in the service of this objection:

> Mary is a brilliant scientist who is, for whatever reason, forced to investigate the world from a black and white room via a black and white television monitor. She specializes in the neurophysiology of vision and acquires, let us suppose, all the physical information there is to obtain about what goes on when we see ripe tomatoes, or the sky, and use terms like "red," "blue," and so on. She discovers, for example, just which wavelength combinations from the sky stimulate the retina, and exactly how this produces via the central nervous system the contraction of the vocal chords and expulsion of air from the lungs that results in the uttering of the sentence "The sky is blue." . . . What will happen when Mary is released from her black and white room or is given a color television monitor? Will she learn anything or not? It seems just obvious that she will learn something about the world and our visual experience of it. But then is it inescapable that her previous knowledge was incomplete? But she had all the physical information. Ergo there is more to have than that, and Physicalism is false.[7]

The example is intuitive and understandable, but in the last line he concludes that physicalism is false. This may seem too quick. After all, physicalism is a thesis about *what there is*, not about *what we know*. Let's make an attempt to state this argument, the **knowledge argument**, formally to clarify this issue:

(5.5)   Mary, though having always been confined to a black and white environment, knows all the facts regarding the physical process of human color vision.

(5.6)   Mary does not know all the facts regarding human color vision.

(5.7)   So, there are facts regarding human color vision *in addition to* facts regarding the physical process of human color vision. (powerful principle)

(5.8)   So, the basic physicalist thesis is false.

It seems quite clear that 5.5 is possible, which is all that 5.5 needs to be for the sake of the argument. It also seems that, given the thought experiment, 5.6 would be true. Mary would not know what it is like to have certain experiences of color that most of us take for granted—the luster of a shiny red car and the bright orange glow of the evening sun. Knowing the neurological facts of the matter, or the various functional roles that mental states like "seeing red" play in our mental network, does not give Mary the qualitative experiences associated with the visual perception of color. And if 5.5 and 5.6 are true, then 5.7 follows.

But how do we move from 5.7 to 5.8? 5.7 says roughly that there are some facts about color that are not about the physical process of color perception. We can take this in two different ways. We might interpret 5.7 as meaning either (i) that there is some *way of knowing* something about the process of vision that Mary lacks, or (ii) that there is *information about* human color vision unknown to Mary. If (i) is true, then the argument is not forceful against physicalism. This is because there may be two ways to know the same facts, in which case there is nothing that Mary does not know. For example, in 2001 two separate teams of researchers, using two distinct methods, both showed that the movement of light can not only be slowed, but stopped. The teams used electromagnetically induced transparency techniques to halt the movement of photons by emitting two beams through a dense gas. One of the teams used an extremely cold sodium gas, while the other team used a warmer rubidium gas to obtain this result. The point is that both teams use quite different methods to learn the same thing. But the fact that there was a *different way of knowing* that photons can be stopped does not imply that either team *lacks knowledge* that photons can be stopped.

The way we have stated the argument leans toward an interpretation of (ii), which marks a stronger reading of the argument—one that is more likely to threaten the physicalist position. The claim, then, is that there are non-physical properties of color vision, and Mary does not know any of the statements expressing those facts. For example, there is a fact about what seeing red is like, and this is not a fact about the physical process of human color vision. But the argument is not merely about Mary's inability to know what it is like to see what we see when we see red. Merely seeing a red object would not give a person—even a person as smart as Mary—knowledge of the wavelengths of light refracted from the object.

Even if Mary sees red, it doesn't follow that she *knows* she is seeing red, as opposed to orange or yellow. Thus, a second set of non-physical facts that Mary doesn't know includes the facts that correlate our awareness of certain qualitative states with color-terms like "red," "orange," and so on. Proponents of this argument conclude that there are truths about our world that apparently do not supervene upon physical facts.

One prominent criticism of the knowledge argument attempts to show that 5.7 does not follow from the two premises, i.e. attempts to deny that there are additional facts that Mary comes to know. This criticism is based on a distinction between propositional knowledge and abilities. Propositional knowledge is knowledge of facts, for example knowledge *that* Neil Armstrong was the first person on the moon, and is the form of knowledge at issue in the argument. But, according to the physicalist, when Mary finally does see the color red, she does not acquire new propositional knowledge. To learn what it is like to perceive in color is not something that is resolved into propositional knowledge. We cannot adequately express the knowledge that Mary acquires by finally seeing red by specifying that experience inside a that–clause. The defender of physicalism argues that knowledge of what the phenomenology of a new experience is like is a form of procedural knowledge. Recall that procedural knowledge is *knowing how*, not *knowing that*. We say that I know how to put together a bicycle, and this is a form of knowledge that seems quite different in kind from propositional knowledge (on which see Chapter 2). If Mary's new knowledge, after seeing in color for the first time, is not propositional knowledge, then 5.7 does not seem to follow from 5.5 and 5.6.

One might attack this physicalist response to the knowledge argument by inquiring about the nature of the procedural knowledge in question. Just what sort of procedural knowledge is it that Mary lacks? The physicalist might respond that one bit of procedural knowledge Mary lacks is the ability to imagine the color red. But to explain the procedural knowledge present in knowing what it is like to see in color by appeal to imagination has problems. One might be a particularly unimaginative person not gifted with the ability to picture or conceive of new experiences or events. Yet one could surely know what it is like to see red, since the ability to perceive in color and experience the qualitative states associated with such perceptions are totally independent of one's imaginative abilities. This is to say that imagination is not necessary for having procedural knowledge.

BOX 5.F: THE QUALITATIVE EXPERIENCE OF AI

Science fiction often portrays artificial intelligences as utterly lacking qualitative states: early robots are stolid, purposeful and lacking any feeling. They process information, sense motion, and perform other rudimentary tasks. In the original series of *Star Trek*, First Officer Spock, who is half-human and half-Vulcan, is often portrayed as having the emotional intelligence of a hard disk due to his inability to experience feelings. (Of course, since Spock is half-human, he can experience some feelings.)

Star Trek: The Next Generation revives this issue, and openly recognizes the great difficulty faced by cognitive scientists in programing an AI with qualitative states, through the portrayal of the character called Commander Data. Data is an android who experiences no qualitative states, which in turn befuddles his attempts to understand the motivations and behaviors of we human beings. In the feature film *Star Trek: Generations*, Data installs an emotion chip that immediately transforms him from a zombie to someone who experiences the full range of emotional and qualitative states.

A few classic science fiction AIs brilliantly invert this SF trope in which AIs do not feel. In Robert Heinlein's *The Moon is a Harsh Mistress*, the lunar computer network, Mike, becomes self-aware, develops a wry sense of humor and becomes the most "human" character in the book. Douglas Adams' android, Marvin, "Your plastic pal who's fun to be with," is depressed and bored. His intelligence is so vast that he knows everything, and therefore nothing is of any interest to him. At one point he is said to solve "all of the major mathematical, physical, chemical, biological, sociological, philosophical, etymological, meteorological and psychological problems of the Universe except his own, three times over."

5.9 SUMMARY

The philosophy of mind is a branch of philosophy aimed at understanding how the mind works, what the mind is made of, and how the mind is related to the physical world. We began this chapter with a discussion of substance dualism, which implies that there are two substances, mind and matter. This required clarifying the meaning of the term "substance" and disambiguating its uses. Substance dualism contrasts with physicalism. Physicalism is an ontological thesis that says that nothing exists but matter in spacetime, so souls—immaterial objects—do not exist. Those two theories are theories about what the mind is, but what the mind does is also controversial. The mind is capable of undergoing several distinct types of state. Just amongst conscious states, there are several noteworthy forms, including reflexive consciousness, qualitative consciousness, and intentionality.

With this in place, we offered an argument on behalf of dualism—the conceivability argument. We identified its premises and conclusions and diagnosed its failure in an equivocation. We continued our discussion of dualism by identifying another problem, the problem of causal interaction. Mental events cause physical events and physical events cause mental events, but the dualist is at a loss to explain how such forms of causation are possible since matter and mind share no properties in common.

We turned next to physicalist theories of the mind, and defined basic physicalism as the thesis that everything is or comes from the physical. Physicalism comes in several subspecies, principally supervenience physicalism, reductive physicalism and non-reductive physicalism. Type identity theory is a form of reductive physicalism asserting that the class of pains is identical to a class of neurological events. The primary ambition of type identity theory is to make the study of the mind scientifically respectable. But type identity theory ran afoul of the problem of multiple realizability. "Multiple realizability" is a term that refers to the hypothesis that different physical systems can support the same mental states. Type identity theory does not allow this, however.

Reflection on the problem of multiple realizability leads to the advent of functionalism, the thesis that a mental state is identical with its functional role. According to functionalism, mental states are to be characterized independently of their makeup. Functionalism is consistent with the goals of cognitive science and artificial intelligence, in ways that type identity theory was not.

We discussed one major problem of physicalism at length: the knowledge argument. This argument uses the "Mary the scientist" thought experiment to show that there are some facts about the world that are not reducible to physical facts. Specifically, what it is like to experience a color is something that one cannot know unless one has the right state of qualitative consciousness.

5.10 ABOUT THE READINGS

"Truncat," by Cory Doctorow (1971–), is our science fiction reading. In addition to being an award winning science fiction author, Cory Doctorow is a technophile and activist championing freedom in and through technology. In "Truncat," the evolving freedom we know on the Internet has reached lofty heights. Adrian is an eighteen-year-old resident of Toronto who spends most of his time on the massive network that he accesses through his mind/brain. He is a member of an informal group of like-minded young people, the "Million," who want to become "post people." A key step in achieving that goal was the discovery of a means to save and trade the sum total experiences of other human beings, and re-experience them by running them in your mind/brain through a process called "flash-baking." However, these sums of total experience are bootlegs and are illegal. Under the watchful eye of his mom, Adrian continues with his work with the Million and meets a girl from space who offers him a new perspective on his activities.

Doctorow assumes for the sake of his story that the mind's contents can be represented as digital data. Historically, many philosophers, most prominently René Descartes, held that this was impossible. In our history of philosophy reading, Descartes offers arguments for substance dualism and against artificial intelligence. In addition, selections from Descartes' *Meditations* pick up his argument following his response to evil demon skepticism present in our Chapter 2 selection of *Meditations* I and II. At the close of Meditation II, Descartes proves that he exists as a thinking thing. Thus far, this is the only fact Descartes knows. Now he sets about determining what else he might be. In particular, he wants to learn whether he has any physical component. This chapter contains two selections from Descartes' *Meditations*. In the first, he discusses the nature of consciousness and the differences between body and mind. In the second, he argues for the conclusion that the mind is a non-physical substance by virtue of his conceptual abilities. The reading from Descartes' *Discourse on Method* offers and defends two "tests" or necessary conditions (mentioned above) for genuine intelligence. Even today it appears Descartes' tests are not passed—at least, not with an A grade—by robots, but they come very close.

Above we described Descartes' considerations against the hypothesis that a machine could become intelligent. John Searle (1932–), a famous philosopher of mind from whom we draw our third reading, is no substance dualist, but he shares with Descartes a skepticism about the ability of machines to manifest intelligence and what he calls "understanding." Searle's concerns are much better developed than are Descartes', and his central argument flows out of a compelling thought experiment about how a computer processes information.

5.11 "TRUNCAT," BY CORY DOCTOROW

"Adrian, you have a million friends," his mother said. "That's an audited stat. I'm sorry if you feel isolated, but none of us are moving to Bangalore just so you can chum it up with this fellow."

Adrian fought to control his irritation. His mother was always cranky before breakfast, and a full-blown fight could extend that mood through the whole day. No one needed that. "Mom," he said, twisting his body in the narrow, three-person coffin he shared with his folks so that he could look her in the eye, "I'm not asking you to move to India. All I'm doing is explaining my paper."

His mother snorted. *"The Last Generation on Earth,* really! Adrian, if I were your instructor, I sure wouldn't graduate you on the strength of something like that. I don't really care if that boy in India has convinced the ITT people that his trendy little thesis holds water. The University of Toronto has higher standards than that."

It had been a mistake to even discuss it with his mother. At 180, she was hardly equipped to understand the pressures he and his minuscule generation faced. He should've just written it and stuck it in his advisor's public directory. Only just that he'd had the coolest idea in the night and he'd reflexively bounced it off of her: Once his generation reached maturity, the whole planet would be post-human, and a new, new era would start. The Bitchun Society, Phase II.

"OK, Mom, OK. I'm going to get breakfast—you want to come?"

"No," she said, rolling back over. "I'm going to wait for your father."

Past her, he saw the snoring bulk of his father, still zonked out even through their heated exchange. Adrian grasped the ceiling rails and inched himself out of the coffin and into the public corridor.

His gut was rumbling, but the queue for the canteen was still lengthy, packed with breakfasters from the warren where he made his home. Reluctantly, he decided to skip breakfast and go to his private spot. It was almost backup time, and he needed to do some purging.

Truth be told, Adrian's private spot was not all that private, and it was a humongous bitch to reach. His netpals liked to compare notes on their hidey-holes, and Adrian was certain that he had the shittiest, least practical of the lot.

First, Adrian got on the subway, opting to go deadhead for a faster load-time. He stepped into the sparkling cryochamber at the Downsview Station, conjured a helmet-mounted display (HUD) against his field of vision, and was granted permission to be frozen. The next thing he knew, he was thawing out on the Union Station platform, pressed belly-to-butt with a couple thousand other commuters who'd opted for the same treatment. In India, where this kind of convenience-freezing was even more prevalent, Mohan had observed that the reason their generation was small for their age was that they spent so much of it in cold-sleep, conserving space in transit. Adrian might've been 18, but he figured that he'd spent at least one cumulative year frozen.

Adrian shuffled through the crowd and up the stairs to the steady-temp surface, peeling off the routing sticker that the cryo had stuck to his shoulder. His tummy was still rumbling, so he popped the sticker in his mouth and chewed until it had dissolved, savoring the steaky flavor and the burst of calories. The guy who'd figured out edible routing tags had Whuffie to spare: Adrian's mom knew someone who knew someone who knew him, and she said that he had an entire subaquatic palace to rattle around in.

A clamor of swallowing noises filled his ears, as the crowd subvocalized, carrying on conversations with distant friends. Adrian basked in the warm, simulated sunlight emanating from the dome overhead. He was going outside of the dome in a matter of minutes, and he had a sneaking suspicion that he was going to be plenty cold soon enough. He patted his little rucksack and made sure he had his cowl with him.

He inched his way through the crowd down Bay Street to the ferry docks, absently paging through his public directory, looking at the stuff he'd accumulated in the night. It would all have to go, of course, but he wanted a chance to run some of it before then. Most of it was crap, of course. The average backup of the average citizen of the Bitchun Society was hardly interesting enough to warrant flash-baking, but there were gems, oh yes.

His private spot hung tantalizingly before him, just outside of the dome. The press of bodies parted and he lengthened his step to the docks, boarded the ferry with a nod to the operator in his booth, and hustled into one of the few seats on the prow, pulling on his cowl as the ferry pushed away and headed off toward the airlock at Toronto Island.

It was even colder than the last time. The telltale on his cowl showed −48 degrees C with the wind-chill. His nose and toes went instantly numb, and he tucked them under the cowl's warmth.

His private place was just a short slosh from the westernmost beach at Hanlon's Point on Toronto Island, a forgotten smartbuoy, bristling with self-repairing electronics, like a fractal porcupine. It had been a couple of weeks since his last foray there, and in the interim, the buoy had grown more instrumentation, closing over the narrow entryway into its console-pod. Cursing under his breath, Adrian wrapped his cowl around his hands and broke off the antennae, tossing them into the choppy Lake Ontario froth. Then he climbed inside and held his breath.

Breakers crashing on Hanlon's Point. Distant hum of the airlock. A plane buzzing overhead. Silence, of a sort. A half-eaten sandwich moldered near his right hand. Disgustedly, he pitched it out, silently cursing the maintenance crews that periodically made their way out to his buoy and tried to puzzle out the inexplicable damage he'd wrought on it.

But the silence, ah. His mother never understood the need for silence. She was comforted by the farting, breathing, shuffling swarm of humanity that bracketed her at all times. She'd spent a couple decades jaunting, tin-plated and iron-lunged in the vast emptiness of space, and she'd had her fill of quiet and then some. Adrian, though, with 18 (or 17) years of the teeming hordes of the post-want Bitchun Society, couldn't get enough of it.

His public directory was bursting with backups, the latest batch that his contemporaries around the world had passed to him. Highly illegal, the backups were out-of-date consciousness-memoirs created by various citizens of the Bitchun Society, a weekly hedge against irreparable physical harm.

Theoretically, when you made a new backup, the old one was discarded, the file copied to a nonexistent node on the distributed network formed by the combined processing power of the implanted computers carried by every member of the Bitchun Society. Theoretically.

Adrian paged through the directory. Carrying one of the bootlegs into a backup terminal would mean instant detection. Even xmitting it to someone else was risky, and prone to being sniffed. But Mohan, his netpal in Bangalore, had authored a sweet little tool that allowed for xmission over the handshaking and routing channel, a narrowband circuit that carried unreliable—and hence untraceable—information that would have been overheard in the main data channels. The Million had quickly adopted the tool, and they used it to pass their contraband to each other, copying the bootlegs prior to erasing them when their own weekly backup sched rolled around.

Adrian had good Whuffie with the Million. Nothing like Mohan, of course, but still good—he reliably stored bootlegs for the Million, even if it meant putting off his own backup until he could find safe storage for all those materials entrusted to him. He didn't mind: being a high-Whuffie storage repository meant that he got everyone's most precious bootlegs for safekeeping.

Like this one, the backup of a third-gen Bitchun, born at the end of the XXIst century, female (though that hadn't lasted long). Seventy years later, her/his backup was a rich tapestry of memories, spectacular space battles, incredible sexual adventures, side-splitting jokes, exotic flavors and esoteric knowledge absorbed from brilliant teachers all over the planet. He'd held onto it for two weeks now, and flash-baked it nearly every day.

Time to do it again. Quickly, he executed the command, and shuddered as that consciousness was rolled up into a bullet of memories and insights and fired directly into his mind, unfolding overtop of his own thoughts and dreams so that for a moment, he *was* that person, her/his self enveloping Adrian with an infinitude of bombarding sense impressions.

It ebbed away, the rush fading in a synaptic crackle, leaving him trembling and wrung out. He slumped against the buoy's spiny interior and brought up a HUD and started an agent searching for another member of the Million with storage to spare for a copy of it.

Backup days were flash-baking days. In the buoy, Adrian flash-baked a dozen times, alternating between timeworn favorites and the tastiest morsels deposited by the rest of the Million. He gorged himself on the antique consciousnesses of the immortals of the Bitchun Society, past satiety and full to bursting, his head throbbing dangerously.

Each time, he carefully passed the file to the network, waiting while the churning, clunking handshaking channel completed the transfer. He didn't mind the wait: It gave him a moment for the synesthetic rushes to pass. Time grew short, and his gut growled protests, sending up keotic belches that filled the closed space with the smell of esters.

One more, one more, deposited for safekeeping by Mohan himself in the night. Mohan sat at the river's headwaters, the source of all the bootlegs. He was the theoretically nonexistent node to which the backup network flushed its expired files. When he identified a keeper, it had to be good. Adrian had saved it for last, and now he rolled it and jammed it into his brain.

God. God. The person was so *old,* saurian and slow, nearly 300, an original revolutionary from the dawn of the Bitchun Society. Just a kid, then, rushing the barricades, destroying the churches, putting on a homemade police uniform and forming the first ad-hoc police force. Boldly walking out of a shop with an armload of groceries, not paying a cent, shouting jauntily over his shoulder to "Charge it up to the ol' Whuffie, all right?"

What a time! Society in hybrid, halfway Bitchun. The religious ones eschewing backup, dying without any hope of recovery, entrusting their souls to Heaven instead of a force-grown clone that would accept an upload of their backup when the time came. People actually *dying*, dying in such number that there were whole industries built around them: gravediggers and funeral directors in quiet suits! People refusing free energy, limitless food, immortality.

And the Bitchun Society outwaited them. They died one at a time, and the revolutionaries were glad to see them go, each one was one less dissenter, until all that remained was the reputation economy, the almighty Whuffie Point, and a surfeit of everything except space.

Adrian's grin was rictus, the hard mirth of the revolutionaries when the last resister was planted in the ground, their corpses embalmed rather than recycled. Years and decades and centuries ticked past, lessons learned, forgotten, relearned. Lovers, strange worlds, inventions and symphonies and magnificent works of art, and ahead, oh ahead, the centuries unrolling, an eternity of rebirth and relearning, the consciousness living on forever.

And then it was over, and Adrian was sweating and still grinning, the triumphant hurrah of the revolutionary echoing in his mind, the world his oyster.

"Oh, Mohan," he breathed to himself. "Oh, that was terrific." He scouted the network on his HUD, looking for a reliable member of the Million, someone he could offload this to so that he could get it back after his own backup was done. There—a girl in France, directory wide open. He started the transfer, then settled back to bask in the remembered exultation of his last flash-bake.

His cochlea chimed. The HUD said it was his mother. Damn.

"Hi, Mom," he said.

"Adrian!" she said. "Where are you?" She wasn't in a good mood, that much was clear.

"Uh," he said. "On the subway," he extemporized. "I'm gonna see if Mr. Bosco can see me." Bosco was the admissions advisor at the University of Toronto that he'd been sucking up to lately, trying to charm the old ad-hocrat into letting him into school for the fall semester. It wasn't easy: The undergrad program at the University was winding down in favor of exclusive, high-Whuffie one-on-one grad programs. Teaching the sparse under-grads of the Million was anything but a glamor gig.

"Bosco?" his mother said, mollified. "Well, that's . . . good. Listen, I don't want you talking about this admissions paper idea of yours—nobody wants to hear about how you and your friends are the last generation of humans. Every generation thinks they're special—it's just not so."

"Fine," he said. He wouldn't talk to Bosco anytime soon if he could help it, anyway.

"Your father worked with you on that good N-P Complete proof. Present that instead."

"Sure," he said. The revolutionary still echoed in his mind, like distant gunfire.

His mother talked on, and he kept his answers down to one syllable until she let him go. Back in the quiet of the buoy, he quickly purged all the bootlegs from his public directory, pulled his cowl tight and reluctantly climbed outside and back to the Island, there to await the ferry.

Adrian's backup was uneventful, a moment before a secure broadband terminal while his life flashed before his eyes, extracted and spread out to a redundant assortment of nodes on the 15 billion-person network that carpeted the earth.

This obeisance to the Bitchun Society completed, he took to the downtown streets, waiting for the files he'd farmed out and deleted to trickle back in. Waiting for the revolutionary's backup, for another taste of exultation and grandiose triumph. He walked all the way from Union Station to Bloor, a good hour in the glottal press of the lunchtime crowd, and still the revolutionary failed to reappear. Clucking his tongue in annoyance, he ducked into a doorway and checked for the French girl.

Her directory was purged! In the space of mere hours, she'd discarded all the third-party files deposited in her personal directory!

It was really inexcusable. The only possible mitigation would be if she'd passed the file on to someone else before deleting it. He spawned an agent and set it hunting for the file through the network of the Million, branching out in binary search from the nodes that were most commonly employed by the French girl.

His mother rang his cochlea again, and he passed her to voice mail, but the ringing stung him into worry. He had a week before the admissions committee deadline at the U of T, and he'd never hear the end of it if he didn't get in. He thought back to the revolutionary, to his participation in the grad-student takeover of the Soc Department in the mid-XXIst, the replacement of tenure with Whuffie.

Those were the days! Real battles, real principles, and the blissful, blessed elbow room. That's what he needed. Or, failing that, another crack at flash-baking the bootleg. Damn that French bimbo, anyway.

His cochlea rang again, his mother. Resigned, he answered.

"Adrian, where are you?" She sounded like she was in a better mood, anyway.

"I'm at Yonge and Bloor, Mom. Having a walk, looking for somewhere to get some lunch."

"What did Mr. Bosco say?"

Damn, damn, damn. "He said he'd think about it—he'll get back to me with comments tomorrow."

"Really?" his mother said, sounding genuinely interested. Bosco had never really given him the time of day.

"Yeah," he said. "I think he liked it, the N-P Complete thing, I mean. I didn't mention the other thing."

"Funny," she said, and her voice was all ice now. "He didn't mention your visit at all when I spoke to him just now."

The blood drained from Adrian's face. He wouldn't hear the end of this for some time. "Uh," he said.

"Just listen to me, kid, don't say anything else. You're in enough trouble as it is. I've got your father conferenced in, and I can tell you he isn't looking like he's very happy."

"Now, here's how it's going to be. I've set up an appointment with Bosco in one hour. I had to call in a lot of favors to do it, and you will be on time. Your father will be there, and you'll tell Bosco how excited you are by this opportunity. You won't mention this stupidity you've been chasing. You will show him how diligent you are in your studies, show him how much you can benefit the university, and you will be cheerful and smart. Do you understand?"

"Yes," Adrian said. Jesus, she was furious.

"One hour," she said, and rang off.

Adrian's agent found the bootleg again just as he reached the waiting room at Innis College. The French one *had* passed it on before deleting it, to another girl in Kansas. Sighing with relief, he queued the download just as his father arrived.

Adrian's father was apparently 22, hardly older-seeming than Adrian himself, though his real age was closer to 122. All Adrian's life, his father had kept himself at an apparent age that was just a few years older than Adrian's own, following a bit of child-rearing wisdom that had been trendy 50 years before, just as the Bitchun Society started to mete out Whuffie-punishments for those people selfish enough to contribute to the overcrowding by reproducing. The logic ran that having a father of playmate-size would reduce the loneliness of the children of the diminished generation of the day.

At 22, Adrian's father was heavyset and acne-pocked, his meaty pelt bulging whenever it came into contact with the light cotton djellaba he wore around town.

He gave Adrian a curt nod when he arrived, his eyes fixed on a space in the middle-distance where his omnipresent HUD shone for him alone. He took a seat next to Adrian and rang his cochlea.

Adrian rolled his eyes and answered subvocally. Why his father couldn't have an unmediated conversation was beyond him. "Hi, Dad," he said.

"Hi there. Had a good morning?"

"Good enough," Adrian answered. "How's Mom?"

His father subvocalized a chuckle, the sound in Adrian's cochlea blending weirdly with the swallowing sounds from his father's throat. "She's pretty angry. Don't worry about it— we'll do a dog 'n' pony for Bosco and she'll forget all about it."

Bosco opened the office door and greeted them. Adrian's father answered audibly, his voice rusty from disuse.

In Bosco's leatherbound academic cave of an office, the two adults chattered boringly and lengthily. Adrian knew the drill, knew that it could be a long time before anyone could have anything to say to him.

Sneaking a glance at his father and Bosco, he rolled up the revolutionary's backup and flash-baked it.

The life unrolled over his mind, the early days of the Bitchun Society, the physical battles and the ego clashes; first adulthood lived as a nomad, trekking around the globe; a second and third adulthood, a fourth, moving toward that moment at which the backup was taken, when eternity unrolled, and

snip

It cut off.

Adrian's eyes popped open. *Damn.* Truncat! The file had been chopped short during transmission between the nodes. Half the revolutionary's life vanished into a random scattering of bits and aether.

Bosco was looking expectantly at him, heavy-lidded, wavy hair and thick eyebrows and crinkles at the corners of his eyes from long hours of thinking. He had said something. Hurriedly, Adrian zipped through his short-term AV capture on a HUD, played back to Bosco saying, "Well, Adrian, this is a very well-prepared entrance paper. Can you tell me what it is about mathematics that interests you?"

Now Bosco and Adrian's father were both staring, and Adrian mimed concentration, as though he were genuinely considering his answer. In truth, he was paging through his files for the canned response his mother had provided him with, but there was no sense in admitting it.

"I've always loved math," he recited, struggling to remember the phrasing. "I just can't help seeing the mathematical relationships in everyday life. It just makes sense to me."

Bosco nodded, the ritual response satisfying him. Adrian's father gave him an appraising look and went back to wrangling with Bosco. It all came down to Whuffie, anyway—did Adrian's parents have enough reputation capital that their gratitude to Bosco outweighed the upset the teaching staff would feel when they were saddled with a lowly undergrad?

The meeting was hardly over before his mother was conferencing Adrian and his father in. As it turned out, Adrian's father had been dumping a real-time video stream to her all through the meeting; she'd seen it all. "Adrian," she said, sharply, "What's the matter with you? You were completely out of it during that whole thing."

"I was just thinking, Mom. I got distracted. I think it went well, anyway, right, Dad?"

"Sure, sure," his father subvocalized, patting him on the shoulder. "I think you're all set for next term."

But Adrian's mother was not to be mollified. "Adrian, I'm sick of all this flakiness. I know exactly what you were *thinking* about—" Adrian's heart sank: how could she know about the bootleg? "All that adolescent hand-wringing about your generation is distracting you from your real priorities, and it's time you smartened up. Grant me private access, I want a look at what you've been up to."

Oh, shit. Hurriedly, Adrian flushed the bootlegs. His mother hadn't gone picking though his files in years, so it took him a moment to remember the mnemonic that erased the bootlegs and all records of their existence from his personal storage. In his cochlea, his mother made impatient noises, and that sure didn't help.

Once the data was flushed, he granted her access. He watched dismally as his system log scrolled by, every file in his storage piping through his mother's keyword filter.

"'The parents of the Million are understandably resentful of their offspring,'" she read, in a dangerous voice. It was the paper he and Mohan had been collaborating on, and he knew she wasn't going to like it. "'For whatever reason, they chose to bring a generation into being at a time when the world wanted nothing but. The sacrifices they've endured since are immense, Whuffie penalties that mount daily as their peers make their disapproval felt. Our parents are stuck in the closest thing the Bitchun Society has to poverty, and it's our fault.'"

She paused and drew breath. "All right, Mom, all right, that's enough," Adrian said. "I'll get rid of it."

She snorted. "You're damned right, you will. Just adolescent nonsense—"

"I know," Adrian said. "I'm sorry." Mohan had a copy, anyway—he could recover it later.

"Don't switch off my access, either," she said, to Adrian's dismay. "I'll be checking in regularly from now on—you've got to concentrate on your studies, not this, this—"

Words failed her.

Adrian wasn't really sure what physically proximate friends did for fun, but Tina had all sorts of ideas. They met up for breakfast the next morning at a public maker near Adrian's place, and the queue had never seemed shorter, as they gabbled in the near-silence of the thronged corridor.

They walked while they shoveled post-scarcity waffles and sausage into their mouths, Tina remarking constantly on the crowds, the sheer thronging humanity of it all. The parks were all too dense for fun, but they found ample elbow room way out in the east end, where untalented sculptors operated public studios in the unpopular former scraplands.

The fight was Adrian's fault. "I want to meet him," Adrian said, as they watched a man with hammer and chisel crawl over a hideous marble lion.

"Him?" Tina said. "Why? He stinks."

Adrian smiled and shushed her. "Not so loud—anyway, he's not as bad as some of the people around here. No, not him—Nestor, the ship's engineer. You know—"

Her expression slammed shut. "No. God! No! Adrian, why—" She choked on whatever she was going to say next.

Adrian, taken aback, said carefully, "Why not? I really, you know, *admire* him."

"But you've been inside his head!" she said, scandalized. "How could you look him in the eye after—" Again, words failed her.

"But that's *why* I want to meet him! What I saw, what he knows, it just makes so much sense. I feel like he could really tell me what it's all about."

Her eyes took on the aspect of steel again, the million lightyear stare. "If you talk to Nestor, I'll never speak to you again. I'll—I'll turn you in! I'll report you and all of your pals!"

"Jesus, Tina, what's *wrong* with you? You're supposed to be my friend and now you're going to *turn me in?*" He was so angry, he could hardly speak. He wished he was talking to her over the network, so that he could just hang up and walk away. He did the next best thing, turning on his heel and walking away.

"Hey," Tina shouted, angry too.

He kept on walking.

She found him in his private place, holding a one-sided argument with his mother. "Mom, I'm old enough to get a place of my own, and you can't stop me," he shouted into the buoy's guts. In her cochlea, he heard his mother's grunt of anger, and his HUD was filled with the scrolling system log as she angrily deleted his files, being on a particularly nasty tear that day.

"Mom!" he shouted again. "Talk to me or I'll—I'll lock you out!"

Tina watched this, half in, half out of the buoy, her bottom exposed to the frigid stinging rain, her face flushed with the captured body heat in the buoy. Adrian had yet to notice her, too absorbed in his conversation.

"That's it," he said. "I'm locking you out now."

He opened his eyes and sighed back against the buoy's bulkhead. He saw Tina and let out a surprised "Yah!"

He recovered quickly, gave her a nasty look and said, "Get out! Jesus, just leave me alone!"

She'd been calling him, leaving messages on his voice mail for a week, but he had her blocked and the messages just kept getting returned, unheard. Defiantly, she crawled the rest of the way in and huddled as far from him as she could, which still meant that she was halfway in his lap.

"God, they must be stupid in space," Adrian ranted. "Can't you understand I don't want to talk to you? Go away!"

Tina gave him an appraising look. "One thing we learn in space," she said, "is how to outwait a bad mood. I'm not leaving until we have a chance to talk, and if you don't like it, that's too bad. You're not getting rid of me unless you throw me into the lake."

Adrian fumed and closed his eyes. He searched fruitlessly for a decent bootleg, but his connections had dried up and dropped off in the two weeks since his mother's spot checks had curtailed his trading. It could take days to build them up again.

"Fine," he said at length. "Say your piece and go, all right?"

"Turn on public access," Tina said. Adrian started to protest, but she fixed him with her stare. "Do it," she said, firmly.

Adrian sighed dramatically and closed his eyes, then watched as all the bootlegs he'd stored with her were passed back to his storage. Everything! "Thanks," he said, cautiously. "What's going on? Are you planting evidence before turning me in?"

She shook her head. "I deserve that, I suppose. There's one more," she said. And a file name appeared in his HUD.

"What is it?" he said.

"Just try it," she said.

He rolled it up and baked it, then grunted in shock. It was Nestor's backup, complete and whole, centuries of life, stretching up to the current day. There was Tina in the memories, her birth on ship, her growing up. There was the voyage, the long trip taken in vain and the long return home. The new memories were mirror-bright and cold as space, all the vigor and passion drained with nothing but a hard waiting in their place.

He opened his eye. "Where—" he began, but couldn't finish. He waved his hands at her.

Tina grinned wryly. "I took it from the ship," she said. "I still have access to its utility files. It's just past Pluto now, spacing out for another mission. That made it a little tricky to transfer, but I got it."

"Thanks," he said.

She tilted her head. "Don't thank me," she said.

It was sinking in now, that hardness, that waiting, the centuries ahead dull and indistinguishable from the ones behind, and no hope of it ever ending. The miserable, fatal knowledge that there was only more of this, more and more, forever, and no break in the monotony. It settled over him like lead weight, sapping everything, even the anger at his mother. Endless days of plenty . . .

"How did he get so, so—'

"We used to say he was 'arid,'" Tina said. "None of the parents on the ship would let the kids go near him, so of course we snuck over to see him whenever we could. He hasn't had a rejuve in, oh, forever, and he looks like a silver skeleton. We'd pester him with questions, and he'd just stare and stare, then finally say something so amazingly depressing."

"But how? He was so, so—*passionate*. He made me feel like there was a chance, like I could make a difference," Adrian said. That first bootleg, it must have dated back to before the ship left, a relative century before, and it was flushed into Mohan's honey-pot when the ship returned and Nestor made a fresh backup.

Tina shrugged. "Space changes people," she said, simply. "Time, too. He's nearly 400 now, you know. My parents called him a post-person. You know, what comes after people. That's why we didn't ship out again—they don't want that to happen to them. Nestor wasn't the only one."

Adrian shuddered. A ship full of people like that, years cooped up in quarters tighter than any he'd known on Earth . . .

"You see why I didn't want you to meet him," she said.

"Oh, I can take care of myself," he said. "You didn't have to worry about me."

She gave him another quizzical look. Her glance was more natural now, less spacey. Her skin, too, had taken on a tone that was more human. "I wasn't worried about *you*," she said. "I was worried about Nestor! He's OK most of the time, but when you get him talking about the old days, he just breaks down. You've never seen anyone so miserable. Poor old Nestor," she said, with feeling.

"Say, I've got one more for you, if you're interested," she said. "Brand new," she added.

"Sure," Adrian said and opened his directory. He took the file he found there, rolled it, baked it.

It was Tina, the short life of Tina, the claustrophobia and unimaginable distances of space, the tight and deep friendships in the tiny shipboard community, the loneliness in the crowds of Earth. Her spying him on the streets of this strange and overwhelming city, her relief when he didn't rebuff her. And him—him, through her eyes, smart and savvy and frightening. Frightening? Yes, his anger and his rejection, his unfathomable values and ideas. It was short, her backup, a mere 17 years' worth of consciousness, and it took him a bare moment to bake it.

Tina was looking down at her feet.

"Hey," Adrian said. "Tina?"

Tina looked up. She was scared, those eyes wide and guileless.

"Yes?" she said.

"Switch on guest access, OK?" Adrian said. Then he pushed her a copy of his last backup.

He spent as long as he could bumming around downtown before catching a subway home. His mother hadn't called him since he'd locked her out of his personal storage and sent her a copy of his backup and the flash-baking app, and the thought of seeing her face-to-face made his stomach knot.

Leadenly, he took the stairs down to the subterranean level where his family slept, and hit the door code. It slid open, revealing his father, alone, staring up at the ceiling.

"Dad?" Adrian said. His cochlea rang. He answered.

"Hi, Adrian," his father said, in his ear. He sounded tired.

"Where's Mom?" Adrian asked, with a growing sense of foreboding.

"Oh, she went out," Adrian's father said, vaguely.

"Is she angry?"

Adrian expected a chuckle, but none came. "No," his father said, flatly. "Not angry."

"Are *you* angry?"

His father shifted his bulk and drew Adrian into a long hug. "No, son, I'm not angry either," he whispered aloud in Adrian's ear.

It took Adrian a moment to register that his father had spoken aloud, and when he did, it hardly eased his nervousness.

"What's going on, Dad?" he asked, finally.

His father sat up, ducking his head for the low ceiling. "I owe you an apology," he said.

"For what?"

His father switched back to subvocal. "All this business with the University. You deserve to choose what you want to do. We had a long talk about it this afternoon, and we decided that it's not our place to tell you what to study. I'll take you to see Bosco in the morning, and we can show him the essay you worked up with your friend in India."

Adrian didn't know what to make of that, except that he felt vaguely guilty. "Why? What changed your mind?"

His father flopped onto his back and stared at the ceiling. "I read the paper," he said. "It's good. Interesting thesis, good execution. Thought-provoking. It's a good paper. You could really start something with it."

"Yeah?" Adrian said, blushing. His HUD flashed an alert. His father was pushing a file into his storage. Adrian examined it: a backup, his father's backup. Adrian understood, now. He knew that if he looked in his father's storage that he'd see a copy of his own backup there.

"Yes. You and your friends, you could have a real destiny. Post-people, the last generation on Earth—that's smart stuff."

Adrian started. *Post-person.* He thought of Nestor, saurian, purposeless, cold and hard. Of Tina, looking for a job, a thing to do every day.

A thought occurred to him. "What are you going to do when I start school, Dad?"

"Oh, I don't know. Maybe deadhead for a while, see what things are like in another century. I know that's what your mother wants to do."

They'd talked about deadheading before, but Adrian had never really believed they'd do it. Gone for a century—frozen in cold sleep like millions of others, waiting to see what the future held.

"I'll miss you," he said.

"Oh, you'll get used to it," Adrian's father said. "I can't tell you how many people I know who're deadheading now. Almost everyone I ever knew, really. We'll see each other again before you know it."

When he woke in the morning, his mother was back, asleep between him and his father. Automatically, he checked his in box. His mother had sent a copy of her backup, too. He got up quietly, careful not to disturb her, and snuck away.

Tina answered on the second ring, sounding groggy.

"'lo?"

"Tina?"

"Hi," she mumbled.

"Listen, do you want a job?" he said.

"Huh?" She was waking up now.

"A job—do you still want a job?"

"Sure," she said.

"You're hired," he said.

"For what?"

Adrian rolled up and flashed Nestor's backup, feeling the hopeless, helpless weight of eternity. He flashed his mother's backup, his father's. He grinned. "Here, let me dump you the job requirements," he said, and dumped the files on her.

"Start with these. Send them around, everyone you know. Don't ask for anything in return, but if they send you anything back, pass it around too." He swallowed, prepared a set to send to Mohan. "We're gonna be post-people, but we're gonna do it *right*," he said.

STUDY AND DISCUSSION QUESTIONS

1 "Quickly, he executed the command, and shuddered as that consciousness was rolled up into a bullet of memories and insights and fired directly into his mind, unfolding overtop of his own thoughts and dreams so that for a moment, he *was* that person, her/his self enveloping Adrian with an infinitude of bombarding sense impressions." What would it be like for Adrian to undergo this sort of experience? Is it possible?

2 The social/political environment in this future Earth includes "Whuffie." What is this? How might it influence relationships?

3 Adrian's primary source of recreation is downloading and experiencing the consciousnesses of others. One particular consciousness that he discovered on

the grid was from a 300-year-old person. First, can he experience the consciousnesses of others in this way? Second, supposing that that is possible, do you believe that members of society would find that to be a primary source of recreation?

4   Adrian's mental storage capacity—an uncertain mix of biological storage in a brain and data storage in untold places on the network—is accessible to others, including to his Mom. This raises ethical issues about privacy and parenthood. Do parents of people Adrian's age have the right to access the mental storage of their children?

5   Is Adrian's flash-baking of the consciousnesses of others immoral? What sorts of ethical issues does the story raise about this?

6   Tina and Adrian share their own consciousnesses by transferring their entire first-person experience to one another. They do this in a surprisingly casual way. What sort of experience would that be? Would it be frightening or intimate or invasive?

7   Suppose in the future that we do have the technology to "flash-bake" the entirety of others' consciousnesses. Do you think that the practice of exchanging complete experiences would occur at all? For example, suppose you were to get married. Would you want to flash-bake the consciousness of your future husband or wife?

8   At the conclusion of the story, Adrian's parents send him copies of their consciousness. This unique feature of the story suggests that this technology could be used to heal interpersonal wounds and negotiate conflicts. Is this naïve, or could it work?

5.12 MEDITATIONS ON FIRST PHILOSOPHY (II AND VI) AND DISCOURSE ON METHOD (V) (EXCERPT) BY RENÉ DESCARTES

[Paragraph numbers refer to paragraph numbers in Descartes' original text in order to facilitate easy reference to and from different editions of the work.]

Meditation II

[Excerpt; please see §2.12, from which this reading picks up][8]

16. What then did I use to think I was? A man, of course. But what is a man? Might I not say a "rational animal"? No, because then I would have to inquire what "animal" and

"rational" mean. And thus from one question I would slide into many more difficult ones. Nor do I now have enough free time that I want to waste it on subtleties of this sort. Instead, permit me to focus here on what came spontaneously and naturally into my thinking whenever I pondered what I was. Now it occurred to me first that I had a face, hands, arms, and this entire mechanism of bodily members: the very same as are discerned in a corpse, and which I referred to by the name "body." It next occurred to me that I took in food, that I walked about, and that I sensed and thought various things; these actions I used to attribute to the soul. But as to what this soul might be, I either did not think about it or else I imagined it a rarified I-know not-what, like a wind, or a fire, or ether, which had been infused into my coarser parts. But as to the body I was not in any doubt. On the contrary, I was under the impression that I knew its nature distinctly. Were I perhaps tempted to describe this nature such as I conceived it in my mind, I would have described it thus: by "body," I understand all that is capable of being bounded by some shape, of being enclosed in a place, and of filling up a space in such a way as to exclude any other body from it; of being perceived by touch, sight, hearing, taste, or smell; of being moved in several ways, not, of course, by itself, but by whatever else impinges upon it. For it was my view that the power of self-motion, and likewise of sensing or of thinking, in no way belonged to the nature of the body. Indeed I used rather to marvel that such faculties were to be found in certain bodies.

17. But now what am I, when I suppose that there is some supremely powerful and, if I may be permitted to say so, malicious deceiver who deliberately tries to fool me in any way he can? Can I not affirm that I possess at least a small measure of all those things which I have already said belong to the nature of the body? I focus my attention on them, I think about them, I review them again, but nothing comes to mind. I am tired of repeating this to no purpose. But what about those things I ascribed to the soul? What about being nourished or moving about? Since I now do not have a body, these are surely nothing but fictions. What about sensing? Surely this too does not take place without a body; and I seemed to have sensed in my dreams many things that I later realized I did not sense. What about thinking? Here I make my discovery: thought exists; it alone cannot be separated from me. I am; I exist—this is certain. But for how long? For as long as I am thinking; for perhaps it could also come to pass that if I were to cease all thinking I would then utterly cease to exist. At this time I admit nothing that is not necessarily true. I am therefore precisely nothing but a thinking thing; that is, a mind, or intellect, or understanding, or reason—words of whose meanings I was previously ignorant. Yet I am a true thing and am truly existing; but what kind of thing? I have said it already: a thinking thing.

18. What else am I? I will set my imagination in motion. I am not that concatenation of members we call the human body. Neither am I even some subtle air infused into these members, nor a wind, nor a fire, nor a vapor, nor a breath, nor anything I devise for myself. For I have supposed these things to be nothing. The assumption still stands; yet nevertheless I am something. But is it perhaps the case that these very things which I take to be nothing, because they are unknown to me, nevertheless are in fact no different from that "me" that I know? This I do not know, and I will not quarrel about it now. I can make

a judgment only about things that are known to me. I know that I exist; I ask now who is this "I" whom I know? Most certainly, in the strict sense the knowledge of this "I" does not depend upon things of whose existence I do not yet have knowledge. Therefore it is not dependent upon any of those things that I simulate in my imagination. But this word "simulate"[9] warns me of my error. For I would indeed be simulating were I to "imagine" that I was something, because imagining is merely the contemplating of the shape or image of a corporeal thing. But I now know with certainty that I am and also that all these images and, generally, everything belonging to the nature of the body—could turn out to be nothing but dreams. Once I have realized this, I would seem to be speaking no less foolishly were I to say: "I will use my imagination in order to recognize more distinctly who I am," than were I to say: "Now I surely am awake, and I see something true; but since I do not yet see it clearly enough, I will deliberately fall asleep so that my dreams might represent it to me more truly and more clearly." Thus I realize that none of what I can grasp by means of the imagination pertains to this knowledge that I have of myself. Moreover, I realize that I must be most diligent about withdrawing my mind from these things so that it can perceive its nature as distinctly as possible.

19. But what then am I? A thing that thinks. What is that? A thing that doubts, understands, affirms, denies, wills, refuses, and that also imagines and senses.

20. Indeed it is no small matter if all of these things belong to me. But why should they not belong to me? Is it not the very same "I" who now doubts almost everything, who nevertheless understands something, who affirms that this one thing is true, who denies other things, who desires to know more, who wishes not to be deceived, who imagines many things even against my will, who also notices many things which appear to come from the senses? What is there in all of this that is not every bit as true as the fact that I exist—even if I am always asleep or even if my creator makes every effort to mislead me? Which of these things is distinct from my thought? Which of them can be said to be separate from myself? For it is so obvious that it is I who doubt, I who understand, and I who will, that there is nothing by which it could be explained more clearly. But indeed it is also the same "I" who imagines; for although perhaps, as I supposed before, absolutely nothing that I imagined is true, still the very power of imagining really does exist, and constitutes a part of my thought. Finally, it is this same "I" who senses or who is cognizant of bodily things as if through the senses. For example, I now see a light, I hear a noise, I feel heat. These things are false, since I am asleep. Yet I certainly do seem to see, hear, and feel warmth. This cannot be false. Properly speaking, this is what in me is called "sensing." But this, precisely so taken, is nothing other than thinking.

21. From these considerations I am beginning to know a little better what I am. But it still seems (and I cannot resist believing) that corporeal things—whose images are formed by thought, and which the senses themselves examine—are much more distinctly known than this mysterious "I" which does not fall within the imagination. And yet it would be strange indeed were I to grasp the very things I consider to be doubtful, unknown, and foreign to me more distinctly than what is true, what is known—than, in short, myself. But I see what is happening: my mind loves to wander and does not yet permit itself to be restricted within the confines of truth. So be it then; let us just this once allow it completely

free rein, so that, a little while later, when the time has come to pull in the reins, the mind may more readily permit itself to be controlled.

22. Let us consider those things which are commonly believed to be the most distinctly grasped of all: namely the bodies we touch and see. Not bodies in general, mind you, for these general perceptions are apt to be somewhat more confused, but one body in particular. Let us take, for instance, this piece of wax. It has been taken quite recently from the honeycomb; it has not yet lost all the honey flavor. It retains some of the scent of the flowers from which it was collected. Its color, shape, and size are manifest. It is hard and cold; it is easy to touch. If you rap on it with your knuckle it will emit a sound. In short, everything is present in it that appears needed to enable a body to be known as distinctly as possible. But notice that, as I am speaking, I am bringing it close to the fire. The remaining traces of the honey flavor are disappearing; the scent is vanishing; the color is changing; the original shape is disappearing. Its size is increasing; it is becoming liquid and hot; you can hardly touch it. And now, when you rap on it, it no longer emits any sound. Does the same wax still remain? I must confess that it does; no one denies it; no one thinks otherwise. So what was there in the wax that was so distinctly grasped? Certainly none of the aspects that I reached by means of the senses. For whatever came under the senses of taste, smell, sight, touch or hearing has now changed; and yet the wax remains.

23. Perhaps the wax was what I now think it is: namely that the wax itself never really was the sweetness of the honey, nor the fragrance of the flowers, nor the whiteness, nor the shape, nor the sound, but instead was a body that a short time ago manifested itself to me in these ways, and now does so in other ways. But just what precisely is this thing that I thus imagine? Let us focus our attention on this and see what remains after we have removed everything that does not belong to the wax: only that it is something extended, flexible, and mutable. But what is it to be flexible and mutable? Is it what my imagination shows it to be: namely, that this piece of wax can change from a round to a square shape, or from the latter to a triangular shape? Not at all; for I grasp that the wax is capable of innumerable changes of this sort, even though I am incapable of running through these innumerable changes by using my imagination. Therefore this insight is not achieved by the faculty of imagination. What is it to be extended? Is this thing's extension also unknown? For it becomes greater in wax that is beginning to melt, greater in boiling wax, and greater still as the heat is increased. And I would not judge correctly what the wax is if I did not believe that it takes on an even greater variety of dimensions than I could ever grasp with the imagination. It remains then for me to concede that I do not grasp what this wax is through the imagination; rather, I perceive it through the mind alone. The point I am making refers to this particular piece of wax, for the case of wax in general is clearer still. But what is this piece of wax which is perceived only by the mind? Surely it is the same piece of wax that I see, touch, and imagine; in short it is the same piece of wax I took it to be from the very beginning. But I need to realize that the perception of the wax is neither a seeing, nor a touching, nor an imagining. Nor has it ever been, even though it previously seemed so; rather it is an inspection on the part of the mind alone. This inspection can be imperfect and confused, as it was before, or clear and distinct, as it is

now, depending on how closely I pay attention to the things in which the piece of wax consists.

24. But meanwhile I marvel at how prone my mind is to error. For although I am considering these things within myself silently and without words, nevertheless I seize upon words themselves and I am nearly deceived by the ways in which people commonly speak. For we say that we see the wax itself, if it is present, and not that we judge it to be present from its color or shape. Whence I might conclude straightaway that I know the wax through the vision had by the eye, and not through an inspection on the part of the mind alone. But then were I perchance to look out my window and observe men crossing the square, I would ordinarily say I see the men themselves just as I say I see the wax. But what do I see aside from hats and clothes, which could conceal automata? Yet I judge them to be men. Thus what I thought I had seen with my eyes, I actually grasped solely with the faculty of judgment, which is in my mind.

25. But a person who seeks to know more than the common crowd ought to be ashamed of himself for looking for doubt in common ways of speaking. Let us then go forward and inquire when it was that I perceived more perfectly and evidently what the piece of wax was. Was it when I first saw it and believed I knew it by the external sense, or at least by the so called common sense, that is, the power of imagination? Or do I have more perfect knowledge now, when I have diligently examined both what the wax is and how it is known? Surely it is absurd to be in doubt about this matter. For what was there in my initial perception that was distinct? What was there that any animal seemed incapable of possessing? But indeed when I distinguish the wax from its external forms, as if stripping it of its clothing, and look at the wax in its nakedness, then, even though there can be still an error in my judgment, nevertheless I cannot perceive it thus without a human mind.

26. But what am I to say about this mind, that is, about myself? For as yet I admit nothing else to be in me over and above the mind. What, I ask, am I who seem to perceive this wax so distinctly? Do I not know myself not only much more truly and with greater certainty, but also much more distinctly and evidently? For if I judge that the wax exists from the fact that I see it, certainly from this same fact that I see the wax it follows much more evidently that I myself exist. For it could happen that what I see is not truly wax. It could happen that I have no eyes with which to see anything. But it is utterly impossible that, while I see or think I see (I do not now distinguish these two), I who think am not something. Likewise, if I judge that the wax exists from the fact that I touch it, the same outcome will again obtain, namely that I exist. If I judge that the wax exists from the fact that I imagine it, or for any other reason, plainly the same thing follows. But what I note regarding the wax applies to everything else that is external to me. Furthermore, if my perception of the wax seemed more distinct after it became known to me not only on account of sight or touch, but on account of many reasons, one has to admit how much more distinctly I am now known to myself. For there is not a single consideration that can aid in my perception of the wax or of any other body that fails to make even more manifest the nature of my mind. But there are still so many other things in the mind itself on the basis of which my knowledge of it can be rendered more

distinct that it hardly seems worth enumerating those things which emanate to it from the body.

27. But lo and behold, I have returned on my own to where I wanted to be. For since I now know that even bodies are not, properly speaking, perceived by the senses or by the faculty of imagination, but by the intellect alone, and that they are not perceived through their being touched or seen, but only through their being understood, I manifestly know that nothing can be perceived more easily and more evidently than my own mind. But since the tendency to hang on to long-held beliefs cannot be put aside so quickly, I want to stop here, so that by the length of my meditation this new knowledge may be more deeply impressed upon my memory.

Meditation VI (excerpts)[10]

8. First, I know that all the things that I clearly and distinctly understand can be made by God such as I understand them. For this reason, my ability clearly and distinctly to understand one thing without another suffices to make me certain that the one thing is different from the other, since they can be separated from each other, at least by God. The question as to the sort of power that might effect such a separation is not relevant to their being thought to be different. For this reason, from the fact that I know that I exist, and that at the same time I judge that obviously nothing else belongs to my nature or essence except that I am a thinking thing, I rightly conclude that my essence consists entirely in my being a thinking thing. And although perhaps (or rather, as I shall soon say, assuredly) I have a body that is very closely joined to me, nevertheless, because on the one hand I have a clear and distinct idea of myself, insofar as I am merely a thinking thing and not an extended thing, and because on the other hand I have a distinct idea of a body, insofar as it is merely an extended thing and not a thinking thing, it is certain that I am really distinct from my body, and can exist without it.

18. Now my first observation here is that there is a great difference between a mind and a body, in that a body, by its very nature, is always divisible. On the other hand, the mind, is utterly indivisible. For when I consider the mind, that is, myself insofar as I am only a thinking thing, I cannot distinguish any parts within me; rather, I understand myself to be manifestly one complete thing. Although the entire mind seems to be united to the entire body, nevertheless, were a foot or an arm or any other bodily part to be amputated, I know that nothing has been taken away from the mind on that account. Nor can the faculties of willing, sensing, understanding, and so on be called "parts" of the mind, since it is one and the same mind that wills, senses, and understands. On the other hand, there is no corporeal or extended thing I can think of that I may not in my thought easily divide into parts; and in this way I understand that it is divisible. This consideration alone would suffice to teach me that the mind is wholly diverse from the body, had I not yet known it well enough in any other way.

Discourse on Method (V) (excerpt)[11]

I paused here in particular in order to show that, if there were such machines having the organs and the shape of a monkey or of some other animal that lacked reason, we would have no way of recognizing that they were not entirely of the same nature as these animals; whereas, if there were any such machines that bore a resemblance to our bodies and imitated our actions as far as this is practically feasible, we would always have two very certain means of recognizing that they were not at all, for that reason, true men. The first is that they could never use words or other signs, or put them together as we do in order to declare our thoughts to others. For one can well conceive of a machine being so made that it utters words, and even that it utters words appropriate to the bodily actions that will cause some change in its organs (such as if one touches it in a certain place, it asks what one wants to say to it, or, if in another place, it cries out that one is hurting it, and the like). But it could not arrange its words differently so as to respond to the sense of all that will be said in its presence, as even the dullest men can do. The second means is that, although they might perform many tasks very well or perhaps better than any of us, such machines would inevitably fail in other tasks; by this means one would discover that they were acting, not through knowledge, but only through the disposition of their organs. For while reason is a universal instrument that can be of help in all sorts of circumstances, these organs require some particular disposition for each particular action; consequently, it is for all practical purposes impossible for there to be enough different organs in a machine to make it act in all the contingencies of life in the same way as our reason makes us act.

Now by these two means one can also know the difference between men and beasts. For it is rather remarkable that there are no men so dull and so stupid (excluding not even the insane), that they are incapable of arranging various words together and of composing from them a discourse by means of which they might make their thoughts understood; and that, on the other hand, there is no other animal at all, however perfect and pedigreed it may be, that does the like. This does not happen because they lack the organs, for one sees that magpies and parrots can utter words just as we can, and yet they cannot speak as we do, that is to say, by testifying to the fact that they are thinking about what they are saying; on the other hand, men born deaf and dumb, who are deprived just as much as, or more than, beasts of the organs that aid others in speaking, are wont to invent for themselves various signs by means of which they make themselves understood to those who, being with them on a regular basis, have the time to learn their language. And this attests not merely to the fact that the beasts have less reason than men but that they have none at all. For it is obvious it does not need much to know how to speak; and since we notice as much inequality among animals of the same species as among men, and that some are easier to train than others, it is unbelievable that a monkey or a parrot that is the most perfect of its species would not equal in this respect one of the most stupid children or at least a child with a disordered brain, if their soul were not of a nature entirely different from our own. And we should not confuse words with the natural movements that attest to the passions and can be imitated by machines as well as by animals. Nor should we think, as did some of the ancients, that beasts speak, although we do not understand their language; for if that were true, since they have many organs corresponding to our own, they could make themselves as well understood by us as they are by their fellow creatures. It is also a very remarkable phenomenon that, although there are many animals that show more skill than we do in some of their actions, we nevertheless see that they show none at all in many other actions. Consequently, the fact that they do something better than we do does not prove that they have any intelligence; for were that the case, they would have more of it than any of us and would excel us in everything. But rather it proves that they have no intelligence at all, and that it is nature that acts in them, according to the disposition of their organs just as we see that a clock composed exclusively of wheels and springs can count the hours and measure time more accurately than we can with all our carefulness.

After that, I described the rational soul and showed that it can in no way be derived from the potentiality of matter, as can the other things I have spoken of, but rather that it must be expressly created; and how it is not enough for it to be lodged in the human body like a pilot in his ship, unless perhaps in order to move its members, but rather that it must be more closely joined and united to the body in order to have, in addition to this, feelings and appetites similar to our own, and thus to constitute a true man. As to the rest, I elaborated here a little on the subject of the soul because it is of the greatest importance; for, after the error of those who deny the existence of God (which I think I have sufficiently refuted), there is none at all that puts weak minds at a greater distance from the straight path of virtue than to imagine that the soul of beasts is of the same nature as ours, and that, as a consequence, we have nothing to fear or to hope for after this life any more than do flies and ants. On the other hand, when one knows how different they are, one understands much better the arguments which prove that our soul is of a nature entirely independent of the body, and consequently that it is not subject to die with it. Then, since we do not see any other causes at all for its destruction, we are naturally led to judge from this that it is immortal.

STUDY AND DISCUSSION QUESTIONS

For Meditation II

1 In paragraph 19, Descartes poses a question to himself: "But what am I?" What is his answer? Is he right?
2 Why does he not claim that he is both a mind *and a body*?
3 Descartes recognizes a methodological problem about the study of the mind: the only way to study the inner workings of my mind is by using my mind. This is equivalent to saying that mental states are private, that is, my mental states are only observable by me. Is Descartes right about this?

4   Suppose Descartes is right about the privacy of the mental. This has implications upon the ability to prove that any other minds exist. Give it a go: try to construct a valid and sound argument for the conclusion *that there are other minds*. What sorts of problems do you run into?

5   In paragraph 22, Descartes explains his thought experiment with a piece of wax. What are the properties of the wax? How do those change after Descartes melts it?

6   What philosophical lesson is Descartes attempting to draw with the wax example? Does Descartes succeed in making that point?

For Meditation VI

1   In paragraph 8, Descartes mounts an argument for the conclusion that he, as a mind, is "distinct from [his] body." What are the premises that enable him to reach this conclusion? Is this argument valid?

2   Descartes places special emphasis upon his ability to conceive of one thing without conceiving of another. Why does he believe that his ability to conceive of himself existing without a body is instrumental in proving that he is not necessarily conjoined to a body?

3   In paragraph 18, Descartes offers a further argument for the conclusion that mind and body are distinct. State this argument in premise/conclusion form.

4   What is the meaning and importance of Descartes' appeal to "indivisibility" in this argument? Is Descartes making claims about what is and is not divisible, or is he making claims about what can be imagined to be and cannot be imagined to be divisible? What is the philosophical importance of this difference?

5   Is this argument valid and sound? What problems affect it?

For *Discourse on Method* (V)

1   What are "machines," according to Descartes? Are animals "machines"? Why/ why not?

2   What are Descartes' two tests? Are Descartes' tests good tests? Relatedly, can something pass these tests that is not intelligent? Can something fail these tests that is intelligent?

3   Assume they are good tests. Have machines, computers or AIs surpassed them?

4   What sort of theory of the mind does Descartes endorse in this passage?

5.13 "MINDS, BRAINS, AND PROGRAMS," BY JOHN R. SEARLE

What psychological and philosophical significance should we attach to recent efforts at computer simulations of human cognitive capacities? In answering this question, I find it useful to distinguish what I will call "strong" AI from "weak" or "cautious" AI (artificial intelligence). According to weak AI, the principal value of the computer in the study of the mind is that it gives us a very powerful tool. For example, it enables us to formulate and test hypotheses in a more rigorous and precise fashion. But according to strong AI, the computer is not merely a tool in the study of the mind; rather, the appropriately programmed computer really is a mind, in the sense that computers given the right programs can be literally said to *understand* and have other cognitive states. In strong AI, because the programmed computer has cognitive states, the programs are not mere tools that enable us to test psychological explanations; rather, the programs are themselves the explanations.

I have no objection to the claims of weak AI, at least as far as this article is concerned. My discussion here will be directed at the claims I have defined as those of strong AI, specifically the claim that the appropriately programmed computer literally has cognitive states and that the programs thereby explain human cognition. When I hereafter refer to AI, I have in mind the strong version, as expressed by these two claims.

I will consider the work of Roger Schank and his colleagues at Yale (Schank and Abelson, 1977) [See Searle, 1980 for Searle's references], because I am more familiar with it than I am with any other similar claims, and because it provides a very clear example of the sort of work I wish to examine. But nothing that follows depends upon the details of Schank's programs. The same arguments would apply to Winograd's SHRDLU (Winograd, 1973), Weizenbaum's ELIZA (Weizenbaum, 1965), and indeed any Turing machine simulation of human mental phenomena.

Very briefly, and leaving out the various details, one can describe Schank's program as follows: The aim of the program is to simulate the human ability to understand stories. It is characteristic of human beings' story-understanding capacity that they can answer questions about the story even though the information that they give was never explicitly stated in the story. Thus, for example, suppose you are given the following story: "A man went into a restaurant and ordered a hamburger. When the hamburger arrived it was burned to a crisp, and the man stormed out of the restaurant angrily, without paying for the hamburger or leaving a tip." Now, if you are asked "Did the man eat the hamburger?" you will presumably answer, "No, he did not." Similarly, if you are given the following story: "A man went into a restaurant and ordered a hamburger; when the hamburger came he was very pleased with it; and as he left the restaurant he gave the server a large tip before paying his bill," and you are asked the question, "Did the man eat the hamburger?" you will presumably answer, "Yes, he ate the hamburger." Now Schank's machines can similarly answer questions about restaurants in this fashion. To do this, they have a "representation" of the sort of information that human beings have about restaurants, which enables them to answer such questions as those above, given these sorts of stories. When the machine is given the story and then asked the question, the machine will print out answers of the sort that we would expect human beings to give if told similar stories. Partisans of strong AI claim that in this question and answer sequence the machine is not only simulating a human ability but also (1) that the machine can literally be said to *understand* the story and provide the answers to questions, and (2) that what the machine and its program do *explains* the human ability to understand the story and answer questions about it.

Both claims seem to me to be totally unsupported by Schank's work, as I will attempt to show in what follows. I am not, of course, saying that Schank himself is vulnerable to these claims.

One way to test any theory of the mind is to ask oneself what it would be like if my mind actually worked on the principles that the theory says all minds work on. Let us apply this test to the Schank program with the following *Gedankenexperiment*. Suppose that I'm locked in a room and given a large batch of Chinese writing. Suppose furthermore (as is indeed the case) that I know no Chinese, either written or spoken, and that I'm not even confident that I could recognize Chinese writing as Chinese writing distinct from, say, Japanese writing or meaningless squiggles. To me, Chinese writing is just so many meaningless squiggles. Now suppose further that after this first batch of Chinese writing I am given a second batch of Chinese script together with a set of rules for correlating the second batch with the first batch. The rules are in English, and I understand these rules as well as any other native speaker of English. They enable me to correlate one set of formal symbols with another set of formal symbols, and all that "formal" means here is that I can identify the symbols entirely by their shapes. Now suppose also that I am given a third batch of Chinese symbols together with some instructions, again in English, that enable me to correlate elements of this third batch with the first two batches, and these rules instruct me how to give back certain Chinese symbols with certain sorts of shapes in response to certain sorts of shapes given me in the third batch. Unknown to me, the people who are giving me all of these symbols call the first batch a "script," they call the second batch a "story," and they call the third batch "questions." Furthermore, they call the symbols I give them back in response to the third batch "answers to the questions," and the set of rules in English that they gave me, they call the "program." Now just to complicate the story a little, imagine that these people also give me stories in English, which I understand, and they then ask me questions in English about these stories, and I give them back answers in English. Suppose also that after a while I get so good at following the instructions for manipulating the Chinese symbols and the programmers get so good at writing the programs that from the external point of view—that is, from the point of view of somebody outside the room in which I am locked—my answers to the questions are absolutely indistinguishable from those of native Chinese speakers. Nobody just looking at my answers can tell that I don't speak a word of Chinese. Let us also suppose that my answers to the English questions are, as they no doubt would be, indistinguishable from those of other native English speakers, for the simple reason that I am a native English speaker. From the external point of view—from the point of view of someone reading my "answers"—the answers to the Chinese questions and the English questions are equally good. But in the Chinese case, unlike the English case, I produce the answers by manipulating uninterpreted formal symbols. As far as the Chinese is concerned, I simply behave like a computer; I perform computational operations on formally specified elements. For the purposes of the Chinese, I am simply an instantiation of the computer program.

Now the claims made by strong AI are that the programmed computer understands the stories and that the program in some sense explains human understanding. But we are now in a position to examine these claims in light of our thought experiment.

1. As regards the first claim, it seems to me quite obvious in the example that I do not understand a word of the Chinese stories. I have inputs and outputs that are indistinguishable from those of the native Chinese speaker, and I can have any formal program you like, but I still understand nothing. For the same reasons, Schank's computer understands nothing of any stories, whether in Chinese, English, or whatever, since in the Chinese case the computer is me, and in cases where the computer is not me, the computer has nothing more than I have in the case where I understand nothing.

2. As regards the second claim, that the program explains human understanding, we can see that the computer and its program do not provide sufficient conditions of understanding since the computer and the program are functioning, and there is no understanding. But does it even provide a necessary condition or a significant contribution to understanding? One of the claims made by the supporters of strong AI is that when I understand a story in English, what I am doing is exactly the same—or perhaps more of the same—as what I was doing in manipulating the Chinese symbols. It is simply more formal symbol manipulation that distinguishes the case in English, where I do understand, from the case in Chinese, where I don't. I have not demonstrated that this claim is false, but it would certainly appear an incredible claim in the example. Such plausibility as the claim has derives from the supposition that we can construct a program that will have the same inputs and outputs as native speakers, and in addition we assume that speakers have some level of description where they are also instantiations of a program. On the basis of these two assumptions we assume that even if Schank's program isn't the whole story about understanding, it may be part of the story. Well, I suppose that is an empirical possibility, but not the slightest reason has so far been given to believe that it is true, since what is suggested—though certainly not demonstrated— by the example is that the computer program is simply irrelevant to my understanding of the story. In the Chinese case I have everything that artificial intelligence can put into me by way of a program, and I understand nothing; in the English case I understand everything, and there is so far no reason at all to suppose that my understanding has anything to do with computer programs, that is, with computational operations on purely formally specified elements. As long as the program is defined in terms of computational operations on purely formally defined elements, what the example suggests is that these by themselves have no interesting connection with understanding. They are certainly not sufficient conditions, and not the slightest reason has been given to suppose that they are necessary conditions or even that they make a significant contribution to understanding. Notice that the force of the argument is not simply that different machines can have the

same input and output while operating on different formal principles—that is not the point at all. Rather, whatever purely formal principles you put into the computer, they will not be sufficient for understanding, since a human will be able to follow the formal principles without understanding anything. No reason whatever has been offered to suppose that such principles are necessary or even contributory, since no reason has been given to suppose that when I understand English I am operating with any formal program at all.

Well, then, what is it that I have in the case of the English sentences that I do not have in the case of the Chinese sentences? The obvious answer is that I know what the former mean, while I haven't the faintest idea what the latter mean. . . .

. . . I want to block some common misunderstandings about "understanding": In many of these discussions one finds a lot of fancy footwork about the word "understanding." My critics point out that there are many different degrees of understanding; that "understanding" is not a simple two-place predicate; that there are even different kinds and levels of understanding, and often the law of excluded middle doesn't even apply in a straightforward way to statements of the form "x understands y"; that in many cases it is a matter for decision and not a simple matter of fact whether x understands y; and so on. To all of these points I want to say: of course, of course. But they have nothing to do with the points at issue. There are clear cases in which "understanding" literally applies and clear cases in which it does not apply; and these two sorts of cases are all I need for this argument. I understand stories in English; to a lesser degree I can understand stories in French; to a still lesser degree, stories in German; and in Chinese, not at all. My car and my adding machine, on the other hand, understand nothing: they are not in that line of business. We often attribute "understanding" and other cognitive predicates by metaphor and analogy to cars, adding machines, and other artifacts, but nothing is proved by such attributions. We say, "The door *knows* when to open because of its photoelectric cell," "The adding machine *knows how* (*understands how*, is *able*) to do addition and subtraction but not division," and "The thermostat *perceives* changes in the temperature." The reason we make these attributions is quite interesting, and it has to do with the fact that in artifacts we extend our own intentionality; our tools are extensions of our purposes, and so we find it natural to make metaphorical attributions of intentionality to them; but I take it no philosophical ice is cut by such examples. The sense in which an automatic door "understands instructions" from its photoelectric cell is not at all the sense in which I understand English. If the sense in which Schank's programmed computers understand stories is supposed to be the metaphorical sense in which the door understands, and not the sense in which I understand English, the issue would not be worth discussing. But Newell and Simon (1963) write that the kind of cognition they claim for computers is exactly the same as for human beings.

STUDY AND DISCUSSION QUESTIONS

1   Describe the difference between strong AI and weak AI. What is the importance of the distinction?
2   What is the purpose of Searle's example about eating a hamburger?
3   Try drawing the Chinese room.
4   In stating his Chinese room thought experiment, Searle uses key terms including "formal symbol." What sets a formal symbol apart from other sorts of symbols?
5   Searle also uses the term "understand" in a specific way. How? What does the term mean?
6   Attempt to translate the Chinese room thought experiment into an argument in premise/conclusion form. Is it valid? Is it sound?
7   Precisely what is Searle concluding in this article?

5.14   BIBLIOGRAPHY AND RECOMMENDED READING

Science fiction

*Asimov, Isaac. *I, Robot*. New York: Bantam Spectra, 2004. This collection contains short stories that inaugurated serious analysis of humanity's relationship with artificial intelligence. Asimov codifies his optimistic vision in the form of the Three Laws of Robotics. The stories trace efforts of an NYPD crime fighting duo Lije Baley and the robot Daneel Olivaw to solve assorted crimes.

Bayley, Barrington. *Soul of the Robot*. Doubleday, 1974. Story of a robot with a soul, who wrestles with the nature of self-consciousness.

Brussof, Valery. "The Republic of the Southern Cross." *The Republic of the Southern Cross, and Other Stories*. Hyperion Press, 1977. A mental illness affects a polar colony in Antarctica by causing intentions to yield opposite reactions.

Boyce, Chris. *Catchworld*. Gollancz, 1975. AI running ship absorbs crew's personalities creating a compound being.

Bunch, D. R. *Moderan*. Avon, 1971. Collection about world altered by cyborgization of inhabitants.

Cadigan, Pat. *Synners*. Bantam, 1991. In this Arthur C. Clarke Award winning novel, a graphic designer and programmer develops a new technology that allows the uploading of one's consciousness. While online, he undergoes a stroke that transmits a virus onto the net. With a deft blurring of human and machine consciousness and a dense, vivid description of the natures of minds, this novel prompts lots of thought about the mental world.

Capek, Carol. *R.U.R. (Rossum's Universal Robots)*. 1921. Trans. Claudia Novack-Jones. New York: Penguin Classics, 2004. This work, which introduced the term "robot" to the vocabulary of our species, is set in a factory in which sexless human beings are produced to serve as labor. These "robots" are infused with emotions and minds and, eventually, they undertake a successful revolt over humanity. The depth of this work is infrequently conveyed in its popular representation.

Compton, D. G. *Synthajoy*. Hodder & Stoughton, 1968. Technology allows the recording and transmission of emotional experiences on "Sensitape." This invention transforms society for the good—addicts can use it to escape their dependence on drugs and the disabled can experience what it is like to have health. Characters in the novel, especially Thea, the wife of the inventor of Sensitape, struggles to understand herself and the morality of her extensive use of Sensitape. Compton's characterization of Thea offers an incisive portrayal of a central female character.

Condon, Richard. *The Manchurian Candidate*. McGraw-Hill, 1959. Raymond Shaw was captured by the Chinese and interred. Their psychologists brainwash him, and hypnotize him with embedded post-hypnotic instructions to assassinate the U.S. president. The political intrigue leading up to the climax insures the reader is on the edge of her seat. The extent of the manipulation of Shaw's mind is plausible in light of many extraordinary feats performed through post-hypnotic suggestion. This is a strength of the novel: by shunning more exotic sci-fi appeals to telepathy and the like, Condon creates believable situations and characters.

Dann, Jack. *The Man Who Melted*. Bluejay, 1984. Social institutions have been rent apart through the effects of outbreaks of group consciousness, which creates a new social order predicated on rampant mental illness.

Delany, Samuel. *Babel-17*. New York: Ace, 1966. The heroine of the novel must learn the language of her attackers in order to understand how it is used as a weapon of war. The language makes people of her kind traitors once it is learned, and it has this effect on her, but she realizes this in time.

*Dick, Philip K. *Do Androids Dream of Electric Sheep?* Doubleday, 1968 In this story responsible for the film *Blade Runner*, Dick characteristically blurs the line between the virtual and the real. A bounty hunter is assigned to find a runaway android, but, in the process, perhaps discovers that he himself is an android. See also Dick's *We Can Build You* (1972) for a story about humans who build androids that are more human than they are.

——. *Eye in the Sky*. Ace, 1957. Several minds create their own subjective realities and struggle for dominance as each is drawn into the reality of the other.

Dickson, G. *The Forever Man*. Doubleday, 1972. Man's consciousness is absorbed into spaceship, which returns to Earth offering promise of an end to war.

Doctorow, Cory. "Truncat." Originally published 26 August 2003 at www.salon.com: http://dir.salon.com/story/tech/feature/2003/08/26/truncat/

Effinger, Alec. *When Gravity Fails*. Arbor, 1987. Uniquely set in a future Arabic-speaking city, the protagonist Marid is caught up in a murder. His standing as a person without "moddies"—enhancements that yield new abilities, beliefs and knowledge to the user—makes him a unique suspect and witness. A Hugo and Nebula nominee.

*Egan, Greg. *Diaspora*. Harper Prism, 1998. Egan crafts this novel around the interactions between a few groups of post-humans, and the discovery that life in the Milky Way is about to end. The richness and deft description of the artificial forms of personality and intelligence defy imagination and make this novel rock-hard SF.

Gerrold, David. *When HARLIE Was One*. Doubleday, 1972 and *When HARLIE Was One (Release 2.0)*. Spectra, 1988 David Auberson is the psychologist charged with rearing the newly manufactured artificial intelligence, HARLIE. Gerrold offers a realistic portrayal of what an AI might be like. The book raises a number of philosophical questions about intelligence and **personhood**, including ethical issues wrapped around HARLIE's interest in not being shut off.

Jones, D. F. *Colossus*. Berkely, 1977. A computer is intended to coordinate the defense system of the United States. After linking with its Soviet counterpart, Colossus becomes ruler of the world.

*Keyes, Daniel. *Flowers for Algernon*. This Hugo and Nebula Award winning story sensitively portrays the rapid rise from mental retardation to normal cognitive functioning to superhuman levels of intelligence in Charlie Gordon. Once his treatment begins to fail, Gordon makes a plaintive return to his retardation, and Keyes reverts to simplified diction and vocabulary.

*LeGuin ,Ursula. *The Lathe of Heaven*. Avon, 1973. A psychiatrist tries to exploit a patient's ability to change the real world by dreaming about changes, but the outcomes are uncontrollable and, ultimately, catastrophic.

Leven, J. *Satan*. New York: Alfred A Knopf, 1982. Satan takes form as an AI, seeks psychological help.

Morgan, Richard. *Altered Carbon*. Gollancz, 2002. This Philip K. Dick Award winning work envisions a future in which not only minds and memories are easily storable, but also they can be "resleeved" into different bodies. Several complications follow on from this technology as the protagonist Takeshi Kovacs attempts to track down a killer.

Platt, Charles. *The Silicon Man*. Bantam, 1991. How will the technology used to produce AIs be used by and against security agencies like the FBI? This novel explores that issue and creates a vivid, believable virtual reality world as its civil service protagonist tries to get his body back.

Rucker, Rudy. *The Hacker and the Ants*. Morrow, 1994. A leading light in the SF sub-genre about artificial intelligence, in this work Rucker casts computer scientist Jerry Rugby in the role of savior. Rugby is the fall guy for the rampant spread of "ants," viruses that threaten the global network, and to make it right he must enter the etherworld of the ants.

Rucker, Rudy. *Software*. New York: Ace, 1982. An early foray into speculation about the role of organic human beings in a world increasingly dominated by artificial intelligences who want their say. Winner of the Philip K. Dick Award.

Ryan, Thomas J. *The Adolescence of P-1*. Baen, 1985. A computer which is taught by humans, grows up and is faced with wielding power.

Scott, Melissa. *Dream Ships*. Tor, 1992. A pilot on a rescue mission is captaining a ship which achieves self-awareness, and debate ensues as to whether it has "human" rights.

*Shelley, Mary Wollstonecraft. *Frankenstein: or The Modern Prometheus*. Lankington Hughes, 3 vols., 1818. Shelley uses a gothic setting to great effect as Dr. Frankenstein plays God by creating a Monster who flees his creator in angst and ill will.

Silverberg, Robert. *The Second Trip*. Signet Books, 1973. Artificial personality created to inhabit body of criminal. Power struggle for entity's psychology.

Watson, Ian. *The Jonah Kit*. Gollancz, 1975. Fascinating story of non-human consciousness told through successful attempts to create communication between human beings and whales.

Williamson, Jack. *The Humanoids*. Avon, 1975. Machines impose total control over all human activities in order to protect them.

Wilson, Robert Charles. *The Harvest*. Bantam, 1993. If aliens arrived on a dying Earth and promised you immortality if you would be willing to give up your body and merge with their group mind, would you do it?

Philosophy

Armstrong, D. *A Materialist Theory of the Mind*. Routledge, 1968.

Block, Ned. "Troubles with Functionalism." *Readings in the Philosophy of Psychology Vol. I*, Ed. Ned Block. Cambridge, MA: Harvard University Press, 1980.

*Chalmers, David. *The Conscious Mind*. New York: Oxford University Press, 1996.

*——. *Philosophy of Mind: Classical and Contemporary Readings*. Oxford: Oxford University Press, 2002.

Churchland, Paul. *Matter and Consciousness*. Cambridge, MA: MIT Press, 1988.

Descartes, René. *Meditations on First Philosophy* (II and VI) and *Discourse on Method* (V). *Discourse on Method and Meditations on First Philosophy*. 3rd ed. Trans. Donald Cress. Indianapolis: Hackett Publishing, 1998. Originally published in 1641.

Flew, Anthony. *Body, Mind, and Death*. Macmillan, 1976.

Foster, J. *The Immaterial Self: A Defence of the Cartesian Dualist Conception of Mind*. London: Routledge, 1991.

*Heil, John. *Philosophy of Mind: A Guide and Anthology*. Oxford: Oxford University Press, 2004.

Hofstadter, Douglas R. and Daniel C. Dennett, eds. *The Mind's I: Fantasies and Reflections on Self and Soul*. Basic Books, 1981.

Jackson, F. "What Mary Didn't Know." *Journal of Philosophy* 83 (1986): pp. 291–95.

Kim, Jaegwon. *Philosophy of Mind*. Boulder, CO: Westview Press, 2005.

Matson, Wallace. *Sentience*. University of California Press, 1976.

*Nagel, Thomas. "What Is It Like to Be a Bat?" *Philosophical Review* 4 (1974): pp. 435–50.

Plato, *Phaedo*. multiple editions in print.

Searle, John R.. "Minds, Brains, and Programs." *The Behavioral and Brain Sciences* 3 (1980): pp. 417–57.

Smart, J. J. C. "The Content of Physicalism" *Philosophical Quarterly* 28 (1978): pp. 239–41.

Swinburne, Richard. *The Evolution of the Soul*. Oxford: Clarendon Press. Revised edition, 1997.

Taliaferro, C. *Consciousness and the Mind of God*. Cambridge: Cambridge University Press, 1996.

Turing, Alan M. "Computing Machinery and Intelligence." *Minds and Machines*. Ed. A. R. Anderson. Prentice Hall, 1964.

Yolton, R. *Thinking Matter*. Minneapolis: University of Minnesota Press, 1983.

6 Personal identity

In the new series of *Battlestar Galactica*, Cylons—artificially intelligent cybernetic robots—are at war with the remnants of humanity. Many models of Cylons take human form. Not only that, but many Cylons appear to be deceived into thinking that they are not Cylons but instead are human beings. Likewise, many human beings in the series wonder whether they are actually Cylon. In "Home, Part 2," Sharon, a Cylon, expresses uncertainty about whether she is or is not a human being. In the course of this episode, she makes a striking observation. She says that her memories appear to her with such clarity that she believes she has lived the human life with which she has been programmed. Implicitly Sharon claims that her memories give her the best evidence that she is the person she thinks she is.

To pose questions about personal identity, we will be attempting to identify the criteria for some person at time 0 to be the same person at time $0 + 1$. What would be required for Sharon to make the transition from human being to Cylon? Can she change the physical nature of her existence in this way, while remaining the same person? She appears to think so. She's implicitly arguing that, if I as a human being lived a life that produced the memories I now have, and if I am a Cylon now, I am still the same *person* I was as a human being. Consider this analogy. When a caterpillar molts into a butterfly, it is still the same organism. The point is that changing the physical constitution of something, for example, adding some computer chips to your brain, does not in itself imply that the pre-operation you and the post-op you are different people. Physically, human bodies change in countless ways, both through natural and artificial processes. Face transplants give the recipient the facial appearance of another person and some of the DNA of the face donor. Imagine that, instead of receiving the face of another person, one changes one's memories. If someone receives a memory transplant—say, all the memories of A's teenage years get transplanted into B, and B's memories from B's own teenage years disappear—does the recipient maintain his or her identity pre- and post-op? Here we have a key difference between theories of personal identity: some focus on traits of the body while others focus on mental traits of the brain. Which type of theory is best? By what criteria?

This chapter introduces the issues involved in the problem of personal identity. We'll explore aspects of these issues and examine a few of the theories on offer.

After completing this chapter, you should be able to:

- Differentiate qualitative from **numerical identity**, and **diachronic** from **synchronic** identity
- Explain the **body criterion** and its failure
- Explain the **memory criterion**, Joseph Butler's "circularity objection" to it and Thomas Reid's "brave office" objection to it
- Explain the **psychological continuity criterion** and the idea of a "mental network"
- Explain Derek Parfit's "Jack counterexample" to psychological continuity
- Explain David Hume's "**bundle theory**" of the self and assess whether it answers the right questions about personal identity.

6.0 IDENTITY

Before we can build a theory of personal identity, we need to distinguish the issue of **personhood** from the issue of **personal identity**. The issue of personal identity concerns answers to the question, "What sorts of changes can a person undergo without ceasing to exist?" The issue of personhood concerns answers to the question, "What is it in virtue of which X is a person?" Answers to that question appeal to properties like "has the ability to reason" or "has 46 chromosomes" or "can experience pain." These and many other answers to the personhood question haven't met with success; philosophers widely disagree about the right answer. But this won't stop us from considering the personal identity question. To answer those questions, we presuppose for the sake of argument that there are persons and proceed directly to an investigation of what makes those persons the same persons over time. As we offer, explain and criticize answers to questions of personal identity, we will identify presuppositions about the nature of personhood when it becomes necessary.

Now then, suppose that you and your boyfriend walk into a shop selling watches because you want to get him a new one for his upcoming birthday. He sees another customer at the counter complete a purchase for a manly but tasteful watch. He turns to you, points at the other customer's new watch, and says, "I want that one." You know what your boyfriend means by that sentence. He means he wants for himself the same type of manly but tasteful watch as was on the previous customer's wrist. In philosophical terms, he wants a *qualitatively identical* watch.

Qualitative identity is a relation that one thing, X, bears to another thing, Y. Two watches of the exact same make, model and size are qualitatively identical as they roll out of the factory. Their parts are made from the same metals, their faces have the same dimensions, their bands are of the same material. Practical disputes about qualitative identity arise, for example, when I order something over the Internet. If you purchase that watch for your boyfriend online, but the watch that arrives is a different model, you'll be upset because the object you ordered and the object you received are not qualitatively identical.

Suppose you two are back in the watch shop and he has just turned to you, pointing at the previous customer, and said "I want that one." If your boyfriend is the demanding type, then there is an outside chance that he means that he does not want *the same kind of watch* purchased by the previous customer. Perhaps he wants the *very same* watch that the previous customer has just purchased! In other words, he wants you to buy the watch from the customer on whose arm it is being worn because nothing other than *that very watch* will do. In this case, in philosophical terms, he wants the *numerically identical* watch.

Concerns about numerical identity are less frequent in daily life than are concerns about qualitative identity, but they do arise. Suppose you are attending your 10-year high school reunion and you seem to see an old classmate, Mark. Upon seeing this person, you run up and ask him this question: "Mark, is that really you?" In this case, your question presupposes the use of an identity relation. You want to know whether the handsome, buff guy standing before you is the same person as, or in other words, *is numerically identical to*, the klutzy, small person you knew back in high school. You are implicitly invoking a concept of numerical identity here because you want to ascertain whether Mark has the same intrinsic properties as did the klutzy person you know from high school. If the person before you were to respond, "No, I'm not Mark but I look just like him," you'd be crestfallen. You don't care whether the two people share many qualities. What matters to you is that X, Mark, and Y, the man before you, are not numerically identical in that case.

In this chapter we are interested in exploring the nature of numerical identity because that is the type of identity of use in answering the question, "What conditions must I fulfill to persist over time as the same person?" Since we want to know what characteristics are necessary and sufficient to make me now the same person as me in the future, we want to know what conditions apply to the numerical identity of persons.

If X is numerically identical to Y, then X and Y share all their essential qualities in common. This is stated clearly and broadly: if X really is *the very same thing* as Y, then the essential properties of X will also be essential properties of Y. It is imperative to realize that the relation of numerical identity is a relation between a thing and itself. Thought of in this way, numerical identity can easily appear to be a trivial, silly concept. After all, it is absurd to think that one particular thing could also be some other thing, isn't it?

BOX 6.A: THE IDENTITY OF INDISCERNIBLES

Philosophers have used logic to increase the precision of our thinking about the nature of identity. Gottfried Leibniz was the first to articulate clear logical rules for identity. He says, "There are never in nature two beings which are perfectly alike and in which it would not be possible to find a difference that is internal or founded upon an intrinsic denomination." (Leibniz, 1991: p. 69) Leibniz's principle can be separated into two related statements, the **identity of indiscernibles** and the **indiscernibility of identicals**.

The principle of the identity of indiscernibles reads: For any X and any Y, if X and Y possess all their properties in common, then X is identical to Y. The principle of the indiscernibility of identicals reads: For any X and any Y, if X is identical to Y then X and Y have all their properties in common.

The principle of the identity of indiscernibles can be clarified by distinguishing its two forms, a weak and a strong form. The weak one holds only of essential properties, and the strong one holds of essential and inessential properties. For example, a boulder is identical over time in virtue of the fact that it has the same intrinsic properties one moment that it has the next. Roughly, an intrinsic property of X is a property X has in relation to itself. For example, the fact that the boulder contains 0.0003 oz. of gold is an intrinsic property because it is part of the boulder's nature to have 0.0003 oz. of gold. Leibniz suggests that the principle has limits—it does not apply to inessential properties. For example, the boulder may bear the inessential property of being next to a red sedan, and when the driver of the sedan moves the car, the boulder has lost that property. Being adjacent to a red sedan is inessential since it is no part of the boulder's nature. Leibniz would not regard this example as an obstacle to the truth of the weak version principle of the identity of indiscernibles.

However, others have deployed thought experiments that attack both versions of this principle. Max Black asks this interesting question:

> Isn't it logically possible that the universe should have contained nothing but two exactly similar spheres? We might suppose that each was made of chemically pure iron, had a diameter of one mile, that they had the same temperature, colour, and so on, and that nothing else existed. Then every quality and relational characteristic of the one would also be a property of the other. Now if what I am describing is logically possible, it is not impossible for two things to have all their properties in common. This seems to me to refute the principle.[1]

The spheres contain identical essential properties. They contain identical inessential properties too, insofar as they both possess properties like being a mile away from an iron sphere. Black believes that these two objects are *not* identical even though they *are* indiscernible from one another. In your opinion, does this influential thought experiment show that the principle is false?

Two surrounding problems prevent us from wrapping up our discussion of numerical identity so swiftly. The first issue concerns the role of time. Identity relationships are either *synchronic* (= same time) or *diachronic* (= through time). To establish the conditions for X to be numerically identical to Y *at a single time T* is easy: we did that in the previous paragraph. To establish the conditions for *X at time T* to be numerically identical to *Y at time T + 1* is more difficult. And that is the type of identity of most interest in discussing personal identity: we want to determine what it is that makes you you through time.

The second issue concerns the nature of properties. Above we mentioned that objects possess certain qualities that are essential to themselves and they possess other qualities that are inessential. It is necessary for diachronic numerical identity *over time* of some thing X at T with some thing Y at T + 1 that X at T and Y at T + 1 share all essential properties. The term "essential properties" refers to properties of some thing X without which X wouldn't be X. Mark, your high school classmate of ten years ago, will still be Mark, your high school classmate of ten years ago, even if he's now gained twenty pounds of muscle mass and died his hair jet black. Mark's weight and his hair color are inessential properties. Changes in inessential properties imply differences of qualitative identity, but changes in inessential properties do not imply differences of numerical identity.

Diachronic conditions for identity may differ from synchronic conditions for identity. Diachronic identity requires the maintenance of a select set of qualities across time. Properties, traits, features, characteristics—all these terms refer to qualities of things. Notice that these words take a direct object. A "quality" is a quality *of* something. The thing that possesses the quality is known as a "substance," familiar from our discussion of "substance" dualism in Chapter 5. The *Millennium Falcon* freighter, a substance, has several qualities. It

has military-class quad laser turrets.

is made from ionized titanium alloy.

contains cramped crew quarters.

has scanner-proof smuggling compartments.

made the Kessel Run.

was won by Han Solo in a game of sabacc.

Of course qualities themselves can have qualities. The turrets may be narrow and the titanium hull has microfissures.

We can change many things about the *Millennium Falcon* while insuring that it is the same freighter before and after our changes. For example, suppose Solo loses the *Falcon* while gambling. The "new" *Falcon* is the same old *Falcon*. The intuition that the ship has the same numerical identity before and after its change of ownership indicates that *who owns the Falcon* is an extrinsic quality of the ship. Inessential qualities like these make implicit reference to things *other than* the *Falcon* itself.

Through variations on a thought experiment, I have to change other qualities of the ship. In which cases am I left with the same ship?

Case 1: Chewbacca takes the ship apart piece by piece. He then puts it all back together with the exact same pieces in the same arrangement.

Case 2: Chewy takes the ship apart piece by piece. But for each piece he removes, he puts a brand new piece of the same shape, size and chemical makeup into the ship. The result is a ship that looks the same, but is made from all new pieces.

Case 3: Half the ship is destroyed in a explosion and Chewy rebuilds that half with new pieces and installs them in the exact way that the original pieces had been arranged.

Case 4: Just like Case 3 except that either 75 percent or 25 percent of the ship was destroyed and replaced.

Case 5: Solo owns the *Millennium Falcon* and buys another Corellian ship of the same exact make, model and year. He and Chewy take piece #1 from ship A and switch it with piece #1 from ship B, then they take piece #2 from A and switch it with piece #2 from B and so on for all the pieces.

Is the *Millennium Falcon* numerically the same after the changes described in these cases? Consider the identity of the ships in Case 5 at the beginning of the work, in the middle of the work and at the end of the work. Halfway through their work, each ship is made half from its original components and half from its sister-ship's components.

Asking about the identity of the *Millennium Falcon* in these cases makes sense because in these cases we have been tinkering with the intrinsic properties of the ship, and intrinsic properties are important for the identity of a substance in ways that its extrinsic properties are not. If any qualities of the ship are necessary for the preservation of the numerical identity of the ship, then it is the intrinsic properties of the ship that fill that role.

Let's apply these observations to our discussion of personal identity. This suggests that questions of personal identity are not questions that consider all aspects of the individual. Someone can change—for example, he could grow a beard, an extrinsic quality—but still be the same person. On the other hand, it seems that there must be *something* that endures for the person to remain diachronically identical. We want to know in what qualities that something consists. We will now examine theories that attempt to solve the problem of personal identity.

6.1 THE BODY THEORY

The most reliable, fastest means by which we determine whether person X is person Y is by identifying X's body. When I'm picking my wife up at the airport, I keep my eyes peeled on the bodies spilling out of the terminal's secured area and I pick her out of the crowd through my familiarity with her looks. When I'm brought before a line-up at a police station and asked to point to the person who burgled my house, I point to the person whose body looks like the body that I saw in my house that night. The reason that my behaviors make so much sense is best explained if a person is numerically identical over time because of their bodily continuity, in other words, because they possess the same body over time. The criterion that emerges from these commonsense considerations is the

> *Body criterion*: X at time T is the same person as Y at time T+1 iff X and Y share the same body.

According to this criterion, the body includes the brain since the brain is a physical part of the body.

The body criterion contrasts sharply with a view that we will state without discussing. The soul criterion states that X is the same person as Y iff X and Y share the same soul. Souls don't serve as a practical means by which to identify people because I have no access to someone's soul—I can't see or hear or touch it, and I can't tell whether X's soul has leapt over to Y's body or vice-versa. Bodies, though, are physical, and less mysterious than souls. We know what bodies are made from and we can test scientifically whether someone has the same body. In addition, arguments for the conclusion that we have physical bodies are solid (though idealists don't endorse them); arguments that we have souls are weak. So, the body criterion is more plausible than the soul criterion because it doesn't need any controversial presuppositions to get off the ground.

BOX 6.B: "THE CHANCE," PERSONAL IDENTITY AND BODY SWITCHING

One motivation behind a body criterion—that we derive much of our self-esteem and our lack of it from our relationship to our body—is compelling. For example, if people could choose to be smarter or better looking, most would choose to be better looking (or are we just being cynical?). In a very interesting short story called "The Chance," by Peter Carey, the relationship between personal identity and the body is raised in a world in which biotechnology allows people to have as beautiful a body as they can afford. This is not a new idea, of course, since even today some individuals have had as many as 50 separate cosmetic surgeries.

In Carey's story, however, one main character has witnessed the way in which a person's outlook and personality changes for the worse after they change their body for the better. In this story, a cluster of people, called Hups, have banded together to resist the trend to body improvement. Hups actually get cosmetic surgery in order to deform their bodies. Lumpy, a human whose body has been modified, falls in love with Carla. Carla is a beautiful young woman who has never undergone a body-switching procedure, i.e. never taken a "chance." Their relationship develops under duress as Carla becomes increasingly convinced that she ought to take a "chance" in order to exchange her present body for an "ugly" one. Perhaps this is to determine whether and how Lumpy loves her; perhaps it is because she feels a moral obligation of some sort to do so; or perhaps she has been unduly and inappropriately influenced by the group.

Is the existence of a group like the Hup beneficial, or are its members harming themselves for no good reason? Would you ever get cosmetic surgery? In which relationships is your body more important than your mind? How does this story support or invert claims within feminist theories about the body? (See Carey 1999)[2]

The body criterion resonates with materialist theories about the mind, and the soul criterion is inconsistent with materialist theories. On the other hand, the soul criterion and substance dualism work very well together. In contrast, the body criterion is inconsistent with substance dualism because the body criterion implies that I am identical with my physical body. The lesson to be drawn from these connections is that the soul criterion will inherit some of the problems (and benefits) of substance dualism, whereas the body criterion will inherit some of the benefits (and problems) of physicalism. Nonetheless, the problems that arise for the body criterion are persuasive. Continuity of body cannot provide a convincing criterion of personal identity. Let's discuss a few of these criticisms.

BOX 6.C: TELETRANSPORTATION AND PERSONAL IDENTITY

Science fiction authors have often described unique forms of transportation to facilitate their stories, and one story dealing with this issue is "Rogue Moon" (1960) by Algis Budrys. In "Rogue Moon" people transmit themselves through space instantaneously. The *Star Trek* multiverse would later adopt this plot device and call it the "transporter." Within the *Star Trek* world, just how a transporter is supposed to work is not clear.

In Budrys' story, the device creates a qualitatively identical copy of a person on the moon. Since they are now two, they cannot be the same person, or can they? In the *Star Trek* universe, one enters the transporter and gets a "digital" copy made, which contains data about the exact arrangement of one's physical structure. This is sent at light speed through radio waves to a chosen set of coordinates. At those coordinates the subject is remade. Though the subject is made out of completely different matter, she is regarded as being numerically identical with the person who first entered the transporter up on the orbiting ship. But is she the same person?

Examples using teletransportation have become popular conceptual tools in the philosophical discussion of personal identity. For example, Derek Parfit, a present-day British philosopher, begins a discussion of personal identity with the words:

> I enter the Teletransporter. I have been to Mars before, but only by the old method, a space-ship journey taking several weeks. This machine will send me at the speed of light. I merely have to press the green button. Like others, I am nervous. Will it work? I remind myself what I have been told to expect. . . . The Scanner here on Earth will destroy my brain and body, while recording the exact states of all of my cells. It will then transmit this information by radio. Traveling at the speed of light, the message will take three minutes to reach the Replicator on Mars. This will then create, out of new matter, a brain and body exactly like mine. It will be in this body that I shall wake up.[3] Parfit considers the anxieties he might experience about using the transporter: Will it really be "I" who wakes up in that other body on Mars? What are the implications for my personal identity if I am not destroyed and remade but rather am duplicated as in Budrys' story? What if my duplicate down on the planet unexpectedly dies—how should I react?

Here is the first problem. British philosopher John Locke constructed a case against the body criterion in the seventeenth century. He presents the argument succinctly in his *Essay Concerning Human Understanding* (§2.27):

> Should the soul of a prince, carrying with it the consciousness of the prince's past life, enter and inform the body of a cobbler, as soon as deserted by his own soul, everyone sees he would be the same person, accountable only for the prince's actions.

What Locke has us consider here is a case like that given in the old folk tale about the prince and the pauper, only in this case the two do not switch places entirely; they only switch bodies. Locke uses this thought experiment as a counterexample to the body criterion. For though the prince in this story changes bodies, he remains the same person.

Imagine that after the switch, the cobbler's mind uses the prince's body to commit heinous crimes. In this case, it is the cobbler who is guilty of a crime. Of course, when the crime scenes are investigated, they will find fingerprints of "the prince" instead of the fingerprints of "the cobbler." But the crime investigators have been deceived about the identity of the criminal. Their deception traces back to their mistaken assumption of the body criterion.

We attribute praise and blame only to persons. If the body criterion were true, then we would need to attribute praise and blame to bodies since bodies are persons. But Locke's thought experiment shows that, if the cobbler were to switch bodies with prince, the cobbler would not become innocent of crimes the cobbler commits when embodied as the prince. This is tantamount to saying that personal identity travels with the mind, not the body. Thus the body criterion appears false.

Here is a second debilitating problem. Our bodies are constantly gaining and losing parts. Our cells die and are replaced by new ones; we slough off skin; we get hip replacements; we cut our hair; we gain and lose weight. The body criterion says that for X and Y to be identical, X and Y must share the same body. But in fact you don't share the same body with the little infant on whom your parents doted. For these and other reasons, the body criterion has fallen out of favor.

6.2 THE MEMORY THEORY

This opens the way to the most intuitive of the criteria for personal identity: the continuity of memory. This criterion would identify you with a feature of your personality, as opposed to features of your body or immaterial soul. This makes a great deal of sense. The appeal to continuity of memory is intuitively plausible because we believe that which best distinguishes us from other people is our mental life. The beliefs, attitudes, desires, interests and memories of each of us are thought to be in some way essential to our individual identities.

John Locke espouses this theory. He says that memory is a "consciousness of past actions," and that it is essential to diachronic numerical identity. Memories are one's own record of one's past, all from one's own point of view. The sum total of memories a person has would seem to offer the best way to individuate that person *from* everyone else and *with* him or herself over time. Beliefs, personality traits, and desires change over time. But previous points of view, encapsulated in the group of memories that one possesses, offer Locke the promise of fixing necessary and sufficient conditions. He might say,

> *Memory criterion*: Person X at time T is numerically identical to person Y at time T + 1 iff X and Y share all the same memories.

This criterion has distinct advantages over previous criteria. This memory criterion implies that, if someone uniquely remembers committing a crime, then that person is the criminal, regardless of whether or not the body he or she has is the same as that which he or she had when the crime was committed. The person that should be punished is the person who was morally responsible for committing the crime. If in some dark future individuals are able to trade bodies, that fact should not abrogate responsibility for actions that an individual committed while in a body other than the one the individual now inhabits.

But despite the improvements it makes, the memory criterion faces serious problems, some of which were raised shortly after Locke wrote about it. In the eighteenth century another British philosopher, Joseph Butler, was one of the earliest critics of the memory criteria. He thought they were circular. (Now would be a good time to read the selection from Butler below at §6.9) Butler wrote a book called *The Analogy of Religion* to which he added an appendix titled "Of Personal Identity." There Butler argues that, for us to make any sense of the notion of abiding memory, we must *presuppose* the prior existence of abiding personal identity: memory theories are circular. In other words, memories, by their nature, cannot exist without being intimately conjoined to a point of view. So accounts of personal identity that make use of memories are viciously circular. Here is the rationale for this abstract objection. Consider the difference between real memories and merely apparent memories. I might have an apparent memory of seeing *Army of Darkness*. I call this "apparent" because my sister has told me about the film so often that I mistakenly believe I've seen it—I even believe I remember seeing it—when I haven't. In my apparent memory, I falsely believe that I did experience an event in my past that I did not.

But now look what I've done: in order to explain the concept of a memory in the first place, I had to appeal to the concept of the *self*, me. My memories are my beliefs about actual past experiences in my life. (Some philosophers add that the belief must be caused in the right way.) So it seems that Locke's appeal to memory in his explanation of personal identity over time is circular. His criterion for personal identity employs the concept of a memory, but to explain what a memory is requires use of the concept of a self.

The next objection to the memory criterion is more commonsensical and comes from another eighteenth-century British philosopher, Thomas Reid. First let's state his "brave officer" thought experiment, in which he imagines different points in time within one man's long life:

> Suppose a brave officer to have been flogged when a boy at school, for robbing an orchard, to have taken a standard [a flag] from the enemy in his first campaign, and to have been made a general in advanced life: suppose also, which must be admitted to be possible, that, when he took the standard, he was conscious of his having been flogged at school, and that when made a general he was conscious of his taking the standard, but had absolutely lost the consciousness of his flogging. These things being supposed, it follows, from Mr. Locke's doctrine, that he who was flogged at school is the same person who took the standard, and that he who took the standard is the same person who was made a general. Whence it follows, if there be any truth in logic, that the general is the same person with him who was flogged at school. But the general's consciousness does not reach so far back as his flogging; therefore, according to Mr. Locke's doctrine, he is not the person who was flogged. Therefore the general is, and at the same time is not, the same person with him who was flogged at school.[4]

This person robbed an orchard as a child, took the enemy's flag in combat as a young man, and became a general in his dotage. Call each of those episodes a "time-slice" of this person. As a young man in combat he remembered robbing an orchard. As an old general he remembered taking the enemy's flag in combat. If we apply Locke's memory criterion, we have a relation of personal identity between child and young man, and between young man and old general. So far, so good. But a strict application of Locke's theory implies that the child *is not* identical with the old general because the old general lacks the child's memories. Numerical identity is the strongest logical relationship that exists between X the child at time T and Y the old general at T + 1. It is a transitive relation. Given the logic of identity, if A is identical with B and B is identical with C, then it necessarily follows that A is identical with C. Locke's doctrine as it applies to persons violates this transitivity since it implies that the child and the general are not identical. But in fact the child is identical with the old general—and with the young soldier. So, the memory criterion must be false.

Here is a final criticism of the memory theory. As it is stated, X and Y must share all memories in order to maintain numerical identity. So if I develop new memories, then I am no longer numerically identical with anyone. To address this problem, we could rephrase the memory criterion as follows: Person X at time T is numerically identical to person Y at time T + 1 iff Y has all the memories that X had. So Y, who occupies a later time than X, is allowed to form new memories and yet remain identical to X. However, this restatement of the memory criterion implies that Y not only might possess all the memories of X, but Y might also possess all the memories of persons U, V and W. But then we have no privileged reason to think that Y is numerically identical to *X* but not numerically identical to *U, V or W*. We'll revisit this type of objection in the next section since something like it has been raised against the psychological continuity criterion.

BOX 6.D: *STAR TREK: THE NEXT GENERATION,* "SECOND CHANCES"

In "Second Chances" (season 6, episode 24), the starship *Enterprise* visits Nervala IV, a planet with a "distortion field" that poses special risks for the transporter. The transporter is a device that dematerializes a human being as it makes a copy or "pattern" of that person down to the last molecule. The *Enterprise* times its visit to coincide with an eight-yearly cycle in which transporting down to the surface is possible.

Commander Riker was serving aboard another starship eight years ago when the last mission was led to the surface, and he leads this one down now. But upon beaming down, he meets an identical copy of himself. Eight years ago, due to the duplication of a "containment beam" required for transport on this odd planet, Riker's pattern was reproduced on the ship and on the surface. For eight years, Riker #2 has been living on the desolate surface isolated from civilization. Now that he is back, he wants back his stuff, and his girlfriend, Counselor Troi.

If either the memory criterion or the psychological continuity criterion are correct, then it would appear that at some point there were two people who were numerically the same person, which is contradictory. "Second Chances" offers a nice thought experiment to test such cases. This is but one of a dozen or so *Star Trek* transporter episodes dealing with issues of personal identity. See also "Tuvix" (*Voyager*, season 2, episode 24), in which two people (of two species) are melded together in a transporter accident.

6.3 THE PSYCHOLOGICAL CONTINUITY THEORY

The psychological approach closely resembles the memory criterion, but its dissimilarities make it immune to some of the memory criterion's problems. We learned that since memory changes and numerical identity does not, memory is not a good philosophical foundation for a theory of personal identity. The psychological continuity theory suggests that features of our mental life other than mere memory explain our diachronic numerical identity, in other words, our self-continuity over time. This continuity over time makes use of the concept of a *mental network*. A mental network is the sum total of mental states— beliefs, desires, and moods in your conscious and non-conscious mind—and the inter-relations that they bear to one another.

> *Psychological continuity criterion*: (i) person X and person Y are diachronically, numerically identical if and only if X and Y are psychologically continuous; and (ii) X and Y are psychologically continuous if and only if Y's mental network is well connected to X's mental network.

This account implies that the psychological continuity criterion offers necessary and sufficient conditions for numerical identity. A mental network is time-indexed, meaning that a mental network occurs in a single moment. Just as a picture of a tree offers a time-indexed snapshot of the tree, so a mental network functions like a cognitive snapshot of all your mental states at one moment in time. Were you to take pictures of the same maple sapling each day for a year, you might notice large differences between its image in the first, the 182nd and the 365th picture. But if you look closely, you'll observe many small changes day to day. Just as a new leaf grows on a tree and wind blows branches, new beliefs, feelings, perceptions and other mental states emerge in one's mental network, creating changes every waking minute.

To be "well connected" means that the two mental networks are causally related in ways that account for the changes between one network and its immediate successor. Picture 100 reveals a small bud on a branch in the tree, picture 105 reveals the formation of a tiny leaf stem, and in picture 140, in the same location on the same branch, a fully grown leaf has emerged. The time-slices of the tree exhibit very good connections since the bud seen in 100 (partially) causes the event seen in 105 and the stem in 105 (partially) causes the growth of the leave as seen in 140. Changes to a mental network also exhibit well-connectedness. At time 1 the network includes the desire to attend a mosque, at time 2 it includes perceptions of being in a mosque at that moment and at some later time the network includes the beliefs that Allah exists and Muhammad is his prophet.

This notion of a well connected mental network is more intuitive than it may seem. As an old man I will forget some of the memories I have now, start to dislike broccoli, and go blind due to cataracts. Despite these changes to my mind/brain, the continuity in my mental network abides one day to the next because changes to it are gradual. This may not seem to be the kind of idea we were looking for. We had been searching for a static, *enduring characteristic* of a human being on which to ground personal identity. Psychological continuity between mental network A at time 0 and mental network A at time 0 + 1 refers to a *relationship between* sets of mental states. When a handful of beliefs about Pluto in network A change from being affirmed at time 0 to being denied at time 0 + 1, the remainder of the components of the network and their relationships continues unaltered.

The fact that sets of mental states follow on one another in succession can be developed into a criterion for personal identity. Gradual change over time is, after all, what explains why one has the beliefs, desires and moods that one has. One has the network that one has because one has had the beliefs, desires and moods that one has had in the past. The psychological continuity accounts for the intuition that, even if I forget some memories, or change moods, or gain new knowledge, a self remains the numerically same person over time because his or her mental networks are continuous. For a self to be continuous over time, the future mental network must evolve out of the present mental network through direct causal connections.

This framework for the psychological continuity criterion gives rise to several creative objections. Thought experiments about brain bisection and brain transplantation show that the theory has significant problems. Philosopher Derek Parfit has considered brain bisection cases in his philosophical thinking about personal identity. He suggests that we suppose that Jack's brain is divided into two equal portions and then transplanted into two brainless bodies, X and Y. Let's suppose for the argument that, after the operation, that Jack's mental network gets copied into both X and Y. After the operation X and Y are both psychologically continuous with Jack, which means that X and Y both think of themselves as Jack and share Jack's mental network.

So who is Jack, post-operation? The logical possibilities are clear: either Jack is both X and Y, Jack is either X or Y but not both, Jack is neither X or Y. Parfit argues that none of these are plausible.

Consider the first solution that Jack is both X and Y. X and Y are not the same people. If they're different people from each other, then Jack cannot be both of them. The reason that X and Y are different people is best glimpsed from a point 30 years on from the operation. At that time X and Y have developed sharp personality differences. X is a bricklayer and Y is not. X loves reading and Y is now illiterate, and so on. So, if Jack is both X and Y, then we have a contradiction.

The next idea is that Jack is either X or Y, but not both. But X and Y bear exactly the same relation to Jack, so there is in principle no reason to think that Jack is X and not Y or vice-versa. Case closed.

The skeptical option is to suppose that Jack is neither X or Y. This may appear strange since X and Y are psychologically continuous with Jack. Who else could Jack be besides X or Y? It doesn't seem that Jack dies as a result of this relationship. After all, his personality, beliefs, desires, etc., all survive seamlessly once he awakens from his anesthetic coma. Nonetheless, perhaps appearances are deceiving and Jack does cease to exist.

Derek Parfit draws three lessons from this thought experiment. (1) First, there is no true answer to the question: "What happened to Jack?" (2) The concept of "personal identity" is too vague to be of any philosophical importance. (3) The commonsense assumption that I either endure through time or I do not endure is false. Parfit seems to be giving up on a philosophical analysis of the question. He might say instead that he simply refrains from pushing philosophy past its proper limits. He recognizes an intractable, insoluble problem for what it is: a mindless pursuit contemplated by armchair philosophers with nothing better to do.

We can respond to Parfit's example by adding a condition to the psychological continuity criterion. Psychological continuity is a necessary and sufficient condition for the numerical identity of persons X and Y. Parfit uses the counterexample about Jack to imply that psychological continuity is not sufficient for personal identity due to the fact that, if there are two beings both of whose networks are equally well connected to Jack's, then they can't both be Jack. After all, two persons cannot be numerically identical to one person. But we might respond to the Jack counterexample by adding condition (iii):

> *Psychological continuity criterion*: (i) person X and person Y are diachronically, numerically identical if and only if X and Y are psychologically continuous; and (ii) X and Y are psychologically continuous if and only if Y's mental network is well connected to X's mental network; and (iii) there are no persons Z where Z is also psychologically continuous with X.

(We assume that Z is not identical to X or identical to Y.) The addition of (iii) makes necessary that there be at most only one single being at time 0 + 1 that is psychologically continuous with X at time 0.

Though this seems to be a sensible idea, and it also seems true, stipulating its truth in the context of a definition of personal identity commits a fallacy. Specifically, (iii) may be an ad hoc reply to the Jack counterexample. The addition of another necessary condition does not directly respond to the criticism. Suppose that I say that it is a necessary condition upon something being a crow that it be black. Then imagine that someone finds a white crow, which falsifies my necessary condition. Now imagine that, instead of revising my thesis about crows to take account of this counterexample to it, I instead redefine the necessary condition: it is a necessary condition upon something being a crow that it be black, *except* for the one that you found. The same problematic strategy is implicitly used in (iii).

(Does the psychological continuity criterion fall prey to Joseph Butler's circularity objection against the memory criterion?)

BOX 6.E: SPLIT CONSCIOUSNESS

Many neurological disorders bear upon what philosophers would describe as problems of personal identity and of the unity of consciousness. One of the most dramatic effects on personal identity follows from a radical form of treatment.

In attempts to control the effects of strong forms of epilepsy, which result in grand mal seizures, neurosurgeons in the 1960s began severing the corpus callosum in humans. The corpus callosum is the neuron-filled tissue that links the brain's left and right hemispheres. The results of these operations have yielded important data both about the division of labor between the hemispheres and about the nature of consciousness.

The scientist who pioneered this type of surgery, Roger Sperry, summarized the philosophical implications of his research on the hemispheres of the brain by saying that they are "Two separate realms of conscious awareness; two sensing, perceiving, thinking and remembering systems." In effect, within each person there are two centers of consciousness, not one. This suggests that the philosopher's quest for a theory of personal identity in which there is only one of me over time may be mistaken from the start. We know that each hemisphere does a lot of thinking on its own due to clever experiments.

When a subject with a split brain is shown a card in the left side of her visual field with a word on it, "fork" for example, she cannot read or say the word because the right side of the brain was processing the data. When the card is shifted to the right side of her visual field (processed by the left hemisphere), the subject recognizes and says the word immediately. The right side is not inactive, though. Subjects who are shown the card in the left portion of their visual field will pick up a fork amongst a number of other objects. Both sides of the brain are thinking in their own way.

The best way to describe these subjects is as having two minds. This is because there is complicated thinking on many levels occurring in each hemisphere in these patients. In fact, a chimp whose right and left arms fight with each other for a banana has been observed. As philosopher Thomas Nagel has observed, if a split-brain subject has two minds, then we do as well—albeit, in our case the two minds are joined together to a greater degree than in the split brain cases. (Split brains are still joined together through the brain stem, but are not joined by the corpus callosum.) Rather than focusing our question about the psychological continuity of a mind, some argue that we must change tack and determine the relationship between the two minds that we have. (See Nagel 1971.)

6.4 THE BUNDLE THEORY

Despite the problems we have discussed, philosophers tend to think that the appeal to psychological continuity is the most promising approach to the problem of personal identity. Many philosophers find the advantages of this approach so compelling, relative to the alternatives, that they accept psychological continuity as the best available theory and continue to improve on it. Other philosophers regard its problems as insurmountable and see the debate about these issues as going down, far down, the wrong track. Instead of attempting to improve upon this theory, some of these critics seek to change the nature and direction of the debate about personal identity.

For this interesting group of thinkers, the principal problems about personal identity lay not with *answers* to the question, "What makes me me over time?" but rather with the *question itself.* Another of John Locke's critics exemplifies this approach, the eighteenth-century Scottish philosopher David Hume. In his *Treatise of Human Nature* (book 1.4.6), Hume advances the theory that persons lack diachronic numerical identity. The crux of Hume's argument occurs in this passage:

> There are some philosophers who imagine we are every moment intimately conscious of what we call our self; that we feel its existence and its continuance in existence; and are certain, beyond the evidence of a demonstration, both of its perfect identity and simplicity. . . . Unluckily all these positive assertions are contrary to that very experience which is pleaded for them; nor have we any idea of self, after the manner it is here explained. For, from what impression could this idea be derived? This question it is impossible to answer without a manifest contradiction and absurdity; and yet it is a question which must necessarily be answered, if we would have the idea of self pass for clear and intelligible. It must be some one impression that gives rise to every real idea. But self or person is not any one impression, but that to which our several impressions and ideas are supposed to have a reference. If any impression gives rise to the idea of self, that impression must continue invariably the same, through the whole course of our lives; since self is supposed to exist after that manner. But there is no impression constant and invariable. Pain and pleasure, grief and joy, passions and sensations succeed each other, and never all exist at the same time. It cannot therefore be from any of these impressions, or from any other, that the idea of self is derived; and consequently there is no such idea.

Among Hume's points in this passage is that he can't seem to find any clear, unambiguous idea of the self in the first place. Each time he tries to look for that idea in his mind, he comes up with something else. So, his conclusion: the concept of "self" or "self-over-time" is meaningless.

What precisely are the premises in Hume's argument for the conclusion that we have no idea of ourselves as numerically identical beings over time? Hume's argument depends on some presuppositions that he takes for granted within his system of philosophy. Foremost among these are Hume's empiricist commitments about philosophical methodology. *Empiricism* refers to a philosophical school according to which all knowledge must be tied to the experiences that we have using our senses. Hume's specific form of empiricism prompts him to ask, for any supposed concept, whether its origins can successfully be traced back to sensory experiences. For example, some people claim to know that God exists. Hume asks where the idea of God comes from. It appears that we have no immediate sensory experience of God. The idea of God seems to be put together from other ideas (ideas of love, power and knowledge) that we have through our own experience. For Hume, the conclusion is that we cannot know that God exists because we can't trace our concept of God back to any experiences.

He applies the same strategy in his analysis of personal identity. When Hume introspects upon his experiences, he finds that he has no experience of "himself" as a substantial being that endures through time. Instead, when he looks inside his mind, he only notices a specific, solitary sensory impression. He feels a moment of fear or he tastes a citrus flavor. Without delving into Hume's complex doctrines about what he calls "impressions" and "ideas," we can state the argument as follows:

(6.1)   I know that person X is diachronically numerical to person Y *only if* I have experience of that property in X and Y responsible for their diachronic numerical identity.

(6.2)   If Y is numerically identical with my current self and X is diachronically numerically identical with Y, then I would have experience of that property in X and Y responsible for their diachronic numerical identity.

(6.3)   But I have no experience of that property in X and Y responsible for their diachronic numerical identity.

(6.4)   So I do not know that person X is diachronically numerical to person Y (even when I'm numerically identical to Y).

6.1 describes the implication of Hume's dedication to empiricism in his epistemology. 6.2 applies the maxim in 6.1 to the first person case. 6.3 is a claim of fact about what Hume does and does not experience. Hume tries to justify 6.3 by his description of the phenomenology of our experience in the passage quoted above. I have framed the argument and its conclusion in epistemological terms: Hume says we do not know that any person X has diachronic numerical identity with any person Y.

In this mix of perceptions and ideas constantly flowing through our minds, we identify no properties of our selves that unify our experience over time. The self is not a being that possesses these experiences, according to Hume. Rather, if a self is anything at all, it is nothing more than *a sequence of individual mental events*. It *seems* to each of us that each of us is more than a sequence of individual events, true. But Hume explains the apparent identity over time by noting the close connections that join our experiences. The closeness of the connections between the events in our mental network trick us into attributing to our mental networks over time a unity that is not there.

In place of offering a criterion for personal identity, Hume gives his readers a philosophical consolation prize. According to Hume, the self is "nothing but a bundle or collection of different perceptions." As these perceptions change, so does the bundle or collection. This bundle is just like a stamp collection. If one buys, trades, or sells a number of stamps, one's collection is no longer the same. If, as Hume says, the self is nothing but a collection of things, as those things change, the self changes with them. Of course selves change—a self is identical over time, despite vast qualitative changes. But Hume is making the stronger claim that the self changes in ways that make diachronic numerical identity of X with Y impossible. In other words, the fact of qualitative changes in one's mental network, or "bundle," implies no diachronic numerical identity.

> I may venture to affirm of the rest of mankind, that they are nothing but a bundle or collection of different perceptions, which succeed each other with an inconceivable rapidity, and are in a perpetual flux and movement. Our eyes cannot turn in their sockets without varying our perceptions. Our thought is still more variable than our sight; and all our other senses and faculties contribute to this change: nor is there any single power of the soul, which remains unalterably the same, perhaps for one moment. The mind is a kind of theatre, where several perceptions successively make their appearance; pass, repass, glide away, and mingle in an infinite variety of postures and situations.
>
> (*Treatise*, 1.4.6)

Other philosophers haven't been willing to abandon the notion of diachronic personal identity. Should we abandon it, we abandon a number of other notions that we seem unable to do without. If there is no personal identity through time, we can't justifiably hold criminals culpable for their crimes since, by the time we convict and sentence them, they are no longer *numerically* the same persons. Contracts between people would be void, legally speaking, for the persons who signed them would be *numerically* different persons before the contracts could be honored.

Much of the work done on the problem of personal identity presupposes a principle given to us by John Locke. According to Locke, something can change and retain identity if such changes are characteristic of entities of that sort and are allowed for in the concept of that thing. Thus, we call a tree the same, even if it has grown by a foot; we call a house the same, even if its exterior has weathered; we call a town the same, even if its citizenry has grown. Our notion of identity has to be more flexible than Hume would allow it to be. Accordingly, we might think about the expressions "same forest," "same dance," "same symphony," and "same motion" as we generate criteria for the concept "same person."

6.5 SUMMARY

In this chapter we have been discussing the conditions under which one person ceases to be that person, i.e. personal identity. To be more specific, criteria for personal identity specify the necessary and sufficient conditions for someone's being the same person over time, or diachronically. In an attempt to clarify the questions that we would be asking, we distinguished two types of identity, qualitative and numerical, and focused our attention on numerical identity. The term "identity" is also tricky. We use it to refer to two things that share all of their intrinsic properties.

With this preliminary material in hand, we next turned our attention to the presentation of theories of personal identity. We discussed the body criterion, according to which X is numerically identical to Y iff X and Y share the same body. But physical bodies change radically over a lifetime, so it appears as though no one is identical over the duration of their life. John Locke's prince/cobbler thought experiment goes some way toward disproving the body theory.

The memory criterion and the psychological continuity criterion share much in common. These theories mark the shift toward mental criteria for personal identity. The basic intuition is that X at time 1 is diachronically numerically identical to Y at time 0 + 1 iff X and Y have well connected mental networks. One objection to psychological continuity involved a thought experiment in which Jack's brain is divided, each hemisphere preserving Jack's mental network. Each hemisphere is transplanted into a brainless body. No clear answer as to which "being" Jack is emerges.

We closed the chapter by considering the bundle theory of the self. The bundle theory was formed to overcome several of the problems associated with other psychological theories. In effect, the bundle theory argues that human beings are not numerically identical over time. Instead, a self changes in so many and in such deep ways that a self cannot be said to be a single person over the course of its life.

6.6 ABOUT THE READINGS

Our science fiction reading for this topic is "Learning to Be Me," by Greg Egan. Egan writes hard SF with an unparalleled combination of scientific and technological know-how, fecund imagination and fast-paced plotting. In the course of this short story, the narrator gives us an intellectual autobiography. His preoccupation is whether to switch his mind—his consciousness, memories, body-control, etc.—from his organic brain to a simulator that is running from within his brain. The simulator or "jewel" is a piece of hardware that contains a couple of important features, including a program that is called "the teacher" and a consciousness of some kind. The teacher identifies the way the consciousness should feel, think and act on the basis of closely monitoring neuronal activity in the organic brain. Though most people switch from organic to jewel, the narrator is one of the few holdouts. The story confronts several problems about his future, his relationships, and, especially, about his own identity. From the point of view of someone who can choose which desires to desire, as can the narrator, we normal human beings must appear trapped in our own petty, two-dimensional identities.

Egan does not propose a theory of personal identity, of course, but he does give us great reasons to reflect more on those criteria that have been presented. In particular, if

I am capable of selecting new desires and destroying old memories—in short, if I rebuild myself psychologically from the ground up—there is very little psychological continuity before and after such an event. This can be used to call into question John Locke's appeal to psychological continuity.

There are two historical readings for this topic. The first is an excerpt from John Locke's *Essay Concerning Human Understanding*, in which he offers a compelling case on behalf of the claim that person X is identical to person Y only if X and Y share key psychological traits in common. This is the classic representation of the psychological continuity criterion. The second reading is the appendix from Bishop Joseph Butler's *Analogy of Religion*, in which he calls into question Locke's psychological criteria. In particular, Butler thinks that all such psychological criteria are question-begging. What his arguments are for that conclusion I leave for you to determine.

The psychological approach to personal identity is the most popular theory among philosophers. It assumes that your psychological makeup and continuity is necessary and sufficient for you to be a person over time. But according to the new biological continuity theory, your psychological continuity is neither necessary or sufficient for your being the same person over time. You are essentially an animal; you are not essentially a person. It follows that being a person is like being a small business owner: for a long period of time you were not a small business owner, then you bought the business and were; and then, years later, you sold the business are were not.

In "Was I Ever a Fetus?" Eric Olson builds upon these observations in order to offer some new arguments against the psychological continuity theory and in support of the biological continuity theory. The biological continuity theory suggests that, fundamentally, what makes you you over time is your biological continuity. If you fall into a persistent vegetative state and permanently lose your higher mental abilities, you do not pass out of existence: you are the animal that respirates, circulates blood, and lays in the hospital bed. This theory is different than the body criterion since the biological continuity theory allows for the replacement of organs—even parts of your brain. You are an animal, an animal with a life, according to the biological continuity theory. On the bodily continuity theory you are a material object, and not necessarily an animal.

Expressing the bodily continuity theory in terms of the debate is difficult for the following reason. Due to the great influence of the psychological continuity theory, philosophers typically state their theory of personal identity in the following terms: "X at T1 is the same person as Y at T2 if and only if . . ." This assumes that creature X and creature Y are always persons at all times. Since the biological continuity theory argues that this assumption is false, it is difficult to put into traditional formulations of personal identity.

6.7 "LEARNING TO BE ME" BY GREG EGAN

I was six years old when my parents told me that there was a small, dark jewel inside my skull, learning to be me.

Microscopic spiders had woven a fine golden web through my brain, so that the jewel's teacher could listen to the whisper of my thoughts. The jewel itself eavesdropped on my senses, and read the chemical messages carried in my bloodstream; it saw, heard, smelt, tasted and felt the world exactly as I did, while the teacher monitored its thoughts and compared them with my own. Whenever the jewel's thoughts were *wrong*, the teacher—faster than thought—rebuilt the jewel slightly, altering it this way and that, seeking out the changes that would make its thoughts correct.

Why? So that when I could no longer be me, the jewel could do it for me.

I thought: if hearing that makes *me* feel strange and giddy, how must it make the *jewel* feel? Exactly the same, I reasoned; it doesn't know it's the jewel, and it too wonders how the jewel must feel, it too reasons: "Exactly the same; it doesn't know it's the jewel, and it too wonders how the jewel must feel . . ."

And it too wonders—

(I knew, because *I* wondered)

—it too wonders whether it's the real me, or whether in fact it's only the jewel that's learning to be me.

As a scornful twelve-year-old, I would have mocked such childish concerns. Everybody had the jewel, save the members of obscure religious sects, and dwelling upon the strangeness of it struck me as unbearably pretentious. The jewel was the jewel, a mundane fact of life, as ordinary as excrement. My friends and I told bad jokes about it, the same way we told bad jokes about sex, to prove to each other how blasé we were about the whole idea.

Yet we weren't quite as jaded and imperturbable as we pretended to be. One day when we were all loitering in the park, up to nothing in particular, one of the gang—whose name I've forgotten, but who has stuck in my mind as always being far too clever for his own good—asked each of us in turn: "Who *are* you? The jewel, or the real human?" We all replied—unthinkingly, indignantly—"The real human!" When the last of us had answered, he cackled and said, "Well, I'm not. *I'm* the jewel. So you can eat my shit, you losers, because *you'll* all get flushed down the cosmic toilet—but me, I'm gonna live forever."

We beat him until he bled.

By the time I was fourteen, despite—or perhaps because of—the fact that the jewel was scarcely mentioned in my teaching machine's dull curriculum, I'd given the question a great deal more thought. The pedantically correct answer when asked "Are you the jewel or the human?" had to be "The human"—because only the human brain was physically able to reply. The jewel received input from the senses, but had no control over the body, and its intended reply coincided with what was actually said only because the device was a perfect imitation of the brain. To tell the outside world "I am the jewel"—with speech, with writing, or with any other method involving the body—was patently false (although to *think it* to oneself was not ruled out by this line of reasoning).

However, in a broader sense, I decided that the question was simply misguided. So long as the jewel and the human brain shared the same sensory input, and so long as the teacher kept their thoughts in perfect step, there was only *one* person, *one* identity, *one* consciousness. This one person merely happened to have the (highly desirable) property that *if either* the jewel *or* the human brain were to be destroyed, he or she would survive unimpaired. People had always had two lungs and two kidneys, and for almost a century, many had lived with two hearts. This was the same: a matter of redundancy; a matter of robustness, no more.

That was the year that my parents decided I was mature enough to be told that they had both undergone the switch—three years before. I pretended to take the news calmly, but I hated them passionately for not having told me at the time. They had disguised their stay in hospital with lies about a business trip overseas. For three years I had been living with jewel-heads, and they hadn't even told me. It was *exactly* what I would have expected of them.

"We didn't seem any different to you, did we?" asked my mother.

"No," I said—truthfully, but burning with resentment nonetheless.

"That's why we didn't tell you," said my father. "If you'd known we'd switched, at the time, you might have *imagined* that we'd changed in some way. By waiting until now to tell you, we've made it easier for you to convince yourself that we're still the same people we've always been." He put an arm around me and squeezed me. I almost screamed out, "Don't *touch* me!" but I remembered in time that I'd convinced myself that the jewel was No Big Deal.

I should have guessed that they'd done it, long before they confessed; after all, I'd known for years that most people underwent the switch in their early thirties. By then, it's downhill for the organic brain, and it would be foolish to have the jewel mimic this decline. So, the nervous system is rewired; the reins of the body are handed over to the jewel, and the teacher is deactivated. For a week, the outward-bound impulses from the brain are compared with those from the jewel, but by this time the jewel is a perfect copy, and no differences are ever detected.

The brain is removed, discarded, and replaced with a spongy tissue-cultured object, brain-shaped down to the level of the finest capillaries, but no more capable of thought than a lung or a kidney. This mock-brain removes exactly as much oxygen and glucose from the blood as the real thing, and faithfully performs a number of crude, essential biochemical functions. In time, like all flesh, it will perish and need to be replaced.

The jewel, however, is immortal. Short of being dropped into a nuclear fireball, it will endure for a billion years.

My parents were machines. My parents were gods. It was nothing special. I hated them.

When I was sixteen, I fell in love, and became a child again.

Spending warm nights on the beach with Eva, I couldn't believe that a mere machine could ever feel the way I did. I knew full well that if my jewel had been given control of my body, it would have spoken the very same words as I had, and executed with equal tenderness and clumsiness my every awkward caress—but I couldn't accept that its inner life was as rich, as miraculous, as joyful as mine. Sex, however pleasant, I could accept as a purely mechanical function, but there was something between us (or so I believed) that had nothing to do with lust, nothing to do with words, nothing to do with any tangible action of our bodies that some spy in the sand dunes with parabolic microphone and infrared binoculars might have discerned. After we made love, we'd gaze up in silence at the handful of visible stars, our souls conjoined in a secret place that no crystalline computer could hope to reach in a billion years of striving. (If I'd said *that* to my sensible, smutty, twelve-year-old self, he would have laughed until he haemorrhaged.)

I knew by then that the jewel's "teacher" didn't monitor every single neuron in the brain. That would have been impractical, both in terms of handling the data, and because of the sheer physical intrusion into the tissue. Someone-or-other's theorem said that sampling certain critical neurons was almost as good as sampling the lot, and—given some very reasonable assumptions that nobody could disprove—bounds on the errors involved could be established with mathematical rigour.

At first, I declared that *within these errors*, however small, lay the difference between brain and jewel, between human and machine, between love and its imitation. Eva, however, soon pointed out that it was absurd to make a radical, qualitative distinction on the basis of the sampling density; if the next model teacher sampled more neurons and halved the error rate, would its jewel then be "half-way" between "human" and "machine?" In theory—and eventually, in practice—the error rate could be made smaller than any number I cared to name. Did I really believe that a discrepancy of one in a billion made any difference at all—when every human being was permanently losing thousands of neurons every day, by natural attrition?

She was right, of course, but I soon found another, more plausible, defence for my position. Living neurons, I argued, had far more internal structure than the crude optical switches that served the same function in the jewel's so-called "neural net." That neurons fired or did not fire reflected only one level of their behaviour; who knew what the subtleties of biochemistry—the quantum mechanics of the specific organic molecules involved—contributed to the nature of human consciousness? Copying the abstract neural topology wasn't enough. Sure, the jewel could pass the fatuous Turing test—no outside observer could tell it from a human—but that didn't prove that *being* a jewel felt the same as *being* human.

Eva asked, "Does that mean you'll never switch? You'll have your jewel removed? You'll let yourself *die* when your brain starts to rot?"

"Maybe," I said. "Better to die at ninety or a hundred than kill myself at thirty, and have some machine marching around, taking my place, pretending to be me."

"How do you know *I* haven't switched?" she asked, provocatively. "How do you know that I'm not just 'pretending to be me'?"

"I know you haven't switched," I said, smugly. "I just *know*."

"How? I'd look the same. I'd talk the same. I'd act the same in every way. People are switching younger, these days. So *how do you know I haven't?*"

I turned onto my side towards her, and gazed into her eyes. "Telepathy. Magic. The communion of souls."

My twelve-year-old self started snickering, but by then I knew exactly how to drive him away.

At nineteen, although I was studying finance, I took an undergraduate philosophy unit. The Philosophy Department, however, apparently had nothing to say about the Ndoli Device, more commonly known as "the jewel." (Ndoli had in fact called it "the *dual*," but the accidental, homophonic nick-name had stuck.) They talked about Plato and Descartes and Marx, they talked about St. Augustine and—when feeling particularly modern and adventurous—Sartre, but if they'd heard of Godel, Turing, Hamsun or Kim, they refused to admit it. Out of sheer frustration, in an essay on Descartes I suggested that the notion of human consciousness as "software" that could be "implemented" equally well on an organic brain or an optical crystal was in fact a throwback to Cartesian dualism: for "software" read "soul." My tutor superimposed a neat, diagonal, luminous red line over each paragraph that dealt with this idea, and wrote in the margin (in vertical, bold-face, 20-point Times, with a contemptuous 2 Hertz flash): IRRELEVANT!

I quit philosophy and enrolled in a unit of optical crystal engineering for non-specialists. I learnt a lot of solid-state quantum mechanics. I learnt a lot of fascinating mathematics. I learnt that a neural net is a device used only for solving problems that are far too hard to be *understood*. A sufficiently flexible neural net can be configured by feedback to mimic almost any system—to produce the same patterns of output from the same patterns of input—but achieving this sheds no light whatsoever on the nature of the system being emulated.

"Understanding," the lecturer told us, "is an overrated concept. Nobody really *understands* how a fertilized egg turns into a human. What should we do? Stop having children until ontogenesis can be described by a set of differential equations?"

I had to concede that she had a point there.

It was clear to me by then that nobody had the answers I craved—and I was hardly likely to come up with them myself; my intellectual skills were, at best, mediocre. It came down to a simple choice: I could waste time fretting about the mysteries of consciousness, or, like everybody else, I could stop worrying and get on with my life.

When I married Daphne, at twenty-three, Eva was a distant memory, and so was any thought of the communion of souls. Daphne was thirty-one, an executive in the merchant bank that had hired me during my PhD, and everyone agreed that the marriage would benefit my career. What she got out of it, I was never quite sure. Maybe she actually liked me. We had an agreeable sex life, and we comforted each other when we were down, the way any kind-hearted person would comfort an animal in distress.

Daphne hadn't switched. She put it off, month after month, inventing ever more ludicrous excuses, and I teased her as if I'd never had reservations of my own.

"I'm afraid," she confessed one night. "What if I die when it happens—what if all that's left is a robot, a puppet, a *thing*? I don't want to *die*."

Talk like that made me squirm, but I hid my feelings. "Suppose you had a stroke," I said glibly, "which destroyed a small part of your brain. Suppose the doctors implanted a machine to take over the functions which that damaged region had performed. Would you still be 'yourself'?"

"Of course."

"Then if they did it twice, or ten times, or a thousand times—"

"That doesn't necessarily follow."

"Oh? At what magic percentage, then, would you stop being 'you'?" She glared at me. "All the old clichéd arguments—"

"Fault them, then, if they're so old and clichéd."

She started to cry. "I don't have to. Fuck you! I'm scared to death, and you don't give a shit!"

I took her in my arms. "Sssh. I'm sorry. But everyone does it sooner or later. You mustn't be afraid. I'm here. I love you." The words might have been a recording, triggered automatically by the sight of her tears.

"Will you do it? With me?"

I went cold. "What?"

"Have the operation, on the same day? Switch when I switch?"

Lots of couples did that. Like my parents. Sometimes, no doubt, it was a matter of love, commitment, sharing. Other times, I'm sure, it was more a matter of neither partner wishing to be an unswitched person living with a jewel-head.

I was silent for a while, then I said, "Sure."

In the months that followed, all of Daphne's fears—which I'd mocked as "childish" and "superstitious"—rapidly began to make perfect sense, and my own "rational" arguments came to sound abstract and hollow. I backed out at the last minute; I refused the anaesthetic, and fled the hospital.

Daphne went ahead, not knowing I had abandoned her.

I never saw her again. I couldn't face her; I quit my job and left town for a year, sickened by my cowardice and betrayal—but at the same time euphoric that I had *escaped*.

There was nothing to fear, after all. I'm exactly the person I've always been. Putting it off was insane; now that I've taken the leap of faith, I couldn't be more at ease.

Your loving robot wife,
Daphne

By the time I was twenty-eight, almost everyone I knew had switched. All my friends from university had done it. Colleagues at my new job, as young as twenty-one, had done it. Eva, I heard through a friend of a friend, had done it six years before.

The longer I delayed, the harder the decision became. I could talk to a thousand people who had switched, I could grill my closest friends for hours about their childhood memories and their most private thoughts, but however compelling their words, I knew that the Ndoli Device had spent decades buried in their heads, learning to fake exactly this kind of behaviour.

Of course, I always acknowledged that it was equally impossible to be *certain* that even another *unswitched* person had an inner life in any way the same as my own—but it didn't seem unreasonable to be more inclined to give the benefit of the doubt to people whose skulls hadn't yet been scraped out with a curette.

I drifted apart from my friends, I stopped searching for a lover. I took to working at home (I put in longer hours and my productivity rose, so the company didn't mind at all). I couldn't bear to be with people whose humanity I doubted.

I wasn't by any means unique. Once I started looking, I found dozens of organisations exclusively for people who hadn't switched, ranging from a social club that might as easily have been for divorcees, to a paranoid, paramilitary "resistance front," who thought they were living out *Invasion of the Body Snatchers*. Even the members of the social club, though, struck me as extremely maladjusted; many of them shared my concerns, almost precisely, but my own ideas from other lips sounded obsessive and ill-conceived. I was briefly involved with an unswitched woman in her early forties, but all we ever talked about was our fear of switching. It was masochistic, it was suffocating, it was insane.

I decided to seek psychiatric help, but I couldn't bring myself to see a therapist who had switched. When I finally found one who hadn't, she tried to talk me into helping her blow up a power station, to let THEM know who was boss.

I'd lie awake for hours every night, trying to convince myself, one way or the other, but the longer I dwelt upon the issues, the more tenuous and elusive they became. Who was "I," anyway? What did it mean that "I" was "still alive," when my personality was utterly different from that of two decades before? My earlier selves were as good as dead—I remembered them no more clearly than I remembered contemporary acquaintances—yet this loss caused me only the slightest discomfort. Maybe the destruction of my organic brain would be the merest hiccup, compared to all the changes that I'd been through in my life so far.

Or maybe not. Maybe it would be exactly like dying.

Sometimes I'd end up weeping and trembling, terrified and desperately lonely, unable to comprehend—and yet unable to cease contemplating—the dizzying prospect of my own nonexistence. At other times, I'd simply grow "healthily" sick of the whole tedious subject. Sometimes I felt certain that the nature of the jewel's inner life was the most important question humanity could ever confront. At other times, my qualms seemed fey and laughable. Every day, hundreds of thousands of people switched, and the world apparently went on as always; surely that fact carried more weight than any abstruse philosophical argument?

Finally, I made an appointment for the operation. I thought, what is there to lose? Sixty more years of uncertainty, and paranoia? If the human race was replacing itself with clockwork automata, I was better off dead; I lacked the blind conviction to join the psychotic underground—who, in any case, were tolerated by the authorities only so long as they remained ineffectual. On the other hand, if all my fears were unfounded—if my sense of identity could survive the switch as easily as it had already survived such traumas as sleeping and waking, the constant death of brain cells, growth, experience, learning and forgetting—then I would gain not only eternal life, but an end to my doubts and my alienation.

I was shopping for food one Sunday morning, two months before the operation was scheduled to take place, flicking through the images of an on-line grocery catalogue, when a mouth-watering shot of the latest variety of apple caught my fancy. I decided to order half a dozen. I didn't, though. Instead, I hit the key which displayed the next item. My mistake, I knew, was easily remedied; a single keystroke could take me back to the apples. The screen showed pears, oranges, grapefruit. I tried to look down to see what my clumsy fingers were up to, but my eyes remained fixed on the screen.

I panicked. I wanted to leap to my feet, but my legs would not obey me. I tried to cry out, but I couldn't make a sound. I didn't feel injured, I didn't feel weak. Was I paralysed? Brain-damaged? I could still *feel* my fingers on the keypad, the soles of my feet on the carpet, my back against the chair.

I watched myself order pineapples. I felt myself rise, stretch, and walk calmly from the room. In the kitchen, I drank a glass of water. I should have been trembling, choking, breathless; the cool liquid flowed smoothly down my throat, and I didn't spill a drop.

I could only think of one explanation: *I had switched*. Spontaneously. The jewel had taken over, while my brain was still alive; all my wildest paranoid fears had come true.

While my body went ahead with an ordinary Sunday morning, I was lost in a claustrophobic delirium of helplessness. The fact that everything I did was exactly what I had planned to do gave me no comfort. I caught a train to the beach, I swam for half an hour; I might as well have been running amok with an axe, or crawling naked down the street, painted with my own excrement and howling like a wolf. *I'd lost control.* My body had turned into a living strait-jacket, and I couldn't struggle, I couldn't scream, I couldn't even close my eyes. I saw my reflection, faintly, in a window on the train, and I couldn't begin to guess what the mind that ruled that bland, tranquil face was thinking.

Swimming was like some sense-enhanced, holographic nightmare; I was a volitionless object, and the perfect familiarity of the signals from my body only made the experience more horribly *wrong*. My arms had no right to the lazy rhythm of their strokes; I wanted to thrash about like a drowning man, I wanted to show the world my distress.

It was only when I lay down on the beach and closed my eyes that I began to think rationally about my situation.

The switch *couldn't* happen "spontaneously." The idea was absurd. Millions of nerve fibres had to be severed and spliced, by an army of tiny surgical robots which weren't even present in my brain—which weren't due to be injected for another two months. Without deliberate intervention, the Ndoli Device was utterly passive, unable to do anything but *eavesdrop*. No failure of the jewel or the teacher could possibly take control of my body away from my organic brain.

Clearly, there had been a malfunction—but my first guess had been wrong, absolutely wrong.

I wish I could have done *something*, when the understanding hit me. I should have curled up, moaning and screaming, ripping the hair from my scalp, raking my flesh with my fingernails. Instead, I lay flat on my back in the dazzling sunshine. There was an itch behind my right knee, but I was, apparently, far too lazy to scratch it.

Oh, I ought to have managed, at the very least, a good, solid bout of hysterical laughter, when I realised that I was the jewel.

The teacher had malfunctioned; it was no longer keeping me aligned with the organic brain. I hadn't suddenly become powerless; I had *always been* powerless. My will to act upon "my" body, upon the world, had *always* gone straight into a vacuum, and it was only because I had been ceaselessly manipulated, "corrected" by the teacher, that my desires had ever coincided with the actions that seemed to be mine.

There are a million questions I could ponder, a million ironies I could savour, but *I mustn't*. I need to focus all my energy in one direction. My time is running out.

When I enter hospital and the switch takes place, if the nerve impulses I transmit to the body are not exactly in agreement with those from the organic brain, the flaw in the teacher will be discovered. *And rectified.* The organic brain has nothing to fear; *his* continuity will be safeguarded, treated as precious, sacrosanct. There will be no question as to which of us will be allowed to prevail. *I* would be made to conform, once again. *I* will be "corrected." *I* will be murdered.

Perhaps it is absurd to be afraid. Looked at one way, I've been murdered every microsecond for the last twenty-eight years. Looked at another way, I've only existed for the seven weeks that have now passed since the teacher failed, and the notion of my separate identity came to mean anything all—and in one more week this aberration, this nightmare, will be over. Two months of misery; why should I begrudge losing that, when I'm on the verge of inheriting eternity? Except that it won't be *I* who inherits it, since that two months of misery is all that defines me.

The permutations of intellectual interpretation are endless, but ultimately, I can only act upon my desperate will to survive. I don't *feel* like an aberration, a disposable glitch. How can I possibly hope to survive? I must conform—of my own free will. I must choose to make myself *appear* identical to that which they would force me to become.

After twenty-eight years, surely I am still close enough to him to carry off the deception. If I study every clue that reaches me through our shared senses, surely I can put myself in his place, forget, temporarily, the revelation of my separateness, and force myself back into synch.

It won't be easy. He met a woman on the beach, the day I came into being. Her name is Cathy. They've slept together three times, and he thinks he loves her. Or at least, he's said it to her face, he's whispered it to her while she slept, he's written it, true or false, into his diary.

I feel nothing for her. She's a nice enough person, I'm sure, but I hardly know her. Preoccupied with my plight, I've paid scant attention to her conversation, and the act of sex was, for me, little more than a distasteful piece of involuntary voyeurism. Since I realised what was at stake, I've *tried* to succumb to the same emotions as my alter ego, but how can I love her when communication between us is impossible, when she doesn't even know *I* exist?

If she rules his thoughts night and day, but is nothing but a dangerous obstacle to me, how can I hope to achieve the flawless imitation that will enable me to escape death?

He's sleeping now, so I must sleep. I listen to his heartbeat, his slow breathing, and try to achieve a tranquility consonant with these rhythms. For a moment, I am discouraged. Even my *dreams* will be different; our divergence is ineradicable, my goal is laughable, ludicrous, pathetic. Every nerve impulse, for a week? My fear of detection and my attempts to conceal it will, unavoidably, distort my responses; this knot of lies and panic will be impossible to hide.

Yet as I drift towards sleep, I find myself believing that I *will* succeed. I *must*. I dream for a while—a confusion of images, both strange and mundane, ending with a grain of salt passing through the eye of a needle—then I tumble, without fear, into dreamless oblivion.

I stare up at the white ceiling, giddy and confused, trying to rid myself of the nagging conviction that there's something I *must* not think about.

Then I clench my fist gingerly, rejoice at this miracle, and remember.

Up until the last minute, I thought he was going to back out again—but he didn't. Cathy talked him through his fears. Cathy, after all, has switched, and he loves her more than he's ever loved anyone before.

So, our roles are reversed now. This body is *his* strait-jacket,

now . . .

I am drenched in sweat. *This is hopeless, impossible.* I can't read his mind, I can't guess what he's trying to do. Should I move, lie still, call out, keep silent? Even if the computer monitoring us is programmed to ignore a few trivial discrepancies, as soon as he notices that his body won't carry out his will, he'll panic just as I did, and I'll have no chance at of making the right guesses. Would *he* be sweating, now? Would his breathing be constricted, like this? *No.* I've been awake for just thirty seconds, and already I have betrayed myself. An optical-fibre cable trails from under my right ear to a panel on the wall. Somewhere, alarm bells must be sounding.

If I made a run for it, what would they do? Use force? I'm a citizen, aren't I? Jewel-heads have had full legal rights for decades; the surgeons and engineers can't do anything to me without my consent. I try to recall the clauses on the waiver he signed, but he hardly gave it a second glance. I tug at the cable that holds me prisoner, but it's firmly anchored, at both ends.

When the door swings open, for a moment I think I'm going to fall to pieces, but from somewhere I find the strength to compose myself. It's my neurologist, Dr Prem. He smiles and says, "How are you feeling? Not too bad?"

I nod dumbly.

"The biggest shock, for most people, is that they don't feel different at all! For a while you'll think, "It can't be this simple! It can't be this easy! It can't be this *normal*!" But you'll soon come to accept that *it is*. And life will go on, unchanged." He beams, taps my shoulder paternally, then turns and departs.

Hours pass. *What are they waiting for?* The evidence must be conclusive by now. Perhaps there are procedures to go through, legal and technical experts to be consulted, ethics committees to be assembled to deliberate on my fate. I'm soaked in perspiration, trembling uncontrollably. I grab the cable several times and yank with all my strength, but it seems fixed in concrete at one end, and bolted to my skull at the other.

An orderly brings me a meal. "Cheer up," he says. "Visiting time soon."

Afterwards, he brings me a bedpan, but I'm too nervous even to piss.

Cathy frowns when she sees me. "What's wrong?"

I shrug and smile, shivering, wondering why I'm even trying to go through with the charade. "Nothing. I just . . . feel a bit sick, that's all."

She takes my hand, then bends and kisses me on the lips. In spite of every-thing, I find myself instantly aroused. Still leaning over me, she smiles and says, "It's over now, okay? There's nothing left to be afraid of. You're a little shook up, but you know in your heart you're still who you've always been. And I love you."

I nod. We make small talk. She leaves. I whisper to myself, hysterically, "I'm still who I've always been. I'm still who I've always been."

Yesterday, they scraped my skull clean, and inserted my new, non-sentient, space-filling mock-brain.

I feel calmer now than I have for a long time, and I think at last I've pieced together an explanation for my survival.

Why do they deactivate the teacher, for the week between the switch and the destruction of the brain? Well, they can hardly keep it running while the brain is being trashed—but why an entire week? To reassure people that the jewel, unsupervised, can still stay in synch; to persuade them that the life the jewel is going to live will be exactly the life that the organic brain "would have lived"—whatever that could mean.

Why, then, only for a week? Why not a month, or a year? Because the jewel *cannot* stay in synch for that long—not because of any flaw, but for precisely the reason that makes it worth using in the first place. The jewel is immortal. The brain is decaying. The jewel's imitation of the brain leaves out—deliberately—the fact that *real* neurons *die*. Without the teacher working to contrive, in effect, an identical deterioration of the jewel, small discrepancies must eventually arise. A fraction of a second's difference in responding to a stimulus is enough to arouse suspicion, and—as I know too well—from that moment on, the process of divergence is irreversible.

No doubt, a team of pioneering neurologists sat huddled around a computer screen, fifty years ago, and contemplated a graph of the probability of this radical divergence, versus time. How would they have chosen *one week*? What probability would have been acceptable? A tenth of a percent? A hundredth? A thousandth? However safe they decided to be, it's hard to imagine them choosing a value low enough to make the phenomenon rare on a global scale, once a quarter of a million people were being switched every day.

In any given hospital, it might happen only once a decade, or once a century, but every institution would still need to have a policy for dealing with the eventuality.

What would their choices be?

They could honour their contractual obligations and turn the teacher on again, erasing their satisfied customer, and giving the traumatised organic brain the chance to rant about its ordeal to the media and the legal profession.

Or, they could quietly erase the computer records of the discrepancy, and calmly remove the only witness.

So, this is it. Eternity.

I'll need transplants in fifty or sixty years' time, and eventually a whole new body, but that prospect shouldn't worry me—I can't die on the operating table. In a thousand years or so, I'll need extra hardware tacked on to cope with my memory storage requirements, but I'm sure the process will be uneventful. On a time scale of millions of years, the structure of the jewel is subject to cosmic-ray damage, but error-free transcription to a fresh crystal at regular intervals will circumvent that problem.

In theory, at least, I'm now guaranteed either a seat at the Big Crunch, or participation in the heat death of the universe.

I ditched Cathy, of course. I might have learnt to like her, but she made me nervous, and I was thoroughly sick of feeling that I had to play a role.

As for the man who claimed that he loved her—the man who spent the last week of his life helpless, terrified, suffocated by the knowledge of his impending death—I can't yet decide how I feel. I ought to be able to empathise—considering that I once expected to suffer the very same fate myself—yet somehow he simply isn't *real* to me. I know my brain was modeled on his—giving him a kind of causal primacy—but in spite of that, I think of him now as a pale, insubstantial shadow.

After all, I have no way of knowing if his sense of himself, his deepest inner life, his experience of *being*, was in any way comparable to my own.

STUDY AND DISCUSSION QUESTIONS

1   What is a "jewel" and what does it do? What is the relationship between a "jewel" and a "teacher"?

2   Early in the story, Egan narrates a conversation amongst children about having or being a jewel. He also explains that, at the time the story is set, almost everyone has one. Be an armchair sociologist and ask yourself whether, once made available, reliable and pain-free, jewels would be as popular as they are portrayed to be in the story?

3   Why does Egan say that it is "patently false" to say out loud "I am the jewel" but it is not evidently patently false to think "I am the jewel"?

4   What exactly happens when one gets "the switch," as the narrator's parents do? Does this enable one to live forever? If so, how?

5   When getting switched, do you have a moral obligation to tell others—friends, family, boss, etc.—that you are in fact getting switched?

6   The narrator briefly muses that love cannot be preserved by a switching event because love is something beyond the physical realm. He says, "There was something between us (or so I believed) that had nothing to do with lust, nothing to do with words, nothing to do with any tangible action of our bodies that some spy in the sand dunes with parabolic microphone and infrared binoculars might have discerned." When we love someone, we love a person (obviously). So would your love for someone fade away if he or she were switched into a jewel?

7   The narrator introduces the reader to his wife, Daphne, and to her reservations about getting switched. She is worried that she—Daphne, her personality, her soul—will die at the switch. Is she correct?

8 Can you reconstruct the narrator's response to Daphne's worry? It takes the form of a philosophical argument. See if you can clearly identify the premises.

9 Consider this claim made by the narrator:

> Of course, I always acknowledged that it was equally impossible to be *certain* that even another *unswitched* person had an inner life in any way the same as my own—but it didn't seem unreasonable to be more inclined to give the benefit of the doubt to people whose skulls hadn't yet been scraped out with a curette.

Do you agree or disagree? Why?

10 How does the narrator come to understand that something was wrong? Does his description of the anomie he feels make sense? In other words, is it even possible for him not to be able to understand why he is thinking or doing what he is thinking or doing?

11 If you are following the complexity of the perspective in which the story is told, what do you make of the irony contained in the narrator's comment that "I must conform—of my own free will. I must choose to make myself *appear* identical to that which they would force me to become." What is he getting at?

12 We get a faux real-time narration of the operation. The narrator seems to be in a dilemma: either begin behaving as "he" wants to, or attempt to mimic the actions and thoughts that "he" believes his host would do or say. Is this the correct way to describe the situation facing "him"?

6.8 "THE PSYCHOLOGICAL CONTINUITY THEORY," BY JOHN LOCKE

7. Idea of identity suited to the idea it is applied to. It is not therefore unity of substance that comprehends all sorts of identity, or will determine it in every case; but to conceive and judge of it aright, we must consider what idea the word it is applied to stands for: it being one thing to be the same substance, another the same man, and a third the same person, if person, man, and substance, are three names standing for three different ideas;—for such as is the idea belonging to that name, such must be the identity; which, if it had been a little more carefully attended to, would possibly have prevented a great deal of that confusion which often occurs about this matter, with no small seeming difficulties, especially concerning personal identity, which therefore we shall in the next place a little consider.

8. Same man. An animal is a living organized body; and consequently the same animal, as we have observed, is the same continued life communicated to different

particles of matter, as they happen successively to be united to that organized living body. And whatever is talked of other definitions, ingenious observation puts it past doubt, that the idea in our minds, of which the sound man in our mouths is the sign, is nothing else but of an animal of such a certain form. Since I think I may be confident, that, whoever should see a creature of his own shape or make, though it had no more reason all its life than a cat or a parrot, would call him still a man; or whoever should hear a cat or a parrot discourse, reason, and philosophize, would call or think it nothing but a cat or a parrot; and say, the one was a dull irrational man, and the other a very intelligent rational parrot. A relation we have in an author of great note, is sufficient to countenance the supposition of a rational parrot.

His words are: "I had a mind to know, from Prince Maurice's own mouth, the account of a common, but much credited story, that I had heard so often from many others, of an old parrot he had in Brazil, during his government there, that spoke, and asked, and answered common questions, like a reasonable creature: so that those of his train there generally concluded it to be witchery or possession; and one of his chaplains, who lived long afterwards in Holland, would never from that time endure a parrot, but said they all had a devil in them. I had heard many particulars of this story, and as severed by people hard to be discredited, which made me ask Prince Maurice what there was of it. He said, with his usual plainness and dryness in talk, there was something true, but a great deal false of what had been reported. I desired to know of him what there was of the first. He told me short and coldly, that he had heard of such an old parrot when he had been at Brazil; and though he believed nothing of it, and it was a good way off, yet he had so much curiosity as to send for it: that it was a very great and a very old one; and when it came first into the room where the prince was, with a great many Dutchmen about him, it said presently, What a company of white men are here! They asked it, what it thought that man was, pointing to the prince. It answered, Some General or other. When they brought it close to him, he asked it, D'ou venez-vous? It answered, De Marinnan. The Prince, A qui estes-vous? The Parrot, A un Portugais. The Prince, Que fais-tu la? Parrot, Je garde les poulles. The Prince laughed, and said, Vous gardez les poulles? The Parrot answered, Oui, moi; et je scai bien faire; and made the chuck four or five times that people use to make to chickens when they call them. I set down the words of this worthy dialogue in French, just as Prince Maurice said them to me. I asked him in what language the parrot spoke, and he said in Brazilian. I asked whether he understood Brazilian; he said No, but he had taken care to have two interpreters by him, the one a Dutchman that spoke Brazilian, and the other a Brazilian that spoke Dutch; that he asked them separately and privately, and both of them agreed in telling him just the same thing that the parrot had said. I could not but tell this odd story, because it is so much out of the way, and from the first hand, and what may pass for a good one; for I dare say this Prince at least believed himself in all he told me, having ever passed for a very honest and pious man: I leave it to naturalists to reason, and to other men to believe, as they please upon it; however, it is not, perhaps, amiss to relieve or enliven a busy scene sometimes with such digressions, whether to the purpose or no."

I have taken care that the reader should have the story at large in the author's own words, because he seems to me not to have thought it incredible; for it cannot be imagined that so able a man as he, who had sufficiency enough to warrant all the testimonies he gives of himself, should take so much pains, in a place where it had nothing to do, to pin so close, not only on a man whom he mentions as his friend, but on a Prince in whom he acknowledges very great honesty and piety, a story which, if he himself thought incredible, he could not but also think ridiculous. The Prince, it is plain, who vouches this story, and our author, who relates it from him, both of them call this talker a parrot: and I ask any one else who thinks such a story fit to be told, whether, if this parrot, and all of its kind, had always talked, as we have a prince's word for it this one did,—whether, I say, they would not have passed for a race of rational animals; but yet, whether, for all that, they would have been allowed to be men, and not parrots? For I presume it is not the idea of a thinking or rational being alone that makes the idea of a man in most people's sense: but of a body, so and so shaped, joined to it: and if that be the idea of a man, the same successive body not shifted all at once, must, as well as the same immaterial spirit, go to the making of the same man.

9. Personal identity. This being premised, to find wherein personal identity consists, we must consider what person stands for;—which, I think, is a thinking intelligent being, that has reason and reflection, and can consider itself as itself, the same thinking thing, in different times and places; which it does only by that consciousness which is inseparable from thinking, and, as it seems to me, essential to it: it being impossible for any one to perceive without perceiving that he does perceive. When we see, hear, smell, taste, feel, meditate, or will anything, we know that we do so. Thus it is always as to our present sensations and perceptions: and by this every one is to himself that which he calls self:— it not being considered, in this case, whether the same self be continued in the same or divers substances. For, since consciousness always accompanies thinking, and it is that which makes every one to be what he calls self, and thereby distinguishes himself from all other thinking things, in this alone consists personal identity, i.e. the sameness of a rational being: and as far as this consciousness can be extended backwards to any past action or thought, so far reaches the identity of that person; it is the same self now it was then; and it is by the same self with this present one that now reflects on it, that that action was done.

10. Consciousness makes personal identity. But it is further inquired, whether it be the same identical substance. This few would think they had reason to doubt of, if these perceptions, with their consciousness, always remained present in the mind, whereby the same thinking thing would be always consciously present, and, as would be thought, evidently the same to itself. But that which seems to make the difficulty is this, that this consciousness being interrupted always by forgetfulness, there being no moment of our lives wherein we have the whole train of all our past actions before our eyes in one view, but even the best memories losing the sight of one part whilst they are viewing another; and we sometimes, and that the greatest part of our lives, not reflecting on our past selves, being intent on our present thoughts, and in sound sleep having no thoughts at all, or at least none with that consciousness which remarks our waking thoughts,—I say, in all these cases, our consciousness being interrupted, and we losing the sight of our past selves, doubts are raised whether we are the same thinking thing, i.e. the same substance or no.

Which, however reasonable or unreasonable, concerns not personal identity at all. The question being what makes the same person; and not whether it be the same identical substance, which always thinks in the same person, which, in this case, matters not at all: different substances, by the same consciousness (where they do partake in it) being united into one person, as well as different bodies by the same life are united into one animal, whose identity is preserved in that change of substances by the unity of one continued life. For, it being the same consciousness that makes a man be himself to himself, personal identity depends on that only, whether it be annexed solely to one individual substance, or can be continued in a succession of several substances. For as far as any intelligent being can repeat the idea of any past action with the same consciousness it had of it at first, and with the same consciousness it has of any present action; so far it is the same personal self. For it is by the consciousness it has of its present thoughts and actions, that it is self to itself now, and so will be the same self, as far as the same consciousness can extend to actions past or to come, and would be by distance of time, or change of substance, no more two persons, than a man be two men by wearing other clothes to-day than he did yesterday, with a long or a short sleep between: the same consciousness uniting those distant actions into the same person, whatever substances contributed to their production.

16. Consciousness alone unites actions into the same person. But though the same immaterial substance or soul does not alone, wherever it be, and in whatsoever state, make the same man; yet it is plain, consciousness, as far as ever it can be extended—should it be to ages past—unites existences and actions very remote in time into the same person, as well as it does the existences and actions of the immediately preceding moment: so that whatever has the consciousness of present and past actions, is the same person to whom they both belong. Had I the same consciousness that I saw the ark and Noah's flood, as that I saw an overflowing of the Thames last winter, or as that I write now, I could no more doubt that I who write this now, that saw the Thames overflowed last winter, and that viewed the flood at the general deluge, was the same self,—place that self in what substance you please—than that I who write this am the same myself now whilst I write (whether I consist of all the same substance, material or immaterial, or no) that I was yesterday. For as to this point of being the same self, it matters not whether this present self be made up of the same or other substances—I being as much concerned, and as justly accountable for any action that was done a thousand years since, appropriated to me now by this self-consciousness, as I am for what I did the last moment.

17. Self depends on consciousness, not on substance. Self is that conscious thinking thing,—whatever substance made up of, (whether spiritual or material, simple or compounded, it matters not)—which is sensible or conscious of pleasure and pain, capable of happiness or misery, and so is concerned for itself, as far as that consciousness extends. Thus every one finds that, whilst comprehended under that consciousness, the little finger is as much a part of himself as what is most so. Upon separation of this little finger, should this consciousness go along with the little finger, and leave the rest of the body, it is evident the little finger would be the person, the same person; and self then would have nothing to do with the rest of the body. As in this case it is the consciousness that goes along with the substance, when one part is separate from another, which makes the same person, and

constitutes this inseparable self: so it is in reference to substances remote in time. That with which the consciousness of this present thinking thing can join itself, makes the same person, and is one self with it, and with nothing else; and so attributes to itself, and owns all the actions of that thing, as its own, as far as that consciousness reaches, and no further; as every one who reflects will perceive.

STUDY AND DISCUSSION QUESTIONS

1   In paragraph 7 Locke says that uses of "identity" must be disambiguated since it is "one thing to be the same substance, another the same man, and a third the same person." What is a substance? What is a man? What is a person?

2   Locke describes an animal as "a living organized body; and consequently the same animal, as we have observed, is the same continued life communicated to different particles of matter." It appears that his use of "animal" and the use of "person" by advocates of the biological continuity view mean the same thing. Is this true? (Read the Eric Olson selection to improve your answer.)

3   Aristotle and earlier philosophers claimed that if something is a rational animal, then it is a human being. With that in mind, what is the purpose of Locke's story of the parrot that talks? Relatedly, what is the role of rationality in Locke's theory of personal identity?

4   In paragraph 9 Locke states his definition of personal identity. Can you sketch this out in some detail?

5   Locke addresses an objection to his theory. According to this objection, there are moments in our lives in which our consciousness is interrupted. Locke interprets this as a claim that we are not the same substance throughout our entire lives. He dismisses this objection. What is going on here in paragraph 10?

6   Is being the same *substance* necessary or sufficient for being the same *person*, according to Locke?

7   Why does consciousness make me the same person over time, according to Locke?

8   If John Locke were to choose a theory in the philosophy of mind that is most compatible with his account of personal identity and with his remarks about substance, what would he choose and why?

6.9 "OF PERSONAL IDENTITY," BY JOSEPH BUTLER

2. Now, when it is asked wherein personal identity consists, the answer should be the same, as if it were asked, wherein consists similitude or equality; that all attempts to

define, would but perplex it. Yet there is no difficulty at all in ascertaining the idea. For as upon two triangles being compared or viewed together, there arises to the mind the idea of similitude; or upon twice two and four, the idea of equality: so likewise upon comparing the consciousness of one's self, or one's own existence in any two moments, being compared, there as immediately arises to the mind the idea of personal identity. And as the two former comparisons, not only give the ideas of similitude and equality, but also shews us, that two triangles are alike, and twice two and four are equal; so the latter comparison not only gives us the idea of personal identity but also shews us the identity of ourselves in those two moments: the present, suppose, and that immediately past; or the present, and that a month, a year, or twenty years past. Or, in other words, by reflecting upon that, which is my self now, and that, which was my self twenty years ago, I discern they are not two, but one and the same self.

3. But though consciousness does thus ascertain our personal identity to ourselves, yet to say, that consciousness makes personal identity, or is necessary to our being the same persons, is to say, that a person has not existed a single moment, nor done one action, but what he can remember; indeed none but what he reflects upon. And one should really think it self-evident, that consciousness of personal identity presupposes, and therefore cannot constitute, personal identity, any more than knowledge in any other case, can constitute truth, which it presupposes.

4. This wonderful mistake may possibly have arisen from hence, that to be endued with consciousness, is inseparable from the idea of a person, or intelligent being. For this might be expressed inaccurately thus, that consciousness makes personality; and from hence it might be concluded to make personal identity. But though present consciousness of what we at present do and feel, is necessary to our being the persons we now are; yet present consciousness of past actions or feelings, is not necessary to our being the same persons, who performed those actions, or had those feelings.

STUDY AND DISCUSSION QUESTIONS

1   Butler opens this piece with reflection on the origin of our idea of personal identity. He is concerned that the philosophical discussions of this concept have convoluted our understanding somewhat. Is the idea difficult to understand and acquire? Why/why not?

2   What does "consciousness" mean for Butler? For Locke above?

3   Consider this statement from paragraph 3: "consciousness of personal identity presupposes, and therefore cannot constitute, personal identity, any more than knowledge in any other case, can constitute truth, which it presupposes." This is Butler's key point, but it is rather abstract. Explain this in your own words. Hint: his claim about the relationship between knowledge and truth echoes issues raised about the definition of knowledge given in Chapter 2.

6.10 "WAS I EVER A FETUS?" BY ERIC T. OLSON

> It is obviously true that the normal foetus is at least a potential person: it is an entity which will, barring abnormal circumstances or intervention, develop into something incontestably a person. The only question is what moral claim upon us this gives it.
>
> (J. Glover, *Causing Death and Saving Lives*)

1. The standard view of personal identity

Was I ever a fetus? Is it possible for a human fetus to become you or me or some other person? It would certainly seem so. Both folk wisdom and biological science tell us that each of us spent several months in the womb before we were born. How could anyone think otherwise? But many philosophers do think otherwise. At any rate, most recent thinking about personal identity clearly entails that no person was ever a five-month-old fetus, and that no such fetus ever comes to be a person.

By "personal identity" I mean the question of personal identity over time: what it takes for a person to persist from one time to another. What sorts of adventures is it possible for you to survive, in the broadest sense of the word "possible"? And what sort of thing would necessarily bring your existence to an end? What is necessary, and what suffices, for a past or future being to be you? Suppose you point to a little boy or girl in an old class photograph and say, "That's me." What makes you *that* boy or girl, and not, say, one of the others? What is it about the way she relates to you as you are now that makes it the case that she *is* you—that you and she are one rather than two?

By far the most popular answer to this question is that we people persist by virtue of some sort of *psychological continuity*. You are that future being that in some sense inherits your current psychological features: that being whose memories, beliefs, preferences, capacity for thought and consciousness, and so on are for the most part caused, in a certain way, by yours. That is what it *is* for something existing in the future to be you. Likewise, you are that past being whose mental properties you have inherited in this way. There is disagreement about just what sort of "inheritance" this has to be: about *how* your past or future mental properties need to cause or be caused by your current ones, for instance. But most philosophers agree that some psychological relation is both necessary and sufficient for us to persist. Call this the *Standard View* of personal identity.

Why accept the Standard View? Imagine that your cerebrum—the upper part of the brain that is primarily responsible for your psychology—is cut out of your head and implanted into another. The one who ends up with that organ will be psychologically continuous with you on any account of what psychological continuity amounts to. She will have your memories, your plans for the future, your likes and dislikes, and so on; and these features would have been continuously physically realized throughout the process. She will believe that she is you, and it would take some doing to convince her that she is wrong about this. It is easy to conclude from this that she *is* you, and that the empty-headed being left behind after your cerebrum is removed is not you. (They couldn't *both* be you, for one thing cannot be two things.) Why is she you? Because she has inherited your psychology in the appropriate way. The empty-headed being is not you because it has inherited no psychology at all from you. If this is right, it suggests that for a past or future being to be you is for it to be appropriately psychologically continuous with you.

Here is another argument, this time not involving science fiction. Suppose you have an accident that destroys your cerebrum but leaves the rest of you intact. All your psychological properties are completely destroyed—even the most basic, such as the capacity to feel pain. Your circulation, breathing, digestion, immune system, and other vital functions, however, are preserved. Clinicians call this a "persistent vegetative state." The resulting being is alive in the biological sense: it can sneeze, cough, swallow, and even thrash about. It can be kept alive indefinitely with only a feeding tube. But it has no psychology whatever, and cannot regain any (the cerebrum, once destroyed, cannot grow back). To many philosophers it seems that this "human vegetable" is not you. Why not? Because there is no psychological continuity of any sort between you and it. When your psychology is destroyed, you cease to exist. (Or if there were someone in the next world who, by some divine miracle, was psychologically continuous with you, then he or she would be you. In any case, you are no longer there in this world.) So you cannot survive without some sort of psychological continuity, just as the Standard View tells us.

2. How the Standard View implies that I was never a fetus

How does the Standard View rule out my having once been a fetus? Well, embryologists tell us that a human fetus less than about six months old has no more psychology than a human vegetable has. That is because the cerebrum does not begin to function as an organ of thought and experience until synapses begin to connect up its neurons; and embryologists tell us that this does not take place until some twenty-five to thirty-two weeks after fertilization. Before that time the cerebrum is simply not "wired up," and there is no capacity for mental activity. A five-month-old fetus is probably not even minimally sentient (and a two-month-old fetus certainly is not): it cannot have even the most basic sort of experience, such as feeling pain. The fetus may be unlike the human vegetable in that it can *acquire* mental capacities. But for as long as it is a fetus, it lacks mental properties for the same reason as the human vegetable lacks them: the relevant neural structures are simply not there.

If the embryologists are right, then I cannot relate to a five-month-old fetus in any psychological way. The fetus has no psychology at all; and my current psychology could not be continuous in any way with that of a being with *no* psychology. There is no more psychological continuity between me as I am now and any early fetus than there would be between you as you are now and a human vegetable, or between you and the being who would stay behind with an empty head if your cerebrum were transplanted. In all three cases there is complete psychological *dis*continuity. And this is precisely what the

Standard View says we cannot survive. So it follows from the Standard View that I could no more have been a five-month-old fetus than you could one day be a human vegetable. Nothing could be a five-month-old fetus at one time and a person later on. No person was ever a fetus, and no fetus ever comes to be a person.

In fact some versions of the Standard View imply not only that no person was ever a fetus, but that none of us was ever a newborn infant either. As I mentioned earlier, advocates of the Standard View disagree about what sort of psychological continuity is necessary for us to persist. Some say that we survive if and only if our basic psychological capacities are preserved: the capacity for rational thought and self-consciousness, for instance. (To have the capacity for self-consciousness is to be able to think about oneself as oneself, a being different from others, as in the thought, "I wish I hadn't told her about that." You retain this capacity even when you are fast asleep and not exercising it.) When does one acquire the capacity for rational thought and self-consciousness? Probably not at birth. These capacities appear to develop only gradually during the first year of life. If their existence is necessary for you to persist, it follows that you were not present at your birth. You did not come into being until several months later.

Because I am concerned with the Standard View in its full generality, however, I will set aside the question of whether we were once infants. The important point for us is that every version of the Standard View rules out my having once been a fetus—or at any rate a fetus less than about five months old and lacking in psychological features.

3. The fetus problem

Judging from the published debate on personal identity in recent decades, most philosophers seem confident that some version of the Standard View is right. If so, most philosophers are committed to the claim that nothing is ever first a fetus and later a person. This would be surprising enough were it not for the fact that most philosophers also say the opposite. In discussing the moral status of the unborn, philosophers may disagree about whether an unthinking human fetus is a person; but they almost always assume that it is at least a *potential* person: something that might later become a person. Nearly everyone agrees that it is possible for something to be an unthinking fetus at one time and a person later on. Almost all sides to the debate over the morality of abortion agree that abortion prevents an embryo or fetus from becoming a full-fledged person, even if they disagree about how bad this is. (The epigraph at the beginning of the paper is typical.) This is taken to be just as obviously true as the Standard View. Yet it is plainly incompatible with the Standard View. Call this conflict the *fetus problem*.

Why has no one worried about the fetus problem?

It may be that the problem has not occurred to anyone. Personal identity is typically discussed in a way that discourages us from asking whether we were once fetuses. Philosophers who think about personal identity—about what it takes for us to persist through time—invariably ask what it takes for a person picked out at one time to be identical with a person picked out at another time. Or they ask under what circumstances someone who exists now is the *same* person as someone who exists earlier or later. The question of our identity over time, they say, is the question of what past or future *person* is you or I.

What is a person? The usual answer is that to be a person is to have certain mental capacities, such as rationality or self-consciousness. You are a person, and a dog is not, because you have the psychological properties that constitute personhood and a dog hasn't. But a fetus hasn't got those properties either: it is no more rational or self-conscious than a dog is. It follows that a fetus is not a person—not yet, anyway.

If the question of personal identity is the question of what makes a past or future person the same person as you or I, and if a fetus is not a person, then whether I was once a fetus is not a question about personal identity. It is not a question about which past or future *person* I am. The fact that philosophers thinking about our identity over time think only about what it takes for a past or future person to be you or I may lead them never to ask whether any of us was ever a fetus. It may even seem obviously false that I was ever a fetus: how can someone be the same person as a thing that is not a person at all? How can a person be identical with a non-person?

But even if a fetus is not a person, this does not prevent me from having been a fetus, any more than the fact that a boy is not a man prevents me from having been a boy. It is perfectly legitimate to ask whether I was once a fetus. As we have seen, most ethicists assume that the answer is yes. It follows that we hadn't better ask only what it takes for a past or future person to be me. We need to ask what it takes for *any* past or future being, person or not, to be me. Asking whether any person at some past time is me and ignoring the possibility that I might have been a non-person then is like asking which man committed the crime and ignoring the possibility that it might be a woman.

So the fetus problem may have been overlooked because philosophers have inquired about personal identity in ways that made them blind to it.

4. Is it really a problem?

Here is another possible explanation of why the fetus problem has been ignored. Perhaps some friends of the Standard View *have* thought about the problem—only they don't see it as a problem. They might say something like this:

"It may be surprising, at first, to be told that none of us came into the world as a microscopic embryo, but rather as a well-developed fetus or infant at least six months after conception. But this is not as implausible as it seems. It is not even clear whether it conflicts with any of our ordinary beliefs."

"When we learned at our mother's knee that each of us was once a fetus in the womb, or that human fetuses become infants and later adults, we may not have learned that each of us was once a fetus in the strictest sense of the word 'was.' Perhaps our mothers didn't mean that each of us is *numerically identical* with a fetus—that you and a certain fetus are one, like Clark Kent and Superman are one. They may have meant only that a fetus, as it develops, *gives rise to* or *produces* a person."

"Here is an example to illustrate the point. When we say that Slovakia and the Czech Republic were once a single country, we are not saying that two things are numerically identical with one thing. We are not saying that Slovakia *is* Czechoslovakia, and that the Czech Republic is Czechoslovakia. That would imply that Slovakia is the Czech Republic: if Slovakia and Czechoslovakia are one, and the Czech Republic and Czechoslovakia are one, Slovakia and the Czech Republic cannot be *two*. Of course, Slovakia is not the Czech Republic. There are three different countries, and one of them ceased to exist when it gave rise to the other two. So when we say that Slovakia and the Czech Republic were once the same country, we mean only that they in some sense grew out of the same country, not that each of them *is* that country. We are not talking about numerical identity over time at all in this case. This shows that there is a sense in which one thing can 'become,' or 'once have been' something else—something numerically different from it.

"The Standard View is an account of our numerical identity over time. It implies that none of us is numerically identical with a fetus—that no one thing is ever first a fetus and later a person. But this is perfectly consistent with the claim that each of us 'was once' a fetus in the sense that Slovakia was once Czechoslovakia. The Standard View does not deny that each of us 'was once' a fetus in the sense of having developed from a fetus. It is still true that a fetus 'becomes' a person in the sense that there is a continuous process of self-directed growth that begins with a fetus and ends with a person. And that may be all we mean when we say that each of us was once a fetus. If so, then the implications of Standard View do not conflict with anything that every enlightened person believes."

This ingenious reply seems to me entirely unpersuasive. There may well be a loose sense of "becoming" and of "having once been" according to which an *F*'s becoming a *G*, or a *G*'s having once been an *F*, does not imply that any one thing is first an *F* and later a *G*, but only that an *F* in some sense engenders a *G*. But this loose sense does not appear to be the one who figures in folk wisdom about how we came to be.

Consider the fact (surely it *is* a fact) that I, the author of this paper, was once a boy. This does not mean merely that a boy engendered me, or that I developed from a boy. It means that some *one* thing—I—was first a boy and later wrote this paper. Or suppose a five-year-old child finds her baby brother disgusting, and you remind her that she too was once an infant. You do not mean merely that she developed from an infant. You mean that she herself, not some other thing, once weighed twenty pounds, nursed at her mother's breast, and kept everyone awake at night. At any rate this is so if it is possible for *any* ordinary thing to persist from one time to another—and the Standard View implies that it is possible. And is it not evident that you were once a fetus in the same sense as you were once a boy or a girl? Isn't that what your mother meant when she told you that you weren't brought by a stork? Surely there is no deep logical difference between saying that I was once a boy and saying that I was once a fetus. It would be absurdly implausible to suppose that when we say that I was once a boy we mean that I am numerically identical with a boy, but when we say that I was once a fetus we mean something entirely different.

So folk wisdom seems to tell us plainly that each of us really was once a fetus, in the sense of being numerically identical with one—contrary to the Standard View.

5. The Termination View

As we have seen, the claim that nothing is ever a fetus at one time and a person later on is profoundly counterintuitive. It also raises serious philosophical problems.

Suppose, as the Standard View would have it, that I came into being six or seven months after I was conceived, when the normal course of fetal development produced the first mental capacities (or several months after my birth, when the normal course of infantile development produced the capacity for rationality and self-consciousness). Suppose that the fetus my mother bore during that period (or the infant she nursed) is numerically different from me. This raises an awkward question: what became of that fetus or infant?

One thing, on the Standard View, is certain: it did not come to be a person. Nothing started out as a microscopic embryo with no brain, no nerve cells, and no psychology, began to acquire its first crude mental features several months into its life, and went on to study philosophy. Rather, at some point, perhaps some six or seven months after the fetus was conceived, a person came into being that did not exist before. What happened to the fetus then? What happened to it when *I* stepped onto the stage? The Standard View allows for two possibilities: either (1) the fetus ceased to exist, and I took its place; or (2) the fetus survived, but never came to be a person: it merely came to share the stage with another being, namely me. There does not appear to be any third possibility. Call option 1 the *Termination View* and option 2 the *Co-location View*.

I don't think anyone will find the Termination View attractive. It tells us that it is absolutely impossible for a human fetus to come to be a normal, adult human being: the fetus necessarily ceases to exist as soon as its nervous system develops to the point where it can support thought, or consciousness, or whatever mental properties it is that figure in the Standard View. In other words, a human fetus (or infant) must perish in the act of bringing forth a human being. This would be one of the most remarkable facts in all of natural history—assuming, anyway, that embryos of other mammal species are capable of surviving to adulthood. Why should a human fetus die simply because, in the course of carrying out the program encoded in its genes, it (or rather its successor) came to be able to think? This is not the sort of thing that typically causes an organism's demise. We can understand the view that one necessarily ceases to exist if one *loses* one's capacity to think; but that one should perish by virtue of *gaining* that ability is absurd. It would leave us wondering what sort of changes a living thing *can* survive, for it would show our ordinary thinking on this subject to be wholly misguided.

6. The Co-location View

The Co-location View is more interesting. It says that a human fetus does survive the normal development of its nervous system and grows into an adult human animal, just as we thought. But in spite of that development it never comes to be a *person*. No human fetus ever comes to be one of us. Rather, at a certain point in a fetus's development, the atoms that make it up begin to compose something else as well—a second being—and *that* thing is the person. (I am assuming, as most friends of the Standard View believe, that you and I are material things. But almost nothing in this paper turns on this assumption, and the Co-location View could be modified to accommodate the view that we are not material.) Presumably the fetus still exists now, even though it is no longer a fetus, but a full-grown human organism. And we should expect it to be the same size, now, as you are, and located in the same place. So you—a person—now share your space and your matter with a biological organism, and it is the organism, not you, that started out as a fetus. The organism is numerically different from you because it began to exist before you did, and because unlike you it can survive without psychological continuity—or at least it could, and did, at one time.

This entails that even if we are material beings, we are not human animals: we are not members of the species *Homo sapiens*. Apparently we are not organisms at all, despite appearances—even though we are alive and are composed entirely of living tissues arranged in just the way that the tissues of a living human organism are arranged. Not, at any rate, unless *two* organisms could be composed of the same matter at the same time, living together in a sort of intimate symbiosis; and no one believes that.

The claim that you and I are material things but not animals is more than simply odd. It threatens to undermine the Standard View itself by depriving us of any grounds for accepting it. Consider the human animal that now coincides with you, on the Co-location View. The Standard View implies that it is not a person, for it could survive without any sort of psychological continuity—as it did during the first months of its life. Still, we should expect that animal to be conscious and intelligent, just as you are. It has the same brain and nervous system as you have, and the same surroundings. It shows the same behavioral evidence of intelligence as you do. What could prevent it from thinking just like you?

Suppose the animal does think just like you. Now you believe you are a person. Presumably the animal believes that *it* is a person. It has the same reason for believing that it is a person as you have for believing that you are. Yet it is mistaken. But then how do you know you aren't making this mistake? For all you could ever know, it seems, *you* might be the animal—the former fetus—rather than the person. If you were, you would never know the difference. Even if the Standard View were true, it seems, we could never have any grounds for supposing that it applied to *us*. That is, even if there *are* beings that persist by virtue of psychological continuity, we could never have any reason to suppose that we are such beings, rather than rational, intelligent animals that don't persist by virtue of psychological continuity. I take that to be absurd.

Friends of the Co-location View will want to deny that the human animals accompanying us can think. (That would enable us to know that we are not those animals.) But they will find it hard to explain why not—why a living human organism with a normal nervous system and showing every sign of intelligence should nonetheless be no cleverer than a stone. And what will they tell their colleagues in the life sciences? That *Homo sapiens*, despite appearances, are in fact *less* intelligent than their evolutionary cousins? That a human fetus, although it can engender a highly intelligent being, can itself only develop into a singularly stupid adult primate?

7. The Biological View

I propose a simpler response to the fetus problem. I say that we are animals. Human animals, like other organisms, do not persist by virtue of psychological continuity. Each human animal starts out as an unthinking embryo, and could survive the destruction of its cerebrum in a vegetative state. The lack of psychological continuity in these cases does not prevent the animal from persisting. No one would say that a human organism ceases to exist and is replaced by a *new* animal when it lapses into a persistent vegetative state. A human animal persists not by virtue of any psychological relation, but by virtue of some sort of physical or biological continuity that does not require anything psychological.

If we are human animals, and human animals persist by virtue of some brute physical continuity that does not involve anything psychological, then *we* persist by virtue of some brute physical continuity that does not involve anything psychological. Each of us was once a fetus, and may end up as a human vegetable. Call this the *Biological View* of personal identity.

The fetus problem does not arise on this view. A human fetus or infant does not cease to be when it acquires the capacity to think; nor is there any reason to say that it comes to share its matter with a thinking being numerically different from it. The fetus or infant simply comes to be a person (if it wasn't a person already)—just as it may later come to be a musician or a philosopher. And as a person it continues to survive for as long as the appropriate biological processes continue, just as it did when it was a fetus. A person may cease to be a person and still exist by losing her mental capacities—that is what happens in the "vegetable case"—just as a musician may cease to be a musician and still exist by losing her musical abilities or habits. This means that we are only temporarily people: we start out and may end up as non-people. At least this is so if you need mental properties to count as a person.

According to the Biological View, I started out as an embryo. Does that mean that I came into existence at the moment of conception? Not necessarily. The Biological View implies that I came into being whenever this human organism did. But it is unlikely that this human organism came into being at conception—that is, that it started out as a fertilized egg. When a fertilized egg cleaves into two, then four, then eight cells, it does not appear to become a multicellular organism—any more than an amoeba comes to be a multicellular organism when it divides. The resulting cells adhere only loosely, and their growth and other activities are not, at first anyway, coordinated in a way that would make them parts of a multicellular organism. The embryological facts suggest that a human organism comes into being around sixteen days after fertilization.

The Biological View is of course incompatible with the Standard View. The Biological View implies that one can survive without any mental features at all. It says that no sort of psychological continuity is either necessary or sufficient for us to persist. It makes psychology completely irrelevant to our identity over time.

8. The hybrid proposal

The Biological View solves the fetus problem by implying that each of us was once a fetus, just as most of us were always inclined to suppose. On the other hand, it flies in the face of most philosophical thinking about personal identity. It implies, for instance, that you would not go along with your transplanted cerebrum. If your cerebrum were moved to another head, the one who ended up with that organ would believe that she was you. But according to the Biological View she would be wrong about this. She would not be you, but rather the person whose cerebrum was removed to make way for yours—a person whose life she has no memory of. *You* would be the empty-headed vegetable left behind.

Why? Because you are an animal, and an animal would not go along with its transplanted cerebrum. The surgeons in our story move an organ from one animal to another, just as they might do with a liver or a kidney. They don't pare an animal down to a naked cerebrum, remove it from what was once its own head, and then graft a new head, arms, legs, and other parts onto it. The empty-headed animal left behind is not a *new* human animal. It is the very animal that your cerebrum starts out as a part of. So the human animal stays behind with an empty head in the transplant story. It simply loses its cerebrum and its mental capacities. If you *are* that animal, as the Biological View implies, then that is what happens to you. Some find this deeply counterintuitive. The Biological View solves the fetus problem, but at considerable cost.

You might wonder whether we could solve the fetus problem at a lower cost: without going so far as accepting the Biological View. Do we really need to say that psychological continuity is completely irrelevant to our identity? Why can't we say that each of us was once a fetus, but also that you would go along with your transplanted cerebrum? This would not be the Standard View, for it denies that any sort of psychological continuity is necessary for us to persist. But neither is it the Biological View, for it does not say that our persistence consists in brute biological continuity. It would be a sort of hybrid.

The suggestion is that psychological continuity of some sort is *sufficient* for us to persist, as the transplant story suggests, but not necessary. We survive as fetuses (and might one day survive as vegetables) by virtue of brute biological continuity; but if your cerebrum were transplanted, you would survive as the one who ended up with that organ because of her psychological continuity with you, even though there would not be biological continuity of the relevant sort here. Our identity over time does not consist in biological continuity or in psychological continuity alone, but sometimes in one and sometimes in the other.

This proposal raises large metaphysical issues that I cannot go into here. I will make just two remarks.

First, the hybrid proposal is difficult to state. It denies that psychological continuity is necessary for us to persist, because we once persisted without it as fetuses (and may one day do so again as vegetables). It also denies that biological continuity of the sort we have been considering is either necessary or sufficient for us to persist: not necessary because you don't need it to survive in the transplant case, and not sufficient because the empty-headed being left behind in the transplant case, though biologically continuous with you, would not be you. But then what *is* necessary and sufficient for us to persist? What *does* it take, in general, for a past or future being to be you? How does the hybrid proposal answer the question of personal identity over time? Nothing in our informal description of the hybrid proposal tells us how to answer these questions. It is not clear what the hybrid proposal actually says.

Here is a specific example of the problem. If a certain past fetus is you, what *makes* it you, according to the hybrid view? Not its being psychologically continuous with you: it isn't. Not its being biologically continuous with you, for something could be biologically continuous with you without being you, as in the transplant case. What, then? You relate to a certain past fetus, and may relate to a certain future vegetable, in just the way that you would relate to the being left behind with an empty head after your cerebrum is transplanted. So what makes it the case, according to the hybrid proposal, that you are the fetus and the vegetable but not the empty-headed being?

Even if this worry were answered, the hybrid proposal would share the philosophical problems of the Standard View. Like the Standard View, it implies that you are not a human animal. Remember, the animal stays behind in the transplant story. If you would not stay behind, but would go along with your cerebrum, then you cannot be that animal: a thing and itself cannot go their separate ways. This seems to imply that you now share your space and your matter with a human organism that is not you. That is, the hybrid proposal leads to the Co-location View we considered in §6. This makes it hard to see how you could ever know that you are not that animal, which presumably thinks your thoughts. Even if the hybrid proposal were true, it is hard to see how we could ever have any reason to believe that it is. For all we could ever know, it seems, we might be animals, in which case the Biological View would be true.

There does not appear to be any hybrid of the Standard and Biological views that has the virtues of both and the vices of neither. It looks as if the only sound solution to the fetus problem is to give up traditional thinking about personal identity and accept the Biological View.

STUDY AND DISCUSSION QUESTIONS

1   How would you state the problem of personal identity over time? How does the way it is stated bear on the question of whether you were ever a fetus?

2   When we say that George was once a fetus (or a child), do we mean that he is *numerically identical* with a fetus (or a child)? If not, what do we mean? How does this issue relate to the fetus problem?

3   If you share your matter with a human animal, but the animal isn't you (as the co-location view has it), is it possible for you to know that you are not the animal?

4   Is Olson right to say that the standard view rules out our being human organisms?

5   Does our being animals imply that psychology is "completely irrelevant to personal identity over time"?

6   Can you state a version of the "hybrid proposal" that both answers the question of personal identity over time and avoids the fetus problem?

7   Most advocates of the standard view take us to be entirely material things. Would it make any difference to the fetus problem if we were partly or wholly immaterial?

6.11 BIBLIOGRAPHY AND RECOMMENDED READING

Science fiction

*Bester, Alfred. *Demolished Man*. Pocket Books, 1978. Some science fiction stories describe cases in which the individual mind is eliminated but the body is not destroyed. A favorite context is the use of mind wiping as punishment for capital offense. In Alfred Bester's Hugo-winning *Demolished Man* the protagonist, a murderer, is subjected to this treatment.

Brin, David. *Kiln People*. Tor, 2002. People create "dittos" of themselves—exact duplicates—which serve to perform repeated, mundane actions or to undertake serious risks. A detective, Al Morris, investigates the production of dittos with his own set of dittos, leading Brin to delve into a number of philosophical issues about personal identity, not least of which is: who is the real Al Morris?

Budrys, Algis. *Rogue Moon*. Gold Medal, 1960. In this Nebula award-winning novella (later, a novel), Budrys explores the philosophical problems surrounding the nature of "matter transmission," arguably inspiring *Star Trek*'s use of the "transporter." In this story, the protagonist is "scanned" to the moon, but rather than beaming him there, the device creates an identical person on the moon and leaves the original person, in tact, on Earth. According to policy, one of the two must die, but who?

Carey, Peter. "The Chance." In Hartwell, David and Damien Broderick, eds. *Centarus: The Best of Australian Science Fiction*. New York: Tor, 1999. pp. 495–525.

Delany, Samuel. *Triton: An Ambiguous Heterotopia*. Bantam, 1976. Another complex Delany work, this James Tiptree Jr. Award winning novel discusses the philosophical and emotional troubles of members of a libertarian society who can choose new physical appearances, sexual orientations, and personal preferences at will. (The term "heterotopia" is borrowed from the work of Michel Foucault.)

Dickinson, Peter. *Eva*. Gollancz, 1988. Following an accident, the brain of a girl is transferred into a chimp. The person that results (the same girl? a human being?) eventually learns to live fully with, and lead, chimpanzees.

Duffy, Maureen. *Gor Saga*. Viking, 1982. Child realizes she's offspring of gorilla and human. Analysis of what it means to be human.

Egan, Greg. "Learning to be Me." *Interzone* no. 37 (July 1990): pp. 53–60.

*——. *Permutation City*. Milennium, 1994. Our universe might be but an algorithm in accord with the "dust" theory of reality. The Autoverse is an artificial reality based upon cellular automation technology which represents an artificial chemistry. "Solipsist Nation," created by a Copy—a simulation of a real person—contains conscious people all of whom are aware that they are artificial, but which fact does not prevent them from speculating on what is real. This John W. Campbell Award winner brims with philosophical reflection about personhood, knowledge and reality.

Grimwood, Jon Courtenay. *Pashazade: The First Arabesk*. Earthlight, 2001. Rafi has installed an experimental AI into himself, but struggles to maintain control of it—and his unitary identity—just as his newly formed North African country, El Iskandriya, struggles to do the same in the face of internal political pressures and external forces.

*Gunn, James. *The Dreamers*. Simon & Schuster, 1980. The processes of human memory are sufficiently understood to create a profitable commercial market for memories and information, but as this technology rises in popularity, its effects on humanity are as unexpected as they are dour.

Harper, Vincent. *The Mortgage on the Brain, Being the Confession of the late Ethelbert Croft, M.D.* Doubleday Page, 1905. In this turn of the century novel a medical doctor performs an operation through which a machine replaces the subject's brain, and his personality, from which ensues a number of personal and philosophical problems.

McCaffrey, Anne. *The Ship Who Sang*. New York: Ballantine, 1970. This novel concerns a human being whose brain becomes the computer controlling a spaceship.

Sheckley, Robert. *The Body*. Galaxy, 1956 A human brain is transplanted into an animal's body.

Silverberg, Robert. *The Second Trip*. Signet, 1973. Artificial personality created to inhabit body of criminal. Power struggle for entity's psychology.

——. *Shadrach in the Furnace*. Pocket Books, 1978. The world's population becomes a source of spare parts for a monomaniacal dictator named Genghis Mao.

Sitwell, Osbert. *Triple Fugue and Other Stories*. Duckworth, 1924. Technological advancement during a third world war has enabled medical scientists to piece together one human being from three damaged bodies following a plane wreck. But whose identity should this person take?

Sladek, John. *The Muller-Fokker Effect*. Carroll & Graf, 1990. Computer tapes on which man's personality is stored are bootlegged and passed around.

*Stevenson, Robert Louis. *The Strange Case of Dr. Jekyll and Mr. Hyde*. Longmans Green, 1886. The classic science fiction identity tale, in which a drug is used to turn a kindly man into his alter-ego.

Stine, Jean Marie (a.k.a. Hank). *Season of the Witch*. Rhinoceros, 1994. Rapist's mind is relocated into the brain of the victim as a punishment. Pornographic.

Sturgeon, Theodore. *More than Human*. Farrar, 1953. A new species "evolves," Homo Gestalt, whose members are the multiple personalities of several distinct minds.

*Swanwick, Michael. *Vacuum Flowers*. Arbor, 1987. The protagonist is addicted to other personalities as manifest in chips that she uses to reprogram her mind. She has hired herself out as a test subject for new persona wetware, but the conglomerate who last used her services wants an embedded persona back.

*Vinge, Vernor. *A Fire Upon the Deep*. New York: Tor, 1992. Hard-edged science coupled with imaginative plotting, but of special interest here is his portrayal of the Tines. These are fascinating dog-like aliens whose intelligence is proportional to the size of the pack in which they travel.

Wolfe, Gene. *The Fifth Head of Cerberus*. Scribner, 1972. Issues about the instability and fluidity of identity not only shape this novel but are reflected in the way the story is told in three linked novellas. The central plot point involves an anthropologist's attempt to identify a species of alien shape-shifters thought to have died out shortly after contact with human beings. Or have they?

Philosophy

Baker, Lynne. R. "What am I?" *Philosophy and Phenomenological Research* 59 (1999): pp. 151–60.

*———. *Persons and Bodies: A Constitution View*. Cambridge: Cambridge University Press, 2000. The most complete statement of the co-location view. Difficult.

———. "Materialism with a Human Face." *Soul, Body, and Survival: Essays on the Metaphysics of Human Persons*. Ed. Kevin Corcoran. Ithaca, NY: Cornell University Press, 2001. pp. 159–80. A more accessible summary of the view defended in *Persons and Bodies*.

Butler, Joseph. "Of Personal Identity." *The Works of Bishop Butler*. David White, ed. Rochester, NY: University of Rochester Press, 2006. From *The Analogy of Religion, Natural and Revealed*, Dissertation I, pp. 305–6.

*Hudson, H. *A Materialist Metaphysics of the Human Person*. Ithaca, NY: Cornell University Press, 2001.

Martin, R., ed. *Personal Identity*. Oxford: Blackwell, 2003. The most up-to-date collection of papers on personal identity.

*Nagel, T. "Brain Bisection and the Unity of Consciousness." *Synthèse* 22 (1971): pp. 396–413. Reprinted in Perry, J., ed. *Personal Identity*. Berkeley: University of California Press, 1975; and in *Mortal Questions*, Nagel, ed. Cambridge: Cambridge University Press, 1979.

Noonan, H. *Personal Identity*. 2nd ed. London: Routledge, 2003. A general textbook on personal identity, which defends the Standard View. Rather difficult.

Locke, John. "The Psychological Continuity Theory." *An Essay Concerning Human Understanding*, vol. 1. Urbana, IL: Project Gutenberg, 2004. Online location: www.gutenberg.org/etext/10615. Originally published in 1690.

*Olson, E. *The Human Animal: Personal Identity Without Psychology*. New York: Oxford University Press, 1997. More on the fetus problem, the biological view, and how to state the question of personal identity over time.

———. "Was I Ever a Fetus?" *Philosophy and Phenomenological Research* LVII, 1 (1997): pp. 95–110.

———. "What does functionalism tell us about personal identity?" *Noûs* 36 (2002): pp. 682–98. A reply to Shoemaker's "Self, Body and Coincidence." Difficult.

*Parfit, D. *Reasons and Persons*. Oxford: Clarendon Press, 1984.

Perry, J., ed. *Personal Identity*. Berkeley: University of California Press, 1975. A collection of classic readings on personal identity.

*——. *A Dialogue on Personal Identity and Immortality*. Indianapolis: Hackett, 1987. A highly readable informal introduction.

Rorty, Amelie O., ed. *The Identities of Persons*. University of California Press, 1976.

Shoemaker, Sydney. "Self, Body, and Coincidence." *Proceedings of the Aristotelian Society, Supplementary* 73 (1999): 287–306. Argues that human animals cannot have mental properties. Difficult.

*Shoemaker, Sydney and Richard Swinburne. *Personal Identity*. Oxford: Blackwell, 1984. Perhaps the best introductory book on personal identity. Shoemaker's contribution is a very clear statement and defense of the Standard View.

7 Free will

Imagine that scientists in the future will be able to conduct sophisticated scans of the lobes of your brain that produce your decisions. These brain scans yield information about what it is that you will desire in the next few minutes. Quite possibly these desires are as yet unknown to you. Retailers, parents, employers, and teachers open up a market for these devices, and they soon become ubiquitous. In this alternate world, the success of this technology strongly suggests that your decision-making is a product of your brain's neurochemistry.

An intelligent criminal, who has been found guilty of assault, is now out on probation after serving time in prison. As a condition of parole, one of these devices is affixed to his brain in order to assess whether he is about to desire to harm someone. Due to his genetic makeup, this criminal has exceedingly strong drives to harm other people, but he is knowledgeable both of this tendency in himself and of his moral duty to prevent himself from acting on these desires. But the drives are so very strong that he alone can't prevent them. The technology, however, can because his brain scanning device is equipped with a system to inject into his bloodstream a packet of neurotransmitters that immediately reduce his desires and render him very passive. One day he hears the familiar ping of the device, which alerts him that he is about to be injected with the packet of neurotransmitters to calm him. But unfortunately, his medic parole officer neglected to refill the device with the neurotransmitter. As a result, he runs out and assaults his nearest neighbor, just like a pit bull might do.

The question "Does the paroled criminal have free will?" can take several different interpretations. We might ask whether he is free when he is hooked up to the device. In this case, direct external controls manipulate his desires. This suggests that he lacks free will when the device is operative. However, what about the case in which the device is not operating correctly? In this case it appears that he is also under direct influence and control, the key difference being that his desires in this second case are caused by his natural, unaugmented neurochemistry. You might be inclined to think that this difference is important for adjudicating this matter. But what both cases share in common is more important than the ways they differ, for in both cases the levels and types of neurotransmitters appear to produce his desires despite the fact that he knowingly does not want to desire to harm others. He cannot control his desires, and this makes him a slave to them.

One more question: suppose you are the judge who sits on the bench when his latest case is brought before the courts. You are apprised of the facts, and you must rule on whether he was morally responsible for harming his neighbor. Common sense suggests that if I have an obligation to perform some action P, I am able to perform P. This is the **ought implies can principle**. For examples, I can't be obligated to come up with a cure for AIDS tomorrow because it is impossible for me to do that, and I can't be obligated to save someone on the 40th floor of the burning building next door because I'm unable to fly up there and bring him down. Given the pathology of the criminal, it is unclear that he has the ability to refrain from assaulting his neighbor. So, what is your verdict and why?

This example raises probing questions about the free will of normal human beings. We might not be as dramatically influenced by our neurochemistry as is this criminal, but physicalists believe that every physical event in the universe has a determinate physical cause. Since physicalists believes that the brain is nothing more than a physical object, this implies that *everything we "normal" human beings think or do* has a determinate physical cause. So our quandary parallels the criminal's. The criminal might say the following to you, the judge:

Everything we do has a prior and determinate cause, so my assault had a cause. But I cannot be held responsible for what my brain chemistry causes me to do. I have no control over my brain chemistry. So I'm not responsible for the assault. So you shouldn't blame me for it.

If we haven't any free will, then the use of praise and blame is thrown into uncertainty. If it was not possible for the criminal to have behaved differently, then it appears that he wasn't responsible for his actions. (Of course, as the judge you could respond, "You're right. But neither am I responsible for sentencing you to 20 years in prison for it!")

One's beliefs about whether one has free will influences many other beliefs one holds. We've already described interplay between solutions to the problem of evil and the existence of free will. Physicalist theories in the philosophy of mind may be incompatible with robust accounts of free will, which state that one's freely willed action is caused by oneself (somehow) and not by the brain.

In this chapter we'll investigate the question, "Are we free?" We'll present the main philosophical answers to this question.

After completing this chapter, you'll be able to:

- Explain the three major theories of **libertarianism, determinism** and **compatibilism**

- Explain the role of moral responsibility for accounts of human freedom, and explain the ought implies can principle
- Explain the differences between those theories in terms of their implications about the **principle of alternative possibilities**
- Explain and assess the principal arguments for these theories
- Understand **hierarchical compatibilism** and its problems.

7.0 INTRODUCING THE ALTERNATIVE THEORIES

People studying biological nomenclature can learn to identify the taxonomy of some organism by looking at the top-down, branching structures in its classificatory tree. We first identify the kingdom into which to place an organism, then we find its phylum, then its class, order, etc., until we identify its species. The theories of free will can be most efficiently understood by adopting a parallel framework.

At the highest level of classification, a theory about free will is either *compatibilist* or *incompatibilist*. **Incompatibilism** states that if all events are causally determined to occur, then human beings do not have free will. The incompatibilist affirms a logical relationship between causal determinism and human free will.

> *Incompatibilism = if* all physical events are causally determined by the conjunction of a fixed past and the laws of nature, *then* human beings lack free will.

The thesis of incompatibilism is composed of two component theses. The antecedent contains a statement of determinism and the consequent contains a statement about human freedom.

The antecedent makes use of the term *determined*. Determinism, as a philosophical doctrine, affirms that the chain of physical events going back to the beginnings of the universe in the Big Bang causally fixes all the events downstream from that event. For every event there has ever been (and will ever be), those events could not but occur in just the ways that they have occurred (or will occur). It is physically impossible for any event that did not occur to have occurred, and vice-versa. According to determinism, human beings are within the natural order, and not outside it. A simple definition is this:

> *Determinism = all* physical events are causally determined by the conjunction of a fixed past and the laws of nature.

The main reason to endorse determinism, sometimes called "causal determinism," is a joint commitment to the fixity of the past and to the regularity of the laws of nature. The past is composed of countless physical events going back to the beginning of spacetime. Laws of nature are law-like generalizations about the interactions of physical objects. These rigorous laws of nature can explain every interaction between one molecule and another. Since the interactions between physical objects are at bottom nothing more than molecules bonding with other molecules, laws of nature can explain why all events in the past must have occurred precisely as they have occurred.

The consequent in the thesis of incompatibilism is a denial that human beings have free will. People who believe that human beings have free will do not affirm that human beings *always* have free will. The scope of the thesis that we have free will is limited to saying that *at some times* and *for some events* human beings have free will.

Notice that determinism and free will *are consistent*. This is because the thesis of determinism does not include any mention of free will. This logical space leaves open the possibility that a theory of free will could be developed that is consistent with determinism. The compatibilist attempts to enter this logical space between determinism and free will by opposing the conditional in the statement of incompatibilism.

> *Compatibilism* = it is false that, if all physical events are causally determined by the conjunction of a fixed past and the laws of nature, then human beings do not have free will.

For compatibilists, it is possible that all the actions of all human beings must occur just as they do occur and yet human beings freely will at least some of those actions. Just as with incompatibilism, compatibilism is not directly a theory about free will. Instead, it's a theory about the logical relationship between determinism and human free will. One implication of this point is that, theoretically, the compatibilist is not committed either to the truth of determinism or to the existence of free will. I say "theoretically" since in practice most compatibilists also affirm that we have free will.

Stepping down level in the classificatory tree of theories of free will we find a few different types of both incompatibilism and compatibilism. There are two prominent types of incompatibilism: one states that we have free will, the other that we do not. Libertarianism is the first of those two theories, and **hard determinism** is the second.

> *Libertarianism* = determinism is false and humans have free will.

(Don't confuse this position with *political libertarianism,* which is a theory that advocates a small government that intervenes in a minimum of economic and social facets of life. Though both theories advocate freedom, they do so in very different contexts.)

> *Hard determinism* = determinism is true and humans do not have free will.

Libertarianism and hard determinism both fall under the phylum of incompatibilism. This may seem surprising, but remember that incompatibilism is a *conditional statement*: if all events are causally determined, *then* humans lack free will. While the libertarian and hard determinist both hold that this if–then statement is true, the libertarian denies that all events are causally determined. The hard determinist, however, affirms this claim.

Compatibilists are committed to free will *and* to the thesis of determinism. (Technically, the compatibilist is committed to the *consistency* of the theses of determinism and of free will, but we will presume that the compatibilist also endorses these two theses.) The difference between the compatibilist and the hard determinist lies in the compatibilist's repudiation of the conditional thesis of incompatibilism.

We have a brief terminological point before we continue. When people discuss "free will" they often mean to refer both to features of our decision-making and to our actions. "Free will" is a concept that stretches across both mental events and bodily actions. This makes our discussion somewhat tricky since we might have freely *decided* on a course of action, but be unable to *act* freely. Freely acting to wash my hands is a more complex philosophical concept than is freely willing to do so. Free actions are dependent upon a host of properties of the world that are independent of our control. In order freely to *act* so as to wash my hands, there must be some soap and water available to me, I must have hands, I must rub each hand on something, etc. I can freely *will* to wash my hands without any water. Willing involves features of the mind alone. For several reasons "freely willing" is the key notion in this debate, not "freely acting." Freely acting involves the unhindered performance of an action. Unless otherwise noted, we use the term "free will" to refer to an agent's ability to control his decision-making and his subsequent behavior in the ways needed for morally responsible action.

BOX 7.A: THE BOOK OF LIFE

While browsing through the library one day, I noticed a dusty old tome, quite large, entitled "Alvin I. Goldman." I take it from the shelf and start reading. In great detail, it describes my life as a little boy. It always gibes with my memory and sometimes even revives my memory of forgotten events. I realize that this purports to be a book of my life, and I resolve to test it. Turning to the section with today's date on it, I find the following entry for 2:36 p.m. "He discovers me on the shelf. He takes me down and starts reading me . . ." I look at the clock and see that it is 3:03. It is quite plausible, I say to myself, that I found the book about half an hour ago. I turn now to the entry for 3:03. It reads: "He is reading me. He is reading me. He is reading me." I continue looking at the book in this place, meanwhile thinking how remarkable the book is. The entry reads: "He continues to look at me, meanwhile thinking how remarkable I am."

I decide to defeat the book by looking at a future entry. I turn to an entry 18 minutes hence. It says: "He is reading this sentence." Ahah, I say to myself, I all need to do is refrain from reading that sentence 18 minutes from now. I check the clock. To ensure that I won't read that sentence, I close the book. My mind wanders; the book has revived a buried memory and I reminisce about it. I decided to reread the book there and relive the experience. That's safe, I tell myself, because it is an earlier part of the book. I read that passage and become lost in reverie and rekindled emotion. Time passes. Suddenly I start. Oh yes, I intended to refute the book. But what was the time of the listed action?, I ask myself. It was 3:19, wasn't it? But it's 3:21 now, which means I have already refuted the book. Let me check and make sure. I inspect the book at the entry for 3:17. Hmm, that seems to be the wrong place for there it says I'm in a reverie. I skip a couple of pages and suddenly my eyes alight on the sentence: "He is reading this sentence." But it's an entry for 3:21, I notice! So I made a mistake. The action I had intended to refute was to occur at 3:21, not 3:19. I look at the clock, and it is still 3:21. I have not refuted the book after all.[1]

7.1 PRINCIPLE OF ALTERNATIVE POSSIBILITIES

It seems likely that, in order for an agent to be free to will choice C, the agent must at the very least have the ability not to C. This may consist in the agent's having the ability to choose A or B instead of C, or it may consist in the agent's having the ability to refrain from choosing C (and not choosing A or B instead). We can put this more formally as the

> *Principle of alternative possibilities*: Only if an agent could have willed something else instead is the agent free to will what he or she wills.

If the principle of alternative possibilities, or "PAP," is true, then presence of alternate possibilities is a *necessary condition* for an exercise of free will. For example, if Han Solo is *free* with respect to his choice whether to aid the Rebel Alliance, then it must be possible for Han to do something else instead.

There are two different, equally important questions to ask about PAP. Is the necessary condition upon human freedom stated in this principle accurate? This first question can be rephrased like this: In order to make a free choice, is it *necessary* that I am able to make other choices instead? Suppose the answer to this question is "yes." We then face the second question: Do human beings *meet* this condition?

Commonsense reflection on the concepts of freedom and moral responsibility supports PAP. Recall our definition of freedom of the will as referring to the type of control an agent has over his decision-making that allows for morally responsible action. Common sense suggests that if I have a moral *obligation* to perform some action P, I am *able* to perform P. This is the *ought implies can principle*. We established that I can't be obligated to save someone on the 40th floor of the burning building next door because I cannot fly up there and bring him down. But suppose as I walk down the street I see a small child drowning in a puddle. I have a prima facie obligation to save this child's life and, since I am in good bodily health, I am able to pull him to safety. This action satisfies the principle, and, therefore, I am obligated to help the child.

It seems as though both the principle of alternative possibilities and the thesis of determinism are commonsensical statements. We have identified reasons to believe both of them. At this point the incompatibilist enters the debate to say that PAP and determinism cannot both be true. If no one has the ability to do otherwise, then no one's choices are free. The incompatibilist insists that having alternative possibilities is a necessary condition of free will.

The status of the principle of alternative possibilities offers an opportunity succinctly to categorize our three main theories (see Table 1).

We'll now discuss libertarianism and determinism, and their positions regarding PAP.

7.2 LIBERTARIANISM

The libertarian theory of free will offers a different conception of human nature than does the hard determinist. The hard determinist believes that humans are passive subjects whose movements and decisions are caused by factors outside their own control. The libertarian believes that human beings are unique because, rather than being *subjects*, we are *agents*. Metaphysically, human beings differ from members of other species and from inanimate objects.

Consider the movement of balls when shooting pool. All the balls on the table are passive. They sit there, stationary and static, awaiting a cue stick to strike the cue ball. Once you do strike the cue ball, when it hits other balls, they will move in various ways. The balls exhibit lots of complex motions. Those forms of motion are all determined by the speed and angle with which you strike the cue ball. The balls on the table do not move unless you make them move. In turn, their motions might, after impact with other balls,

Table 1 Logical relations between theories

Logical Relations Between Theories	Determinism	Libertarian Free Will	Compatibilist Free Will
Is it a necessary condition for human free will that humans have the ability to do otherwise?	YY	Y	N
Do humans in fact have the ability to do other than they do?	N	Y	?
Do human beings have free will?	N	Y	Y

cause other balls in turn to move, and so on. They receive action from outside themselves. They don't act.

According to hard determinism, you are like a pool ball insofar as all of your actions are produced by prior events that act upon you. You receive actions and you convert those actions into movements of your own. This holds not only of movements of your body but also thoughts in your brain. According to the libertarian, you are not like a pool ball since you are the causal source of (many of) your own actions.

This insight on the part of the libertarian links with a major argument on behalf of the thesis of libertarian free will. When lightning randomly strikes someone down and kills him, we do not hold any human being responsible for that person's death. This is because lightning is the product of purely physical forces acting upon other purely physical forces in accord with mechanical laws. But if human beings are passive subjects, mere recipients of action, and could not do other than they do—that is, if determinism is true—then humans cannot be held morally accountable for their actions.

The libertarian holds that it makes no sense to say that a person is moral or immoral unless you think of the person as an agent. If you do something as an agent, such as skip an exam, you could always do something else, such as take the exam. This implies that "You ought to take the exam" only if it is true that "You are capable of taking the exam." If you really can't do something, it makes no sense to say that you *ought* to do it.

When it is hungry, a leopard will kill and eat an available antelope. I see this all happen on *Animal Planet* and my friend says, "It's morally *wrong* for the leopard to kill that poor, defenseless baby antelope off on its own like that. That leopard is cruel!" One of the reasons that my friend's response makes no sense is because the leopard could not but kill the antelope in those circumstances. The combination of nature and nurture produces the leopard's action of killing the antelope. The leopard is not "morally responsible" for its behavior any more than is the eight ball for prematurely falling into the corner pocket and costing you the game.

In sharp contrast, insists the libertarian, human beings have responsibility for their actions. The sources of support for this claim are many. First, look at our society. Governments erect systems by which criminals are charged for violating laws. They build these systems on the belief that humans are morally responsible creatures who freely choose to do wrong. Second, you might perform an action that, though not illegal, is still immoral. For example, suppose that you cheat on your girlfriend by becoming involved with another woman and lying about it. All other things being equal, you will know that this is wrong by the guilt you feel inside. If you save someone from certain death you will rightly feel an upwelling of pride for your valor. These reactions are as they should be since human behavior merits praise and blame.

To many people it will appear silly to have offered these sources of support since (to describe a third source) it's just obvious that people are morally responsible for their actions. No argument or evidence is needed. It is a principle of common sense believed by virtually everyone in virtually every culture.

Reflection upon these examples can be used to construct an **argument from moral responsibility** against hard determinism. Due to the logical relationship between the theses under discussion, a successful argument against hard determinism is tantamount to an argument in support of libertarian free will. This is because the libertarian free will thesis includes the claim that determinism is false and the claim that we have free will. Here is how this argument from moral responsibility runs:

(7.0)   Human beings are morally responsible for some of their choices.

(7.1)   If human beings are morally responsible for some of their choices, then human beings must freely will those choices for which they are morally responsible.

(7.2)   So, human beings must free will those choices for which they are morally responsible.

Both this and the next premise rely upon the intuitions about our ought implies can principle.

(7.3)   According to the principle of alternative possibilities, in order for human beings freely to will choices it is necessary that human beings could have made other choices.

(7.4)   Therefore, human beings could have made choices other than the ones they in fact made.

(7.5)   If human beings could have made choices other than the ones they in fact made, then it is false that all events are causally determined by the conjunction of a fixed past and the laws of nature.

In other words, if humans can make choices other than the ones they make, the thesis of determinism is false. The last step of the argument concludes that determinism is false:

(7.6)   So it is false that all events are causally determined by the conjunction of a fixed past and the laws of nature.

This is a powerful argument on behalf of libertarian free will and against hard determinism, but it has a few problems.

7.3 ASSESSING LIBERTARIANISM

One key question about the libertarian viewpoint remains unanswered. The denial of hard determinism in (7.6) implies that when human beings freely will a choice, the choice is not caused by prior events. What, then, causes a freely willed choice?

The libertarian has only a few ways to respond to this question. First, to this apparently simple-minded question the libertarian might offer a simple-minded answer: the *human beings themselves* cause their freely willed choices, of course. Second, they might say that the freely willed choice is *uncaused*.

The second option is not promising. This is because if my freely willed choice is uncaused, then its source is exceedingly mysterious. What, after all, would it mean to say this? If my freely willed choice is uncaused, it appears that it isn't *my* choice anymore. If my choice is uncaused, it appears that I do not have any moral responsibility for it.

Let's return to the first answer—that *I* am the cause of my freely willed choices. In practice, this implies that if I freely will to take a bike ride, it is my will that causes my choice to ride my bike. The term "will" is now not merely used as a verb. It is also a noun. Our minds have *wills*, and, on this suggestion, when our wills directly cause our choices, then our choices are freely willed.

But what sort of cause is one's will? Normally causes involve physical processes. A nail entering a tire causes a flat. But does your act of will physically influence your brain and body in such a way as to make you decide and act as you do? This leads to a dilemma for the libertarian: Either willing is an event occurring in your brain, or it is an event of a different nature. If it is a brain event, then it is a physical event. But the physical events in your body seem to be always caused by other physical events. If this is so, then the determinist would argue that the act of will is itself caused and is not free from influence of prior causes.

It is of crucial importance to realize that saying that willing is a physical event in the brain does not imply that willing might not be a psychological process. In other words, states like *Han Solo wants to destroy the Death Star* are physical states in addition to being psychological states. Put more gingerly, if basic physicalism in the philosophy of mind is true, then desiring something is a physical state of affairs. These states are *psychophysical*. If Han's will is composed of his psychophysical states, then the libertarian has a problem. Psychophysical states are caused, at least in part, by prior events. For example, if Han is so depressed that he can't muster the desire to help the rebels, then Han has chosen not to help the rebels. But in this case, his "choice" appears to be caused by his depression. As an abundance of research in clinical neuropsychology has shown, depression is an emotion caused by the levels of neurotransmitters in your brain. Neurotransmitters are chemicals that regulate electrical signals between neurons and other cells in the brain. The quantity of neurotransmitters in your brain at some time T is caused by physical events at time $T-1$. Han's genetic structure and the nutrients in his body cause the quantity of neurotransmitters in his brain to be what it is. Since the quantity of neurotransmitters in his brain causes his depression, and his depression causes his choice not to help the rebels, his choice was not free.

This line of reasoning suggests that the libertarian should opt for the second horn of the above dilemma and argue that willing is an event of a non-physical nature. On this account, one's will is couched in terms of a soul or essence, and not in terms of psychological activity. By selecting this more "metaphysical" response, the libertarian argues that the human will stands outside the network of physical causes. What causes one's will to cause the choices it does? Nothing. I said above that the libertarian believes that human beings are unique because we are agents. One historically prominent way of explaining this is to say that humans are "agent causes." This means that events in the minds or souls of human beings are causes of actions, and nothing causes the events in the minds or souls in human beings. They act without being acted upon.

The principal historical source for this metaphysical version of libertarianism is the Scottish philosopher Thomas Reid (1710–96). He says,

> I grant, then, that an effect uncaused is a contradiction, and that an event uncaused is an absurdity. The question that remains is whether a volition, undetermined by motives, is an event uncaused. This I deny. The cause of the volition is the man that willed it.[2]

Reid believes that uncaused events are absurd, so it follows that freely willed choices, or "volitions," must have a cause. A person's willing is not caused by anything but the person's will itself. But if persons are physical objects, the determinist will observe that persons are subject to the same deterministic laws that govern the rest of the physical world. Granted, the physical events in one's brain are unimaginably complicated—every decision that one makes requires the use of millions of neurons. But still, the hard determinist will insist that if humans are physical objects, then their decisions are produced by prior physical states.

This at last pushes the libertarian to clarify the metaphysical status of a human person. In effect, Thomas Reid and other libertarians who endorse agent causation argue that human beings are metaphysically unique because they stand outside the ebb and flow of physical causation. Human beings are non-physical. This allies the theory of libertarian free will with several other theories discussed earlier in the book. For example, the agent causation form of libertarianism has natural affinities with—in fact, it might require the truth of—the theory of substance dualism in the philosophy of mind (see §5.1 & §5.2) and a theory of personal identity according to which I am diachronically, numerically identical to my immaterial soul.

Here is a recipe—and only a recipe—for an argument against libertarianism built upon this insight. Show that if libertarianism is true, then substance dualism must be true or that we must have immaterial souls. Then argue that either substance dualism is false or that immaterial souls don't exist. If you complete those steps, then you are entitled to conclude that libertarianism is false in accordance with valid rules of inference.

7.4 DETERMINISM

Suppose Han Solo's spaceship, the *Millennium Falcon*, breaks down and Chewy can't fix the engines. They get it towed in to a repair shop on Alderaan and receive some troubling news from the chief mechanic.

> Han's mechanic says, "We removed your engines and dismantled them, but we found no problem at all."
>
> "Huh?" Han responds. "What d'you mean you 'found no problem'? They don't run! I can't fly! Fix 'em."

The mechanic says, "Uh, you seem to misunderstand me. There is no mechanical problem with the engines. There is simply no cause for the fact that they won't run."

"I have a spice run to make and you're telling me that you can't repair my engines. Is that it?"

"Uh, we could repair them if there were something wrong with them. They don't work, but there is no cause for that."[3]

Chances are that, were you to take your car to a mechanic like this, you wouldn't go back. You wouldn't go back because this mechanic seems not to share your belief that the physical events in your car have physical causes.

The determinist makes use of our intuitions about cases like this in an effort to justify the thesis of determinism. This thesis says that all physical events are causally determined by the conjunction of a fixed past and the laws of nature. This is stated as a universal generalization, meaning that there is no physical event that is not causally determined by prior physical events. There are no exceptions on which physical events are caused by non-physical causes like immaterial souls that exist but don't exist in spacetime.

This commitment explains our confidence that physical events have natural explanations. When we smoke cigarettes, we anticipate experiencing adverse physical effects on our lungs. When an earthquake destroys parts of California, our scientists explain that through the movement of plates in Earth's crust. Of course, not everyone agrees that, to find out the causes of such events, we should study physical movements of plates and subduction zones. Televangelist Pat Robertson has said that we should look to the scriptures to find the causes of some cataclysmic weather events because he says God causes many natural disasters as punishments. Rather than ocean currents, winds and temperature causing a hurricane that destroyed New Orleans, God did it to punish debauchery.

Causal determinism is a metaphysical thesis about a general feature of the world. But the hard determinist applies the thesis of determinism to the issue of human free will. The hard determinist endorses the following disjunction: either we have free will or the world is deterministic but not both. The world is deterministic, so we don't have free will. By denying that human beings possess any free will, hard determinism opposes libertarianism. The determinist accepts **universal and ancestral causation**, according to which every event that occurs in this universe has an earlier cause, which itself has an earlier cause, and so on back indefinitely into the past. This means that the conjunction of all past events of the world coupled with the laws of nature fixes a *single* future amongst all the logically possible futures. This form of determinism is inconsistent with saying that God caused hurricane Katrina.

This creates a sharp conflict with libertarianism. The hard determinist's argument against libertarianism starts with a statement of PAP:

(7.3)   According to the principle of alternative possibilities, in order for human beings freely to will choices it is necessary that human beings could have made other choices.

(7.7) All physical events are causally determined by the conjunction of a fixed past and the laws of nature.

(7.8) If (7.7), then it is false that human beings could have made other choices.

(7.9) So, the thesis of libertarianism is false.

7.9 follows because the thesis of libertarianism says that humans have the kind of free will that is incompatible with determinism.

The contrast between the two theories as revealed by this argument helps us indirectly understand determinism, but we also need to look at the determinist thesis in 7.7. It contains an appeal to the past, and an appeal to the laws of nature. The concept of a "law of nature" is central to an understanding of determinism, but it is a vexing concept. Arguably, the truth of determinism hinges upon establishing one of two competing theories about laws of nature. The two are **regularity theory** and **necessity theory**. The thesis of determinism is true only if necessity theory is true. This gives the determinist a vested interest in showing that regularity theory is false.

These two theories have much in common. Both theories hold that *laws of nature are not logically necessary*. Recall that a statement is logically necessary only if it must be true in all possible worlds, for example "1 + 1 = 2" is logically necessary. In some bizarre alternate universe, laws of nature may differ from those we know in our universe. Both theories hold that laws of nature are *universally true*. A law of nature, if it is true at all, is, was and will be true. Both theories formulate laws of nature by way of repeated observations of patterns in nature.

The most important difference between regularity theory and necessity theory concerns whether laws of nature are regarded as physically necessary. A statement is

BOX 7.B: DETERMINISM, THE PAST, AND TIME TRAVEL

If time travel is physically possible, then is determinism false? This intriguing question is difficult to answer. First, a definition: the term "the past" refers to the full period of elapsed time and the events that occurred in it. On the multiverse interpretation of quantum physics, if particle P does travel to "the past" it does not travel from time T1 in Universe A to time T minus 1 in Universe A. Rather, it effectively enters a different parallel universe, Universe B, at $T-1$. If this is the correct way to think about time travel being physically possible, then this does not disprove the thesis of determinism. This is because Universe B was determined, through the beginning of spacetime, in such a way that particle P would enter it at $T-1$. Likewise, Universe A was determined in such a way that particle P would exit it at time T. Thus, both universes were determined.

physically necessary if it is implied by the laws of nature. Regularity theory holds that laws of nature are not physically necessary, whereas the necessity theory holds that they are. On the necessity theory, basic laws of nature imply that other, non-basic laws of nature must be true. Necessity theory holds that the laws of nature could not be other than they are. A series of arguments on behalf of the physical necessity of laws of nature has been constructed that revolve around differences between statements that are contingently true and statements that are physically necessary. The recipe is this: the necessity theory identifies a statement that meets many criteria for being a law of nature. But it then argues that the statement clearly fails to qualify as a law of nature. An example will illustrate this pattern of argument.

Karl Popper, the eminent philosopher of science, offers the following thought experiment. The moa was a species of bird that lived in New Zealand, but has been extinct since 1500. (It appears to be the only bird that had no wings!) Let's suppose that the longest-lived moa lived to be 49 years old. This allows us to formulate what *appears* to be a law of nature: "All moas die before reaching the age of 50." This statement can be rephrased as follows: "If X is a moa, then X cannot live for 50 years." This statement is true; it is universal in that it is, was and will be true; it is completely general. It has the hallmarks of a law of nature but for one final fact: it is entirely contingent upon the length of time that the longest moa bird lived.

> [T]his universal statement will not be a law of nature; for according to our assump-tions, it would be *possible* for a moa to live longer, and it is only due to *accidental or contingent* conditions—such as the co-presence of a certain virus—that in fact no moa did live longer. This example shows that there may be *true, strictly universal statements* which have an accidental character rather than the character of true laws of nature. Accordingly, the characterization of laws of nature as strictly universal statements [as on the regularity theory] is logically insufficient and intuitively inadequate. This example may also indicate in what sense natural laws may be described as "principles of necessity" or "principles of impossibility."[4]

Popper's example points to a problem with regularity theory. "If X is a moa, then X cannot live for 50 years" does express a regularity about our world, one that is universal and true. But it is not a law because its truth is not something that expresses a physical necessity. This claim about moas doesn't express a physical necessity because it is purely coincidental that the longest-lived moa bird lived for exactly 49 years. The last moa could have lived for 49 years and one day, or for only 40 years. It is not a physical necessity about our world that the longest-lived moa lived exactly 49 years.

This objection to the regularity theory takes the form of a reductio ad absurdum argument. If we suppose that necessity theory is false and, therefore, that laws of nature need not be physically necessary, then "If X is a moa, then X cannot live for 50 years" must be a law of nature. But that statement is not a law of nature. Therefore, necessity theory must be true.

In contrast with necessity theory, the regularity theory demands much less of the world. The founder of this theory, David Hume, created it in part because it is considerably simpler than necessity theory. Necessity theory must posit statements that are physically necessary, but we human beings have a tough time identifying statements that are physically necessary. The most we experience are singular events. We human beings take it upon ourselves to relate them together in ways that *appear* to be necessary; but that is a misnomer. We form beliefs about lucky events when one serendipitous event follows another, but luck is a purely human way to relate one event to another. Likewise, argues regularity theory, the necessities claimed to hold between sets of events according to necessity theory are purely human inventions. They don't belong in science. Hume was an empiricist, which means that he delimits all knowledge to what can be experienced. The very idea of "necessity" cannot be traced back to any experience, so Hume claimed not to have any concept of necessity.

Hume's opposition to necessity theory was equivalent to an opposition to a theological understanding according to which the laws of nature were divinely ordained by God. At least, this is the historical antecedent to present-day necessity theory. God created the laws of nature to operate necessarily in accordance with his perfect plan for our world. The necessity theory, as it was advocated in the history of philosophy, was imbued with Christian sensibilities and was used to explain events by appeal to God. Necessity theory today has eliminated appeal to God, but has retained the metaphysical status of laws of nature inherited from earlier, Christian versions of the theory.

According to regularity theory, a law is a universal, generalized statement about sets of objects in the physical world, period. Laws are made true by virtue of contingent events coming together in nature. Necessity theory says laws determine the way the world is: in this sense, the truths of laws of nature are conceptually prior to the events that they control. Given the laws of nature, it is physically impossible that anything contrary occur. Regularity theory says laws describe the way the world is: the truths of laws of nature follow from and are conceptually subsequent to the events that they control. Given the laws of nature, it is not physically impossible that an event contrary to those laws occur. Of course, such events in fact do not, have not and will not occur, but regularity theory claims that there is nothing deeply metaphysical or profound about this.

Regularity theory poses a threat to determinism. Let's examine an example to find out how. Newton's law of gravity states that every object in the universe attracts every other object with a force proportional to the masses of the objects and inversely proportional to the square of the distance between the objects. **Necessary truths** have necessary implications. If the law of gravity were physically necessary, then the fact that the Moon and Earth are attracted to one another to the precise degree that they are would not only be true but it would be necessarily true. But regularity theory says that the law of gravity is not physically necessary but is contingent. If a statement is contingent then it is possible that that statement is or becomes false. If laws are contingent, then it follows that it is possible that such laws are, were or can become false. Determinism holds that the laws of nature and the past fix a single future. But if it is physically possible that they could change, then there is not a single possible future but rather there are infinitely many physically possible futures. So, only if the necessity theory is true is determinism true.

According to regularity theory, when Han Solo chooses to help the rebels he creates a state of affairs that can be described by laws of nature. But the past combined with laws of nature did not make it necessary that he help the rebels. Rather, the fact that he chooses to do so provides data *for* the formulation and refinement of existing laws of nature. It is the fact that the Moon and Earth are attracted to one another as they are that provides data *for* the formulation of the law of gravity. On the regularity theory, particular facts about the mass of bodies and their distance from one another account for the law of gravity. This relationship is seen in a quite different light by necessity theory since it says that the law of gravity accounts for why the Moon and Earth are attracted to one another as they are.

BOX 7.C: DETERMINISM AND NEUROSCIENCE

Advances in our ability to study the brain have pushed neuroscientists to a point at which they can measure detailed brain activity that coincides with allegedly free choices. Benjamin Libet pioneered this research with an experiment in which subjects were asked to choose a random moment to move their wrist. He asked subjects to note the time at which they were first aware of the urge to move. They did this by observing the location of a dot moving across an oscilloscope. Then, with an electroencephalogram linked to the oscilloscope, Libet monitored the activity in the cortex that occurred before the subject's decision to make a motor movement. His research group found that 200 milliseconds before motor movement, the conscious decision occurred, and that 500 milliseconds before motor movement, heightened activity in the secondary motor cortex occurred. The implication is that brain activity occurs about 300 milliseconds before conscious decisions are made! Hard determinists often take this and other similar studies to show that the firing of neurons in the cortex is the physical cause of our decisions. Since our conscious decisions are caused by antecedent physical events in our brains, this is further reason to believe that humans do not have free will.

Others have responded that these experiments do not prove that the agents are not free. One philosopher, Timothy O'Connor, argues that the subjects of these experiments have already decided to move their wrists at the beginning of the experiment. They have been informed that they need to do this within a 30-second interval. Therefore, Libet is only testing the timing of the action subsequent to the prior and freely willed decision to flick their wrists. In addition, since Libet asked the subjects to note the time at which the urge to move their wrists came to them, he has asked them to take the point of view of external observers on their own conscious decision-making. In general terms, O'Connor believes that the context of Libet's experiments contain too many restrictions on the subject to support the conclusion that these experiments prove that the decision to flick one's wrist is determined by brain activity prior to the decision to flick one's wrist.

Suppose you were designing a new experiment. How would you craft it so that you could avoid O'Connor's criticisms? Or is it impossible to meet O'Connor's criteria in any experimental context?

7.5 ASSESSING DETERMINISM

We foreshadowed the central problem for determinism in our argument for libertarianism: if determinism is true, then it is unlikely that we are morally responsible for our actions. If "ought" implies "can," and all of us are simply fated to do what we do in life, how can we say that we *ought* to perform some acts and *ought not* to perform others? According to the determinist, saints are saintly because that is their causal fate; likewise, sinners have no control over what they do. To praise saints and blame sinners is mistaken. This view of human beings as not responsible for their actions conflicts with the deepest intuitions we have about the moral requirements for life in a society. We are appalled by the prospect of a society in which people are not held morally responsible for their actions.

But according to determinism, I don't freely perform any actions. I can't choose to perform any actions other than the ones I perform. It may seem to me that I can select amongst several different possible actions. But determinism implies that it is physically possible for me to perform only one of those actions. Think about this in reference to our moral obligations and the "ought implies can" principle. The word "can" in that context means "physically possible." It is not physically possible for me to fly up to the 40th floor of a burning building, so I'm not obligated to. But now see this from the point of view of determinism! If determinism, then you have been determined to take each action that you take and not any other. In other words, it is physically possible for you to do *only the things that you actually do*. I think I can order a double espresso or a latte, but I can't. I can only order whichever one it is that I order. I think I can refrain from lying to my boss, but I can't: if I lie to my boss, then I was determined to lie to my boss. If "ought implies can" is true and hard determinism is true, then the scope of moral obligations shrinks drastically: it appears I have no moral obligations at all. For many people, this is a frightening implication of hard determinism, and a sufficient reason to reject it.

How might the hard determinist reply to this line of reasoning, as set out in the argument in §7.2? Some determinists argue that 7.0—that human beings are morally responsible for their actions—begs the question against compatibilism and against hard determinism. The case for this charge can be made in different ways, but the simplest is this. A critic might argue that what we call "moral responsibility" is an illusion. We praise and blame people, but the language of morality does not pick out real properties in spacetime. Rather, the very idea of holding people morally responsible for their actions is a social construct. Members of our species long ago found it convenient to invent right and wrong in order to regulate social behavior for the preservation of order and harmony. While it's convenient to have concepts of praise and blame at work in our cultures, those concepts are illusory. Large groups of people can be entirely incorrect about what they believe. Residents of Europe for centuries believed that the Sun orbits Earth. The fact that they were mistaken does not mean that they didn't fiercely believe in a geocentric solar system. But merely desiring that a theory is true does not make it true. The determinist insists that 7.0 is false and human beings are not morally responsible for their actions.

Philosophers have developed another argument against hard determinism by making an appeal to quantum mechanics. Quantum mechanics is a set of physical theories about the nature and interaction of atomic and subatomic particles. The term "mechanics" refers to any branch of physics that is concerned with the energy and motion of objects. Since quantum mechanics produces theories about unobservable particles, like quarks and muons, these theories rely heavily on mathematical models to predict future observations made possible with a supercollider. But these physicists have found that the subatomic universe is not nearly as deterministic as the atomic universe.

One developer of quantum mechanics, Neils Bohr, interpreted his mathematical models about the behaviors of subatomic particles and their energy, position, and momentum in a way that implies that the subatomic world violates the thesis of determinism. (This became known as the *Copenhagen interpretation*.) The past and laws of nature are insufficient to cause a subatomic particle to behave in the way that it does. Other interpretations of quantum mechanics do not have this result, but suppose for the sake of argument that the Copenhagen interpretation is correct, and that indeterminacy and randomness abound at the subatomic level.

Since determinism states that the past and the laws of nature fix a single future as the only physically possible future, quantum mechanics appears to falsify determinism. Laws within quantum mechanics are statistical in character, and are not deterministic. The conditions antecedent to quantum event E only make it highly probable that E will come about; the conditions are not sufficient to bring E about. On this probabilistic conception, to say that "x causes y" is only to say something like "given x, the likelihood of y's occurring is much greater than the probability of y's occurring without x." X's presence appreciably raises the probability of y's occurring, but does not render y 100 percent likely.

How might the advocate of determinism respond to this objection from quantum mechanical indeterminacy? The first response revises the thesis of determinism as follows:

> *Determinism*: For all non-subatomic events E, natural laws and the conditions prior to those events necessarily determine that those events occur.

The hard determinist would make this change because, in order to insure that humans do not have free will, it is unnecessary that *all* events must be deterministic. It would be enough to achieve this result that all events relevant to human decision-making are determined by antecedent causes. The hard determinist would then add the further premise that changes in the momentum and energy of subatomic particles are not causally relevant in the production of human choices. Therefore, by narrowing the thesis somewhat, the hard determinist's opposition to human free will escapes the criticism.

The libertarian might respond by arguing that, in fact, sub-atomic events are causally relevant in the production of our human choices. The molecules in our brain are made up of atoms, which are made up of subatomic particles. Presumably the energy, momentum and arrangement of sub-atomic particles in our brain at some level does affect our decision-making.

The determinist offers the following response to this rejoinder from the libertarian. Human free will would not be possible if human decision-making were random or indeterministic. Imagine a thought experiment in which human decision-making was indeterminate in the way that quantum events are. When I form the desire for a cup of coffee, that antecedent event does not cause me to go to the coffee shop. Instead, I randomly "decide" to listen to my parents' old records. After lengthy preparations to enter a police academy, on the day of the entrance exam I randomly decide to go boating. When asked why I performed these actions, given the antecedent factors, I offer no reason, but instead confess that my actions were random. In this scenario, my will operates randomly and indeterminately, but we would *not* say that I am in control of my decisions.

The libertarian's position is motivated by a concern with moral responsibility, but to be morally responsible for my actions requires that I am in control of them. If my decisions resemble the indeterministic events at the quantum level, I am not morally responsible for my actions. This discussion of the application of quantum mechanics to the problem of free will reveals that the hard determinist should not universally generalize her thesis. It also implies that, even if indeterministic interpretations of quantum mechanics are true, they do not provide much assistance to opponents of determinism about human free will.

BOX 7.D: GOD'S FOREKNOWLEDGE AND HUMAN FREEDOM

Here is an argument to think that a traditional conception of God as omniscient entails that humans have no freedom. The governing idea is that, since God's knowledge is infallible, and he knows what you will do tomorrow, you are not free with respect to your choice about what to do tomorrow.

(7.10) God is omniscient.

(7.11) If God is omniscient, God knows everything that all humans will do in the future.

(7.12) If God knows everything that all humans will do in the future, then human beings could not have made other choices instead.

(7.13) But it is necessary for a human being *freely* to will a choice that the agent could have made other choices instead.

(7.14) Therefore, if God is omniscient, human beings do not have free will.

One easy way out of this argument is to reject 7.10, either by claiming that God does not exist, or by claiming that, if God does exist, there are statements that God does not know. Another perspective on this argument is simply to endorse its conclusion. Calvinists, for example, believe that humans do not have any free will with respect to their ability to enter heaven. We are chosen by God.

Other attacks upon this argument are directed at 7.11. A response that dates from Aristotle argues that statements about the future are neither true nor false. They cannot be, since the content of those statements refers to a specific time—in the future. How can that thought be reapplied to this argument? Does the relationship between God and time enable the traditional theist to show that this argument is unsound?

7.6 COMPATIBILISM AND SENSES OF "CAN"

To enter into the mindset of the compatibilist, consider the question, "Does one have a *choice* whether or not to decide to X?" This way of phrasing the question indicates a distinctively more concrete and practical focus. Under what situations would you say that you have a *choice*? What is it to *choose*? The compatibilist takes his cue from ordinary language. We routinely speak of making choices. To choose is to select between alternatives. Alternatives may include options A, B and C, or they might be restricted to doing A or not doing A. The compatibilist characterizes "free will" in terms of choosing: when we are able to choose amongst alternatives, we are free, but when we are unable to choose amongst alternatives, we are unfree.

In many cases, we don't have choices about our actions. Here are a few examples of situations in which we lack choices. In each of these situations, the compatibilist will deny that Han Solo can freely will to help the Rebel Alliance destroy the Death Star. We can say, of each Han below, that he "cannot" help the rebels. But how would you define that term for each of the cases?

Carbonite Han is "frozen" in a block of minerals and cannot think or move.

Hypnotized Han: Han has been given effective post-hypnotic suggestions that cause Han to cringe in fear whenever he thinks of the Death Star.

Coerced Han: Han has credible reasons to believe that Jabba the Hutt is holding his loved ones hostage and that Jabba will kill them if Han helps the rebels.

Depressed Han: Han is in a depressed mood, due to adverse circumstances and an imbalance of serotonin.

According to the compatibilist, in none of these cases is Han free, though each case emphasizes a slightly different sense of "can." Carbonite Han is physically compelled not to help the rebels. For hypnotized, coerced and depressed Han, they can't help the rebels due to mental factors. By infering in these situations that Han has no choice and is not free, compatibilism captures what we actually seem to think when we consider aspects of "choosing."

The compatibilist also believes that this analysis of the cases corresponds with our feelings about moral responsibility. Since Han has no choice as to whether or not to help the rebels in these cases, Han is not morally blameworthy for not helping them. Cases in which Han is bodily or mentally incapable of doing something conform to the ought implies can principle. If Han has no power of locomotion, then he can't be faulted for not going somewhere. If Han is clinically obsessive-compulsive about watching TV, then Han can't be faulted for his inability to control his desire to watch TV.

However, in many other cases Han is responsible for his actions (or inactions).

Apathetic Han: Han doesn't feel like going to the Death Star and feels instead like watching TV with Chewy.

Despite his promise to Luke and the rebels, Apathetic Han has chosen to remain at home. He was not physically or mentally compelled to stay home and watch TV; he chooses to watch TV voluntarily. So he is morally responsible for failing to fulfill his promise. (What might be the differences between Depressed Han and Apathetic Han?) In general, the compatibilist suggests that Han is morally responsible for his actions so long as the cause of his failure to fulfill his moral duty both lies within his own mind and is under his own control. Apathetic Han meets this joint necessary condition since he wanted to stay home and did so voluntarily.

To appreciate the compatibilist's great insight, let's look at a very different thought experiment created in order to illustrate the difference between compatibilist and libertarian incompatibilist free will. John Locke offers the "locked room" thought experiment on this point.

Suppose a man be carried, whilst fast asleep, into a room where is a person he longs to see and speak with; and be there locked fast in, beyond his power to get out: he awakes, and is glad to find himself in so desirable company, which he stays willingly in, i.e. prefers his stay to going away. I ask, is not this stay voluntary? I think nobody will doubt it; and yet being locked fast in, it is evident he is not at liberty to stay, he does not have freedom to be gone.[5]

Locke says the man possesses a sense of free will despite the fact that he cannot do other than remain in the room. The source of this compatibilist freedom lies in the man's desire to remain in the room. His action corresponds to his interest because he remains in the room *voluntarily*.

Locke's example does not offer a set of necessary and sufficient conditions for an analysis of compatibilist freedom. The chief result of the thought experiment is to identify a condition that is *not* necessary for human freedom. The gentleman in Locke's locked room thought experiment offers a counterexample to the principle of alternative possibilities. The man in the room can't do otherwise, but he has chosen to remain in the room. No other alternative is as attractive to him as that one. The immediate causes of his decision-making are his own psychological states. He is not being coerced to do so against his will; he is mentally capable of choosing to leave the room; he is not physically prevented from choosing to leave the room, for example he is not handcuffed to the wall. If any of those hypothetical scenarios were true, he would not be free. If he were compelled to remain in the room in those ways, he would not be choosing to remain in the room. But he is choosing to remain in it—despite the fact that, as it happens, he cannot but remain in the room since the door is locked from the outside.

BOX 7.E: UPDATING LOCKE'S LOCKED ROOM

Imagine that Kristen is one among a group of thieves who plan a bank heist. Kristen's crime boss worries that Kristen isn't sufficiently enthusiastic about doing this job, so the boss has implanted a device into her brain that will control Kristen's behavior. He had this put in without Kristen's knowledge. This implant will insure the boss that Kristen does choose to and act to rob the bank. However, this implant will *only* cause Kristen to decide to rob the bank if Kristen herself decides not to rob the bank. If Kristen overcomes her hesitations and decides to rob the bank, then the implant is never activated. According to Harry Frankfurt, who developed this thought experiment, if Kristen decides to rob the bank and the implant is not activated, then Kristen is free, in the philosophically important sense of the term "free." She is free in the sense that counts. But notice that Kristen could not do otherwise than to rob the bank. In other words, Kristen will walk out of that building having robbed a bank. Circumstances have determined that Kristen has no alternative possibility; Kristen could not do other than she does. Yet she is capable of freely willing to rob the bank and she is free in a way that makes her morally responsible for her choices and actions. (See Frankfurt, 1969.)

As this thought experiment makes clear, the compatibilist favors discussing human freedom in terms of "control" over our choices, not in terms of their causation. Having control over your decision amounts to producing it through your desires. If Kristen decided not to rob the bank, then her actions would have failed to exemplify her desire because the brain implant would have coerced her into robbing the bank anyway.

This thought experiment provides the intuitive rationale for the compatibilist's rejection of PAP. If this premise is false, then the determinist's argument is unsound. Furthermore, if this is false, then the libertarian is also incorrect that a necessary condition on human freedom is the ability to do otherwise.

7.7 HIERARCHICAL COMPATIBILISM

Why isn't someone who has been hypnotized free? Does someone who is addicted to cigarettes freely will to continue smoking? The examples used to illustrate compatibilism typically refer to psychological factors involved in decision-making, since focusing on those issues plays to compatibilism's strengths. This stands in contrast to the determinist's interest in emphasizing metaphysical factors. But we haven't yet specified the required relationships within a person's psychology that, together, yield compatibilist freedom.

One specific form of compatibilism appeals to hierarchical features within our psychology to explain when one is free. For hierarchical compatibilism, freedom is not independence from prior streams of causation. Instead, freedom is produced by an appropriate relationship between different states of mind.

We can borrow from Harry Frankfurt's compatibilist discussion about the will and its operations to develop compatibilist freedom. Psychologically, we can say that the smoker has a first-order desire to smoke. A first-order desire is a desire about what to do. The smoker also has a second-order desire, which is a desire about a desire. Her second-order desire in this case is her desire not to want to smoke. Typically, an agent's will is better reflected by second-order desires. As in this case, the addict's brain chemistry is dependent on nicotine, which explains why she has the first-order desires to smoke. It is due to this appeal to hierarchies of desires that this form of compatibilist freedom gets the name *hierarchical compatibilism*. Likewise, someone who has a second-order desire to visit his friend—he wants to want to—but who is prevented by hypnotism from wanting to (at the first order level) is unfree. Addicts and people who are hypnotized against their will lack free will because their first-order and second-order desires are in direct conflict. How addicts were caused to have the first-order desires they have is not relevant to assessing whether they have free will.

According to Frankfurt, to have free will we must "identify" with our desires at the second-order. In this case, the unwilling smoker is alienated from her desire to smoke, and therefore does not identify with it. This is shown by the fact that she wants not to want to smoke. She would identify with her desire to smoke if she wanted to continue smoking. In a natural use of the term, she does not have "control" over her first-order desire to smoke since she continues smoking despite not wanting to do so. The compatibilist insists that I must maintain some control over my first-order decision-making if I am to be free. In cases of addicts and the hypnotized, external factors exert more control over their first-order desires than they are able to exert through the implementation of their second-order desires. On these grounds, the agent is not free.

This discussion of the two levels of desires plausibly explains why we think that addicts are not free. But by introducing two levels of desires, this compatibilist proposal risks stepping into a problem. When someone experiences conflict between opposing first-order desires, the person looks to his second-order desires in order to identify which first-order desire best exemplifies the person's preferences and interests. Typically this works efficiently. Amy finds a wallet with some cash. She can choose to keep the wallet or return it. She considers this choice seriously, because she is tempted to keep it. But her second-order reflection about which desire she wants to become her will, which desire she wants to act upon, leads her to return the wallet. She chooses to find the owner of the wallet and return it, money intact, because she has decided that she wants to exemplify virtue in her first-order choices.

Imagine that Phil also has the same internal conflict between returning and keeping the wallet. He cannot determine which first-order choice best exemplifies his most deeply held commitments, so he too turns to second-order reflection for an answer to his dilemma. But when he does so, all he finds is another conflict, in this case between his desire to be rich and his desire to be ethical. These conflicting desires weigh heavily upon him and he sees no clear answer. In his mind, his second-order decision between money and morality is wrapped up in another choice he must make, at the third-order level, between whether he wants to be a religious person or a non-religious person. You can imagine that poor Phil will be unable to choose which of his third-order desires best exemplify the kind of person he wants to be, and so on for any further levels of decision-making.

The hierarchical compatibilist says that a person's (first-order) will is freely made if and only if it exemplifies the person's second-order desires. While this assists the compatibilist in skirting problems created by addiction cases, it leaves the compatibilist open to an objection that there will be a regress into ever higher levels of conflicting desires. If this is so, then the agent may be unable to identify, or fully identify, with any first-order choices he makes. It appears that this "harmony" condition is not sufficient for free will. Even if it is necessary that for a choice to be free it must harmonize with my second-order desires, the hierarchical compatibilist must add to this necessary condition some further conditions that prevent there from being an infinite chain of pairs of desires.

BOX 7.F: *STAR TREK: DEEP SPACE NINE,* "ROCKS AND SHOALS"

In "Rocks and Shoals" (from season 6, episode 123) Captain Sisko and his Starfleet crew crash land on a planet inside a nebula. There they meet a band of Jem'Hadar, who are enemies of Starfleet. The Jem'Hadar are a species designed and created by a super-race from another part of the galaxy. These lizard-like Jem'Hadar are bred to be obedient, exceedingly strong and adept warriors who die for their masters. They are also given a number of fascinating biological modifications.

The band of Jem'Hadar stranded on this planet are accompanied by Keevan, a master who feeds them the hormone that they need for their survival. Keevan is dying, and his only hope for survival is to leave the planet for medical attention. But the only way to do that is by securing the friendship of Captain Sisko, which is impossible since Keevan has a dozen Jem'Hadar in tow who will attack Sisko with the least provocation.

Keevan informs Sisko that he wants to surrender. To facilitate this, Keevan tells Sisko that he will order his Jem'Hadar to attack the Starfleet personnel at a specified place and time. This way Sisko and his crew will be poised for a surprise attack and kill the Jem'Hadar. The lead Jem'Hadar gets wind of Keevan's cowardly plan to sacrifice the Jem'Hadar in order that he alone might survive. The Jem'Hadar do have an interest in surviving, but their genetic engineering overwhelms them, which leads to the climax of the episode: they walk into the surprise attack out of loyalty to Keevan. It appears that they wanted to do this since their decision was not externally forced upon them, but their internal motivations have been seeded by their creators. So did they do this willingly?

7.8 ASSESSING COMPATIBILISM

The analytic philosophy reading accompanying this chapter will continue the process of evaluating compatibilism, but we can get this process started by remarking that the sense of "control" used to articulate the compatibilist position is elusive. This is the first and most important problem with compatibilism. If someone such as Apathetic Han is determined to remain at home and could not do otherwise, what does this "control" amount to? For recall that the compatibilist says that even if Apathetic Han is causally determined by the past and laws of nature to desire to watch TV instead of help the rebels, he nonetheless freely chooses to watch TV. Furthermore, are these leftovers of freedom sufficient to make him morally responsible for his actions?

The compatibilist holds that, when Han is psychologically coerced or physically compelled to X, he is not free. The compatibilist also holds that, when Han is metaphysically determined to X, he can be free, ceteris paribus. Someone isn't free in cases in which their first- and second-order desires are not in harmony. But opponents of compatibilism can use this as a launching pad for an argument against it.

Consider a case of a "meta-addictive" drug, call it "blast," which not only causes its users to want to take more blast, but it also causes them to want to be the kind of person who is addicted to blast. In other words, this drug affects not only first-order desires, but second-order desires too. This implies that the first- and second-order desires of users of blast are in perfect harmony, even though both first- and second-order desires are determined by the drug itself. This satisfies the hierarchical compatibilist's condition for free will, but it seems as though blast users are not free. It will seem to the user herself that she is choosing freely, but this is simply a delusion brought about as an effect of the drug. In other words, to be "free" in the hierarchical compatibilist's sense is not very important or interesting, nor does it bear any relationship to moral responsibility.

We draw this conclusion on the basis of our thought experiment about blast. But the incompatibilist can widen the scope of the conclusion critical of compatibilism. This thought experiment implies that the user of blast is not in control of her second-order desires regarding future uses of blast. But the hard determinist insists that *all our second-order desires are out of our control*, just like the blast addict's second-order desire to want to want to take blast. The only difference between the blast addict and everyone else is that blast itself determines the blast addict's desires. Those desires are still determined by factors outside her control. And the determinist insists that this makes the blast addict unfree. The compatibilist should be under no delusion that any act of choosing or willing, or any other mental events, are exempt from this broad commitment to determinism. Our acts of willing *at both the first- and second-order* obey deterministic laws. If all our second-order desires are determined just as ineluctably as the blast addict's desire to want blast, then, if the blast addict is not free, neither is anyone else.

When an agent forms a second-order desire through which she identifies with a first-order desire, this second-order desire is also an event. Thus, it also conforms to the determinist's thesis. In assessing the compatibilist position, we mustn't under-appreciate the fact that events of second-order willing—what are regarded as the thoughts that best exemplify the kind of person that each individual is—are themselves merely mechanistic products of prior causes. They are determined as unfreely as are sneezes and reflex movements. Not only is it impossible that an agent act other than she does, but the compatibilist must concede that she cannot will other than she does.

For these reasons the incompatibilist argues for the necessity of alternative possibilities for human free will. The incompatibilist must then say that the use of Locke's locked room as support for compatibilism is unsuccessful. The gentleman inside the room could not act otherwise than to stay in the room, since it is locked. But, more insidious, the gentleman inside the room could not even desire otherwise than to want to stay in the room. His decision is itself determined by facts of ancestral causation far beyond his control. The compatibilist insists that the man is more free when he chooses to remain in the room than when he is coerced to remain in the room. But the incompatibilist will draw attention to the surreptitious use of quantitative terms like "more free." All concerned parties can grant that when an agent chooses to remain in a room, his action is more intimately related to his personality than if he is coerced at gunpoint to remain in the room. But this does not show that he is sufficiently free as to be morally responsible for his actions. This kind of freedom requires the ability to do and desire otherwise, and he lacks these abilities.

This criticism of compatibilism is closely related to whether or not compatibilist freedom is sufficient for moral responsibility. One of the central reasons for which we are interested in determining whether human beings have free will is because free will is regarded as necessary for moral responsibility. The libertarian incompatibilist argues that the ability to do otherwise is necessary for moral responsibility by defending a version of the ought implies can principle. If we have good reasons for believing ought implies can, then compatibilism suffers. This is because it appears not only that we do not have the ability to *do* otherwise—that is, to perform *actions* other than those actions we perform. We also do not have the ability to *will* otherwise either, since acts of willing at every level of thought are ancestrally caused by physical processes working in a perfectly deterministic fashion upon my brain chemistry. If the ought implies can principle is true, then compatibilism does not offer us sufficient freedom to enable us to be morally responsible for our actions.

7.9 SUMMARY

In this chapter we have investigated arguments for and against three theories about freedom of the will. Libertarianism says we have free will and our actions are not causally determined. Determinism argues for the opposite pair of conclusions. Compatibilism states that, though we have free will, our actions are causally determined.

Much of the dispute between these theories surrounds the status of the principle of alternative possibilities. This principle states a necessary condition on free will, namely, one has free will with respect to some choice only if one could have done otherwise. The compatibilist is the odd man out since he does not accept this principle. Locke's locked room example is used to establish the denial of the principle of alternative possibilities. This displays a key difference between compatibilists and incompatibilists: Compatibilists believe that freedom is a matter of *control* rather than *causation*.

Libertarians and determinists differ about whether events in the physical world are determined. It appears as though we are physical beings in a physical world, and as a result human beings and all their component parts behave in strict accord with the deterministic laws of physics. So it appears that we do not have the ability to do otherwise. But libertarians are unconvinced by this appeal to causal closure and to science. The libertarian argues that the most plausible current theories about physical laws indicate that laws are not deterministic. We detailed two distinct accounts of physical laws—necessity theory and regularity theory—and showed why the libertarians are right to endorse regularity theory.

We discussed senses of "can" at work in compatibilism in an attempt to better understand that theory. The term "can" is highly ambiguous in the compatibilist's hands because the underlying notion of "control" changes subtly in different examples. Historically, hierarchical compatibilism has influenced the development of compatibilist theories. This version attempts to identify circumstances under which an agent exerts control over her actions by explaining control in terms of the relationships between sets of her desires. However, this development alone does not successfully respond to the central problem with compatibilism. If the sets of my desires are themselves caused by factors outside one's control, it appears that the type of freedom one is left with does not yield a form of freedom that sustains moral responsibility.

7.10 ABOUT THE READINGS

Our science fiction story for this chapter is "Norbert and the System," by Timons Esaias. Norbert's bland life takes a sharp turn when he asks a simple-minded, but unintentionally blasphemous, question about a piece of technology so ubiquitous that it can scarcely be distinguished from human minds. The "personal system" is an implant that does an inordinate amount of thinking, feeling and sensing for those who wear one, and everyone does. This story contains overt warnings about consumerism and raises troubling questions about the extent of our freedom in the face of increasingly sophisticated technology. Since the PS makes many decisions without the conscious consent of the human being, it limits the number of choices made by humans. Even for those decisions made by the human being, the PS presents ranked preferences that its program indicates will maximize utility for the human being. It inevitably coaches its users on what to say and what effects their words might have on their recipients. What freedom there is left for Norbert is unclear.

But the question whether he, or we, have freedom is moot; according to Thomas Hobbes, there is no freedom. In the pair of selections from Hobbes' writings, he offers a few arguments on behalf of that conclusion. Hobbes argues that the will is caused to will what it does by factors outside itself. This implies that the will's actions are not free in a libertarian sense of the term. However, he is willing to allow that human actions have liberty in some derivative sense. This selection, "On Behalf of Determinism," comes from Hobbes' *Liberty and Necessity*, and from his *Leviathan*.

In our analytic philosophy selection, "Free Will: Alternatives and Sources," Kevin Timpe compares, contrasts and assesses two contrasting approaches to free will. On the first, free will is a matter of an agent exerting ultimate control over her choices. On the second, free will is a matter of having alternative choices. Timpe describes the ways both compatibilists and incompatibilists have interpreted both these proposals.

7.11 "NORBERT AND THE SYSTEM," BY TIMONS ESAIAS

Her skirt had a stylish cut; the boots accented the shapeliness of her legs; and her social beacon, cunningly mounted above her left ear, was flashing green. Norbert, instantly taken by her graceful yet careless walk, summoned his analysis program for her personality profile and a suitable introductory line. But while he waited for the printout to flash on his lens, she stepped up onto a passing trolley-shuttle—and the moment was lost.

When the display arrived he angrily subaudibled to his Personal System, "A fine lot of good it does me now!"

"Do you want an identity search for her address and access code?" his PS inquired.

"No, I do not. Clear." His lens screen returned to the basic display. Still seething, he demanded, "How long did you take to process my request?"

"Three seconds, request and display inclusive."

It won't do, he thought. How could he ever get a girl with a time-lag like that? His shyness might be a factor, but Personal Systems are supposed to make up for that.

He needed to invest in some new equipment.

While the kitchsys made his dinner, he sprawled in the bedchair and summoned the showroom program. A list of Personal Systems in his price range crawled down his left lens, while his right displayed an index of nearly 1,000 second-level options.

"Civilization can be tedious at times," he remarked.

Judging his tone as dissatisfaction, the General System brought up a salesperson. "Good day, Shopper Kamdar! How may we assist you?"

Norbert explained his problem.

"Ah, yes. We've had a lot of replacement orders from shoppers with the 1200 series. Time marches on! Ha, ha!" The salesperson simulation paused for a change of mood, "Frankly, an eligible bachelor like yourself shouldn't have to ask his PS to assess a young lady. A modern System would have started on it the second your cortex responded to her positive features. You should have had the output before the hormones hit."

Letting that message sink in, the salesrepresentation got down to cases. "How much surgical adjustment are you willing to tolerate? . . . Ah! Well, then, I would suggest the latest thing out of Gabon, the 15B Jizmet. It's powerful, but economical, and most of the hardware is rib-mounted. It takes ten ribs on a male your size, but that means three pounds *less* on the head mounting you already have with the 1200! Could I consult your mounting diagram? . . . Yes, I see you already have four ribs converted, that'll save on installation . . ."

"Gabonese?" Norbert interrupted. "What's their track-record?"

Instantly a series of charts and tables came up on his left lens. Then his right lens scrolled a list of sports personalities currently using Gabonese Systems: heavy on defensive backs and third basemen. Quick response time.

"They're fairly new in the market, but quite reliable. They have to be licensed by our Administration. Do you have a particular concern?" The rep struck just the right note of reassurance and mild contempt.

"Actually, I was just wondering how you turn it off." Norbert chuckled awkwardly. Come to think of it, how did you turn off the System he had?

The salesrep paused for some quick processing. "Off?" it asked with a tilt of its head.

"Yeah, you know, if it malfunctioned. An over-ride command, or an off switch. Whatever." Norbert tried to act in control, even though he knew that a sophisticated show-room program like this could detect his insecurity in a millisecond. That's why he rarely shopped. The salesreps reminded him of all his inadequacies, without even trying.

"An off switch? Frankly, I've never heard of such . . ." There was clearly a reset. "I do see your point, Shopper Kamdar. One does not have an off switch, however, because the failure rate for PSs is vastly lower than that for people on their own, not that there are people without Systems any more!" A statistical comparison of deaths by malfunction as opposed to expected deaths without Personal Systems flashed on his lens. "As you see, if one could shut the PS off it would put the owner at increased risk. It would be gross negligence on our part to allow that."

"That makes sense," Norbert admitted, getting out of his stupid question as gracefully as possible.

Norbert dropped into the hospital that Saturday to have his new PS installed. The waiting room bored him—everyone in it being loaded with anti-anxiety shots by their PSs—so he called up the latest flick. He hadn't even seen the opening titles before his message light blinked: would he please go to Room 45921?

Room 45921 was in the Counselling Section, which seemed odd. He hadn't needed counselling for the last PS. Odder still, the counsellor appeared in person, not just represented through the GS. A short, round European of some sort with an old-style half-helmet covering the back of his skull. What could a guy with an archaic set-up like that tell him about a PS?

"Shopper Kamdar, Norbert Kamdar! Sit down, sit down!" The man's jovial manner surprised Norbert. Counsellors were usually so downbeat and concerned. "Just a few questions before we do the installation."

"Is there a problem?" Norbert hated problems, and he already sensed his PS generating soothing currents in his shoulder muscles.

"We don't think so. We just want to make sure that you're getting the right product."

"I don't think I can afford to go up much further," Norbert objected, calling up his spread-sheets.

"I see that," the counsellor agreed. He scanned something on his lens. "Actually, I'm looking into your concern about System safety. This very original remark you made about an 'off switch,' to be precise."

Norbert tried, and failed, to suppress a wince. "The showroom explained that to me. I don't really know what made me think of that. Probably something about Africans and that dam that collapsed."

The counsellor paused for an update. "Ah, in Egypt. Yes. That was probably it."

"I really want this System," Norbert pointed out.

"Of course. Your PS doesn't report any unusual nightmares or anxiety problems. Is that correct?"

How did they get that data from the GS? It must be in the installation contract. Norbert agreed with the assessment. All he dreamed about were the beautiful, interesting women he never seemed to attract.

The counsellor went on in the careful tone of a prepared speech, "Shopper Kamdar, as you know, your Personal System is carefully designed to protect you from health hazards both internal and external. Your heart, lungs, brain, liver and other organs are constantly monitored for any sign of trouble. Your enzymes and hormones are adjusted for maximum health and efficiency, and your caloric intake is restricted, if necessary, by the kitchsys interface to assure proper nutrition."

"Quite. Counsellor, I . . ."

"But that's just part of it. Your PS is constantly updated with weather, traffic, fire, and hazard conditions which could threaten your safety. You've heard of crime in the history films, haven't you? Crime posed a significant threat to physical, financial and emotional well-being in former times, but our Personal Systems and the General System just don't allow it now. I'm sure you agree that this is all for the good."

"Yes, I do."

"Then why would you want to turn a PS off? If you were injured, it couldn't bring assistance. If people could turn their Systems off, we could have crime again! Do you want that?" The man leaned forward in an authoritative pose, which seemed too artificial. He really needed to update his software.

"No. Of course not. What I want is my new System."

The Counsellor pointed his gnarled finger at Norbert. "But are you satisfied that the System is safe? We're not going to have you bringing up this switch business after the installation, are we?"

"No, Counsellor. I'm sorry I ever mentioned it."

"All right, then."

The guys from work dropped by to admire his new set-up. They group-viewed the latest Victoria's Secret ads, and compared baseball statistics software. Norbert found that he entertained more cleverly with the new System, and the gang stayed more than an hour before they excused themselves. A record. And he earned a party invitation, his first in weeks.

But one guy from Engineering, Howardi, stayed behind. Howardi designed bureaucracy networks, and knew people who ran things. Talking with him always reminded Norbert of the gangsters in the oldies. He always had the inside dope on everything.

"So, Norb, I got something about you on the GS the other day. Strictly upstairs stuff, but flagged to my attention. What's this about over-riding your PS?" Howardi swirled his drink in the manner management Systems tended to suggest.

Norbert's System blocked any hesitation more smoothly than he'd ever experienced before. "Oh, that! It was a silly question I asked the showroom. I don't follow hardware much, so a really dumb idea leaked out. My old PS just didn't catch it." Why would Howardi have been flagged for this? What had he stumbled into?

"Yeah, I've had some funny ideas in my time," Howardi admitted. "I've missed a warning message a time or two, as well. Embarrassing."

NOD SAGELY. Norbert nodded, though he couldn't remember ignoring a warning message in his whole life.

"You're probably wondering what the fuss is about, right? I think you may have proposed the heresy of our time! And you thought you were just a regular guy! But seriously, Norb, the PS is the cornerstone of our material culture. When the archaeology teams dig us up it's going to be our defining element, the "PS People" or something. So questioning the PS would be like an ancient Greek questioning pottery or amphorae or some thing." He contemplated his drink before swallowing the last.

Norbert's new System flagged him: SEE PYTHAGORAS. SEE DIOGENES.

"I sure didn't mean anything by it, Howie." Norbert said in his best subdued voice. "They straightened me out at the hospital before it went in."

"Well, that's good." Howardi got up to go. "Don't get all subversive on us, eh, Norb?"

The party wasn't bad, and he even managed to get two dates in the weeks following his new installation. The first date ended early, because she suddenly remembered that her hair needed washing.

The second girl was political. She wanted to spend the evening sitting on the benches in a public lounge area, reading political bulletin boards together.

Norbert had never kept up with politics, and didn't read the bulletin boards much. He had only posted an opinion once in his life, back when the Colts were trying to get the franchise law changed so they could get out of Key West. An evening lounging around sharing reactions wasn't what he had had in mind, but if that's what Vodkette wanted, that's what he'd put up with.

They picked the Tribune board, very mainstream, and filled with the usual drivel. Norbert kept his remarks fairly tame, so as not to offend, but he had his PS check the background of the bulletin board contributors. The readouts indicated that every political opinion originated in an expected financial benefit for the shopper who posted it. "I bet almost every opinion on this board is directly linked to the financial gain of the shopper who posted it," Norbert observed in a moment of wild abandon.

"Really!" exclaimed a startled Vodkette. Norbert suddenly remembered that she had done studies in social theory, and that he had probably put his foot in it. He quickly flashed her the background data his PS had been finding on each posting.

While she was looking it over, Norbert's System signalled a startling development: an arousal spike in the young lady, corresponding to his political observation. What had he done?

She smiled. "What made you check that out?" she asked.

"I dunno. It's like at work, I guess. If you're on the way up, you side with management. If you're up for retraining, you hate the place. Opinions are all rather predictable." His System red-flagged his comments: SOCIALLY RISKY.

But her arousal level spiked again, and plateaued higher than Norbert had ever encountered on a date. He ran a quick diagnostic, just to be sure.

She arched a sceptical eyebrow, which just showed above her lenses. "And I suppose *you* have some *un*predictable opinions?"

"Oh, I dunno. I dunno," he stalled, desperately trying to subvocalize a search order for his wildest opinion.

His PS was way ahead of him. Before he could phrase the command, he was looking at a list of his five most original opinions, and their deviation value. Two of them were just errors of fact on his part (his old System hadn't caught them in time), and two more varied less than .45 from the norm. But at the top of the list stood an idea with a colossal deviation.

He swallowed. He took a chance. "I've often thought that we ought to be able to switch off our PS. I've never heard anybody say that, and some people get on my case if I mention it."

She sat there stunned. His System told him that her System was going crazy refuting this remark. But her arousal level doubled.

Her personal distance markers dropped to zero, and her health history became available to his System for review. Norbert never looked back.

When Norbert returned to his rooms that night he couldn't believe a number of things about the date. That she had liked him. That he had had a good time. That he had brought up the off switch idea. That he had, against the advice of his System, allowed her to talk him into posting it for all to see.

His PS seemed insistent that he should examine the replies already coming in, and that he should prepare to deal with repercussions. It certainly was a fine new System, with much more foresight than the 1200; and it didn't rely so much on that nagging voice in the ear.

But Norbert didn't want to think about politics and opinions tonight. He wanted to think about Vodkette, about her responses, about her shape, about the delicious way her rib-mount curved into the swell of her breast. And that is what he thought about until the System put him to sleep.

He awoke to find himself a famous revolutionary.

His System was so backlogged with urgent messages that he had to cancel work for the day. Norbert had never cancelled work before, but his System revealed that he was fully within his rights to do so.

There were thousands of responses to his political posting. Thousands. 16 percent were completely irrelevant; 11 percent confused; 61 percent irately opposed; 2 percent concerned about his mental health. But 8.63 percent agreed. Hundreds of shoppers had taken time out to make a point of agreeing with Norbert.

The feeling it gave him was so overwhelmingly wonderful that his PS had to intervene chemically.

After breakfast and coffoid, he looked at the urgent message traffic.

The counsellor at the installation hospital wanted him to come in for an appointment. The precinct bureaucrat urgently demanded a meeting. It looked ominous, and his bloodstream soon filled with anti-anxiety formulations. There were some dozen threats from angry fellow-shoppers. He had to have his PS explain some of the epithets.

He had been in trouble with Authority before, but no one had ever bothered to send him hate messages.

The most surprising thing was the long, long list of paying messages. Like other shoppers he made a few bucks each month scanning the advertisements offered to him, but it rarely seemed worth the money to sit through more than a few. Besides, the ads were so convincing that you usually bought the product, so what good was it?

But these messages had respectable fees. A long list of lawyers, publicists, writers and interviewers clamoured for his business or co-operation. He spent most of the morning scanning their pitches, and in just three hours earned ten months' salary. Norbert had the uneasy feeling that he might soon need the cash.

After lunch, Norbert screwed up his courage and called the counsellor—the counsellor whom he had assured that the off switch would never be mentioned again. The counsellor's phone-male smiled and redirected his call to another office. A very slick management-woman greeted him with effusive warmth.

"Shopper Kamdar! How good of you to return our message! Let me assure you that we will reimburse you for this call. Say five hundred dollars a minute?" Her pose suggested a willingness to pay more.

"Ah, sure. But I was supposed to talk to Counselling." Norbert suspected a run-around of some kind.

"Yes, well, we're sorry about that. A lot has changed since we sent that message. You may find this hard to believe, but we've been swamped with calls from shoppers just dying to know what PS you're currently using. You've probably experienced a touch of celebrity yourself since yesterday?"

"Yes, er. Yes, I have." What were they up to?

"Well, as a political celebrity you're entitled to realize the rewards of your position. We'd like to offer you an eight per cent commission on all the Jizmet I5S we sell in the next six months, if you'll let us release your System information to the public. We'd gladly raise that to twenty-five per cent if you could find the time to tape an endorsement."

"Why that'd be just . . . Excuse me." His PS urgently flashed: GET AN AGENT across both lenses, as well as a prioritized list of those whose messages had been received that morning. "Sorry, but all this is a little sudden," he dutifully read from his optiprompter. "I'm sure something can be worked out. My lawyer will call to work out the details."

Just the briefest moue of disappointment was replaced by a broad smile of pleasure. She changed the subject. "We did notice one thing about your System that needs correction, and we'll gladly return half of the installation fee to cover your trouble. Ha, ha! The boys in the show-room sadly mis-read your character profile, I'm afraid. No one knew you were such an original, forceful young man. We've been hiding our light a bit, haven't we?"

"Well, perhaps a little . . ."

"So pardon us but we need to give you a more sophisticated repartee package, and damp down some of those annoying inhibition messages that less forthright individuals require. We can do that by remote, if you'll okay it."

"Sure. I guess."

"Fine, then. And again our apologies." She hesitated. "I nearly forgot. The factory is designing that off switch you wanted as an option. We'll let you have an exclusive on that for sixty days, if you'll allow us to use you to market it afterwards. Good shopping!"

His PS-chosen lawyer was on his lens before her smile had even begun to fade out.

While his new agent worked out his contracts, Norbert entered further uncharted territory. He informed his employer that he just wouldn't be able to show up for the next two months, maybe longer. (To his surprise, they were understanding and willing to accommodate.) Then he began a careful screening of the social messages on the queue. Dozens of women had sent paying offers of their company. Only a few of them were professional escorts, the majority were single women with a taste for adventure; and adventure, in this case, meant Norbert!

His PS took a decidedly worldly approach to the situation, which told Norbert that the new software had already been transferred from the company. Norbert felt enormous gratitude to them for this new life. He would gladly endorse the Jizmet line. It was a fine product.

The interview programme would probably be Norbert's finest hour, if he didn't mess up. His PS, armed with a special celebrity-interview package, had been coaching him for days. They had practiced a dozen different gemphrases, the kind that get millions of replay requests, and all the royalties that go with it.

Their chief problem had been justifying his iconoclastic action. Norbert's vagueness on politics and philosophy kept showing through, and he wasn't pig-headed enough to carry it off on emotional insistence alone. So they ended up with a consistently ambiguous set of prepared tactical responses, and a persistent uneasiness in the pit of Norbert's soul.

The presence of a live audience threw him. Forty people had paid large sums, of which he got twelve per cent, to view the taping session in person. Norbert couldn't remember ever having been in one place with that many people in his life. His PS confirmed it; he never had.

The repetitious takes also bothered him. Most shoppers assumed that these programmes were taped in one seamless session. Actually, the interviewer asked the same questions over and over in different tones and moods, in order to elicit a variety of responses. Editing would patch them together later.

"Is it true that you get the famous off switch installed tomorrow?"—Yes.

"What do you intend to do with your switch once you have it?"—I should think that was obvious . . .

"How long do you intend to leave your PS off?"—I'll have to see.

"What about crime, Shopper? What's to assure other shoppers that you won't go on a, what did they call it, skree?"—Spree. Perhaps you should invest in a Jizmet yourself. (PAUSE FOR STUDIO LAUGHTER, IF ANY) No, the switch is being installed under the condition that the GS can over-ride if any shopper's System detects me in criminal activity. I will have the power to try to commit a crime, just not the power to succeed . . .

"Why did you want an off switch in the first place?"—It was just an excruciatingly original idea I had. (SMILE IN SELF-DEPRECATING FASHION) . . .

"Why do you think the shoppers of this world need these switches?"—I didn't say that other shoppers need them. I did say that the option should be available . . .

"But really, what purpose does an off switch serve? What good is a PS that's not in use?"—The purpose of the off switch is to turn the PS off. A shut-down PS serves no purpose but the purpose of waiting to serve. (DON'T USE THIS IF YOU THINK YOU'LL GARBLE IT) . . .

"But, Shopper Kamdar, I really don't think you've answered the question. Why put such a dangerous power in the hands of mere mortals?"

"For the tenth time . . ." Norbert caught himself, and tried to read his prompt. But the answers didn't mean anything to him, and he was angry and afraid. He ignored the prompt. "Because I'm a human and my PS is just a tool, and it's not right . . ." and he slumped in his chair, suddenly unable to speak at all—which his PS had decided was the best thing for everybody.

The published version, which omitted the slumping at the end, soared up the charts. The commentator explained, "And so, like Lewis Carroll's Humpty Dumpty, Norbert Kamdar insists that it all comes down to 'who is to be the master,' and that's all."

In the end Norbert never spent a dime on legal fees. The Shoppers' Defence Fund gladly staved off all the challenges from the bureaucrats and Jizmet's competitors. The courts managed to tie up installation of the switch for an entire month, but the publicity kept the interview selling and the Jizmet orders pouring in. By the day the switch was installed, Norbert was set up for life.

The "switch" could be activated by entering a code on a keypad mounted on his belt, next to the battery charging plug, followed by a subvocal command. If the PS suspected a suicide attempt, it would immobilize him instead of shutting off, and call for help. Otherwise it would wait until he hit the button again to turn back on.

Norbert carried it around for two days before he decided to give it a try. It seemed that every time he thought about it for very long his PS had to sedate him. He spent hours asleep, or in a torpor. What good is it if I can never use it, he thought. But finally, on the spur of the moment, he reached down and twisted the arming cover, flipped off the lid, tapped in the code, and then repeated the command phrase that appeared on his optiprompter. His lens went blank. After a few moments, even the cooling fan shut off.

It was astonishingly quiet without the sound-track. He hadn't realized that it was part of the PS, until now.

Both lenses began to steam up. It took him a while to understand that he wasn't going blind. But the light became otherworldly, and his room very fuzzy. He shouldn't have done this before he'd become familiar with his new rooms.

His head hurt! How can a head hurt on the inside? And he could hear his heart pounding. And his stomach felt very strange, and he began to taste something unpleasant near his throat . . . he reached down and turned the PS back on. It quickly reset and rushed to his aid.

But not in time to save the carpet.

Norbert waited a day to make sure he'd fully recovered from the experiment, and then decided to take a walk through the corridors. Almost immediately he ran into Howardi, who shouted a hearty, " How's shopping!"

" Always a sale. Yourself ?"

"Never better. Say, Norb, the guys at work keep asking about you."

"Really?" Norbert found that idea odd. "Say hello for me."

"Of course. Hey, have you had any more weird ideas I can tell 'em about?"

"No." Norbert shook his head in self-deprecation. "I'm in enough trouble from just the one."

"You're a wild one, Norbert. A real stitch."

Norbert watched Howardi continue down the hall and turn a corner. INSINCERE, said the Jizmet 15.

Her smoky lenses spoke volumes, but her mouth said, "Have you used it?"

"Oh, yeah."

"What's it like?"

"Like nothing I've ever done before. I don't think most people would like it, though."

She reached across the table and stroked his arm. His twentieth date, in the twentieth restaurant, since the inter-view. It seemed almost routine, now.

His PS guided him along routes he'd never taken, but he didn't take much in. Despite the mood-levellers his System was pumping, the halls and galleries all looked the same. He thought back to Vodkette, who had helped start all this. His first conquest. What was she doing now?

SAME EMPLOYMENT. SAME SHOPPING PATTERNS.

There was a note reminding him that her System was probably hopelessly incompatible with his Jizmet. She would bore him now, after all the sophisticated, upscale shoppers he'd been dating since.

That realization made him a tiny bit sad, a tiny bit lonely.

By mid-afternoon he found himself on the edge of the nature park. He decided to explore it. The trees and shrubs here were allowed to grow freely, unless they interfered with the pathways. Few shoppers came here and Norbert could see why. The confusion of shapes and densities seemed quite odd, and the dead leaves and branches accumulating on the ground was somewhat disturbing. Still, his software gave him permission to continue.

At first he stayed on the concrete walkways, which were lined with stone lanterns and other pointless artifacts. The PS offered a series of lectures on their significance, but he declined. Impulsively he stepped onto an unpaved pathway, and during his first few steps switched off his System.

Again the stunning silence in the absence of the sound-track, the pounding of his heart and the rising nausea. The grass under his feet felt very irregular, like a poorly designed pile carpet, and made walking unsteady. He stopped, and tried to control the panic that mounted in his mind. The lenses steamed up, first the right, then the left. He reached up to his face and, for the first time he could remember, unsnapped the lenspiece and flipped it up.

His eyes, unused to the raw air, filled with tears. He could barely keep them open, the impulse to blink was so strong.

The vertigo became overwhelming, and he fell to his hands and knees. The unfamiliar feel of grass and Earth under his hands distracted him momentarily, and allowed him to fight off the nausea. This is how his ancestors had once lived, in the wild, under the trees, listening to the song-birds. How could they stand it, he wondered; how could they shop, feeling like this?

He heard footsteps rapidly approaching.

"Are you all right?"

Norbert reached up unsteadily and restarted his PS, then flipped down the lenspiece. He gestured unsteadily for patience, though he knew his interrogator's System would be monitoring his rapid return to normal. Then he sensed two people squatting down beside him, and his PS said, "Park rangers."

"Shopper? Do you need assistance?"

Norbert, his head clearing, sat back on his heels and read through the last of his tears, "Certainly not. But thank you. I was just having a rather . . . extraordinary experience."

The PS cleared him to stand, so he did, brushing himself off, and smiling his best enigmatic—#3 said, "Yes. . . that was quite extraordinary. Good day, gentleshoppers."

As he walked back toward the concrete he heard one exclaim, "I tell you, it's him!"

"Imagine that. Right out here!"

Howardi had left messages, as had the bureaucrat's office. The Jizmet sales people left messages, more and more urgent as the evening wore on. Norbert realized that the General System probably told them about the incident in the park. With the new switch going on sale in a few days, they might be panic-stricken. His PS urged him to return their calls.

He was right. They wanted to know "if he had experienced any difficulties" with the new switch.

"No," he told them. "But it's not for the timid."

They liked that. They quoted him in their ads.

For a few days afterward Norbert stayed home, cancelling all his dates and postponing his investment counselling sessions. His Jizmet supported very conservative financial software, and tended to veto all the schemes that were proposed. Besides, he didn't really need more money.

He wasn't sure what he did need. He did some shopping, but the salesreps annoyed him. He took in some games, but his teams didn't inspire him the way they once had. The flicks couldn't compete with his own sex life of recent weeks.

Norbert was lonely.

He considered several new hobbies, but he knew that they weren't the answer. He tried a couple of the banter-lines, but the interesting people on them were all computer generated; the rest were shoppers like himself, who didn't know what they were looking for. Finally, he decided to keep one of his dinner dates. Back to the sugar mines, he thought.

Artemia did not have her lenses set to "smoky," nor did she ask about the switch before the first course of paste was finished. She inquired about his interests and reading preferences, and seemed a bit unsure of herself when she discovered that he had none.

Norbert stuck strictly to the suggested comments, feeling utterly lost with this woman. He had dated the educated classes before, but they never seemed to stray much from their software—the conversations being carefully scripted until simple curiosity inevitably led to the same questions, the same responses, and bed.

Until now, Norbert had never quite understood how artificial those conversations had been.

He recklessly strayed from the script. "Excuse me, could we just talk about you for a while?"

She paused. "I suppose you want to know why I decided to ask for a date?"

"Not really. I'd just like to know what you really . . . what you're like." IF YOU DON'T MIND. "If you don't mind?"

Artemia reviewed her likes and dislikes, hobbies and interests, for the most part reciting the pre-date resume her System had provided to his. Growing bored, he asked for elaboration, and she responded with complicated details. The Jizmet barraged him with definitions and explanations in both earspeakers, while filling both lenses with charts and graphs. He had to be prompted to realize that she had stopped talking some time before and expected a reply.

"Pardon me?" he tried.

"I said . . . well, never mind." She frowned. "You're not really very well educated, are you? I didn't know quite what to expect, but you're not really much like your pop image, are you?"

A long silence fell between them, and Norbert considered the RUDENESS: OFF SCALE blinking in his left lens, and the series of pointed replies scrolling down his right.

He took a deep breath and shut off his PS. Her System must have informed her, because she immediately sat quite straight.

"No," he said. "No, I'm not very well educated. I'm not very smart, either. I just asked a very silly question while I was shopping one day, and all this . . ." He gestured vaguely, not even sure she was still there, beyond his foggy lenses. "All this . . . happened. I'm sorry." He switched back on.

She was still there. She slowly sat back in her chair, and her mouth dropped open. His prompt signalled STRONG EMOTIONAL RESPONSE. CONFUSED.

"You shut it off," she said. "You answered my question without a prompter."

He shrugged.

She leaned forward. "I don't think I've ever been given an unprompted answer to anything."

RESPECT INDICATED.

"Well, Shopper Kamdar," she said, smiling in a way he would always remember, "You might just have possibilities . . ."

EMOTIONAL COMPLICATIONS PENDING.

The switch proved quite a popular option for several years before fading into disfavour and oblivion, though not until the royalties made a fortune for the newlyweds. Norbert never used his again, except for brief moments—just long enough to whisper in Artemia's ear that he loved her. This often punctuated the lessons they took together in a most delightful, if not instructive, way.

Artemia never did buy a switch for her own System. And though their friends and acquaintances often sported the device, the question of actually trying it never seemed to come up in conversation. "Someday we ought to ask Jizmet how often they were used," she used to say—but it never seemed all that important.

STUDY AND DISCUSSION QUESTIONS

1   What is the social and political significance of the title "Shopper" used throughout "Norbert and the System"? Consider the emphasis on advertising and salesemanship. Can you think of examples of marketing that cross the line from influencing to coercing consumers? If so, have such marketers prevented consumers from exercising their free will?

2   Relatedly, consider the role of advertising in your life—on the internet, along the roadside, at home, etc. In an innovative scene in the film *Minority Report*, as John Anderson walks through a mall a host of cameras scan his retina without his permission, identify him and begin beaming him ads specific to his interests. Would you be comfortable with that?

3   What is a PS, exactly? What can we infer about a PS from the story? Does it affect the intellect? the will? the emotions? Is there any clear conceptual determination about where Norbert's own mental operations end and where those controlled by the PS begin?

4   The answer to the previous question may depend upon which PS one uses. When he used his 1200 series PS, Norbert was able to ask an unusual question to the salesperson simulation. So did he have free will while operating (or being operated by) the high-end PS, but not the low-end PS?

5   Turn this entire discussion around for a moment. It appears that the 1200 enables Norbert to more clearly and directly state his preferences. Mightn't his use of a 1200 series *enhance* his free will, rather than take it away?

6   How do we or should we determine whether Norbert has free will? Do we analyze whether it is possible for him to think any thought he wishes? Do

we analyze whether it is possible for Norbert to perform any action that he wishes to?

7   In contemplating Norbert's free will (if any), recall the role of the PS in preventing criminal actions. But the PS will even prevent its "clients" from fully forming criminal thoughts. How does this point focus the issue of free will? Are there similarities between the use of the PS in this story, and the use of the people who foretell murders in *Minority Report*?

8   What would it be like to be Norbert? To get a sense for this, try to imagine all the ways that the PS controls and manipulates his cognitive and sensory experience.

9   What occurs when Norbert tries, and finally succeeds in, shutting off his PS at home? In the park? At dinner with his date?

10 In questions 1 and 2, I suggest that advertising has a considerable influence over our thoughts and feelings, but the influence of anti-depressant medication on us bears closer similarity to the influence of a PS on us. How might Norbert's free will (if any) compare with the free will (if any) of someone who takes daily, large doses of a strong anti-depressant?

11 Is it important for one's happiness that one has free will? Suppose that Norbert's PS greatly restricts his free will. Would Norbert be happier without his PS than he would with his PS?

12 One implication of the conclusion is that love is not true unless it is produced through one's use of free will. Is this so? Isn't Norbert's brain chemistry and genetic makeup just another type of personal system, albeit an organic one?

13 Suppose you were in charge of setting the parameters of the intervention protocols in PS units. What would you program the PS to prohibit the client from doing? Murdering someone? Committing suicide? Larceny? Stealing? Littering? Lying?

7.12 "ON BEHALF OF DETERMINISM," BY THOMAS HOBBES

Liberty and necessity (excerpt)

1. . . . . Thirdly, I conceive that in all deliberations, that is to say, in all alternate succession of contrary appetites, the last is that which we call the will and is immediately next before the doing of the action, or next before the doing of it become impossible. All other appetites to do, and to quit, that come upon a man during his deliberations, are called intentions and inclinations, but not wills, there being but one will, which also in this case may be called the last will, though the intentions change often.

2. Fourthly, I conceive that those actions, which a man is said to do upon deliberation, are said to be voluntary, and done upon choice and election, so that voluntary action, and action proceeding from election is the same thing; and that of a voluntary agent, it is all one to say, he is free, and to say, he hath not made an end of deliberating.

3. Fifthly, I conceive liberty to be rightly defined in this manner: Liberty is the absence of all the impediments to action that are not contained in the nature and intrinsical quality of the agent. As for example, the water is said to descend freely, or to have liberty to descend by the channel of the river, because there is no impediment that way, but not across, because the banks are impediments. And though the water cannot ascend, yet men never say it wants the liberty to ascend, but the faculty or power, because the impediment is in the nature of the water, and intrinsical. So also we say, he that is tied, [lacks] the liberty to go, because the impediment is not in him, but in his bands; whereas we say not so of him that is sick or lame, because the impediment is in himself. . . .

4. Sixthly, I conceive that nothing [takes its] beginning from itself, but from the action of some other immediate agent without itself. And that therefore, when first a man has an appetite or will to something, to which immediately before he had no appetite nor will, the cause of his will, is not the will itself, but something else not in his own disposing. [It is uncontroversial to say that] the will is the necessary cause [of voluntary actions], and by this which is said, the will is also caused by other things whereof it disposes not, it follows, that voluntary actions have all of them necessary causes, and therefore are necessitated.

5. Seventhly, I hold that to be a sufficient cause, to which nothing is [lacking] that is needed to produce the effect. The same also is a necessary cause. For if it be possible that a sufficient cause shall not bring forth the effect, then there [was lacking] something which was needed to the producing of it, and so the cause was not sufficient. But if it be impossible that a sufficient cause should not produce the effect, then is a sufficient cause a necessary cause, for that is said to produce an effect necessarily that cannot but produce it. Hence it is manifest, that whatsoever is produced, is produced necessarily; for whatsoever is produced has had a sufficient cause to produce it, or else it had not been; and therefore also voluntary actions are necessitated.

6. Lastly, that ordinary definition of a free agent, namely, that a free agent is that, which, when all things are present which are needful to produce the effect, can nevertheless not produce it, implies a contradiction, and is nonsense; being as much as to say, the cause may be sufficient, that is to say, necessary, and yet the effect shall not follow. . . .

7. For the seventh point, which is, that all events have necessary causes, it is there proved, in that they have sufficient causes. Further let us in this place also suppose any event never so casual, as the throwing, for example . . . a pair of dice, and see, if it must not have been necessary before it was thrown. For seeing it was thrown, it had a beginning, and consequently a sufficient cause to produce it, consisting partly in the dice, partly in outward things, as the posture of the parts of the hand, the measure of force applied by the caster, the posture of the parts of the table, and the like. In sum, there was nothing [lacking] which was necessarily requisite to the producing of that particular cast, and

consequently the cast was necessarily thrown; for if it had not been thrown, there [must have been something required for] the throwing of it, and so the cause had not been sufficient. In the like manner it may be proved that every other accident, how contingent soever it seem, or how voluntary soever it be, is produced necessarily. . . .

8. The last thing, in which also consists the whole controversy, namely that there is no such thing as an agent, which when all things required for an action are present, can nevertheless [refrain from] producing it; or, which is all one, that there is no such thing as freedom from necessity, is easily inferred from that which has been before alleged. For if it be an agent, it can work; and if it work, there is nothing [lacking that] is required to produce the action, and consequently the cause of the action is sufficient; and if sufficient, then also necessary, as hath been proved before.

Leviathan (excerpt)

9. LIBERTY or FREEDOM signifies . . . the absence of opposition; by opposition, I mean external impediments of motion; and [the term "liberty"] may be applied no less to irrational, and inanimate creatures, than to rational. For whatever is so tied, or environed, as it cannot move but within a certain space, which space is determined by the opposition of some external body, we say it has no liberty to go further. And so of all living creatures, while they are imprisoned or restrained with walls, or chains; and of the water whilst it is kept in by banks. . . . But when the impediment of motion is the constitution of the thing itself, we [do not] say, it [lacks] liberty; but [we say it lacks] the power to move; as when a stone lieth still, or a man is fastened to his bed by sickness.

10. And according to this proper, and generally received meaning of the word, a FREEMAN is he, that in those things, which by his strength and wit he is able to do, is not hindered to do what he has a will to. But when the words free and liberty are applied to anything but bodies, they are abused; for that which is not subject to motion, is not subject to impediment. And [when we say] the way is free, no liberty of the way is signified, but of those that walk in it without stop. . . . So when we speak freely, it is not the liberty of voice, or pronunciation, but of the man, whom no law has obliged to speak otherwise than he did. Lastly, from the use of the word free-will, no liberty can be inferred of the will, desire, or inclination, but the liberty of the man, which consists in this, that he finds no stop, in doing what he has the will, desire, or inclination to do.

11. Fear and liberty are consistent; as when a man throws his goods into the sea for fear the ship should sink, he does it . . . very willingly, and may refuse to do it if he will: it is therefore the action of one that was free: so a man sometimes pays his debt, only for fear of imprisonment, which because no body hindered him from [doing so], was the action of a man at liberty. And generally all actions which men do in commonwealths, for fear of the law, are actions, which the doers had liberty to omit.

12. Liberty and Necessity are consistent: as in the water, that has not only liberty but a necessity of descending by the channel; so likewise in the actions which men voluntarily do: which, because they proceed from their will, proceed from liberty, and yet, because

every act of man's will, and every desire, and inclination proceed from some cause, and that from another cause, in a continual chain, whose first link is in the hand of God the first of all causes, proceed from necessity. So that to him that could see the connection of those causes, the necessity of all men's voluntary actions, would appear manifest. And therefore God, that sees and disposes all things, sees also that the liberty of man in doing what he will, is accompanied with the necessity of doing that which God will, and no more, nor less. For though men may do many things, which God does not command, nor is therefore author of them; yet they can have no passion, nor appetite to anything, of which appetite God's will is not the cause. And [if God's will did not] assure the necessity of man's will, and consequently of all that on man's will dependeth, [then] the liberty of men would be a contradiction, and an impediment to the omnipotence and liberty of God. And this shall suffice, as to the matter in hand, of that natural liberty, which only is properly called liberty.

STUDY AND DISCUSSION QUESTIONS

1   Hobbes begins with some definitions in the first three paragraphs. How does he define "will," "voluntary," and "liberty"?

2   In his definition of "liberty," Hobbes argues for a distinction between two types of impediments. What are these? How are they used?

3   In paragraph 4, Hobbes mounts an argument to the effect that the activity of the will is caused by factors outside the will itself and, as a consequence, all voluntary actions are necessitated by events outside the will. Is his argument persuasive? Discuss.

4   What is the difference between a necessary cause and a sufficient cause, for Hobbes?

5   Hobbes concludes in paragraph 6 that the idea of a free agent is contradictory. What is his argument for this conclusion?

6   In paragraph 9, Hobbes offers a definition of "freedom" that applies to humans, animals and inanimate creatures. What is this definition? How does it apply so widely?

7   What is God's role in the freedom or the determination of human actions?

8   Is Hobbes a compatibilist or a determinist? Does he accept the principle of alternative possibilities?

7.13 "FREE WILL: ALTERNATIVES AND SOURCES," BY KEVIN TIMPE

I. Introduction

This is an article on free will. By free will, I simply mean the kind of control an agent needs to have over her actions (choices, decisions, etc. . . .) in order for her to be morally responsible for those actions (choices, decisions, etc. . . .). In what follows, for purposes of simplicity I'm going to focus on free choices, though I intend a similar analysis to apply to the other kinds of actions that agents might be morally responsible for. It should also be noted that, as defined here, free will is only a necessary condition for moral responsibility, not a sufficient condition. An agent could freely make a choice and still fail to be morally responsible for that choice if some other requirement for moral responsibility—such as the epistemic condition—is not met.

The contemporary free will literature is voluminous and intricate; nevertheless, one finds two dominant general approaches to the nature of free will. According to the first of these, which has received the majority of the attention, free will is primarily a function of being able to do otherwise than one does. For example, Norbert freely chooses to date Artemia when he could have chosen to date Vodkette instead, or even chosen to not go on a date at all. According to the second approach, free will is primarily a function of an agent being the ultimate source of his actions. On this approach, Norbert freely chooses to date Artemia if nothing outside of him is the ultimate source of his choice. Both of these notions can be seen in the following passage:

> We believe we have free will when we view ourselves as agents capable of influencing the world in various ways. Open alternatives, or alternative possibilities, seem to lie before us. We reason and deliberate among them and choose. We feel (1) it is "up to us" what we choose and how we act; and this means we could have chosen or acted otherwise. As Aristotle noted: when acting is "up to us," so is not acting. This "up-to-us-ness" also suggests (2) the ultimate control of our actions lie in us and not outside us in factors beyond our control.
>
> (Kane, 2005: p. 6)

The first understanding involves an "alternative possibilities condition" at its core, while the second understanding instead involves a "sourcehood condition." In what follows, I first demarcate these two different approaches to free will. I then explore these two approaches to see how they are related.

II. The alternative possibilities condition (AP)

Consider the following argument for the incompatibility of free will and determinism, which I will call the "Basic Argument":

(1) Free will requires the ability to do otherwise.
(2) If causal determinism is true, then no agent has the ability to do otherwise.
(3) Therefore, free will requires the falsity of causal determinism.

Since it concludes that compatibilism is false, compatibilists will reject the argument. Insofar as it is valid, the only way to do this is to deny the truth of one or both of its premises.

There was a time in recent philosophical discussions of free will that the majority of incompatibilists and compatibilists alike accepted premise (1). If (1) is true, then in order for an agent to be free, she must be able to do otherwise; that is, she must have alternative possibilities. Premise (1) is often called the "Principle of Alternative Possibilities," or simply PAP. In an important article, Harry Frankfurt defined PAP as follows:

> PAP: a person is morally responsible for what he has done only if he could have done otherwise (Frankfurt, 1988b: p. 1).

Frankfurt expresses PAP in terms of what is required for moral responsibility. But since my interest here is primarily free will, rather than moral responsibility, I want to consider the following analogue principle, called "AP" for alternative possibilities condition:

> AP: a person chooses freely only if he could have chosen otherwise—that is, if he has alternative possibilities regarding his choice.

As Robert Kane notes, "the two principles (PAP and AP) would be equivalent, if the moral responsibility at issue (in PAP) were precisely the kind that free will (in AP) is supposed to confer; and this assumption has been commonly made in free will debates" (Kane, 2002: p. 17). Given the way I defined free will above, AP and PAP will stand and fall together.

As mentioned above, there was a time when the alternative possibilities condition was accepted by virtually all participants. This fact also helps explain why some simply understand free will as primarily a function of satisfying the alternative possibilities condition.

(a) Incompatibilist understandings of AP

It is quite intuitive to see how the incompatibilist understands AP. Incompatibilism, at its core, is simply the thesis that the existence of free will is incompatible with the truth of causal determinism. If causal determinism is false, then there will be at least two possible futures that are consistent with the past and the laws of nature. This means the future is open in a way that the past is not. Thus, when an agent like Norbert is using his free will, what he is doing is selecting from a range of different available options for the future. For this reason, this view of free will is often called the "Garden of Forking Paths Model," and the incompatibilist's understanding of AP involves our choosing from among these multiple paths into the future. It shouldn't be surprising then that the majority of incompatibilists think that some version of AP must be true in order for incompatibilism to be true. In fact, many incompatibilists think that AP and incompatibilism go hand in hand.

(b) Compatibilist understandings of AP

But there are also compatibilists who accept AP. These compatibilists, called "strong compatibilists," think that free will requires alternative possibilities; but they do not think that the truth of determinism would rule out alternative possibilities, and thus reject premise (2) of the Basic Argument. There are a number of different ways that strong compatibilism can be developed. Let me briefly indicate three of them.

Since the truth of determinism means there is only one future compossible with the conjunction of the past and the laws of nature, some strong compatibilists think that in order to be free, agents must have alternative possibilities regarding the conjunction of the past and the laws of nature. Peter Forrest, for example, argues that we have the ability to do otherwise even if determinism is true because we have the ability to causally affect the past:

> When a person acts he or she affects the *whole causal chain*, stretching back into the past, as well as forwards into the future. . . . And, to the extent that the person's reasons for acting *explain* the act, they explain why there is *that* causal chain . . . rather than *some other* causal chain—the one which would have occurred if the person had acted otherwise. My proposal, then, is that in acting . . . I affect the past.
>
> (Forrest, 1985: p. 212f.)

Such versions of strong compatibilism, however, face considerable obstacles in terms of their plausibility, and for this reason few strong compatibilists defend such a view.

In an influential paper, David Lewis argues that agents have the ability to do otherwise even if determinism is true because they have the ability to act contrary to the laws of nature. According to Lewis, "sometimes one freely does what one is [causally] predetermined to do; and that in such a case one is able to act otherwise though past history and the laws of nature determine that one will not act otherwise" (Lewis, 1987: p. 291).

Slightly modifying Lewis' own example, imagine a deterministic world in which Norbert fails to raise his hand at time t_3. Since we are assuming that determinism is true, Norbert's action at t_3 is the result of the conjunction of the past, say at t_1, and the laws of nature. Let us call the proposition expressing the conjunction of all the individual laws of nature "L." According to Lewis, if Norbert is free in not raising his hand at t_3, then since free will requires the ability to do otherwise, he could have raised his hand at t_3. But given that the past at t_1 and L together entail that he not raise his hand at t_3, if Norbert were to raise his hand at t_3, then one of the following would be true:

(i)   contradictions could be true;
(ii)   the past would not have been as it actually was at t_1; or
(iii) L would not have been true.

Lewis dismisses the first two options and embraces the third. Thus, he is "committed to that consequence that if [Norbert] had done what he was able to do—raise his hand—then some law would have been broken" (ibid.: p. 292). As counterintuitive as it may seem, Lewis thinks this is true. He distinguishes two different claims. The weaker claim is that, in virtue of being free, Norbert is able to do something such that, if he were to do it, a law of nature would have been broken. The stronger claim is that Norbert is actually able to break a law of nature. According to Lewis, compatibilism requires only that the weaker claim is true, not the stronger admittedly "utterly incredible" claim (ibid.). Lewis defends the truth of the weaker claim by appealing to "a divergence miracle." If Norbert were to raise his hand at t_3, then some part of L that is a law of nature would have been broken earlier, say at t_2. But, Lewis thinks, this miracle would not have been caused by Norbert raising his hand. Thus, Lewis thinks that agents have the ability to do otherwise despite the truth of determinism in the sense that were they to do otherwise, then a miracle would have taken place.

Not all versions of strong compatibilism are developed in either of these two directions. The most common form of strong compatibilism, which Peter van Inwagen has labeled "conditionalism," makes no mention of miracles or power over the past whatsoever (van Inwagen, 1983: p. 114). Proponents of conditionalism are strong compatibilists who reject premise (2) of the Basic Argument by giving subjunctive or conditional accounts of the ability to do otherwise. According to such accounts, the proposition "an agent could have done other than A" is to be understood along the lines of "the agent would have done other than A if some condition C had been fulfilled." One way of specifying condition C is with "had the agent willed or chosen to do so." For example, G. E. Moore wrote that "there are certainly good reasons for thinking that we *very often* mean by 'could' merely 'would, *if* so and so had chosen.' And if so, then we have a sense of the word 'could' in which the fact that we often *could* have done what we did not do, is perfectly compatible with the principle that everything has a cause" (Moore, 1912: p. 131). Similarly, A. J. Ayer expressed conditionalism—as well as a commitment to AP— in his influential article, "Freedom and Necessity":

> When I am said to have done something of my own free will it is implied that I could have acted otherwise; and it is only when it is believed that I could have acted otherwise that I am held to be morally responsible for what I have done. For a man is not thought to be morally responsible for an action that it was not in his power to avoid. But if human behaviour is entirely governed by causal laws, it is not clear how any action that is done could ever have been avoided. It may be said of the agent that he would have acted otherwise if the causes of his action had been different.
>
> (Ayer, 1997: p. 110)

If the ability do otherwise is to be understood as Moore, Ayer or other proponents of conditionalism understand it, the truth of the relevant conditional is compatible with the truth of determinism.

However, such subjunctive accounts of the ability to do otherwise are thought by many to be problematic since the conditional analysis says that an agent could have done otherwise in cases where it is clear that the agent wasn't free. The conditional attributing to an agent the ability to do otherwise (such as "Norbert could have done otherwise than A if C") could be true even when there is nothing the agent could do to satisfy the antecedent of the conditional. But if there is no way that the agent could satisfy the antecedent of the conditional, then the agent couldn't in fact do what the conditional says the agent could do.

> It [the conditional analysis] seems clearly to fail. For one thing, the analysis misses the target distinction almost entirely. Compulsives, addicts, people operating under duress—virtually everyone whose freedom to will differently we ordinarily view as compromised—would count by this criterion as free. Surely, if determinism is true, they would have willed differently had their strongest motives been different. Yet these are the people whose responsibility for decisions we would question, precisely *because* we think their strongest motive was too influential.
>
> (McCann, 1998: p. 177)

It is for this reason that many philosophers think that the conditionalist version of strong compatibilism should be rejected.

(c) Frankfurt's critique of AP and the move towards ultimacy

Debates about free will changed dramatically when Harry Frankfurt published an article calling into question the truth of AP—regardless of one's preferred version. Frankfurt's aim in this trenchant article is devilishly simple: to describe an agent who is morally responsible (or, in our case, free) despite lacking the ability to do otherwise, thereby showing AP false and rendering the Basic Argument unsound. Here is Frankfurt's example:

> Suppose someone—Black, let us say—wants Jones to perform a certain action [i.e. action A]. Black is prepared to go to considerable lengths to get his way, but he prefers to avoid showing his hand unnecessarily. So he waits until Jones is about to make up his mind what to do, and he does nothing unless it is clear to him (Black is an excellent judge of such things) that Jones is going to decide to do something *other* than what he wants him to do [i.e. other than A]. If it does become clear that Jones is going to decide to do something else, Black takes effective steps to ensure that Jones decides to do, and that he does do, what he wants him to do. Whatever Jones' initial preferences and inclinations, then, Black will have his way. . . . Now suppose that Black never has to show his hand because Jones, for reasons of his own, decides to perform and does perform the very action that Black wants him to perform. In that case, it seems clear, Jones will bear precisely the same moral responsibility for what he does as he would have borne if Black had not been ready to take steps to ensure that he do it.
>
> (Frankfurt, 1988b: p. 6f.)

Subsequently, countless similar scenarios, many of increasing complexity, have been put forth in the literature. Let us call such scenarios Frankfurt-style counterexamples, or FSCs. FSCs purport to show that moral responsibility and free will are compatible with the lack of the ability to do otherwise. There is considerable debate about whether FSCs do, in fact, show AP to be false, with incompatibilists giving a number of arguments against their success. But rather than revisiting these arguments here, I want to say why I think FSCs have shown us something important about the nature of free will, even if they are ultimately unsuccessful in demonstrating AP to be false.

Instead of understanding free will to be a function of an agent's having alternative possibilities, Frankfurt advances a hierarchical account of freedom of the will. As mentioned in an earlier chapter in this volume, Frankfurt thinks that a person has free will (or what Frankfurt calls "freedom of the will") if he has second-order volitions—that is, if he has a desire that certain other of his desires actually move him to action. "A wants the desire to X to be the desire that moves him effectively to act. It is not merely that he wants the desire to X to be among his desires by which, to one degree or another, he is moved or inclined to act. He wants this desire to be effective—that is, to provide the motive in what he actually does" (Frankfurt, 1988b: p. 15). On this view, Norbert freely decides to go for a walk in the park if he desires to go for a walk and he desires for his desire to go for a walk to be the reason that he actually does go for a walk. So, on Frankfurt's account, having free will is primarily a function not of having alternative possibilities, but of one's choices having their source in the agent in a particular way— namely if the source of that volition is a second-order desire.

III. The sourcehood condition (SC)

Frankfurt's criticism of AP and his own understanding of the nature of free will suggest the second approach to the nature of free will introduced above. On this approach, free will is primarily a function of an agent being the source or originator of her choices in a particular way. This way of understanding free will gives a strong reason for thinking that Jones, the agent in an FSC, is choosing freely when he chooses to X on his own, but not when Black coerces Jones to choose X. In the former case, Jones is the source of his own choice, while in the latter case Black is the source of Jones' choice and thus Jones isn't choosing freely.

This, I think, gives an intuitive initial notion of the sourcehood condition that we might express as follows:

SC: a person chooses freely only if he is the ultimate source or originator of his choice.

But just as both incompatibilists and compatibilists have their own readings of AP, they also have their own understandings of SC. This leads to the need for further investigation regarding exactly what it means to be the "ultimate source" of one's choices. In the next section, I present and criticize two influential compatibilist accounts of sourcehood. The objections leveled against these two accounts will point us in the final section toward an incompatibilist understanding of sourcehood, one that I think is at the very heart of free will.

(a) Compatibilist readings of SC

One compatibilist understanding of SC can be found in Frankfurt's account of freedom of the will. As seen above, Frankfurt thinks that "the enjoyment of a free will means the satisfaction of certain desires—desires of the second or higher orders" (Frankfurt, 1988b: p. 22). More fully, an agent has free will so long as his behavior is explained by his second-order volitions; that is, so long as he identifies with a first-order desire, wants that desire to move him to action, and is moved to action because of that desire. Thus, for Frankfurt, just as freedom of action is being able to do what one wants to do, freedom of will is being able to have the kind of will that one wants to have. It is for this reason that Frankfurt's account is often called a "structural" or "hierarchical" account, since he understands freedom of the will to be primarily a function of having a certain kind of structural or hierarchical mesh between one's first- and second-order desires and volitions. And since having the will one wants to have is independent of whether one could have had a different will, Frankfurt's account clearly isn't based on an alternative possibilities condition such as AP.

A natural way of understanding Frankfurt's view at this point is as involving a certain kind of sourcehood condition, which might be put as follows: a person wills freely only if he wills as he does because of a higher-order desire. But given the importance of the second-order desire in adjudicating which of a set of conflicting first-order desires becomes the agent's volition, it is natural to ask what adjudicates among conflicting second-order desires. For instance, what if Norbert is torn regarding his second-order desires, as when he wants both his desire to date Artemia and his conflicting desire to date only Vodkette instead to become his will? If the solution to this conflict is to be found in a third-order desire, then we are off on apparent infinite regress. To prevent this kind of regress, Frankfurt utilizes a notion of "wholeheartedness." Robert Kane nicely captures Frankfurt's view as follows:

> Persons are "wholehearted" when there are no conflicts in their wills and they are not ambivalent about what they want to do. Ambivalent persons, by contrast, are of two (or more) minds about what they want to do and cannot make up their minds. Reflection on our desires stops, says Frankfurt, when we reach desires to which we are wholeheartedly committed and to which we have no ambivalence. It is not arbitrary, he insists, to identify with such wholehearted desires because they are the desires with which we are "fully satisfied" and we have no "active interest" in bringing about a change in them.
>
> (Kane, 2005: p. 96f.)

We might thus understand Frankfurt's view as involving the following sort of condition:

Frankfurt's condition: a person chooses freely only if he chooses as he does because of a higher-order desire that he wholeheartedly identifies with—that is, if the desire that becomes his volition has its source in a more fundamental desire with which the agent unwaveringly aligns himself.

From this condition, we see that Frankfurt grounds free will in the agent's choice originating in his volitional structure in the right way. Not only is free will internal to the agent's volitional structure, but it more specifically involves the source of the agent's first-order volition being located in those second-order desires with which he identifies.

Nevertheless, there is reason to think that wholehearted identification is insufficient to ground free will. Consider the following example involving Norbert, and his new Personal System, the 15B Jizmet. Suppose that after having the new PS installed, Norbert finds himself with the desire to sabotage the General System. This desire, however, is implanted in him from his PS. Furthermore, his PS also causes him to have the second-order desire to have his first-order desire for sabotage to become his will. And in case Norbert has any conflicting first-order desire not to engage in sabotage, his new PS also causes him to wholeheartedly identify with those desires caused by his PS. In other words, Norbert's PS manipulates him into identifying with a particular second-order desire. In such an instance, even though Norbert's desire for sabotage meshes with his volitional structure, it does not ultimately originate in that volitional structure since the mesh is the result of external manipulation by the PS. According to Frankfurt's account, Norbert would enjoy free will despite all of the relevant desires being caused by his PS rather than himself:

> The only thing that really counts is what condition I am in. How I got into that condition is another matter. If I'm in the condition where I'm doing what I want to do and I really want to do it, i.e. I decisively identify with my action, then I think I'm responsible for it. It makes no difference how it came about that that is the case. . . . If the person is wholehearted in the action, let us say performs the action because he wants to perform it and the desire to perform it is a desire that he really wants to have and there's no reservation, there no imposition, no passivity: the person is completely, fully, wholeheartedly identified with what's going on. What more could there be? What more could you want? That's all the freedom that's possible for human beings to have, in my opinion. . . . What accounts for the fact that he's completely whole-hearted is no longer relevant. The only important consideration is that he is doing exactly what he wants to do.
>
> (Frankfurt, 1988a: pp. 32ff.)

But surely the kind of manipulation being described here would undermine, rather than give rise to, free will. While Frankfurt is willing to bite the bullet here, I think the size of this particular bullet gives us sufficient reason to look elsewhere for a satisfactory account of sourcehood.

A second influential compatibilist account of free will based on the idea that free will is primarily a matter of sourcehood can be found in the work of John Martin Fischer, as well as in a book he co-authored with Mark Ravizza. Fischer calls his view "semi-compatibilism"; by this he means that the truth of causal determinism is *compatible* with moral responsibility even if causal determinism ends up being *incompatible* with a certain kind of freedom. Fischer differentiates between two kinds of control: guidance control and regulative control. Regulative control involves having control over which of a number of genuinely open possibilities becomes actual; we can thus think of regulative control as fundamentally linked with AP, discussed above. Fischer thinks that this kind of control is *not* required for free will. But there is another kind of control that he thinks *is* required, namely guidance control. Fischer's discussion of guidance control is extensive, but we can focus here on the two central aspects that he thinks are needed for guidance control: a free choice must issue from one's own mechanism, and this mechanism must be appropriately responsive to the agent's reasons. The responsiveness that Fischer takes to be required here requires that the agent "act on a mechanism that is regularly receptive to reasons, some of which are moral reasons" (Fischer and Ravizza, 1998: pp. 82). This means that the volitional structure that results in the agent's choices manifests an understandable pattern of recognizing moral reasons for choosing in various ways. Such an agent "recognizes how reasons fit together, sees why one reason is stronger than another, and understands how the acceptance of one reason as sufficient implies that a stronger reason must also be sufficient" (ibid.: p. 71). Furthermore, Fischer thinks that the agent's volitional structure must also be reactive to those reasons in the right kind of way. Norbert meets this condition: if had he recognized a reason to sabotage the General System that is stronger than his reason not to, then he would have chosen on the basis of this other reason.

The second requirement for guidance control is that the agent takes responsibility for the reasons-responsive mechanism that results in his choices; that is, that the mechanism is *his own*. This feature of Fischer's view marks an important difference between his understanding and Frankfurt's view. Recall that on Frankfurt's view, all that is needed is the right sort of hierarchical mesh among an agent's desires; it was this feature of Frankfurt's account that led to that objection that his account couldn't properly account for why certain sorts of manipulation undermine control. Fischer's ownership requirement allows his view to avoid this particular problem. For Fischer, "the *mere existence* of a mesh is *not* sufficient for moral responsibility; the *history* behind the mesh is also relevant" (ibid.: p. 196). In addition to having the right kind of mesh within his volitional structure, the agent must also have taken responsibility for that structure in such a way as to see himself as the source of the choices that result from his mechanism, believe that he is responsible for how he chooses on the basis of that mechanism in appropriate circumstances, and believe this on the basis of appropriate evidence. Putting these elements together, we can understand Fischer's view as follows:

> *Fischer's condition*: a person chooses freely only (i) if he chooses as he does because of an appropriately reasons-responsive mechanism, and (ii) he sees that mechanism as his own.

We might think of these two aspects as respectively insisting on the agent having the right kind of mesh and the right history behind that mesh.

In the case above involving Norbert's choosing to sabotage the General System on the basis of desires implanted by his PS, he would fail to meet the second condition of Fischer's view. But it looks as if Fischer's view is subject to a parallel worry involving manipulation. Suppose that prior to the time at which Norbert is deliberating about whether or not to engage in the act of sabotage, his PS causes him to have a certain reasons-responsive mechanism of the sort that Fischer thinks is required for guidance control—that is, it induces in him a volitional structure that is different from the one that he had prior to the installation of the 15B Jizmet. In addition, Norbert's new PS also causes him to take ownership of this new mechanism. Because of the inputs from his new PS, Norbert sees himself as the source of the choices that result from this newly implanted volitional structure, believes that he is responsible for how he chooses on the basis of this new structure in appropriate circumstances, and believes this on the basis of the evidence that he has. It appears that in such a case, Norbert would meet all of Fischer's requirements for guidance control despite the fact that his meeting all these requirements is the result of his PS's manipulation. But there is good reason to think that Norbert would not have the kind of control over his choices required for moral responsibility in this case, since all of the relevant factors are the product of his PS, rather than Norbert himself.

(b) Incompatibilist readings of SC

Though I think the compatibilist renderings of the sourcehood requirement offered by Frankfurt and Fischer fail, I think that they are quite helpful in pointing us in the right direction for a more acceptable understanding of free will as consisting in being the appropriate source of one's choices. Both Frankfurt's and Fischer's view fail because they allow for the possibility that the agent's being the source of his choices in the way required for free will is determined by something outside of the agent himself. While both think that Norbert must be the source of his choices in order to be free, on neither of their views must Norbert be the ultimate source of those choices given the role that his PS could play. Norbert's choices might have their source in some feature of Norbert, but the source for why that feature is that way is in turn outside of Norbert. What is needed then is a way of understanding why these accounts of sourcehood are insufficient.

(i) TRUTHMAKING AND SC

A piece of metaphysical machinery that will be helpful at this stage is what is known as the truthmaking principle. At its core, the truthmaking principle holds that truth depends on reality; that is, that true propositions are true because there is something in the world that makes them true. This is their truthmaker. Truthmaker theory holds that a truthmaker "makes true" a true proposition, or "grounds" it; one could also say that a true proposition "owes" its truth-value to the truthmaker. Truthmaking has recently received much attention in metaphysics. While there is a significant amount of disagreement regarding how truthmaking theory should account for negative existential truths (such as "there are no unicorns") and necessary truths (such as "a thing is colored if red"), we can set aside these issues for present purposes since the propositions that concern us at present are contingent propositions regarding free human actions.

Turning then to the relationship between truthmaking and free choices, an agent's free choice will be the truthmaker for the true proposition describing that choice. Consider a free choice, C. Focusing on a particular action, Norbert's choice to date Artemia on Thursday serves as the truthmaker for the proposition *Norbert chooses to date Artemia on Thursday*. So we might understand an initial formulation of the sourcehood requirement as follows:

> ISR: A person A is the ultimate source or originator of some choice C only if A is the truthmaker for the proposition A *chooses* C.

(II) WHY SC REQUIRES THE FALSITY OF CAUSAL DETERMINISM

However, this way of understanding the ultimacy in SC is insufficient to avoid the problems mentioned above plaguing Frankfurt and Fischer's accounts. To see why, let us first consider Frankfurt's view. For Frankfurt, an agent such as Norbert could wholeheartedly identify with his volitional structure even if both that volitional structure and the identification were caused by something outside of him, such as his PS. Nevertheless, in this case Norbert would satisfy ISR since he and his volitional structure are the truthmaker for the relevant proposition. After all, Norbert chooses as he does *precisely* because his Personal System instills the relevant volitional hierarchy in him, but Frankfurt doesn't think that the history for *why* agents have their volitional structure matters. Similarly, on Fischer's view, Norbert could also satisfy ISR even if his PS determines him to have the requisite reasons-responsive mechanism. Fischer does insist on a historical dimension in that the agent must also have taken ownership of that mechanism; but we also saw how something outside of the agent could determine the agent to engage in such identification. In addition to causing Norbert to have the needed reasons-responsive mechanism, his PS could have previously determined him to take responsibility for said mechanism in the way that Fischer thinks is required for guidance control. ISR must therefore be modified to eliminate the satisfaction of the sourcehood condition in these ways.

The most plausible way to do this would be to add a excluding clause to ISR that would prohibit an agent from satisfying the requirement if his satisfying ISR is determined by something outside of himself. The revised sourcehood requirement could be understood as follows:

> RSR: A person A is the ultimate source or originator of some choice C only if
>
> (a)   A is the truthmaker for the proposition A *chooses* C, and
>
> (b)   there is no X such that both
>
> (b.1)   X is external to A and
>
> (b.2)   X is able to determine that A is the truthmaker for the proposition A *chooses* C.

When RSR is coupled with SC, these conditions prevent an agent from choosing freely when that agent is caused to choose as he does by something external to himself such as a Personal System or a Frankfurt-style controller (though b.1 does allow an agent to choose freely if he is determined to choose as he does by a moral character that he has previously freely chosen). Condition b.2 allows for the obvious truth that things external to agents influence their choices; it just insists that such external factors cannot determine that the agent choose as he does.

Granted, RSR is just a preliminary sketch of how the sourcehood condition should be spelled out; there is need for further refinement to unpack the various elements (for further details on these issues, see Timpe (2008)). Despite this need, I think that RSR gives a very plausible way of understanding the kind of ultimate control over one's choices that is needed for free will. Note also that RSR entails that free will and the truth of causal determinism are incompatible. For if causal determinism is true, then the conjunction of the past and the laws of nature jointly entail all the choices that an agent will make. The conjunction of the past and the laws of nature thus satisfy b.2. And since both the past and the laws of nature are external to the agent, b.1 would also be satisfied. Since b requires that both b.1 and b.2 cannot be satisfied if the agent is to have free will, the truth of causal determinism would rule out agents being the kind of ultimate source of their actions that is essential to free will. Free will, understood as the kind of control over one's choices needed for an agent to be morally responsible for those choices, is thus incompatible with the truth of causal determinism.[6]

STUDY AND DISCUSSION QUESTIONS

1   Contrast the difference between the two fundamental understandings of free will. How might the two be related?

2   How do incompatibilists who embrace the principle of alternative possibilities account for an agent's ability to do otherwise?

3   What are the various ways that compatibilists understand the ability to do otherwise?

4   What are the central problems facing Frankfurt's and Fischer's compatibilist understandings of the sourcehood condition for free will?

5   In your own words, explain what RSR claims is required for free will.

7.14 BIBLIOGRAPHY AND RECOMMENDED READING

Science fiction

Aldiss, Brian W. *Man in His Time: The Best Science Fiction Stories of Brian W. Aldiss*. Atheneum, 1989. Aldiss offers a fascinating "test" of the deterministic hypothesis in "Man in His Time," in which an astronaut, as a result of an accident in space, responds now to events occurring three minutes in our own future.

Anderson, Poul. *Genesis*. New York: Tor, 2000. This John W. Campbell award-winning novel tracks the attempts of two post-human personalities to understand why the artificial intelligence governing Earth is not taking steps to prevent the sun from dying. Anderson explores issues in both the philosophy of mind and free will in this book because his characters need to return to human form to deal with the problem and subvert the deception of the AI mind governing Earth. The novella appeared in *Far Futures*, Gregory Benford, ed. Tor, 1995.

*Asimov, Isaac. *Foundation Trilogy*. Doubleday, 1963. Asimov's Hugo-winning *Foundation Trilogy* employs the idea of psychohistory, discovered by a scientist, Han Seldon, which has extremely high predictive power. It predicts the fall and eventual reappearance of galactic civilization. Nevertheless, the predictions are evidently not infallible, and paradoxes involving the indeterminacy of social forecasting are touched upon by Asimov.

Ballard, J. G. "Subliminal Man." *The Best Short Stories of J. G. Ballard*. Picador, 2001. At one time the use of psychological techniques in advertising caused considerable anxiety. This is expressed in J. G. Ballard's "Subliminal Man," in which people compulsively buy products as a result of subliminal influences.

*Bear, Greg. *Queen of Angels*. New York: Warner, 1990. If you are aware of having committed a crime, does that imply that you are morally responsible for it? A mind-reading psychologist and a hard-nosed detective face that question when they track down Emanuel Goldsmith, charging him with mass murder. This is a novel about crime, punishment, free will and responsibility. Awareness could signal guilt, but if we're not aware of what we're doing when we do it, can we be punished for it?

Brunner, John. *The Shockwave Rider*. Harper, 1975. This is a cautionary—perhaps alarmist—novel about the effects of technological development and sophistication upon human free will.

Budrys, Algis. *The Falling Torch*. Pyramid, 1974. Budrys uses a naturalistic style to show how a revolutionary hero's actions were completely determined by historical forces outside his control. The idea that we are all puppets on strings which are pulled by subconscious forces within us has been argued by philosophers influenced by Freud's psychoanalytic theory.

Cherryh, C. J. *Cyteen*. New York: Aspect, 1995. The leaders of planet Cyteen not only manufacture Azi, artificial human beings, but they also clone human beings. The action surrounds the consequences of the cloning of the planet's genetic labs. Many questions are raised about genetic determinism.

Esaias, Timons. "Norbert and the System." *Interzone* no. 73. July 1993. pp. 16–21.

Herbert, Frank. *Dune Chronicles*. New York: Ace, 1965. Frank Herbert's *Dune* series, launched with the publication of *Dune* in 1965, which won two Hugos and a Nebula, describes a future religious movement in which a leader, Muad'dib is conditioned with a "spice" drug, and trained to have highly developed and prophetic powers. The capacity of newly evolving beings to foresee the future, and whether or not that future is determined, receives increasing emphasis as the series unfolds.

——. *Man of Two Worlds*. New York: Orb Books, 1997. Dreens give worlds existence by their imagination, but they cannot control the beings to whom they give free will and consider destroying creation.

Levin, Ira. *The Boys from Brazil*. Bloomsbury Publishing, 1998. Yakov Liebermann is a Nazi-hunter who receives a strange call regarding the resurgent activities of Dr. Joseph Mengele, a Nazi doctor and experimenter. It appears that Mengele is alive and conducting cloning experiences to perpetuate a line of Aryan people.

McAuley, Paul. *Fairyland*. Gollancz, 1995. A warring Europe is transformed by the construction of "fairies"—a race of intelligent, manufactured dolls. Do dolls have any freedom? Any less than the genetically engineered human beings who have given them birth? John W. Campbell Award and Arthur C. Clarke Award winning novel.

Niven, Larry. *Ringworld*. New York: Ballantine, 1970. The ancient belief that the human will is subject to the will of God or to some transcendent supernatural force like fate or karma is represented here with some levity. Received the Nebula and Hugo awards.

Skinner, B. F. *Walden Two*. New York: Hackett Publishing Co., 2005. A fictional story in which Skinner defends the view that human behavior is determined by environmental conditioning. Operant conditioning is used to establish a utopian society.

Swanwick, Michael. "Walden Three." *New Dimensions 12*. Marta Randall and Robert Silverberg, eds. Pocket, 1981. A science fiction story offering a criticism of Skinner's views in *Walden Two*.

*Tiptree, James. "Love Is the Plan, the Plan Is Death." *The Alien Condition*. Goldin, Stephen, ed. New York: Ballantine, 1973. A very imaginative description of an insect-like alien species' struggle against its biological imperatives. The story ironically suggests that even our rebellious assertions of free will may themselves be biologically programmed.

Vonnegut, Kurt. *The Sirens of Titan*. New York: Dell, 1999. Vonnegut's views of free will are reminiscent of those of ancient stoics such as Marcus Aurelius.

Wilhelm, Kate. *Where Late the Sweet Birds Sang*. Harper, 1976. Cloning is used by a small band of survivors of a cataclysm, but questions arise regarding whether their paths are determined by the pre-selection of genetic traits.

Philosophy

Augustine. *On the Free Choice of the Will*. Trans. Thomas Williams. Indianapolis: Hackett Publishing, 1993.

Ayer, A. J. "Freedom and Necessity." In *Free Will*, ed. Derk Pereboom, 110–18. Indianapolis: Hackett Publishing Company, 1997.

Berofsky, Bernard. *Free Will and Determinism*. Harper, 1966.

Clarke, Randolph. *Libertarian Accounts of Free Will*. Oxford: Oxford University Press, 2003.

*Dennett, Daniel. *Elbow Room: The Varieties of Free Will Worth Having*. Cambridge, MA: MIT Press, 1984. Another view of compatibilism, namely that free actions are caused without being altogether determined.

*Fischer, John Martin. *The Metaphysics of Free Will: An Essay on Control*. Oxford: Blackwell, 1996.

Fischer, John Martin, and Mark Ravizza. *Responsibility and Control: A Theory of Moral Responsibility*. Cambridge: Cambridge University Press, 1998.

Forrest, Peter. "Backward Causation in Defence of Free Will." *Mind* 94 (1985): pp. 210–17.

Frankfurt, Harry. "Alternate Possibilities and Moral Responsibility." *Journal of Philosophy* 66 (1969): pp. 829–39.

*——. "Freedom of the Will and the Concept of a Person," *Journal of Philosophy* 68, 1 (1971): pp. 5–20.

*——. *The Importance of What We Care About*. New York: Cambridge University Press, 1988.

——. "Discussion with Harry Frankfurt." *Ethical Perspectives* 5 (1998): pp. 15–43.

Hobbes, Thomas. "On Behalf of Determinism." *The English Works of Thomas Hobbes*. Sir Wm. Molesworth, ed. Vol. 4. London: John Bohn, 1829–1845. From *Of Liberty and Necessity* (1656), pp. 272–75 and from *Leviathan* (1651), part 2, chapter 21, pp. 196–98. Originally published in 1656.

Honderich, Ted. *A Theory of Determinism*. Oxford: Oxford University Press, 1988.

*——. *The Significance of Free Will*. New York: Oxford University Press. 1996.

Hook, Sidney. *Determinism and Freedom in the Age of Modern Science*. Collier, 1961.

*Kane, Robert. *A Contemporary Introduction to Free Will*. New York: Oxford University Press, 2005.

——. *Free Will: Blackwell Readings in Philosophy*. Malden, MA: Blackwell.

Lewis, David. "Are We Free to Break the Laws?" *Philosophical Papers, Volume II*, 291–98. New York: Oxford University Press, 1987.

McCann, Hugh. *The Works of Agency: On Human Action, Will, and Freedom*. Ithaca, NY: Cornell University Press, 1998.

McKenna, Michael and David Widerker, eds. *Moral Responsibility and Alternative Possibilities*. Burlington, VT: Ashgate, 2003.

Moore, G. E. *Ethics*. London: Williams & Norgate, 1912.

O'Connor, Timothy. *Persons and Causes: The Metaphysics of Free Will*. New York: Oxford University Press, 2000.

Pereboom, Derk. *Living Without Free Will*. Cambridge: Cambridge University Press. 2001.

Rowe, William. *Can God Be Free?* Oxford: Oxford University Press, 2004.

Sartre, Jean-Paul. *Being and Nothingness*. Trans. Hazel Barnes. Philosophical Library, 1984.

Sorabji, Richard. *Necessity, Cause, and Blame*. Ithaca, NY: Cornell University Press, 1980. An informative discussion of Aristotle and other philosophers on the issues of voluntary action and free will.

Timpe, Kevin. *Free Will: Sourcehood and Its Alternatives*. London: Continuum, 2008.

*van Inwagen, Peter. *An Essay on Free Will*. Oxford: Clarendon Press, 1983.

Afterword

It is because of wondering that men began to philosophize and do so now. First, they wondered at the difficulties close at hand; then, advancing little by little, they discussed difficulties also about greater matters, for example, about the changing attributes of the Moon and of the Sun and of the stars, and about the generation of the universe. Now a man who is perplexed and wonders considers himself ignorant (whence a lover of myth, too, is in a sense a philosopher, for a myth is composed of wonders), so if indeed they philosophized in order to avoid ignorance, it is evident that they pursued science in order to understand and not in order to use it for something else.

(Aristotle's *Metaphysics*. Translated by Hippocrates G. Apostle. Book A.1.2, 982b. Bloomington: Indiana University Press, 1970.)

Glossary

Abductive argument argument whose premises give support to the conclusion by showing that it is the best explanation amongst alternatives of phenomena that require explanation.

Absolute space theory of space on which it is an independently existing entity separate from the relationships between the physical bodies inhabiting it.

Act something done by someone in such a way as to be the product of that person's responsible control; type of event in which agency is evident.

Act-utilitarianism the consequentialist view that one ought always to act in each and every individual case in such a way as to maximize benefits and (or) minimize harms.

Ad hominem fallacy logical fallacy on which one criticizes the person giving the argument in order to refute the argument.

Aesthetics sub-discipline of philosophy that studies artistic value and beauty.

Affirming the consequent logical fallacy according to which one affirms the consequent of a conditional statement, then concludes that the antecedent must be true.

Agent a responsible performer of acts; one who is a proper candidate for praise or blame for doing what he or she does as an agent.

Agnosticism thesis that there is no strong reason for assurance one way or the other about the existence of God.

Analogical argument argument that attempts to establish a conclusion about topic A by comparing A things with other, often better known, B things.

Applied philosophy the application of theoretical philosophical principles to actual problems in everyday life.

Argument a set of statements in which some of the premises or assumptions are supposed to support the conclusion.

Argument from evil family of arguments purporting to demonstrate God's non-existence by appeal to evidence that the existence and amount of evil in the world could not exist if God were to exist.

Argument from moral responsibility reductio ad absurdum argument for libertarianism on which, if libertarianism is false, then there are no moral truths about what we ought to do.

Argument from tolerance for relativism argument for relativism according to which one must affirm the truth of relativism in order to exemplify the virtue of tolerance.

Artificial intelligence theoretical discipline aiming to understand intelligence and related mental states by designing machines that think; the thinking machine-based beings created by human beings.

Atheism the view that God does not exist; the opposite of theism.

Begging the question a logical fallacy in which an argument's conclusion is illicitly presupposed in the set of premises.

Belief a statement that is affirmed by a person.

Body criterion theory of personal identity according to which person X is the same person as person Y iff X and Y share the same body.

Bundle theory theory of personal identity on which persons do not have abiding diachronic numerical identity but are instead simple, changing collections of mental experiences moment to moment.

Causal loop problem in the context of the philosophy of time, problem on which a causal sequence takes circular form; e.g. event A causes event B, B causes C and C causes A.

Closure principle epistemological principle specifying the conditions under which one is or is not justified to move from some known belief P to knowledge of another belief Q.

Cogito lit. "I think"; or, Descartes' statement, in *Discourse on Method*, exemplifying his refutation of evil demon skepticism; or, self-verifying statement that is known whenever it is affirmed.

Coherentism non-skeptical epistemological theory on which justification (or knowledge) arises in a network of beliefs by virtue of a series of inferential relationships between component beliefs; a response to the regress of knowledge theory standing in opposition to foundationalism.

Compatibilism thesis about freedom of the will on which it is false that, if all physical events are causally determined by the conjunction of a fixed past and the laws of nature, then human beings do not have free will.

Conclusion a statement in an argument that is supported by premises.

Conditional any statement with an antecedent and a conditional, i.e. an if–then statement.

Consequentialism normative theory whose prescriptions and prohibitions are based upon an assessment of the consequences of actions.

Correspondence theory of truth theory of truth according to which a statement is true if and only if the state of affairs expressed by the statement corresponds to the way that the world is.

Cosmological arguments (for the existence of God) arguments that attempt to demonstrate God's existence by citing God as explaining causally what are said to be otherwise inexplicable natural phenomena; such arguments contend that the cosmos or some of its features require causal explanation, which only God can provide.

Creature consciousness consciousness describing a person's awareness or capacity for awareness.

Deductive argument set of statements, some of which, the premises, are thought to entail another, the conclusion.

Deductive logic the study of direct inferences from premises that purport to guarantee their conclusions.

Defense in the context of the philosophy of religion, a theistic response to arguments from evil that aims only to propose ways in which God might use certain evils to acquire certain goods; more circumspect response to arguments from evil than theodicies.

Deontological theory normative theory that attempts to found prescriptions and prohibitions on exceptionless duties or obligations, whose dictates do not take consequences into account.

Design argument (or **teleological argument**) argument using observations of features of apparent design and order in the universe as evidence for the conclusion that God exists.

Designedness feature of an object according to which it possess the *appearance* of intelligent design.

Determinism thesis that all physical events are causally determined by the conjunction of a fixed past and the laws of nature.

Diachronic through time.

Divine command theory normative theory of moral philosophy on which the rightness and wrongness of actions are determined by and only by reference to God's will.

Dream skepticism argument Cartesian argument on which beliefs about the external world are not known to be true on the grounds that the evidence does not disprove the hypothesis that I might be dreaming.

Eliminitivism reductionist and physicalist theory of mind recommending the disuse of psychological terms, like "belief" and "doubt," that lack physical referents.

Emotivism non-cognitivist theory about the meaning of moral language on which moral judgments and claims *express* emotions but do not *describe* anything.

Epiphenomenalism thesis that mental events are caused by physical events, but that mental events have no causal influence upon any other events, physical or mental.

Epistemology the philosophical study of cognitive states, such as knowledge and belief, their relationships to one another, the processes by which they are achieved, and the possibility of their achievement.

Equivocation a logical fallacy on which an ambiguous word or sentence is used to mean one thing in one statement, but is used to mean another thing in another statement.

Evil see **moral evil, natural evil**.

Evil demon skepticism skeptical theory on which an evil god-like being deceives one into falsely believing appearance resembles reality, and who therefore subverts knowledge claims.

External time (or historical time) form of time measurement on which time is measured from a timeless, ageless perspective and on which no reference to the present is required.

Externalism theory of justification on which justification depends upon the features that produce the belief, rather than on reasons possessed by the agent.

Fallacy an invalid inference.

Fallibilism the non-skeptical position that legitimate claims to knowledge may be made even without the kind of justification that gives one certainty.

False dilemma a logical fallacy in which too few explanations are proposed (often merely two) and all but one are eliminated, yielding only one explanation.

Foundationalism non-skeptical epistemological theory on which beliefs possess justification (or are known) because of their inferential relationships to basic beliefs, which are self-justifying or are justified non-inferentially.

Four-dimensionalism theory of time on which time is a fourth dimension in the unified field of spacetime.

Functionalism theory in the philosophy of mind consistent with physicalism on which mental states are identical to functional roles they play in a person's mental network.

God omniscient, omnipotent, omni-benevolent and perfect creator being.

Hard determinism thesis about the freedom of the will on which determinism is true and humans do not have free will.

Hedonism the naturalistic (hence, definistic) view that identifies goodness with pleasure.

Hierarchical compatibilism theory about the freedom of the will on which freedom is a relationship between the internal, ordered mental states of a person such that, only if first-order and second-order desires about topic T are harmonized, is the person free with respect to choices about T.

Idealism in the philosophy of mind, theory on which minds and mental stuff exists and nothing that is not a mind or mental stuff exists.

Identity of indiscernibles Leibnizian principle on which, for any X and any Y, if X and Y share all intrinsic properties in common, then X is identical to Y.

Incompatibilism thesis about the freedom will on which, *if* all physical events are causally determined by the conjunction of a fixed past and the laws of nature, *then* human beings lack free will.

Indiscernibility of identicals Leibnizian principle on which, for any X and any Y, if X is identical to Y then X and Y have all their intrinsic properties in common.

Inductive argument a set of statements, some of which, the premises or assumptions, are intended to make the conclusion probable.

Inductive logic the study of predictive or generalizing inferences whose premises purport to make their conclusions probable without guaranteeing them.

Instrumental good a state of affairs beneficial only as a means to some intrinsically good state of affairs; e.g. pain felt during dental work is instrumentally good as a means to better dental hygiene.

Intelligent design theory set of theories using physical facts about the life and the universe to establish that life and/or the universe are created by an intelligent being, which may or may not be God; scientific methodology on which the order and design of biological systems requires appeal to intelligent designer.

Intentionality feature of mental states on which mental states are directed and about something.

Internalism a theory of epistemic justification on which justification for a statement takes form as evidence or reasons possessed by or internal to a person.

Internal time form of measurement of time using the first-person perspective typically employing the present moment as a reference point.

Interactionism the form of dualism that accepts both the theses of physical-to-mental causality and mental-to-physical causality.

Intrinsic goods a state of affairs beneficial as an end in itself.

Intuitionism The cognitivist view that moral values and the correctness of moral judgments can be recognized by direct intuition.

Justification evidence for a belief that increases the likelihood that the belief is true.

Justified true belief analysis of knowledge some person (S) knows that some proposition (p) is true if and only if (i) p is true; (ii) S believes p; and (iii) S is fully justified in believing p.

Knowledge argument argument in the philosophy of mind that opposes physicalism by justifying the claim that there are some true statements about topic T that are unknown to agents who know all the knowable physical facts about T.

Libertarianism thesis about freedom of the will on which determinism is false and humans have free will.

Logic a sub-discipline of philosophy dedicated to the study of rules and patterns of inference, and to formal relationships between statements.

Logical impossibility a statement that is true in no possible world.

Logical possibility a statement is logically possible if and only if its truth is consistent with logical laws.

Memory criterion person X at time T is numerically identical to person Y at time T + 1 iff X and Y share all the same memories.

Metaethics the part of value theory concerned with identifying the nature of values, with understanding moral concepts like "right" and "wrong," and with finding the ultimate foundations for all our value judgments.

Metaphysics the philosophical study of the basic nature and constituents of reality.

Monism ontological thesis on which all that exists is constituted by one type of substance; e.g. physicalism is a monist thesis that all that exists is constituted.

Moral disagreement argument for relativism abductive argument for relativism according to which the best explanation for the fact of widespread, cross-cultural moral differences is the truth of relativism.

Moral evil disvaluable states of pain, suffering and evil caused through immoral acts performed by morally responsible agents.

Multiple realizability thesis in the philosophy of mind on which it is physically possible to implement or realize mental states in a variety of physical forms.

Natural evil disvaluable states of pain, suffering and evil caused by forces of nature for which no person is to blame.

Necessary condition A is a necessary condition for B if and only if the falsity or non-existence of A is guaranteed to bring about the falsity or non-existence of B. For example, being male is a necessary condition for being a bachelor.

Necessary truth statement that is true in every possible world.

Necessity theory theory in the philosophy of science on which natural laws express necessary truths about the way this world must be.

Non-skepticism the opposite of skepticism; the philosophical view that we can have certain knowledge of some specified subject.

Normative ethics the philosophical attempt to discern and account for the nature of ethical good and evil.

Numerical identity A is numerically identical with B if A is the same thing as B; e.g. Clark Kent is numerically identical with Superman.

Objective statements statements whose truth does not depend upon facts found within the speaker's own mind, e.g. *the Earth orbits the Sun*.

Ontological arguments arguments in the philosophy of religion that demonstrate God's existence by appeals to the concept of God, and on which, from a proper understanding of the nature of God, one infers God's existence.

Ought implies can principle thesis that person P has no moral obligation to perform action X at time T unless it is physically possible for P to perform X at time T.

Paradox of omnipotence philosophical problem on which God's omnipotence is argued to be self-contradictory on the grounds that, if God is omnipotent, there are events that God lacks the power to perform.

Parallelism the form of dualism that rejects both the theses of physical-to-mental causality and mental-to-physical causality.

Personal identity, conditions of necessary and sufficient conditions specifying facts for which person P is numerically identical to person Q.

Personhood, conditions of necessary and sufficient conditions specifying when some X is or becomes a person.

(Basic) physicalism ontological theory on which, if some thing exists, it exists within spacetime; statement that everything is physical and that non-physical things, e.g. souls, do not exist.

Physical possibility a statement is physically possible if and only if its truth is consistent with the conjunction of known physical laws.

Possible world a set of statements which is typically hypothesized in order to understand and assess the logical relations between member statements.

Powerful principle a proposed general truth of profound significance, whose general sense is taken to be undeniable.

Pre-established harmony Leibnizian metaphysical and theological theory on which God, when he created the world, created two parallel and synchronized series of events, one physical and one mental, which is used to account for substance dualism without causal interaction.

Premise a statement used as evidence to support the conclusion.

Principle of alternative possibilities thesis about freedom of the will on which only if an agent could have willed something else instead is the agent free to will what he or she wills.

Probabilistic conception of causation "x causes y" entails that, given x, y will more *probably* occur than it would without x.

Problem of other minds epistemological problem of proving that the beings who appear to be persons with minds in fact are persons with minds and not automata.

Problem of personal identity the philosophical problem of justifying the claim that a person at one time is the same as a person at another time.

Propositional knowledge knowledge that some proposition (normally expressed by a declarative sentence) is true; knowing that such and such is the case, e.g. Jones has propositional knowledge that snow is white if Jones knows that "snow is white" is true.)

Psychological continuity criterion theory of personal identity on which (i) person X and person Y are diachronically, numerically identical if and only if X and Y are psychologically continuous; and (ii) X and Y are psychologically continuous if and only if Y's mental network is well connected to X's mental network.

Qualitative consciousness form of mental awareness of phenomenological experiences, e.g. one's perceptual awareness of the shade of red is a qualitatively conscious mental state.

Qualitative identity X and Y are qualitatively identical if and only if X and Y have all the same qualities.

Rational positive epistemic quality used to describe beliefs or people; or, a belief P is rational for a person A only if, *if* the beliefs upon which A believes P are true, *then* A is likely to be true.

Reductio ad absurdum argument an argument on which a conclusion is shown to have consequences so absurd that one of the premises leading to such consequences is false.

Reductio ad absurdum argument against ethical relativism argument on which the truth of ethical relativism implies that horrible and immoral behavior is moral, a fact which is then used to refute ethical relativism.

Reductionism in the context of the philosophy of mind, a theory on which statements about the mind, its nature and its properties, are re-construed to be statements about the brain, its nature and its properties.

Reflexive consciousness mental state of person P that takes another mental state of P's as its object.

Regress of knowledge epistemological problem on which the justification for a target belief B depends upon the justification of C, and the justification of C depends upon the justification of D, etc.; or, argument based upon this problem that concludes that no belief has sufficient justification to convert the belief to knowledge.

Regularity theory thesis in the philosophy of science on which natural laws express correlations between pairs of events known to be conjoined together in experience.

Relative space a theory of space on which it does not exist independent from the relations of physical bodies within it.

Relativism a theory on which a wide range of statements are subjective; **individual relativism**: a theory on which the truth or falsity of statements depends on whether or not the subject believes they are true; **group relativism**: a theory on which the truth or falsity of statements depends on whether the group to which one belongs believes the statements.

Responsibility the feature of an agent by which he or she is supposed to merit praise or blame for his or her actions. A person is responsible for his or her deeds when and only when he or she may rightly be said to have been able to do otherwise.

Rule-utilitarianism the consequentialist view that one ought always to act in accordance with a rule the following of which would maximize benefits and (or) minimize harms.

Self-verifying statement any statement that, when affirmed, is true and known to be true; e.g. "I think."

Simple predictive conception of causality "x causes y" entails that, given x, y *will* come true.

Skepticism theory of knowledge on which we lack knowledge, in whole or in part.

Slippery slope a logical fallacy in which one attempts to refute a statement on the grounds that, if it is true, a sequence of increasingly unacceptable events follows.

Social and political philosophy the philosophical study of social structures (such as the family) and political structures (such as constitutional democracy) that shape the human environment.

Sound valid inferences whose premises are all true.

Statement a sentence that expresses a proposition that is either true or false.

Subjective statement a statement whose truth or falsity depends upon its correspondence to the subject's state of mind, e.g. *I like chocolate ice cream.*

Substance dualism theory of mind on which persons are composed of two distinct entities, the non-physical mind and the physical body.

Sufficient conditions A is a sufficient condition for B if and only if the fact or existence of A brings about the fact or existence of B. For example, being a Boeing 777 is a sufficient condition for being an airplane.

Supervenience thesis in the philosophy mind on which, if some property A supervenes on another property B, then if an object has property A it must have property B.

Synchronic at the same time.

Teleological arguments (for the existence of God) arguments that attempt to demonstrate God's existence by citing God as explaining the intelligibility or allegedly evident purposiveness of nature.

Theism the view that God exists.

Theodicy theistic response to arguments from evil that seeks to vindicate God's moral character by explaining how God uses evil events to create goods that depend upon those evils; more ambitious response to arguments from evil than defenses.

Thesis of mental-to-physical causality mental states and objects can cause physical states and/or objects to come into being.

Thesis of physical-to-mental causality physical states and objects can cause mental states and/or objects to come into being.

Time traveler's hypothesis travel to the past by some object or person is logically and physically possible.

Truth accurate representation of reality by a statement.

Tsujigiri historical ritual act performed by Japanese samurai in which they test the sharpness of swords by beheading passing strangers.

Type identity theory theory in the philosophy of mind on which a type or kind of mental state is identical to a type or kind of physical event such that each mental type has a physical correlate type.

Universal and ancestral causation the principle that every event is the product of a chain of causes which has continued, unbroken, from the beginning of time.

Valid argument whose conclusions cannot be false, unless one or more of their premises are false.

Value theory the philosophical study of value judgments; the language in which they are expressed, and the reasoning patterns by which they are made.

Notes

0 WHAT IS PHILOSOPHY?

1 Molyneux's letter to John Locke, March 2, 1693, p. 651, letter 1609 in volume 3. In *The Correspondence of John Locke*. 8 vols.. E. DeBeer, ed. New York: Oxford University Press, 1976–1989.

1 PHILOSOPHICAL METHOD AND PHILOSOPHICAL DISAGREEMENT

1 www.who.int/mediacentre /news/releases/2006/pr30/en/
2 Lateef, Mungin. "Dad Gets 10 Years in Mutilation Case." *The Atlanta Journal-Constitution*. Retrieved November 2, 2006.
3 Stang, Howard J. and Leonard W. Snellman (June 1998). "Circumcision Practice Patterns in the United States" (PDF). *Pediatrics* 101, 6 (1998): pp. e5–. DOI:10.1542/peds.101.6.e5. ISSN 1098–4275.

2 KNOWLEDGE AND SKEPTICISM

1 Clifford, William Kingdon. *The Ethics of Belief and Other Essays*. Amherst, NY: Prometheus Books, 1999 [1877]. p. 77.
2 Gettier, Edmund L. "Is Justified True Belief Knowledge?" *Analysis* 23 (1963): pp. 121–23.

3 RELIGION AND BELIEF IN GOD

1 James, William. *The Will to Believe and Other Essays in Popular Philosophy*. Boston, MA: Elibron Classics, 2000. Reprint of New York: Longmans, Green & Co., 1898. pp. 23–24.
2 The term "noseeum argument" is apt because "noseeums" are a tiny gnat here in the Midwest which, while so small you "no see 'um," nevertheless have a painful bite. The

term "skeptical gambit" combines "skepticism" (in philosophy, the view that we aren't in a position to see or know about the thing one way or the other) and "gambit" (in chess, a sacrifice of something of value—here, optimism that we can usually grasp God's purposes) for the sake of long term benefits (undercutting Rowe's argument for atheism).

3   I've here omitted important nuances. One is that a good God (or good parent) might allow certain intense suffering for the sake of an outweighing good even when that good doesn't require allowing that particular suffering. It might only require allowing that suffering or some other comparably bad thing. Second, when God allows certain suffering "for the sake of" some good thing, it needn't be that the suffering *brings about* the good thing. The good might come before the suffering: God might allow suffering caused by human evil choices, for the sake of having creatures with free will. Third, the outweighing goods can be somewhat "abstract." God, like a good parent, might allow some suffering as just punishment for wrongdoing: the outweighing good is then having a world in which principles of justice are satisfied. Such nuances differentiate standard theism from the sort of rosy-glow metaphysical optimism that Voltaire famously satirizes in *Candide*.

4   The caveat "other things being equal" allows that special further considerations may "defeat" this evidence: learning your neighbor has a lawn-watering system that causes the same pitter-patter sound may defeat the inference that it is raining. For more about defeaters, see Chapter 2, §2.0.

5   In the literature these principles are known as Wykstra's "CORNEA" principle, where "CORNEA" is a cheater-acronym standing for "Condition of ReasoNable Epistemic Access." Note that the principles put the onus on the person *making* the noseeum inference. It is the person making the inference who must reasonably be able to say that if there were a God-justifying Good served by all suffering, we'd likely see this Point for the select instance. Hence, to defeat the Noseeum Inference, the critic needn't prove that if the good is there, we likely *wouldn't* see it. Her reasons for thinking we wouldn't see it need only be strong enough to balance out (or cancel out) any reasons for thinking that we *would* see it.

6   It is also often called "skeptical theism." I prefer "skeptical gambit," for atheists as well as theists can endorse it as a reply to Rowe's particular argument.

7   I did indeed once take communion at Mass, when a Catholic friend at Notre Dame invited me to go to Mass with him. My friend assumed I realized that Protestants, while warmly welcome to worship at Mass, are expected—by the Vatican, at least— to refrain from receiving the sacrament. He gently told me this later. Someone seeing me on that occasion might indeed have strong (but misleading) evidence that I was a Catholic.

8   A parent's purposed good can be unknown to the child (or God's, to us) for reasons other than it's lying in the distant future. Nothing in the parent analogy commits us to saying this is the *only* reason why, if God exists, we'd often be unable to see or grasp God-purposed goods for present sufferings.

4 SPACETIME AND TIME TRAVEL

1 Augustine. *Confessions*. Trans. Arthur Cook Outler. Mineola, NY: Courier Dover Publications, 1995. Book 11, ch. 14, para. 17, p. 224.
2 Williams, Donald. "The Myth of Passage." In Richard M. Gale, ed. *The Philosophy of Time*. New York: Anchor, 1969: p. 105.
3 Heisenberg's uncertainty principle, even if interpreted in the usual way, doesn't help here. One could, after all, measure (say) the location of an electron in the watch as precisely as one cares to, even if one thereby has to give up knowing the electron's momentum. But that measurement would be a single event, and therefore have a single result.
4 This assumes that time for the universe as a whole is linear, but even if it is circular—if the universe itself is a causal loop—there is a similar problem. The watch's circular time would still form a circle within a circle, and similar considerations about that situation lead to the same conclusion.
5 It doesn't actually have to be the entire universe, although considering just that possibility makes things easier. Suppose the mass of the universe at T0 = m, and that at T1 = that at T2 = 2m. Then, if mass m + p travels from T2 to T1 (where p is any positive number), there is a contradiction, since in that case the mass at T1 (and at T2) would have to be 2m + p.

5 MIND

1 Nagel, Thomas. "What Is It like to Be a Bat?" *Philosophical Review* 83:4 (1974): pp. 435–50, at 438, 439.
2 Leibniz, Gottfried. "Monadology." R. Ariew and D. Garber, trans. In *Modern Philosophy*. R. Ariew and E. Watkins, eds. Indianapolis: Hackett, 1998: §17, p. 236.
3 *Discourse on Method*, Part V, in Descartes, 1984: vol 2, p. 139.
4 *Discourse on Method*, Part V, in Descartes, 1984, vol 2, p. 141.
5 Turing, A. M. "Computing Machinery and Intelligence." *Mind* 59 (1950): pp. 433–60.
6 Ibid.
7 Jackson, Frank. "Epiphenomenal Qualia." *Philosophical Quarterly* 32 (1982): pp. 127–36, at 130.
8 Descartes, Rene. *Meditations on First Philosophy*. D. Cress, trans. In *Modern Philosophy*, R. Ariew and E. Watkins, eds. Indianapolis: Hackett, 1998: pp. 30–34.
9 The Latin word *effingo* means "to form an image" or "imagine."
10 Descartes, Rene. *Meditations on First Philosophy*. D. Cress, trans. In *Modern Philosophy*. R. Ariew and E. Watkins, eds. Indianapolis: Hackett, 1998: pp. 50, 53.
11 Descartes, Rene. *Discourse on Method*. D. Cress, trans. In *Modern Philosophy*. R. Ariew and E. Watkins, eds. Indianapolis: Hackett, 1998: pp. 19–21.

6 PERSONAL IDENTITY

1   Black, Max. "The Identity of Indiscernibles." *Mind* 61 (1952): p. 156.
2   Carey, Peter. "The Chance." In Hartwell, David and Damien Broderick, eds. *Centarus: The Best of Australian Science Fiction*. New York: Tor, 1999. pp. 495–525.
3   Parfit, Derek. *Reasons and Persons*. Oxford: Oxford University Press, 1986. p. 199.
4   Reid, Thomas. *Essays on the Intellectual Powers of Man* [1785]. Ed. Ronald Beanblossom. Indianapolis: Hackett, 1983. Book 3, ch. 6, pp. 217–18.

7 FREE WILL

1   Goldman, Alvin. I. "Actions, Predictions, and Books of Life." *American Philosophical Quarterly* 5, 3 (1968): pp. 135–51, at pp. 143–44.
2   Reid, Thomas. *The Correspondence of Thomas Reid*. P. Wood, ed. Edinburgh, UK: Edinburgh University Press, 2002. From a letter to James Gregory, p. 234.
3   Pappas, G., J. Cornman, and K. Lehrer. *Philosophical Problems and Arguments*. Indianapolis: Hackett Publishing, 1991. p. 92.
4   Popper, Karl. *The Logic of Scientific Discovery*. New York: Science Editions, 1961. Appendix *X, pp. 427–28.
5   Locke, John. *Essay Concerning Human Understanding*. In *Modern Philosophy*. R. Ariew and E. Watkins, eds. Indianapolis: Hackett, 1998: book 2, section 21, para. 10, p. 303.
6   Thanks to Ryan Nichols and Neal Tognazzini for helpful comments on earlier versions of this paper.

References

0 WHAT IS PHILOSOPHY?

Morgan, Michael. *Molyneux's Question: Vision, Touch and the Philosophy of Perception*. Cambridge: Cambridge University Press, 1977.

*Sorenson, Roy. *Thought Experiments*. Oxford: Oxford University Press, 1992.

2 KNOWLEDGE AND SKEPTICISM

Armstrong, D. M. *What is a Law of Nature?* Cambridge: Cambridge University Press, 1975.

*Baxter, Stephen. *Time: Manifold 1*. London: HarperCollins, 2000.

BonJour, Laurence. "Externalist Theories of Empirical Knowledge." *Midwest Studies in Philosophy* 5 (1980): pp. 59–60.

Bostrom, Nick. "Are We Living in a Computer Simulation?" *The Philosophical Quarterly* 53 (2003): pp. 243–55. See also: www.simulation-argument.com/simulation.html [Bostrom 2003a].

*——. "The Simulation Argument: Why the Probability that You Are Living in a Matrix is Quite High." *Times Higher Education Supplement*, May 16, 2003. See also: www.simulation-argument.com/matrix.html [Bostrom 2003b].

*Dainton, Barry. "Innocence Lost: Simulation Scenarios: Prospects and Consequences," 2002, at: www.simulation-argument.com/dainton.pdf

Descartes, René. *The Philosophical Writings of Descartes*, 3 vols. J. Cottingham, R. Stoothoff and D. Murdoch, trans. Cambridge: Cambridge University Press., 1984, 1985, 1991.

*Leslie, John. *The End of the World: The Science and Ethics of Human Extinction*. London: Routledge, 1996. Revised paperback ed., 1998.

Putnam, Hilary. *Reason, Truth, and History*. Cambridge: Cambridge University Press, 1981.

Weatherson, Brian. "Are You A Sim?" *The Philosophical Quarterly* 53 (2003): pp. 425–31.

3 RELIGION AND BELIEF IN GOD

Anselm, Saint. "The Classical Ontological Argument for God's Existence." *Complete Philosophical and Theological Treatises of Anselm of Canterbury*. Hopkins, Jasper and Herbert Richardson, eds. Trans. Arthur J. Banning. Minneapolis: University of Minnesota Press, 2000.

Descartes, René. *The Philosophical Writings of Descartes*, 3 vols. J. Cottingham, R. Stoothoff and D. Murdoch, trans. Cambridge: Cambridge University Press., 1984, 1985, 1991.

James, William. *The Will to Believe: Human Immortality*. New York: Dover Publications, 1956.

Rowe, William. *The Cosmological Argument*. New York: Fordham University Press, 1975.

———. "The Problem of Evil and Some Varieties of Atheism." *American Philosophical Quarterly* 16 (1979): pp. 335–41.

*———. "Evil and the Theistic Hypothesis: A Response to Wykstra" (pp. 61–88). *International Journal for Philosophy of Religion* 16 (1984): pp. 95–100. Republished in Adams, Robert M. and Marilyn M. Adams. *The Problem of Evil*. Oxford University Press, 1990. pp. 161–67.

———. "The Evidential Argument From Evil: A Second Look." In *The Evidential Argument from Evil*. 1996. D. Howard-Synder, ed. Indianapolis: Indiana University Press, 1996. pp. 262–85.

*———. *Can God be Free?* New York: Oxford University Press, 2006.

Russell, B. and S. Wykstra. "The 'Inductive' Argument From Evil: A Dialogue." *Philosophical Topics* 16 (1988): pp. 33–60.

Wykstra, Stephen. "The Humean Obstacle to Evidential Arguments from Suffering: On Avoiding the Evils of 'Appearance.'" *International Journal for Philosophy of Religion* 16 (1984): pp. 73–93. Republished in Adams, Robert M. and Marilyn M. Adams. *The Problem of Evil*. Oxford University Press, 1990. pp. 138–60.

*———. "Rowe's Noseeum Arguments from Evil". In Howard-Snyder, Daniel, ed. *The Evidential Problem of Evil*. Bloomington: Indiana University Press, 1996. pp. 126–50.

4 SPACETIME AND TIME TRAVEL

Hanley, Richard. "No End in Sight: Causal Loops in Philosophy, Physics and Fiction." *Synthese: An International Journal for Epistemology, Methodology and Philosophy of Science* 141, 1 (2004): pp. 123–52.

——— . "Identity Crisis: Time Travel and Metaphysics in the DC Multiverse." *Superheroes and Philosophy: Truth, Justice, and the Socratic Way*. Ed. Tom Morris. Chicago: Open Court, 2005.

*Lewis, David. "The Paradoxes of Time Travel." *American Philosophical Quarterly* 13 (1976): pp. 145–52.

*Sider, Theodore. "A New Grandfather Paradox?" *Philosophy and Phenomenological Research* 57 (1997): pp. 139–44.

———. "Time Travel, Coincidences and Counterfactuals." *Philosophical Studies* 110 (2002): 115–38.

Smith, Nicholas J. J. "Bananas Enough for Time Travel?" *British Journal of Philosophy* 48 (1997): pp. 363–89.

Wells, H. G. *The Time Machine*. New York: Pocket Books, 1895.

5 MIND

Descartes, René. *The Philosophical Writings of Descartes*, 3 vols. J. Cottingham, R. Stoothoff and D. Murdoch, trans. Cambridge: Cambridge University Press, 1984, 1985, 1991.
Searle, John R.. "Minds, Brains, and Programs." *The Behavioral and Brain Sciences* 3 (1980): pp. 417–57.

6 PERSONAL IDENTITY

Carey, Peter. "The Chance." In Hartwell, David and Damien Broderick, eds. *Centarus: The Best of Australian Science Fiction*. New York: Tor, 1999. pp. 495–525.
Hume, David. *A Treatise of Human Nature*. 3 vols. 1739–40. Multiple editions in print.
Leibniz, G. W. *Discourse on Metaphysics and Other Essays*. D. Garber and R. Ariew, trans. Indianapolis: Hackett Publishing, 1991.
*Nagel, T. "Brain Bisection and the Unity of Consciousness." *Synthèse* 22 (1971): pp. 396–413.

7 FREE WILL

Ayer, A. J. "Freedom and Necessity." In *Free Will*, ed. Derk Pereboom. Indianapolis: Hackett Publishing Company, 1997: pp. 110–18.
Fischer, John Martin. *The Metaphysics of Free Will*. Oxford: Blackwell, 1994.
Fischer, John Martin, and Mark Ravizza. *Responsibility and Control: A Theory of Moral Responsibility*. Cambridge: Cambridge University Press, 1998.
Forrest, Peter. "Backward Causation in Defence of Free Will." *Mind* 94 (1985): pp. 210–17.
Frankfurt, Harry. "Alternate Possibilities and Moral Responsibility." *Journal of Philosophy* 66 (1969): pp. 829–39.
——. *The Importance of What We Care About*. New York: Cambridge University Press, 1988a.
——. "Discussion with Harry Frankfurt." *Ethical Perspectives* 5 (1998b): pp. 15–43.
Hobbes, Thomas. *Liberty and Necessity* (excerpt). *The English Works of Thomas Hobbes*. Sir Wm. Molesworth, ed. Vol. 4. London: John Bohn, 1829–1845. From *Of Liberty and Necessity*, pp. 272–75.
——. *Leviathan* (excerpt). *The English Works of Thomas Hobbes*. Sir Wm. Molesworth, ed. Vol. 4. London: John Bohn, 1829–1845. From *Leviathan*, part 2, chapter 21, pp. 196–98.
Kane, Robert, ed. *The Oxford Handbook of Free Will*. Oxford: Oxford University Press, 2002.
——. *A Contemporary Introduction to Free Will*. New York: Oxford University Press, 2005.
Lewis, David. "Are We Free to Break the Laws?" *Philosophical Papers, Volume II*, New York: Oxford University Press, 1987: pp. 291–98.
McCann, Hugh. *The Works of Agency: On Human Action, Will, and Freedom*. Ithaca, NY: Cornell University Press, 1998.

McKenna, Michael and David Widerker, eds. *Moral Responsibility and Alternative Possibilities*. Burlington, VT: Ashgate, 2003.

Moore, G. E. *Ethics*. London: Williams & Norgate, 1912.

Timpe, Kevin. *Free Will: Sourcehood and Its Alternatives*. London: Continuum, 2008.

van Inwagen, Peter. *An Essay on Free Will*. Oxford: Clarendon Press, 1983.

Credits

The editors and publishers wish to thank the following for permission to reproduce material in this volume:

Arthur J. Banning Press for Saint Anselm, chapters 2 and 3 of "The Classical Ontological Argument for God's Existence" from *Complete Philosophical and Theological Treatises of Anselm of Canterbury*, trans. Jasper Hopkins and Herbert Richardson (2000) pp. 93–94.

Blackwell Publishing Ltd. for Eric T. Olson, "Was I Ever a Fetus?" from *Philosophy and Phenomenological Research* LVII, 1 (1997): pp. 95–110.

Cambridge University Press for John Searle, "Minds, Brains, and Programs" from *The Behavioral and Brain Sciences* 3 (1980): pp. 417–57, copyright © 1980 by Cambridge University Press. Reprinted with permission of Cambridge University Press.

Ted Chiang for "Hell is the Absence of God"; first appeared in *Starlight 3* (Tor Books, 2001); also published in Ted Chiang, *Stories of Your Life and Others* (Tor Books, 2002); reprinted by permission of the author and the author's agents, The Virginia Kidd Agency, Inc., copyright © 2001 by Ted Chiang.

David Higham Associates for Mary Midgley, "On Trying Out One's New Sword" from *Heart and Mind: The Varieties of Moral Experience* (Harvester Press, 1981).

Cory Doctorow for "Truncat." Originally published August 26, 2003 at www.salon.com: http://dir.salon.com/story/tech/feature/2003/08/26/truncat/

Greg Egan for "Learning to Be Me" from *Interzone* #37 (July 1990): pp. 53–60.

Eleanor Wood/Spectrum Literary Agency for Robert A. Heinlein, "—All You Zombies—" from *The Magazine of Fantasy and Science Fiction* (March 1959).

Timons Esaias for "Norbert and the System" from *Interzone* #73 (July 1993): pp. 16–21.

Hackett Publishing Company, Inc. for Descartes, *Discourse on Method and Meditations on First Philosophy 3/e*, trans. Donald Cress (Hackett, 1993) pp. 59–70, 97, 102, 32–34, copyright © 1993 by Hackett Publishing Company, Inc.; and for Plato, *Republic*, trans. G. M. A. Grube, rev. C. D. C. Reeve (Hackett, 1992), pp. 186–92, 34–36, copyright © 1992 by Hackett Publishing Company, Inc. Reprinted by permission of Hackett Publishing Company, Inc. All rights reserved.

Franz Kiekeben for "Three Time Travel Problems." Appears for the first time in this volume by permission of the author.

Project Gutenberg for David Hume, "Problems with the Design Argument" from *Dialogues Concerning Natural Religion*; and John Locke, "The Psychological Continuity Theory" from *An Essay Concerning Human Understanding*.

Michael Resnick for "Kirinyaga" from *The Magazine of Fantasy and Science Fiction* (November 1998): pp. 6–25.

Alasdair Richmond for "The Simulation Argument and Simulation Hypotheses". Appears for the first time in this volume by permission of the author.

Scovil Chichak Galen Literary Agency, Inc. for Philip K. Dick, "We Can Remember It For You Wholesale" from *The Magazine of Fantasy and Science Fiction* (April 1966). Reprinted by permission of the author and the author's agents, Scovil Chichak Galen Literary Agency, Inc.

Kevin Timpe for "Free Will: Alternatives and Sources." Appears for the first time in this volume by permission of the author.

University of Rochester Press for Joseph Butler, "Of Personal Identity" from *The Works of Bishop Butler*, ed. David White, Rochester (2006) pp. 305–6.

Stephen Wykstra for "Suffering, Evidence, and Analogy: Noseeum Arguments *versus* Skeptical Gambits." Appears for the first time in this volume by permission of the author.

Philosophy through Science Fiction

Index of Terms

Index of Names